Acting as if Tomorrow Matters:
Accelerating the Transition to Sustainability

March 2012

*For students and faculty
at Harrisburg Area Community
College — a great institution.*

John C. Dernbach
Principal Author

FSC
www.fsc.org
MIX
Paper from
responsible sources
FSC® C005010

ENVIRONMENTAL LAW INSTITUTE
Washington, D.C.
2012

ELI publishes books that contribute to education of the profession and disseminate diverse points of view and opinion to stimulate a robust and creative exchange of ideas. These publications, which express opinions of the authors and not necessarily those of the Institute, its Board of Directors, or funding organizations, exemplify ELI's commitment to dialogue with all sectors. ELI welcomes suggestions for book topics and encourages the submission of draft manuscripts and book proposals.

Copyright © 2012
Environmental Law Institute
2000 L Street NW, Washington, DC 20036

Published September 2012.

Printed in the United States of America.
ISBN 978-158576-158-6

Contributing Authors

Robert Adler, University of Utah, S.J. Quinney College of Law (Freshwater)

Rachel Armstrong, University of Denver, Sturm College of Law, Class of 2012 (Forests)

Jennifer Baka, Yale University, School of Forestry & Environmental Studies (Industrial Ecology)

Athena Ballesteros, World Resources Institute (International Financing of Sustainable Development)

Gary D. Bass, Bauman Foundation (Information, Participation, and Access to Justice)

Donald A. Brown, Pennsylvania State University (Climate Change)

Carl Bruch, Environmental Law Institute (Information, Participation, and Access to Justice)

Wynn Calder, Association of University Leaders for a Sustainable Future (Higher Education)

Federico Cheever, University of Denver, Sturm College of Law (Forests)

Marian R. Chertow, Yale University, School of Forestry & Environmental Studies (Industrial Ecology)

Jaimie P. Cloud, Cloud Institute for Sustainability Education (K-12 Education)

Ilona Coyle, Environmental Law Institute (Information, Participation, and Access to Justice)

Robin Kundis Craig, University of Utah, S.J. Quinney College of Law (Oceans and Estuaries)

Julian Dautremont-Smith, University of Michigan (Higher Education)

Michael DiRamio, Corporation for a Skilled Workforce (Green/Sustainable Jobs)

Catherine Easton, World Resources Institute (International Financing of Sustainable Development)

Anne H. Ehrlich, Stanford University, Center for Conservation Biology (Population)

Joel B. Eisen, University of Richmond, School of Law (Brownfield Redevelopment)

Jonathan Barry Forman, University of Oklahoma, College of Law (Economic Development & Poverty)

Lynn R. Goldman, George Washington University, School of Public Health & Health Services (Chemicals and Pesticides)

Kirk Herbertson, World Resources Institute (International Financing of Sustainable Development)

Dieter T. Hessel, Presbyterian Minister (Religion & Ethics)

Keith H. Hirokawa, Albany Law School (Green Building)

Leo Horrigan, Johns Hopkins University, Center for a Livable Future (Sustainable Agriculture)

Frances Irwin, Policy Analyst and Writer (Information, Participation, and Access to Justice)

Kevin Kennedy, Michigan State University, College of Law (International Trade)

Jeannine M. La Prad, Corporation for a Skilled Workforce (Green/Sustainable Jobs)

John A. ("Skip") Laitner, American Council for an Energy-Efficient Economy (Resource Economics)

Amy E. Landis, University of Pittsburgh, Department of Civil and Environmental Engineering (Production and Consumption of Materials)

Robert Lawrence, Johns Hopkins University, Center for a Livable Future (Sustainable Agriculture)

Mark D. Levine, Lawrence Berkeley National Laboratory (Production and Consumption of Energy)

Reid Lifset, Yale University, School of Forestry & Environmental Studies (Industrial Ecology)

Roberta Mann, University of Oregon, School of Law (Economic Development & Poverty)

Brian McNamara, Chicago-Kent College of Law, Class of 2010 (Biodiversity)

Joel A. Mintz, Nova Southeastern University Law Center (Hazardous Waste & Superfund)

Craig Oren, Rutgers University, School of Law-Camden (Air Quality)

Bradley C. Parks, College of William and Mary (Official Development Assistance)

Trip Pollard, Southern Environmental Law Center (Transportation)

David Rejeski, Woodrow Wilson Institute (Science and Technology)

Ed Richards, Louisiana State University, Law Center (Public Health)

J. Timmons Roberts, Brown University (Official Development Assistance)

K.W. James Rochow, Trust for Lead Poisoning Prevention (International Lead Poisoning & Prevention)

Patricia E. Salkin, Albany Law School, Government Law Center (Land Use)

Jim Salzman, Duke University, Law School & Nicholas School of the Environment (Population)

Brent Steel, Oregon State University, School of Public Policy (State Governance)

Kurt A. Strasser, University of Connecticut, School of Law (Business & Industry)

Susanna Sutherland, City of Knoxville, Tennessee (Local Governance)

Dan Tarlock, Chicago-Kent Law School (Biodiversity Conservation)

Michael J. Tierney, College of William and Mary (Official Development Assistance)

Jonathan Weiss, ManTech SRS Technologies (Local Governance)

Christopher Williams, Lawrence Berkeley National Laboratory (Production and Consumption of Energy)

For Tess, Becky, and all those in the next generation

"This nation behaves well if it treats the natural resources as assets which it must turn over to the next generation increased, and not impaired, in value."

Theodore Roosevelt (1910)

Contents

Preface

This book is the product of a unique collaboration among more than four dozen contributing authors who have extraordinary expertise and experience in their fields. Each of them is part of the growing community of sustainability practitioners in the United States—people who translate the vision of sustainability into reality in specific settings. The ideas expressed here are based on the collective thinking of all of the contributing authors of this book.

Each contributing author or team of authors was asked to answer five questions about a particular sustainability topic (forestry, for example, or business and industry). Answering these questions required an assessment of sustainability efforts in the United States over the past 20 years, an explanation of the reasons sustainability has taken root (to the extent it has), a description of obstacles to sustainability, and an explanation of how to accelerate sustainability and overcome obstacles. The answers were separated, organized, and grouped based on patterns in the responses. We then employed a collaborative process to refine these groupings, make sure that nothing of importance was omitted, and review and clarify our understanding of the common patterns. The contributing authors were asked to answer these questions in a narrative form that includes citations to sources, and the book is presented in a single voice.

This book is part of an ongoing project reviewing sustainability in the United States—the only project of its kind in this country. The project is premised on the view that both the opportunities and challenges of sustainability are enormous. While climate change, declining global biodiversity, and other adverse effects of unsustainable development loom large, the economic and social opportunities of sustainable development are equally great. A second premise is that the United States has an important responsibility, not only to get its own house in order but also to support and help lead the global effort. The economic and military power of the United States, its scientific and technological capacity, and the historical leadership role it has played on many issues all underscore the importance of the United States in this effort. Those premises were solid when the project started, and they are still true.

The book is being published on the twentieth anniversary of the United Nations Conference on Environment and Development, or Earth Summit, which took place in Rio de Janeiro in 1992. Nearly 110 heads of state participated in that gathering, a greater number than had attended any prior international conference. In simple and direct terms, the world's leaders described the challenge we face: "Humanity stands at a defining moment in history. We are confronted with a perpetuation of disparities between and within nations, a worsening of poverty, hunger, ill health and illiteracy, and the continuing deterioration of the ecosystems on which we depend for our well-being." They then described the opportunity that sustainable development provides, asserting that it "will lead to the fulfillment of basic needs, improved living standards for all, better protected and managed ecosystems and a safer, more prosperous future."

For the first time, the nations of the world endorsed sustainable development. Each nation made a commitment at the Earth Summit: to work to achieve sustainable development within its own borders and as part of its international activities. One of those countries was the United States.

This book is the fourth review in this ongoing project. The prior reviews have occurred on or after the fifth, tenth, and fifteenth anniversaries of the Earth Summit. These anniversaries were worth marking because the Earth Summit was not just another international meeting; it put sustainability front and center on the world's stage. All of these reviews focused on environmental sustainability because that is the way that sustainability has most commonly been described and understood.

The first review, conducted with the help of my students in a seminar at Widener University School of Law, was published as an article in the *Environmental Law Reporter*.[1] The second review, *Stumbling Toward Sustainability*, was published by the Environmental Law Institute just before the World Summit on Sustainable Development in Johannesburg in 2002.[2] It was written by more than three dozen experts with a wide range of backgrounds and disciplines from universities, non-governmental organizations, and the private sector. The third review, *Agenda for a Sustainable America*, was published by the Environmental Law Institute after the 15-year anniversary of the Earth Summit.[3] The contributors to that volume were substantially the same as those in *Stumbling Toward Sustainability.*

This fourth review is somewhat different. To begin with, it examines U.S. efforts for the entire 20 years that have followed the Earth Summit, not just the most recent five-year period. The passage of a generation-length period provides an appropriate opportunity to assess where we have come from, and where we need to go next. Also unlike the two prior reviews, this book does not focus on policy prescriptions for particular topics, such as hazardous waste, international trade, or higher education. With rare exceptions, most of what is now being advocated for sustainability is more or less what we advocated in prior books. It is increasingly clear that the problem is not the absence of specific and feasible policy recommendations; we've provided those in prior books.

The problem is that, to a very large degree, relatively little has occurred. This volume is thus focused thematically on how to make sustainability happen more rapidly and at a larger scale. Using the last 20 years as a baseline, it looks for patterns in the progress we have achieved, identifies obstacles, and explains how we can accelerate progress and overcome obstacles. Because the book is conceptual and thematic, the examples we use are intended to illustrate particular points. We do not purport to provide an exhaustive description or list of examples for every theme or development that is discussed.

A great many people have inspired and supported this project over the years. The Environmental Law Institute (ELI) continues to be the publisher; its support has made this effort possible. Special thanks to Scott Schang, Rachel Jean-Baptiste, Bill Straub, Graham Campbell, and Brett Kitchen at ELI and Jason Leppig at Island Press. For this volume, Peter Whitten once again proved to be an exceptionally capable editor, and did much to improve the manuscript. Jessica Schuller at Widener University Law School was an unfailing and positive source of secretarial and administrative support. Jeffery Higgins, Richard Katsifis, and Jim Strupe provided research assistance. Research librarian Ed Sonnenberg was enormously helpful in finding difficult sources. Thanks also to Robert Altenburg, Dionne Anthon, Lorene L. Boudreau, Helen Delano, Becky Dernbach, Stephanie Engerer, Kristie Falbo, Jeremy Firestone, Tom Graedel, Neil Hawkins, Anna Hemingway, Timothy Lavin, Amye Kenall, Tricia Lontz, Lauren McLane, Barbara Mindell, Kourtney Myers, Bob Power, Dawn Shiang, Jim Strock, and Mary Ellen Ternes. My wife, Kathy Yorkievitz, has been a constant source of support and useful advice. Finally, as always, the contributing authors to this book are its greatest strength, and they have my deepest gratitude.

Biographies of Authors

John C. Dernbach is Distinguished Professor of Law at Widener University in Harrisburg, Pennsylvania, and codirector of Widener's Environmental Law Center. He leads the only project in the United States that comprehensively assesses American sustainability efforts and makes recommendations for future efforts. As part of that project, he previously edited *Agenda for a Sustainable America* (Environmental Law Institute 2009) and *Stumbling Toward Sustainability* (Environmental Law Institute 2002). His scholarship focuses on environmental law, climate change, sustainable development, and legal writing. Professor Dernbach has written more than 40 articles for law reviews and peer-reviewed journals, and has authored, coauthored, or contributed chapters to 14 books. He was a member of the committee that wrote the 2011 National Research Council report, *Sustainability and the U.S. EPA*. Before taking his teaching position at Widener, Professor Dernbach worked in a variety of positions at the Pennsylvania Department of Environmental Protection, and served most recently as that agency's policy director.

* * * * *

Robert Adler is the associate dean for academic affairs and James I. Farr Chair in Law at the University of Utah S.J. Quinney College of Law. Prior to entering academia, he practiced environmental law for 15 years. His most recent books are *Restoring Colorado River Ecosystems: A Troubled Sense of Immensity* and, with David Driesen, *Environmental Law: A Conceptual and Pragmatic Approach*.

Rachel Armstrong is a member of the Class of 2012 at the University of Denver Sturm College of Law. She holds a B.S. from the University of Wisconsin Madison in both wildlife ecology and biological aspects of conservation. She founded and directs Farm Commons, a nonprofit legal services organization that provides sustainable farmers with the resources to become the stable, resilient base of a healthy food system.

Jennifer Baka is completing her Ph.D. at the Yale School of Forestry and Environmental Studies. She holds a master's degree in public policy from the Goldman School of Public Policy at the University of California Berkeley.

Athena Ballesteros is manager of the International Financial Flows and Environment Project at the World Resources Institute. She has been working on national and international climate policy with a particular focus on climate finance, sustainable energy, and reform of international financial institutions for more than 10 years. Since 1997, she has been one of the technical and policy advisors to the Philippine negotiating team at the U.N. Framework Convention on Climate Change (UNFCCC) negotiations. She is one of the founding members of the Asian NGO Forum on the Asian Development Bank (ADB), which has grown to a coalition of over 200 organizations working on ADB reform.

Gary D. Bass is the executive director of the Bauman Foundation and an affiliated professor at Georgetown University's Public Policy Institute, where he teaches about advocacy and social change. For 28 years, he ran OMB Watch, an organization that addresses government accountability and citizen participation. He serves on numerous nonprofit boards and advisory committees, and has received numerous awards, including recognition as one of the *NonProfit Times* Power and Influence Top 50 for more than 10 years, induction in 2006 into the National Freedom of Information Hall of Fame, and selection as one of the 2007 Federal 100, which recognizes those who had the greatest impact on the government information-systems community. In 1989, Dr. Bass started RTK NET (www.rtknet.org), a searchable website providing information about toxic chemicals released into our communities.

Donald A. Brown is an associate professor in the Environmental Ethics, Science, and Law Program in the Program on Science, Technology, and Society at The Pennsylvania State University. Professor Brown has held a number of senior positions in law and policy for the Pennsylvania and New Jersey environmental protection programs and the U.S. Environmental Protection Agency. During the Clinton Administration, He was the program manager for United Nations organizations at EPA's Office of International Environmental Policy. In this position, he represented EPA in U.S. delegations to the United Nations during negotiations on climate change, biodiversity, and sustainable development. Professor Brown's latest book is *American Heat: Ethical Problems With the United States' Response to Global Warming*. Professor Brown has written over 80 books, book chapters, and articles on the ethical dimensions of climate change.

Carl Bruch is a senior attorney at the Environmental Law Institute, where he codirects ELI's international programs. He has worked on public participation, compliance and enforcement, and environmental governance in the United States and internationally.

Wynn Calder is director of the Association of University Leaders for a Sustainable Future (ULSF) and principal of Sustainable Schools, LLC. ULSF conducts research on sustainability in higher education and serves as secretariat for signatories of the Talloires Declaration (1990). Sustainable Schools consults with colleges, universities, and K-12 schools to build environmental sustainability into strategic planning, teaching, and institutional practice. Mr. Calder has spoken widely on sustainable operations and sustainability in the curriculum, consults on strategies to green campuses, and conducts campus sustainability assessments. He is review editor for the *Journal of Education for Sustainable Development*, news editor for the *International Journal of Sustainability in Higher Education*, and has written extensively on education for sustainability. He is a cofounder of the U.S. Partnership for Education for Sustainable Development. Mr. Calder also serves on the senior council of the Association for the Advancement of Sustainability in Higher Education and on the advisory council of the Cloud Institute for Sustainability Education.

Federico Cheever is director of the Environmental and Natural Resources Law Program and professor of law at the University of Denver Sturm College of Law. Professor Cheever is also chair of the Sustainability Council for the University of Denver. He began teaching at the Sturm College of Law in 1993, specializing in environmental law, wildlife law, public land law, land conservation transactions, and property. Professor Cheever writes extensively about the Endangered Species Act, federal public land law, and land conservation transactions. He coauthored a natural resources casebook, *Natural Resources Law: A Place-Based Book of Problems and Cases*, with Christine Klein and Bret Birdsong. Over the years, Professor Cheever has represented environmental groups in cases under the Endangered Species Act, the National Forest Management Act, the National Environmental Policy Act, the Wilderness Act, and a number of other environmental laws.

Marian R. Chertow is a professor of industrial environmental management at the Yale School of Forestry and Environmental Studies. Her research and teaching focus on industrial ecology, business/environment issues, waste management, and environmental technology innovation. Prior to joining Yale, Professor Chertow spent 10 years in the environmental business and in state and local government, including service as president of a large state bonding authority charged with developing a billion-dollar waste infrastructure system. She led Yale's Environmental Reform: The Next Generation Project for four years and edited a book on the future of environmental policy with Prof. Daniel Esty. She also holds appointments at the Yale School of Management and the National University of Singapore, and serves on the National Advisory Council for Environmental Policy and Technology (NACEPT), which advises EPA.

Jaimie P. Cloud is the founder and president of the Cloud Institute for Sustainability Education in New York City. The Cloud Institute is dedicated to the vital role of education in creating awareness, fostering commitment, and guiding actions toward a healthy, secure, and sustainable future. Ms. Cloud has written several book

chapters and articles, teaches extensively, and writes and facilitates the development of numerous instructional units and programs that are designed to teach core
courses across the disciplines through the lens of sustainability. She is a member
of the advisory committee of the Buckminster Fuller Institute, the international
advisory committee for the Tbilisi+30 Conference, the co-chair of the Commission
on Education for Sustainability of the North American Association for Environmental Education, and a member of the advisory committee of Greenopolis and
the Sustainability Education Planning Committee for the National Association of
Independent Schools.

Ilona Coyle is a consultant and visiting attorney at the Environmental Law Institute.

Robin Kundis Craig is professor of law at the University of Utah S.J. Quinney
College of Law, where she is associated with the Wallace Stegner Center for Land,
Resources, and Environment. She specializes in all things water—the Clean Water
Act, water law, ocean and coastal law, the intersection of fresh and salt water
regulation, marine protected areas, the public trust doctrine, and climate change
and water resources. Professor Craig is the author or co-author of five books,
including *The Clean Water Act and the Constitution* (Envt'l Law Inst., 2d ed. 2009)
and *Environmental Law in Context*, and over 50 book chapters and law review
articles. She served on three successive National Research Council Committees
on the Clean Water Act and the Mississippi River and is currently a member of
the Executive Council of the American Bar Association's Section on Environment,
Energy, and Resources.

Julian Dautremont-Smith is an expert on sustainability in higher education. He
co-founded the Association for the Advancement of Sustainability in Higher Education (AASHE) and served as the organization's associate director from 2004 to
2009. In that capacity, he played leadership roles in creating the American College
& University Presidents' Climate Commitment and the Sustainability Tracking,
Assessment & Rating System (STARS), a rating system for institutions of higher
education that is in use at almost 300 colleges and universities. As an undergraduate at Lewis & Clark College, he spearheaded a successful effort to make the
college the first in the United States to declare compliance with the greenhouse
gas emissions reductions stipulated in the Kyoto Protocol. Mr. Dautremont-Smith
has been a Fulbright Scholar, Harry S. Truman Scholar, Doris Duke Conservation
Fellow, National Wildlife Federation Campus Ecology Fellow, and *USA Today*
Academic All-Star.

Michael DiRamio is program director for sustainable communities at the Corporation for a Skilled Workforce (CSW) in Ann Arbor, Michigan. He leads CSW's
research and development of strategies to integrate community-based job creation,
entrepreneurship, and strategies for human capital development and to accelerate

the adoption of a sustainability mindset and triple-bottom-line business policies by businesses and communities. Mr. DiRamio is working with partners in Detroit to create jobs for city residents, grow sustainable innovation-driven industries, and involve a broader community in policy decisionmaking processes, and was a strategic advisor to the state of Michigan on implementation of its signature Green Jobs Initiative. At the national level, he works with the National Governor's Association to provide technical assistance to green jobs partnership and training grantees of the U.S. Department of Labor. He has contributed to international award-winning books and articles. He serves on several national and regional steering committees focused on promoting sustainability in economic development, education, and workforce development. Mr. DiRamio also teaches sustainability science and technology at Oakland Community College.

Catherine Easton is a project coordinator for the Institutions and Governance Program at the World Resources Institute. Her publications include "Summary of Developed Country 'Fast-Start' Climate Finance Pledges," available on WRI's website, and "The Conservation Campaign Guide," available on the Conservation Campaign's website.

Anne Ehrlich is the policy coordinator for the Center for Conservation Biology at Stanford University. She has carried out research and coauthored many technical articles in population biology and has written extensively on population control, environmental protection, and the environmental consequences of nuclear war. Ms. Ehrlich served as one of seven outside consultants to the White House Council on Environmental Quality's *Global 2000 Report*, and has served on the boards of directors of The Sierra Club; Friends of the Earth; The Ploughshares Fund; and the Pacific Institute for Studies in Development, Environment, and Security. She is a member of the American Academy of Arts and Sciences and has been awarded several prizes for environmental achievement. Her most recent book is *The Dominant Animal: Human Evolution and the Environment* (2008), coauthored with Paul Ehrlich.

Joel B. Eisen is a professor at the University of Richmond School of Law, where he teaches environmental law, energy law, and climate change law. He also teaches a course on environmental law and policy to undergraduate students in the University of Richmond's Environmental Studies Program. Professor Eisen has published extensively in law periodicals on renewable energy, China's environmental and energy laws, and brownfields redevelopment. He is a coauthor of *Energy, Economics and the Environment*, the 2010 edition of which has been adopted in over 40 energy law and policy courses. In 2009, Professor Eisen was a Fulbright professor of law at the China University of Political Science and Law in Beijing.

Jonathan Barry Forman is the Alfred P. Murrah Professor of Law at the University of Oklahoma. Professor Forman is active in the American Bar Association, the Association of American Law Professors, and the National Academy of Social Insurance. Professor Forman has also lectured around the world, testified before Congress, and served on numerous federal and state advisory committees. He has more than 250 publications, including *Making America Work*. In addition to his many scholarly publications, Professor Forman has published articles and op-eds in numerous newspapers and magazines. Prior to entering academia, he served in all three branches of the federal government, most recently as tax counsel to the late Sen. Daniel Patrick Moynihan of New York.

Lynn Goldman is the dean of the School of Public Health and Public Health Services at George Washington University. She was previously a pediatrician and professor of environmental health sciences at Johns Hopkins Bloomberg School of Public Health, where she specialized in environmental risks to children. Prior to joining Hopkins, she was the chief of the Division of Environmental and Occupational Disease Control at the California Department of Health Services, and the assistant administrator of the Office of Prevention, Pesticides, and Toxic Substances at the Environmental Protection Agency. She is a member of the Environmental Defense Fund's board of trustees, acting chair of the Institute of Medicine Roundtable on Environmental Health Sciences, and a member of the National Academy of Sciences Report Review Committee.

Kirk Herbertson is based in Southeast Asia with International Rivers, a California-based organization that monitors the impacts of large hydropower projects. Previously, he worked at the World Resources Institute, where he focused on reform of the World Bank and other international financial institutions.

Dieter T. Hessel is a Presbyterian minister specializing in social ethics who resides in Cape Elizabeth, Maine, where he directs the ecumenical Program on Ecology, Justice, and Faith, and is an adjunct professor at Bangor Theological Seminary. From 1965 to 1990, he was the social education coordinator and social policy director of the Presbyterian Church (USA). His recent books include *Earth Habitat: Eco-Injustice and the Church's Response*; *Christianity and Ecology: Seeking the Well-Being of Earth and Humans*; and *Theology for Earth Community: A Field Guide*.

Keith Hirokawa is an associate professor of law at Albany Law School, where he teaches courses in land use, property, natural resources, and environmental law. His scholarly interests include environmental ethics and policy, ecosystem services, and drivers for local governments in community building. Professor Hirokawa is the author or coauthor of dozens of articles, book chapters, book reviews, and essays on these subjects. Before entering academia, Professor Hirokawa practiced law for eight years in Oregon and Washington.

Leo Horrigan is a food system correspondent for the Johns Hopkins Center for a Livable Future. He is a coauthor of *How Sustainable Agriculture Can Address the Environmental and Human Health Harms of Industrial Agriculture*, an extensive literature review that details problems with industrial agriculture and potential solutions. He also coauthored "Antibiotic Drug Abuse: CAFOs Are Squandering Vital Human Medicines," a chapter in *CAFO: The Tragedy of Industrial Animal Factories*.

Frances Irwin is a policy analyst and writer on issues ranging from public access to information and participation, environmental governance, and environmental policy reform to chemicals and materials policy and people and ecosystems. She has worked with state, national, and international civil society groups, including the Vermont Natural Resources Council, The Conservation Foundation, and the World Wildlife Fund. As a fellow at the World Resources Institute, she most recently coauthored an action agenda and a guide for decisionmakers and coedited a volume of papers on governance of ecosystem services.

Kevin Kennedy is a professor of law at Michigan State University College of Law. Before joining the Michigan State faculty, he practiced law in Hawaii for four years, then served as a law clerk at the U.S. Court of International Trade in New York. After his clerkship he was a trial attorney for the U.S. Department of Justice, where he represented the Department of Commerce and the then-U.S. Customs Service in international trade litigation. In addition to nearly 60 law review articles and book chapters on international law and international trade regulation, Professor Kennedy is the author of *Competition Law and the World Trade Organization* and coauthor, with Raj Bhala, of *World Trade Law*.

John A. Laitner has been involved in the environmental and energy policy arenas for 40 years. He focuses on improving the way we understand and represent energy efficiency technologies and behaviors for use in energy and climate economic policy models. He joined the American Council for an Energy-Efficient Economy in 2006. Prior to that, Mr. Laitner worked for the Environmental Protection Agency as a senior economist for technology policy; in 1998, he was awarded EPA's Gold Medal for his work with a team of EPA economists to evaluate the impact of different strategies for implementing policies to reduce greenhouse gas emissions. In 2003, he received an award from the U.S. Combined Heat and Power Association for contributions to the policy development of that industry. He is the author of more than 280 reports, journal articles, and book chapters.

Jeannine M. La Prad is president and CEO of Corporation for a Skilled Workforce (CSW) in Ann Arbor, Michigan. She is responsible for helping CSW advance its mission of catalyzing transformative change in education, economic, and work-force development through research and action. She was the director of CSW's collaborative project with the Midwestern Governors Association to develop a new energy economy jobs platform. Ms. La Prad advises the Interstate Renewable Energy Council (IREC) on its administration of the Solar Instructor Training Network (SITN) and is a member of the board of directors for Creative Change Educational Solutions, a nonprofit organization focused on sustainability education.

Amy E. Landis is assistant professor of sustainability and green design in the Department of Civil and Environmental Engineering at the University of Pittsburgh. Her research and teaching interests in the arena of sustainable environmental engineering encompass topics such as bio-based production, bio-based and alternative fuels, modeling environmental variability and uncertainty, product end-of-life management, industrial ecology, and life-cycle analysis.

Robert Lawrence, M.D., is the Center for a Livable Future Professor in the Department of Environmental Health Sciences at the Johns Hopkins Bloomberg School of Public Health, with joint appointments as a professor of health policy, international health, and medicine. He is the founding director of the Johns Hopkins Center for a Livable Future, which supports research and develops policies on the public health impacts of industrialized food animal production, improved food security, and healthier diets. He is a member of the Institute of Medicine of the National Academy of Science; a founding director of Physicians for Human Rights; serves on the board of directors of the Albert Schweitzer Fellowship; and is a member of the Global Health Advisory Committee of the Open Society Foundation.

Mark D. Levine leads the China Energy Group at Lawrence Berkeley National Laboratory, a group he created in 1988. From 1996 to 2006, he was director of the Environmental Division, which included 400 people working on energy-efficiency policy analysis and R&D. He is a board member of several leading nonprofits in the United States and is a member of the Energy Advisory Board of Dow Chemical Company, the board of directors of CalCEF, an energy venture capital firm, and the advisory board of the Asian Pacific Energy Research Centre in Tokyo. In 1999, Mr. Levine was elected a fellow of the California Council on Science and Technology. In 2008, he received the Obayashi Prize for his contributions to sustainable urban development. In addition to authoring numerous technical publications, he has led or co-led teams for the Intergovernmental Panel on Climate Change and major energy scenario studies of the United States, China, and the world.

Reid Lifset is resident fellow in industrial ecology and associate director of the Industrial Environmental Management Program at the Yale School of Forestry & Environmental Studies. His research and teaching focus on the emerging field of industrial ecology, the study of the environmental consequences of production and consumption. He is editor-in-chief of the *Journal of Industrial Ecology*, a peer-reviewed journal owned by Yale University and published by Wiley-Blackwell. He serves on the Science Advisory Board of the U.S. EPA and is a member of the governing council of the International Society for Industrial Ecology and the editorial advisory board for the Springer book series Eco-efficiency in Industry & Science.

Roberta Mann is the Frank Nash Professor of Law at the University of Oregon School of Law. She is a tax expert who has written numerous law review articles on how tax policy affects the environment, including several articles on tax policy and climate change. Prior to entering academia, she practiced in the Office of Chief Counsel of the Internal Revenue Service and served on the staff of the Joint Committee on Taxation.

Brian McNamara is a member of the Class of 2010 at the Chicago-Kent College of Law. He holds a B.A. from Bradley University.

Joel A. Mintz is a professor of law at Nova Southeastern University Law Center, a member of the American Law Institute, a fellow of the American Bar Foundation, and a member scholar of The Center for Progressive Reform. His scholarly interests include environmental enforcement, hazardous waste regulation, and state and local government finance. Professor Mintz is the author or coauthor of eight books and numerous articles, book chapters, book reviews, essays, and op-ed pieces. Before entering academia, he was an attorney and chief attorney with the U.S. Environmental Protection Agency. He is a recipient of Nova University's President's Faculty Scholarship Award, EPA's Special Service Award, and the EPA Bronze Medal for Commendable Service.

Craig Oren is a professor of law at Rutgers University School of Law-Camden. He is a nationally known expert on the Clean Air Act and has written extensively about it. He has also served on three different National Academy of Sciences committees on clean air issues. Before becoming an academic, he was assistant counsel for the U.S. House of Representatives subcommittee with legislative jurisdiction over the Clean Air Act.

Brad Parks is co-executive director of AidData and Research Faculty at the College of William and Mary's Institute for the Theory and Practice of International Relations. He is also a Visiting Research Associate at the Center for Global Development. He is currently a Ph.D. candidate at the London School of Economics and has written and contributed to several books and articles on aid allocation, aid effectiveness, and development theory and practice. Most recently, he coauthored *Greening Aid? Understanding the Environmental Impact of Development Assistance* with Michael Tierney, J. Timmons Roberts, and Robert Hicks. He is also the coauthor, with J. Timmons Roberts, of *A Climate of Injustice: Global Inequality, North-South Politics, and Climate Policy*.

Trip Pollard is a senior attorney with the Southern Environmental Law Center (SELC). He is the director of SELC's Land and Community Program, which uses public education, policy reform, and legal advocacy to promote smarter growth and sustainable transportation. Mr. Pollard is involved in shaping policies and decisions throughout the Southeast. He also has written dozens of reports and articles on transportation, land use, energy, and environmental issues. He has lectured widely, and he has served on numerous governmental commissions, advisory bodies, and the boards of many organizations.

David Rejeski directs the Science and Technology Innovation Program (STIP) at the Woodrow Wilson International Center for Scholars. STIP explores the scientific and technological frontier, stimulating discovery and bringing new tools to bear on public policy challenges that emerge as science advances. Between 1994 and 2000, he worked at the White House Council on Environmental Quality and the Office of Science and Technology on a variety of technology, R&D, and policy initiatives, including the development and implementation of the National Environmental Technology Strategy, the Greening of the White House, and the Education for Sustainability Initiative. He sits on the advisory boards of a number of organizations, including the Board on Global Science and Technology of the National Academy of Sciences and the National Science Foundation's Advisory Committee on Environmental Research and Education.

Edward P. Richards is the Clarence W. Edwards Professor of Law at the Louisiana State University Law Center, and the director of the Program in Law, Science, and Public Health. Professor Richards works in health and public health law, and since 2001, he has worked on law and policy related to national security and disaster response. He is currently researching the impact of ocean rise and climate change on coastal disaster risks. He has worked on projects with the Centers for Disease Control and Prevention, the Department of Justice, the Department of Homeland Security, and several state health departments.

J. Timmons Roberts is director of the Center for Environmental Studies and professor of sociology and environmental studies at Brown University. The coauthor or editor of eight books and over 60 articles and book chapters, his current research focuses on climate change and international development. As a cofounder of Aid-Data.org, he is part of an international effort to increase transparency in climate finance, and foreign aid more broadly. His Climate and Development Lab at Brown provides research support to the Least Developed Countries Group (the world's 49 poorest nations) in U.N. negotiations. He is a leader in Rhode Island's efforts to plan for adapting to climate changes, serving on the Rhode Island Climate Change Commission, created in 2010 by legislation written by him and his Brown students. Most recently, he was appointed to the Board on Environmental Change and Society of the National Academy of Sciences.

K.W. James Rochow is president of the Trust for Lead Poisoning Prevention and an environmental law and policy consultant based in Washington, D.C. He has helped orchestrate the global phaseout of leaded gasoline and initiate integrated approaches to toxics pollution and environmental health. Most recently, Mr. Rochow has worked on reform of the natural resource sector and reconstruction of failed states in West Africa for the World Bank, the U.N. Development Program, and the Government of Liberia. He has also taught international environmental law and policy at numerous universities in the United States and abroad, most recently at the University of Pennsylvania Law School.

Patricia E. Salkin is the Raymond and Ella Smith Distinguished Professor of Law, associate dean, and director of the Government Law Center at Albany Law School. She teaches courses in land use law, Chinese law, current legal issues in government, and government ethics. She is also on the adjunct faculty at the University at Albany's Department of Geography and Planning, where she teaches planning ethics. Dean Salkin is a past chair of the American Bar Association's State & Local Government Law Section and the Municipal Law Section of the New York State Bar Association, where she is also a founding member and past-chair of the State Bar's Standing Committee on Attorneys in Public Service. She serves as chair of the Amicus Curiae Committee for the American Planning Association and is an appointed member of EPA's National Environmental Justice Advisory Council. She is a coauthor, with John R. Nolon, of *Climate Change and Sustainable Development Law in a Nutshell*, as well as dozens of books, articles, and book chapters on land use and sustainable development.

Jim Salzman holds joint appointments at Duke University as the Samuel Fox Mordecai Professor of Law and as the Nicholas Institute Professor of Environmental Policy. In more than 50 articles and five books, his scholarship has addressed topics spanning trade and environment conflicts, the history of drinking water, environmental protection in the service economy, wetlands mitigation banking, and the legal and institutional issues in creating markets for ecosystem services. Elected a Fellow of the Royal Geographical Society, he has delivered lectures on environmental law and policy on every continent except Antarctica, and has been a visiting professor at Yale, Harvard, and Stanford, as well as at Macquarie (Australia), Lund (Sweden), and Tel Aviv (Israel) Universities.

Brent Steel is professor and director of the Public Policy Graduate Program in the School of Public Policy at Oregon State University. He is coeditor of *Oregon Politics and Government: Progressive Versus Conservative Populists* with Richard Clucas and Mark Henkels, and is coauthor of *State and Local Government: Sustainability in the 21st Century* with Chris Simon and Nicholas P. Lovrich.

Kurt Strasser is the Phillip I. Blumberg Professor of Law at the University of Connecticut Law School, where he teaches environmental law, natural resources law, and contracts. His scholarly writing is primarily concerned with the law of corporate groups and with environmental law and policy. Professor Strasser coauthored the second edition of *Blumberg on Corporate Groups* with Philip I. Blumberg, Nicholas L. Georgakopoulas, and Eric J. Gouvin. He has recently published *Myths and Realities of Business Environmentalism: Good Works, Good Business or Greenwash?* As well as his teaching at the University of Connecticut Law School, he served as associate dean for academic affairs from 1996 to 1999 and as interim dean for the academic year 2006-2007. He has twice been a visiting professor at Exeter University in England, served as the DAAD Guest Professor of Anglo-American Law at the Free University of Berlin in the summer of 2003, and was the Gilhuis Professor on the Future of Environmental Law at Tilburg University in the Netherlands during the spring of 2008.

Susanna Sutherland is the first sustainability program manager for the city of Knoxville, Tennessee, where she has been charged with using more than $2 million in funding from the U.S. Department of Energy to design and implement a program that balances economic, social, and environmental considerations into city operations and community growth. She also co-chairs a nine-state southeastern city sustainability network. Sutherland was a member of the committee that wrote the 2011 National Research Council report *Sustainability and the U.S. EPA.*

Dan Tarlock is Distinguished Professor of Law at the Chicago-Kent College of Law and honorary professor of law at the UNESCO Centre for Water Law, Policy, and Science at the University of Dundee, Scotland. He teaches land use, property, energy and natural resource law, and international environmental law. He has published a treatise about water rights and resources, coauthored four textbooks on related subjects, and recently coauthored, with Holly Doremus, *Water War in the Klamath Basin: Macho Law, Combat Biology, and Dirty Politics.* His current research focuses on the legal aspects of domestic and international aquatic bio-diversity protection and drought management. Professor Tarlock is one of three U.S. special legal advisors to the North American Free Trade Agreement, and is a frequent consultant to local, state, federal, and international agencies. He was the chair of a National Academy of Sciences/National Research Council committee to study water management in the western United States, and was the principal drafter of the Western Water Policy Advisory Review Commission report.

Michael J. Tierney is the Mary and George Hylton Associate Professor of Government and International Relations at the College of William and Mary, where he also directs the International Relations Program. He has published two books: *Delegation and Agency in International Organizations* and *Greening Aid? Understanding the Environmental Impact of Development Assistance.* He is a principal investigator on the AidData research project, which maintains the most comprehensive data set in the world on development finance projects. He has published articles in a range of journals including *International Organization, International Studies Quarterly, Review of International Political Economy, Foreign Policy*, and *World Development*.

Jonathan Weiss is Director of Sustainability at ManTech International Corporation, a global consulting firm based in Fairfax, Virginia, where he advises clients on emerging sustainability issues. His work focuses on developing cutting-edge policy initiatives and collaborative partnerships on such issues as climate change, renewable energy, and sustainable land use. Weiss has lectured in more than a dozen countries on sustainability, and has been published widely. His chapter in the book, *Agenda for a Sustainable America*, was recognized by the Environmental Law Institute as one of the top writings in the environmental field. He formerly held positions in the Clinton Administration, at the White House, and the U.S. Environmental Protection Agency.

Christopher Williams is a researcher at the Lawrence Berkeley National Laboratory's China Energy Group, where he concentrates on municipal and building-level energy efficiency programs.

Introduction

This book is about how to seize the opportunities that sustainability presents and how to minimize the risks of the environmental challenges that confront us. It is, in other words, about making environmentally sustainable development happen in the United States as rapidly as possible and on the broadest scale. On most issues, we already have a pretty good idea of *what* to do.[1] This book focuses instead on *how* to achieve sustainability. It provides a broad conceptual framework for fostering sustainability in all aspects of American life.

Over the past several decades, we have made some progress toward sustainability but have also encountered major obstacles. This book teases out those patterns that account for the progress, albeit modest, that we have made to date. Similarly, it describes the obstacles to sustainability. The book then outlines an approach for accelerating progress and overcoming obstacles.

While this book is about the environment, it is also about a great deal more. It is about the kind of community, nation, and world in which we wish to live. It is about how to maintain and improve our quality of life, protect our freedom, and create opportunity. And it is about our children and grandchildren and all those who will live here after we are gone.

Sustainable development—or sustainability for short—will make the United States more livable, healthy, secure, and prosperous. Policies that promote sustainability will reduce risks to our national security, improve our economic efficiency and productivity, enhance our health and communities, improve the lives of the poorest among us, and foster greater human well-being. Sustainability can provide these multiple benefits while protecting and restoring the environment for our generation and for generations that follow.

This book is premised on a fact that we have known for a long time, and which we ignore at our peril. The National Research Council opened its recent report on sustainability at the U.S. Environmental Protection Agency this way:

> Everything that humans require for their survival and well-being depends, directly or indirectly, on the natural environment. The environment provides the air we breathe, the water we drink, and the food we eat. It defines in fundamental ways the communities in which we live and is the source for renewable and nonrenewable resources on which civilization depends. Our health and well-being, our economy, and our security all require a high quality environment.[2]

Americans tend to trace such thoughts back to great conservationists, including George Perkins Marsh, John Muir, Aldo Leopold, and Theodore Roosevelt. But they actually go back further, to the founding of the nation. Our first four presidents—George Washington, John Adams, Thomas Jefferson, and James Madison—owned farms or plantations. They differed in many ways (three were slaveholders, and one, Adams, was not), yet all were convinced that the health of the soil is essential to the health of the nation.[3] After James Madison's presidency, he was elected as first president of the Agriculture Society of Albemarle, Virginia. In 1818, he gave an address to the society in which he explained that preservation of adjoining forests and woodlands, use of manure as fertilizer, horizontal plowing on hill sides, and other conservation techniques were all essential to ensuring soil fertility. Failure to do these things, he emphasized, meant degraded soil, low yield, and a weaker nation. The "happiness of our country," he added, depends not just on its "soil and climate" and its "uncrowded situation" but also on actions that maintain and enhance soil fertility.[4]

It was just such thinking—applied to a broader set of problems—that motivated the United States and other countries at the 1992 U.N. Conference on Environment and Development (known widely as the Earth Summit) in Rio. The twin problems addressed at the Earth Summit were high levels of global poverty and increasing environmental degradation. It was widely recognized that each problem helped to make the other worse; environmental degradation makes it hard for people to stay healthy and earn a living, and poverty deprives individuals of the time and resources needed to protect the environment.

Twenty years later, these problems are no less pressing. Our actions as a species and as a nation are not sustainable. The situation we face at the global level is both simple and daunting: humans are making greater demands for natural resources and causing widespread environmental degradation on a planet with a finite capacity to meet those demands or absorb their effects. In addition, some people have access to abundant resources at an affordable price, and some do not. Sadly, many conditions, including climate change, are now worse than they were two decades ago.

At Rio the countries of the world, including the United States, under the far-sighted leadership of President George H.W. Bush, endorsed a broad and ambitious plan to move toward sustainability (Agenda 21)[5] and a set of principles to guide the effort (Rio Declaration).[6] The United States endorsed this plan and these principles because, to a great degree, they were based on longstanding U.S. laws and policies. Indeed, sustainability is anchored in conservation concepts that have been employed in the United States for more than a century to preserve forests, soil, fish, and game.

Sustainability Is . . . .

We use the terms "sustainability" and "sustainable development" more now than we did two decades ago. Still, it is far from clear that most of us understand what sustainability and sustainable development mean. For many, perhaps most, these are just vague words in the "green" vocabulary. For more than a few others, sustainability means something negative, like tree hugging. Yet sustainability is distinctive—and positive—in at least seven ways.

First, sustainability provides a framework for humans to live and prosper in harmony with nature rather than, as we have tended to do for centuries, at nature's expense. It is about finding ways to make our goals for environmental protection, economic growth, peace and security, and social well-being mutually reinforcing—rather than treating environmental degradation as the necessary price of progress. It is about quality of life and well-being. Although the terms *sustainability* and *sustainable development* were first used in an environmental context, they are not about the environment alone or the environment before everything else. The Venn diagram in Figure 1 is a common way of expressing the nexus of environmental, social, and economic goals. These are sometimes also called the three pillars of sustainability. Corporate sustainability efforts are often described in terms of a triple bottom line of, for example, "profit, people, and planet."[7]

The three pillars and triple bottom line are used so often that a fourth dimension—peace and security—is often omitted. Yet most activities are difficult or impossible in the absence of peace and security. As the Rio Declaration states, "Peace, development and environmental protection are interdependent and indivisible."[8] Some sustainability issues more obviously involve security than others. The use of petroleum for transportation, for instance, involves foreign oil supplies, and thus has national security implications. In this book, we discuss security when it is appropriate to do so, but more often we refer to three goals or the triple bottom line.

Figure 1
Sustainability and Three Circles

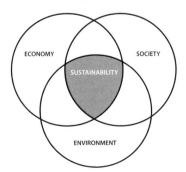

As Figure 1 suggests, the object of sustainability is to maximize the positive contribution of human activities to the environment, the economy, and society at the same time. The reuse and recycling of materials provides an example. If we buy things and then throw them out, we contribute to economic growth and job creation but the environmental impact is negative. If nearly everything is recycled or reused, on the other hand, we not only contribute to economic growth but also create more jobs than if materials were simply landfilled, save energy used to make and refine those materials that would otherwise be lost, and have almost no negative environmental impact. If we mined existing disposal facilities for metal and other materials, and converted the land to park or other use, we would have a positive environmental impact. Sustainability is not just about minimizing environmental damage; it is also about the restoration of environmental quality.

Sustainability is thus about *integrating* environmental protection and restoration into economic, social, and national security decisions and goals. If the risks of environmental degradation are accounted for, sustainability will be more efficient and less costly than making a development decision first and then figuring out what to do about the environment afterward, or addressing the environment as a costly add-on to a development project or manufacturing process. In principle, a dollar spent on sustainability will yield more benefits—and a greater variety of benefits—than a dollar spent only on economic development or the environment. In fact, sustainability is consistent with the fiscal discipline that current economic circumstances require. And for energy efficiency and conservation in particular, sustainability can, and usually does, also mean lower economic costs.

Second, sustainability focuses on both the short-term and long-term effects of decisions. The most widely accepted definition of sustainable development— "development that meets the needs of the present without compromising the ability of future generations to meet their own needs"[9]—captures this point precisely. It is reinforced by one of the principles in the Rio Declaration—intergenerational equity. It is also consistent with much American political rhetoric that focuses on protecting the interests of our children and grandchildren. Sustainability is inconsistent with decisions that lead to long-term debts or problems that can only be resolved, if at all, by future generations—such as the federal budget deficit, climate change, overpopulation, depletion of resources, destruction of biodiversity, and the global accumulation of toxic materials.

Third, sustainability is about exercising precaution and making commonsense decisions in the face of known or likely risks. Sustainable development is not based on what we want to believe or not believe; it is anchored in reality and risk. Because sustainability is premised in part on avoiding or limiting risks, it does not require complete certainty before we act. That is how we ordinarily behave, and we should treat risks related to sustainability in the same way.

Fourth, sustainability is also a moral, ethical, and even a religious issue, not just a matter of policy or law. Environmental quality and the availability of natural resources directly affect human well-being; environmental damage hurts individuals, forcing them to breathe unhealthy air, drink filthy water, or ingest toxic chemicals. Environmental degradation also damages the vast ecological commons on which life depends. To address this problem, the Rio Declaration mirrors a basic principle of U.S. environmental law, stating that "the polluter should, in principle, bear the cost of pollution," rather than imposing that cost on others or the environment.[10] For those who recognize the existence of God, or another deity or force larger than themselves, environmental degradation also can be an offense against God, creation, or the natural order.

Fifth, sustainability is not directed just to government or industry, but to all parts of society, all ages, and all economic sectors. The Rio Declaration identifies public participation, access to information, and access to justice—key principles of American governance—as essential to sustainability.[11] It is also directed to individuals, not simply as participants in the development of government policy but also as consumers and users of goods and services. The problems are so large, and the opportunities so many, that virtually every individual, organization, institution, corporation, and government needs to contribute to a more-sustainable world.

Sixth, sustainability requires considerable innovation in all spheres of public and private life. Many of the legal, policy, and other tools we need to achieve sustainability do not yet exist, are only now being attempted, or have only been tried for a short time. Sustainability is an effort to change the environmental habits, scripts, and patterns that have dominated the American landscape over the past several decades, and even longer. Day after day, at home, at work, and in school, most of us act in many ways that are not environmentally sustainable. We will need to change those habits, either through the use of new technologies, new options for doing things, new or different infrastructure, new or modified laws, or changes in personal habits.

Seventh, sustainability's objectives are human freedom, opportunity, and quality of life in a world in which the environment is protected and restored and in which natural resources are readily available. The objectives of sustainable development are in many ways the same as those of conventional development. It is easy to forget that sustainable development is, after all, a form of development. In *Our Common Future*, a landmark report on sustainable development, the World Commission on Environment and Development stated: "The satisfaction of human needs and aspirations is the major objective of development."[12] International lawyer Rumu Sarkar explains that, "for most practitioners and theorists, the overall objectives of alleviating poverty and human suffering and of improving the human condition more generally are the desired end product of the development process."[13] She adds that, "development aims at enlarging the opportunities people have in their lives."[14] Amartya Sen, a professor of economics and philosophy at Harvard who has won the Nobel Prize in economics, describes development as a process that enlarges individual freedom.[15]

Sustainability Is Not . . .

To be clear about what sustainability *is*, we also need to make clear what sustainability is *not*. This is particularly important because many people believe that sustainability does not fit into their own view of the world or personal values and aspirations. As John Maynard Keynes once said, "the difficulty lies not with the new ideas, but in escaping from the old ones."

Sustainability is not about less freedom and opportunity. In fact, it is about providing people choices they do not now have. In the broadest sense it includes the opportunity to enjoy a high quality of life regardless of income, without interference from environmental pollutants or climate change. On a more mundane level it includes the freedom to purchase affordably priced vehicles that obtain high gas mileage and the opportunity to get to school or work conveniently by walking, biking, or using mass transit. Or the ability to buy locally grown fruits and vegetables conveniently and for an affordable and fair price.

Sustainability is not about bigger government. While government needs to steer society in particular directions, sustainability cannot be accomplished by government or regulation alone. Government needs to repeal or modify laws that inhibit progress toward sustainability, and not simply adopt new laws. And while regulation has a role to play, sustainability is primarily about unleashing the creative energies of individuals, families, entrepreneurs, businesses, nongovernmental organizations, colleges and universities, and many others to make a contribution toward our collective present and future well-being.

Sustainability is not about mindless implementation of an international plan. As Agenda 21 made clear, sustainable development needs to be realized in the particular economic, natural, and historical settings of each country. The United States will not embrace sustainability because we agreed to it at an international conference or because we care about the environment. We will move toward sustainability only if it is more beneficial to us than conventional development. We will move toward sustainability only if—and then because—it makes both us and our descendants better off.

Sustainable development is not about economic development or economic growth for its own sake. Sustainability is also not the same thing as sustained economic growth, although sustainability and sustained economic growth can certainly occur at the same time. The ultimate objectives, again, involve human well-being and environmental quality. Economic development and economic growth are means to that end, but they are not ends in themselves. On the other hand, as already suggested, sustainable development does not mean a lower standard of living.

A Destination or a Journey?

Is sustainability a destination, or is it a journey? In a sense, it is both. Its goal is a society in which the ordinary effects of human activity protect and restore the environment and minimize or eliminate large-scale poverty. That is plainly not the world we have today, and in that sense sustainability is a destination. To reach this destination, however, we must embark upon a long journey, one that is likely to take more than a generation.[16] While it is appropriate to focus our efforts on the journey, we should nonetheless not lose sight of the destination.

The destination-versus-journey question goes to the heart of what sustainability means. In a world where a great many of our activities cause some environmental damage, actions that merely reduce our negative environmental impacts are better—and could be labeled as steps toward sustainability. By themselves, however, those steps may not represent true sustainability. To make that distinction clear, this book uses the term "more-sustainable" to describe an alternative that is better than business as usual, but not necessarily "sustainable." A building that uses 25% less energy is a more-sustainable building, for example, but not the same as a "net zero energy" building or a building that uses renewable energy to produce more power than it uses.

In a fully sustainable society, the ordinary effect of human behavior will be to protect and restore the environment. We know that human societies will never be fixed and unchanging, but we hope to reach a point where changes within human society will always occur within the boundaries of sustainability.

However, words like "journey" and "destination" mask a hard fact about sustainability that is more challenging. If the destination were a fixed point, any progress we made toward sustainability would put us closer to the target. But sustainability is not a fixed target because it is constantly moving—or, worse, in many respects we are actually moving *away* from the target. Continuing and growing damage to the environment increases the distance between where we are and the goal of a sustainable society. To reach the destination, we need to first slow down the rate at which things are getting worse, then start making things better. When the destination is moving away from us even as we make progress toward it, it is possible to be farther away after we have started than before we began.

On issues where unsustainable activities continue to accelerate—and climate change is the most important example—there is a discrete and real risk that we will never catch up. Positive feedback loops for greenhouse gas emissions (for example, warming in the Arctic leading to large methane releases, which create more warming and more methane releases) could cause climate change to accelerate even more rapidly. At some point, climate change *could* outpace human mitigation efforts even if human societies around the world are doing everything they can to reduce their emissions.

That is the real challenge of progress toward sustainability: to make sustainability happen on a scale large enough, and at a pace fast enough, to overtake the rate at which things are getting worse. When we describe progress in this book, we are describing it in this context.

Sustainability Embodies American Values

The goals of sustainable development—human freedom, opportunity, and quality of life—are quintessential American goals. The American colonies sought independence for these purposes, and the new nation established a legal and economic system premised on their importance, endured a civil war to protect that system and expand its opportunities to others, and fought two world wars and numerous other conflicts to protect us and help make those same opportunities available to others. At Memorial Day ceremonies throughout the United States, veterans almost inevitably talk about preservation of freedom as a key reason they were proud to serve our country. In the decades ahead, with a growing global population and economy, and growing demands on our environment, sustainability can provide a foundation on which to base continued freedom, opportunity, and quality of life.

Sustainable development would lead to a stronger and more efficient America because we would be pursuing social, economic, environmental, and security goals in ways that are mutually reinforcing or supportive, not contradictory or antagonistic. The result would be a stronger, more efficient country that provides its citizens and their descendants increasingly more opportunities in a quality natural environment. In his 1818 address to the Agriculture Society of Albemarle, Virginia, James Madison described enhancement of soil fertility as a patriotic act. During World War II, the American public was encouraged to save energy and to recycle metal and rubber, so that these resources would be available for the war effort. In recent decades, Congress has adopted legislation to limit dependence on foreign oil and thus protect national security.

Sustainable development would also lead to a safer, more stable and secure world outside American borders. The world is deeply divided between the wealthy and the desperately poor, and there is a real risk of evolving toward an unstable world of haves and have-nots, with a huge global underclass. Such a world would pose serious threats to our security. None of the goals that this country has pursued around the world—peace and stability, human rights and democracy, expansion of trade and markets, environmental protection, or putting an end to hunger and extreme deprivation—can be accomplished if the world is not on a path of sustainable development. We can be quite sure that unsustainable development will lead to a world with less freedom, fewer opportunities, and lower quality of life.

The ethical and religious concerns that characterize the sustainability movement are also quintessentially American. The country's history is full of circumstances that combined national self-interest with doing the right thing. The Civil War did not simply preserve the Union; it also ended slavery. We created the national parks because of pride in our natural heritage and also for the public's benefit. We led the effort to create the United Nations to make both our country and the rest of the world more secure. The challenges of sustainability require a response that is similarly motivated. Moreover, the texts and beliefs of each of the world's major religions teach responsibility toward other humans as well as the environment.

Because unsustainable actions adversely affect others, more-sustainable actions are not simply better for us; they reflect our ethical and religious values. Greenhouse gas emissions from the United States, for example, do not adversely affect us alone; they have an even greater impact on developing countries that lack the money and technology to cope with drought, famine, and other effects of climate change. What we do about sustainability, in other words, is not simply a policy question or a question of national self-interest. It is also—and more fundamentally—about who we are, what we value, and how we fulfill our obligations to others.

Finally, sustainable development is not just about us, the current generation of Americans. It is, in the Constitution's words, about "ourselves and our posterity," our children, grandchildren, nieces, nephews—all of those not yet born who will someday inhabit this country. We pride ourselves on providing our descendants greater opportunities and a better quality of life. Sustainable development will do precisely that. Without it, we cannot assure our children and grandchildren a better life, and are likely to leave them a poorer one.

The United States has survived and prospered only because each generation looked after the next. When John Dernbach's maternal grandparents died in the years after World War II, their children had these words put on their gravestone: "They gave their today for our tomorrow." Art and Clara Retzlaff were not reformers or activists; they were hardscrabble people who knew war, poverty, and unemployment first hand, and who worked hard for their children. These words may connote more sacrifice than we are comfortable with today. But there is a bigger problem. We say we care about tomorrow, yet all too often our actions tell a different story. This book's title captures both the dissonance and the challenge: acting as if tomorrow matters.

Looking Back, Looking Forward

The 1992 Earth Summit is both a reasonable and imperfect date for marking a review of U.S. activities on behalf of sustainable development. It is reasonable because the United States made an international commitment to sustainability at the conference, and because that conference represented an endorsement of sustainability by virtually every nation in the world. It is imperfect because, as the following chapters describe, a great many steps toward sustainability in the United States were taken before the Earth Summit, and we need to acknowledge them. Across a broad range of topics—environmental and public health protection; population, consumption, and technology; poverty, unemployment, and social equality; development of the built environment; governance; public education and engagement; and international activity—the United States has made *some* progress in the two decades since the Earth Summit. On balance, however, Part I suggests that the sustainability destination is now farther away than it was in 1992.

Yet there is nonetheless an emerging sustainability movement in the United States. It includes dedicated practitioners in a wide variety of fields who have thought deeply about what sustainability means in different contexts and why it is attractive, and whose day-to-day job is to make it happen, fix what doesn't work, and improve results. They are engaged in a wide variety of fields, including agriculture, energy, manufacturing, technology, community planning and development, business and industry, government, education, building construction, engineering, and law.

They understand that the global economy, population, and environmental degradation are all growing, and that there are huge unmet human needs due to extreme poverty throughout the world. They all see that we have no choice but to make economic development, job creation, environmental protection, and national security work together rather than against each other. And they seek to translate those basic realities into reduced risks and greater opportunities in the work that they do and in the way they live.

Across their many and varying activities, there are three broad patterns. First, they have been supported and encouraged by citizens, consumers, investors, students, parents, and other stakeholders. There is also growing support from a wide variety of corporations and nongovernmental organizations, including the religious and ethical community. Second, more-sustainable decisions have become easier to make because of the growing availability of more-sustainable alternatives, and these alternatives are increasingly attractive. And third, government lawmaking for the past two decades has emphasized economic development on behalf of sustainability—renewable energy and energy efficiency, tax incentives, and a wide range of other laws—and has not been limited to environmental regulation. These patterns are described in Part II.

To be very sure, there are also obstacles to greater progress. It is important to "call out" the forces and circumstances that stand in the way—partly to understand them, partly to recognize that legal and policy recommendations for environmental sustainability won't necessarily happen simply because they are based on good ideas. One set of practical obstacles is the sheer force of existing unsustainable habits—personal, social, organizational, and governmental—that are reinforced by both lack of urgency and uncertainty about what more-sustainable behavior would entail. Another set of obstacles are legal and policy impediments. They include laws and policies that support or encourage unsustainable development, and thus inhibit progress toward sustainability, as well as the lack of a bipartisan consensus about critical environmental issues. Finally, and perhaps most visibly, there are political obstacles—the direct opposition of influential economic interests and the growing economic and political influence of developing countries that are more interested in pursuing conventional development than sustainable development. These obstacles are discussed in Part III.

How do we build on the progress made to date, overcome these obstacles, and thus accelerate the transition to sustainability? Four broad approaches are needed. First, we need better sustainability choices—options that make even greater progress toward sustainability than currently available options, and more options and tools for a greater number and variety of activities. Second, the United States needs to move from an almost exclusive reliance on environmental regulation to a greater variety of legal and policy tools, including economic development, the repeal of laws that foster unsustainable development, and the like. In addition, the United States needs to adopt legislation that directly and fully addresses climate change. Visionary and pragmatic governance for sustainability is a third needed approach—at all levels of government. This kind of governance requires a bipartisan national strategy that can guide the nation's sustainability efforts over a long period, an equally strong commitment to research and development of innovative technology, an intensified focus on public education, and greater public participation in decisionmaking for sustainability.

Finally, and perhaps most fundamentally, to achieve the kind of effort needed to create a sustainable America, we need a national movement that builds on the many local, state, organizational, and sector-specific movements described in this book. The businesses, religious organizations, educational institutions, communities, families, individuals, government agencies, and others who work for sustainability on particular issues in specific places all do so for their own reasons, responding to their particular constituents. The integration of economic, social, environmental, and security goals lends itself to partnerships or coalitions of organizations and individuals that otherwise would not likely work together. For those discouraged by the rancorous state of national politics, this movement—which appears to be growing—provides reason for hope.

These four approaches—more and better choices, law for sustainability, visionary and pragmatic governance, and an American movement for sustainability—reinforce each other. A sustainability movement makes it more likely that the needed legal and governance changes will happen and encourages the availability of more-sustainable options and greater use of those options. Public satisfaction with more-sustainable options would, in turn, lead to even more choices and greater support for changes in law and governance that would further contribute to sustainability. Taken together, these four approaches provide a way to build on our progress to date, overcome obstacles, and thus accelerate the transition to a sustainable America. Part IV discusses these approaches.

The question in front of us is not whether we will make a transition to sustainability. Unsustainable activities cannot continue indefinitely and will come to an end sooner or later. Instead, the question is whether that transition will be smooth or jarring. By accelerating progress toward sustainability, and by overcoming the obstacles to its accomplishment, we can make that transition more seamless and constructive, and thus ensure a high quality of life for present and future generations. We can act, in short, as if we really believe that tomorrow matters.

PART I

Modest Progress Toward an Increasingly Distant Goal

CHAPTER 1

Environmental and Public Health Protection: Steps Forward and Steps Back

Environmental laws and policies are a key part of the foundation for sustainability. Many of these laws offer important public health benefits. Pollutants and wastes that damage the environment also tend to injure human health, and vice versa.[1] In general, our environmental and natural resource laws have provided a basic level of protection to human health and the environment; without them, we can be very sure that environmental quality—including the air we breathe and the water we drink—would be in much worse shape.

The past two decades have seen some steps forward and some steps back in environmental and public health protection. This chapter includes some good news. Particular areas of progress include improvements in air quality and reductions in pesticide use. The chapter also describes issues where less change in longstanding practices and laws (but often some progress nonetheless) has been made over the last two decades. These include agriculture, fresh water, hazardous waste and Superfund remediation, and oceans and estuaries.

There is also bad news. In some areas, especially climate change, we are moving in the wrong direction on emissions even as new information unfolds about the seriousness of the risks climate change presents and the fact that it is already occurring. There are also new challenges, where our activity has tended to get ahead of our ability to manage for sustainability. These include nanotechnology, corn ethanol, and hydraulic fracturing of shale for oil and gas.

Good News

In recent years good news has been relatively scarce in the world of environmental protection. But there have been some striking environmental successes over the past two decades in the improvement of air quality, control of chemicals and pesticides, and prevention of lead poisoning.

Air Quality

All too frequently, the quality of our air falls short of what is needed to protect public health and the environment. The 1970 Clean Air Act establishes a regulatory program to achieve these goals. Every pollutant regulated under the act is known to

15

cause significant adverse effects to human health, the environment, or both, when present in excess concentrations. Ozone, for instance, not only injures public health but also damages crops, vegetation, and trees.

The basic accomplishment of the Clean Air Act, as shown in Figure 1.1, is both simple and fundamental: unhealthy air has substantially diminished over the past two decades, even as the economy has grown. The six criteria air pollutants—the pollutants primarily targeted by the act (sulfur dioxide, carbon monoxide, lead, ground-level ozone, particulate matter, and nitrogen dioxide)—declined by 59% while GDP grew 65%. What makes this reduction remarkable is that population, energy consumption, and vehicle miles traveled all increased during the same period. Only carbon dioxide emissions, which have only recently been regulated and not in a comprehensive manner, increased.

Figure 1.1
Comparison of Growth Measures and Air Emissions, 1990–2010[2]

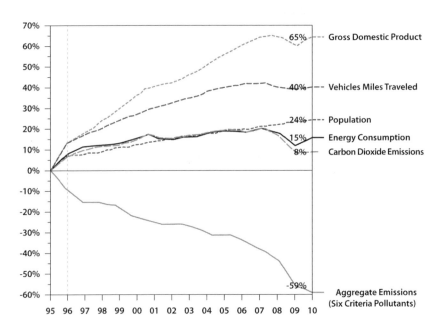

The United States has made a great deal of progress toward achieving air quality since 1970, when the basic framework of the Clean Air Act was first adopted, and particularly after the enactment in 1990 of comprehensive amendments to the Act. Carbon monoxide concentrations in the air have decreased significantly as cleaner cars have replaced older, more-polluting vehicles.[3] No areas in the country are currently classified as in violation of the air quality standards for carbon monoxide[4]—quite a contrast with 1990, when 30 million Americans lived in areas that exceeded the ambient air quality standards for carbon monoxide.[5] The phaseout of leaded gasoline has caused a 99% reduction in total emissions of lead,[6] lowering the risk of anemia and IQ loss in children. The control of lead in the air is truly one of the greatest, and most successful, public health measures of our time.

Progress also has been made in regulating stationary sources of air pollution (power plants and factories, primarily). Sulfur dioxide, which is emitted into the air mainly from the combustion of coal at electricity-generating units, decreased by nearly 50% between 1992 and 2008.[7] These reductions are due in part to the acid deposition control program established by the 1990 amendments to the Clean Air Act.[8] The amendments led to significant reductions in acid deposition, especially in Western Pennsylvania and the Ohio River valley, where the concentrations of sulfates and nitrates were the greatest. There has also been marked progress in the Northeast, where lakes were dying due to acid rain.[9] Overall there appear to be no areas that are actually violating the ambient air quality standards for sulfur dioxide.[10]

The benefits from these improvements have far outstripped their costs. EPA has estimated that the benefits from 1970 to 1990 amounted to trillions of dollars.[11] According to a 2011 EPA report required by Congress, in 2010 alone the Clean Air Act prevented more than 160,000 early deaths, 13 million lost work days, and 3.2 million lost school days. These benefits are projected to be even greater in 2020. In addition, the benefits of the legislation exceed its costs by a ratio of 30 to 1 ($2 trillion in benefits to $65 billion in costs). Apart from improved public health, benefits from the implementation of the Clean Air Act include improved agricultural productivity, higher visibility, greater quality of life, and healthier ecosystems.[12] Earlier studies drew similar conclusions—that the costs are frequently far less than initially estimated and the benefits of control often are orders of magnitude greater than the costs.[13] These benefits have largely come from the regulation of particles and pollutants such as sulfur dioxide and nitrogen oxide that contribute to the formation of particles.

But there is still a long way to go. More than one-third of the nation's population live in areas where the air quality standards for ozone are violated.[14] Areas in the Northeast and California will, under the most optimistic scenarios, need years, perhaps decades, to meet those standards. Worse, it appears that the present standards are inadequate. EPA's own scientific advisory board has said the standards are too lax to protect public health and the environment, and the agency has proposed that the standards be tightened.[15] But after pressure from industry and states, President Obama, in 2011, vetoed efforts to tighten the standards for the time being.[16]

Chemicals and Pesticides

The management of chemicals is at the very heart of sustainable development because chemicals are responsible for both a great deal of our social and economic progress and much damage to human health and the environment. Principles of sustainable development that are particularly relevant to chemicals include the precautionary principle (willingness to take action in the face of uncertainty to avert irreversible and serious threats to health and the environment); intergenerational equity (avoiding the imposition of large costs for future generations); access to information; and integrated decisionmaking.

Progress over the past two decades has been based on a public-private partnership and a new statute, the 1996 Food Quality Protection Act. EPA's voluntary High Production Volume (HPV) Chemicals Program, begun in 1998 in partnership with the Environmental Defense Fund, the American Petroleum Institute, and the American Chemistry Council, has yielded an enormous amount of new information.[17] More than 2,200 HPV chemicals were "sponsored" by industry—which means that industry agreed to collect basic information about their risks—resulting in the submission of 6,500 published studies, 8,100 unpublished studies, and a large number of new tests conducted on existing high-volume chemicals. In 2010, companies that had not volunteered to provide data on HPV chemicals were directed to do so by regulation. In addition, the U.S. National Toxicology Program and EPA have collaborated to put forward the Tox 21 initiative, an effort to develop and deploy high-throughput in vitro methods (which involve many simultaneous tests on biological material) to reduce the costs and time required for assessing the hazards of the tens of thousands of chemicals about which we know very little.[18]

Information generated from the HPV program is helping to support EPA's Enhancing Chemical Management Program, an effort launched by the agency in September 2009. The program has yielded EPA action plans, built on prior efforts, to address risks of a number of high-priority chemicals. State laws had already achieved some regulation of certain high-priority chemicals, particularly polybrominated diphenyl ether flame retardants (PBDEs), which appear to reduce fertility in women.[19] EPA worked with the only U.S. manufacturer of two PBDE commercial products (pentaBDE and octaBDE), and this manufacturer voluntarily agreed to phase out production by the end of 2004. States have also begun to regulate the polycarbonate polymer compound bisphenol A (BPA), which is widely used in making plastics. A variety of studies raise "questions about its potential impact, particularly on children's health and the environment."[20] At the federal level, EPA took a number of steps to limit use of the persistent and toxic polyfluorinated compounds, most notably perfluorooctanoic acid (PFOA), which is used to make nonstick coatings and many other industrial products. EPA also prosecuted reported violations by the manufacturers of both PFOA and a related compound, perfluorooctyl sulfonoate (PFOS), which was once used to make stain repellents.

For pesticides, there has been much more progress. In 2008, EPA completed the reregistration of pesticides already on the market, as required under the 1988 amendments to the Federal Insecticide, Fungicide, and Rodenticide Act. Reregistration was required for pesticides registered before 1984 to make sure they met current standards. EPA also reassessed pesticide food regulations as required under the Food Quality Protection Act (FQPA) of 1996. Registration renewal—a relicensing program established under the FQPA—now is underway. The FQPA resulted in many changes in U.S. pesticide use, the best-documented being reduced use of the very toxic organophosphate pesticides. Their production peaked at 131 million pounds per year in 1980. While use already had fallen to 80 million pounds per year by 1990, it did not continue to decline. After passage of the 1996 law and a 10-year period the government was given to fully implement that law, use fell to 33 million pounds per year in 2007 and may still be declining.[21] Another significant change in pesticide usage has resulted from implementation of the 1990 Organic Foods Act and subsequent establishment of organic food standards (discussed in more detail in Chapter 10).

Prevention of Lead Poisoning

Lead impedes the neurological development of children—their readiness to learn, their intellectual potential, their ability to participate in society—and hence compromises society's future, one of the driving concerns of sustainable development. Although no one is immune to lead poisoning by virtue of income and status, it disproportionately affects impoverished and minority communities. The control and elimination of the two primary sources of lead exposure (gas and paint) has resulted in a demonstrable decrease in the incidence of lead poisoning. Since the elimination of leaded gasoline, the decrease has reached the point where the median blood level in children is 1.4 micrograms per deciliter, below the Centers for Disease Control 10-micrograms-per-deciliter threshold of concern.[22]

Public-awareness campaigns catalyzed by EPA's prevention strategy and the Residential Lead-Based Paint Hazard Reduction Act of 1992, which established a "hot line" for public inquiries, have increased public vigilance of potential lead hazards. Articles and alerts on a range of possible lead hazards continue to be prominently featured in U.S. media. Reflecting and reinforcing this heightened degree of public awareness, the Consumer Product Safety Commission continues to issue highly publicized recalls and warning notices for a range of lead-containing products, especially imported toys for infants and children. These ongoing consumer protection actions highlight both the momentum established for continued progress on the prevention of lead poisoning and the need to complete the job by continuing to identify and address new sources of lead exposure.

Little News/Mixed News

Environmental legislation of the type that was enacted in the early years of the modern environmental movement has ground to a halt. The most recent major environmental legislation is the Clean Air Act Amendments of 1990, signed into law by President George H.W. Bush. The lack of more recent legislation is one reason why many environmental objectives are far from met—perhaps most especially true for agriculture.

Agriculture

If there is to be a sustainable form of agriculture in the United States, it will have to be embedded within a more-sustainable food system—one that will look dramatically different from the dominant food system of today. We must produce and distribute food in a way that preserves natural resources for the future production of food and does not exceed nature's capacity to absorb our wastes. Although this book is focused primarily on environmental sustainability, it is important to recognize that sustainable agriculture would also sustain farmers economically by providing them with a fair share of the food dollar, and meet the standards of equity by providing living wages for farm workers as well as reasonable access to healthy food for all consumers.[23]

Today, by contrast, we produce and distribute most of our food through an industrialized system of agriculture that uses large amounts of mostly nonrenewable inputs (pesticides, fertilizers, irrigation water, fossil fuels); relies on long-distance networks for distribution; and stresses high yields of commodity crops such as corn, soybeans, and wheat, grown in monoculture (one plant species per plot of land). Most of this output then becomes inputs to animal agriculture as animal feed, the processed food industry, or the biofuels industry.[24] The use of commodity grains as animal feed is inherently wasteful of resources: the feed-to-animal-weight ratio for beef is 7:1, for pork 4:1, and for poultry 2:1.[25]

One way to gauge our progress toward sustainable agriculture is to conduct an inventory of the resources we need for agriculture and determine how well we are conserving them. We should acknowledge the importance of farmers and their knowledge base, inputs to agriculture that are often overlooked when we discuss sustainability. The farming population in the United States has been dwindling as a consequence of the mechanization and industrialization of agriculture, which tends toward fewer farms with more acreage per farm and more animals per farm.[26] The other main ingredients in agriculture include land, soil quality and quantity, water quality and quantity, energy, and biodiversity.

Farmland

According to the Natural Resources Conservation Service, the United States lost 15% of its farmland between 1982 and 2007, although half of this loss was accounted for by environmentally sensitive cropland being enrolled in the federal

Conservation Reserve Program.[27] This voluntary program for agricultural landowners, inaugurated in 1985, provides annual payments in return for growing specific plants that attract wildlife, reduce soil erosion, and improve water quality.[28]

Soil Quantity

The National Resources Inventory, conducted by the Natural Resources Conservation Service of the U.S. Department of Agriculture (USDA), reports both good news and bad news on soil erosion on U.S. cropland. The good news is that the rate at which we are losing topsoil in the United States has been declining; between 1982 and 2007 the rate decreased by 43%. The bad news is that we are still losing topsoil at a rate much faster than nature can replenish it; in 2007, U.S. cropland was still losing topsoil at an average rate of 4.8 tons per acre per year.[29]

More U.S. farmers have been practicing conservation tillage (a system that leaves crop residues on the surface to control erosion); the percentage of planted acreage managed under the system increased from 26% to 41% between 1990 and 2004.[30] However, conservation tillage systems—which often mean a no-till approach—are often heavily dependent on herbicides for controlling weeds, where tillage (turning over the soil and burying weeds) was once used to control them. According to EPA, "Pesticides are used on the vast majority of U.S. cropland.... [H]erbicides were applied to 98% of corn acreage and 96% of soybean acreage in 2001."[31]

Soil Quality

A National Research Council report has described how industrialized agriculture affects the quality of soil:

> Some modern agricultural practices adversely affect soil quality by affecting soil physical, chemical, and biological factors through erosion, compaction [by heavy machinery], acidification, and salinization. They also reduce biological activity as a result of pesticide applications, excessive fertilization, and loss of organic matter.[32]

The report also points out that modern farming methods might be reducing the nutrient content of our soils: "The nutrient density of 43 garden crops (mostly vegetables) has been shown to have declined between 1950 and 1999 in the United States, suggesting possible tradeoffs between yield and nutrient content."[33]

Synthetic fertilizers are used as a substitute for natural fertility in the soil and are dependent on a fossil fuel (natural gas) as their feedstock. Based on these factors, synthetic fertilizers are not regarded as a long-term solution to soil fertility needs.

USDA's Economic Research Service found that in 2006, about two-thirds of U.S. cropland was not meeting all three criteria for good nitrogen management, which are related to the rate, timing, and method of application.[34]

Water Quantity

Agriculture accounts for 80% of all water use in the United States, primarily through irrigation. Only 16% of U.S. cropland is irrigated, but that acreage accounts for nearly half of the value of all crops.[35] Most irrigation depends on groundwater withdrawals from aquifers such as the High Plains Aquifer (also known as the Ogallala Aquifer), which lies under eight U.S. states and provides water to more than 15 million irrigated acres, or about one-quarter of all irrigated acres in the United States.[36] Between 1950 and 2009, the aquifer was depleted by about 9%.[37] The Texas portion of the aquifer had lost even more—nearly 1% of its water in storage each year between 1990 and 2004.[38]

On a more positive note, U.S. farmers have increased their adoption of pressurized irrigation systems, which usually achieve 75-85% efficiency in water use (compared to a typical 40–65% efficiency in gravity-flow systems). Between 1979 and 2003, acreage under pressurized systems increased from 37% to 57% of all irrigated acreage. Acreage using low-flow systems such as drip irrigation (which has an application efficiency of 95% or greater) increased tenfold, but it represented only 6% of all irrigated acreage.[39]

Water Quality

Water quality can be affected by soil erosion and the runoff of pesticides, excess fertilizer, and animal waste into watersheds. It has been estimated that crops only take up 30–50% of the nitrogen fertilizer applied to farm fields, and about 45% of applied phosphorus. Some of the excess is absorbed by soils, but some runs off the land and harms our watersheds.[40]

Between 1996 and 2008, an additional 383 million pounds of herbicides were used in the United States because of the widespread adoption of crops that are genetically engineered to tolerate herbicides; Monsanto's Roundup Ready soybean seeds, for example, now make up about 95% of commercial soybean plantings. By contrast, insecticide use decreased significantly during that same 13-year period because some major crops have been genetically engineered to produce their own insecticide, a toxin derived from *Bacillus thuringiensis* (Bt), a bacterium found in soil. These Bt crops present a serious danger, though, because their widespread use virtually ensures that insects will develop resistance to Bt, which has been a valuable tool in organic agriculture.[41]

Despite the successes of no-till farming in reducing soil loss, the system has not stemmed the tide of excess nutrients entering waterways and causing dead zones in water bodies, most prominently the Gulf of Mexico and the Chesapeake Bay. These dead zones are places where excess nutrients have caused blooms of algae, which as they die off and decompose, absorb most of the oxygen in the water and make it uninhabitable for aquatic life.[42] As sustainable agriculture advocate Wes Jackson explains: "The water coming off a minimum-till or no-till field looks a lot better than the water coming off a conventional-till field. There's only one problem:

The nitrogen level of the water from that no-till land is still three times above the acceptable level determined by the Environmental Protection Agency."[43]

The concentrated animal-feeding operations (CAFOs) that produce most of the nation's meat, milk, and eggs have severed the connection between animals and the land. Traditionally, animal manure was valuable fertilizer for farmers. Today, because so many animals are now produced in each CAFO and many CAFOs tend to be concentrated in certain areas of the country, animal manure often poses problems of air and water pollution—or, at the very least, a waste management problem. In 1997, 152 U.S. counties produced more phosphorus from animal manure than their cropland could absorb, and 68 counties produced more manure nitrogen than their land could absorb. The largest farms (more than 1,000 "animal units," each equal to 1,000 pounds of live weight) constituted only 2% of all farms but were responsible for half of the excess nutrients.[44] Excess manure from CAFOs is stored in cesspits in the ground that the industry calls "lagoons." During heavy storms or floods, these storage pits can overflow or rupture and release excess nutrients into local waterways, killing fish and other aquatic life.[45]

Energy

An estimated 7.3 units of energy are expended for every unit of food produced in the United States. Most of this energy input comes from nonrenewable fossil sources.[46] Fossil fuels are used in the production of pesticides and fertilizers; the pumping of irrigation water; the use of heavy machinery for tilling, planting, and harvesting; the processing of foods; and the shipping of raw materials and finished products, often across great distances. This industrialized food system cannot be sustained into the future using the same energy sources it now depends upon.

Although agriculture is still largely dependent on nonrenewable energy sources, it is using energy more efficiently. In 2004, the Congressional Research Service (CRS) reported that "since the late 1970s, the direct use of energy by agriculture has declined by 26%, while the energy used to produce fertilizers and pesticides has declined by 31%." The CRS attributed these declines to improved energy efficiency inspired by the petroleum price shocks of the 1970s.[47] The Natural Resources Conservation Service adds: "Direct energy use has been reduced as a result of advances in equipment efficiency, irrigation efficiency, adoption of no-till or conservation tillage, and other practices and technologies."[48]

Biodiversity

Biodiversity can be defined as the "variety of life on Earth at all its levels, from genes to ecosystems, and the ecological and evolutionary processes that sustain it."[49] Agriculture both depends on biodiversity and impacts it. Industrial agriculture, in particular, erodes biodiversity among domesticated plants because it relies on a small number of high-yielding crop varieties, to the exclusion of other varieties.

The United Nations Food & Agriculture Organization (FAO) points out that about three-quarters of the world's plant genetic diversity was lost during the 20th century, "as farmers worldwide have left their multiple local varieties and landraces for genetically uniform, high-yielding varieties." The FAO also reports that 30% of livestock breeds are threatened with extinction and that "75% of the world's food is generated from only twelve plants and five animal species." In addition, 60% of all the plant-based calories we eat come from just three crops—rice, corn, and wheat.[50] This uniformity in agriculture—and therefore our food supply—puts us at risk when there are disruptions such as extreme weather, insect infestations, or outbreaks of plant diseases.

On a brighter note, the U.S. Department of Agriculture's Conservation Reserve Program (CRP), which has helped reduce soil loss, is also the major federal land conservation program that has a positive influence in the protection of biodiversity. Federal farm bills have been a major source of the dedication of land for biodiversity conservation purposes, through the CRP and several different programs. The 2002 Farm Bill continued the CRP and created the Wildlife Habitat Incentives Program, which pays farmers for biodiversity conservation on private land, primarily enhancement and restoration of fish and wildlife habitat.[51] The 2008 farm bill provided a total of $733 million over five years for the Farm and Ranch Lands Protection Program, which pays for up to 50% of the price of acquiring conservation easements or other interests to preserve private agricultural land.[52] The legislation also reestablished the Grassland Reserve Program, which supports "working grazing operations, enhancement of plant and animal biodiversity, and protection of grassland under threat of conversion to other uses," and has a goal of protecting 1.22 million acres.[53] However, the 2008 bill will expire in 2012, and all of these programs will be reviewed through the lens of the drive to reduce federal spending.

Freshwater

In the interrelated fields of water quality/aquatic ecosystem health and water quantity/water resources management, some progress has been made over the past 20 years. The Clean Water Act, which established a permitting and regulatory program to protect water quality, continues to serve as a reasonably effective tool for reducing pollution from major sources such as factories and sewage treatment plants, and to a lesser degree for more difficult challenges such as urban stormwater and other sources of runoff pollution. Statutes such as the Resource Conservation and Recovery Act,[54] which regulates solid and hazardous waste, and the Safe Drinking Water Act also help to protect groundwater from new sources of pollution and to ensure the safety of the tap water consumed by most Americans. Especially when compared with much of the world, most of the United States is served by modern collection and treatment systems for sewage (at secondary treatment levels or higher), and by modern treatment and conveyance systems for drinking water.

Yet there is a long way to go. Surface water and groundwater pollution remains a significant problem. In urban areas, waterways remain impaired due to the physical and chemical effects of stormwater runoff, especially after intensive storms. Urban waters can also be severely impaired by combined sewer overflows and sanitary sewer overflows, which cause the discharge of untreated waste into waterways. Suburban watersheds are impaired by intensive sprawl development, which changes the flow characteristics of many streams in addition to generating pollution by nutrients, toxic metals, and organic chemicals. Surface water and groundwater in rural watersheds, especially those with intensive row-crop agriculture, continue to be polluted by pesticides and herbicides that can contaminate fish and wildlife or directly impair drinking water sources. In many coastal regions, saltwater intrusion is already impairing or threatening the utility of groundwater supplies for domestic and other use, or requiring expensive advanced treatment systems (such as reverse osmosis filtration) to make them potable; and rising sea levels may exacerbate those problems.

Even areas served by modern infrastructure face health risks from water pollution. On a national scale there are as many as 2.5 million cases of giardia and 300,000 cases of cryptosporidiosis each year, both of which are waterborne diseases. Warnings on fish consumption and beach closures continue to provide evidence that water pollution can cause significant threats to human health, from both pathogens and toxics. Despite massive investments in municipal sewerage and stormwater management facilities in recent decades, wastewater collection and treatment infrastructure in the United States faces tremendous challenges due to aging systems, urban and suburban growth, and new or strengthened water quality standards. EPA estimates it will cost almost $300 billion to meet these needs over the next 20 years.[55]

The Clean Water Act and other tools to protect aquatic ecosystems, such as the Endangered Species Act, have also been less effective in protecting the biological integrity of aquatic ecosystems from threats such as the filling of wetlands, loss of riparian areas, stream channelization and diversion, and other kinds of habitat impairment. In the 1990s, the federal government adopted a "no net loss" policy for wetlands protection, reflecting a pledge to ensure that any future wetland loss or degradation be offset by equal or greater wetlands gains through wetland restoration or creation efforts. Wetlands improve water quality, help store flood waters, and are excellent wildlife habitat.[56] Although this policy has slowed the rate of wetlands loss, there is considerable uncertainty about the effectiveness of wetlands restoration and creation, and therefore the success of the "no net loss" policy. Moreover, a series of judicial decisions has injected additional uncertainty about which waters are covered by the Clean Water Act program. Many other activities that result in aquatic ecosystem degradation, such as dam construction and operation, stream channelization, bank stabilization, and floodplain and watershed development, are not regulated directly by federal law. Intensification of this kind of land use change can lead to significant degradation of aquatic ecosystems due to the aggregate impacts of a large number of activities that are difficult to regulate or modify individually. Those kinds of pervasive impacts have presented significant barriers to even large, heavily funded, and well-designed aquatic ecosystem protection and restoration programs, such as the Chesapeake Bay Program.

Growth has also stressed water supplies in many parts of the United States, including in eastern states usually considered to have water. A protracted drought in the Southwest has left major reservoirs such as Lake Powell and Lake Mead half full, posing threats to water supplies from Denver to Los Angeles. While many have believed since the early 1990s that the era of large water projects was over, recent shortages have given rise to calls for renewed construction of storage reservoirs and other water-supply infrastructure, including some projects involving major water transfers from water-rich to arid regions. Climate change makes these challenges even harder.

Hazardous and Toxic Wastes

A sustainable hazardous waste regime requires, if possible, that the use of chemicals that produce hazardous wastes be eliminated entirely. Where that is not possible, the use of such chemicals must be minimized, and a cycle of use and reuse must be created to minimize or eliminate their release. Hazardous wastes that were improperly disposed of in the past must be remediated in order to remove the dangers they may pose to human health, water resources, land, and wildlife. Sustainable management of hazardous waste creates genuine opportunities for industries to reduce the costs of purchasing raw materials, decrease workplace risks and accidents, minimize industrial liability, improve community relations, and ease the costs of waste management.

Two major federal statutes govern this effort—the Resource Conservation and Recovery Act (RCRA), which established a regulatory program for the management of hazardous wastes, and the Comprehensive Environmental Response, Compensation, and Liability Act (CERCLA),[57] or Superfund law, which established a program for cleaning up contaminated sites. Over the past 20 years, progress toward sustainability under these two laws has been limited and inconsistent at best. Beginning in 2002, EPA created and promoted an entirely voluntary program designed to encourage industries to minimize their generation of hazardous wastes. This program achieved anecdotal progress in some areas. And in 2007, the U.S. Supreme Court handed down a decision that encouraged firms to be more proactive in cleaning up contaminated hazardous waste sites.[58] This ruling removed confusion over which parties engaging in a cleanup could recover some or all of their costs from other responsible parties.

These salutary developments aside, however, further necessary steps that would represent progress toward sustainability have been stalled, and in some cases, new measures have been adopted that move us away from a sustainable approach. In

1995, Congress ended the petroleum tax that had been the source of money for Superfund cleanups at sites where no solvent responsible party can be found. Since then, the Fund has been chronically underfinanced with general tax revenues. Moreover, in 1996, Congress took another step away from achieving sustainable development by removing a significant source of private financial pressure on hazardous waste site operators/debtors to manage their facilities in an environmentally sound fashion. It did so by expanding CERCLA's existing liability exemption for secured creditors (primarily banks) so long as they do not actively participate in facility operations and decisions.[59]

These and other statutes have not been amended in ways that would make them more sustainable. Although the EPA-sponsored voluntary hazardous waste minimization programs sparked some marginal advances, they are a far cry from new environmental legislation that would require industrial hazardous waste generators to decrease their generation of such wastes, in phased increments, by fixed dates. Between fiscal years 2007 and 2010, industrial, federal, state, and local sources reduced nearly 16 million pounds of 31 hazardous compounds and metals that EPA defines as "priority chemicals" from their waste streams—mostly by cutting releases of lead and lead compounds. Yet in 2007 (the latest year for which comparable statistics are available), those same sources continued to generate almost 85 million pounds of priority chemicals.[60] In 2010, sources in the United States released into the environment more than 3.92 billion pounds of a more comprehensive set of toxic chemicals.[61]

RCRA has not been amended to include a consistent, straightforward, and comprehensive definition of hazardous waste. Longstanding exclusions from statutory coverage—irrigation return flow waters containing pesticides and domestic sewage containing toxic chemicals—continue to exist. Similarly, while EPA continues efforts to make constructive use of the 1976 Toxic Substances Control Act to manage the introduction and use of new chemicals in the marketplace, the statute has not been amended since 1992, and there is an increasing consensus among many parties that reform is needed.[62]

Oceans and Estuaries

Sustainable use of the oceans requires that all human activities preserve water quality sufficient to support the biological, chemical, and physical processes of the oceans without stress, so that oceans can support a variety of healthy ecosystems; dissolve excess carbon dioxide from the atmosphere; and circulate in currents that aid human navigation, drive relatively predictable weather patterns, and cycle heat and nutrients throughout the depths and around the world. Sustainable development further requires that humans remove only the amount of biological resources—such as algae/seaweed, fish, marine mammals, and corals—that those species can comfortably replace between human harvests and that will not disrupt the greater food webs and ecosystems of which those species are a part.

The United States is not managing its oceans, coasts, and estuaries in a sustainable manner. One key stressor is overfishing, which not only removes target species in an unsustainable manner but also results in by-catch of nontarget species and in shifting food webs (that is, shifting predator-prey relationships, as target predator or prey fish are caught). As a result, overfishing can alter or destroy basic components of marine ecosystem functioning. Certain fishing methods, such as bottom trawling, can destroy marine habitat, further interfering with overall ecosystem function and productivity. In 2005, the National Oceanic and Atmospheric Administration (NOAA) instituted its Fish Stock Sustainability Index (FSSI), a performance measure for the sustainability of fish stocks selected for their importance to commercial and recreational fisheries.[63] The index provides valuable data about sustainable ocean fisheries. Although NOAA's reporting methodology has changed over time, its figures show only limited progress toward sustainability in fisheries management. Between 1997 and 2010 the number of stocks not overfished declined from 183 to 136. Yet in 2010, 43 fish stocks were considered overfished, and another 72 were considered not to be sustainable. Moreover, much remains unknown regarding U.S. fish stocks, especially species that support only minor fisheries. In 2010, the sustainability status of 51 other major fish stocks was simply unknown.

While overfishing is one major challenge to the sustainability of oceans and estuaries, another is land-based marine pollution, which remains the last major category of marine pollution not subject to effective regulation, either in the United States or internationally. One of the most critical land-based contaminants of marine ecosystems is nutrient runoff from agricultural activities. For example, the Mississippi River drains more than two-thirds of the United States, and much of the runoff entering the river comes from farms. Nutrient runoff has been deemed a major cause of the hypoxic (low-oxygen) zone in the Gulf of Mexico. The U.S. Geological Survey's yearly summer measurements of the size of the Gulf of Mexico hypoxic zone shows that the average size of the Gulf "dead zone" continues to be very high (Figure 1.2).

Figure 1.2
The Size of the Gulf of Mexico Hypoxic Zone, 1985–2009[64]

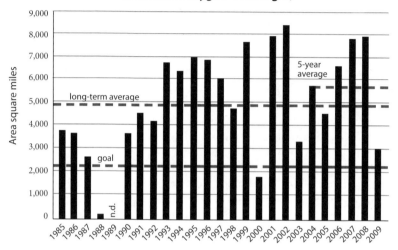

Area of Mid-Summer Bottom Water Hypoxia
(Dissolved Oxygen < 2.0 mg/L)

Other forms of land-based marine pollution include run-off of toxics and fertilizers, intentional discharge and dumping of pollutants into the ocean, the accumulation of plastics into "garbage patches" at the gyres in the Pacific and Atlantic Oceans, and atmospheric deposition of mercury.

Bad News: Climate Change

For some critical environmental issues, the problem is not that our progress has been too little or too slow. Rather, the problem is that we are moving in the wrong direction in spite of what we have learned in the past several decades about the magnitude of the damage being done, the risks we face, and the challenge to achieve sustainability. Climate change is the most pressing environmental, health, economic, social, and national security issue on which we are moving in the wrong direction.

Greenhouse gas pollution has steadily increased since 1990 despite U.S. agreement to the 1992 United Nations Framework Convention on Climate Change to avoid serious harm to human well-being and the environment. It is increasingly evident that climate change is having, and will continue to have, adverse effects not only on other countries but on the United States, including its biodiversity and water supplies. But the United States has not been able to adopt comprehensive national legislation to address climate change.

Risks

As scientific information has developed over the past several decades, it is increasingly clear that humans are causing climate change and that climate change presents enormous risks to life, human health, property, biodiversity, plants, animals, species, and ecosystems. [65] It threatens people in the United States and around the world with rising seas, reduced agricultural production, lower water supply, drought, floods, lethal heat waves, and increases in vector-borne disease. It is also increasingly clear that climate change is already underway, as sea levels rise, growing seasons change, the number and scale of unusual weather events increases, and glaciers disappear.[66] And it is not just the environmental and human health risks of climate change that present sustainability challenges. Because most greenhouse gas emissions derive from the use of fossil fuels to produce energy, it is also important to be mindful of the economic costs and security risks inherent in supporting a global fossil fuel infrastructure.

Climate change is likely to have an adverse impact on biodiversity. If nothing is done to mitigate global climate change, impacts to biodiversity may include shifts in migration and breeding patterns of species; expansions or contractions of natural species ranges; a rise in sea level, water temperature, and acidity; increases in disease transmission and pest infestations; and unpredictable fluctuations in populations and habitat conditions. Climate change may also contribute to the proliferation of invasive nonnative species, which can lead to the endangerment and extinction of native species. The most immediate threat is that current habitats for species, including those protected by the Endangered Species Act, may become unsuitable and species will be forced to migrate or face increased stresses in their original habitats.[67] Thus existing reserves may no longer serve their intended purpose and new ones will have to be created.

Models suggest that climate disruption is likely to induce higher water demand due to rising temperatures, increased frequency and intensity of droughts in some parts of the United States, and more intensive rain leading to flooding in others. That will likely place significant additional stress on America's aquatic ecosystems, water supply, and water infrastructure.

Agriculture is also being increasingly impacted by climate change as droughts, floods, hurricanes, and tornadoes become more frequent and more severe. These extreme events diminish crop yields and damage our natural resource base. The U.S. Global Change Research Program has summed up some of the impacts to be expected:

- Many crops show positive responses to elevated carbon dioxide and low levels of warming, but higher levels of warming often negatively affect growth and yields.
- Extreme events such as heavy downpours and droughts are likely to reduce crop yields because excesses or deficits of water have negative impacts on plant growth.

- Weeds, diseases, and insect pests benefit from warming, and weeds also benefit from a higher carbon dioxide concentration, increasing stress on crop plants and requiring more attention to pest and weed control.
- Increased heat, disease, and weather extremes are likely to reduce live-stock productivity.[68]

The relatively stable climate that has existed on the planet for most of agriculture's history has been a key element of agriculture's success,[69] even though a stable climate is not something we usually think of as an "input" to agriculture. In the coming decades, though, climate change will be the norm.

The United States also has not grappled with the fact that climate change will have a tremendous impact on marine resources as the oceans become warmer and chemically less basic (the result of dissolved carbon dioxide causing "ocean acidification") and as ocean current patterns change. Warmer oceans mean that species will shift poleward to cooler waters, a phenomenon that has already been documented for some fish species, such as Atlantic cod. Changing ocean temperatures also affect ocean current patterns, which can alter ocean nutrient upwellings and species patterns. For example, a hypoxic zone that appeared rather suddenly off the coast of Oregon has been attributed to changing current patterns. Finally, ocean acidification interferes with the basic chemistry of biological processes, such as shell-building, for many marine species.

International Agreements and U.S. Emissions

Though most Americans are unaware of it, the United States ratified the United Nations Framework Convention on Climate Change in 1992.[70] The treaty provides an international framework for addressing climate change; it does not establish quantitative emissions reduction requirements. Yet the convention provides several ways to measure whether U.S. greenhouse gas emissions are moving toward or away from sustainability. Chief among them is Article 2, which establishes the convention's ultimate objective—"stabilization of greenhouse gas concentrations in the atmosphere at a level that would prevent dangerous anthropogenic [human] interference with the climate system."[71] As one of the parties to the convention, the United States also agreed to "protect the climate system for the benefit of present and future generations of humankind, on the basis of equity" and other factors.[72] Developed countries such as the United States agreed to take the lead in reducing greenhouse gas emissions because of their greater technological and economic resources and because of their large historical contribution to higher atmospheric greenhouse gas levels.[73] This promise entails addressing the global consequences of climate change in developing climate change policy, not just pursuing national interests, because climate change is a threat to people and ecological systems around the world.

The acknowledgement in the Framework Convention of historical responsibility has particular importance for the United States. Between 1857 and 2007, the United

States emitted 28.77% of the entire world's greenhouse gas emissions, more than any other developed country, and far more than any other developing country.[74] While China has today overtaken the United States as the world's greatest emitter of greenhouse gases in absolute quantity, about one-fourth of the overall increase in global greenhouse gas concentrations over the past century and a half is attributable to the United States.

It now appears that global emissions of greenhouse gases need to be reduced by as much as 80% by 2050 to achieve nondangerous levels.[75] Because the United States remains one of the highest per capita emitters and some nations emit greenhouse gas emissions at levels significantly below average international per capita emissions, the United States will eventually need to reduce its greenhouse gas emissions by greater amounts than most of the rest of the globe in order to achieve "equity." Although the term "equity" in the Convention is without a precise legal definition, it is usually understood to connote an obligation to fairly share needed global greenhouse gas emissions reductions burdens.[76]

Because the convention did not contain enforceable national-reduction targets that would translate these general provisions into concrete numbers, the next major step was to negotiate a protocol to do just that. The Kyoto Protocol, named after the Japanese city in which it was negotiated, grew out of a conviction, underscored by the emerging science on climate change, that developed nations needed to be bound by numerical emissions reductions targets.[77] Under the Kyoto Protocol developed countries agreed to reduce their net greenhouse gas emissions by at least 5% from 1990 levels by 2008 to 2012; the European Union agreed to an 8% reduction, and the United States would have reduced its emissions by 7%.[78] The protocol now has 193 parties,[79] although it will end by its own terms at the end of 2012. The United States is the only developed country that did not ratify the Kyoto Protocol or adopt quantifiable greenhouse emissions targets (although Canada announced its withdrawal from the Protocol at the end of 2011).

Since ratifying the convention, the United States has failed to reduce emissions below levels that existed in 1990, the common measuring point for a country's progress. In 2009, total U.S. greenhouse gas emissions (including not only carbon dioxide but also methane, nitrous oxide, and other gases) were 6,633.2 teragrams (or million metric tons) of carbon dioxide equivalent. U.S. emissions increased by 7.3% between 1990 and 2009 (Figure 1.3). This overall increase occurred in spite of an emissions decrease from 2008 to 2009 by 6.1% (427.9 teragrams of carbon dioxide equivalent).[80] This recent dip in emissions was primarily due to a decrease in economic output resulting in reduced energy consumption across all sectors and a decrease in the carbon intensity of fuels used to generate electricity due to fuel switching as the price of coal increased and the price of natural gas declined.[81]

Figure 1.3
Cumulative Change in Annual U.S. Greenhouse Gas Emissions
Relative to 1990[82]

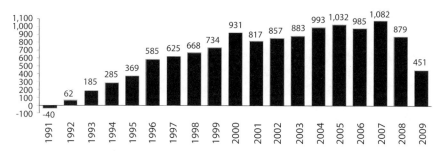

U.S. emissions have increased since 1990 at an average annual rate of 0.4%.[83] There have been significant differences in the annual change, with the two most recent years showing decreases (Figure 1.4).

Figure 1.4
Annual Percentage Change in U.S. Greenhouse Gas Emissions[84]

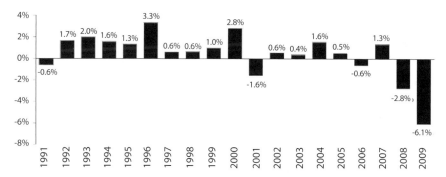

When President Obama was elected in 2008, there was widespread international hope that the United States would change course on climate change. Yet the United States approached international climate negotiations under the convention in Cancun in 2010 and the year before in Copenhagen by making a voluntary commitment only to reduce its greenhouse gas emissions by 17% below 2005 emissions levels by 2020. The U.S. promise is the weakest of all of the developed country promises, falls far short of what is required of global greenhouse gas emissions reductions necessary to prevent dangerous climate change, and is without any response to what equity would require for U.S. emissions reductions.[85]

National Measures

President Obama's commitment on greenhouse gas emissions was based upon the proposed American Clean Energy and Security Act (also known as the Waxman-Markey bill after its two primary House sponsors), comprehensive cap-and-trade legislation that passed the House of Representatives in 2010 but was not passed in the Senate.[86] In the 2010 mid-term elections, control of the House of Representatives passed to the Republicans, many of whom deny the scientific consensus that humans are contributing to climate change. As of this writing, it is unlikely in the near future that Congress will take action that achieves even the weak U.S. commitment made in Cancun.

Although Congress has failed to enact legislation directly limiting greenhouse gas emissions, the Obama Administration has taken action in response to the 2007 U.S. Supreme Court decision in *Massachusetts v. EPA*.[87] The case arose out of a petition to EPA to regulate greenhouse gas emissions from motor vehicles under the Clean Air Act. EPA refused, saying among other things that greenhouse gases are not pollutants under the Clean Air Act. The Court, in what is widely recognized as a landmark decision, held that greenhouse gases are air pollutants subject to regulation under the Clean Air Act. The Court also interpreted the act as requiring EPA to regulate greenhouse gases unless EPA determined that greenhouse gases are not endangering human health and the environment.[88] The case means that new federal legislation is not required to regulate greenhouse gas emissions, even though many believe that new legislation more specifically tailored to greenhouse gases is preferable. Moreover, because an air pollutant under the Clean Air Act is an air pollutant for all purposes, the EPA's newly recognized authority is not limited to motor vehicles but also applies to factories, power plants, and other stationary sources.

In 2009, EPA found that greenhouse gases, including those emitted from new motor vehicles, endanger human health and the environment[89] (and subsequently refused to reconsider that finding after petitioned to do so).[90] Since then, EPA and the Department of Transportation have worked together to both reduce greenhouse gases from motor vehicles and improve their fuel efficiency. The Department of Transportation has authority to establish corporate average fuel efficiency (CAFE) standards for motor vehicles under the Energy Policy and Conservation Act, which was adopted in 1975 in response to national security challenges raised by the 1973 and 1974 oil embargoes by the Organization of Petroleum Exporting Countries.[91] Efficiency improvements lagged in the United States for many years, however, and the average fuel economy of new cars and trucks was higher for model year 1985 than 2005.[92]

Fuel efficiency for motor vehicles has begun to improve again, and new standards set by Congress and advanced by the Obama Administration for passenger cars and light-duty trucks will provide the biggest increase in efficiency in 30 years—and substantial cuts in emissions—by model year 2016.[93] The Supreme Court's decision played a lead role in prompting these standards, as well as

California's efforts to advance low- and zero-emission vehicles. An agreement between the federal government and 13 automakers will accomplish even more in future model years.[94] The new proposal would increase the CAFE standard to 49.6 miles per gallon by model year 2025 on an average industry fleetwide basis, and the proposed greenhouse gas standards are projected to require vehicles to get 54.5 miles per gallon if the standards are met solely through improvements in fuel efficiency.[95] These standards are expected to trim oil consumption by 4 billion barrels and greenhouse gas emissions by 2 billion metric tons over the life of vehicles sold in model years 2017 to 2025.[96] This approach harmonizes CAFE standards and limits on greenhouse gas emissions from motor vehicles to produce much cleaner, more efficient vehicles. Although the proposed standards would increase the purchase price of vehicles, they also would result in far greater savings in fuel costs, which should strengthen the competitive position of the U.S. auto industry. In addition to these provisions, EPA and the Department of Transportation in 2011 announced the first program to reduce greenhouse gas emissions and fuel use in heavy-duty trucks and buses. This program will also result in significant additional reductions in air pollution and oil consumption.[97]

Using its authority under *Massachusetts v. EPA*, EPA has also adopted greenhouse gas regulations based on the best available control technology for large stationary sources such as factories and power plants.[98] Since January 2, 2011, some new stationary sources or modifications to those sources that increase greenhouse gas emissions have been subject to permitting.[99] EPA has issued guidance emphasizing the importance of energy efficiency in meeting these best available control technology requirements for greenhouse gases.[100] EPA also agreed to adopt by 2012 new performance standards for greenhouse gas emissions from electricity-generating units[101] and refineries.[102] As part of that agreement, EPA proposed new source performance standards for electricity-generating units in March 2012.[103]

New Challenges

A major challenge to sustainability is the fact that new environmental issues continue to arise, and will always continue to arise. Prominent among the recent developments that present challenges to sustainability are nanotechnology, increased production of corn-based ethanol for fuel, and the use of hydraulic fracturing to extract natural gas or oil from shale.

The field of nanotechnology emerged over the last 20 years, and nanomaterials have now entered the market. Nanomaterials (materials made of particles with at least one dimension of 100 nanometers or less; a nanometer is one billionth of a meter) occur in nature. Engineered nanomaterials (those made by people) have a wide array of chemistries, including fullerenes (C60 or Bucky Balls, hollow carbon molecules that are unusually stable), carbon nanotubes, metal and metal oxide particles (such as the nanozinc sunscreens and nanosilver substances that kill or resist bacteria and other microorganisms), polymers, and quantum dots (nanoscale semiconductors). Such materials are used in industrial coatings, paints, fabric treatments, pharmaceutical delivery systems, sunscreens, and cosmetics. Rapid commercialization has occurred despite a lack of knowledge about how these materials move and transform in the environment, how they affect biological systems, and what their potential for harm to human health and ecosystems might be. The assessment, indeed even the identification, of these as unique materials pose challenges for safety evaluations. During the Bush Administration, the federal government opted to use only voluntary approaches for managing risks of nano-materials, and did not think it necessary to consider their potential risks to health and the environment.[104] More recently, the EPA has announced steps to regulate nanotechnology under its chemicals program through a new rule under the Toxic Substances Control Act (TSCA), and as pesticides under the Federal Insecticide, Fungicide, and Rodenticide Act. The proposed TSCA rule was scheduled for release for comment at the end of 2010 but had not come forward by the time of writing.[105] The proposed new policies for pesticides were released for public comment in June 2011.[106] Also in June 2011, the White House issued a memorandum to all government agencies emphasizing the promise of nanotechnology to help address multiple societal needs, and the ability of the agencies to address nanotechnology risks using existing statutory authorities and "risk-based approaches."[107]

Increased production of biofuels, particularly ethanol made from corn, is a second major issue that has emerged in recent years. Higher fuel prices have led to an increasing adoption of renewable energy technologies such as wind and solar. However, this has also led to expanded use of biofuels; their use grew at an annual average rate of 1.8% between 1992 and 2009.[108] While biofuel energy use increased by more than a factor of 10 between 1992 and 2009, wood energy use declined by 19%.[109] Of particular concern is the fact is the dramatic growth in corn-based ethanol production. The United States has been the world's largest producer of ethanol fuels since 2005,[110] with output nearly doubling between 2005 and 2009.[111] The current high use of corn-based ethanol is of concern because of the low energy return on energy invested in making corn-based ethanol, the low energy density of ethanol, the inflationary impact on food and energy prices, and the ecological limitations of U.S. and global corn production.[112] Despite these significant drawbacks, the 2007 Energy Independence and Security Act mandates that the United States annually produce a certain amount of corn-based ethanol into the next decade[113]—a goal that was supported until the end of 2011 with tax incentives.[114]

The economic development of natural gas and oil from shale formations such as the Barnett in Texas and the Marcellus in the Appalachian Basin has been made possible by improved technologies in directional drilling and hydrofracturing, known as "fracking." Gas production from shale predates the 1859 Drake oil well in Pennsylvania, which gave birth to the American oil industry, but deep targets such as the Marcellus were considered uneconomical. Hydraulic fracturing, using high water pressure to open cracks in reservoir rocks and sand to keep the fractures open when pressure is released, is a long-established technique. What is new is the way operators drill horizontally to expose more shale to the wellbore, use millions of gallons of water/fluids to perforate and stimulate the wells, complete several wells on a given pad, and produce millions of cubic feet of gas per day.

This new "unconventional" gas play, as it is called, combines three distinctive and challenging features for sustainability: it has emerged with breathtaking speed, it has enormous economic potential, and it raises a host of environmental and social issues that are not yet resolved. No one knew for sure that gas development from Marcellus shale was even economically and technologically feasible until it was successfully attempted in western Pennsylvania in 2004. Already, billions of dollars have been invested, thousands of wells have been dug, and gas is already being sent to market in considerable volumes. The rapid development of shale gas is transforming the gas market by substantially increasing the gas supply. Nobuo Tanaka, executive director of the International Energy Agency, recently described "unconventional gas" as "unquestionably a game-changer in North America with potentially significant implications for the rest of the world."[115]

The environmental and social effects of shale gas drilling are considerable. Water management is a key issue because of the large volumes required for drilling and hydraulic fracturing, and because most of the water is returned to the surface. This "spent frac water" contains dissolved solids from the rock and brines present at depth as well as any additives used to enhance fluid and sand penetration into fractures and control bacterial growth in the well. Finding sufficient supplies of water and disposing of or treating wastewater are both challenging. There is also considerable controversy over whether fracking can cause migration of drilling fluids into near-surface groundwater. The combination of bad casing installation, which can allow well fluids to migrate out of the wellbore, and naturally occurring gas and brine in near-surface rock, raise additional problems. These issues are addressed primarily through state regulations that vary considerably in their requirements and enforcement.[116]

While new domestic sources of energy are good for energy security, the overall effect on greenhouse gas emission is not clear. Increased gas production and lower gas prices could be damaging to the coal industry (thus reducing greenhouse gas emissions because coal produces more carbon dioxide than gas), the renewable energy industry (thus increasing greenhouse gas emissions), or both. In addition, although some shale gas exploration and development is occurring in areas with prior drilling, much of it is occurring in areas where residents and local government are not familiar with the petroleum industry. The learning curve for all of the steps—from leasing to drilling to production to transporting product, not to mention their environmental effects—can be steep. And an influx of transient workers requires difficult social adjustments for both the workers and the communities where they operate.[117] Even newer development of oil from the Bakken and Three Forks shale formations in North Dakota raises similar environmental and social issues. More troubling, perhaps, is that few appear to be seriously asking what sustainable development of unconventional shale even means.

Conclusion

Environmental law and policy have played a significant role in moving the United States toward sustainability over the past two decades, although less through the adoption of new legislation than the administration of existing statutes. As a result, some significant improvements in environmental quality have occurred, particularly in air quality and reduced use of some toxic chemicals and pesticides. In many other areas, including agriculture, freshwater, oceans and estuaries, and hazardous and toxic chemicals, relatively little change in longstanding practices has occurred. In many cases, that means continued worsening conditions. Climate change is an especially important but controversial issue that requires a more substantial effort than the United States has been willing to muster. We have been moving away from sustainability in spite of growing scientific information about the severity and certainty of the risks of climate change. And new issues are arising—including nanotechnology, ethanol, and shale gas—before there is a policy or legal structure to address them.

CHAPTER 2

Growing Consumption and Population

Environmental degradation around the world was a major impetus for the 1992 Rio Earth Summit. And the problems we face today are daunting, even depressing—depleted fisheries, diminishing biodiversity, air and water pollution, a changing climate, and the list goes on. We tend to think about these problems as separate and mostly unrelated issues and tend to deal with them one at a time. And there is some truth to this: overfishing, improper waste disposal, destructive land-use policies, deforestation, and polluting emissions each differ in both their immediate causes and their specific remedies.

But there are two factors that underlie and explain these seemingly separate issues: unsustainable patterns of production and consumption of material goods and population growth. Essentially, too many of us consume too many resources. Indeed, at the Earth Summit, the United States and other countries agreed that these two factors are the root causes of environmental degradation. For Americans—and everyone else—these root causes are immensely important. Mathis Wackernagel, president of the Global Footprint Network, and Professor William Rees of the University of British Columbia have estimated that it would take three Earths to supply the resources the world's population would need to live at the American standard of consumption.[1]

A helpful way to express environmental impact is through the equation I = P $\times$ A $\times$ T. Environmental impact (I) is the product of population size (P), affluence measured as consumption per person (A), and the technology, economic, and political arrangements used to supply the consumption (T).[2] The equation reminds us of these basic underlying issues of consumption and population. Professor Arnold Reitze, who teaches at the University of Utah Law School, argues that U.S. environmental law sidesteps these basic issues.[3] While environmental law can and does address the symptoms—unclean water and dirty air, for instance—it does not fully and directly address their underlying causes. Chapter 1's description of the successes and failures of environmental law in protecting human health and the environment, in other words, does not tell the complete story. The equation is also useful because environmental impact is not based on just one factor; it is not just about population, consumption, or technology but about all three. We can manage some increase in one or two of these if there are more-than-offsetting developments in the others.

American levels of consumption, population size, and resource-consuming technology all contribute to a very high—and growing—environmental impact. In brief: consumption and population have grown over the past two decades, and technological changes have not offset the effects of that growth. The recent economic downturn has dented these trends, but there is no evidence that it has permanently changed them. And the environmental impacts of American consumption extend far beyond the nation's borders; the nation's energy use is a major component of global environmental change.[4]

Overall, the nation's consumption of energy, water, and materials remains very high. With just 4.5% of the world's population, the United States accounts for 20% of the world's energy consumption[5] and as much as one-third of the world's consumption of raw materials.[6] The United states also accounts for roughly 20% of the world's greenhouse gas emissions (closely correlated with fossil fuel energy use)—now behind China in total emissions but well ahead in per capita emissions.[7] Over most of the past six decades, as U.S. energy consumption has grown so have its greenhouse gas emissions. Moreover, the United States has become increasingly dependent on imported energy resources, especially petroleum, thereby increasing pressure on global supplies of a depleting resource and to the detriment of the U.S. trade balance. Only since the recession of 2008-2009 have U.S. energy use and emissions dropped, but this is more a reflection of the struggling economy than of efforts to reduce consumption.

While the United States has abundant supplies of fresh water, its high per capita water use contributes to the threat of regional water shortages because of growing population and climate change. Materials consumption in the United States is harder to measure because the federal government does not conduct a systematic material-flow analysis. A nongovernmental assessment of materials consumption shows steady increases in materials consumption until 2000, but there has been no comprehensive assessment since then. Analyses for some key materials (such as aluminum and cement) show decreases, mostly in recent years, and due in significant part to the economic downturn.

The United States has a large and growing population—309 million in 2010 and behind only China and India. Unlike most industrialized nations, however, the U.S. population is still growing and is likely to exceed 400 million before 2050.

At the same time, there have been only modest changes in the technologies involved in supplying most U.S. consumption over the past two decades. A national strategy for developing technologies needed for sustainability was released in 1995 but never implemented, largely because of political and cultural obstruction.

Production and Consumption of Energy

Progress toward energy sustainability in the United States can be measured by answering four questions: Are we on a path to consume less energy over time? Are we using more renewable energy and less fossil fuel? Are we reducing both conventional air pollutants and greenhouse gas emissions? Are we substantially improving energy efficiency (so that we consume less energy every year, not more) and reducing the amount of energy that is wasted? Because the environmental impact of U.S. production and consumption is so great, rapid progress on all these issues is needed.

Between 1992 and 2009, energy consumption per dollar of GDP declined, many air pollutants were significantly reduced, and America became active in the development of alternative energy technologies such as wind and solar photovoltaics (but not the leader as befits its large economy, heavy energy use, and capacity for industrial innovation). However, overall energy consumption increased, fossil fuel use continued to rise until the recent recession forced a decline, and energy efficiency policies have been set at levels or provide incentives that are much below achievable levels. In addition, a national carbon market is still far off, and energy producers are increasingly exploiting new unsustainable fuels as energy prices rise. In sum, the United States has seen limited success in improving the sustainability of its energy system in the 20 years since the Rio Summit—far less than it could have achieved. Certain states and regions have led in the implementation of energy efficiency and renewable energy technologies, and their efforts have in many cases had a marked effect. Yet the lack of a federal consensus to transform our energy system has resulted in relatively few large-scale policy achievements.

A look at the data shows four salient trends. First, absolute energy consumption has continued to grow. Figure 2.1 shows steady growth in energy demand from 1992 until 2007, only falling during the financial crisis. Of the four major categories of energy consumption—industrial, residential, commercial, and transportation—most of the reduction in energy demand from 2007 to 2009 took place in the industry sector.

Figure 2.1
U.S. Primary Energy Consumption by Sector
(Quadrillion BTU), 1992–2009[8]

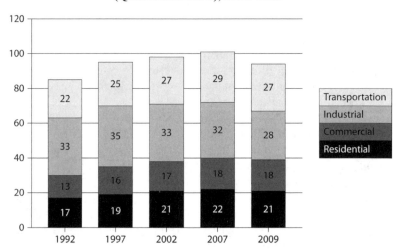

Second, the United States has seen only a small reduction in the share of fossil fuels in its fuel mix, and only small changes overall. In 2009, fossil fuels constituted 83% of primary energy consumption, down only 2% since 1992. Coal's share of primary energy consumption also was virtually unchanged, decreasing by only 1% over 20 years. The share of renewables and nuclear energy remained nearly unchanged until very recently. Nuclear power increased from 8% to 9% of total primary energy consumption in the past 20 years. Total renewables (including biomass and hydroelectric power) increased from 7% to 8%, mostly because wind generation has become market-competitive in many areas.[9]

States have tried to change the fuel mix by requiring that a greater fraction of their electricity production come from renewable sources. While these efforts have not had much impact on the national fuel mix, there have nonetheless been some significant achievements at the state level. Texas has achieved the most remarkable success in implementing wind power, reaching 8% of total delivered energy in 2010, with installed capacity growing 54 times in the 11 years since 1999.[10] The Texas case is instructive because it shows how government-structured economic incentives can drive renewable energy development despite a traditional reliance on fossil fuels, even in a state with large fossil fuel interests and a conservative government. Texas has achieved its successes by streamlining regulatory processes, targeting the concerns of land owners and communities in planning, and supporting the expansion of transmission infrastructure.[11] Perhaps most influential has been Texas' pursuit of an aggressive renewable portfolio standard, which mandates that utilities deliver a certain percentage of electricity from renewable sources.

Third, conventional pollutants from energy consumption have declined, but the emission of greenhouse gases has increased. A large proportion of air pollution originates from the combustion of fuel. To a much greater degree than for energy-related carbon dioxide emissions (for which no control technology at present exists), the United States has had considerable success in reducing the amount of emissions of other harmful air pollutants. Overall, air quality in the United States has improved since 1992, as monitored by emission monitoring stations throughout the country. Some of the most positive results are for carbon monoxide, nitrogen oxide, volatile organic compounds, particulate matter, and sulfur dioxide, all of which can have significant adverse public health effects. (These improvements are described in more detail in Chapter 1.)

It should be noted, however, that between 1992 and 2009 absolute carbon emissions rose by 6.6%. Over the past two decades, these emissions increased in the residential, commercial, and transportation sectors, but declined in the industrial sector.[12] Recently, China has overtaken the United States as the world's leader in carbon dioxide emissions. At the same time, U.S. greenhouse gas emissions from energy consumption are almost four times greater than those of China on a per capita basis and over 15 times greater per capita than those of India.[13]

Fourth, both energy consumption and pollution from energy consumption are increasingly decoupled from economic growth. That is, they are rising more slowly than GDP, or better still (at least for air pollution), they are declining in absolute terms even as GDP grows. These are modest positive signs for sustainability. Yet notwithstanding these improvements, most energy produced in the United States continues to be wasted. There are enormous opportunities to further improve the efficiency with which energy is used, although these opportunities are all too often simply ignored. Kurt Vonnegut had it right back in 1952, when he wrote, "You, the engineers and managers and bureaucrats, almost alone among men of higher intelligence, have continued to believe that the condition of man improves in direct ratio to the energy and devices for using energy put at his disposal."[14]

This modest decoupling of energy consumption from economic growth is most evident in the change in economic intensity of energy consumption. The economic intensity of energy consumption—the amount of energy used to produce one dollar of gross domestic product (GDP)—provides a standardized approximation of how well our economy uses energy to produce goods and services. On a per dollar basis, the U.S. economy has become less energy intensive and more energy-efficient since 1992, with the amount of energy used to make $1 GDP decreasing by nearly 30% (Figure 2.2).

Figure 2.2
U.S. National Energy Intensity (MBtu/$GDP)
1992–2009, Indexed to 1992 (1992=100)[15]

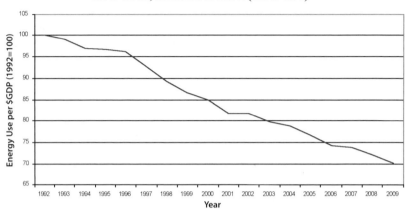

In spite of improvements such as this, however, our economy remains, on the whole, extremely inefficient. Economists and policy analysts have formulated many of their insights based on the data provided here, which was collected by the Energy Information Administration (EIA). But the EIA data provide only part of the story of how energy moves the economy forward. EIA routinely gathers annual data on physical units such as tons of coal, cords of wood, gallons of gasoline, therms of natural gas, or kilowatt-hours of electricity. All of these different energy forms have an equivalent heat value that allows us to compare a gallon of gasoline with, say, one kilowatt-hour of electricity. In all of the various methods of tracking energy consumption, in other words, energy is measured as heat, using the BTU.

But the real issue is the ability of energy to do work. From an economic perspective, work is defined as the energy that is used to create goods and services. As energy physicist Robert Ayres and sustainability analyst Benjamin Warr have noted, it is the raw energy converted to useful work that drives economic activity as typically measured by the nation's GDP. They calculate that less than 14% of the energy produced in the United States is actually used to produce goods and services and that 86% is wasted.[16] In some ways this is not significantly better than we were doing more than a century ago. In 1900, the United States wasted more than 97% of the energy it produced to maintain its economy. Admittedly, not all of that energy can be recovered and put to more productive uses in a cost-effective manner. Yet a large number of studies suggest we can do much better if we make better choices and smarter investments.[17]

Americans waste enormous amounts of energy. Every day of the year, we burn off 100 million cubic feet of natural gas from U.S. oil fields, enough to heat 500,000 homes for a day.[18] Our electrical generation system by itself squanders almost 30 quadrillion BTUs of heat a year (more than the primary energy consumption of Japan).[19]

What the national data on energy use show, in sum, is considerable waste. Consumption is growing. There are only small changes in a fuel mix dominated by fossil fuels. While emissions of conventional pollutants from energy use have declined, greenhouse gas emissions are growing. But the national data also conceal important differences among states—differences that have remained largely unchanged since 1992.[20] In 2009, the five states with the lowest energy use per dollar of GDP were New York, Connecticut, Massachusetts, Hawaii, and California (ranging from $3.91 to $4.61 per thousand BTUs), while the five highest were Kentucky, Arkansas, Wyoming, North Dakota, and Louisiana ($13.53 to $17.53 per thousand BTUs). The national average was $7.33.[21]

Similar results occur when states are analyzed for lowest and highest per capita energy use. In 2009, New York, Rhode Island, Hawaii, Massachusetts, and California had the lowest energy use per capita (ranging from 196 to 217 million BTUs per capita), while Indiana, North Dakota, Louisiana, Arkansas, and Wyoming had the highest (ranging from 472 to 956 million BTUs per capita). The national average is 308 million BTUs.[22]

While the rankings of many states—whether in leading or lagging positions—remained relatively stable, a number showed considerable progress in improving their energy intensity. The five states with the largest reductions in energy use per dollar of GDP over this period were Oregon, Indiana, Washington, Texas, and Rhode Island (ranging from a 40% to 53% decrease between 1992 and 2009, while the U.S. average was a 29% decrease).[23] For a different indicator—energy use per capita—some states experienced reductions during this same period, and others experienced increases. The five states with the largest reduction in energy use per capita were Washington, Delaware, Hawaii, Texas, and Rhode Island (ranging from an 18% to 26% reduction). They were well ahead of the U.S. average of an 8% reduction. By contrast, the states with the largest percentage increase in energy use per capita were Minnesota, North Dakota, Nebraska, Iowa, and South Dakota (ranging from a 7% to 50% increase).[24]

The varying degrees of success of state-led energy efficiency programs are due in part to historical, social, economic, and climatic contexts. Some states are simply more reliant upon energy-intensive industries than others. Others use a large share of their energy for residential and commercial building uses, which are more amenable to energy savings programs. Nonetheless, the most important lesson from these figures is that there are many ways to improve the sustainability of an energy system, and states continue to experiment and to learn which policies are most effective for their particular needs. Despite significant variation in local conditions, many good practices can be gleaned from the states' experiences (described in more detail in Chapter 5).

Production and Consumption of Water

While the United States has abundant supplies of fresh water, it also has a very high per capita rate of water use. Water supplies are subject to regional shortages, particularly in arid areas in the South and West where there are large populations, heavy water usage, or both. Water scarcity is likely to become an even greater problem because of climate change and will likely have its greatest effects on cooling of hydroelectric power plants, on agriculture, and on public water supplies.

Along with the atmosphere, water is the most fundamental of resources. Adequate supplies of safe drinking water are essential for human health and welfare, and water is the lynchpin of every ecosystem on which humans and other species depend. A reliable supply of good water is also necessary to grow food and fiber (including forests), to support livestock and other sources of food, and to manufacture essential products. Other important but not necessarily essential uses include energy production (for example, hydroelectric power and power plant cooling), transportation, wastewater processing, recreation, and irrigation for aesthetic purposes (such as fountains or decorative ponds).[25]

The United States is blessed with a large supply of fresh water in rivers, lakes, and underground aquifers, and replenishment by precipitation is sufficient in many regions. North America enjoys four times as much fresh water per capita as Europe and Asia, and about three times as much as Africa (although less than South America and Australia).[26] As a result, on a national basis the United States uses a smaller percentage of its renewable water supplies than many other countries when measured as both per capita withdrawals (650 cubic meters per person, or m^3/person, roughly 26% of renewable water resources)[27] and total consumption (one-fifteenth of renewable supplies).[28] Approximately 80% of water withdrawals are from surface water, and 20% from groundwater.[29]

By some measures, sustainability of water use appears to have improved in the United States over the past several decades. The population has grown steadily since the 1950s, when the U.S. Geological Survey (USGS) began to publish detailed information on national water use every five years. Total water withdrawals from surface and groundwater peaked in 1980 and declined in the 1980s and 1990s, although withdrawals increased slightly between 1995 and 2005 (but not to 1980 levels).[30] Some water experts attribute these declines in water use to efficiency improvements, changes in the structure of the U.S. economy, the federal Clean Water Act (which led to significantly reduced industrial withdrawals as a discharge reduction strategy), and declining access to new water supplies due to physical, environmental, and other constraints.[31] That said, the United States is still profligate in its use of freshwater. On a per capita basis, U.S. water use is among the highest in the world, even by reference to other economically developed countries (Table 2.2).

Table 2.1
Per Capita Water Use in the United States and Selected Countries[32]

Country	Per capita annual water withdrawals (m³/person/year)
United States	1834
Canada	1607
Spain	884
Japan	735
Italy	730
Germany	579
Turkey	558
France	547
Norway	489
China	439
South Africa	366
Sweden	340
Israel	287
Denmark	233
World average	650

The data in Table 2.1 must be interpreted in context. Water withdrawals in a particular country depend on climate, the amount of irrigated acreage for agriculture, and other economic and physical factors. Still, this information suggests that there is considerable room for improvement in water efficiency in the United States without sacrificing economic prosperity.

In some regions of the United States, water use is often not sustainable because demand exceeds available supplies or because water is used faster than it can be naturally replaced.[33] This imbalance can become severe in some regions during a drought, but in certain parts of the country it is a chronic problem. For example, for many years water has been overdrawn at rates that exceed natural recharge in agricultural regions such as those served by the Ogallala Aquifer in the western portion of the Great Plains.[34] Surface water systems are also increasingly stressed in arid regions such as the Colorado River Basin,[35] and even in typically wetter regions in eastern states where rapid urban growth has outstripped water supplies.[36] Significant seasonal variations in precipitation can also cause imbalances between supply and demand, especially where high summer demand for crops and other irrigation water occurs during drier months of the year.[37]

These conditions are likely to be exacerbated by climate change. Available models predict that climate-induced changes in precipitation will further stress water supplies in some regions (most likely, areas that are already arid), while increasing the amount and intensity of precipitation in other regions, leading to increased flooding.[38] A recent U.S. Geological Society report indicated that "[o]f all the potential threats posed by climatic variability and change, those associated with water resources are arguably the most consequential for both society and the environment."[39]

Efforts to reduce water use will affect some economic sectors more than others, and will affect some kinds of water uses. The largest consumptive water use (use that reduces the supply from which it is provided, as opposed to nonconsumptive water uses such as recreation and hydroelectric power) in the United States is for cooling of thermoelectric power plants (49%), followed by irrigation (31%) and providing the public water supply (11%).[40] Some water uses are inherently sustainable from the perspective of conserving the freshwater resource itself. For example, water generates electricity by running through turbines in hydroelectric projects and is returned immediately to the river. By contrast, water used to cool thermal electric power plants evaporates and is lost to the water system from which it is taken, although it will eventually replenish the system through subsequent precipitation. Of course, even nonconsumptive water uses that are sustainable from a water use and conservation perspective (such as hydroelectric power) may degrade water resources through contamination, or the underlying projects might degrade ecosystems through habitat alteration.

Production and Consumption of Materials

Sustaining the flow of materials in an economy requires knowing the size of the virgin stock of materials available and working to conserve them during production. Sustainability is determined by the ability to consume as few raw materials as possible to sustain essential services and nonessential material desires, replace less-sustainable products with more-sustainable counterparts, and use consumer goods longer and more productively. An issue in materials consumption that is not as prominent in energy sectors is disposal of materials that cannot be eliminated and cannot be reused.[41] It is not only the quantity of materials that we use, but also the way in which those materials are processed, delivered, used, and disposed of that greatly affects environmental quality and human health.

The United States is the world's largest absolute consumer of most natural resources and, in many cases, the world's largest consumer of natural resources on a per capita basis.[42] There have been some improvements to the intensity of resource use in the United States, in part due to improvements in the efficiency with which materials are used, and in part because of state recycling laws. Yet much of the reduction in materials consumption in recent years appears to be caused by the economic downturn rather than conservation efforts. (The caveat here, however, is that these conclusions are extrapolated from limited data. For materials production and consumption, there is no federal counterpart to the EIA's comprehensive energy reports.)

Materials flows analysis (MFA) is a growing field of research that calculates the flows of materials in an economy using data from the U.S. Census Bureau and other government agencies. Studies in MFA are beginning to show the "metabolism of materials" within our system—their sources, manufacture, uses, and disposal, including traditionally ignored issues such as waste flows and stocks of obsolete products. MFA aims for a total accounting—from virgin natural resources to final disposal. An MFA study typically looks to three indicators to judge materials intensity: (1) material consumed per dollar of GDP, (2) materials use per capita, and (3) total materials use. MFAs can help to organize and simplify a large body of information for policymakers looking to prioritize limited governance resources towards tackling those materials and uses that have the greatest potential to harm the environment or human health. Such information can be invaluable when environmental, human health, or resource-availability issues occur without apparent cause.

The most comprehensive MFA of the U.S. economy was undertaken by the World Resources Institute in 2008.[43] Between 1975 and 2000, materials consumed per dollar of GDP declined by 31%. However, per capita materials consumption increased by 23% over the same period, while total consumption of materials increased by 57%. As Figure 2.3 shows, the greatest increases in per capita and total materials consumption occurred after 1992, whereas throughout that period materials consumed per dollar of GDP continued to slowly decrease.

Figure 2.3
Total and Per Capita U.S. Materials Consumption, 1975–2000[44]

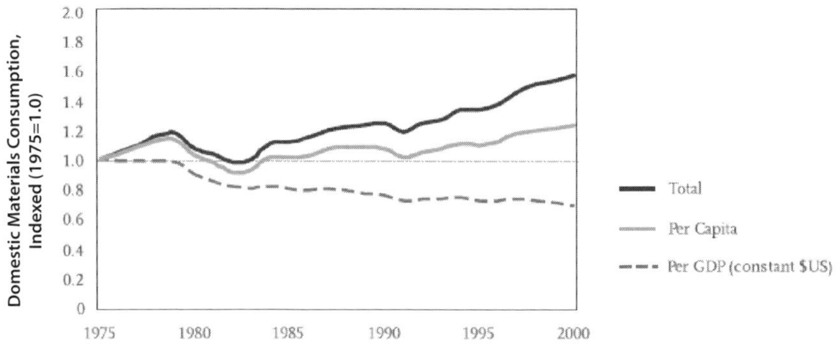

More recent data show that although the United States appears to have achieved real progress in reducing materials consumption for some materials by 2009, this progress must be understood within the context of the global financial crisis. Apparent consumption of key materials has declined since 1991, as seen in Figure 2.4. (Apparent consumption is calculated by adding production and imports, then subtracting exports; any other change in available stock is also added or subtracted.[45]) The sharp change in materials intensity indicates the effects of the economic changes that have occurred since the financial crisis. Without the large drops in materials consumption in the construction sector and in industrial production that have occurred since 2008, the U.S. economy would very likely have surpassed the total consumption rates seen in 2006. It is also possible, however, that the construction asset bubble created by the loose monetary policy of most of the post-Rio period may have resulted in dramatically higher consumption rates than would have been experienced under less aggressive expansion in the construction sector.

Figure 2.4[46]
U.S. Total Apparent Consumption
for Certain Mineral Commodities, 1991-2009
(1991 = 1)

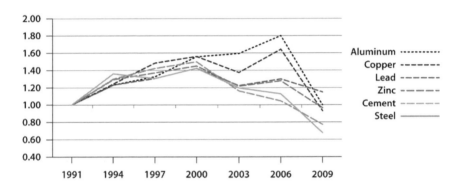

In summary, the dominant factor changing U.S. materials consumption in recent years appears to be the economic downturn. But it is not the only factor. As Figures 2.4 shows, apparent consumption of certain important mineral commodities was already declining by 2000.

Population

The U.S population is the third-largest in the world, behind only China and India, and it continues to grow steadily. Although Americans commonly view population as a problem for other countries, the data on birthrates show that world population growth has begun to slow while the U.S. population continues to grow. To understand this discrepancy in perception, it is worth sketching global trends before describing what is happening in the United States.

The world's population roughly quadrupled during the 20th century and passed 7 billion in 2011. Demographers at the United Nations project that it will exceed 9 billion by 2050 and reach 10 billion by 2100.[47] Even so, the pace of population growth is slowing. Birthrates nearly everywhere around the globe fell throughout the 1990s, and by 2010 the global average population growth rate was 1.2% per year, having fallen from its highest rate of about 2.0% in the 1960s. By the 21st century, the great majority of population growth was in the developing world, where the average growth rate was 1.4%.[48] Accordingly, the average family size in the developing world dropped from 6.2 children per woman in 1950 to 2.7 in 2010.[49] Changes in population growth rates also lag behind fertility changes because of "population momentum," caused by the higher birthrates of previous generations.[50] That momentum is why population growth is likely to continue throughout the 21st century.

Over the last decade the United States added some 27 million people to its population by natural birth and immigration, an increase of just under 10%.[51] The United States today is the *only* major industrialized country in the world experiencing significant population growth.[52] Projections of future U.S. population size by demographers vary under differing assumptions about future immigration and fertility trends. Assuming no significant change in either factor, most indicate a population of considerably more than 400 million by 2050,[53] and no hint of an end to growth in subsequent decades.

It is not a large U.S. population alone that presents challenges to sustainability; it is a large population coupled with high rates of consumption. With some 309 million people in 2010, and with one of the world's largest per capita incomes, the global reach and impact of the United States through trade, greenhouse gas emissions, and extraction of resources is unparalleled.

In 2010 the average number of children born per woman in the United States was 2.0, slightly below the replacement rate of 2.06.[54] The total fertility rate has been at or below replacement level for more than 30 years, yet the population is continuing to grow significantly, in part because of population momentum and in part because of a high rate of immigration. The natural increase (births minus deaths) of the U.S. population is 0.6 % annually, but it is growing at nearly 1.0 % when immigration is included.[55] Since 2000 the U.S. population growth rate has fallen from 1.3% per year, mainly because of a lower rate of immigration. Immigration today contributes roughly 30% of the annual population growth, having declined from a 40% share in 2000.[56] The Census Bureau estimated that some 38 million foreign-born persons were living in the United States in 2007, amounting to about 12.7% of the total population.[57]

Technology

The environmental impacts of U.S. production and consumption of energy, materials, and water are large because of the technologies we use. The impact of technology is a function of both the available technologies and human behavior in deploying and using them. More-sustainable technologies—not just prototypes but reliable technologies being deployed at a large scale in the real world—would reduce environmental impacts and help restore the environment. We are a long way from the widespread use of such technologies, largely because we have never systematically tried to develop them. Although a national sustainable technologies strategy was adopted in 1995, it was never fully implemented.

The United States is a country awash in waste—an embarrassing abundance that goes largely unutilized. The U.S. economy is based on what some industrial ecologists have termed a linear model, where resources are viewed as unlimited and very high waste flows are produced (Figure 2.5). On the other hand, a sustainable system is one in which those materials are recycled or reused, and there is no waste.

Figure 2.5
Three Types of Resource Flow Systems[58]

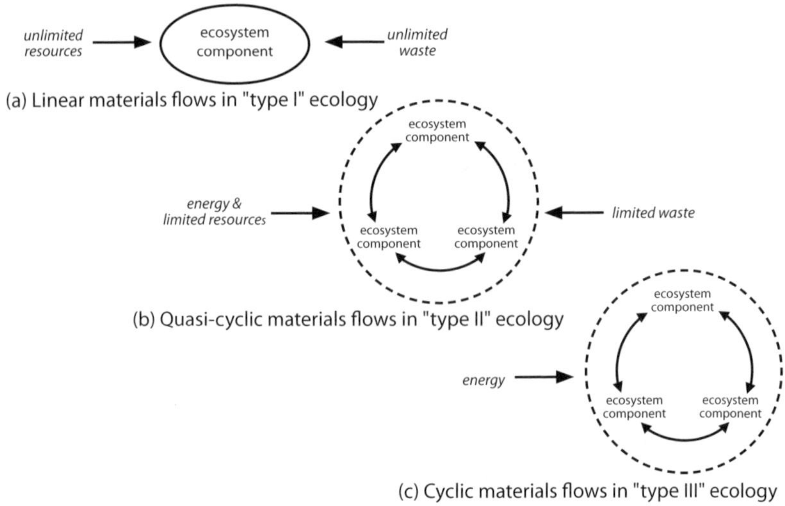

(a) Linear materials flows in "type I" ecology

(b) Quasi-cyclic materials flows in "type II" ecology

(c) Cyclic materials flows in "type III" ecology

The 1995 National Environmental Technology Strategy,[59] an effort by the U.S. government to bring science and technology into alignment with sustainability, has been lost in the backwaters of memory. That strategy, which was built on six years of interagency work and 25 workshops held around the United States, laid out a vision of the technological transformation needed to move the U.S. towards greater levels of sustainability. The specific goals of the strategy were "to generate 40 to 50 percent less waste, use 30 to 40 percent less energy, and 20 to 25 percent less materials per unit of gross domestic product."[60] Figure 2.6 depicts the strategy as an evolution from pollution control (the current model) to sustainable communities. Describing the challenge, John Gibbons, the advisor to the president for science and technology, noted:

Together we must transform our technological infrastructure to use less energy and less materials, to cause less environmental harm, and, at the same time, to provide those goods and services we all desire. In this joint endeavor, we seek more than small steps down the familiar technological paths. Instead, we seek a transformation of our industrial economy, a transformation involving technological ingenuity and a people committed to stewardship.[61]

Figure 2.6
Moving Toward Sustainable Solutions[62]

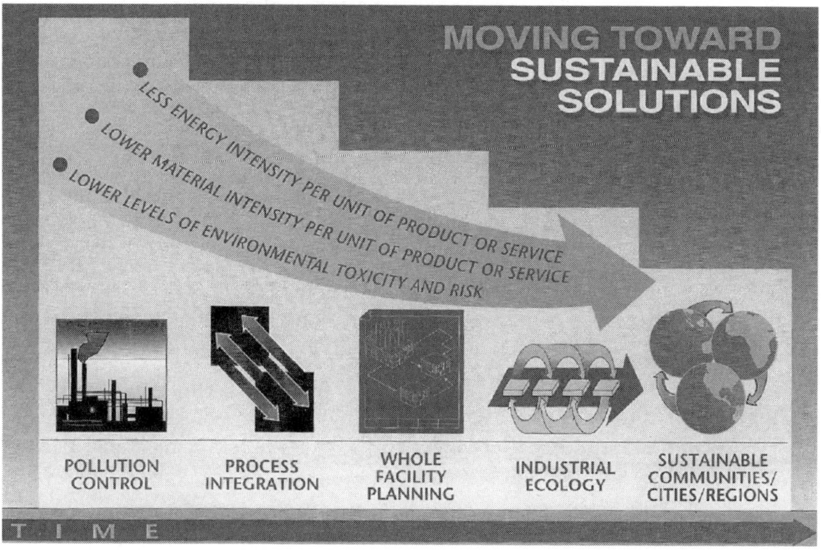

That never happened. There were small successes, such as those in green chemistry. In 1994, EPA and the National Science Foundation established the Technology for a Sustainable Environment program, which invested $57 million over a 10-year period in 205 research projects, most of them focused on supporting green chemistry and increasing the energy and material efficiency of industrial processes.[63]

Because of the absence of a push from the public or catalyzing events (think catastrophes) and poorly defined institutional responsibilities, coordinated federal efforts languished, and many of the initiatives launched under the National Environmental Technology Initiative waned during the Bush years. Only recently have we seen increased federal focus on science and technology linked to sustainability.

Several recent developments provide some reason to be more hopeful about technology for sustainability. In 2010, the National Science Foundation launched a new multi-year program called Science, Engineering, and Education for Sustainability, to address challenges in climate and energy research and education, using a systems-based approach to understand, predict, and react to change in the interwoven natural, social, and built environments.[64] The EPA has just announced its Chemical Safety for Sustainability Research Program.[65] The agency also received a report from the National Research Council (part of the National Academy of Sciences (NAS)) on how to incorporate sustainability into agency programs, which includes the development of better metrics, analytical tools, and an operational framework.[66] The NAS is also undertaking a nationally focused study, Sustainability Linkages in the Federal Government, to identify and describe the linkages among domains such as energy, water, and health that are not usually considered in decisionmaking.[67]

Energy research and development has also been undervalued and underfunded. The paucity of research and development funds for clean energy technologies and inconsistent funding from the federal government makes research and development difficult to carry out and causes inefficient use of the funds that are provided. In addition, governmental research and development tends to work on a different time frame. Unlike the private sector, which seeks short-term results, the government is interested in technologies that will become mature in three to five years. Inadequate and inconsistent funding thus causes the national effort to be even less effective than it might be. The difficulty in achieving lasting private-public partnerships and close collaborations with other countries on research and development for clean energy has also slowed progress in addressing achievements needed over the long term.

Another good sign is that federal research and development funding for renewable energy more than doubled between 2007 and 2010, and that research and development funding to improve the energy efficiency of various end-use technologies (for example, buildings and vehicles) nearly doubled in the same period.[68] Federal research and development funding for nuclear power, coal, and natural gas also increased during that time, though by lesser percentages.[69]

Still another hopeful sign—and one with the potential for considerable benefit over the long term—is the Department of Energy's 2011 report on its first quadrennial technology review.[70] This report, which is modeled on the long-term planning embodied in the Defense Department's quadrennial review, identifies six priority strategies: increasing vehicle efficiency, electrification of light-duty motor vehicles, deployment of alternative fuels, increasing the energy efficiency of buildings and industry, modernizing the electric grid, and deploying clean electricity. The Department of Energy report also found that the agency had underinvested in transportation research even though "reliance on oil is the greatest immediate threat to U.S. economic and national security" and contributes to climate change. Improvements in vehicle efficiency and the use of electricity to power vehicles, the report said, could reduce oil consumption.[71] The agency said it would use this review to make changes in its energy research and development funding and that it hoped this review would lead to a government-wide quadrennial energy review.[72]

Conclusion

Americans tend to frame their understanding of environmental protection in terms of specific causes and specific effects. When we limit our focus in this way, we miss the big picture. The $I = P \times A \times T$ equation provides a way of understanding the underlying reasons for the growing environmental impact of the United States over the past two decades—both within this country and as experienced globally. We consume large and generally growing amounts of energy, water, and materials, although some materials consumption appears to have declined recently for reasons other than the economic slowdown. Our population continues to grow. And we have not been effective in developing technology to reduce the effects of a growing population that consumes more and more resources.

There are, of course, signs of progress. Over the past several decades, per capita energy consumption and air pollution from energy use have declined, and the efficiencies with which materials and energy are used (per dollar of GDP) have improved. There have also been noticeable improvements in the efficiency with which water is used. The Obama Administration has recently made efforts to fund research to accelerate the development of new technologies, including energy technologies. Still, we have not seen a systematic effort to address these underlying issues—much less any comprehensive effort to use improvements in technology or resource efficiency to address poverty and unemployment.

CHAPTER 3

Greater Poverty, Unemployment, and Attention to Environmental Justice

In addition to environmental degradation, a key motivation for the Earth Summit was poverty—particularly poverty in developing countries. Nearly 3 billion people live on less than two dollars per day and lack services that are taken for granted in developed countries, such as access to clean water and education. In its report, *Our Common Future*, the World Commission on Environment and Development explained how poverty and environmental degradation are related. Poverty reduces the time and resources that people have to protect and restore the environment in which they live. Environmental degradation contributes to poverty because people who breathe unhealthy air, drink unclean water, and live in environmentally unsafe areas are less likely to be able to earn a living to support themselves and their families.[1]

The Earth Summit delegates were aware that there is a growing and pronounced trend toward greater economic and social inequality around the world. By addressing poverty and the environment together, it was hoped the condition of the world's poorest would be improved and inequality would be reduced. For developing countries in particular, there was another worry. Because high levels of consumption in developed countries such as the United States were already causing significant global environmental problems, developing countries did not want an environmental protection agenda to lock them into existing levels of poverty and underdevelopment. If developed countries moved in a more-sustainable direction by reducing their overall environmental impact (through changes in consumption, population, and technology), there would be more economic opportunity for all of the world's people.

Of course, poverty in the United States is quite different from poverty in developing countries. Even the poorest Americans ordinarily live on much more than two dollars per day, and nearly everyone has access to reasonably clean water and a free public education. But even poverty in affluent America is inconsistent with human opportunity and quality of life, longstanding American policy objectives that also happen to be major objectives of sustainable development.

This chapter provides an overview of the relatively high unemployment and poverty rate in the United States and the country's growing gap between rich and poor. It reviews some of the efforts over the past two decades to address the relationship between poverty and environmental degradation. The basic method for protecting all people from the adverse effects of pollution and environmental degradation, including low-income people and the unemployed, continues to be environmental law. While these laws have achieved some significant improvements over the past two decades, they have not fully or effectively addressed many problems—including some that are longstanding and others that have only recently emerged. Because this book is written from an environmental sustainability perspective, this chapter focuses on ways in which environmental degradation contributes to poverty and unemployment, and on ways that environmental protection and restoration can reduce them. But to understand the part of the poverty and unemployment problem that environmental sustainability can address, it is first important to review the problem as a whole.

Poverty, Unemployment, and Inequality

The recession that began with the financial crisis of 2008 led to increases in both unemployment and poverty. The unemployment rate is now higher than at any time in the past 40 years, except for 1982 (Figure 3.1). The poverty rate is approaching, but has not yet reached, the highest levels reached during this same period. According to the United States Census Bureau, the poverty rate has increased each year from 2007 to 2010.[2] In 2010, 46.2 million people were in poverty, representing 15.1% of the U.S. population.[3]

Figure 3.1
Poverty and Unemployment, 1970–2010[4]

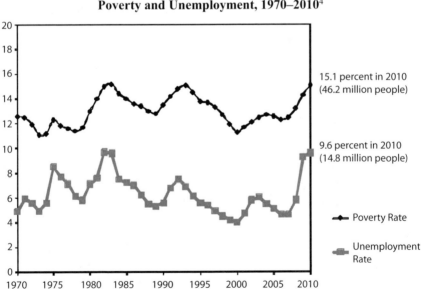

15.1 percent in 2010
(46.2 million people)

9.6 percent in 2010
(14.8 million people)

Poverty Rate

Unemployment Rate

Economic inequality has also increased over the past few decades. In 2010, households in the top income bracket earned more than 15 times the income of those in the lowest income bracket (Table 3.1). The top 20% of households received 50.3% of all household income that year, while the bottom 20% got just 3.3%.

Table 3.1
Measures of Household Income Dispersion, 2010 (2010 dollars)[5]

Percentile of Household Income Quintile	Mean Household Income ($)	Share of all Household Income (%)
Lowest	11,034	3.3
Second	28,636	8.5
Middle	49,309	14.6
Fourth	79,040	23.4
Highest	169,633	50.3

Household income inequality has grown significantly in the past few decades, as measured by the Gini index, a mathematical measure of income inequality that can range from 0, indicating perfect equality (where everyone has the same income), to 1.0, indicating perfect inequality (where one person has all the income and the rest have none). The Gini index of income inequality for the United States was 0.469 in 2010, up from 0.462 in 2000, 0.428 in 1990, 0.403 in 1980, and 0.394 in 1970.[6] Pertinent here, income inequality in the United States also tends to be larger than in other industrialized nations. For example, according to one recent survey, the most recent Gini indices of household income inequality were just 0.23 for Sweden, 0.327 for France, 0.27 for Germany, and 0.34 for the United Kingdom.[7]

Figure 3.2 shows how family income levels have changed from 1970 to 2010. Of note, income growth in recent decades was strongest among families in the top 1% of household income.[8] A report by the Center for Budget and Policy Priorities (CBPP) determined that after-tax incomes for the top 1%—after adjusting for inflation—rose by 281% between 1970 and 2007. The Congressional Budget Office data analyzed by the CBPP suggests "greater income concentration at the top of the income scale than at any time since 1928."[9]

Figure 3.2
Family Income by Percentile, 1970-2010[10]

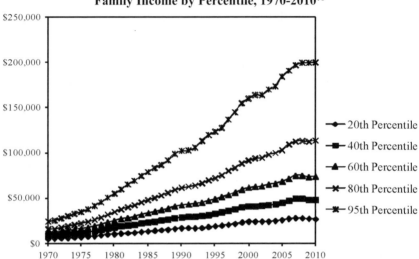

Another way to measure changes in earnings inequality is to study the ratio of average earnings for those in the highest 10% of earners and the average for those in the lowest 10% of earners over time. The 90/10 earnings ratio of male workers increased from 3.85 to 1 in 1970 to 5.50 to 1 in 2010.[11] Top-earning women earned 4.94 times as much as bottom-earning women in 2010, up from just 3.41 times as much in 1970.[12] All in all, earnings inequality increased by about 25% from 1970 to 2008.[13]

Environment and Poverty

Nearly all pollution and environmental degradation involves making some people worse off than they would otherwise be. Those who breathe polluted water, drink unclean water, bathe in contaminated rivers, or live next to substandard waste landfills are worse off for doing so. On the other hand, because polluters are not forced to bear the costs of preventing or controlling their damage, they are better off financially. So in some profound and perverse sense, pollution and environmental degradation redistribute the burdens and benefits of life. To be sure, activities that cause pollution can often have economic benefits and even create jobs, but the benefits often do not go to the same people who are harmed, and the resultant environmental degradation can counteract and even outweigh those benefits.

The poor tend to bear a higher share of the burdens of environmental degradation. To some degree this burden has been ameliorated over the past two decades. Environmental laws have significantly reduced the scope and severity of air and water pollution, improper waste disposal, and many other environmental problems.

Because the protection required does not vary based on the income of those living in a particular place, these laws have reduced, but not eliminated, much of the pollution burden on the poor. (These measures are described in more detail in Chapter 1.)

Four other significant activities and measures have also been undertaken to address the remaining pollution burdens on the poor. The first and most prominent general expression of this objective is the environmental justice movement, an effort to integrate environmental justice into federal programs. Integrating the concerns of low-income people into environmental policies is consistent with the sustainable development principle of addressing environmental, economic, and social concerns. Second is the creation of green jobs, the concept that environment-related industries can help create jobs, including jobs for the unemployed and those with low incomes, and thus boost the national and global economy. Third is climate justice, a political and social movement based on the view that those who contribute to climate change are causing or contributing to serious problems for others, particularly the poor and those in developing countries. Fourth is the continuing effort to prevent lead poisoning, especially from lead-based paint.

Environmental Justice

Environmental justice is a critically important component of sustainability. The uneven impact of environmental laws spawned the environmental justice movement, which mobilized to protect adversely affected communities and make lawmakers and other decisionmakers aware of the potential consequences.

Environmental justice (EJ) is based on the conviction that minority and low-income individuals, communities, and populations should not be disproportionately exposed to environmental hazards and that they should share in making the decisions that affect their environment.[14] EPA defines environmental justice as "the fair treatment and meaningful involvement of all people regardless of race, color, national origin, culture, education, or income with respect to the development, implementation, and enforcement of environmental laws, regulations, and policies."[15]

Many view the 1982 protest in Warren County, North Carolina, as the beginning of the environmental justice movement, when people protested the state's plan to dump more than 6,000 truckloads of PCB-contaminated soil into a "secure" landfill in an area with a high poverty rate populated mostly by African Americans. Galvanized by community struggles countrywide, activists have created a multiracial grassroots movement aimed at achieving environmental and social equality.[16] Following a number of influential studies indicating that government agencies disproportionately located hazardous waste landfills near low-income, minority populations, EPA created the Office of Environmental Equity (now the Office of Environmental Justice) in 1992.[17] The National Environmental Justice Advisory Council, a federal advisory committee, was established by charter in 1993 (and rechartered in 2008) to bring together representatives of community, academic, industrial, environmental, indigenous, and government groups at all levels to provide advice to EPA on integrating environmental justice principles into EPA actions.[18] In 1994, President Bill Clinton issued Executive Order 12898, mandating that federal government agencies incorporate environmental justice as part of their missions.[19]

In September 2010, after a decade of what many advocates saw as slow movement on the part of the federal government to address environmental justice in any meaningful way, EPA Administrator Lisa Jackson and Council on Environmental Quality Chair Nancy Sutley reconvened the then-dormant Federal Interagency Working Group on Environmental Justice. This was followed by a historic White House meeting in December 2010 between administration cabinet members and about 100 environmental justice advocates. Administrator Jackson has made environmental justice a priority, announcing Plan EJ 2014[20] (to mark the 20th anniversary of President Clinton's 1994 executive order) to further help EPA integrate environmental justice into the agency's programs, policies, and activities. The effort is designed to result in a strategy, not a regulation, to protect health in communities overburdened by pollution; to empower communities to take action to improve their health and environment; and to establish partnerships among local, state, tribal, and federal organizations to achieve healthy and sustainable communities.[21]

One of the principles of the EJ movement is that communities impacted by environmental degradation need the tools—access to information and skill building—to be able to advocate for themselves. Since 1994 the EPA's EJ Small Grants Program has awarded more than 1,200 grants totaling more than $20 million to help affected communities create self-sustaining, community-based partnerships that will continue to improve local environments.[22]

While the EPA definition of environmental justice and Executive Order 12898 focus on potential disproportionate harm from environmental hazards, environmental justice also requires that environmental benefits be equitably distributed. cause minority and low-income populations tend to live in the most polluted areas, environmental benefits such as cleaner air and water tend to be lower there than in more affluent areas.[23] Yet EJ should result in better public health, higher environmental quality, and improved job opportunities in those communities.[24] While this has proven true to a significant degree over the past two decades, it is not always true. As Professor Richard Lazarus of Harvard Law School notes:

> Inequities in the ultimate distribution of environmental protection benefits may also result, paradoxically, from environmental improvement itself. A cleaner physical environment may increase property values to such an extent that members of a racial minority with fewer economic resources can no longer afford to live in that community.[25]

Some studies have shown a similarly neutral or regressive distribution of benefits from pollution reductions.[26] A study of the cleanup of contaminated sites by economists H. Spencer Banzhof and Randall P. Walsh, for example, found evidence of gentrification[27] as wealthier people "move into cleaner neighbor-hoods," while "poorer families pay higher rents," frequently "leaving the original residents worse off."[28]

Moreover, despite the fact that most Americans are served by modern infra-structure for sanitation and drinking water, there is evidence that surprisingly large numbers of people in some areas predominantly inhabited by disadvantaged minor-ity groups face high public health risks, comparable even to what one might find in the developing world. A recent article by Dr. Peter Hotez, of the Baylor College of Medicine, identified five regional "communities" in the United States where substandard plumbing, water, or sanitation lead to disease burdens similar to those in developing nations.[29] In Appalachia in 2000, for example, an estimated 169,000 households had no indoor plumbing whatsoever. Almost 3% of the population in the region lived in housing that lacked complete plumbing (in some counties up to 25%). These conditions can lead to significant rates of illness. As of the late 1970s, infection rates for ascariasis (a parasitic worm that is virtually nonexistent in most parts of the developed world) in schoolchildren were in the 13-14% range in some counties, and no surveys have been conducted since that time to determine whether the situation has changed. Hotez identified high rates of tuberculosis and parasitic infections such as ascariasis and roundworm in the Mississippi Delta and former Cotton Belt region and high rates of rat-borne and louse-borne bacterial infections and toxacaria infections in disadvantaged urban areas. In the Mexican borderland region he found high rates of substandard housing and an estimated 30,000 hous-ing units without indoor plumbing, not including mobile homes, leading to high infection rates of vector-borne diseases, including dengue fever and Chagas disease. And in some Native American tribal regions up to 20% of all homes lack complete indoor plumbing, causing high rates of trachoma (bacterial eye infection) and cystic echinococcosis (tapeworms).

There can be conflicts between environmental justice and environmental protec-tion. For example, restrictions on rebuilding in the highest flood-risk areas in New Orleans after Hurricane Katrina were defeated by EJ concerns about preventing poor and ethnic communities from returning to their low-lying neighborhoods. A smaller, higher footprint—the result if they had relocated elsewhere—would have greatly reduced the size and scope of levee systems and limited the consequent destruction of the remaining coastal wetlands.

Green Jobs

The "green economy"—generally defined as the sector that produces goods and services with an environmental benefit—is a compelling vision for many com-munities and regions around the country. Many individuals and organizations are working to increase the likelihood that the green economy will generate jobs in their communities. While estimates vary about how many green jobs are available, the potential growth in this part of the economy appears to be considerable.

While the green economy initially stemmed from environmental concerns, sustainability and new market opportunities are now driving the creation and reinvention of industries and jobs focused on reducing negative environmental and social impacts. It is difficult to define boundaries and scope of the green economy because green activities and jobs related to environmental goals cut across all sectors of the economy. The green economy is not only about wind farms and solar parks. It also includes parts of existing industries such as food production and materials recycling where the environmental activities are not easily counted.[30] A 2011 study by the Brookings Institution and Battelle's Technology Partnership provides a solid base for defining the green economy and job creation trends during the last 7-10 years and projecting what the future might bring if certain policies, programs, and practices are implemented. The study found that jobs in the clean-energy economy are on the rise while jobs in many other sectors are slipping away or moving overseas. And these green jobs tend to pay well. The study also found 2.7 million existing jobs in the "clean economy," which it defined to include energy and resource efficiency, agricultural and natural resources conservation, renewable energy, greenhouse gas reduction, recycling, environmental management, and education and compliance.[31] This part of the economy employs more people than the fossil fuel industry and is more manufacturing intensive than the rest of the economy. The green economy is also, perhaps most importantly, capable of considerable additional growth,[32] which can provide increased employment for minority and low-income populations to perform such jobs in their own communities.

In addition:

- The clean economy—including transportation, restoration, efficiency, and clean energy—grew at an annual rate of 3.4% from 2003 to 2010, adding half a million new jobs.[33]
- The part of the clean economy that is focused on clean energy in particular—the wind, solar, fuel cell, smart grid, biofuel, and battery companies—grew at an average rate of 8.3%, which is nearly twice the growth rate of the economy as a whole.[34]
- Roughly 26% of all clean economy jobs lie in manufacturing establishments, compared with just 9% in the broader economy. This figure includes jobs in electric vehicles, green chemical products, and lighting, which are both manufacturing and export intensive.[35]
- The clean economy offers more opportunities and better pay for low- and middle-skilled workers than the national economy as a whole. Median wages are 13% higher in green energy jobs than the overall economy average.[36]
- "Almost half of all jobs in the clean economy are held by workers with a high school diploma or less, compared to only 37.2% of U.S. jobs." At the same time, "only 32.5% of clean economy jobs are weak-wage (paying below the U.S. median) and low-skill, compared with 41.4% nationally."[37]

The clean economy has continued to grow even while industries across America have had to lay off workers or close up shop. Venture capital investment in clean technology is increasing, and investors are directing billions of dollars into American businesses in the clean energy economy.[38] Investments in the U.S. energy infrastructure are creating green jobs and expanding employment opportunities while reducing pollution, providing an alternative to foreign oil, and increasing exports. Continued investment in the clean economy and the growth of green jobs has the potential to result in greater productivity and long-term economic prosperity.[39]

While the clean economy holds promise for the growth of new technologies, processes, industries, and jobs, the clean economy does not represent a specific set of occupations that can be easily counted. Green jobs span huge numbers of industries and occupations and touch nearly every sector of the economy. They can be found in research and development, manufacturing, construction and installation, operations and maintenance, and retail and service.

Another way of looking at the pervasiveness of the emerging green economy is to look at the growth of what Collaborative Economics, Inc. (CE), refers to as the "core green economy." The core green economy "consists of businesses that provide the products and services that leverage clean energy sources, conserve energy and all natural resources, reduce pollution, and repurpose waste."[40] These companies are the core, CE says, "because they provide the means for all other businesses as well as households and public entities to transition to a cleaner and more resource efficient economy." The "adaptive green economy," in partial contrast, is composed of companies that are adopting more-sustainable practices and are "using the products and services of the Core Green Economy in order to improve the resource efficiency of their own operations." Given the emergence of companies in both the core and adaptive parts of the green economy, there is a wider range of job opportunities across the skills spectrum and greater potential for continued growth in green business.[41]

Job growth is a key reason why in the past decade many states adopted legislation encouraging or requiring the greater use of renewable energy and energy efficiency. (These laws are described in more detail in Chapter 5.) When Pennsylvania persuaded a major Spanish wind turbine manufacturer, Gamesa, to locate its North American headquarters and a manufacturing plant in the state, it created hundreds of new jobs.[42] Many of these new jobs have gone to laid-off workers from other manufacturing plants.[43]

At the federal and state level, much of the recent interest in laws on renewable energy and energy efficiency has been due to their potential to create or retain jobs. The American Recovery and Reinvestment Act of 2009 (ARRA)[44] was intended in part to stimulate energy efficiency and renewable energy, thus helping to create jobs in those industries. The act authorized $16.8 billion for energy efficiency and renewable energy.[45] A significant portion of this funding is in the form of tax incentives.[46] This and other recent legislation has made energy efficiency and renewable energy more attractive.[47] ARRA also included $5 billion for home weatherization grants to low and middle-income families; $1 billion for energy efficiency upgrades to federally supported and public housing, including new insulation, windows, and frames[48]; and $8 billion for high-speed rail.[49] The act was designed as a temporary measure, providing temporary funding. Still, the Council of Economic Advisors estimated that the number of people employed in 2011 because of the legislation was between 2.2 and 4.2 million.[50] A significant number of these jobs were due to the clean energy and infrastructure funding. Somewhat similarly, the famous "cash for clunkers" legislation in 2009, which provided rebates for trade-ins of less fuel-efficient vehicles for more fuel-efficient ones, produced modest fuel savings and greenhouse gas reduction benefits but saved or created more than 60,000 jobs in automobile manufacturing and sales and in related industries such as auto parts suppliers.[51]

There has not been any formal governmental reporting about green jobs, much less an officially recognized definition of green jobs. But the Labor Department's Bureau of Labor Statistics (BLS) has begun an initiative to "develop information on (1) the number of and trend over time in green jobs, (2) the industrial, occupational, and geographic distribution of the jobs, and (3) the wages of the workers in these jobs."[52] To collect data on green jobs, BLS defines them as either "[j]obs in businesses that produce goods or provide services that benefit the environment or conserve natural resources" or "jobs in which workers' duties involve making their establishment's production processes more environmentally friendly or use fewer natural resources."[53] The definition will be used in surveys covering 2.2 million of the nation's 9 million establishments, where most of the green jobs are believed to exist.[54] The collected data will be used to evaluate the labor-market effect of various environmental policy initiatives—something BLS has not previously been able to do. The first publication of green jobs data is planned for summer 2012.[55]

Climate Justice

Although the initial focus of the environmental justice movement was on unfair exposure to toxic substances or facilities in poor communities, its attention has expanded to include human-induced climate change. Around the world, governments, nongovernmental organizations, and individuals have been organizing to respond to the threat of climate change as a matter of justice. Most of the greenhouse gas emissions are coming from wealthier developed nations and richer people in developing nations, but the world's poorest people, who have done little to cause the problem, are experiencing the impacts most gravely.[56] The harshest impacts of climate change are predicted for parts of the world where millions of already impoverished people struggle to survive, such as the Horn of Africa. The poor lack the financial resources to respond to climate change's threats. Wealthier people in developed countries can afford to pay more for rising food prices caused by local droughts, but poor people starve when food prices rise.

For many poor countries or people living in poverty, climate change is not a future problem; it is already the cause of great human suffering and death.[57] The World Health Organization has estimated that by 2004 global warming was causing more than 140,000 excess deaths annually,[58] a number that is projected to increase in the years ahead. Tens of millions of poor people around the world have already suffered from droughts and floods, which are increasing in intensity and frequency in a warming world. Although science cannot attribute recent disastrous floods and droughts solely to human-induced climate change, the increase in intensity and frequency of damage now being experienced is predicted by climate change science.[59]

As a result of the inequality between those causing the problem and those experiencing its harshest impacts, climate change is being understood as a problem of justice. Representatives of some of the world's most vulnerable people are appearing more frequently at the annual meetings of the conference of the parties to the U.N. Framework Convention on Climate Change, demanding that high-emitting countries reduce their emissions to their fair share of safe global emissions.[60] There are also growing demands by developing countries for funding to help developing countries adapt to climate change problems that, they insist, they did not cause. These demands are likely to grow in the years ahead. Many organizations in the United States, including the National Association for the Advancement of Colored People, have put forward climate justice initiatives.[61]

Lead Poisoning

Although no income strata is immune to lead poisoning, low-income communities that have substandard housing with deteriorating lead-based paint surfaces, or located near polluting highways and waste dumps, are especially susceptible to lead poisoning. As a consequence, identification, control, and elimination of lead poisoning has been incorporated into community-improvement programs, ranging from healthy housing initiatives and abatement-contractor training to community gardening (plantings that uptake lead in soil) and Superfund site remediation.

The effort to address lead poisoning in the United States began decades ago with the phase-out of lead from paint and then gasoline. More recently, the Residential Lead-Based Paint Hazard Reduction Act of 1992[62] requires that prior notification of possible lead-based paint hazards be provided at the point of real estate sales and rentals. The act also promotes the development through funding and standard setting of the lead-based paint hazard assessment, inspection, and remediation industry that is needed to provide an effective lead-poisoning prevention program. As part of its EJ initiative, EPA instituted its State Environmental Justice Cooperative Agreements Program to support, among other things, "projects that utilize collaborative problem solving to address environmental and public health issues, such as childhood lead poisoning and exposure to air pollution."[63]

Conclusion

Just as environmental degradation and pollution contributes to poverty and unemployment, environmental protection and restoration can help reduce poverty and even create jobs. While environmental laws have improved environmental quality for nearly everyone, the benefits of environmental protection and the burdens of pollution have not been evenly distributed.

The background picture of U.S. poverty and unemployment at present is not pretty, although there are signs of improvement in unemployment as this book goes to press. The recession that began in 2008 has pushed poverty and unemployment in the United States to some of the highest levels in recent decades. Even before the recession began, however, income inequality had been growing for many years.

Regardless of the state of the economy, however, pollution and environmental degradation worsen living conditions, particularly those of poor people, leading the federal government to pay greater attention to environmental justice. There is also growing interest in green jobs that could employ a great many people, including the poor and unemployed. Perhaps the largest environmental justice issue, however—and one that could profoundly affect the United States—is caused by the adverse effect of U.S. greenhouse gas emissions on poor countries around the world.

CHAPTER 4

The Built Environment:
Shifting Toward Sustainability

Some would argue that economic growth is incompatible with the principles of sustainability. Yet making economic growth and development sustainable is one of the central objectives of the sustainable development movement. And a key component of sustainable development is to make the built environment—our homes, neighborhoods, and cities, as well as supporting infrastructure such as transportation, water, and energy systems—more sustainable. Laws and policies dealing with the environment, land use, and transportation impose some limitations on development of the built environment in order to protect, or at least reduce damage to, the environment. But halting or limiting destructive development is only part of the challenge. The greater task is to promote more-sustainable development. In a world that is experiencing growing competition for resources, depletion and impairment of resources, higher and fluctuating prices for fossil fuel, a growing economy, and an increasing population, more-sustainable development policies and practices are essential. More-sustainable development also provides important opportunities for economic growth, green jobs, and reduced costs to taxpayers—all of which are recurring themes in this book.

Efforts to promote sustainable development of the built environment over the past two decades have tended to focus on a small cluster of issues. Two of them—transportation and land use—seek to address the longstanding challenge of moving existing economic activities and infrastructure that are largely unsustainable in a more-sustainable direction. Two other areas—green building and brownfields redevelopment—are comparatively new. They involve development or redevelopment that is, by definition, more sustainable than conventional development.

The last two decades have seen the creation and deployment of a suite of legal and policy tools that move development in each of these sectors in a more-sustainable direction. In all of these areas, work of considerable sophistication is being done—transportation and land-use planning for livable communities, certification programs for green building, and a legal structure for voluntary cleanup of brownfield sites. These new approaches have been tested and successfully applied in a variety of ways. While these approaches have yet to become the norm within their fields, much of the groundwork for that to happen has now been laid.

Transportation

Definite progress toward sustainable transportation has occurred in the past 20 years. Key indicators of change include increased use of rail and public transit, a leveling off of the number of vehicle miles traveled per capita, reduced emissions of some pollutants, and long-overdue policy changes that promote cleaner transportation, increased fuel efficiency, and better connection between transportation and land use. Progress has been made at the national level and in many states, metropolitan areas, and localities, although most steps thus far are comparatively modest given the magnitude of the problem.

The bottom line is that our transportation system is not sustainable.[1] It is heavily dependent on fossil fuels, is a leading and growing source of carbon pollution, degrades our air and water, chews up farmland and natural areas, and contributes to a host of other environmental problems. Moreover, momentum for more-sustainable transportation is in danger of stalling in the face of recent proposed budget cuts, political polarization, and opposition from special interests.

The six indicators discussed below illustrate our progress—or lack of progress—toward more-sustainable transportation.

Greater Transportation Choices and Usage

Funding for alternatives to driving has increased significantly in the past 20 years, providing a greater range of less-polluting transportation choices. Although transportation policies and spending at all levels of government continue to focus primarily on roads and motor vehicles, a great many new rail, public transit, bicycle, and pedestrian projects have been completed. Even more importantly, use of these modes has surged, reflecting strong demand and a willingness of many people to change their travel behavior when alternatives to driving are available. Most new light-rail and streetcar systems have proven to be very successful in cities such as Charlotte, Dallas, Denver, Houston, Minneapolis, Phoenix, and Salt Lake City.[2] The number of public transit trips nationwide has ebbed and flowed, but overall rose more than 33% between 1995 and 2009.[3] Transit ridership has continued to increase on the whole, even in the face of an economic downturn and widespread fare hikes and service cutbacks.[4] Amtrak had the highest ridership in its 40-year history in 2011, rising 5% in that year alone to reach almost 30.2 million passengers.[5] There has also been an increase in bicycle and pedestrian projects and use. For example, New York City has expanded its network of bicycle paths and taken other steps to encourage cycling, resulting in a 14% increase in bicycle commuting between 2010 and 2011, and a 262% increase since 2000.[6]

Federal and state funding for freight rail has increased, helping to upgrade facilities to shift freight from trucks to rail and significantly reducing fuel consumption and air pollution. Norfolk Southern's Heartland Corridor project to improve the route from Virginia to the Midwest was funded by the railroad, the federal government, and the states of Virginia and Ohio.[7] The improvement is expected to remove

1.9 million trucks from Virginia's highways, save 189 million gallons of fuel, and cut carbon emissions by 700,000 tons in the first 15 years of operation.[8]

Linking Transportation and Land Use, Promoting Smarter Growth

Efforts have increased to promote more-sustainable development patterns and to better coordinate transportation and land-use planning by, for example, providing incentives for mixed-use, walkable, and transit-oriented development that better integrates where people live, work, and shop and reducing the number and length of vehicle trips.[9] Arlington County, Virginia, has been a leader in transit-oriented development, adopting a suite of policies to encourage development near transit stations, mixed-use development, and pedestrian-oriented design. The county now has one of the highest levels of public transit ridership in the country. Almost 40% of county residents in transit corridors commute by transit while another 10% bike or walk to work.[10] Motor vehicle traffic has held steady or even declined despite a growing population.[11] Portland, Oregon, has made multiple efforts to link transportation and land use, resulting in per capita vehicle travel well below the national average, as well as bicycling and transit rates far above average; one study estimates that the resulting savings in transportation and time total $2.6 billion annually.[12]

At the federal level, a significant effort to link transportation and land use is the collaboration between the Environmental Protection Agency, the Department of Transportation, and the Department of Housing and Urban Development (HUD) to form the Partnership for Sustainable Communities. To maximize the impact of each dollar spent by the three agencies, the program coordinates funding for promoting affordable, sustainable communities served by public transit.[13] To guide the administration of the program, the agencies have adopted a set of livability principles based on multiple transportation choices, equitable and affordable housing, enhanced economic competitiveness, coordination and leveraging of available funds, support for existing communities and neighborhoods, and investment "in healthy, safe, and walkable neighborhoods."[14] Investments can simultaneously lower transportation costs, reduce greenhouse gas emissions and other air pollution, decrease traffic congestion, encourage healthy walking and bicycling, and spur development of new homes and businesses around transit stations.[15] Despite those benefits, the program was opposed by Republicans in the House of Representatives in 2011, and HUD's funding for the partnership was eliminated by Congress for fiscal year 2012.[16]

Cleaner, More Efficient Vehicles

There has been some progress in reducing the direct impacts of vehicles, including increasing fuel efficiency, reducing tailpipe emissions, and promoting alternative-fuel vehicles, as Chapter 1 explained. The federal government has combined standards for fuel efficiency and limits to greenhouse gas emission for motor vehicles. In addition, there has been accelerated investment in advancing electric, hybrid, hydrogen, and other clean-fuel vehicles. The federal government, and many states and localities, have provided a range of tax credits, direct investments, and other incentives for producing alternative fuels, purchasing alternative-fuel vehicles, and developing fueling stations and other infrastructure.[17] Governments at all levels also have adopted purchasing requirements for their vehicle fleets to help drive the market, and have invested in research and development.[18]

New Approaches to Roads and Driving

Most states, and many localities, have adopted policy changes to build more efficient and less destructive roadways. Several innovations have been adopted: building narrower streets, creating "road diets" that reduce the number and width of lanes on existing streets, increasing the use of roundabouts, designing "complete streets" for all users (rather than just drivers), and starting "green street" programs that capture storm water and filter pollutants. Although the level of commitment varies widely, more than one-half of the states have adopted a context-sensitive policy to seek transportation solutions appropriate for the physical setting while preserving scenic, aesthetic, historical, and environmental resources.[19] The federal government, particularly the Department of Transportation, has primarily played a supporting role, encouraging these trends by providing project funding through its Transportation Enhancements program, technical assistance, and other measures.[20]

In addition to these policies, steps such as congestion pricing, charging for parking, and reducing minimum parking requirements can help reduce current subsidies for motor vehicle use. Such policies send price signals for the cost of driving, thus reducing driving rates and increasing the use of more-sustainable forms of transportation.[21]

Driving Rates

Americans drove almost 3 trillion miles in 2010. The amount of miles driven rose nearly 40% between 1990 and 2010[22]—almost twice the rate of population growth. But the rate of increase in miles driven has begun to slow, increasing only 9% between 2000 and 2010. In addition, vehicle miles traveled per capita actually decreased slightly nationwide between 2000 and 2010. The recent rise in gasoline prices and the economic downturn certainly have contributed to this drop, but demographic and other factors are at play as well, and the shift in driving rates began even before these recent events.[23]

Pollution Reduction

As a result of federal efforts to reduce tailpipe emissions and some of the trends noted above, the level of certain pollutants from transportation has dropped significantly since 1990. Annual emissions of smog-causing nitrogen oxides from highway vehicles declined by 42% between 1990 and 2007.[24] On the other hand, carbon dioxide emissions from transportation rose more than 27% during that period.[25]

In short, as these six indicators show, there are success stories throughout the country in moving toward more-sustainable transportation, but tremendous challenges remain.

Land Use

Two movements directed at regulating land use—smart growth and climate change/green development—have helped to shape the landscape of sustainability over the last 20 years. Both contain elements of environmental justice.

Smart Growth

The smart growth movement is driven by a series of principles that includes mixed land uses, walkable communities, preservation of open space, maintenance or creation of distinctive communities with a sense of place, and choice of transportation options. Its goal is to reenergize communities for growth and infill (development in unoccupied parts of a municipality's existing footprint) and to encourage public involvement in development decisions. The movement comprises myriad "creative strategies to develop in ways that preserve natural lands and critical environmental areas, protect water and air quality, and reuse already-developed land," which stand in opposition to the existing patterns of sprawl-centered development.[26]

There seem to have been more studies, executive orders, and legislation on smart growth between 1991 and 2005 than at present. But the quality of what is being enacted and implemented today under the smart growth framework is arguably better because of lessons learned from earlier efforts. The American Planning Association's *Growing Smart Legislative Guidebook*,[27] a manual for drafting and passing smart growth laws published in 2002, has been responsible for dozens of statutory and regulatory changes across the country.[28]

Concern that the smart growth movement would be nothing more than a passing phase has been mostly put to rest because it has been entrenched in federal policy. For example, EPA has created an entire office and on-line presence devoted to promoting smart growth and sustainable communities through publications, case studies, links to resources, technical assistance, and grant opportunities.[29] EPA has also provided sustained leadership through the Smart Growth Network[30] and its participation in the three-agency Partnership for Sustainable Communities described above.[31] The federal government as a whole is also providing sustained leadership for smart growth. A government-wide smart growth policy is being implemented, and funding is available to encourage smart growth at other levels of government.[32] Congress still maintains an interest in smart growth through the House Livable Communities Task Force.[33]

However, many states have not continued the same level of sustained leadership on smart growth as the federal government. The Florida Legislature in 2011 eliminated funding for the Department of Community Affairs, nationally known for its commitment to smart growth principles.[34] State-level smart growth offices specifically identified as such number less than 10. To some degree, smart-growth policies are being implemented and more-sustainable development is occurring even if the smart growth label is not used.[35] Colorado, for example, has been characterized as "arguably a smart growth state without a comprehensive state-level growth management program" because of a combination of residential land-use regulations, limited access to water (which promotes regional cooperation), and the role of mountains in both attracting and concentrating development.[36]

More broadly, major demographic trends and changing individual and business needs are creating a market for smarter growth patterns, placing a premium on well-designed, mixed-use, compact, walkable communities.[37] For example, the fastest growing age groups in the United States are young adults of the Generation Y or the "echo boomer" generation (ages 20-34) and seniors as the baby boomer generation gets older. Younger households often seek to rent rather than to own, particularly in the current economic climate, and many members of Gen Y are opting for a more urban lifestyle. An aging population means many people are seeking a smaller residence that requires less upkeep and often has lower property taxes and energy bills, as well as transportation options that offer mobility to those no longer able to drive. Other trends and impacts are contributing to changing market preferences as well. A national real estate assessment noted that "energy prices and road congestion accelerate the move back into metropolitan-area interiors as more people ... want to live closer to work and shopping without the hassle of car dependence."[38]

Market surveys consistently show strong interest in more compact, walkable communities.[39] The shortage of such options has led to price premiums for houses in mixed-use neighborhoods compared to those in single-use subdivisions nearby. The recent mortgage foreclosure crisis tended to hit suburban areas harder than cities, and housing values now tend to be higher in cities and inner suburbs than in far-flung suburbs.[40] Although it is difficult to predict future preferences, and some sprawl is likely to continue, a recent national real estate report concluded that "next-generation projects will orient to infill, urbanizing suburbs, and transit-oriented development."[41]

Climate Change and Green Development

While sustainability issues were framed predominantly under the smart growth movement in the 1990s and early 2000s, the focus has shifted to climate change and green development, especially after the release of the U.N. Intergovernmental Panel on Climate Change's *Fourth Assessment Report* in 2007.[42] The same year, the U.S. Supreme Court's decision in *Massachusetts v. EPA,*[43] which essentially ruled that greenhouse gases must be regulated under the Clean Air Act, provided additional support for federal and state agencies to consider emissions impacts under the National Environmental Policy Act (NEPA) and similar state legislation.

NEPA and its state-level counterparts require preparation of an environmental impact statement for major actions and consideration of alternatives to those actions. So far, only a few states have applied these laws to climate change. In 2007, Massachusetts became the first state to officially incorporate the impacts of climate change into its environmental review procedures. The regulations, which apply to a variety of local land-use and transportation projects, direct agencies to "consider reasonably foreseeable climate change impacts, including additional greenhouse gas emissions, and effects, such as predicted sea level rise." Project applicants must submit analyses of projected emissions and must consider mitigation options to the extent feasible. If options that are more energy-efficient are rejected, applicants must explain why.[44] In July 2009, the New York Department of Environmental Conservation followed Massachusetts' lead and amended its regulations to guide state and local agencies in the process of assessing and mitigating greenhouse gas emissions from large-scale land-development projects. The department's guidance lists a number of mitigating measures for land-use agencies to consider when they undergo the process mandated by the state's Environmental Quality Review Act (SEQRA), including green roofs, energy-efficient building envelopes, high-albedo roofing (which reflects solar energy and thus reduces the need for air conditioning), maximum interior day lighting, reuse of building materials, on-site renewable energy, and combined heat and power technologies.[45] In California, similar guidelines for evaluating climate change impacts went into effect in March 2010 under the California Environmental Quality Act (CEQA).[46]

While only a few states have incorporated considerations of emissions and energy efficiency into their environmental review procedures, a majority of states and a significant number of municipalities have enacted climate action plans. These plans generally start with the completion of an inventory of greenhouse gas emissions. Based on this inventory, a realistic target for emissions reduction is set and an analysis of energy-saving opportunities is performed. Finally, climate action plans recommend strategies and policies to meet stated emissions reductions goals. Many of these strategies are directly related to land use, such as recommendations for increasing energy and water efficiency in buildings, reducing vehicle miles traveled, siting renewable energy facilities, increasing development density, and preserving farmland.[47]

In focusing on land use, climate action plans recognize that sustainable neighborhood development is integral to efforts to reduce vehicle miles traveled and preserve open space. Some states have sought to influence and encourage municipalities to adopt these types of regulations through their comprehensive planning enabling acts. For example, a 2008 amendment to Florida's comprehensive planning enabling act, which provides legal authority for local government planning, specifically rejects policies that support low density, single-use, and automobile-reliant development by directing local governments to consider methods of discouraging urban sprawl, supporting energy-efficient development patterns, and reducing greenhouse gas emissions. Since 2007, Arizona's larger cities and counties have been required to include an energy element in their plans, which must describe incentives and other strategies to encourage the efficient use of energy and increased renewable energy production.[48] And in 2008, New Jersey amended its comprehensive planning laws to direct local governments to develop strategies for green building and sustainability.[49]

The strength of climate change as a driver for sustainability policy is also illustrated by the U.S. Conference of Mayors' Climate Protection Agreement, which currently has more than a thousand signatories.[50] The agreement commits these cities and towns to work toward meeting the U.S. Kyoto Protocol target (reducing greenhouse gas emissions to 7% below 1990 levels by 2012) through actions taken in their own communities.[51] Many U.S. cities have also joined the International Council for Local Environmental Initiatives (ICLEI), which promotes smart planning, sustainable development, and initiatives focused on slowing global warming.[52] And counties have been invited to join the Cool Counties campaign, which asks them to commit to four actions: "(1) reducing our own contributions to climate change through our internal operations; (2) demonstrating regional leadership to achieve climate stabilization and protect our communities; (3) helping our community become climate resilient; [and] (4) urging the federal government to support our efforts."[53]

While the actions described here are not yet business as usual, they provide a foundation of experience and practice that can be copied or adapted by other municipalities and state governments. Because the impacts of climate change are increasingly experienced by state and local governments, it is likely that climate change will drive local land-use planning and decisionmaking more than smart growth.

Brownfields Redevelopment

Brownfields are abandoned or underused urban sites that federal law defines as "real property, the expansion, redevelopment, or reuse of which may be complicated by the presence or potential presence of a hazardous substance, pollutant, or contaminant."[54] An estimated 1 million brownfields sites exist in the United States.[55]

Remediating and reusing these sites has become an important sustainability strategy since the 1990s. Many brownfields sites are in cities' central areas, and their dramatic transformation from vacant or blighted sites to centerpieces of redevelopment has been a core achievement of urban revitalization.[56] For more than 20 years, programs designed to promote brownfields redevelopment have led to remediation and re-use of thousands of sites that lay abandoned for years and are now being used as industrial, commercial, residential, and even recreational properties. Some (but not all) re-uses of these sites promote green and sustainable practices.

To be sure, there is still a long way to go. According to one recent estimate, only 1-2% of the national inventory of brownfields sites has been successfully remediated.[57] In many communities, interest in redeveloping brownfields is still low, and this is especially true for small brownfields or those in cities with "little interest from developers and a lack of knowledge on how to proceed with redevelopment."[58] Still, the programs developed over the past two decades provide a foundation for greater future progress.

Brownfields redevelopment programs are a response to provisions of the Comprehensive Environmental Response, Compensation, and Liability Act of 1980 (CERCLA) on landowner liability,[59] which were intended to make those who caused or allowed dumping of hazardous substances on their property pay for the cleanup of that property. In a great many cases, the act worked exactly as it was intended, and these provisions led to the cleanup of a great many sites. Because the statute tended to make new owners of the same property liable for the cleanup of that property, however, CERCLA meant that many old industrial sites, or sites that were contaminated for other reasons, could not be marketed and hence remained unused. These sites also tend to be in urban areas, where there are already roads, utilities, and other infrastructure. To avoid liability for these brownfields, developers tended to build in undeveloped areas at the edge of municipalities (or greenfields), where there was no infrastructure, and thus contribute to sprawl.

The federal and state governments have promoted redevelopment activities on brownfields sites[60] through state voluntary cleanup programs (VCPs) and federal liability protection for brownfields developers.[61] According to one recent estimate, state VCPs have addressed more than 50,000 brownfields sites, and they evaluate another 7,000 to 8,000 sites each year.[62] The EPA's brownfields website cites a number of redevelopment success stories achieved with assistance from federal brownfields programs.[63] In Bridgeport, Connecticut, for example, the abandoned Jenkins Valve site was remediated and transformed into a 5,500-seat stadium for the Bridgeport Bluefish, a professional baseball team. A 10,000-seat arena and parking garage were built nearby.

The environmental and economic benefits of remediating and rehabilitating a brownfields site go well beyond reversing the adverse impacts of consuming previously undeveloped land at a greenfields location.[64] At five sites, EPA found a 32-57% reduction in vehicle miles traveled, a 47-62% reduction in stormwater runoff, a 2-3% increase in adjacent property values, creation of jobs in urban communities, improvements in air and water quality, and increases in tax revenues and property values.[65]

Brownfields redevelopment has gone beyond remediation to pursue a broader agenda more closely related to sustainability—occupying "center stage in a sustainable planning strategy of thwarting sprawl, preserving open space, reducing greenhouse gas emissions, and reinvesting in urban areas and their communities."[66] Building on urban sites can often conserve the land at greenfields locations and lessen the impacts of suburban and exurban sprawl.[67] According to one study, redeveloping one acre of brownfields can conserve as much as 6.2 acres of greenfields.[68] Since 2002, EPA has awarded smart growth grants to city projects that incorporate brownfields redevelopment strategies in their planning for the future.[69]

Green Building

Buildings can have impacts on water and materials use, land-cover changes, waste production, construction practices, building systems, and transportation needs. EPA estimates that the U.S. building industry creates 170 million tons of construction and demolition waste annually.[70] The U.S. Energy Information Administration reported that in 2009 the building sector (residential and commercial) was responsible for more than 50% of total annual U.S. energy consumption.[71] In addition, there is growing evidence that green buildings are more attractive places to live and work, and even that they appreciate in value faster than other buildings.[72]

Green building, which is still a new and emerging approach to the built environment, embodies the idea that buildings can use less to accomplish more. EPA defines green building as

> the practice of creating structures and using processes that are environmentally responsible and resource-efficient throughout a building's life-cycle from siting to design, construction, operation, maintenance, renovation and deconstruction. This practice expands and complements the classical building design concerns of economy, utility, durability, and comfort. [A g]reen building is also known as a sustainable or 'high performance' building.[73]

Green building principles seek to curtail a broad range of health, environmental, and economic impacts that are directly and indirectly caused by physical characteristics of buildings, and in the process make those buildings more attractive to prospective and existing users.

The building industry has produced several models and rating systems for green building: the Leadership in Energy and Environmental Design (LEED) standards developed by the U.S. Green Building Council (USGBC),[74] the Green Globes green rating program,[75] the Energy Star program administered by EPA,[76] guidelines of the National Association of Homebuilders (NAHB),[77] the International Green Construction Code of the International Code Council,[78] and CalGreen in California, the first statewide green building standards.[79]

There is a growing recognition of the need to consider not only a building itself but how it relates to transportation, land use, and community design in order to assess its full environmental impact. In short, green building needs to be connected to promoting more-sustainable transportation and smarter growth. Green-building designers have begun to recognize the relevance of location, walkability, transit accessibility, and other features of the green building concept, and to incorporate these considerations into the various rating systems.[80]

November 2010 marked a landmark in green building certification, as measured by adherence to LEED standards. At that time, "the total footprint of commercial projects certified under the USGBC's LEED Green Building Rating System worldwide surpassed one billion square feet. Another six billion square feet of projects are registered and currently working towards LEED certification around the world."[81] These figures represent more than 36,000 commercial projects and 38,000 single-family homes. Given these numbers, projections for future growth in the green building market tend to be optimistic, as exemplified by the projection by the USGBC that green building will contribute $554 billion to the U.S. gross domestic product by 2013.[82]

The American Institute of Architects has found that 24 of the 25 most-populated metropolitan areas benefit from some form of green building policy, and there are more than 53 million Americans living in cities that have green building programs.[83] Even now, despite the recent economic downturn, the green building industry continues to grow.[84]

Conclusion

The face of conventional economic development in the built environment is beginning to shift toward sustainability. In four prominent areas—transportation, land use, brownfields redevelopment, and green building—conventional development is being redirected toward greater quality of life, achieving economic, social, and environmental goals at the same time. While the federal government is encouraging and enabling this shift, it is being driven primarily at the state, local, and regional levels as government officials and the private sector work together on shared goals. Some of this activity, including cleaner vehicles and more comprehensive planning, is required by environmental and other laws. But a great deal of it—especially green building and brownfields redevelopment—is authorized and encouraged, but not mandated, by law. And this more-sustainable development is also reducing consumption, particularly energy consumption, by improving energy efficiency and encouraging more compact and walkable communities. Activities at the cutting edge, in each case, are not necessarily indicative of what is occurring in industry as a whole. Still, these activities provide a foundation for broader and more far-reaching efforts.

CHAPTER 5

Governance:
Communities as Sustainability Leaders, States as Energy Leaders (and the Federal Government Catching Up?)

As the past four chapters have shown, sustainability raises a much bigger set of questions than those typically addressed by EPA or state environmental regulatory agencies. Because sustainability would integrate our environmental, economic, security, and social goals, it raises questions that can be addressed only by government as a whole. This is not to say that sustainability is only about government or governance—far from it. But when issues do need to be addressed by government, one or two agencies with relatively limited cross-governmental responsibility will not be able to do the job.

Governance for sustainability is like all other governance in many respects. It requires effective governmental institutions and laws, a favorable investment climate, public access to information, informed and science-based decisionmaking, and public participation. Yet governance for sustainability is also different from governance for other issues and purposes. It is directed at a broad, long-term goal—moving from the current condition of unsustainable development to a future condition of sustainable development. And it requires the deep integration of environment with development, and thus raises problems with which we have relatively little experience.[1]

Achieving sustainability will likely take a long time. A 1999 report by the National Research Council (NRC), *Our Common Journey*, stated that "a successful transition toward sustainability is *possible* over the next two generations."[2] The major climate change bills that Congress has considered (but not passed) include goals for reducing greenhouse gas emissions to specified levels by 2050.[3] Even this time horizon of 40 to 50 years falls short of the full length of the transition. The NRC report observed: "It is over this period that serious progress in a transition toward sustainability will need to take place if interactions between the earth's human population and life support systems are not to significantly damage both."[4] The two-generation time frame is also a feasible and imaginable planning and analysis period for individuals, governments, and other entities.[5] Yet the actual length of the journey could even be longer.

Some scientists ask whether we have even that much time, emphasizing our limited understanding of how much stress physical and ecological systems can take without collapsing or changing in ways that would be disastrous to humans.[6] They point out that we could overshoot the tolerance level of these systems without even knowing it, leading to irreversible outcomes. That story line, which does not contradict the magnitude of the required changes, nonetheless adds considerable urgency to the task.

Sustainable development requires that we reverse certain paths we have followed for decades and will likely take decades to overcome. For the United States, these include high consumption levels for materials, energy, and water—and land use that has encouraged sprawl and dependence on the automobile. We have little if any experience with law in conceiving and carrying out multigenerational projects of this scale. While the United States has considerable experience and success in maintaining policy goals over long periods of time in foreign policy (e.g., Monroe Doctrine against foreign colonization or intervention in Latin America) and domestic policy (e.g., reduction and prosecution of crime), few of our national goals involve a long-term project for moving from an unacceptable or less acceptable situation to an acceptable or more acceptable situation (balancing the budget may be an exception).

By contrast, political life in the United States is organized around two-, four-, and six-year election cycles.[7] Sustainable development will not happen if every new president or congress starts all over again or revisits basic premises. We thus need to develop the capacity to set and achieve long-term objectives and create the institutions and political ownership necessary to realize them.

Sustainable development also requires the systematic integration of environmental concerns and goals into decisionmaking. Conventional development decisions by governments and private actors—transportation projects or economic development, for example—should include environmental considerations and result in environmental protection and even restoration.[8] While these challenges are sometimes addressed in environmental law, they are broader. Environmental law tends to target a discrete set of problems—air and water pollution, waste management and remediation, and endangered species—with a set of legal tools that are primarily regulatory. But sustainability involves much more than regulation. "Environmental policy as a whole," Prof. Richard Andrews of the University of North Carolina explains, "includes all government actions that alter natural environmental conditions and processes, for whatever purpose and under whatever label."[9] This includes subsidies, economic development programs, international trade, land use, taxation, and other policies and laws.

So sustainable development is different from ordinary governance issues in two profound ways—by looking ahead over a much longer period of time and by systematically integrating the environment into decisionmaking through the use of a wide variety of legal and policy tools. Yet governance for sustainability is not an entirely different form of governance; it is a set of perspectives that should inform all governance. It would provide tools, a legal structure, and support for more-sustainable alternatives.

Among the three levels of governance in the United States—local, state, and national—local governments have made the most progress toward sustainability. Many municipalities even have sustainability directors or coordinators. While many state governments have engaged in a variety of sustainability activities, only a few have made a systematic effort to address sustainability. Still, states have long been doing more to advance renewable energy, energy efficiency, and reduced greenhouse gas emissions than the federal government. While the federal government has used sustainability concepts in some strategic planning and has incorporated sustainability in the planning and operations of many agencies, it does not employ a strategic process for understanding threats to national sustainability or opportunities that sustainability might provide. In recent years, the federal government appears to be catching up to state and local governments, although it is unclear whether it will continue to do so. And one of the inherent challenges for sustainability governance continues to be the lack of coordination among different levels of government.

Local Governance

In the past 20 years, some communities have made great strides toward becoming more sustainable, growing their local economies while minimizing damage and maximizing access to their natural environments. This effort has been aided in large part by visionary mayors and by nonprofit organizations, funding foundations, and collaborative stakeholder networks that have sprung up to offer support to local governments.

Cities pursuing sustainability strive to bring together all three components of sustainability—environment, economics, and social equity—in an integrated decisionmaking process in both internal operations and community initiatives.[10] Cities that are successful in this endeavor have found and speak the language of the sustainability component (social, economic, environmental) that resonates most with their leaders and populace. The message of improving the bottom line and growing the tax base, for example, is most powerful in conservative portions of the country. Showing energy reduction in dollars rather than carbon, or having a new company state it relocated to an area because of its commitment to sustainability, has a huge impact on otherwise skeptical leaders.

Other cities have taken only small steps or faced challenges that have made progress more difficult—lack of political will, chronic budget shortages, or an unclear understanding of what sustainability looks like in practical application. When a city is charged with providing key services such as garbage and trash collection, other items that deal with quality of life—greenway development or public transit, for example—are often the first to be cut when the tax base declines or doesn't grow with the rate of inflation.

Sustainable communities are attractive because the mutually reinforcing policies that protect the environment, create jobs, and build social equity are most obvious at the local level, where people actually live, work, and play. Sustainable communities are "cities and towns that prosper because people work together to produce a high quality of life that they want to sustain and constantly improve. They are communities that flourish because they build a mutually supportive, dynamic balance between social well-being, economic opportunity, and environmental quality."[11] Put differently, sustainable communities strive to have thriving inhabitants with sustainable livelihoods that fit into, rather than undermine, the local web of life; they achieve social equity and ecological integrity together, in ways that value both biological wealth and cultural wealth. A company recruiting top graduates is concerned about employee diversity and retention; its prospective employees can move anywhere, so locating the business in a city that provides a sustainable lifestyle—transit and housing options, local food, proximity to green space—is key for that company. The city in turn benefits from the company, whose employees give back through taxes and support of local charities and businesses.

To date, at least eight sustainability rankings have been issued for North American cities: Green Cities Index, Nalgene Least Wasteful Cities, Popular Science Greenest Cities, Price Waterhouse Cooper's Cities of Opportunity, SustainLane, Our Green Cities, National Resource Defense Council Smart Cities, and Corporate Knights. Each ranking organization features different criteria, methodologies, categories, and weightings. Some are more quantitative than qualitative, some account for population size while others do not, and most ignore ready access to resources (such as hydropower) that would allow one city to prosper while others remain inherently unsustainable. Very few consider education as a tool to long-term sustainability, but many count categories not directly relevant to sustainable living, such as cultural events. This variety in evaluations can result in very different rankings for the same city. For example, New York City was recently ranked 39th in the nation in the "waste" category by SustainLane and 3rd in the same category by the Green Cities Index. None of these rankings is a definitive index to measure the progress cities have made toward sustainability, and there is no federal or accepted standard of measurement. Still, the existence of so many different rating systems indicates how much work to achieve sustainability is being done at the local level.

SustainLane has conducted research since 2005 to rank the 50 most populous cities in the United States. In its most recent ranking in 2008, cities were compared and ranked across 16 different indicators of sustainability. Success in sustainability, according to SustainLane, includes city leadership and commitment to sustainability initiatives, as well as consensus and buy-in from residents and the local business community.[12] SustainLane and others have found that in recent years many cities have created environmental or sustainability offices or hired sustainability coordinators.

Larger cities that have made particular progress in advancing local sustainability include Chicago, Denver, Seattle, and Portland. Seattle and Chicago lead the nation in development of a climate action plan and have adopted a broad array of sustainability initiatives, including urban greening, energy efficiency, and private-sector engagement. King County in Washington State, Arlington County in Virginia, and Sarasota County in Florida have been recognized for their innovative sustainability efforts. Smaller, more progressive towns like Santa Monica, California, and Burlington, Vermont, have perhaps the longest history on sustainability among U.S. localities, steadily building on their progress in the past two decades. In the Southeast, municipalities tend to be more active on sustainability and climate change than the states in which they are located.[13]

The most successful cities have viewed sustainability broadly, adopting policies, funding initiatives, partnering with other sectors, engaging their community members, setting specific targets and goals, and developing tracking metrics. Most important, they have tied sustainability to the community's economic and social health and have set up governing and community systems that affect everyone in the long term.[14] Many of their stories are recounted throughout this book. Nonetheless, most localities have found it difficult to integrate the different aspects of sustainability, and many of the local initiatives are not broad enough or empowered to make a large difference. Best practices are often a combination of what is most commonly successful in other municipalities around the country adapted to local circumstances.

Two issues related to local sustainability have gained significant traction. The first, climate change, illustrates some of the challenges communities face as they try to reduce their city's carbon emissions. As noted earlier (Chapter 4), the fact that more than 1,000 mayors across the country have joined the Mayors' Climate Protection Agreement and committed to reducing their greenhouse gas emissions 7% below 1990 levels[15] makes a strong political statement. The U.S. Conference of Mayors has recommended several policies to implement this commitment: conducting local greenhouse gas inventories, adopting anti-sprawl land-use regulations, encouraging alternative modes of transportation, promoting production of renewable energy, increasing the use of green building techniques for new construction as well as retrofits, purchasing fuel-efficient vehicles for municipal fleets, increasing the efficiency of water pumping systems, promoting the growth of urban forests, and educating the public about climate change and the need to reduce greenhouse gas pollution. Many cities have put action to words, making regulations, providing incentives, educating, collaborating, and improving their operations; these cities tend to be thriving even in difficult economic times, and capturing what remains of federal funds for sustainable initiatives. On the other hand, many of these cities have not actually made concrete steps toward reducing carbon emissions; nor have they undertaken broad sustainability measures.

The second issue is economic development, particularly in the areas of renewable energy, energy efficiency, recycling, and transportation. As Professor Joan Fitzgerald, an urban planner who directs the law and public policy program at Northeastern University, describes in her recent book, *Emerald Cities: Urban Sustainability and Economic Development*, municipalities across the country have begun to use economic development to improve quality of life, create jobs, and foster new technologies.[16] Toledo, Ohio, which has long been a glass technology and manufacturing center, has begun to use this expertise to produce thin-film solar panels. These solar panels are made by placing a thin layer of photovoltaic material between two layers of glass. The city government is not alone in this effort; it is assisted by the Wright Center for Photovoltaics Innovation and Commercialization at the University of Toledo, the Regional Growth Partnership (a nonprofit economic development organization), and the Ohio Department of Development's Green Places Initiative. As a result, First Solar, a leading thin-film solar panel manufacturer, is located in Toledo; more than 6,000 people are employed at First Solar and other solar-related businesses in the Toledo area.[17]

Much of the funding for staffing local sustainability initiatives, however, has been based on unreliable federal funding sources. City sustainability surveys have found that a significant portion of member offices have been originally staffed through grants. The most notable of these were the 2009 American Recovery and Reinvestment Act Energy Efficiency and Conservation Block Grants from the Department of Energy, which expire in 2012. Encouraging trends show more and more cities bringing these fledgling offices onto general funds as grants are expended.[18]

In addition, many cities have simply not developed the necessary comprehensive sustainability planning. One key challenge is that for all the progress being made in cities like Chicago and the increasing examples of energy-efficient and new urbanist development, sprawl in the largely auto-dependent suburbs in metropolitan areas has carried on. And almost every city making progress on sustainability still faces enormous social equity challenges. Of course, some of the challenges to advancing sustainability at the local level are inherently embedded in our governance system, as communities are often dependent on coordination with neighboring jurisdictions and other levels of government.[19] While cities can accomplish much on their own, they are ultimately limited in achievement by the need for support from and coordination with the state and federal levels.

State Governance

Supportive state governance is essential to sustainability. As Profs. Kirsten Engel and Marc Miller of the University of Arizona College of Law explain:

> There is an almost total overlap between the major topics of sustainability discourse and the traditional functions of states in areas such as environmental protection, health, education, public safety, economic development, water policy, the provision or regulation of

various natural monopolies, and social and public goods. States also continue to serve as policy innovators in our federal system. The uncertainties and variation involved in seeking a sustainable society (and even our conceptions of sustainability) counsel in favor of variation and experimentation. It is in the states where experimentation takes place—in, for example, environment, education, and health care.[20]

A growing number of states have moved toward sustainability by adopting a variety of green practices—to the point where there are now national sustainability rankings for states. For more than a decade, states have in many ways been a stronger force in advancing renewable energy and energy efficiency than the federal government. Of perhaps equal importance, the states have provided a forum for experimentation in energy policy, learning from each other, and improving performance. States have also been active, to some degree, on a variety of other specific sustainability issues; the brownfields redevelopment and smart growth efforts described in Chapter 4 are based to a great extent on state laws. Yet on the broader question of sustainability in general, and not just energy policy, brownfields, or smart growth, only a handful of states have adopted systematic policies, and they have had to do so through executive orders rather than legislation.

Various nongovernmental organizations (NGOs) and media organizations rank states for their sustainable environmental practices. Greenopia, an online consumer's directory for "green, sustainability and socially conscious, daily purchase decisions," annually ranks states in terms of sustainability.[21] Using data from various federal and state government agencies and some NGOs, Greenopia compiles an index of sustainability based on air quality, water quality, recycling rate, number of green businesses, LEED buildings, per capita emissions, per capital energy consumption, per capita water consumption, and per capita waste generation. Based on this index, Greenopia's 10 greenest states in 2011 were California, Maine, Massachusetts, Minnesota, Nevada, New Hampshire, New York, Oregon, Vermont, and Washington. The 10 least green states were Alabama, Alaska, Delaware, Indiana, Kentucky, Louisiana, Mississippi, North Dakota, West Virginia, and Wyoming.

In 2007, *Forbes Magazine* ranked states in terms of greenness using the six equally weighted indicators of air quality, carbon footprint, hazardous waste management, energy consumption, policy initiatives, and water quality.[22] The top-ranked states include Vermont, Oregon, and Washington (three states also identified as among the greenest states by Greenopia; see Table 5.1). These states, *Forbes* said, "have low carbon dioxide emissions per capita, strong policies to promote energy efficiency and air quality," and the highest number of LEED-certified buildings per capita. As with the Greenopia rankings, many southern states can be found in the lower half of the rankings. While there are striking differences in the rankings of some states, the existence of these two ranking systems indicates considerable activity at the state level.

Table 5.1
Two Rankings of States on Sustainability

State	2011 Greenopia Ranking	2007 Forbes Ranking
Vermont	1	1
New York	2	9
Washington	3	3
Oregon	4	2
Minnesota	5	15
California	6	14
Nevada	7	17
New Hampshire	8	19
Massachusetts	9	11
Maine	10	25
Hawaii	11	4
Arizona	12	10
Colorado	13	13
South Dakota	14	21
Idaho	15	12
Florida	16	20
Connecticut	17	6
Iowa	18	35
Maryland	19	5
Rhode Island	20	8
Georgia	21	29
Wisconsin	22	16
Arkansas	23	44
Michigan	24	24
North Carolina	25	26
Virginia	26	23
Illinois	27	27
New Mexico	28	18
Missouri	29	41
Texas	30	34
Pennsylvania	31	32
Ohio	32	39
Oklahoma	33	38
South Carolina	34	36
Tennessee	35	43
Montana	36	22
Kansas	37	31
New Jersey	38	7
Utah	39	28
Nebraska	40	33
Mississippi	41	46
Alabama	42	48
Delaware	43	30
Alaska	44	40
North Dakota	45	42
Kentucky	46	45
Wyoming	47	37
Indiana	48	49
Louisiana	49	47
West Virginia	50	50

Only four states—Minnesota, New Jersey, Oregon, and Washington—have addressed sustainability in a holistic fashion through the use of executive orders, planning, and periodic reporting on progress.[23] Instead, states tend to be focusing principally on energy. Many of these states are focused entirely on promoting renewable energy and energy efficiency, with little or no emphasis on climate change. Other states include energy within an explicit commitment to address climate change.

For more than a decade, state governments have done more to foster renewable energy, increase energy efficiency, and reduce greenhouse gas emissions than the federal government, especially during the presidency of George W. Bush. In the Obama Administration, states still maintain their lead on many issues. As Magali Delmas, from the UCLA Institute of Environmental and Sustainability, and Maria Mones-Sancho, of the University of Madrid, Department of Business Administration, have argued:

> While there are current debates about the implementation of federal renewable policy, U.S. states have taken the leading role in establishing renewable energy policies since the 1990s. These include Renewable Portfolio Standards, the requirement to sell green products, disclosure policies, and subsidies.[24]

The scope and intensity of state activity on energy efficiency, renewable energy, and climate change is so great that there are now at least two websites devoted to tracking and displaying this work: the Department of Energy's Database of State Incentives for Renewables & Efficiency (DSIRE)[25] and the Center for Climate and Energy Solutions (C2ES) (formerly the Pew Center on Global Climate Change).[26] The C2ES site, for example, describes 26 different kinds of state activities in four categories—climate action, energy, transportation, and buildings. For each of these, the site identifies the specific states that have taken action and the number of states that have acted. For each of these 26 categories of policy actions, at least 5 states, and as many as 45, have taken action.[27] Several examples illustrate the range of state actions.

In the field of energy, one of the most common state actions is adoption of a renewable energy portfolio standard. According to the U.S. Department of Energy, 29 states and the District of Columbia have adopted a renewable portfolio standard (RPS).[28] Seventeen of these states have an RPS of 20% or higher, with Maine having the highest at 40%. These states, in other words, are seeking to increase the percentage of their overall electricity that comes from renewable sources to at least 20% of their total portfolio. Southern states appear to be least likely to adopt an RPS (although the Texas law described in Chapter 2 is a notable exception).

Another promising policy at the state level is energy efficiency resource standards, which are analogous to renewable portfolio standards. Energy efficiency standards require utilities to reduce their electricity use by a specified percentage by a specified year. So far, 27 states have adopted some form of energy efficiency resource standard, including not only most Midwestern, Northeastern, and West

Coast states but also Texas, Arkansas, Florida, North Carolina, Virginia, and Colorado.[29] Some of these states have promulgated regulations to decouple utilities' earnings from electricity sales volume. Traditionally, utilities received profits based on the quantity of electricity or gas sold. Using their utility regulatory power, some states have ended this practice and instead have offered financial incentives to utilities that reduce sales (save energy).[30]

Some states have taken the lead in developing energy-efficiency building codes and appliance standards. Since California implemented the nation's first building energy code, 35 states have mandated residential building codes and 36 have mandated commercial codes.[31]

California has long been a leader in implementing statewide efficiency standards for appliances such as refrigerators, influencing other states and national product suppliers to improve codes and performance. California initiated appliance standards in the mid-1970s (the first state to do so) and has continued to promulgate standards on some products in spite of the jurisdiction of the federal government in this policy area. California's standards, in fact, prompted the federal government to adopt energy efficiency standards for a wide range of household appliances as well as industrial equipment (such as pumps).

Oregon and many other states also subsidize energy efficiency through the use of public-benefit fund programs. These programs impose a small charge on the distribution cost in an electric bill, ranging from 0.03 to 3 mills per kilowatt hour. (A mill is one-tenth of a cent.) Revenue is then used for energy efficiency programs like building retrofits, codes and standards, research and development, and public awareness campaigns.[32]

States have also adopted tax policies that incentivize individuals and businesses to use renewable energy. This is a preferred policy for most states, with all but three states having some form of property, sales, business, or income tax incentive to encourage renewable energy development and use.[33] Other states have successfully utilized tax credits for energy efficiency purchases and upgrades.[34] Since 1979, Oregon's business energy tax credit has offered significant tax savings for purchases of products that meet minimum energy savings targets. In Oregon, the tax credit (equal to 50% of eligible costs) is for those businesses, trade groups or rental property owners who invest in recycling, energy conservation, renewable energy resources, and less-polluting transportation fuels.

The effect of state programs that use multiple legal and policy tools can be quite dramatic. Since the early 1970s, per capita electricity consumption in California and New York has been relatively flat, even as per capita U.S. consumption has increased by about 50% (Figure 5.1). To accomplish that, California adopted stringent building and appliance standards, decoupled utility profits from sales of electricity, imposed a charge of 0.3 cents per kilowatt hour to fund energy efficiency and other public benefit activities, and established energy efficiency goals along with incentives for utilities to achieve those goals.[35] New York used a somewhat similar set of legal and policy tools that also includes considerable funding for research and development.[36]

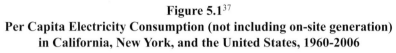

Figure 5.1[37]
Per Capita Electricity Consumption (not including on-site generation) in California, New York, and the United States, 1960-2006

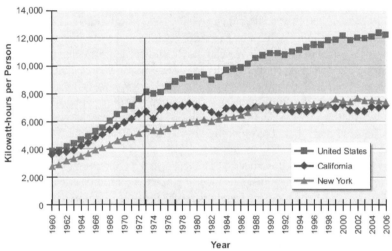

Many states have also explicitly addressed climate change. In fact, observers have argued that state climate change efforts also far exceed those of the federal government. John Byrne, of the Center for Energy and Environmental Policy, wrote in 2007:

> In contrast to mostly inaction at the national level, U.S. states and localities have crafted innovative, cooperative, and increasingly bold strategies to address climate change.... Their motivations and strategies vary, but together suggest a sizable and growing divergence from national policy, with significant implications for the country and for international strategy.[38]

The Center for Climate and Energy Solutions reports that 43 states have developed an inventory of their greenhouse gas emissions, 36 have developed or are developing climate action plans, 20 have set greenhouse gas reduction targets, and 15 have climate change adaptation plans.[39] Such plans help state policymakers plan for the future in ways that meet their own unique economic, resource, and social needs. The Center observes that over the last decade two trends are visible at the state level: more states are taking climate change seriously, and they continue to adopt more types of climate-change policies.[40]

California has the nation's most far-reaching climate change legislation. California's Global Warming Solutions Act of 2006 (known as AB 32, after its bill number in the legislature) requires the state to reduce its greenhouse gas emissions to 1990 levels by 2020.[41] AB 32 assigns to the California Air Resources Board (CARB) the task of choosing legal and policy tools to meet that goal.[42] CARB has elected to proceed with an economy-wide cap-and-trade program.[43] California's program launched January 1, 2012, but is in an unenforceable testing stage for the first year.

The program caps overall greenhouse gas emissions, and then reduces the overall emissions limit annually until the 2020 goal is met. Sources covered under the cap—which emit 85% of California's greenhouse gas emissions—are each subject to their own declining emissions caps. For each budget year, the state will issue allowances equal to the state-wide cap. Each allowance represents one metric ton of carbon dioxide or its equivalent. Every year, covered sources will need to turn in allowances equal to their emissions. For 2013, CARB will allocate allowances to cover about 90% of emissions for free. Covered sources may then purchase additional allowances at auction. In addition, sources that achieve reductions in emissions beyond what is required by law can sell "offset credits" that represent those reductions. In theory, as the cap declines and the number of allowances decreases, the price of allowances will increase, and it will become more economical for sources to reduce emissions than to purchase additional allowances.

The cap-and-trade program is only part of California's comprehensive plan for achieving the maximum technologically feasible and cost-effective reductions in greenhouse gas emissions that AB 32 mandates.[44] For example, CARB developed low carbon fuel standards, which reduce greenhouse gas emissions by reducing the carbon intensity of transportation fuels used in the state by at least 10% by 2020.[45] Implementation of the low carbon fuel standards is being delayed while a federal court decides whether the rule is unconstitutional on the ground that it discriminates against out-of-state ethanol producers and crude oil sources.[46] California also limits the carbon intensity of new long-term electricity supply agreements so that the supplier cannot generate emissions greater than a combined-cycle natural gas-fired power plant, which is approximately one-half the emissions of a coal-fired plant.[47]

Some states have collaborated to develop regional climate action strategies. California is a member of the Western Climate Initiative, a collaboration with four Canadian provinces that is working to address climate change. In addition, nine states in the Mid-Atlantic and Northeast are members of the Regional Greenhouse Gas Initiative, the "first market-based regulatory program in the United States to reduce greenhouse gas emissions.... [It] will reduce CO_2 emissions from the power sector 10% by 2018."[48] The states participating in this initiative are Connecticut, Delaware, Maine, Maryland, Massachusetts, New Hampshire, New York, Rhode Island, and Vermont.

In summary, many states have taken a leadership role—in comparison to the federal government—in the pursuit of sustainability in renewable energy, energy efficiency, and climate change policy. Vermont, Oregon, and Washington are noteworthy in their pursuit of sustainability. There also has been much progress in many other states in the West, Midwest, and East Coast. However, Southern states tend to be lagging far behind other regions.

National Governance

Whatever state and local governments do, effective and supportive national governance is an essential requirement for sustainable development. In the United States, none of the broad goals of sustainable development—environmental protection and restoration, economic development, security, and social development or human rights—can be achieved unless the federal government also works effectively to achieve those goals. Sustainability also requires the development and implementation of a national strategy that includes the articulation of goals and a planning process for defining and achieving them. A sustainable development strategy also requires bipartisan support by the country's national leaders, a capable governmental implementing or coordinating agency or entity, sustainable development indicators to measure progress, and an effective means of involving and educating the public. More generally, a meaningful strategy requires a level of national effort and support, as well as international cooperation, that corresponds to the problems and opportunities of sustainable development.[49]

Over the last two decades, the United States has taken some modest steps toward sustainability—in strategic planning, in the incorporation of sustainability in agency missions and operations, and in environmental reporting and indicators. Energy efficiency and renewable energy legislation, and administrative efforts to reduce greenhouse gas emissions and implement the legislation, have increased in recent years. Still, the United States lags far behind most developed countries and a great many developing countries in its sustainability efforts.

Strategic Planning

At the World Summit on Sustainable Development in Johannesburg in 2002, the United States and other countries agreed that nations should take "immediate steps to make progress in the formulation and elaboration of national strategies for sustainable development and begin their implementation by 2005."[50] But the United States has never had an overall national strategy for sustainable development, and there appears to be no prospect for such a strategy in the near future.

The federal government engages in strategic planning on other issues, however, particularly for national security and defense. Congress requires the President to submit an annual report on the country's national security strategy.[51] Congress also requires the preparation, every four years, of the Quadrennial Defense Review that sets out "the defense strategy of the United States" as well as "a defense program for the next 20 years."[52] The usefulness of the long-term, multi-year, nationwide scope of the Quadrennial Defense Review has led to proposals for such reviews in other areas. Though not required by law, quadrennial reviews were issued in

2010 for the first time by the Department of Homeland Security[53] and the State Department/U.S. Agency for International Development,[54] both modeled on the Department of Defense review.

Also in 2010, the President's Council of Advisors on Science and Technology recommended the establishment of a quadrennial energy review to "establish governmentwide goals, coordinate actions across agencies, and identify the resources needed for the invention, translation, adoption, and diffusion of energy technologies."[55] In response to that report, as noted in Chapter 2, the Department of Energy in 2011 issued its first Quadrennial Technology Review, identifying six priority strategies to guide that agency's work in developing and deploying new energy technologies over the next five years.[56] The United States is thus moving in the direction of more comprehensive strategies. It is also beginning to link national defense with climate change. Congress recently required the national security strategy and the Quadrennial Defense Review to consider the effect of climate change on Defense Department "facilities, capabilities, and missions."[57]

But there is no strategic planning, risk assessment, or long-term review for the challenges and opportunities of sustainable development. This is also true on such issues as climate-change funding, where, according to a recent General Accountability Office report, the lack of a government-wide strategic planning process means that priorities are not articulated or understood across agencies, that there appear to be mismatches between funding levels and priorities, and that many existing programs are less effective than they could be.[58]

The closest the United States has come to a national sustainability strategy was the creation in 1993 of the President's Council on Sustainable Development (PCSD), with the mandate to develop "bold, new approaches to achieve our economic, environmental, and equity goals." The PCSD, which was terminated in 1999, brought together stakeholders and made many thoughtful recommendations in a series of reports.[59] The Council was only an advisory body, however. It did not lead to a national strategic process, the use of sustainability goals or indicators, a governmental implementing or coordinating entity, or any corresponding changes in law.[60] Today, the work of the PCSD is barely remembered; in a recent survey conducted by the Woodrow Wilson International Center for Scholars and the Environmental Law Institute to list our greatest environmental policy accomplishments, the PCSD came out 26th in a list of 31 items.[61]

Sustainability in Agency Missions

Some progress has nonetheless occurred at the federal agency level through the Government Performance and Results Act of 1993 (GPRA).[62] The GPRA obligates federal agencies to develop and implement multi-year strategic plans that include a mission statement, goals and objectives for major agency activities, a description of how those goals and objectives will be achieved, and an explanation of the evaluation method that will be used to assess the achievement of those goals and objectives.[63] The act also requires each agency, as part of its annual budget submission, to prepare and submit to the Office of Management and Budget a performance plan that is consistent with its strategic plan.[64] In addition, the act requires agencies to publish a report after each fiscal year comparing the agency's goals for that fiscal year with its actual achievements, evaluating successes in achieving goals, and where performance goals were not met, explaining why.[65]

In January 2011, President Obama signed into law the Government Performance and Results Modernization Act of 2010, which updated and refined the GPRA.[66] The intent of the new legislation is to better define governance structures by integrating and connecting the programs, plans, and outcomes of agencies across the federal government. The new law requires quarterly reports instead of annual reports and explicitly requires fact-based decisionmaking approaches for program implementation and management.

Environmental and sustainable development goals are contained in some, but not all, agency strategic plans under GPRA. As this book goes to press, 7 of 15 federal agencies (the 14 cabinet agencies and EPA) identify environmental or natural resources protection, environmental stewardship, environmental responsibility, or sustainability as strategic goals. These agencies are the Departments of Agriculture, Commerce, Energy, Housing and Urban Development, the Interior, and Transportation, and EPA.[67] Additionally, the State Department and U.S. Agency for International Development can be considered as an agency with some form of environmental sustainability goal. Their plans are prepared as a single report because, to some degree, the Agency for International Development operates under the umbrella of the State Department. The combined GPRA plan of the two agencies identifies promotion of economic growth and prosperity as a goal, and identifies energy security and environment as two of the strategic priorities for achieving that goal.[68]

Agencies that address sustainability tend to link environmental protection with economic development, job creation, and quality of life, both in the United States and in developing countries. Themes include sustainability and environmental protection as a way to provide opportunity to the poor (State/USAID); revitalize neighborhoods and create livable communities (EPA); sustain the economy, environment, and culture of the American West (Interior); provide economic benefits (Commerce); avoid congestion and improve motor vehicle fuel efficiency (Transportation); help farmers find new ways to make money by protecting the environment (Agriculture); and build a sustainable and competitive clean energy economy (Energy).

The question of how to institutionalize sustainability in an agency's mission was addressed in a 2011 report by the National Research Council. The report was in response to a request from EPA for recommendations on how the agency could more systematically integrate sustainability into its overall mission and programs.[69] As the NRC recognized, EPA has for some years been applying specific sustainability concepts and tools in individual programs. The NRC recommended that EPA adopt an overall sustainability management system to guide agency priority setting and decisions. Under this management system, EPA would articulate specific sustainability principles, develop a clear statement of the agency's sustainability vision, set short-term objectives and ways of measuring whether these objectives have been met, create a sustainability assessment process for new or priority issues, and conduct periodic evaluation and public reporting on how the system is working.[70] Recognizing that the immediate adoption of such a system across the entire agency would be impossible, the NRC recommended that it be phased in as appropriate over time. The NRC also made clear that this management system could be implemented only to the extent that EPA had the statutory authority to do so; the NRC did not recommend any changes in law. Finally, the NRC suggested that this management system could be applied by other federal agencies as well.

Sustainability in Agency Buildings and Operations

The federal government has also taken steps toward sustainability in the operations of federal agencies. Executive Order 13514, signed by President Obama in fall 2009,[71] directs federal agencies to set sustainability goals for their buildings and operations. Among other things, the order requires agencies to set goals for reduction of greenhouse gases from sources they own or control; from electricity, steam, or heat they purchase; and from vendors, suppliers, and agency travel. Agencies are also required to set long-term goals (for 2015 or 2020) to reduce energy intensity, potable water intensity, and fleet petroleum use and to construct and use high-performance (green) buildings. The executive order requires each agency to "develop, implement, and annually update an integrated Strategic Sustainability Performance Plan that will prioritize agency actions based on lifecycle return on investment."[72] These plans are to be integrated into agency GPRA plans and be publicly available.[73] The Office of Management and Budget is required to periodically post agency performance scorecards on a website.[74] The executive order also requires agencies to begin planning for climate change adaptation.[75] Since the executive order was promulgated, the Council on Environmental Quality has issued instructions to federal agencies for incorporating climate change adaptation into their strategic planning, including their GPRA planning.[76] In April 2011, OMB issued a summary of progress that each agency has made thus far in implementing the executive order.[77]

Environmental Reporting and Indicators

Periodic national reports on the state of the environment have made a comeback in recent years. The National Environmental Policy Act of 1969 required the Council on Environmental Quality to publish an annual report on the condition of the environment, but Congress repealed that requirement in 1995.[78] In 2003, EPA published a draft report on the environment,[79] and followed that with a final report in 2008.[80]

The report uses environmental indicators to assess the environmental and public health impacts of specific human activities and to describe general environmental conditions (air quality, water quality, waste, forest conditions). In addition to the full report, EPA's website enables users to find updated information.[81]

EPA is considering the use of sustainability indicators,[82] which unlike environmental indicators, blend social, economic, and environmental information. For sustainable communities, such indicators might include the fraction of the population that is within walking distance of public transportation or progress toward a goal of reducing potable water consumption by a specific percentage.[83]

The federal government as a whole is also beginning to consider, once again, the use of sustainability indicators, or at least something akin to such indictors. An interagency work group published an experimental set of sustainability indicators in 1998,[84] but nothing came of it. In the absence of governmental action, State of the USA (SUSA), a nonprofit organization advised by the National Academy of Sciences, began developing a set of key economic, social, and environmental indicators. SUSA's mission is "to help the American people better assess for themselves the progress of the United States, providing scientifically selected measures, supporting statistical data and appropriate editorial context."[85] Over the same period, a series of General Accountability Office reports helped lead to bipartisan support for legislation that would create a key national indicator system.[86] Because they address environmental, social, and quality of life measures, these indicators address a longstanding concern that one economic indicator—gross domestic product—"has become a singular measure of national performance."[87] The Patient Care and Affordable Care Act, the comprehensive health care legislation which was signed into law in March 2010, created the Commission on Key National Indicators to work with the National Academy of Sciences to create just such a system.[88] Appointments to the commission, which were made by majority and minority leaders in the House and the Senate, were completed at the end of 2010.[89] As anticipated and authorized in the legislation, the Academy is working with SUSA to develop proposed measures and a website for public access to the key indicators.[90]

Energy and Climate Legislation

Recent congressional and administrative efforts on renewable energy and energy efficiency represent the most significant national movement toward energy sustainability that has occurred in the two decades since Rio. After a long period of little activity on energy efficiency and conservation, from 2007 to 2009 Congress adopted a series of tax incentives for energy efficiency and renewable energy and provided significant additional funding for both. As previously explained, the Obama Administration has used that and other legal authority to significantly improve fuel efficiency standards for cars and trucks. The Supreme Court's 2007 decision in *Massachusetts v. EPA* gave EPA explicit authority to regulate greenhouse gas emissions under the Clean Air Act—authority it has used for mobile sources as well as factories and power plants. Still, Congress has thus far failed to adopt comprehensive climate change legislation.

Lack of International Leadership

It is a truism that the United States can lead internationally only by what it does at home, that actions speak louder than words. There have been two comparative reviews of various countries' environmental performance that include the United States. Neither viewed the United States as having particularly impressive environmental or sustainability programs. They also pointed out our continued unwillingness to participate fully in international agreements.

The first review, by the Organization for Economic Cooperation and Development (OECD), is part of a periodic review of each member country's environmental performance. The most recent report for the United States was issued in 2006.[91] The OECD acknowledged that the United States has a robust and well-developed set of laws to protect the environment and natural resources. It also concluded that the United States had made some progress in reducing pesticide use and the emission of some toxic air pollutants, that GPRA has fostered cooperation among federal agencies, that many "federal agencies have points of contact on sustainability," and that the Office of the Federal Executive (which is part of the Council on Environmental Quality) provides coordination on sustainability.[92] Nonetheless, OECD asserted:

> The pollution, energy, water and material intensities of the US economy remain high in OECD terms, and the fuel supply is still among the most carbon intensive. Neither municipal waste generation nor land conversion has been decoupled from population growth. The lack of full internalization of environmental costs in transport and energy pricing structures causes market distortions that undermine efforts to encourage energy conservation and enhance energy security through programs such as Energy Star and incentives for development of low-emission energy sources.[93]

The report added that integration of environmental concerns into tax policy was uneven, and that there continue to be environmentally damaging subsidies.[94]

The other report, the annual Environmental Performance Index, is a comparative global review of environmental performance by the Yale University Center for Environmental Law and Policy and the Columbia University Center for International Earth Science Information Network. In the most recent report,[95] issued in 2011, the United States ranked 61 out of 163 countries, bracketed by Paraguay (60) and Brazil (62).[96] Breaking down the overall ranking into specific components, the United States had comparatively good scores for forestry, fisheries, and air and water pollution effects on humans, but comparatively low scores for climate change and air pollution effects on ecosystems.[97]

Another measure of U.S. sustainability efforts is our willingness to ratify international treaties relating to the environment.[98] The Framework Convention on Climate Change and the Convention on Biological Diversity—both of which were opened for signature at the 1992 Earth Summit, are suffused with sustainability principles and concepts. Treaties that have been negotiated since then also represent an effort to work out the meaning of sustainable development in specific contexts or on specific issues. It follows that ratification of these treaties, and full legal participation in the regimes they create, is an essential part of any serious U.S. sustainability effort. While the United States in 1992 was the fourth country in the world to ratify the Framework Convention on Climate Change, this country has failed to ratify a number of other international agreements that would provide greater protection of human health and the environment, or greater public access to information. These include:

- The Convention on Biological Diversity, which creates an international framework for protection of biodiversity.
- The Stockholm Convention on Persistent Organic Pollutants, which requires parties to reduce or eliminate long-lived pollutants that have significant adverse environmental and human health effects.
- The Rotterdam Convention on the Prior Informed Consent Procedure for Certain Hazardous Chemicals and Pesticides in International Trade, which bans the export of listed chemicals unless the importing country has consented.
- The Basel Convention on the Control of Transboundary Movements of Hazardous Wastes, which aims to prohibit the export of hazardous waste to (mostly developing) countries that lack the capacity to deal with those wastes in an environmentally sound manner.
- The Aarhus Convention on Access to Information, Public Participation in Decision-making and Access to Justice in Environmental Matters, even though U.S. statutes served as a source of inspiration for its implementing guidelines.
- The 1997 Kyoto Protocol, which would have committed the U.S. to reducing its greenhouse gas emissions by 7% below 1990 levels by 2008-2012. The United States is the only developed country that never ratified the protocol. While the United States could still ratify or accede to the other treaties, it is far too late for the U.S. to ratify Kyoto.

Conclusion

Governance for sustainability is a much bigger task than regulating environmental pollutants. It requires governments at all levels to encourage and foster an ongoing long-term reduction in our overall environmental footprint at the same time as they improve opportunities for greater quality of life. And it requires a much greater range of legal and policy tools than environmental regulation alone. The United States has made some progress toward governing for sustainability over the past two decades at the local, state, and national levels, though not to the extent needed.

Local governments, which are closer to their citizens and see directly how the environmental, social, and economic impacts of specific problems are intertwined, have done the most. State governments have also been active, particularly on renewable energy, energy efficiency, and even climate change. The federal government has been more active in recent years, but not to the extent of many state and local governments, nor many other countries.

CHAPTER 6

Improving Opportunities for Sustainability Education and Engagement

Governance for sustainability is impossible without an informed and engaged public, demanding more-sustainable laws, insisting that each political party and elected official work for a more-sustainable America, moving toward sustainability wherever they work, and making sustainable decisions for themselves and their families. Public education and engagement are indispensable to the transition to a sustainable society—both in the United States and around the world.

Formal education is essential to sustainability. Education provides people with the skills and knowledge they need to hold a job, raise a family, vote, and participate in society. Education for sustainability raises an additional dimension to these objectives. It is not just about providing information concerning the environment and environmental problems; it is also and more fundamentally about the connections between the environment and everything else we care about. A starting point is having students see the connections—how wetlands can reduce flooding, why a relatively stable climate matters to agriculture, how sustainable fishing practices protect and create jobs, how energy efficiency can save money—that they might not otherwise understand. But of equal and even greater importance is acquiring the skills and knowledge needed to move toward sustainability—to practice green chemistry, to design zero energy buildings, to install green roofs, to develop web-based applications for solving sustainability problems, to better understand how to encourage appropriate behavior, to write better laws and counsel clients to make more-sustainable decisions, and to integrate environmental goals into decisionmaking.

Public participation, access to governmental information, and access to justice are also essential. Public participation in decisionmaking allows different sectors of the public to have their voices heard and bring additional information to the attention of the decisionmakers, and ultimately to improve the quality of decisions and their implementation. Similarly, the American people need information—not just in school but also from various levels of government—to fully understand the environmental challenges the country faces, to advocate for the commitment of resources necessary to address those challenges, and to track progress toward meeting the goals of sustainable development. Access to the judicial system ensures that people's procedural and environmental rights are respected.

Public participation, access to information, and access to justice also enhance the likelihood of the kind of integrated decisionmaking that sustainable development requires. Public participation and lawsuits, based at least in part on publicly available information, are likely to bring environmental, social, and economic perspectives into decisionmaking processes that might not otherwise consider them. Participation, information, and access to justice, which are rooted deeply in American law and history, are so central to sustainability that they are contained in Principle 10 of the Rio Declaration.[1]

This chapter reviews efforts over the past two decades in two critical areas: formal education, particularly higher education and kindergarten through 12th grade (K-12); and public information, participation, and access to justice. In formal education there is evidence of substantial progress toward sustainability in every significant aspect of college and university activity—institutional mission, campus operations, curriculum, research, community outreach and service, and student life. At the K-12 level there is now an established set of standards and practices for education for sustainability, and while these standards and practices are not as widespread as those for higher education, they are being employed by a growing number of states and school districts. They also tend to link education with the environment in the place where schools are located, and there is evidence that they improve learning outcomes.

Over the past two decades, access to information, participation, and access to justice have been dramatically changed by communications technology, especially the Internet and social media. These nongovernmental trends may be more significant than governmental developments. At the national government level, public access to information has fluctuated from administration to administration. Standing to sue in federal court has also become somewhat more difficult for nongovernmental organizations.

Formal Education

Both higher education and K-12 education have taken significant steps toward sustainability over the past two decades, although there is much more evidence of progress in colleges and universities.

Higher Education

Fostering a more-sustainable world is an important outcome of higher education. Nearly every college and university mission statement holds the institution to a purpose higher than simply the creation and dissemination of knowledge. They aspire to instill in graduates such qualities as good citizenship, moral integrity, leadership, critical thinking, and care for the environment—the very qualities needed for building a sustainable world. Colleges and universities are uniquely equipped to help achieve sustainability through innovation in teaching, research, and institutional practice. Overall, there has been significant progress toward sustainability in higher education over the past 20 years. Some areas of college and university life have moved faster than others, and in recent years several organizations have endeavored to monitor progress and identify areas of strength and weakness. These surveys and their "report cards" evaluate progress in six critical dimensions of higher education.

Institutional Mission, Policy, and Planning

Various indicators show a strong shift toward sustainability at the administrative level of U.S. colleges and universities. According to the National Wildlife Federation's *Campus Environment 2008: A National Report Card on Sustainability in Higher Education*, 65% of the institutions surveyed either have a written commitment to promote environmental sustainability or stewardship or have plans to develop one, representing a 50% increase since 2001.[2] Fifty-three percent of the colleges and universities either have a written declaration that educating students about environmental responsibility is part of their academic mission or plan on developing one, up from 34% in 2001. The number of coordinators, directors, and offices of environment or sustainability has also grown significantly.[3]

Since it was created in 2006, more than 670 presidents and chancellors have signed the American College & University Presidents' Climate Commitment (ACUPCC),[4] committing their institutions to develop and implement long-term institutional action plans for becoming climate neutral. As a result, the ACUPCC is expected to be a major driver of higher-education sustainability activities in the coming years. The number of signatories represents about 20% of U.S. colleges and universities and 35% of the student population.

Campus Operations

Sustainable campus operations are the poster child of the movement for sustainability in higher education. Increasing numbers of projects and programs are reported both in surveys and on daily discussion lists and e-bulletins devoted to the topic. Sustainable operations include recycling, energy and water conservation, green purchasing, transportation initiatives, sustainable landscaping, and green buildings. Sustainability staff, whose numbers have increased dramatically in recent years, are mainly responsible for greening their schools' operations. Fostering sustainable operations presents far fewer barriers than attempting to integrate sustainability into teaching and research because the practices and technologies bring tangible, environmentally responsible results, and they can save money. In 2011, the Sustainable Endowments Institute's annual report card of sustainability in higher education showed dramatic progress in several aspects of campus operations since 2006, including campus farms or gardens, trayless dining, waste reduction, recycling, and sustainable transportation.[5] The National Wildlife Federation's *Report Card* also reported significant progress in campus operations, particularly in energy and water conservation.

Curriculum

Various efforts appear to be underway to transform academic programs to foster interdisciplinary thinking, a hallmark of education for sustainability. Bachelor's and master's degrees in sustainability studies—sustainable design, sustainable agriculture, sustainability education, and sustainable business—are emerging at several schools around the country. Professional schools are also responding to the sustainability challenge, the most promising being business and law schools.[6]

According to the Association for the Advancement of Sustainability in Higher Education, "green studies" and environmental science are the fastest growing trends in higher education. In 2009 alone, more than 100 new energy and sustainability-focused degree programs were created across the nation. This is a drastic increase from 2005, when only three new programs were added in these fields.[7]

Research

Particularly critical to advancing sustainability globally is the advancement of research. Sustainability-oriented research is increasingly funded in the sciences, but initiatives are also underway to include the social sciences and humanities. "Sustainability science" is beginning to emerge as a legitimate area of research; the *Proceedings of the National Academies of Sciences* has created a new section of the journal devoted to the field.[8]

Likewise, the academic community has seen a rise in peer-reviewed journals focused on education for sustainable development in higher education and on sustainability generally. The *International Journal of Sustainability in Higher Education* (Emerald) was launched in 2000; *Environment and Sustainable Development* (Inderscience) in 2002; and both the *Journal of Education for Sustainable Development* (Sage Publications) and *Sustainability: Research and Practice* (Mary Ann Liebert) in 2007. Within professional education, business and law journals now discuss sustainable development or include sustainability themes, and American University's Washington College of Law has created the student-run publication *Sustainable Development Law and Policy*.[9]

Growth in other research areas is less clear. According to the 2008 National Wildlife Federation study, 19% of the colleges and universities surveyed had research institutes that study sustainability, climate change, or clean energy issues. Although that figure is lower than the 23% in 2001, this finding is not significantly different from 2001 by statistical standards.

Community Outreach and Service

Many universities and colleges promote sustainable development in their surrounding communities and beyond,[10] efforts that typically involve service learning projects, student internships, and student and faculty research. Now considered mainstream in higher education, service learning is also an effective pedagogical strategy for integrating sustainability into class work. However, Elizabeth Coleman, president of Bennington College, argues that "despite the [growing] attention paid to service these efforts remain emphatically extracurricular and have had virtually no impact on the curriculum itself. In effect, civic-mindedness is seen as residing outside the realm of what purports to be serious thinking and adult purposes."[11]

Student Life

Student environmental activism has risen over the past 20 years, and students are very often the major drivers of sustainability on campus. The Energy Action Coalition is a national organization of student-focused organizations that work on energy and climate change issues. The Real Food Challenge is a coalition of organizations working to improve food sustainability on campus. Sustainable living programs, in which students engage in some form of peer-to-peer education to encourage energy and water conservation, recycling, and waste reduction in dormitories, are also increasingly popular at schools across the country.[12] As with energy and climate issues, student interest in sustainable food and recycling initiatives continues to grow. Student demand for local, organic, and fair-trade food options has led more than 200 campuses to initiate farm-to-college programs that match farmers with local universities. Many of these schools offer menus on which 30% or more of the food is locally grown.[13] Participation in RecycleMania—a friendly competition among campuses to increase recycling and reduce waste—has grown from 2 participants in 2001 to 630 in 2011.[14]

Sustainability in colleges and universities appears to be increasingly attractive to prospective students. According to the Princeton Review's *Guide to 311 Green Colleges* (2011), 66% of respondents (among nearly 16,000 college applicants and parents of applicants surveyed) said they would value having information about a college's commitment to the environment.[15] Of that group, 24% said such information would "very much" impact their decision to apply to or attend the school.

Kindergarten Through 12th Grade

Twenty years ago, there was no "field" of Education for Sustainability (EfS) at the K-12 level. It was a glimmer in a few people's eyes. There was first a draft set of competencies, but no EfS standards and performance indicators for individuals, organizations, buildings, or communities. Nor were there curriculum exemplars, model schools, or student work providing evidence of the knowledge, skills, attitudes, behaviors, and outcomes that characterize EfS. Today, all of these exist. There is also growing recognition that a sustainable community initiative cannot be sustained without the participation and leadership of all the children, young people, and their teachers within the school systems.

Twenty years ago there was no evidence that a comprehensive approach to EfS could contribute to student achievement and be correlated with improved sustainable-community indicators at the local or regional level. Today there is more and more evidence that the two are correlated and that the effect of EfS on sustainability can be measured. Although EfS is less widely practiced than sustainability in higher education, and local budget shortfalls due to the economic slowdown have impeded EfS, there is nonetheless a solid core of expertise and experience.

Where It Is Working

There is growing evidence that significant numbers of both public and independent schools around the country are engaged in educating for sustainability. Some states, such as Vermont and Washington, have explicit EfS standards, which give credibility and "permission" for schools and teachers to educate for sustainability. At the same time, many schools and districts without explicit EfS state standards are engaging in those teaching, learning, organizational, and operational practices that characterize EfS.[16] For example, even in the absence of state standards, 17 districts in the Putnam/Northern Westchester Board of Cooperative Educational Services in New York State have made the commitment to EfS.[17]

EfS principles and practices are also reinforced through professional organizations and networks. More than 1,000 people gathered at the first Green Schools National Conference in 2010 to discuss their work and to advance the field of EfS. The National Association of Independent Schools has taken on EfS with a fervor. Many private schools are shifting their practices on school lunch, energy use, green building materials, gardens, composting, overall waste reduction and elimination, and even curriculum and instructional practices.

New Jersey combines EfS with community sustainability. School districts in Cherry Hill, Maplewood/South Orange, and Cranford, among others, are registered with Sustainable Jersey, which is the nation's first certification program for sustainable communities.[18] Points are awarded to municipalities for their green or sustainable actions. Municipalities that educate for sustainability receive points toward their Sustainable Jersey certification, a public recognition and grant program for communities aspiring to leadership on community sustainability. In all these municipalities, students engage in real-world research, data collection, project design, and actions that increase student achievement while measurably contributing to the sustainability of their communities.[19]

Evidence of Success

In locations that have engaged in educating for sustainability—such as New York City, New Hampshire, and Vermont—there is evidence of improved air quality, positive changes in children's food consumption, reduced waste and increased materials recycling, and overall reductions in energy consumption in the schools.[20] In addition, EfS has multiple, positive effects on student achievement, school culture, community vitality, and ecological integrity.[21] Student-centered effects include improved achievement, support for humans' innate affinity for holistic learning, attention to the needs of the whole person, provision of a safe and secure space in which to take risks and develop skills of active participation, and encouragement to make connections between the self and the larger systems of which one is a part. EfS has teacher-centered effects as well, especially an attitudinal impact and the ability of both new and veteran teachers to yield strong academic outcomes from their students. Finally, there are also school- and community-centered effects, including improved relationships among the school, parents, and the community and modeling of actions and attitudes that promote sustainable living.

Information, Participation, and Access to Justice

Since the Rio Summit, transparency, participation, and access to justice in the U.S. have experienced both advances and setbacks, even as technology has transformed how information is shared and how people participate in environmental decisionmaking.

Transformative Effect of Technology on Information and Participation

The biggest changes in public information and participation in the United States since the Rio Summit have resulted more from the expansion of technology than new legislation. Principle 10 of the Rio Declaration was adopted as excitement grew over the potential of public electronic databases demonstrated by the U.S. Toxics Release Inventory, established under the Emergency Planning and Community Right-to-Know Act (1986).[22] Under this act, manufacturers are required each year to publicly report their releases of toxic chemicals to water, land, and outdoor air and to publicly report offsite transfers of these chemicals. As the environmental community was preparing for the Rio Summit, the information technology community was developing and launching the World Wide Web. Since then, the Internet has transformed how people collect and disseminate information and how they communicate. This is true not only of Internet sites and e-mail, but also of social media such as Facebook and Twitter.[23] Most government agencies now have their own YouTube posts, Facebook pages, and Twitter accounts, and some even have wikis and blogs.[24]

Increasingly, government agencies communicate environmental information over the Internet. Environmental information that previously would have been time-consuming and expensive to obtain—requiring a Freedom of Information Act (FOIA) request and the review of thousands of pages of data—is now instantly available on websites such as MyEnvironment, an EPA website that allows users to search information about the state of the environment in their communities[25] and Data.Gov, which links to public information on a variety of topics from the restoration of the Gulf to EPA's environmental civil penalties policies.[26] Databases such

as these were first made user friendly in the early 1990s by nongovernmental organizations that created user interfaces and online services to make environmental
information from EPA more easily accessible to the public.[27] Today, federal, state,
and local agencies have websites providing a great deal of information about their
activities—information that would have been routinely available without an FOIA
request two decades ago, but would have required a phone call or letter to obtain
if one was even aware that it existed. This information can now be downloaded
without charge from any location in the world.

While most environmental legislation does not yet require the dissemination of
public information online,[28] the proliferation of publicly available data has largely
been undertaken voluntarily by government agencies. These agencies are guided
by Office of Management and Budget (OMB) Circular A-130, which calls on agencies to "provide for public access to records where required or appropriate."[29] The
circular instructs agencies to "use electronic media and formats, including public
networks, as appropriate and within budgetary constraints, in order to make government information more easily accessible and useful to the public." The concept
of agencies affirmatively making information publicly accessible was reinforced
under OMB's Open Government Directive, issued December 8, 2009.[30] Moreover,
the E-Government Act of 2002 requires that federal court dockets and decisions
and all information posted in the Federal Register be posted online.[31]

The federal government's track record of disclosure and encouraging public
participation has varied immensely depending on presidential leadership. When
one contrasts the policies of the administrations of Presidents Bill Clinton, George
W. Bush, and Barack Obama, one sees how elastic existing legislation is and how
much depends on leadership and worldview.

While President Clinton generally maintained the status quo with respect to
transparency and access to information, President Bush used his prerogatives as
president to actively limit access to information. In 2002, Attorney General John
Ashcroft issued a memorandum to federal agencies assuring them that the Department of Justice would defend any decision to withhold information in response
to an FOIA request if it had a "sound legal basis."[32] This resulted in a drop in full
disclosure. A report by the nonprofit Right to Know Committee stated that "in 2007,
only a little more than a third of all FOIA requests (35.6 percent) were granted full
disclosure, the lowest level since 1998."[33] From 2001 through the end of 2007,
President Bush used the state secrets privilege to withhold documents from Congress, courts, and the public a reported 45 times.[34] By contrast, the privilege was
invoked only six times from 1953 to 1976 during the height of the Cold War.[35]

The Obama Administration has reversed the trend of the Bush years and has
placed a high priority on transparency and public participation. Immediately following his inauguration on January 20, 2009, President Obama authorized creation
of the first White House blog with a post that said that he is committed to "making his administration the most open and transparent in history."[36] On January

21, 2011, President Obama issued the Memorandum on Transparency and Open Government to establish "a system of transparency, public participation, and collaboration" as principles to guide his administration.[37] The memorandum also stated that the Freedom of Information Act (FOIA) "should be administered with a clear presumption: In the face of doubt, openness prevails."[38] Agencies under the Obama Administration have also made significant progress in reducing FOIA backlogs; however, they use certain exemptions from FOIA disclosure even more than under the Bush Administration.[39]

Administrations are not always consistent on issues of transparency, and questions of transparency do not always follow party lines. Although the Obama Administration has generally encouraged transparency, it has supported the continued use of the state secrets doctrine. In 2009, the Administration continued to apply 4 of the 45 Bush Administration decisions to invoke the state secrets exemption.[40] The Department of Justice also invoked the state secrets exemption at least once in 2010.[41] The Department of Justice issued a formal policy on the state secrets doctrine that claims to limit its use through procedural safeguards within the department.[42] The press release accompanying the policy stated: "In order to facilitate meaningful judicial scrutiny of the privilege assertions, the Department will submit evidence to the court for review."[43] However, the policy itself does not expressly provide any opportunity for judges (even judges with security clearances) to review the information claimed to be secret.

Access to Justice

Access to administrative and judicial redress is also essential for sustainable development. Often, as we know, government and private decisionmakers do not follow the law. To the extent that it is available, administrative and judicial review helps ensure integrated decisionmaking, and thus enhances the likelihood that decisionmakers will fulfill their legal obligations in the first place.

Access to justice has faced both progress and setbacks since 1992. Citizen standing to sue in federal court has continued to expand and contract. Congress has considered taking steps to keep citizens and nongovernmental organizations from collecting attorney fees when they prevail in litigation against the government under the Equal Access to Justice Act. States likewise have a mixed record in this regard; while some have expanded standing in recent years, others are trying to limit it.

Citizen lawsuits provide access to justice for citizens and organizations that claim in good faith that government or private decisionmakers have not complied with environmental and other laws. Citizen standing to sue under federal environmental statutes in the United States has fluctuated since 1992 and is currently on a more restrictive path. In 1992, the Supreme Court established limits on who would have standing to sue under the Constitution,[44] limiting those who could sue over environmental issues to people who could show that they were challenging an activity which either could or had injured them "in fact," that the injury was caused by the defendant's action or inaction, and that winning the suit would address their injury.[45] This meant that nonprofit organizations had to make sure they were suing on behalf of people who were harmed or would be harmed. Between 1992 and 2000, the rules of standing continued to become more restrictive.[46] The Court started to expand citizen access to the courts in 2000,[47] continuing through the landmark case of *Massachusetts v. EPA*,[48] in which the Court recognized the standing of states, cities, and environmental organizations to compel EPA to promulgate regulations for greenhouse gas emissions from motor vehicles. Since 2009, however, the Court appears to have started shifting back to a more restrictive course, although the general rules of standing remain relatively constant.[49]

Congress has been trying to limit access to justice by limiting the ability of non-profits and environmental plaintiffs to obtain lawyers. Under the Equal Access to Justice Act of 1980, the prevailing party in an administrative adjudication or lawsuit against a government agency is awarded legal fees if the agency's position was not "substantially justified."[50] This is important because it often allows citizens and nonprofits to recoup the significant legal expenses of challenging agency actions. In 2011, the House of Representatives unsuccessfully attempted to limit the ability of citizens to collect attorney fees when they prevail in suits against the government.[51]

At the state level, trends vary. While New York is moving to expand access to justice, Maryland and Louisiana are taking steps to limit it. In 2009, the New York Court of Appeals expanded its formerly restrictive standard on standing.[52] Maryland and Louisiana considered steps to keep environmental litigation clinics from representing citizens whose lawsuits could affect local business interests.[53] These measures did not pass; however, the experiences do demonstrate that some members of Congress and certain state legislatures are hostile to the principle of access to justice, at least in these contexts.

Conclusion

An informed and engaged public is a fundamental requirement for sustainability. There is some evidence that the institutional changes needed to inform and engage the public are being made, though we are a long way from where we need to be.

Colleges and universities, as well as K-12 schools, can provide information and skills for sustainability by teaching them. In these institutions, a body of practice and experience has been developed and applied, particularly at the college and university level, with growing sophistication and success.

Another key aspect of public engagement is public participation, access to information, and access to justice, all of which focus on the relationship between citizens and their government. Governments can also create information and make it publicly available. The dominant trend in public information over the past two decades has been the availability of the Internet, personal computers, and social media. In these and other ways, governments and educational institutions are providing citizens with the information and tools to make more-sustainable decisions and to participate more fully in governmental decisionmaking. Governments can also improve access to justice to foster more-sustainable decisions when litigation is necessary, and recent actions have enhanced and limited access in different ways.

CHAPTER 7

International Activity: A More-Sustainable Direction but Reduced Influence

The United States influences international activities related to sustainability largely through the example it sets at home. Because of the communications revolution, people watching BBC television in a restaurant in Kenya's Great Rift Valley or surfing the Web at an Internet cafe in Jeonju, South Korea, can learn a great deal about what Americans think and do, including their views and actions on sustainability. The force of our example—our domestic decisions about energy, environment, climate change, consumption, and other sustainability issues—has as much international impact, for better and for worse, as our explicit international activities. As explained previously, our domestic example is not impressive. One need look no further than U.S. domestic decisions concerning climate change to see that our decisions have discouraged some other countries from taking action, or at least provided an excuse for those countries to take no action.

As a global power, the United States should be, and is, active outside its borders on a great variety of sustainability issues. This chapter describes four: official development assistance, international financing of sustainable development, international trade, and prevention of lead poisoning. These issues have a profound effect on sustainability throughout the world because they affect the international rules under which the United States conducts international trade and because they encourage and support sustainable actions by other countries, including developing countries. Because the fate of the United States is, in important ways, bound up with the fate of the rest of the world, U.S. actions on behalf of international sustainability can also contribute to U.S. security and well-being.

While the United States has been moving in a more-sustainable direction over the past two decades, the effect of this shift has been limited by reduced U.S. influence internationally. There has been a dramatic decline in the official development assistance provided to environmentally damaging projects (or what some call "dirty" projects) over the past two decades, and an increase in the assistance provided to more environmentally beneficial projects. Because other donors, including Russia and China, are now providing more aid than they did previously, however, and because these donors are willing to support projects that the United States no longer supports, U.S. policy changes may have less environmental impact in recipient countries.

For international financial institutions, particularly the World Bank and export credit agencies, a somewhat similar story has played out over the past two decades. Thanks in significant part to early U.S. leadership, these institutions have improved their environmental and social performance. But the United States has been less able to exercise leadership as the voices of other governments have become more important, and as U.S. domestic environmental policies have fallen behind the environmental policies of other countries.

On trade, U.S. influence appears to be weaker within the World Trade Organization (WTO) than with various regional and bilateral trade agreements to which the United States is a party. Sustainability is an explicit objective of the WTO, and is slowly working its way into WTO's policies. Environmental protection provisions have also been included in the North American Free Trade Agreement as well as virtually all recent U.S. bilateral trade agreements.

Lead poisoning is an issue where the United States has exercised notable leadership for many decades. Great strides have been made in eliminating lead from paint and gasoline, in part because of U.S. domestic and international efforts. Yet lead continues to be used in many other ways that lead to human exposure, and the residual effects of leaded gasoline and paint continue to be significant.

Official Development Assistance

Official development assistance (ODA) is financial support from developed countries to developing countries, usually to promote economic development or social well-being. There has been a persistent effort over the years, most importantly at the 1992 Earth Summit, to encourage developed countries to provide an amount equal to 0.7% of their gross domestic product for ODA, based on the argument that such levels of funding are needed to enable developing countries to achieve sustainable development. But the United States has never agreed to that level of ODA.

That said, there are any number of reasons why the United States should ensure that its ODA fosters sustainable development, or at least does not encourage or support unsustainable development. There are humanitarian and strategic reasons, such as improving human well-being in developing countries and achieving national security.[1] More generally, it makes sense for the United States to support environmentally sustainable economic and social development in developing countries.

By financing more environmental remediation and environmental protection, U.S. foreign assistance appears to do less environmental damage today than it did in past years. The amount of explicitly environmental aid has increased only slightly over the past three decades, but the amount of "dirty" aid has declined dramatically. Figure 7.1 shows the amount of dirty, neutral, and pro-environmental aid allocated by the United States from 1980 to 2008 by "environment code." This figure represents $543 billion in U.S. foreign aid over those 30 years. U.S. environmental aid—aid that is expressly intended to address environmental purposes, such as assistance in complying with multilateral environmental agreements like the Montreal Protocol (which phases out chemicals that deplete the stratospheric ozone layer)—is the smallest component of overall U.S. foreign aid and has risen slowly to nearly $1 billion a year in the final five years of the past decade.[2]

Figure 7.1[3]
U.S. Aid by Environment Code, 1980-2008

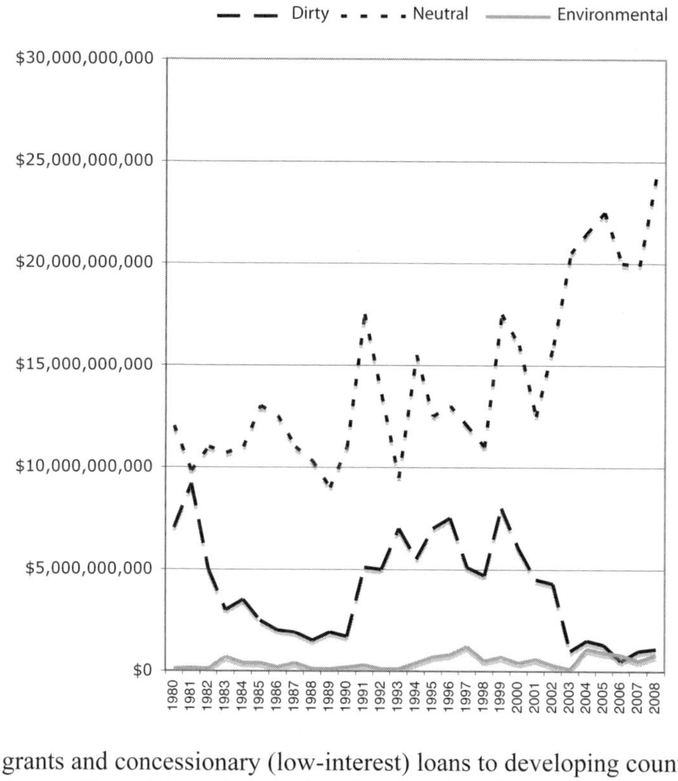

U.S. grants and concessionary (low-interest) loans to developing countries for dirty projects—like mining, clear cutting, highway building, and other infrastructure—fell, rose, and then fell again over the nearly three decades. Overall, it has fallen from over $5 billion a year in the early 1980s to levels that are slightly higher than those for environmental aid, about $1 billion a year at present. Environmentally neutral aid—social aid that is likely to have neither a good nor bad environmental impact—is now about 15 times larger than the other two categories combined. Environmentally neutral aid saw a steady increase over the three decades, from just above $10 billion a year to above $20 billion a year by the end of the period.[4]

However, the fact that U.S. development finance has greened over the past 20 years does not necessarily mean that recipient countries are pursuing more environmentally sustainable policies and practices. Nor does it mean that multilateral agencies like the World Bank have eliminated the funding of coal-burning power plants or other dirty projects in developing countries. They have not. Progress has been incremental and uneven, but nonetheless U.S. taxpayers are not financing environmental destruction abroad to the same degree they were in the past. However, when the U.S. government refuses to bankroll environmentally damaging development projects, developing countries often manage to substitute alternative sources of funding from private banks and nontraditional donors such as China, Russia, and Iran. In short, U.S. foreign aid is now much greener than it was in previous decades, but it is not obvious that the development policies, practices, and projects of low- and middle-income countries are substantially less damaging to the environment.

Recent U.S. foreign assistance has focused on helping developing countries avoid new greenhouse gas emissions and adapt to the impacts of climate change. In 2009 and 2010, direct climate assistance for these purposes through the U.S. Agency for International Development, the Treasury Department, and the State Department tripled from $316 million to about $1 billion, while adaptation assistance increased tenfold, from $24 million to $244 million. These funding increases represent an effort on the part of the Obama Administration to honor pledges that were made at the December 2009 Copenhagen meeting of the parties to the Framework Convention on Climate Change. Nevertheless, current funding levels remain significantly lower than the levels recommended by most scientists. Climate finance has also become a target of criticism in recent congressional appropriations, and the likelihood of meeting those promises may be reduced.[5]

International Finance for Sustainable Development

International financial institutions (IFIs) exist throughout the world to provide financial support for development projects. They include government-owned banks, such as the World Bank, regional development banks, export credit agencies, and numerous private-sector banks that invest jointly with governments.[6]

To finance sustainable development, environmental and social considerations need to be integrated into the investment decisions of financial institutions. Over the past 20 years, IFIs have focused more on improving their environmental and social performance. The U.S. government provided early leadership in this shift but has gradually been less influential as other governments' voices have emerged and as U.S. domestic environmental policies have stalled.

U.S. Role at the World Bank

Multilateral development banks—such as the World Bank, Asian Development Bank, and Inter-American Development Bank—play a significant role in channeling public funds towards emerging economies. They provide low-interest loans to developing countries for structural and policy reforms and technical assistance where capacity to implement reforms is low. Jointly with other financiers (including commercial banks), they often support large infrastructure and energy projects. The World Bank is the most prominent of the development banks.

The World Bank is considered to be a specialized agency of the United Nations (U.N.) because it collaborates with the U.N. on behalf of international development, but it acts separately—and sometimes at odds—with the U.N.[7] It operates as a bank, applying the principles of finance and development rather than of environment and human rights. When governments created the Bank in 1944, they envisioned it as one part of a system of international institutions in which the U.N. would focus on political issues and the Bank on economic growth; Bank interference in political affairs was prohibited.

Today our understanding of development has changed, and economic growth alone is no longer sufficient. The current approach to development recognizes that the protection of environmental and human rights is closely linked with economic growth and stability. The Rio Declaration captured this linkage by stating that "the right to development must be fulfilled so as to equitably meet developmental and environmental needs of present and future generations."[8] Over time, the World Bank has made more investments in activities that promote the environment and human rights, although its legal mandate has not changed to reflect this broader understanding.

What has changed instead is the World Bank's view of how to accomplish its development mission.[9] After heavy criticism in the 1980s and 1990s for imposing what many deemed unduly harsh economic reforms on countries, the Bank has reversed its approach to become a "demand-driven" institution. An important part of the Bank's institutional culture is not to impose development on a government but rather to allow the borrowing government to choose what is most appropriate for its needs. Sometimes this is in line with sustainable development as governments seek to tackle climate change and food insecurity. Other times, this approach is not in line with sustainable development when governments seek funds to build projects that are environmentally destructive, violate human rights, or deny the participation of local stakeholders.

Early U.S. Leadership

Since the Bank's creation the U.S. government has been its largest shareholder and has often been the most influential member of the board. The influence of the U.S. government on the World Bank's board is complex—as the largest shareholder, it has a strong voice in policy reforms but cannot dictate specific investments. Each year, the United States votes against or abstains from about one-tenth of proposed investments, many of which go forward anyway. At the same time, the U.S. government has been a driver behind many of the Bank's largest policy reforms. This is in part due to its status as the largest shareholder, but also a result of being well staffed. The U.S. executive director (1 of 25 executive directors with voting power on Bank activities, who form, along with the World Bank Group president, the Bank's board of directors) has extensive staffing support to enter policy debates at a depth that most other countries cannot match.

Around 20 years ago, the U.S. government—at the urging of civil society organizations and Congress—began to use this leverage to push the Bank toward promoting environmental and social reforms. Within the United States, Congress has the authority to authorize financial support that the U.S. government provides to international organizations such as the World Bank. In the 1980s and 1990s, public criticism grew over the World Bank's involvement in controversial projects, such as the Narmada Dam in India, which displaced more than 300,000 people, and Polo-noroeste's BR-364 Amazon highway program in Brazil that uprooted indigenous communities. Civil society organizations asked Congress to make appropriations to the Bank conditional on stronger environmental and social performance. As a result, the Bank began a series of reforms.

The 1989 International Development and Finance Act required the U.S. government to abstain from supporting any investment by the World Bank or multilateral development banks that has not undergone an environmental impact assessment.[10] This law, combined with U.S. leverage, led to the adoption of environmental and social safeguards for Bank investments in the form of an assessment process based on the procedures established in the 1969 U.S. National Environmental Policy Act. In 1993, the Bank also established the Inspection Panel, to investigate whether its projects meet social and environmental standards as a condition of U.S. financial support. The panel provides a way for communities affected by Bank projects to bring complaints when the Bank's policies are not followed.

These steps helped to spark further reforms at the Bank, often encouraged by the U.S. government and Congress. Some examples include:

- *Safeguards*. Over the past two decades, the Bank has established increasingly robust environmental and social safeguards to cover a range of issues such as involuntary resettlement and indigenous peoples' rights. The U.S. government has consistently been a champion of stronger safeguards.

- *Climate Investment Funds.* The Bank has managed several climate change funds while U.N. negotiations tried to agree on a new climate-finance mechanism. These funds are intended to scale up funding to assist developing countries in mitigating greenhouse gas emissions and adapting to climate change. The United States, United Kingdom, and Japan initiated the creation of these funds.

- *Mitigating the Risks of Controversial Projects.* On the Bank board, the U.S. government has promoted stronger scrutiny of several environmentally and socially controversial projects, such as the Bujagali dam in Uganda, the Nam Theun 2 dam in Vietnam, and the China Western Poverty Reduction Project. The China Western Poverty Reduction Project was the collective name for several projects, one of which, the Qinghai project, involved the relocation of close to 60,000 Chinese farmers to Tibet. Although the project was opposed from the start by the United States, the Bank initially approved the relocation project. However, following a high-profile campaign by nongovernmental organizations to stop the project, the Bank decided to delay its start until it could review the Inspection Panel's findings. Ultimately, the Bank withdrew from the Qinghai project.[11]

- *Access to Information.* In 2010, the Bank adopted a progressive access-to-information policy, which contains a presumption of disclosure for many Bank documents and allows communities and civil society watchdogs to learn more about the Bank's investments.

Falling Behind

Despite these reforms, the World Bank does not measure its overall impact on sustainable development. Environmental and social policies do not apply in all cases and have not consistently prevented controversial investments from going forward.[12] Some Bank activities are supportive of sustainable development, and some are opposed.

On the supportive side, the World Bank has had a significant presence at the U.N. negotiations on climate change. Between 2008 and 2010, the Bank managed $6.3 billion in climate investment funds. At the Cancun conference of the parties to the Framework Convention on Climate Change in December 2010, governments created the Green Climate Fund as a new central mechanism for financing the global response to climate change and selected the World Bank to manage the trust fund. In the coming years, the Bank will play a leading role in directing finance to address climate change and in setting the precedents for future financing. The Bank's performance will be crucial to the success of the U.N. agreement on climate change.

On the other hand, the Bank does not measure how its investments contribute to greenhouse gas emissions and has not committed to reducing the overall climate footprint of its lending portfolio. Indeed, the portfolio of fossil-fuel-related projects has grown.[13] In 2008, research by the World Resources Institute revealed that 60% of the Bank's financing for the energy sector did not take climate change into account. In 2010, a follow-up survey showed that only a limited number of the Bank loans to the electricity sector support clean energy.[14] By contrast, the Asian Development Bank measures the carbon footprint in proposed projects, provides technical support for countries to undertake low-carbon strategies, and helps countries determine energy-efficient options.[15]

The World Bank's recent investment in a South African coal-fired power plant illustrates the perception within the Bank that countries face a choice between clean energy and economic development, rather than considering these goals to be mutually reinforcing. In April 2010, the Bank's board of directors voted unanimously to approve a $3.75 billion loan to South Africa for the project, which was seen as a necessary response to the South Africa electricity crisis that had begun two years earlier. The coal plant, part of the national utility Eskom's program to expand generation capacity, is expected to provide 4,800 megawatts of electricity. Yet, there was little open debate within the South African government over whether coal was the most viable of the available energy options.[16]

Throughout the world, journalists and policymakers debated whether it is more important to promote economic development or prevent climate change. The project's supporters argued that environmentalists were being antidevelopment, and that the power plant would bolster South Africa's economy and create jobs.[17] The project's opponents—climate change activists and local community leaders—argued that the project would triple the greenhouse gas emissions of South Africa's energy sector, contribute to South Africa's water scarcity, and impose heavy costs on some of the country's most impoverished people.[18] They argued that the water and land surrounding the power plant and its 40 coal mines would become heavily polluted. Nevertheless, the project is going forward, and the campaign against it continues.

When the World Bank was considering the financing for the Eskom project, the U.S. Treasury Department released a statement noting that the project was incompatible with the Bank's strategy to "help countries pursue economic growth and poverty reduction in ways that are environmentally sustainable." The United States objected to the project for other reasons as well, including Eskom's inconsistencies with the World Bank's procurement guidelines and subpar environmental impact assessment.[19] Nevertheless, the World Bank board approved the investment.

The contradiction between the World Bank's leadership role in the U.N. climate negotiations and its unwillingness to manage its own climate footprint raises questions about the overall legitimacy of its approach to climate change. It also raises questions about the U.S. government's influence on the Bank's board of directors. The United States regularly abstains or votes against projects that go forward anyway. In the Eskom project, the United States and four other governments abstained from voting, but the opposition was insufficient for the Bank to revisit its investment. It remains unclear whether this high-profile defeat of the U.S. government will affect future board dynamics.

Next Steps

The World Bank invests in a wide range of development activities to help meet the needs of a broad variety of borrowers. At such a complicated international institution—the Bank has a staff of more than 10,000 and is owned by 187 governments—decisions inevitably become intertwined with global politics. In this setting, the U.S. government is still trying to find ways to be influential in the face of two obstacles:

- In the absence of strong domestic policies, the United States has limited credibility to push for strong reforms (such as a reduction in coal-fired power plants) abroad.
- Among the changing dynamics of global environmental governance, it is not sufficient for the U.S. government to act unilaterally as the largest "purse holder," or even in coordination with European governments. Instead, global financial decisionmaking must account for the voices of both donors and recipient countries[20]—a reality for many years at regional development banks and now extending to World Bank governance as well.

Role of U.S. Export Credit Agencies

Export credit agencies (ECAs) are public institutions that facilitate financing for home-country exporters and investors doing business overseas, particularly in developing countries and emerging market economies. The U.S. government has two ECAs—the Export-Import Bank (Ex-Im Bank) and the Overseas Private Investment Corporation (OPIC). While the primary mandate of the Ex-Im Bank is to promote U.S. exports and job creation, it has begun to take environmental considerations into account, particularly in its leadership role among export credit agencies in countries that are members of the Organization for Economic Cooperation and Development (OECD). OPIC's mandate has evolved to assisting U.S. businesses competing in emerging markets in a manner that is "consistent with sound environmental and worker rights standards."[21]

Reforms by Congressional Mandate and Litigation

As with World Bank reforms, environmental and social reforms at the ECAs were largely initiated by Congress. The U.S. Congress established the Ex-Im Bank in 1934 and OPIC in 1971, and it reauthorizes each institution's charter every few years. In 1992, around the time of the World Bank reforms, Congress for the first time required the Ex-Im Bank to establish environmental procedures for its operations. In subsequent reauthorizations, Congress has often mandated additional reforms; the 2006 Export-Import Bank Reauthorization Act required the bank to promote renewable energy projects.

Litigation against the Ex-Im Bank and OPIC has also led to reforms. In 2002, the Friends of the Earth and Greenpeace, along with the city of Boulder, Colorado, sued both in federal court.[22] They alleged that between 1990 and 2003 the Ex-Im Bank and the OPIC provided more than $32 billion in public financing for overseas projects that cumulatively produced carbon dioxide emissions equivalent to more than 7% of the world's annual emissions in 2003. Three California cities—Arcata, Santa Monica, and Oakland—later joined the suit, arguing that the climate change caused by these overseas projects would harm them.

The federal court ordered the parties to negotiate an agreement. As part of the final settlement announced in February 2009, the Ex-Im Bank agreed to take carbon dioxide emissions into account when evaluating fossil fuel projects and to develop an organizationwide carbon policy in consultation with a group of environmental organizations.[23] The carbon policy—the first of its kind for an ECA—was adopted in 2009.[24] The bank must also provide its board of directors with information about carbon dioxide emissions before the board considers whether to approve transactions related to fossil fuel projects. Under the agreement, the Ex-Im Bank must also set aside $250 million in financing for renewable energy.

OPIC also agreed to establish a goal of reducing its greenhouse gas emissions by 20% over the next 10 years. A full environmental impact assessment is required for projects that emit significant amounts of carbon dioxide, and OPIC must publicly report emissions from these projects annually.[25] (In anticipation of the settlement, OPIC established its Greenhouse Gas Initiative in 2007, which included many of the terms later agreed upon.[26])

Early Leadership at OECD

As the Ex-Im Bank moves forward with environmental reforms, it must do so with the consensus of other ECAs. Under the rules of OECD, to which the United States and other developed countries belong, ECAs negotiate common terms of financing in order to ensure a level playing field among governments promoting their country's exports. Beginning in the early 2000s, the Ex-Im Bank initiated discussions on common approaches to the environment. During the George W. Bush Administration, however, the bank's negotiators were not given authorization to discuss climate change or other issues openly. In 2003, and again in 2007, ECAs agreed to the Common Approaches on the Environment and Officially Supported Export Credits, but with less-supportive U.S. involvement.[27] Today, the Ex-Im Bank is once again playing a leadership role in promoting environmental standards for OECD export credit agencies.

Next Steps

The Ex-Im Bank and OPIC continue to struggle with the challenge of promoting U.S. competitiveness and jobs, as their mandates require, while also enhancing environmental and social sustainability. There are several policy debates, some of them outside of these institutions' control:

- OECD export credit agencies have begun to see China and other emerging economies as formidable competitors. Greater participation of China in the OECD—even if not as a member obligated to OECD standards—would generate positive economic and environmental benefits. Will the U.S. government encourage the Chinese government to participate?
- Can the ECAs demonstrate that job creation and environmental protection can occur together?
- Will the ECAs become a part of U.S. commitments to provide climate finance to the U.N. negotiations, and if so, which investments will count?

International Trade

At the World Summit on Sustainable Development in Johannesburg, South Africa, in 2002, countries from around the world, including the United States, agreed to work toward "mutual supportiveness between the multilateral trading system and the multilateral environmental agreements, consistent with sustainable development goals."[28] The principle of mutual supportiveness is based on the assumption that the overall objective of environmental and trade legal regimes should be the same—namely, the improvement of the human condition in ways that also protect human, animal, and plant life and health. Put differently, the principle is that trade can and should become an instrument of sustainable development, not merely economic development. Ten years after Johannesburg, and two decades after the Rio Earth Summit, the concept of sustainability has taken root at both the international and regional levels of trade. This is not to say that trade has become environmentally sustainable; rather, the first steps in that direction have been taken. The United States has played a role in making that happen, particularly at the regional level and in bilateral trade agreements.

At the global level, with the establishment of the World Trade Organization in 1995 as the successor organization to the 1947 General Agreement on Tariffs and Trade, sustainable development at last has a place on the multilateral trading system's agenda. In the agreement establishing the WTO, the parties emphasize the importance of

> expanding the production of and trade in goods and services, while allowing for the optimal use of the world's resources in accordance with the objective of sustainable development, seeking both to protect and preserve the environment and to enhance the means for doing so in a manner consistent with their respective needs and concerns at different levels of economic development.[29]

In addition, a decision at the 1994 Uruguay Round of WTO members made the previously temporary Committee on Trade and Environment (CTE) permanent. The CTE's work addresses the relationship between the WTO agreements and multilateral environmental agreements or treaties, including the circumstances under which trade measures may be used on environmental grounds. The CTE is also charged with the task of investigating the links between trade and the environment and making recommendations on how to ease conflicts between trade and environment. In addition, the secretariats of several multilateral environmental agreements, including the Convention on International Trade in Endangered Species, have observer status at the CTE. Finally, the 2001 WTO Doha Ministerial Declaration stresses the links among trade, environment, and sustainable development. In that declaration the world's trade ministers underscored the importance of "enhancing the mutual supportiveness" of trade and the environment, calling for negotiations on the relationship between global trade rules and multilateral environmental agreements. It is safe to say that a link between the two has finally been forged at the WTO. The question remains, however, as to how strong the link is.

The WTO has also tried to better understand the relationship between trade and environmental degradation. In 1999, the WTO secretariat issued its *Report on Trade and Environment*.[30] It concluded the following:

- Most environmental problems result from polluting production processes, certain kinds of consumption, and the disposal of waste products. Trade as such is rarely the root cause of environmental degradation, except for the pollution associated with transportation of goods.
- The competitiveness effects of environmental regulations are minor for most industries. Little evidence exists for the claim that polluting industries tend to migrate from developed to developing countries to reduce the costs of environmental compliance. In other words, there is little empirical evidence to show that tough environmental laws cause capital flight to "pollution havens."
- The effectiveness of unilateral import bans as a means for achieving certain environmental ends is unproven. Trade barriers generally make for poor environmental policy. Environmental degradation occurs because producers and consumers are not always required to pay for the costs of their actions. The "polluter pays" principle, which would have the polluter pay for the cost of cleaning up pollution, needs broader implementation. Environmental degradation is sometimes accentuated by policy failures, such as subsidies to agriculture and fishing that pollute and degrade resources.

At the regional level, the provisions on the environment in the North American Free Trade Agreement (NAFTA) have been a watershed for post-NAFTA bilateral and regional free-trade agreements entered into by the United States. NAFTA's preamble obligates the NAFTA parties (1) "to undertake [the goals of NAFTA] in a manner consistent with environmental protection and conservation," (2) "to promote sustainable development," and (3) "to strengthen the development and enforcement of environmental laws and regulations."[31] The agreement also provides that in the event of a conflict between one of the listed multilateral environmental agreements (MEAs; the Montreal Protocol on Substances that Deplete the Ozone Layer, the Basel Convention on the Control of Transboundary Movements of Hazardous Wastes and their Disposal, and the Convention on International Trade in Endangered Species of Wild Fauna and Flora) and NAFTA, the MEAs prevail. NAFTA permits the ratcheting up of environmental standards, and prohibits the ratcheting down of environmental standards as a way of attracting foreign direct investment. Finally, the NAFTA environmental side agreement, the North American Agreement on Environmental Cooperation, obligates the parties to maintain high levels of environmental protection and establishes the Commission on Environmental Cooperation to oversee the agreement. The Agreement on Environmental Cooperation sets up a process in which private parties can petition the commission to investigate allegations of failure by a NAFTA party to enforce its environmental laws.[32] This process has been actively used. To date, a total of 87 citizen submissions have been filed against Canada (28), Mexico (39), and the United States (10). The commission's secretariat has undertaken 15 investigations and prepared factual records based on those submissions involving the United States (1), Mexico (7), and Canada (7).[33]

The NAFTA environmental provisions have been used as a rough template in all subsequent U.S. free-trade agreements (FTA). Since 2007, all U.S. FTAs contain five core provisions on environmental protection. First, parties to all future FTAs must adopt, maintain, and implement laws, regulations, and all other measures to comply with the following seven MEAs: (1) Convention on International Trade in Endangered Species, (2) Montreal Protocol on Ozone Depleting Substances, (3) Convention on Marine Pollution, (4) Inter-American Tropical Tuna Convention, (5) Ramsar Convention on Wetlands, (6) International Whaling Convention, and (7) Convention on the Conservation of Antarctic Marine Living Resources.

Second, parties "shall not waive" environmental laws in order to attract foreign investment. This is a change from the soft language in NAFTA ("should not" waive) and the Central American Free Trade Agreement for the Dominican Republic ("shall strive to ensure" nonwaiver).

Third, a legal hierarchy is established in favor of MEAs. In the event of an inconsistency between a country's obligations under an FTA and one of the MEAs, a party shall not be precluded from taking a measure to comply with its obligations under the MEA.

Fourth, environment disputes are to be resolved using the same dispute settlement mechanism that is used for trade disputes. That is, trade-environment disputes that arise under post-2007 FTAs are resolved by the parties' trade ministers, rather than by the parties' environment ministers. This is also a departure from the NAFTA model and is intended to strengthen the observance of national environmental laws and MEAs.

Fifth, there is a clarification as to what constitutes an indirect expropriation in connection with the enforcement of environmental law. The issue of indirect expropriations has become an issue under NAFTA because some companies have complained in litigation that NAFTA requires them to be compensated for costs they incur under environmental regulations. The clarification states: "Except in rare circumstances, non-discriminatory regulatory actions by a Party that are designed and applied to protect legitimate public welfare objectives, such as public health, safety, and the environment, do not constitute indirect expropriations."[34]

The Colombia-United States FTA and the Peru-United States FTA contain a unique provision on biodiversity and sustainable development:

> The Parties recognize the importance of the conservation and sustainable use of biological diversity and their role in achieving sustainable development. . . .Accordingly, the Parties remain committed to promoting and encouraging the conservation and

sustainable use of biological diversity and all its components and levels, including plants, animals, and habitat.[35]

Much of this can be traced back to Executive Order 13141, issued by President Bill Clinton in 1999, which requires that environmental considerations be integrated into the objectives and positions of U.S. trade negotiators.[36] Implementing guidelines for the executive order provide for public comment and hearings on the environmental and other impacts of proposed agreements. The main focus of FTA environmental reviews is the potential environmental impacts of FTAs on the United States. However, reviews also include consideration of global and transboundary effects.

Finally, there has been some progress in advancing sustainability in bilateral investment treaties, which establish rules for private investment in one country by companies or individuals in another. In connection with the U.S. bilateral investment treaty (BIT) program, the 2006 Uruguay-United States BIT contains a first-of-its-kind provision on environmental protection. It provides that "each Party shall strive to ensure that it does not waive or otherwise derogate from, or offer to waive or otherwise derogate from, [its environmental] laws in a manner that weakens or reduces the protections afforded in those laws as an encouragement for the establishment, acquisition, expansion, or retention of an investment in its territory."[37] It further provides: "Except in rare circumstances, non-discriminatory regulatory actions by a Party that are designed and applied to protect legitimate public welfare objectives, such as public health, safety, and the environment, do not constitute indirect expropriations."[38]

International Lead Poisoning and Prevention

Lead poisoning is an example of the problem of unsustainable products in global commerce, and the need to address many such issues on a product-by-product or toxin-by-toxin basis. While it is different from the three issues discussed above— official development assistance, international finance for sustainable development, and international trade—it is a reminder that U.S. international sustainability efforts are often focused on a specific issue.

Long before the 1992 Earth Summit, the United States took a leadership role in eliminating lead poisoning. Public health pioneers, mostly from the United States, formed a constituency that warned of the dangers of the continued use of lead-containing products, particularly leaded gasoline and lead-based paint. They kept up a drumbeat for combating lead poisoning that helped overcome cycles of policy inattention and industry resistance.[39] Yet after many decades, there is still a long way to go. News headlines remind us regularly both of the legacy of lead from existing uses and the flow of lead-containing products that still threaten to contribute to continued lead poisoning in the United States and elsewhere.[40]

Leaded gasoline has constituted the most dispersive use of lead. It can be said without exaggeration that leaded gasoline constitutes one of humankind's worst inventions. Its vehicular use provides a perversely efficient delivery system for the environmental deposition of lead through tailpipe emissions. To make matters worse, and contrary to the discredited myth that leaded gasoline improves vehicular performance, leaded gasoline dramatically increases maintenance costs.[41]

Although the United States was not the first country to phase out leaded gasoline, the U.S. phaseout was virtually completed before the 1992 Earth Summit. The process took two decades and provides a rich store of instructive experience that has allowed other countries to telescope their phaseout. There is an almost perfect correspondence between the leaded gasoline phaseout and the decline of lead in children's blood in the United States.[42] In addition, EPA and the U.N. Environment Program carried out the Partnership for Clean Fuel and Vehicles, which accelerated the phaseout of leaded gasoline, especially in sub-Saharan Africa.[43] The worldwide production of leaded gasoline has virtually ceased and it is now legally used in only a handful of countries.[44]

But the phaseout victory remains incomplete. The greatest continuing challenge is the vast reservoir of lead deposited in the environment, primarily through the past use of leaded gasoline. In particular, urban areas often have extremely high levels of lead in the soil. Those high levels are particularly true of poorer and disadvantaged communities, which are more likely to be located near highways and traffic congestion.[45]

Conclusion

U.S. international activities—particularly official development assistance, financial assistance for development projects, bilateral trade agreements, and promotion of unleaded gasoline—have moved in a more-sustainable direction over the past several decades. At the same time, there is evidence that the U.S. ability to exert international leadership on sustainability has diminished, as other countries fund projects that the United States will no longer support and continue unsustainable practices (use of leaded paint and lead in other products) long after they have been banned or eliminated in the United States.

Overall, the U.S. sustainability activities described in this and previous chapters—both domestic and international—show modest progress toward an increasingly distant goal. There are many efforts across a wide range of activities—environmental and public health protection, energy and water conservation, attention to environmental justice, economic development, governance, and public education and engagement. But nearly all of these activities are modest, limited in scope, and not fully sustainable. They represent real progress, to be sure, but are not fully responsive to the scale or importance of the challenges and opportunities of sustainability. And in many ways, the sustainability goal established two decades ago is farther away than ever, because of growing greenhouse gas emissions and population, as well as the cumulative effect of two more decades of unsustainable development and investment.

While it is much harder to say what the future holds, there are reasons to be hopeful. For one, much of the progress that has been made is in demonstrated capacity, know-how, and methods for sustainability. Over the next decade or longer, the deployment of these methods could accelerate very rapidly. If so, we will say in retrospect that the first two decades provided a foundation that, when finally completed, led to closing the distance to a sustainable destination. For another, the United States has not yet been fully engaged in the sustainability effort, has not seen both public and private sectors working together intensively for sustainability, has not had a broad movement of citizens working for sustainability in their own lives and communities and demanding more-sustainable goods, services, and governmental actions. If we made a full-bore commitment of our considerable talents and resources to addressing the challenges and seizing the opportunities of sustainability, we could also say in retrospect that the work of the first two decades was only a sample of what was to come.

PART II

Drivers for Sustainability

CHAPTER 8

Growing Support in
Spite of Mixed Public Opinion

There is simply too much to do to achieve a sustainable society, in too many places, for government to do it by itself. Broad, supportive public opinion, voiced in conversations with neighbors and in the workplace, through the purchase (or not) of goods and services, and also through elections, is an indispensable requirement for sustainability. After all, the people we elect will make decisions about the direction that our municipalities, states, and nation will take.

The Earth Summit delegates made clear that the active participation and engagement of a great many groups—religious bodies, business and industry, workers and trade unions, nongovernmental organizations, the scientific and technological community—is required. Chapter 6 discussed growing opportunities for public education and engagement—higher education, kindergarten through 12th grade education, as well as public participation, public information, and access to justice. This chapter discusses what other people and organizations are actually thinking and doing with regard to sustainability. How are they translating global and national environmental threats, as well as the opportunities provided by sustainability, into specific actions in particular places?

Public opinion, as reflected in national polls, has been mixed on sustainability. It has become less supportive of environmental protection over the past two decades and more inclined to favor tradeoffs of economic development over environmental protection. Much of this, no doubt, reflects the economic downturn of 2008. While an ample majority believes that the Earth is warming and will become warmer in the future, only one-third believe that warming is caused by humans. There is nonetheless substantial public support for specific policies to improve energy efficiency and increase the use of renewable energy. And the Millennium Generation (those born after 1982) appears to recognize the importance of sustainability issues more than do older generations.

That said, support for sustainability has been growing over the past two decades among those most directly affected by, and interested in, specific sustainability issues. Part I of this book provided abundant evidence of growing activity in a wide variety of contexts. Many nongovernmental organizations and corporations have become not simply supportive but, more importantly, have taken up leadership in the effort to achieve sustainability. This chapter discusses two stakeholder communities—organizations concerned with religion and ethics, on one hand, and business and industry on the other. It may seem odd to pair these two; after all, on the surface they seem to reflect very different perspectives. Yet—and perhaps surprisingly to many—they find a decent piece of common ground on sustainability.

Public support is manifest in other ways as well. Advocacy by nongovernmental organizations has played a key role in moving government and other decisionmakers in a more-sustainable direction. Public-private partnerships enable a variety of nongovernmental and governmental entities to combine their strengths and pool resources. Growing market pressure moves companies in a more-sustainable direction, and cities are competing with each other by improving quality of life for their residents. In these and other ways, public support for more-sustainable decisions is growing on many specific issues.

Mixed Public Opinion

In national public opinion polls, Americans are less supportive of environmental protection now than they were two decades ago and more inclined to believe that economic development should be given priority over environmental protection. Ironically, they may view things that way partly because they also perceive that environmental quality is improving.

Climate change emerged only recently as an issue of public concern. The Gallup Organization did not do polling on climate change until 1997, and the Pew Research Center only since 2006. At present, more than three-fourths of respondents believe that the world will be warmer in the future, but two-thirds do not believe that global warming will seriously threaten them in their lifetime, and only one-third believe that humans cause this warming. There are generational differences among the population: younger people are more likely than older people to believe that future environmental conditions will be worse. However, there is currently widespread support for many sustainable energy policies that can be justified from multiple perspectives, including climate change, economic development, and energy security.

Two decades ago, public support for environmental protection was comparatively high. In a comprehensive review of American public opinion about the environment published in 1992, environmental sociologist Riley Dunlap identified three significant trends:

- Public environmental concern developed dramatically in the late 1960s.
- After a slight decline in environmental concern in the 1970s, there was a significant and steady increase in both public awareness of environmental problems and support for environmental protection efforts through the 1980s into the early 1990s.
- By Earth Day in 1990, public concern for the environment had reached unprecedented levels in the United States.[1]

One indicator of strong public support for environmental protection and the environmental movement at this time can be seen in the results of a 1989 Gallup survey, in which 41% of the survey respondents considered themselves to be "strong environmentalists," and another 35% called themselves "environmentalists."[2] Only one in five of the survey respondents stated that they were "not an environmentalist." In addition, 85% of those surveyed indicated that they worry about the loss of natural habitat a "fair amount" to a "great deal" (58% said a "great deal"). This high percentage of Americans calling themselves environmentalists and expressing concern about the environment remained nearly constant throughout the 1990s.[3]

However, after the advent of the 2008 financial crisis and the ensuing recession, concern for jobs and the economy eroded some support for the environment in 2010 and 2011.[4] In 2007, the Gallup Poll found that 55% of Americans would give priority to protecting the environment, while 37% would give priority to economic growth. By 2011, only 36% of Americans would give priority to environmental protection, while 54% would give priority to economic growth (Table 8.1). In addition to the impact of the recession, Gallup also found that another reason for the decline is that "Americans may be less worried about environmental problems [because] they perceive environmental conditions in the U.S. to be improving."[5]

Table 8.1
Gallup Poll Results for Environment-Economic Tradeoffs[6]

Question: With which one of these statements about the environment and the economy do you most agree—protection of the environment should be given priority, even at the risk of curbing economic growth (or) economic growth should be given priority, even if the environment suffers to some extent?

	Environment (%)	Economic Growth (%)	Equally Priority (%)	No Opinion (%)
2011	36	54	6	4
2010	38	53	4	5
2007	55	37	4	4
2005	53	36	7	4
2000	67	28	2	3
1995	62	32	—	6
1990	71	19	—	10

In other surveys Gallup asked a similar tradeoff question on whether Americans prefer environmental protection or development of U.S. energy supplies. In 2001 (the first year the question was asked), 52% of respondents would give priority to environmental protection compared with 36% for the development of U.S. energy supplies. In the most recent 2011 survey, this pattern was reversed, with 41% preferring environmental protection, and 50% preferring energy development (Table 8.2).

Table 8.2
Gallup Poll Results for Environment-Energy Tradeoffs[7]

Question: With which one of these statements about the environment and energy production do you most agree: protection of the environment should be given priority, even
at the risk of limiting the amount of energy supplies—such as oil, gas and coal—which
the United States produces (or) development of U.S. energy supplies—such as oil and
gas and coal—should be given priority, even if the environment suffers to some extent?

	Environment (%)	Development of U.S. Energy Supplies (%)	Both Equally (%)	Neither/ Other (%)	No Opinion (%)
2011	41	50	4	1	4
2010	55	39	3	1	2
2005	52	39	4	2	3
2001	52	36	6	2	4

This trend of declining public concern for environmental issues is also reflected
in opinions about global warming. A recent Gallup report stated:

> The percentage of Americans who now say reports of global warming are generally
> exaggerated is by a significant margin the highest such reading in the 13-year history of
> asking the question. In 1997, 31% said global warming's effects had been exaggerated,
> last year, 41% said the same, and this year (2010) the number is 48%.[8]

The Pew Research Center has been asking the public about global warming in
its surveys for the past six years. In 2006, it found that 79% of Americans believed
there is "solid evidence the Earth is warming," 17% believed there is no evidence,
and 4% had no opinion. Of those believing the Earth is warming, 50% (of the
79% agreeing there is solid evidence of warming) said it was "because of human
activity," and 23% said it was "because of natural patterns" (Table 8.3). By 2010,
the percentage of Americans believing the Earth is warming had dropped to 59%,
while 32% believed there is no evidence. Likewise, the percentage of the public
believing that the warming is caused by human activity had declined to 34%.[9]

Table 8.3
Pew Research Center Poll on Opinions About Global Warming[10]

	2006 (%)	2007 (%)	2008 (%)	2009 (%)	2010 (%)
Is there solid evidence the Earth is warming?					
Yes	79	77	71	57	59
Because of human activity	50	47	47	36	34
Because of natural patterns	23	20	18	16	18
Don't know	6	10	6	6	6
No	17	16	21	33	32
Don't know	4	7	8	10	9

Pew also found that views of climate change are "sharply divided along party lines," with 79% of Democrats saying there is solid evidence of warming compared with only 38% of Republicans in 2010.[11] The Pew poll (Table 8.4) also found that 56% of political independents believe there is evidence of warming. A finding in the 2010 poll that does not bode well for government action to promote sustainability is that 58% of Republicans and 45% of independents believe there is no agreement among scientists that the Earth is warming (compared with 59% of Democrats who believe there is consensus). Meaningful action on climate change, as previously discussed, is necessary for sustainability.

Table 8.4
Pew Center Poll on Party Identification and Opinions
About Global Warming—2010[12]

	Republicans (%)	Democrats (%)	Independents (%)
Is there solid evidence the Earth is warming?			
Yes	38	79	56
Because of human activity	16	53	32
Because of natural patterns	18	18	17
Don't know	3	8	7
No	53	14	31
Don't know	9	6	12
How serious a problem?			
Very serious	14	50	30
Somewhat serious	27	32	32
Not too serious	23	8	17
Not a problem	34	7	18
Don't know	2	3	3
Is it a problem requiring immediate government action?			
Yes	24	68	44
No	39	19	31
Don't know	37	13	25
Do scientists agree the Earth is getting warmer because of human activity?			
Yes	30	59	41
No	58	32	45
Don't know	12	9	14

Gallup periodically asks people if they feel that global warming will be a threat within their lifetime. In 1997, 25% of the public answered that global warming would affect their lives, while 69% said it would not. In 2010, there was a slight increase to 32% believing it would affect their lives, while 67% believed it will not (Table 8.5).

Table 8.5
Gallup Poll Results for Impact of Global Warming[13]

Question: Do you think that global warming will pose a serious threat to you or your way of life in your lifetime?			
	Yes (%)	**No (%)**	**No Opinion (%)**
2010	32	67	2
2006	35	62	2
2001	31	66	3
1997	25	69	6

How people view the likelihood of a future threat—that is, how they assess risk—can be a tricky question. Social scientists have investigated the context of risk perception over the last several decades and have found that it is a complicated dynamic in which social context and culture are important considerations.[14] Mike Hulme, a professor of climate change in the School of Environmental Sciences at the University of East Anglia, explains:

> Rather than being told by experts what risks of climate change "really are," and then believing them, many people project their world-views outwards, thereby shaping sorts of risks associated with climate change in which they are prepared to believe. Someone who views the world's climate as fragile and easily destabilized is more likely to believe intimations that we are approaching a 'tipping point' in relation to ice sheets or ocean currents than is someone who views nature as benign or tolerant. When scientific assessments clash with deeply held values or outlooks, it may not always be science that triumphs.[15]

Not only is culture important in framing our understanding of climate change and its potential risks, public opinion research has found shared patterns of beliefs and values in those who either support or oppose the development of alternative-energy technologies.[16] In a sense, our values and beliefs shape what we believe to be true and untrue, what is or is not a risk, and the role government should play in responding to a perceived risk or problem deserving of action or undeserving of action. This research has found substantial support for alternative-energy technologies among individuals with strong biocentric (natured-centered) values and less support from those with more anthropocentric (human-centered) values. However, other paths to supporting sustainability policies were also found. Some Americans with anthropocentric values didn't believe in global warming, but did support the development of renewable energy sources for economic development and energy security.[17] Such bundles of shared values thus become a consideration when trying to understand how people perceive the risk of climate change and the adoption of alternative energy technologies.

The results of a 2010 Pew Research Center poll on energy policy provide additional support that there is some consensus for policies that promote sustainability, even while there is increased skepticism for global warming (Table 8.6). A majority of Americans favor requiring better fuel efficiency for vehicles (79%), more funding for alternative energy (74%), more spending on mass transit (63%), and providing incentives for buying hybrid or electric vehicles (60%). At the same time, 51% also supported more oil and gas drilling in U.S. waters, and 45% supported more nuclear power use as well.

Table 8.6
Pew Research Center Poll on Public Support for Energy Policies—2010[18]

	Favor (%)	Oppose (%)	Don't Know (%)
Requiring better fuel efficiency for vehicles	79	17	4
More funding for alternative energy	74	21	6
Spending more on mass transit	63	29	8
Providing tax incentives for buying hybrid or electric vehicles	60	34	7
Allowing more oil and gas drilling in U.S. waters	51	41	7
Promoting more nuclear power use	45	44	11

In 2010, the Pew Research Center also asked Americans about possible environmental scenarios in 2050 (Table 8.7). A majority said that the following events "definitely" or "probably will happen": most energy will be from alternative sources (74%); there will be a major world energy crisis (72%); the Earth will be warmer (66%); there will no more gas-powered cars (54%); and there will be severe freshwater shortages in most of the United States (53%). Pew also found that "those who hold more pessimistic views about the future of the environment are also more likely to be pessimistic about the future of the country."[19]

Table 8.7
Pew Research Center Poll on Future Scenarios—2010[20]

	Definitely/Probably Will Happen (%)	Definitely Will Not Happen (%)	Don't Know (%)
In the next 40 years…			
Most energy from alternative sources	74	24	2
Major world energy crisis	72	25	3
The Earth will get warmer	66	30	4
No more gas-powered cars	54	41	4
Severe freshwater shortages in most of U.S.	53	43	3

The same Pew study found that younger respondents (ages 18-29) were significantly more pessimistic about the future than older cohorts (65 and over). Younger respondents were more likely to believe that in the next 40 years the world's oceans will be less healthy than today, that environmental quality will not improve, and that the Earth will get warmer (Table 8.8). These results are consistent with new research by political scientists challenging the notion that youth are not concerned or worried about the future.[21]

Table 8.8
Pew Research Center Poll on Future Environmental Scenarios—2010[22]

	18–29 years (%)	30–49 years (%)	50–64 years (%)	65+ years (%)	Young-Old Difference
In next 40 years…					
World's oceans will be less healthy than today*	74	60	55	51	+23
Environmental quality will not improve*	62	51	43	42	+20
Earth will get warmer*	77	63	65	61	+16

*Percent responding "definitely" and "probably."

Some of the public opinion trends presented here do not bode well for continued public concern for the environment and global climate change—and therefore support for sustainability policies. However, the results concerning cohort differences may offer some hope. Research on the Millennium Generation has found that those born after 1982 are significantly more engaged in their communities through internships, volunteer work, and community action groups; are more tolerant of diversity and diverse opinions; are more concerned about current and future environmental conditions; and are more likely to disagree with older cohorts concerning "their level of faith in the political process to resolve problems and improve things."[23] Therefore, while younger cohorts are cynical about the political process, they are still open-minded and could be an important voice in solving future environmental problems.

Political scientist Russell Dalton has argued that Generation X (those born between 1961 and 1982) and especially the Millennium Generation are uniquely situated to be engaged in politics and civil society through new social networking technologies and new cultural symbols and messages. While voting among American youth has lagged significantly behind older cohorts in recent years because of perceived cynical, polarizing messages of traditional politics, their unprecedented level of community-based citizenship (volunteering) and concern about the planet offers an opportunity for further engagement.[24]

There is thus evidence that the Millennium Generation has adopted the need for sustainability as a core belief and embraces that perspective more firmly than older generations. What that means as they grow older, or for the generations that follow them, is harder to determine.

More-Supportive Public Opinion on Specific Issues

As the polling data indicate, public opinion is more favorable to sustainability when the questions focus on specific policies or issues. For example, there is wide public understanding of the need to have clean air for health reasons,[25] and the awareness often translates into support for specific measures to reduce air pollution. Public demand for a clean environment is also undoubtedly responsible for continued federal support for water pollution control and investments in safe drinking water.

A possible reason for support of water sustainability at a local and regional level is the phenomenon of bioregionalism, a sense of appreciation for and pride in a community's environment.[26] Bioregionalism has generated public support for aquatic ecosystem restoration efforts at all levels, from the clean-up of small urban streams to programs that stabilize rural watersheds to very large watershed restoration programs in places like the Chesapeake Bay, the Great Lakes, the Everglades, and the San Francisco Bay Delta. Some significant progress has been made in restoring aquatic ecosystems under these programs, either by reducing sources of impacts or by restoring habitats degraded by past activities. For example, bioregionalism can increase willingness to support restoration activities financially, through programs such as extra automobile license fees for license plates featuring the Chesapeake Bay and other ecosystems, or individual time and effort (what might be called "environmental sweat equity") spent on citizen water-quality monitoring or watershed restoration efforts.[27] Even with ample funding and the best intentions, however, those programs face significant barriers to success because of development pressures and competition for limited resources.

Sustainable approaches to toxic chemicals have been driven by legitimate public concern about persistent organic pollutants, a class of pollutants that accumulate in the food chain and pose serious risks to human health and the environment, as well as chemicals that cause disruptions to the endocrine system. Another motivator has been the national biomonitoring information generated by the Centers for Disease Control, which has made individuals more conscious of their personal exposure to chemicals. Still another motivator has been concern about risks of chemical exposures to children, high rates of neurological disorders like autism spectrum and attention deficit/hyperactivity disorder in children, and diseases like childhood cancer, even though it is hard to link these health conditions to exposure to any specific chemical.

Favorable public opinion is also translating into greater public involvement in sustainable communities. At the local level, where connections between the environmental, social, and economic aspects of life are experienced most directly, there is growing involvement and public demand for more-sustainable communities. According to a recent USA Today/Gallup poll, the "overwhelming majority of Americans say it's important for them to be involved in their community."[28] Not only do they seek to be involved; they also want their communities to be more sustainable.[29]

Public opinion strongly supports steps to more-sustainable transportation. In a recent national poll, when asked which approach they preferred to accommodate population growth, 75% chose building and improving rail systems such as commuter rail and light rail, while 20% chose new highways.[30]

In addition, demographic shifts are altering transportation and development patterns and creating pressure for further change. The U.S. population is aging, and it has been estimated that by 2030 one of every four Americans will be 65 or older. As the baby boomers age and leave the work force, they tend to drive less. And an aging population has a greater need for alternatives to driving. The Millennium Generation is another fast-growing population, and they so far have tended to prefer urban living and alternatives to driving.[31]

Finally, while it is difficult to measure, there appears to be a broader, growing sense of stewardship and responsibility across all age groups that is favoring greater sustainability. For example, a survey of small-forest owners participating in a Vermont community-based forest organization revealed that the social incentives to adopt forest sustainability certification were stronger than the financial incentives. Participants felt that they were supporting a movement reflecting their core values and promoting sustainability by becoming certified.[32]

Nongovernmental Organizations and Corporations

Nongovernmental organizations (NGOs) and corporations have been at the forefront of a great many efforts to advance sustainability in the United States over the past two decades. Among nongovernmental organizations, one of the most important perspectives comes from religious and ethics-based organizations that value human harmony with the natural world, responsible living within limits, and environmental justice for oppressed communities. Wherever such values are affirmed and followed, there is shared motivation to care for the entire Earth community in ways that foster long-term well-being. The actions and views of these organizations, on one hand, and business and industry, on the other, are, on at least some environmental sustainability issues, beginning to converge.

Ethics and Religion

The overarching moral assignment of our time is to act personally, institutionally, and politically in ways that are both ecologically fitting and socially just. The Earth community's health now depends on humans relating to the natural world so as to maintain its ecological health and aesthetic quality, or as Aldo Leopold wrote in *The Sand County Almanac*, the "integrity, stability and beauty of the biotic community."

We need a supportive ethos that melds respect for diverse life with justice for all life and responsibility to future generations. The vision of a just and sustainable Earth community resonates with major religious traditions of the West, East, South, and Indigenous Peoples, which, at their best, inculcate awareness of the sacred and visions of an interdependent Earth community pivoting around belief in a just, loving God or a benign cosmic order. And it is not just the religious communities themselves who are affected by such a vision; society looks to religious communities as an important source—and, for many, the only significant source—of values.

Communities of faith and doers of ethics continue on a difficult but rewarding pilgrimage to achieve a sustainable way of life that serves the vision and values of ecological justice, or eco-justice. Eco-justice, which is akin to environmental justice, recognizes that environmental harms almost always involve harm to people as well, and it fuses environmental protection and human rights. Even though the environmental crisis has deepened in the two decades since the Earth Summit, three positive developments in religion and ethics are contributing to a more just and sustainable American society.

First, more communities of faith are actively fostering sustainable (green) practices that emphasize simpler living, energy saving, food securing and sharing, and other Earth community-building initiatives that are expected of all who care for creation. For example, Interfaith Power and Light, which began in California, now has 37 state affiliates that respond to climate change by promoting energy conservation, energy efficiency, and renewable energy, in order to secure sufficient sustainable energy for all. Other best practices by communities of faith are similar to those employed at colleges and universities—reducing, reusing, and recycling more of what is consumed; fostering sustainable landscaping; purchasing green products; buying fair-trade food and other items; lowering greenhouse gas emissions; supporting local farmers and engaging in sustainable farming; and eating lower on the food chain. St. Stephen's Episcopal Cathedral in Harrisburg, Pennsylvania, for example, achieved LEED certification when it converted an old parking garage into its community school building. The congregation saw the green building effort as an expression of its faith and an opportunity to save money by reducing energy use.

Ecumenical networks—such as Earth Ministry, Seattle; Faith in Place, Chicago; Green Faith, New Jersey—continue to shape the involvement of numerous congregations, mosques, and groups of laity in the movement toward sustainable living. Mainline religious denominations support their members' efforts to achieve sustainability through voluntary organizations of laity and clergy that are supported by national office staff and the National Council of Churches Eco-Justice Program. Conservative evangelical congregations and student groups support organizations such as the Evangelical Environmental Network and the Evangelical Climate Initiative.

These efforts extend from personal choices to policy advocacy, but with mixed results. Leaders of the evangelical organizations candidly report that their advocacy for environmental sustainability or climate justice often arouses a negative reaction from conservative members, as well as marked opposition from the political right. In mainline faith communities one finds readier support for energetic advocacy to protect both the environment and human health. But the hope to achieve a just, participatory, and sustainable community is shared across the spectrum of liberal to conservative faith. Ecumenically engaged faith groups and organizations also continue to play a special role in asserting human environmental rights and seeking environmental justice for oppressed communities.

The second achievement is research and study in religion and ecology, or religion and ethics to meet the environmental challenge. A series of conferences in the 1990s encouraged more religion scholars and teachers across the United States and Canada to concentrate their attention on this subject. The extent to which religious environmentalism becomes institutionalized as a field of study remains to be seen, however, because this work is so dependent on the charisma of dedicated professors, the creative energy of program staff, and steady foundation support.

In 1993, this process began with Theological Education to Meet the Environmental Challenge (TEMEC), a national gathering of religion scholars at Stony Point, New York, organized by theologian Dieter Hessel and ethicist Richard Clugston. The conference stimulated participating professors and graduate students to pursue teaching, research, and writing in eco-theology, ethics, and ministry. The TEMEC process was continued a dozen years later by the Green Seminary Initiative (GSI), a coalition of more than 45 theological schools that infuse Earth care into all aspects of seminary education.

Complementing TEMEC and GSI, a group of religion scholars led by Mary Evelyn Tucker and John Grim, both of the Yale School of Forestry and Environmental Studies, organized the Forum on Religion and Ecology (FORE), which seeks to bring the resources of 10 major world religions to bear on the environmental crisis and to prod religious communities to reexamine and reform what they say and do about human-Earth relations. Toward this end, FORE produced a set of volumes published by the Harvard University Center for the Study of World Religions.[33] Each volume reflects the deliberations of a scholarly gathering designed to clarify spiritual resources that the world religions offer to meet the environmental challenge.

Respectful mining of major religious traditions exposes environmentally engaged persons to deeply durable worldviews and ethical teachings concerning human-Earth relations. It also stimulates religious adherents to reread their sacred texts with a "view from outdoors" that is attentive to Earth-community relationships (not simply divine-human interaction) and aware of ecological injustice in creation. Traditional stories of human origin and salvation told within faith communities take on new meanings, reinterpreting who we are—ecological beings in kinship with all life—and how we are to live consciously dependent on and responsible for nature's well-being.

More universities now offer multidisciplinary environmental studies, mostly at the undergraduate level, that feature green sciences and, often, an elective course in environmental ethics. Structured opportunities for concentrated study of religion and ecology, or eco-theology and ethics, at the master's degree level are available at only a few universities with divinity schools that collaborate well with that university's school of environmental studies or a science department, such as Yale. Such programs draw on the insights of both theology and science, a crucial interplay because both are needed if we are to value and care for nature. As environmental philosopher and theologian Holmes Rolston III recently reminded us, the sciences are necessary but not sufficient to guide environmental policymaking:

> Science, unaided, does not teach us what we most need to know about nature: *how to value it.* ... There should [also] be consideration of religious convictions about living on the American landscape.... Religious ethicists can, with considerable plausibility, make the claim that neither sustainable development, nor conservation, nor a sustainable biosphere, nor any other harmony between humans and nature can be gained until persons learn to use the earth both justly and charitably. Those twin concepts are not found either in wild nature or in any science that studies nature or human nature. They must be grounded in some ethical authority.[34]

Third, alert leaders of religious communities are teaching the vision and values of eco-justice ethics rooted in scripture and tradition, informed by scientific insights, and sharpened by social experience of eco-injustice or encounters with unsustainable development. Eco-justice ethics articulates basic norms and supporting principles for morally coherent Earth citizenship. At least a million religious and nonreligious nongovernmental organizations around the world, including in the United States, are now "working toward ecological sustainability and social justice."[35]

Four norms—solidarity, sustainability, sufficiency, and participation—offer an ethical frame of reference for these organizations.

The norm of *solidarity* expresses the vision and values of Earth community. We are to live with genuine respect and care for other people and creatures—companions, victims, and allies—in biodiverse creation.

Sustainability, as we have explained, means relating to the natural world so that its stability, integrity, and beauty may be maintained for future generations. It means showing steady concern to preserve biological diversity and to protect the natural processes that support life. Sustainability also refers to fostering healthy social systems that both depend on and affect natural systems.

Sufficiency is a norm of distributive justice that calls for humans and other participants throughout Earth community to obtain adequate sustenance. Sufficiency for all can be achieved and sustained only when the good things of God's creation are shared according to a keen sense of need, not wants. The already excessive demands on nature must be reduced. Those who now have or use too much must learn to live well on less.

Participation means being included in the social process of obtaining, managing, and enjoying the good things of life, setting environmental policies, and living cooperatively within limits. Social systems that are unsustainable or insufficiently participatory cannot be just.

Eco-justice ethics, bringing these four norms to bear, now has global reach and relevance for diverse communities of ethical discourse concerning multiple problems in the natural and built environment. We do not yet know to what extent this perspective will reshape policy decisions by public officials. But religiously and ethically guided actors are increasingly helping to shape an agenda of sustainability-with-justice in ways that reorient daily lives, social institutions, economics, and politics for the well-being of Earth and people.

Business and Industry

When the modern environmental movement began in the late 1960s and early 1970s, business and industry were the most visible and important sources of air pollution, water pollution, and hazardous and toxic wastes and emissions. Environmental law has done much to change that; the air is cleaner, our waterways are healthier, and waste has been reduced and is more safely managed, even as our economy has grown. The views in some segments of the business community have evolved over the years—from compliance with these laws, then to "beyond compliance" and eco-efficiency, and now to sustainability. This part of the business community has moved into a leadership position on sustainability.

This evolution of attitudes and practices is essential for sustainability. Environmental law tends to set a floor of minimally acceptable practices; it is less successful in rewarding or requiring the best or most sustainable practices. Enlightened business practices go beyond mere compliance to active pursuit of sustainability goals.

There is evidence that the pursuit of sustainability by business organizations is growing quite substantially.[36] A 2012 survey of nearly 3,000 business executives and managers from the MIT Sloan Management Review and the Boston Group found that 70% of companies report that sustainability is solidly and permanently on the management agenda, 20% of which have added it in the past two years. Just over two-thirds of the companies involved say their commitment increased in the past year, even in the face of a difficult economy. The reasons for this commitment include the need to remain competitive (67%), customer preferences (41%), and increasing interest in sustainability information from institutional investors.[37] Yet even with this robust group of business drivers, overall the survey respondents report that sustainability, while on the management agenda, was eighth in importance of priority with other goals.

Of the firms reporting that sustainability is on the agenda, 31% see increased profitability from the pursuit of sustainability. For business organizations, this group is of the most interest because these are the firms most likely to pursue the issue durably and energetically. The firms in this group have much more developed and energetic sustainability programs: they are three times as likely to have developed a business case for sustainability, 50% more likely to have CEO commitment, twice as likely to have a sustainability office in each business unit, and two-and-a-half times as likely to have a chief sustainability officer. Further, these firms are twice as likely to have separate employee performance indicators and direct financial incentives tied to sustainability.[38] These companies, in sum, have incorporated sustainability deeply into their management structure, practices, and culture. Two aspects of this point deserve emphasis. First, when companies actually pursue sustainability, they integrate it into their business and management in direct and powerful ways that are likely to generate results, as these companies are reported to be doing. Second, this group is 31% of all the companies claiming pursuit of sustainability. While this represents important progress, it is not yet universal.

Corporate Sustainability Reporting

Voluntary company reporting on sustainability practices was for years an interesting but marginal effort by businesses, but today it has become quite common for most large companies. The reports have evolved from public-relations promotions to more comprehensive efforts to measure and report actual environmental impacts, with substantial reporting standards and use of outside auditors or third-party evaluators. Today, many large corporations are voluntarily compiling and issuing annual reports on their environmental and sustainability performance.[39] One of the striking facts about corporate sustainability reporting is its rapid growth.[40] From 2008 to 2011, reporting by the largest 100 firms in the United States grew from 74% to 83%, and the largest 250 firms in the world, the G250, increased from approximately 80% to 95%.[41] Virtually all of the largest 100 companies in both Japan and the United Kingdom report, with very high rates across Europe. Sustainability reporting is rapidly becoming the norm for large businesses worldwide.

The dramatic increase in corporate sustainability reporting reflects a growing commitment by hundreds of corporations to move in a more-sustainable direction. As the practice of reporting has grown, the coverage of these reports has changed and broadened. While these reports were originally concerned almost exclusively with the company's environmental performance, their coverage has expanded to include the social and economic impacts of the firm's activities.[42] These broader reports are typically referred to as *sustainability reports* or *corporate responsibility reports*. Reporting on environmental performance typically includes the use of materials, energy and water, biodiversity impacts, traditional pollution emissions, effluents, and waste.[43] The social impacts typically covered include labor and human rights practices; economic ones include community impacts, corruption, public policy, and anticompetitive behavior.[44] Increasingly, the largest companies are also reporting on how their internal corporate governance and management structure support their sustainability goals.[45]

When asked why they report, 67% of the world's largest reporting firms said in 2011 it was to enhance their reputation, an increase from 2008.[46] Ethical considerations drove 58% of firms, and 44% claimed employee motivation as well as innovation and learning; each of these figures is a decrease from the motivations reported in 2008, implying shifting company motivations. It appears that being seen as a green, sustainable corporate citizen is increasingly important to both internal and external stakeholders, beyond the wish to portray particular products as green.

Are reporting companies greener? Specifically, do firms that issue environmental or sustainability reports perform better on these matters than do other firms? Taken together, the empirical studies present a mixed picture, although the most recent work does find a positive association.[47] A study of 191 U.S. companies in high-polluting industries concluded: "We find a positive association between environmental performance and the level of discretionary disclosures in environmental and social reports or related web disclosures. In other words, superior environmental performers are more forthcoming in truly discretionary disclosure channels, as predicted by economics based voluntary disclosure theories."[48] This study applied sophisticated empirical methodology and measured environmental performance using Toxics Release Inventory data based on a federal law that requires public disclosure of the releases of toxic chemicals. Similarly, a study of 26 New Zealand firms indicated that firms with strong environmental performance efforts are more likely to report on the results of those efforts, supporting the case for sustainability reporting by business.[49]

The increase in this type of reporting is consistent with broader trends toward greater reporting of environmental information that have been described earlier, including laws requiring public reporting of releases of toxic chemicals. Still, there are countervailing forces. An example is the lack of public disclosure concerning the precise chemicals used in hydraulic fracturing of shale to recover gas. Many state environmental regulators and environmental groups fear that the chemicals used in this process will pollute groundwater and damage public health. Officials and trade associations in the natural gas industry argue, however, that the precise chemical formulas they use are trade secrets and should be protected as such.[50]

Voluntary Environmental Performance Commitments

Corporations sometimes make voluntary commitments to improve their environmental performance, either in partnership with the government, collectively in trade association groups, or on their own.[51] One approach is to set goals. A company, group, or partnership might commit to reducing its carbon dioxide emissions by, say, 20% over the next five years, or reducing its energy or water usage by a similar amount. While individual company commitments appear to be increasing, at least in part because these commitments are reflected in corporate sustainability and corporate social responsibility reporting, there has been no systematic evaluation of how much the commitments have affected their environmental performance.

Another approach is represented by trade association programs. The Sustainable Forestry Initiative, a voluntary certification program that is described in more detail in Chapter 9, and the chemical industry's Responsible Care Program are two well-known examples.[52] In these programs, companies commit to environmental performance standards, usually stated qualitatively rather than quantitatively, as a condition of membership in the sponsoring organization. Technical advice and help from the organization and other members of the group are often part of the program, as is public recognition and an improved public image for the company and the industry. Some of the programs monitor a company's performance and expel or otherwise sanction a poorly performing member; others do not.

Individual companies and industry trade groups have made commitments to reduce the climate impact of their businesses, such as the Climate Principles and Carbon Principles adopted in the finance industry.[53] Part of the motivation may be to get ahead of the curve, because these voluntary efforts are taking place in the shadow of increased public visibility of the problem and a consensus that substantial regulation in the United States and internationally is coming. While the voluntary programs certainly fuel this consensus, they also appear to express a commitment that has the potential to go well beyond compliance with regulatory commands.

A growing number of companies have set up internal governance systems to reduce carbon and other greenhouse gas emissions. A December 2008 study from the Coalition for Environmentally Responsible Economies (CERES) and the RiskMetrics Group provided a comprehensive evaluation of how this management challenge was being taken on by 63 of the world's largest consumer and information technology companies in 11 industry sectors.[54] The study concluded that "setting targets to reduce [greenhouse gas] emissions is becoming a norm for corporate climate change strategies; roughly half of the 63 companies evaluated in this report have established quantitative emission reduction targets for their Scope 1 and 2—and occasionally even some Scope 3—greenhouse gas emissions." (Scope 1 emissions are direct emissions by the company, Scope 2 result from the company's electricity use, and Scope 3 are emissions from the company's supply chain.) Other encouraging results included more use of renewable energy, water conservation, green building certification, and vehicle fleet goals and investments, as well as increased phaseout goals for specific harmful chemicals, including hydrochlorofluorocarbons and perfluorocarbons.[55]

These voluntary programs appear to have the potential for substantial improvement in environmental performance. But they have received little empirical study to date, and the limited evidence of their environmental performance impact is mixed. Most of the small number of studies in this area find that participation in these voluntary programs is not associated with better environmental performance.[56] For example, a 2000 study of the chemical industry's Responsible Care Program concluded that improved environmental performance, measured by other reports outside the program, was not associated with program membership.[57] Although membership in the Responsible Care Program required specified performance targets and management activities, the program required neither monitoring nor enforcement by participants or third parties, and the study's authors hypothesized that this was the reason for its poor performance. Since the study, the Responsible Care Program has been restructured to incorporate both monitoring and program sanctions, and later studies may find improved performance.

The picture is, however, not all bleak. Two studies found that firms that joined a voluntary program at its early stages tended to show better environmental performance than the overall industry, even though this was not true for firms that joined later or for the program overall. One study examined firms that participated in the EPA's Climate Challenge,[58] which seeks to encourage voluntary reductions in carbon dioxide emissions by the largest electric utilities. The early joiners of the program were good prospects for improvement; as a group, they were leaders in reducing their emissions prior to joining, and they were subject to greater political pressure over their emissions. An earlier study of the EPA's WasteWise Program reached broadly similar conclusions.[59] The program seeks to encourage voluntary reductions in waste generation; while it required annual reporting on results, there was no sanction for not reporting. This study found that the earliest to join the program were more likely to report their results than were late joiners. Taken together, these studies offer some support for the idea that voluntary performance programs seem to make a difference for the firms that join early, but that these positive initial results appear to be swamped by a larger group of free riders that subsequently join, effectively taking advantage of the goodwill created by the real efforts of the early joiners.

One study of 400 firms tried to determine which companies join which kinds of voluntary programs. It found that those with a record of superior environmental performance tend to join programs that monitor performance and expel violators, such as the Sustainable Forestry Initiative. In contrast, the firms that join programs that do not monitor and sanction, such as the original Responsible Care program, have worse pollution records than their industry averages.[60] These findings suggest that firms choose programs, and that program design may be quite important for the environmental performance results. But it is unclear whether the improved performance is caused by participation in the program or by self-selection by the participating firms.

Support and Advocacy by Nongovernmental Organizations

In addition to religious groups and corporations, a great variety of organizations have engaged in support and advocacy efforts on behalf of sustainability. These organizations have affected both international and domestic activities.

One of the most direct ways that nongovernmental organizations have played a supportive role is through their purchase of land. Private land conservation has accelerated over the past two decades, and represents a positive development for the protection of biodiversity. In 2010, private landowners participating in the Forest Legacy Program—a partnership between the U.S. Forest Service and private landowners to preserve private forest land as sustainable working forests—had more than 2 million acres of land under protection.[61] According to a 2005 census by the Land Trust Alliance, land trusts in the United States had protected a total of 37 million acres of land through outright purchase of the land or through conservation easements. These purchases, primarily by national, state, and local conservation organizations, have created a patchwork of open space and nature reserves that contribute to conservation of biodiversity. A large but unspecified percentage of that land is forested.[62] This is a positive development even though there has been no systematic effort to assess the contribution of these private reserves to biodiversity conservation.

These purchases have taken place because of the availability of both public and private money. Nature reserves are funded by contributions, while federal tax benefits are available for property owners who restrict the use of their land by imposing conservation easements. Corporate forestland holdings are being sold throughout the Midwest, Northeast, and South, enabling conservation groups to acquire or otherwise protect forestlands. For example, the Nature Conservancy has recently added several large holdings and secured conservation easements on many more acres of forestland.[63]

Most of the work by nongovernmental organizations on behalf of sustainability is probably through advocacy. Over the past 20 years, NGOs' advocacy has led to sustainability-related reforms at international financial institutions. In many cases, the NGOs have raised the awareness of Congress on these issues, which has enabled members of Congress—in particular Rep. Barney Frank, at the time chair of the House Financial Services Committee, and then-House Majority Leader Nancy Pelosi—to use their leverage to initiate reforms. In several instances, Congress has made U.S. financial support for the World Bank conditional upon specific sustainability reforms. Congress has also mandated environmental reforms at the U.S. Export-Import Bank (Ex-Im Bank) and the Overseas Private Investment Corporation (OPIC) as a condition of reauthorization and funding. Where constructive engagement has not worked, NGOs have occasionally litigated. As explained earlier, a 2002 lawsuit against the Ex-Im Bank and OPIC resulted in new climate change policies at both institutions.[64] The Ex-Im Bank now considers the carbon dioxide emissions of potential fossil fuel projects, while OPIC set a greenhouse gas reduction target of 20% over 10 years for emissions linked to its projects. Moreover, both agencies have committed to increased financing of renewable energy.

Nongovernmental organizations also have helped to serve as watchdogs, deterring investments to several controversial, high-impact development projects. In doing so, they have used a combination of public pressure, internal lobbying, and engagement with the U.S. government and other governments. The World Bank's 1992 creation of an accountability mechanism, the Inspection Panel, provided a formal process for investigating complaints brought by NGOs and local communities. In 2007, for example, the Inspection Panel investigated a claim that a Bank-financed project in Albania had contributed to the unlawful demolition of people's homes in coastal areas. The Inspection Panel confirmed that the Bank's involvement had contributed to harm, leading the Bank to suspend financial support for the project.[65] Other development banks have since developed their own accountability mechanisms.

Nongovernmental organizations have also been effective on certain domestic sustainability issues. The existence of national organizations such as the American Association for Sustainability in Higher Education[66] (and groups such as the United States Partnership for Education for Sustainable Development[67] and the Disciplinary Associations Network for Sustainability[68]) have helped to legitimize and provide resources and precedents to those championing college and university sustainability programs. The way colleges and universities market (and sometimes overstate, or "greenwash") their sustainability programs has created pressure for full disclosure and more implementation. This has led to more robust sustainability programming rather than simply making an effort at energy efficiency. The movement toward sustainability is an iterative process that grows because of public commitments fed by transparency.[69]

Efforts by activists are also an important reason industrial ecology, an important new tool for understanding the environmental impacts of products, has taken root in recent years. Examples include a backlash against the Nike shoe company after accusations that it was using child labor, Greenpeace's protests of Shell Oil's decision to sink an obsolete oil rig in the North Sea in the mid-1990s, and, more broadly, the anti-globalization protests at the 1999 World Trade Organization meeting in Seattle. Activist campaigns against products viewed as unsustainable have influenced consumers to think more critically about the impacts of their purchases, which in turn has motivated businesses to adopt more conscientious production patterns. More generally, companies are concerned about their environmental reputations; when asked why they issue corporate sustainability reports, the most frequent answer companies give is concern about their reputation.[70]

Public advocacy campaigns by NGOs have supported and reinforced international and regional initiatives to eliminate leaded gasoline. The Natural Resources Defense Council advocated for including a leaded gasoline phaseout at the Rio Conference in 1992 and follow-up meetings. The Alliance to End Childhood Lead Poisoning (now called the Trust for Lead Poisoning Prevention) prepared the International Action Plan for Preventing Lead Poisoning and subsequently conducted a global leaded gasoline phaseout campaign through its Global Lead Network. The campaign was dedicated to correcting the myths and misperceptions impeding phaseout, such as the purported engine valve coating protection leaded gasoline offered to engines in older vehicles, and rallying local groups to apply bottom-up pressure on national governments to expedite the phaseout.[71]

Public-Private Partnerships

Because sustainability is based on the premise that social, environmental, economic, and security goals should be mutually reinforcing, it can bring together people and organizations that have different perspectives. Public-private partnerships provide a way for organizations, businesses, and governments to work together to address sustainability issues. At the World Summit on Sustainable Development in Johannesburg in 2002, the United States and others advocated the greater use of partnerships in achieving sustainable development. The multidisciplinary nature of sustainability, coupled with the need to integrate environmental protection with other issues, lends itself to an approach in which groups with varied expertise work together. Indeed, a striking characteristic of many of the sustainability partnerships is the diversity of views represented by the organizations that have collaborated on sustainability programs.

The Energy Star program is a public-private partnership involving more than 20,000 public and private entities in developing, identifying, labeling, and promoting energy-efficient products. EPA's voluntary High Production Volume (HPV) Chemicals Program includes the Environmental Defense Fund, the American Petroleum Institute, and the American Chemistry Council. Design for the Environment is a labeling program for environmentally safer products, and WaterSense is a labeling program for water-saving products.[72] Both are public-private partnerships. At the local level, the city of Toledo, the University of Toledo's Wright Center for Photovoltaics Innovation and Commercialization, and the Regional Growth Partnership have joined together to advance solar glass technology.

These partnerships are often coalitions of environmental, business, and labor organizations. The BlueGreen Alliance, for instance, was started in 2006 by the Sierra Club and the United Steelworkers Union. Now expanded to include other environmental groups and labor unions, the Alliance states that it "unites nearly 15 million members and supporters in pursuit of good jobs, a clean environment and a green economy."[73] National environmental groups and major corporations formed the U.S. Climate Action Partnership in 2007 to advocate that Congress "quickly enact strong national legislation to require significant reductions of greenhouse gas emissions."[74] Comparable partnerships between groups with seemingly different worldviews can be found at the state and local level.

Government-led regional partnerships have proven effective. Envision Utah is a voluntary planning collaboration to improve quality of life in the Salt Lake City/Wasatch region of Utah. Bringing together unlikely allies can pay particular benefits. Communities can join with local military installations, for example, to promote smarter growth and sustainability, as has been done in the multicounty region near Fort Bragg, North Carolina.

These partnerships are also global. The Partnership for Clean Fuels and Vehicles (PCFV), which resulted from the World Summit on Sustainable Development, is organized under the auspices of the United Nations Environment Program (UNEP).[75] Completing the global transition from leaded gasoline is one of the PCFV's twin charges (the other is to reduce the sulfur content of fuels). The PCFV has developed an informative website to disseminate technical documents on the benefits of eliminating, and alternatives to using, leaded gasoline and to provide a reference on the status of country-by-country progress on eliminating leaded gasoline.

The initial meeting of the Global Alliance to Eliminate Lead in Paint (GAELP) in 2010 was under the joint auspices of UNEP and the World Health Organization (WHO), with representatives from governments, international organizations, NGOs, and industry.[76] As the availability and use of leaded gasoline has dwindled to a handful of countries, international attention has begun to shift to the hazards of lead-based paint. Participants in GAELP agreed to undertake a broad range of actions, ranging from education outreach to development of recommended policies.

Market and Peer Pressure

Public opinion is reflected in market pressure through the purchasing decisions of individuals, businesses, and governments. A 2009 consumer survey by Mintel Oxygen Reports found that 36% of Americans said that they "almost always" or "regularly" buy green products.[77] This number is triple the figure in 2007. This pressure encourages and even requires businesses to provide more-sustainable goods and services in a remarkable variety of contexts. For example, U.S. consumers rejected toys found to contain lead, causing manufacturers and retailers to develop lists of chemicals that cannot be included in the manufacture of their products. Likewise, the organic foods market in the United States has stimulated the development of an organic agriculture industry that does not use pesticides or biotechnology in production.

In some sectors, producers are working cooperatively with customers to expand their market. Team efforts between farmers and a community of sustainability-minded consumers have developed a market for those willing to pay for products produced more sustainably.[78] These community-rooted projects include community-supported agriculture (CSA), farm-to-school programs, and farmers' markets, all of which have exploded in numbers in recent years. In a CSA program, community members give financial support to a farm before the planting season in exchange for a share of the harvest. Members share some of the risks involved in farming, such as the chance of a poor harvest, and free the farmer from the burden of marketing products during the harvest season. The CSA phenomenon grew from

60 such farms nationwide in 1990 to 1,700 in 2004, and then to more than 4,000 in 2011.[79] There are also more than 2,000 farm-to-school programs, in which farms provide local food to school cafeterias.[80] In addition, more than 7,000 farmers' markets now exist in the United States, more than four times the number in 1994.[81]

Anticipating a growing consumer demand for more water, material, and energy-efficient products, and to benefit from new market opportunities, General Electric launched its Ecomagination Initiative in 2005. Initially, some saw it primarily as a way to reorganize existing product lines, but Ecomagination has shown itself to be an effective way to realign business and environmental values so that more sales also mean greater use of environmentally improved products. In 2009, despite a sluggish global economy, Ecomagination's revenues grew 6% to $18 billion.[82] Further, the initiative has helped GE reduce its greenhouse gas emissions by 22% and its water use by more than 30% since the launch of the program. As a result, GE has committed to investing an additional $10 billion in research and development funding between 2010 and 2015 and to continuing aggressive goals for water use and greenhouse gas reduction.

External pressure and competition help drive a great many decisions toward greater sustainability. Increasingly, cities believe they need to compete with each other on sustainability grounds as a way to improve quality of life and attract employers and employees. Parks and open space, such as Chicago's Millennium Park or New York's High Line, increase an employee's quality of life. Municipal competition has also led to improvements in mass transit systems as a means of furthering local growth, development, and quality of life.

Globalization of commerce has motivated international progress on chemicals sustainability. Precautionary approaches to chemicals management have increasingly been incorporated into the European Union's REACH (Registration, Evaluation, Authorisation, and Restriction of Chemical Substances) program. REACH aims to protect human health and the environment "through the better and earlier identification of the intrinsic properties of chemical substances," and to "enhance innovation and competitiveness of the EU chemicals industry."[83] Programs like REACH affect the United States because many U.S. corporations design their facilities to comply with the most stringent standard existing anywhere rather than attempt to comply separately with a variety of different standards.

Conclusion

Public opinion and support for sustainability present a paradox. On one hand, overall public opinion appears in some ways to be less supportive now than it was two decades ago, even though there is still considerable overall support for environmental protection and strong majorities support more-sustainable energy policies. On the other hand, there is growing public support for a variety of sustainable policies.

All over the country, in a variety of ways, individuals, businesses, governments, and NGOs are working out what sustainability means for their regular activities—what risks they need to minimize or avoid, what opportunities it presents, and what they need to do. The religious and ethical community as well as business and industry have become more active in support. If organizations representing such different views can find some common ground on sustainability, there is reason to hope that public opinion in support of sustainability will strengthen over time. NGOs have also been important advocates for a variety of more-sustainable policies. Public-private partnerships, as well as market and peer pressure, also contribute to, and reflect, this growing support. What is most impressive, perhaps, is the wide variety of ways that the public supports sustainability when the issue is presented in specific terms and with practical outcomes.

CHAPTER 9

More-Sustainable Decisions Are
Easier to Make and More Attractive

To a large degree, the patterns of unsustainable behavior described in Part I of this book have occurred because governments, corporations, individuals, and families have had no other choice or because sustainable options have been more expensive, less functional, or unpalatable. Even where more-sustainable approaches exist, they are often misunderstood or perceived as unattractive. Over the last two decades, the number and variety of attractive and publicly understood choices have grown. Governments, businesses, and individuals are making more-sustainable decisions because more and better choices exist.

More-sustainable decisions are increasingly understood as less expensive; more efficient; better for quality of life; and more consistent with individual, consumer, and public values. This is particularly true for decisions involving the use of energy, where rising energy costs, security concerns, and the availability of options for energy efficiency and renewable energy has made more-sustainable alternatives more appealing. In other cases, particularly with forest certification, the sustainable alternative is attractive in spite of the fact that it tends to command a price premium.

Fundamentally, sustainability is about creating choices that do not now exist and about making those alternatives attractive enough to be implemented. Changes that people want to make are more likely to happen at the necessary scale and speed than are changes that people resist or make reluctantly. The transitions from typewriters to personal computers, and from ordinary telephones to smartphones—both of which have happened in only a couple of decades—are examples of technological transitions that took place at the speed and scale needed for the transition to sustainability. Few if any of today's new practices are fully sustainable. Still, they are perhaps the most obvious and prominent way that progress toward sustainability has manifested itself over the past two decades. And they are in response to the growing public support described in the previous chapter.

Over the past two decades, the number, variety, and sophistication of specific and demonstrated sustainability practices have grown. These practices, beyond simply being available, often provide more attractive opportunities than are provided by many current practices. At the same time, many unsustainable business-as-usual practices are becoming more costly and present greater risks. The availability of new analytical frameworks and approaches, particularly ecosystem services, industrial ecology, and environmental management systems, enable more-sustainable decisions to be made more easily.

Better Practices

A major reason for progress has been the development of specific sustainability practices that can be used in a variety of contexts and across a broad spectrum of quite ordinary, everyday decisions. Because sustainability requires a divergence from the path of business as usual, people want to know what those changes will be. The triple-bottom line of mutually reinforcing social, environmental, and economic goals is simply too abstract to provide guidelines for what one should do. Specific and previously demonstrated practices provide a reliable basis for departing from business as usual and enable interested businesses, governments, and individuals to move in a more-sustainable direction.

These refined and tested practices embrace a range of activities. They include certification and labeling programs, voluntary reporting and auditing standards, and specific sustainability practices.

Certification and Labeling Programs

Certification programs, which provide a set of sustainability-related standards, are typically run by nongovernmental organizations. If a particular entity—a business, for example—has met the appropriate standards or criteria, it is allowed to publicly display a sustainability certification. Labeling programs work in a similar way.

Over the past two decades, a great many third-party certification systems have developed for various economic sectors and activities. Three are highlighted in this chapter: green building (Leadership in Energy and Environmental Design, or LEED), sustainable forestry (Forest Stewardship Council and Sustainable Forestry Initiative), and the Energy Star labeling program run by EPA and the U.S. Department of Energy.

LEED

Perhaps the most visible nongovernmental certification program is the Leadership in Energy and Environmental Design process for green building, discussed in Chapter 4. Like many of the other building rating systems, LEED rates green building performance in six categories of building design, construction, and operation. LEED awards points for sustainable sites (such as where building projects preserve existing topography, retain existing vegetation, and reduce impervious surfaces), water efficiency (water collection and reuse, irrigation, and indoor water efficiency), energy and atmosphere (reduced energy consumption in buildings, such as by insulation and appliance efficiency), materials and resources (materials reuse and use of local materials), indoor environmental quality (reducing levels of volatile organic compounds released from furniture and wall treatments), and innovation and design (such as the use of integrated photovoltaic technology).

Under LEED programs the "greenness" of a building is certified on a progressive scale, with the benchmarks of certified, silver, gold, and platinum. Due to the increasing popularity and rapid success of green-building rating systems, the green building industry now includes experienced builders and building officials equipped to manage development costs and anticipate misunderstandings about green building more efficiently. Experience also has produced more informed buyers of green building products.

Forest Certification

Two major certification programs exist for forestry in the United States: the Forest Stewardship Council (FSC), which operates around the world, and the American Forest and Paper Association's Sustainable Forestry Initiative (SFI). Each has certified millions of acres. Landowners obtain certification by meeting certain standards specified by one of these programs. The standards require protection of old growth, biodiversity, and water quality; specify sustainable harvest levels; require prompt reforestation; recognize the rights of indigenous peoples; minimize the use of chemicals; and allow clearcutting under certain circumstances. The two programs use somewhat different criteria. FSC emphasizes community relations, workers' rights, preservation of old growth, and traditional forestry concepts; SFI emphasizes organizational procedures and flexible performance guidelines.[1] In addition, SFI allows more use of tree plantations (areas where a single species is grown) than FSC and, unlike FSC, allows some use of genetically modified trees.[2]

Forested areas are not certified by FSC or SFI but by a third party, in order to ensure the independence and integrity of the process. By stimulating consumer demand, certification schemes persuade forest managers to adopt sustainable practices. In return, certified products receive a premium price. Although a consumer demanding more-sustainable products is the end customer, printers and homebuilders are influential intermediate customers. The Pinchot Institute for Conservation states that "independent, third party certification is one of the most significant developments in the field of forest management in the last two decades."[3] According to a 2010 status report on forest certification by Dovetail Partners, "the forest certification programs developed by the Forest Stewardship Council (FSC) and the Sustainable Forestry Initiative (SFI) have had a significant and positive impact on forest management in the United States" since 1990.[4]

In the aggregate, commitments from large buyers stimulate forest certification. Time Incorporated's 2007 commitment to use more paper certified by FSC coincided with certification on 11.4 million acres of forest.[5] The commitment of high profile paper buyers encourages forest product suppliers to certify their forests in the expectation that the demand for certified forest products will grow. To date,

however, no large homebuilder or lumber contractor has made a similar commitment to certified lumber sourcing.

In March 2011, 34 million acres of land in the United States were certified under
the FSC program, and 56 million acres were certified under SFI.[6] Even though
millions of acres are "dual certified," this still constitutes an important portion of
the 651 million acres of forestland in the United States.[7]

While most of the certified land is in private hands, certification is also affecting state and federal forestlands. All of Washington State's forest trust lands are
certified by SFI (2.1 million acres), and some are dual certified.[8] Minnesota has
dual certification on 4.84 million acres of state-administered forestlands.[9] Three
million acres of Wisconsin-owned land have dual certification.[10] In 2011, Michigan renewed both certifications on 3.9 million acres of state-owned forestland.[11]
In Pennsylvania, 2.2 million acres of state forestland are certified by FSC.[12] Other
states with recent significant state forest certifications under one or both major
programs include Maryland,[13] New York,[14] Massachusetts,[15] and Ohio.[16] National
forests administered by the U.S. Forest Service now meet many of the requirements of existing FSC and SFI certification standards. The Pinchot Institute for
Conservation has concluded, however, that the "performance gaps" between the
certification standards and national forest management would be difficult to close
without changes in federal law and policy.[17]

The two major certification programs have also developed specialized certifications for particular areas. In 2004, the FSC created a separate certification for small,
low-intensity forest operations with the aim of reducing certification costs and
paperwork. The special certification program has proven successful in adapting to
the needs of small-forest managers. In 2008, for example, 2.2 million acres of forest
in Wisconsin, distributed among 41,000 parcels, earned FSC certification. A "group
entity" actually holds the certificate and coordinates with individual landowners.
In the Wisconsin example, and other similar programs, a state program acts as the
group entity.[18] In other regions, nonprofit organizations and forest cooperatives
act as the group entity.

Energy Star

Energy Star is a partnership between government and industry to promote energy
efficiency. EPA created Energy Star in 1992 "as a voluntary labeling program
designed to identify and promote energy-efficient products to reduce greenhouse
gas emissions." In 2005, after more than a decade of existence as an administrative
initiative, Congress formally authorized Energy Star.[19] Now administered jointly
by EPA and the Department of Energy, Energy Star covers a variety of office and
residential equipment as well as homes and commercial and industrial buildings.[20]

The widely recognized Energy Star label is placed on products that meet certain
efficiency standards. Participation in Energy Star is voluntary, and products will not
ordinarily be allowed to use the Energy Star Label unless they can deliver greater

energy savings than required by the energy efficiency standards established by Congress or the Department of Energy for those products. This typically requires appliances to be 10% to 25% more efficient than applicable minimum requirements.[21] Energy Star criteria also apply to appliances and equipment for which no standards have been set, including personal computers and computer monitors.

Energy Star has grown steadily in scope and effectiveness. In 2010 alone, adherence to Energy Star standards saved enough energy "to avoid greenhouse gas emissions equivalent to those from 33 million cars—all while saving nearly $18 billion on . . . utility bills."[22] Annual energy savings and reductions of greenhouse gas emissions are three times greater than they were in 2000.[23] Americans have purchased nearly 3.5 billion Energy Star-certified products since 2000, and almost 1.2 million homes have certification.[24] Energy Star also provides the basis for a substantial energy-efficiency rebate program. Funded through the American Recovery and Reinvestment Act of 2009,[25] the program provides $300 million worth of $50-to-$200 rebates to consumers who replace old appliances for new more-efficient household devices that have the Energy Star seal.[26]

Voluntary Reporting and Auditing Standards

The increase in corporate sustainability reporting described in Chapter 8 has been facilitated by the standardization of reporting and auditing. To be useful, these reports must be consistent and credible. For stakeholders the reports must cover a common group of core issues, although the reporting standards allow variation to cover topics of concern to a particular industry or geographic area.[27] While reporting standards have been an issue, a consensus is now emerging to use the Sustainability Reporting Guidelines issued by the Global Reporting Initiative (GRI) as the accepted standard for reporting. The project to develop the Global Reporting Initiative Guidelines originated with the Coalition for Environmentally Responsible Economies (CERES) and the Tellus Institute, which are American organizations, but the initiative is now a freestanding entity located in the Netherlands that also operates as a U.N. affiliate. In 2011, 80% of the largest companies, the G250 (the largest 250 countries in the world), applied the GRI guidelines to their reports, and 69% of the largest 100 firms in each of 34 countries studied did so as well; a separate calculation for the United States was not available.[28]

The GRI reporting guidelines are now in their third edition, and a fourth edition is planned for 2013. These guidelines are developed through an extensive process of consultation among a large group of stakeholders. The guidelines specify that all companies using them are to report on core environmental, economic, and social impacts but also allow for supplementary protocols for particular industry sectors as needed. In addition, GRI has indicated willingness to incorporate other reporting standards as needed for particular topics, as it has done with the reporting standards for climate change proposed by the World Resources Institute and the World Business Council for Sustainable Development. In sum, to be credible, sustainability reporting today must either be done to GRI standards or convincingly explain why it is not.

A second credibility issue is whether the reports are consistently audited or otherwise checked to assure their accuracy. An Australian study concluded, unsurprisingly, that the companies with assurance review of their reports provided better environmental information.[29] There has also been substantial progress in developing auditing standards. Two sets of auditing standards for sustainability reports are now in place.[30] Auditing standards are different from reporting standards; they are instructions for auditors who are reviewing and evaluating a company's reporting.

How many companies undertake and report formal assurance either by auditing or some other means? Of the fourth-fifths of the Global 250 firms that report, 46% currently come with an assurance statement, as do 38% of the largest 100 companies in each country; these percentages reflect modest growth since 2005.[31] Major accounting firms do the bulk of this work (70% and 65% for the G250 and the largest 100 companies in each country, respectively) and in 2008, it was reported that most of the assurance is done in accord with auditing standards.[32] Reporting companies that do not use formal auditing practices typically substitute evaluations of other third-party commentators, including prominent nongovernmental organizations, as an alternative.[33] Taken together, formal assurance or third-party commentary is becoming an expected part of corporate sustainability reporting. As more and more companies issue assurance statements, their absence in the reports of others will be all the more glaring and impeaching.

Specific Sustainability Practices and Information Sharing Networks

There is a growing range of practices and programs that move a particular activity in a more-sustainable direction. These include, but are certainly not limited to, green infrastructure, green roofs, pollution prevention, and recycling. They generally have no certification program, although a builder may receive points for implementing some of these innovations in the course of seeking LEED certification. They do not embrace sustainability in the same broad sense as codes of conduct or sustainability programs. Rather, they are practices or sets of practices that can be employed to solve particular problems or as part of an overall project or program. For example, green infrastructure—permeable pavement, greater use of vegetated areas, and the like—has become more widely used by cities to cope with stormwater runoff.

Much of the information about best practices is distributed through networks that rely on conferences, newsletters, regular conference calls, and professional organizations to share information. The U.S. Green Building Council reports that its membership comprises 80 local chapters, 17,000 member companies and organizations, and more than 155,000 individuals certified with LEED professional credentials. Professional organizations for sustainability in education include the

Green Schools National Network and the American Association for Sustainability in Higher Education.

Attendance at the major conferences in the United States that focus on sustainability in higher education has increased steadily. Ball State University in Indiana has hosted the biannual Greening of the Campus conference since 1996; the number of attendees increased from an initial 150 in 1996 to 775 in 2009. Notably, the content of the conference has transitioned from a mix of the theoretical and inspirational to a more how-to focus.

Sustainability efforts are also growing in the practice of law. The American Bar Association, in partnership with EPA, has created the ABA-EPA Law Office Climate Challenge, a program to encourage law offices to conserve energy and resources, as well as reduce emissions of greenhouse gases and other pollutants.[34] The ABA Section on Environment, Energy, and Resources has also developed the Model Sustainability Policy and Implementation Guidelines for Law Organizations, in which a law organization commits to take steps over time toward sustainability.[35] Bar associations in Massachusetts,[36] California,[37] and Pennsylvania[38] have adopted lists of model sustainability practices. Oregon Lawyers for a Sustainable Future has published its own model sustainability policy for law offices, which is directed at reducing their environmental impact.[39]

The American Chemistry Council's Responsible Care Program encourages better environmental management, materials handling, and product stewardship of potentially harmful chemicals.[40] It has the potential to support and encourage environmental performance improvements by member companies, although the empirical results comparing the performance of program participants to the rest of the industry in 2000 were not encouraging.[41] The Council claims a 75% reduction in hazardous air pollutants since 1988, compared with an industrywide reduction of 38%, as well as recent reductions in sulphur dioxide emissions and water usage.[42]

Attractiveness of More-Sustainable Alternatives and Opportunities

Sustainable development increasingly provides new and more attractive opportunities that would not otherwise be available. A core premise of integrated decisionmaking—integrating environmental, economic, and social considerations into decisions—is that the resulting decisions are likely to produce more net benefits than would otherwise occur. Put differently, the environmental, social, and economic aspects of a decision are likely to be mutually reinforcing rather than contradictory or antagonistic. This premise is increasingly apparent to decisionmakers in a wide variety of contexts.

More-sustainable infrastructure, including mass transit systems, helps make many communities more attractive. Perhaps one of the oldest examples is the San Francisco cable cars, which not only reduce congestion and automobile emissions but also serve as a unique identifiable feature of San Francisco. (Other well-known and highly used mass transit systems include the Chicago elevated train, the New York subway, and the Washington, D.C., Metrorail, to name but a few.) Portland, Oregon, and Seattle, Washington, are renowned for their bike paths, and Minneapolis was recently identified by *Bicycling* magazine as the most bike-friendly city in the country.[43] Boulder, Colorado, is known for its vast open spaces and parks. Chicago, the birthplace of the skyscraper, is becoming better known for its lush green roofs, urban forests, and parks.

As steps toward sustainability are taken in more places, awareness of the economic, environmental, health, quality-of-life, and other benefits of these efforts has spurred additional action. The market success of compact, walkable communities has encouraged localities and developers to pursue growth that promotes cleaner transportation choices. And ridership and development sparked by certain transportation projects has increased demand for these projects. Portland, Oregon's streetcar system, for example, was launched in 2001 and has spurred more than $3.5 billion of private investment along the line. Similarly, communities with significant wind and solar resources may be more aware of the opportunities to develop green industries; other local governments may rely on the corollary benefits of climate-change planning, such as lowering costs through gains in energy efficiency.

Brownfields redevelopment also provides a variety of benefits. Apart from cleaning up a property, or reusing it, brownfields redevelopment can create jobs. Most of these jobs are created in the predevelopment (cleanup or site preparation) stage, but a great many of them are created afterwards through the subsequent use of the property. According to the U.S. Conference of Mayors, between 1993 and 2010, 54 cities created nearly 97,150 permanent jobs at brownfields sites and another 64,730 jobs for the predevelopment and remediation of those sites.[44]

At brownfields sites, there are also many opportunities for sustainable reuse. Green technologies, for example, can reduce carbon emissions and produce other benefits.[45] Some sites, for example, have been transformed into urban greenways.[46] An intriguing new use of brownfields sites is "brightfields,"[47] locating renewable energy production equipment at urban sites.[48] In Brockton, Massachusetts, a 425-kilowatt solar array began operating in 2006 on the 3.7 acre site of a former gas works.

On sites where existing buildings are reused, employing green design and construction techniques in conjunction with overhauling the infrastructure may conserve energy and feature sustainable building materials and creative waste-reduction strategies.[49] Recognizing this, the new version of the popular LEED certification system for sustainable buildings awards points for building on a brownfields site and adds points for variables like building close to existing transportation systems.[50]

The drivers for change in building practices—human health, environmental quality, and economic needs—are not really disputed, and the growing number of green construction projects shows that green buildings perform better than their conventional counterparts.[51] Studies report that green buildings often use 25% to 30% less energy than the national average.[52] Green building design and construction minimize the impacts of material needs and reduce construction and building waste. Green building practices result in reduced water consumption both indoors and outdoors, and contribute to improved water quality by incorporating stormwater control into building design.

Green building yields health and productivity benefits in both residential and nonresidential buildings. One report attributed green building with improving employee productivity at an estimated benefit of $6.4 billion in 2010.[53] Green building practices have also supported the notion that healthier spaces for education are also more productive spaces. A review of 30 green schools across the country, "based on a very substantial data set on productivity and test performance of healthier, more comfortable study and learning environments," concluded that "a 3-5% improvement in learning ability and test scores in green schools appears reasonable and conservative."[54]

Green building is also becoming more attractive because the upfront costs—real or imagined—of LEED certification are now much lower. One of the initial hurdles for green building was the perception that the costs of green building design and construction were prohibitively high.[55] Many of the increased building costs were found to be artificially inflated because green design principles were not incorporated early in the building concept.[56] In contrast to early estimates that green building methods would increase building costs as much as 25% over conventional building methods,[57] it has more recently been argued that LEED-certified buildings might increase upfront costs by only 2%.[58] The American Institute of Architects recently noted that "as the cost of green building continues to fall toward parity with traditional building practices, the old excuse of high cost begins to fall by the wayside."[59]

The economic benefits after the building is constructed are also considerable. For example, it is estimated that "an initial upfront investment of up to $100,000 to incorporate green building features into a $5 million project would result in a savings of a million dollars over the life of the building,"[60] and the upfront costs of green building investments are often recoverable within five years.[61] On a broader scale, the U.S. Department of Energy estimates that continued development, adoption, implementation, and compliance with green building standards will generate energy cost savings of more than $2.5 billion per year.[62] For the owners of a green building, the improvements also enhance property values.

Economic benefits have been a primary driver for other decisions as well. For a great many organizations—government at all levels, business and industry, colleges and universities, and even religious bodies—the opportunity to save money through reduced energy use has been an important driver for sustainability decisions. Between 1990 and 2009, IBM saved more than $370 million by reducing its energy use through efficiency and conservation.[63] According to Dow Chemical

Company, the $1 billion it has invested in energy efficiency between 1994 and 2010 has contributed to savings of $9.4 billion.[64]

Adoption of forest certification is motivated by the higher price of certified products. This market premium is most successful at encouraging sustainable practices where it can be captured primarily by the forest managers and directly enhances their bottom line.[65] The market premium available for certified paper is most accessible to northern forests, which are closest to pulp manufacturers. With less shipping cost and a more direct purchasing relationship, northern forest managers feel the benefit of certification.[66] Anecdotal evidence indicates that certified products are maintaining their market premium even in the economic downturn,[67] although weak demand and excess supply has weakened the market for paper and lumber.[68] Yet, in interviews with the Wisconsin Department of Natural Resources, paper and lumber industry executives felt that certified products buffered the impact of falling prices on their companies. Southern forests, by contrast, are already at a competitive disadvantage with higher shipping costs and lower-value wood products. Without efficient access to manufacturing, southern forest managers choose not to certify because the price premium does not translate into greater profits.[69]

At the state and local levels, the attractiveness of more-sustainable decisions includes not only economic returns but a variety of other factors. Many states believe, for example, that more-sustainable decisions will contribute to the preservation of a quality environment, the use of renewable or highly efficient energy resources, the maintenance of a healthy population, the presence of economic and social equity, and the maintenance of an engaged citizenry—all of which means that these states will have better futures. Many local sustainability efforts are being undertaken to address pressing environmental concerns, especially deterioration of air, water, or other resources necessary to the health or public life of the community.[70] Other local sustainability efforts address public health epidemics[71] as well as social and economic inequities,[72] or promote greater civic engagement in the process of monitoring the quality of life in local communities.[73]

Sustainability also provides a way for a decisionmaker to accomplish more than a single goal at one time. Because sustainable development means that one dollar of public expenditures will help achieve more than one purpose, it provides opportunities to improve the cost-effectiveness of government programs. The federal government's recent efforts under Executive Order 13514—which requires federal agencies to move toward sustainability by setting and achieving goals for reducing greenhouse gases, energy intensity, and potable water intensity—also provide opportunities that might not otherwise exist (especially cost savings through energy-use reduction) to enable federal agencies to spend their resources more efficiently and effectively. Much of the funding under recent federal legislation, including the American Recovery and Reinvestment Act, was premised on the view that energy efficiency and environmental protection can, if properly done, also provide opportunities for economic development and job creation.

Success stories—about economic development from the manufacture and use of wind turbines and solar collectors, growing demand for fuel-efficient cars, or the use of green infrastructure to comply with federal pollution-control requirements—all create interest in doing more of the same. Pennsylvania's mandatory recycling program is regarded as successful because it keeps 2 million tons of recyclable material out of landfills every year, supports thousands of businesses that employ more than 50,000 people, has saved more than a billion dollars in disposal costs, and has reduced greenhouse gas emissions.[74] Success stories are one of the most prominent features of sustainability because, by definition, they involve an improvement over business as usual. Success stories do not mean that an improvement in one place is necessarily replicable in another, but they provide abundant evidence that sustainability can and does lead to improvement.

Significantly, the voluntary nature of many of these practices makes them more attractive because it creates a context in which trial and error are more tolerable. LEED was initiated as a voluntary certification program that builders could market in private construction projects, not as a regulatory mandate.[75] In general, green building practices have been designed to overlay (rather than replace) the prescriptions of conventional building codes to add resource efficiency and environmental quality to existing safety requirements. The collaborative and voluntary nature of green building practices generally has avoided major litigation while encouraging private participation.

Growing Cost of, and Limits to, Business as Usual

There is growing evidence of the adverse effects of unsustainable development. These effects, based on national and global trends, include population growth, globalization, a growing gap between rich and poor, the loss of biodiversity, deterioration of ecosystems, and depletion of natural resources around the world. But the most obvious example is climate change, which is identified as a growing issue in many federal agency strategies as well as national defense and security strategies. Business-as-usual measures of success are also increasingly seen as inadequate. The movement to develop key indicators that would better measure national well-being (described in Chapter 5) was prompted by a recognition that GDP is not a complete measure of the nation's health and progress, and that we need a more well-rounded approach. This broader approach is likely to include the impacts of unsustainable development.

Business-as-usual approaches are becoming both more costly and more physically difficult. Rising, volatile gas prices and oil dependence are prompting more-sustainable transportation and land-use policies and also greater efforts for sustainable and reduced energy use in higher education. When gas prices spiked at more than $4 per gallon nationwide in 2008, the impact on the economy and on household budgets was pronounced. Purchases of more efficient vehicles, use of alternatives to driving, and support for more-sustainable transportation poli-cies all rose. Gas prices remain high as this book goes to press, as is awareness of the national security costs of dependence on unstable regimes for fossil fuel and potential limits to available oil supply. Because of growing global demand and the absence of sufficient global reserves that can be released to reduce price peaks, "[g]reat oil price swings are here to stay."[76] Higher and more volatile energy prices have made many operational sustainability efforts at colleges and universities more economical and have also sparked greater investments in education and research related to energy sustainability.

Climate change also makes business as usual less attractive. Higher temperatures as well as more severe and intense storms and droughts can pose serious risks to the availability of food and water, especially in developing countries, where the resulting social breakdown can lead to conflict. Similarly, the demand for fossil fuels from developing countries raises another set of security concerns, particu-larly the protection of supply lines, which can cause or contribute to war. Climate change is thus a major driver of corporate sustainability efforts. As Ira Feldman of Greentrack Strategies has explained:

> Understanding that "business as usual" is an untenable long-term strategy in the face of overwhelming scientific evidence, some businesses are responding to climate change by identifying the opportunities it presents, perhaps "one of the greatest investment, business and job creation opportunities of this generation . . . from carbon trading to renewable and cleaner energy generation and energy efficiency."[77]

A majority of states have recognized the need to reduce the use of fossil fuel and lower greenhouse gas emissions, whether based on concerns about climate change, energy security, or both. This is not to say that all states recognize that business as usual is becoming less attractive. A number of states with strong historical ties to fossil-fuel production, including Texas, Oklahoma, and Wyoming, have yet to enact climate action plans or take other significant steps to plan for greenhouse gas reductions.[78]

Coastal cities and states are recognizing the need to adapt to rising sea levels, warmer temperatures, and other changes. So is the National Park Service. Of the 150 glaciers that existed in Glacier National Park when it was created in 1850, only 26 remain, and these are likely to be gone by 2030.[79] (What will we call that park when it no longer has any glaciers?) Climate change adaptation is even considered serious enough to warrant inclusion in all federal agency strategies.

In the area of water use, improvements have resulted from a combination of scar-city and changes in water pricing that have created incentives for more efficiency. Some water scarcity is periodic (in the case of serious and protracted droughts), and some is due to more permanent shortages (in the case of metropolitan regions as varied as Atlanta and Las Vegas that are outgrowing their natural water supply). Growing urban areas face significant barriers in obtaining new water supplies, as well as legal barriers to new water projects. These legal barriers exist because of the Endangered Species Act, the National Environmental Policy Act, and the Clean Water Act, all of which force consideration of alternatives. As a result, many cities have adopted significant water-efficiency requirements or incentives and invested in alternatives such as wastewater recycling and reuse. The U.S. Geological Survey suggests that "stricter water-quality standards for water discharges, mandated by the Clean Water Act, may have encouraged conservation, greater efficiency, and shifts to technologies that use less water."[80]

Recognition of specific problems with business as usual has prompted different decisions on other issues as well. Experience has shown that we cannot build our way out of congestion, since building or widening highways generates significant new traffic and often fails to provide long-term congestion relief. Moreover, the fiscal, physical, and environmental constraints on road building are becoming increasingly apparent. In Virginia, for example, it has been estimated that 418 lane miles would have to be built in the Washington, Hampton Roads, and Richmond urban areas each year just to maintain current congestion levels. The economic and social costs of traffic congestion and long commutes in rapidly growing areas have become so great that they have generated increased support for transportation alternatives and better links between transportation and land use. In Atlanta, for example, some major employers voiced a reluctance to locate or expand in the region due to severe congestion.

The costs of business as usual also prompted movement toward sustainability on lead poisoning. The phaseout of leaded gasoline and lead-based paint, the two principal sources of lead exposure, occurred in the United States and other countries in considerable measure because of product obsolescence and commercial decisions, facilitated and accelerated by regulatory and advocacy pressures. Similarly, much of the impetus for the international effort to prevent lead poisoning has been based on recognition of the costly problems that lead causes. Although the international effort was not based on mandatory action, the Rio Conference helped catalyze an international front against lead poisoning. Beginning with the 1993 session of the Commission on Sustainable Development—an oversight and review body created by the Rio Conference—the international community has recognized and reinforced the reduction and elimination of lead poisoning as a global priority.[81]

More and Better Tools

More-sustainable decisions are also easier to make because better tools exist to integrate social, economic, and environmental information, and to use that information in decisionmaking. Three key analytical tools are accounting for ecosystem services, industrial ecology, and environmental management systems.

Accounting for Ecosystem Services

Accounting for ecosystem services has emerged as the basis for many conservation and restoration efforts, including biodiversity conservation, watershed management, and water-quality protection. The premise for this accounting approach is that functioning ecosystems are essential to human well-being, and if ecosystems fail, we must build substitutes to ensure human survival.[82] Ecosystem services include air and water filtering, food production, and protection from severe weather events.[83] Ecosystem services also provide value by supporting particular cultural practices and cultural information.

Historically, many ecosystem services were not perceived as having financial value.[84] Not surprisingly, the Millennium Ecosystem Assessment reported that degradation of more than 60% of the ecosystems studied has outpaced their ability to recover.[85] Ecosystem services accounting seeks to capture the value of these previously ignored functions.[86] More specifically, as Gretchen Daily, director of the Center for Conservation Biology at Stanford University, explains, "the main aim in understanding and valuing natural capital and ecosystem services is to make better decisions, resulting in better actions relating to the use of land, water, and other elements of natural capital."[87] Initiatives are now underway to quantify the economic value of these services to humans and to use those values to protect and restore the environment. Many landowners, for instance, are now being paid for actions that recharge aquifers, store flood waters, or decrease the introduction of pollutants into waters, because those actions are now understood to have value. The market value of such agreements was $7 billion in 2007 and is expected to increase considerably in coming decades as demand for water increases and water becomes scarcer.[88]

Accounting for ecosystem services is now used in a variety of federal programs. The EPA has been integrating the valuation of ecosystem services into the assessment of natural resources damages under the Comprehensive Environmental Response, Compensation and Liability Act[89] and the Oil Pollution Act.[90] Ecosystem services have been targeted to assist in the implementation of a provision of the Food, Conservation, and Energy Act of 2008. That Act requires the government to encourage farmers, ranchowners, and landowners to use emerging markets for conservation activities by adopting guidelines "to measure the environmental services benefits" of those activities.[91] EPA's Ecosystem Services Research Program has focused on valuation techniques and capacity building for ecosystem services analysis,[92] and the Secretary of Agriculture has established the Office of Ecosystem Services and Markets to provide assistance in understanding the benefits of ecosystem services and to encourage the participation of farmers, ranchers, and forest landowners in ecosystem services markets.[93] The trend has pervaded state governments as well, as seen in the Oregon Legislature's announcement of a policy "to support the maintenance, enhancement, and restoration of ecosystem services throughout Oregon, focusing on the protection of land, water, air, soil, and native flora and fauna."[94]

Industrial Ecology

Industrial ecology, a field that analyzes the flow of energy and materials through society, offers an alternative perspective to conventional economic analysis. It applies a systems approach to problem solving, which can assess how materials move through space and across time. The development of indicators for sustainability, and tools with which to quantify these metrics, has been one of the major steps toward enabling sustainable production of materials in the past 20 years.

Industrial ecology can evaluate the magnitude of environmental impacts that are often excluded from economic impact studies. The evolution of the subfield of materials flow analysis has highlighted the importance of "hidden flows"—the materials that are extracted or moved, but do not enter the economy, from activities such as mining. Often goods and services imported by one country cause such flows (or impacts) in the exporting country.[95] They are a measure, in other words, of the environmental impact of trade. The recently developed concept of "virtual water" provides another example of an impact not considered in standard economic studies. What makes water "virtual" is its use in production, but not in the final product. When Brazil ships soybeans to China, for example, the water use for growing occurs in Brazil. In that way, China meets part of its need for water, not by having the water exported to China, but rather by having water used in Brazil to produce food that is then shipped to China. Virtual water accounted for approximately 26% of the global water footprint between 1996 and 2005.[96] Virtual water helps us understand the "water footprint," not only of the production of soybeans and other products, but also of nations.

The largest contribution to industrial ecology has been the adoption of a life-cycle perspective to problem solving. In this approach, production systems are analyzed over the life span of a product (the so-called "cradle to grave" or "cradle to cradle" perspective) from raw material extraction, transformation, use, recycling, and disposal. After accounting for the flow of energy and materials of a production system, the environmental impact of that system can be assessed by identifying the emissions and pollutants resulting from the system.[97] These inputs and outputs (called the life-cycle inventory) to the end product are classified into different categories of environmental impact. Thus one can conduct a life cycle impact assessment (LCA) of a product; often these LCA categories of environmental impact include climate-change potential, acidification, eutrophication, resource depletion, ecotoxicity, and human health. The overall goal of life-cycle thinking is to promote efficient resource use and sustainable consumption practices.

"Industrial ecology thinking promises broadly to spur attention to opportunities for cost savings that would otherwise go unnoticed," according to Dan Esty, a Yale law professor who is now Commissioner of the Connecticut Department of

Energy and Environmental Protection, and Professor Michael Porter of Harvard Business School.[98] The information produced from an LCA can be used for product improvement and product comparison. An LCA can enable a manufacturer to improve a product or process by identifying an area with a heavy environmental burden. Often, these areas are targeted for improvements during, say, manufacture or supply-chain management, resulting in better energy efficiency or reduced waste. 3M has saved approximately $1.4 billion since 1974, when the company began focusing on pollution prevention in resource extraction and manufacturing. General Mills saves approximately $500,000 per year by using oat hulls for energy production in its biomass power plant rather than discarding the hulls to landfills.[99] This sort of recycling can involve multiple nearby facilities in a web of exchanges of byproducts, shared waste-management infrastructure, and similar environmental services in an industrial ecology practice known as industrial symbiosis.[100]

An LCA can also compare the environmental impact of different products, enabling a consumer to compare, for example, the environmental impacts from linoleum with those of ceramic/hardwood floors. The adoption of life-cycle thinking has permeated all sectors of the economy, both domestically and internationally, and has given rise to a host of consortiums dedicated to putting life cycle thinking into practice.[101]

Within the last decade, life-cycle analysis has also been incorporated into policymaking, particularly in the area of transportation fuels. In 2007, the state of California established the Low-Carbon Fuel Standard, a first-in-the-world greenhouse gas standard that mandates a "life-cycle carbon intensity" profile for all transportation fuels.[102] The law requires at least a 10% reduction in the greenhouse gas intensity of transportation fuels by 2020. Similar initiatives have been adopted by the European Union,[103] the United Kingdom,[104] and the Canadian province of British Columbia.[105] The Energy Independence and Security Act of 2007, which required that the amount of renewable liquid fuel used for transportation be increased from 9 billion gallons in 2008 to 36 billion gallons in 2022, also directed EPA to employ greenhouse gas performance standards based on life-cycle analysis to ensure that the new renewable fuels resulted in lower greenhouse gas emissions than the fossil fuels they were replacing.[106] Critics of renewable transportation fuels such as corn ethanol have argued that the net effect of these fuels, when land-use changes and other impacts are taken into account, is to increase greenhouse gas emissions rather than reduce them. In 2010, EPA finalized standards for a Low-Carbon Fuel Standard to ensure that the life-cycle greenhouse gas impacts of renewable fuels are significantly lower than those of fossil fuels.[107]

Green chemistry and green engineering are related to industrial ecology. These two fields, which have emerged in the last 20 years, are concerned with the discovery and development of materials and industrial processes that are "benign by design."[108] They focus on energy, water, and other resource inputs; worker and consumer health and safety; and waste generation through the entire product life cycle. EPA is supporting the development of this emerging field though the Annual Presidential Green Chemistry Challenge Awards, established in 1998, and other efforts.

Environmental Management Systems

There has also been a growing use of management systems for sustainability. The International Standards Organization (ISO) has developed a series of standards that can be used to assist corporate sustainability efforts, including the ISO process for certifying a company's environmental management system,[109] which organizes and implements a company's environmental protection efforts. It includes internal policies and procedures designed and implemented to discover more of the company's total impact on the environment, and then to manage its operations as well as its decisions about products and processes to reduce these impacts and continuously improve environmental performance.

Companies can obtain certification of their environment management systems through ISO, and such certification has become increasingly popular.[110] To be certified, a facility must be checked and monitored to ensure that there really is a management system in place that meets the ISO standards and that the system is actually being implemented. Certification is typically done by third-party auditors who have themselves been approved by ISO, although a company may use its own employees if they have been trained and certified as auditors.

One limitation should be noted. These are management systems, not standards of environmental performance. As such, they articulate a commitment to internal processes and activities within the company, but they are not themselves a commitment to any specified level of environmental performance. Still, companies with environmental management systems generally have better environmental performance than other companies, and these systems offer some potential for moving a company toward sustainability.[111]

ISO has also developed a series of environmental standards, including guidelines for environmental auditing, environmental labeling (more commonly referred to as ecolabeling), product standards, and energy management. The standards do not mandate levels of pollution or performance; rather, they focus on evaluating the environmental or energy effects of particular products or activities, both within and outside manufacturing facilities.

Government agencies and businesses have also developed and deployed management systems to enable them to set sustainability goals, monitor progress toward those goals, and achieve them. The 2011 National Research Council report on sustainability at EPA, which recommended a management system that is based in many ways on those used in the private sector, provides an approach that other federal agencies could use to incorporate sustainability into their operations.[112]

These three tools—accounting for ecosystem services, industrial ecology, and environmental management systems—do not exhaust the range of new tools that have been developed. For example:

- The Natural Step (TNS), a nonprofit organization, has developed Toolkits for Sustainability to enable consumers to evaluate sustainable consumption at home, allow communities to plan for sustainable development, and encourage businesses to plan for sustainable wealth creation and sustainable production.[113]
- The United States played an active role in the development of the Strategic Approach to International Chemicals Management (SAICM), a global system for managing chemicals in commerce and designed specifically to address the lack of technical capacity in most countries for assessing and managing the hazards of chemicals. The SAICM provides a specific framework by which international efforts to manage chemicals can be strengthened.[114]
- EPA's Regional Vulnerability Assessment Program uses maps and online data to enable decisionmakers to gauge the extent to which specific actions will result in environmental improvements in specific places.[115]

Conclusion

Progress on sustainability has not occurred because there is now a better or more compelling definition of sustainability in general. Rather, it has come about in great measure because there are a growing number of specific programs, certification systems, checklists, and tools to enable businesses, individuals, and governments to move in a more-sustainable direction. These programs and tools provide decisionmakers with something focused and reliable that they can use with relative ease. At the same time, these more-sustainable programs and tools are increasingly attractive because the costs of business as usual are growing.

The availability of more attractive and sustainable alternatives reinforces, and is reinforced by, growing public support for more-sustainable practices. The existence of these alternatives provides something specific and attractive that can be supported, and growing support prompts the development and deployment of even more alternatives. As the economic and other costs of business as usual become clearer to more people, and as the ethical or religious implications of unsustainable development are better understood, it is likely that more and better alternatives will become available and be widely used.

CHAPTER 10

Lawmaking Is Not Limited to Environmental Regulation

Much of the progress toward sustainability over the past two decades has occurred because of law and legal institutions. While there is growing support for sustainability in other ways—in the work of nongovernmental organizations and corporations, as well as the creation and use of certification systems, reporting and auditing requirements, and various decisionmaking tools for sustainability—they supplement rather than replace law as means of achieving sustainability. Law provides much of the framework within which decisions are made. It can make unsustainable decisions difficult or impossible—at least for those who seek to comply with the law. Law can also create processes that will result in better decisions, or create incentives that make some decisions more attractive.

Environmental law as we know it is a very specialized form of law. It is regulatory and is administered by government agencies with broad rulemaking and enforcement power. Nearly all modern environmental legislation in the United States was adopted over two decades, beginning with the National Environmental Policy Act of 1969 and ending with the Clean Air Act Amendments of 1990; no major environmental legislation has been enacted since then. These laws provide a basic foundation for sustainability, and their adoption and implementation prior to the Earth Summit made an enormous contribution even before the label of sustainable development was used. As Chapter 1 explained, the air is much cleaner than it was even two decades ago, water quality and hazardous waste management have improved because of these laws, and the national economy has grown. These laws also indicate the kind of leadership that the United States and other developed countries with similar laws have employed to address environmental pollution. To the extent there has been progress toward sustainability in environmental law since the Earth Summit, however, it has occurred not because of the adoption of new legislation but because of the implementation of existing laws.

Much of the most significant legislative movement toward environmental sustainability over the past two decades has occurred not in environmental or natural resources law but rather in the law of economic development. It seems increasingly clear to lawmakers at both the federal and state levels that sustainability provides opportunities for economic development and job creation, even when legislators are not using sustainability language. Many of these laws are intended to foster economic development of the renewable energy and energy efficiency industries, but they have also increased waste recycling and the sale of organic food.

Law has also supported sustainability in recent decades by the use of incentives, mostly financial incentives. Many but not all of them have an explicit goal of economic development. A large number of them are in the form of tax credits and tax deductions for the use of renewable energy or the purchase of energy-efficient equipment. Other incentives include grants and local laws that enable permit applicants for more-sustainable projects to get their applications reviewed more quickly than other applicants.

Laws supportive of sustainability can include almost every type of law. Anti-smoking laws in particular have made an enormous contribution to public health over the last two decades. But laws ranging from private contractual and property arrangements to international policies have also played a role. The variety of these laws highlights a central feature of the emerging law of sustainability: it is not another name for environmental regulation. Rather, the law of sustainability is the entire range of local, state, national, and even international laws that have the effect of requiring, encouraging, or enabling more-sustainable decisions.

Implementation of Existing Environmental Laws

Environmental laws protect air, water, land, and ecosystems in ways that the marketplace has not provided. They make environmentally damaging decisions more difficult, if not impossible, and they encourage or require the use of less damaging alternatives. From an economics perspective, they significantly reduce negative environmental externalities—the costs that a polluting entity imposes on other people or the environment when it does not bear the costs of reducing its own pollution. As noted earlier, the Rio Declaration—the Earth Summit's statement of principles for sustainability—explicitly endorses the internalization of environmental costs, and in so doing affirms a longstanding principle of U.S. environmental law.[1]

Moreover, these laws do more than protect the environment. Their dominant purpose, in fact, is not limited to environmental protection; it is also protection of human health.[2] This is particularly true of the Clean Air Act, the Clean Water Act, the Safe Drinking Water Act, and the Resource Conservation and Recovery Act (RCRA), which protects human health and safety from the improper disposal of hazardous and solid waste. These statutes also attempt to ensure the sustainability of certain resources such as ocean fisheries and foster environmental justice by reducing the disproportionate burden of pollution that is borne by the poor and people of color, by improving efficiency in the use of energy and other materials, by promoting the development of better science and technology, by attempting to ensure greater intergenerational equity, and by fostering sustainable communities.[3]

Environmental regulation also plays a role in stimulating business and corporate innovation, with its resulting economic and competitive benefits.[4]

Where there has been progress toward sustainability, it has occurred because of the manner in which existing environmental laws have been implemented—the day-to-day administration of the laws as well as the adoption of new regulations. Two key elements of environmental law—pollution control and pollution prevention—were well established by the time of the Earth Summit and have provided the legal foundation for much of what has been achieved before and since, even though they have not substantially changed over the past several decades.

The direct regulation of water quality through mandatory, technology-based performance standards has played a major role in reducing municipal and industrial point-source pollution. The controls have been effective because they require pollution reductions across entire categories of dischargers, without creating a difficult, uncertain scientific debate about precise impacts at particular locations. At the same time, this form of regulation does not restrict innovation or flexibility. While the numerical limitations contained in effluent limitations (for example, prohibiting a company from discharging more than 25 parts per billion of chromium) are based on the effectiveness of a model control technology, the Clean Water Act does not require the use of that particular technology. Dischargers may choose to use model technology or meet an applicable standard in some other way that is more cost-effective or confers greater benefits. In many cases, industry has complied with these standards through innovations that have rendered industrial processes more efficient and more productive. However, the failings in this form of regulation have been in the limited scope of what they address. For example, the Clean Water Act is relatively effective at controlling point-source discharges (discharges from pipes at industrial facilities and sewage treatment plants) but vastly less effective at controlling nonpoint discharges (runoff from farms). Nonetheless, the statute has not been amended in any significant way for more than two decades.

The basic regulatory structure of the Clean Air Act also has been in place for decades. The act authorizes EPA to establish air quality standards for pollutants that may endanger public health. Primary standards seek to protect public health with an adequate margin of safety; secondary standards seek to protect public welfare, including a broad array of ecological values. Typically, these standards have been set at the same levels. States must submit for EPA approval plans to attain and maintain these standards—plans that must contain permitting programs for new and modified sources. EPA and Congress establish emissions standards for new motor vehicles and for fuel content. In addition, EPA sets categorywide standards for new sources that act as minimal benchmarks for the states. The act requires EPA to administer a cap-and-trade program for utilities for the purpose of decreasing emissions of sulfur dioxides and nitrogen oxides, which form sulfates and nitrates that lead to acid deposition, reduce visibility, and harm public health. Finally, the act directs EPA to regulate hazardous air pollutants—those that contribute to a risk of cancer or similar disorders. Following the Supreme Court's 2007 decision in *Massachusetts v. EPA*, the act is now the primary legislative authority for EPA's regulation of greenhouse gases. Despite arguments that a different or better approach to greenhouse gases is needed, the Clean Air Act has not been amended since 1990.

Similarly, nearly all of the major steps towards sustainability in the field of hazardous waste took place prior to the Earth Summit. The Resource Conservation and Recovery Act in 1976 and the Comprehensive Environmental Response, Compensation, and Liability Act (CERCLA, or Superfund) in 1980 established a foundation for the regulation of hazardous waste and the remediation of abandoned hazardous waste sites. Progress has been achieved under those statutes because, on the whole, they have been implemented effectively by EPA, which—with some exceptions—has taken the mandates of those statutes seriously. The liability provisions of the Superfund statute—combined with generally supportive interpretations of those provisions in the federal courts—have created powerful incentives for hazardous waste generators, transporters, and disposers to clean up contaminated sites. Moreover, EPA and state enforcement of RCRA requirements has induced many regulated companies and individuals to handle and dispose of their wastes in a more-sustainable manner.

Control of water and air pollution and hazardous waste indirectly encourages facilities to reduce the amount of pollution they generate, thus reducing treatment and control costs. Pollution prevention also predates the Earth Summit. The Pollution Prevention Act of 1990, which is also administered by EPA, establishes a formal pollution-prevention program that has also been influential in moving the United States toward sustainability. This program aims to prevent pollution at the source, promote the use of greener substances, and conserve natural resources. In so doing, pollution prevention can be, and usually is, more environmentally protective and more economically efficient than more traditional after-the-fact pollution control. It creates a preference for changes in the manufacturing process to prevent pollution over the installation of treatment technologies for pollutants created by the manufacturing process. As the program has evolved, it has grown more outward-looking, linking pollution prevention and industrial ecology principles. Pollution prevention, as one of EPA's five program goals in its 2011-2015 strategic plan, will continue shaping EPA's overall program in coming years.[5]

The prevention approach has also been important for lead poisoning. Solutions to lead poisoning were historically based on after-the-fact diagnosis and treatment. By contrast, the premise of the primary prevention strategy (PPS) developed by the nonprofit Alliance to End Childhood Lead Poisoning (now called the Trust for Lead Poisoning Prevention) and supported by EPA, is that lead-based paint—the most prevalent source of lead exposure in the United States after the phase-out of leaded gasoline—requires concentrated priority attention. PPS is an integrated interdisciplinary prevention program based on proactively identifying and assessing likely sources of lead-based paint hazards, rather than an after-the-fact screening of individuals and populations for lead poisoning. The PPS process also informed a successful effort to institutionalize the preventive approach to lead poisoning through national legislation. The Residential Lead-Based Paint Hazard Reduction Act of 1992[6] mandated an expedited large-scale prevention effort, based initially on practicably controlling residential lead-based paint hazards through inspection and maintenance, rather than relying exclusively on often prohibitively expensive removal of lead-based paint in all instances.

States continue to play a strong role in the national environmental effort. They exercise most of the day-to-day responsibilities of implementing the major federal pollution control laws, make the vast majority of permit decisions, and conduct an overwhelming part of the enforcement actions. For both better and for worse, efforts to regulate the environmental effects of gas extraction from Marcellus shale depend almost entirely on the effectiveness of state environmental laws and environmental agencies. In addition, states often lead in adopting new legislation. California, for example, has continued to be a leader in enacting environmental regulations, from banning the use of percholorethylene (a carcinogen used in dry cleaning) and brominated flame retardants to launching a carbon cap-and-trade system for greenhouse gases.

New Economic Development Laws for Environmental Sustainability

In the last two decades, much of the progress made in the United States toward sustainability has been made by laws expressly encouraging or requiring specific kinds of economic development that tends to be more sustainable than conventional economic development. Like economic development laws in general, these laws are not just about business development; they also create jobs. In addition, they reduce the use of fossil fuels, foster new technology, and reduce pollution. Much of this new lawmaking, as we saw in Chapter 4, focuses on the built environment, but new economic development laws for environmental sustainability are not limited to the built environment. These new laws tend to fall into the following seven categories:

Laws requiring an increase in a more-sustainable activity. A variety of laws, mostly enacted in the last several decades at the state level, require increases in renewable energy, energy efficiency, recycling, or some other more-sustainable activity. Many, including the renewable energy portfolio standard, which requires an increase in the percentage of electricity that comes from renewable energy, were described in Chapter 5. These laws require a particular kind of economic development that can be understood as more sustainable because, among other things, they save energy and materials, reduce emissions from burning of fossil fuel, create more jobs than conventional economic development, and save money.

Laws creating a legal structure in which a more-sustainable activity can flourish. These laws do not require a specified increase in a particular activity. Rather, they provide legal authorization for a particular activity. State and federal laws authorizing voluntary cleanup of brownfields sites are one example. By providing legal rules for cleanup levels and release of liability when these rules are met, these laws have cleared the way for the remediation and reuse of thousands of contaminated sites. Net metering is another example: 42 states and the District of Columbia now authorize persons with their own energy-generation systems to sell electricity that they do not use to their local electric utility.[7] Because excess electricity can be sold, net metering also provides an additional incentive to develop and use small-scale renewable technologies.[8] Similarly, organic food certification enables organic food to compete in the market. The program of organic food certification and labeling adopted by the U.S. Department of Agriculture in 2000 has helped create a national and even international market for organic foods. Certification has enabled sales of organic food and beverages to increase from $3.6 billion to $26.7 billion between 1997 and 2010, and organic food's share of total U.S. food production to increase to 4.0%.[9]

Laws that remove legal impediments to sustainability. In many cases, existing laws that create roadblocks to sustainability must be modified or repealed, and some have been. Roadblock laws, which exist at all levels of government, effectively privilege less-sustainable forms of economic development by directly or indirectly impeding other and often more-sustainable economic development. When New York City considered requiring the use of hybrid cars in its taxi fleet, officials discovered that hybrids were effectively prohibited because of a law requiring that taxis be of a larger size. The city subsequently changed that law.[10] At the federal level, steps in the right direction over the past two decades include a 1997 amendment to the Internal Revenue Code permitting homeowners to purchase less expensive homes in cities without incurring a capital gains tax for the sale of the more expensive home in the suburbs.[11] The last two reauthorizations of federal transportation laws, in 1991 and 2005, have focused more on repairing existing roads and developing alternatives to driving than on building new roads.[12] Progress here has been halting, but some steps have been taken.

Application of traditional economic development laws to more-sustainable activities. Governments have a variety of tools to encourage business and industry to locate their facilities in a particular jurisdiction, as well as to encourage them to retain and expand existing facilities. These tools include preferential tax treatment, siting assistance and incentives, and workforce development assistance. Historically, governments have often used such tools to lure more-polluting and less-sustainable business and industry to their states and municipalities. Increasingly, however, state and local governments are employing the very same economic development tools to attract clean energy facilities.[13] Pennsylvania used a variety of these economic development tools—and some that had been modified specifically to attract clean energy projects—to persuade a major Spanish wind turbine manufacturer, Gamesa, to locate its North American headquarters and a manufacturing plant in the state.[14]

Laws and policies that overcome market barriers for more-sustainable activities. In many cases, the market for a particular and sustainable activity does not exist, or is not able to flourish because of a variety of market barriers. To move economic development in a more-sustainable direction, these barriers must be overcome. Federal energy-efficiency laws, which have become more stringent over the past two decades, help overcome these barriers by imposing minimum efficiency standards for appliances, industrial equipment, and motor vehicles.[15] Public-benefit fund programs for energy efficiency,[16] which were described in Chapter 5, typically reduce the upfront cost of energy efficiency and minimize a key market barrier for the wider use of energy efficiency. They do so because the small charge attached to the electric bill is then used to offset the up-front cost of a variety of energy efficiency projects and activities.

A market barrier exists for energy upgrades and retrofits for existing residential and commercial buildings, which are responsible for 38% of carbon dioxide emissions in the United States.[17] In fact, 60% of residences are not well insulated, and 70% of commercial buildings lack either roof or wall insulation.[18] Retrofits in the nation's 130 million homes could reduce home energy use and energy bills by as much as 40%, saving $21 billion annually.[19] In spite of these opportunities, there is no large-scale effective market for retrofits and upgrades of such buildings.[20] To address this issue, the U.S. Department of Energy (DOE) has awarded grants under the American Recovery and Reinvestment Act to 40 states, local governments, and other organizations for pilot programs to "ramp-up energy efficiency building retrofits in their communities." DOE plans to make the lessons learned from these programs available to other communities as part of its effort to scale up retrofits across the country.[21] In February 2011, President Obama launched the Better Buildings Initiative "to make commercial buildings 20% more energy efficient by 2020 and accelerate private sector investment in energy efficiency."[22]

Laws that require the creation and public disclosure of information. Markets can work only with good information, and laws that require or regulate information disclosure promote sustainability by improving the working of those markets. With better information, consumers and investors can use the power of markets to pursue their goals.

One of the clearest examples is the Toxics Release Inventory.[23] The Emergency Planning and Community Right-to-Know Act requires industrial facilities to disclose their releases of specified toxic substances, reporting information on standardized forms that are then made available to the public on computerized databases. No action beyond reporting is required, and no reductions in releases are mandated. Still, the experience has been that reductions in toxic substances releases have been a regular, steady occurrence. Between 2001 and 2010, total production-related waste from covered facilities dropped by 19%.[24] Clearly, companies do not want to be seen as leaders in toxic substances releases.

Somewhat similarly, a 2008 appropriations law requires major contributors to greenhouse gas emissions to publicly report their emissions.[25] In 2009, EPA finalized a regulation under this legislation requiring fossil fuel and industrial greenhouse gas suppliers, motor vehicle and engine manufacturers, and facilities that emit 25,000 metric tons or more of carbon dioxide equivalent per year, to report greenhouse gas emissions data to EPA annually.[26] This new program, which covers approximately 85% of the nation's greenhouse gas emissions and applies to roughly 10,000 facilities, began to be employed for 2010 emissions. Public reporting of this information may, or may not, encourage major greenhouse gas contributors to reduce their emissions.

Also recently, the Federal Trade Commission's Green Guides specify requirements for environmental marketing and advertising claims, and several states have similar rules.[27] These rules are necessary because some companies make or have made false or misleading environmental claims about their products, a practice known as "greenwashing." In addition, the FTC regulates third-party endorsements of products, and this regulation could potentially be applicable to such false claims. Federal and state consumer protection and regulatory agencies have broad power to reach much further to protect consumers, although to date they have made only limited use of it.

Much the same can be said of regulation of information provided to green investors.[28] The Securities and Exchange Commission (SEC) has broad power to supervise information that companies choose to provide voluntarily, as well as power to command disclosure of information that investors need. However, the SEC has traditionally seen environmental information as having only limited financial impact and therefore not important in protecting investors. However, this is changing; the SEC has recently issued new guidance on reporting climate change business information.[29] While the guidance is not mandatory, it does recommend that companies consider and disclose their business, financial, and potential future regulatory risks from climate change. It provides some—but limited—direction for determining these risks. At this stage, it should be counted as a real but modest step in the right direction, but not a wholesale policy change.

Economic development legislation that also has environmental and job creation benefits. As explained earlier, a primary driver for state renewable energy and energy efficiency legislation is economic development, including job creation, development of new technology, and support for new and existing businesses. Local sustainability efforts as well as national energy legislation are often similarly motivated.

Even laws that are no longer in effect provide important lessons about how to design and implement this kind of legislation. During the financial crisis in 2008 and 2009, Congress adopted the Consumer Assistance to Recycle and Save (CARS) Act of 2009.[30] This law, also known as the "cash for clunkers" law, provided government-funded rebates of $3,500 to $4,500 for less-fuel-efficient cars and trucks that were traded in for vehicles with better efficiency.[31] The law was widely popular for the short time it existed, but terminated when the allocated $3 billion ran out. The primary beneficiaries of the law were the automobile industry and its suppliers—no small benefit given the precarious state of the U.S. auto industry at the time. Although the exact level of improvement is contested, the law improved fuel efficiency in the vehicle fleet and helped reduce greenhouse gas emissions.[32] Lessons learned from this experience include not only the importance of designing programs that are financially sustainable, but also the need for authoritative evaluation of program outcomes for the full range of economic, social, and environmental benefits that sustainability provides. The enormous popularity of "cash for clunkers" also suggests the tantalizing possibility that a more rapid transition to sustainability is possible if the public is more fully engaged.[33]

Government Financial or Other Support

Government support—particularly but not exclusively financial support—has been an important factor in growing sustainability efforts. Laws thus often include support for more-sustainable public infrastructure, for brownfields redevelopment, for energy efficiency and renewable energy, and for green building.

Much energy is wasted because U.S. infrastructure—including the transportation system and the electric grid—is inefficient. The American Recovery and Reinvestment Act of 2009 provided $8 billion for high-speed rail investments,[34] $1.5 billion for public-transit improvements and infrastructure investments,[35] and $3.4 billion for modernization of the electric grid.[36] Such funding is a small positive step toward a much more energy-efficient, and thereby more sustainable, infrastructure that is capable of supporting economic development at lower cost and with less pollution.

Public funding is often essential for the success of brownfields redevelopment. As the EPA has noted in a recent summary of brownfields trends, an "important element of success" in brownfields projects "depends on the extent that public investments leverage private funds"[37]—to the degree, in other words, in which the availability of public funding encourages private investors to provide funding. This is especially the case when the costs of site assessment and remediation exceed property values.[38] Grants, loans, training and education programs, and tax and other financing incentives are offered by a wide variety of federal and state agencies (Table 10.1).[39]

Table 10.1
Selected Brownfields Financial Assistance Programs[40]

Program/ Incentive	Level of Government	Description	Notes
Brownfields expensing tax incentive	Federal	Allows the developer to deduct environmental cleanup costs in the year that they are incurred, rather than capitalize them over time.	Reauthorized through December, 2011; no further reauthorization.
Historical rehabilitation tax credits	Federal	Tax credits for restoration of certified historical properties and rehabilitation of noncertified sites.	$4.7 billion in work at 1,044 sites in 2009.
Tax-increment financing (TIF) guarantees	States	Guarantees stream of increased property taxes that repay TIF bonds.	Example: Pennsylvania TIF Guarantee Program.
Bond, loan, and/ or grant funding	States	Direct funding programs that differ depending on the state.	Examples: Low-interest cleanup loans (Delaware, Indiana, and Wisconsin); remediation grant funds (New Jersey and Minnesota).
Other programs	Federal/state	Programs designed for other purposes that can be used for brownfields sites.	Examples: State clean water revolving loan funds; renewable energy incentive programs.

Continued public investment is not always guaranteed, however, in the current tight budgetary climate,[41] and the brownfields expensing tax incentive shown in Table 10.1 was not extended past the end of 2011. In addition, cutbacks in governmental resources (particularly at the state level) can also lead to a slower pace of cleanups and less-vigilant oversight of brownfields sites.[42]

Federal tax incentives have been a central part of the effort to improve energy efficiency and encourage the use of renewable energy, as explained in prior chapters. In addition, generous federal and state tax incentives continue to drive the expansion of the number of acres of land preserved through conservation easements and transfers to private land trusts and local governments.

Innovative approaches to problems also facilitate funding. By characterizing aquatic ecosystem restoration as green infrastructure, the U.S. Army Corps of Engineers and other federal agencies enhance the likelihood of funding such projects. Agencies such as the Corps of Engineers can then combine or leverage federal funding with money from local governments and national conservation groups. Significant efforts to involve both the Corps of Engineers and private parties are underway on the upper Mississippi River and in the Florida Everglades.

Many financial incentives exist at the state and local level. Green building practices have been encouraged through tax incentives.[43] The state of New York, for example, allows owners and tenants to claim tax credits for incorporating green elements into new and existing buildings.[44] Harris County, Texas, provides partial tax abatement for costs incurred in the green certification process.[45] The city of Cincinnati offers tax abatements for the value of certain commercial and residential construction in the reinvestment area (for the value of the building, but not the land), and enforces the green benefit by requiring repayment for noncompliance.[46]

Not all financial incentives have been successful. In 2005, the state of Nevada approved sales and property tax exemptions for green buildings. Under the program, buildings meeting LEED-Silver requirements would benefit from a 93% exemption from sales tax on all building materials and a property tax abatement of up to 50% for up to 10 years.[47] It was soon realized, however, that the incentive would cost the state approximately $900 million in lost revenue over the next decade,[48] compelling the legislature to substantially revise and lower the property tax exemption.[49]

Chicago's Green Roof Program is notable for igniting the community-wide adoption of green roofs. Chicago's City Hall was the first building in the city to build a green roof in 2001.[50] Chicago's tourism website reports that, as of 2011, "Chicago has over 400 green roof projects in various stages of development, with 7 million square feet of green roofs constructed or underway (more than all other U.S. cities combined)."[51] This explosion in development is a direct result of the Green Roof Program, a grant program that awarded $5,000 grants to selected commercial and residential projects in 2005. Although Chicago is no longer accepting applications for the grants, the program's momentum has continued, and green-roof construction is still thriving in Chicago.

State and local governments have provided a variety of other incentives to encourage and reward green builders,[52] including expedited or preferred review status. The city of Santa Monica, California, has offered to give priority to plans for new construction and significant remodeling projects that are registered and actively pursuing certain LEED certification.[53] Cities and state agencies have encouraged green building through the innovative use of grants, loans, permit fee waivers, and fee reductions.[54] The city of Gainesville, Florida, offers a cash renovation incentive and a solar water heater incentive to private projects involving multifamily residential retrofitting or remodeling.[55] Some local governments have experimented with density and bulk bonuses,[56] allowing developers of LEED-certified buildings to construct more and taller structures in certain areas than zoning law would otherwise permit. Other local governments have offered to use their Internet and other marketing resources to publicize the efforts of green builders.[57]

Other Legal and Policy Tools

A great variety of other laws have contributed to progress on sustainability over the past two decades. The following three examples illustrate some of the ways that law and policy can positively affect the trajectory toward sustainability.

Anti-smoking measures. Anti-smoking laws have been one of the greatest public health successes of the last 20 years, and account for a large part of the reduction in cardiovascular mortality and morbidity.[58] Anti-smoking legislation is almost completely state and local. Congress has done much more to protect tobacco companies than to protect the public from tobacco injuries. As might be expected, wealthier and more regulation-friendly states such as California and New York, and cities such as New York City, have led the way by limiting smoking in public spaces and by enforcing limitations on the sale of tobacco products. But other states, such as Louisiana and Florida, have also adopted anti-smoking measures.

Anti-smoking measures are driven by three concerns: the need to reduce workers' exposure to smoke in public spaces such as restaurants; the fact that smokers tend to be poorer and more likely to turn to the state for expensive smoking-related medical care[59]; and the fact that the affluent and well-educated tend to smoke at much lower rates and demand smoke-free public spaces.[60] As the percentage of the public that smokes has dropped, it has become harder for tobacco companies to stop state and local anti-smoking initiatives.

U.S. international population policies. United States international population policies also influence sustainability globally. Despite progress in reducing birthrates in most developing regions, 98% of today's population growth is occurring in developing countries, so the need for family planning assistance from overseas donors remains very real.[61] As Agenda 21 and the 1994 Cairo Conference on Population and Development made clear, both bilateral and multilateral funding are essential for successful efforts to address world population growth. The United States has supported international family planning since 1965, providing some $648 million in 2010.[62] The subject has been extremely contentious since the Ronald Reagan presidency, with the domestic abortion debate acting as a political lightning rod. Notwithstanding the annual political controversy in the United States over international family planning funds, this aid has almost certainly played a role in the significant decrease in population growth in developing countries, from an average growth rate of roughly 2.4% in the 1960s to 1.4% by 2010.[63]

Indeed, the United States remains the largest single donor to international family-planning programs. While this may seem generous, however, it amounts to a small fraction of 1% of the national budget. It is important to recall that foreign donors (including the United States) at the 1994 United Nations Conference on Population and Development in Cairo committed to providing one-third of the family planning and reproductive health care costs in developing countries (all of the costs now are about $9.6 billion annually). However, despite increasing demand for services, international funding for contraceptives has remained stagnant for the last decade at about $238 million, and the U.S. share was cut 5% by Congress in 2011.[64] In real terms, the United States funds for family planning assistance are the same as they were 35 years ago.[65] Since the Cairo+5 Conference in 1999, developed and developing countries together have been providing only about one-third of what they had promised.[66] This reduction reflects both a lack of priority for the program and the need to divert funding toward AIDS prevention.

Combination of the tools of public and private law. Collaborative, flexible land-use planning enables community groups and nonprofits to protect forest sustainability. Traditional land-use review boards that take up-or-down votes on fully rendered land-use plans may not provide a genuine opportunity to integrate community concerns for forest health and forest-related uses. And the scale of a subdivision or development proposal may overwhelm rural and small-town planning boards, placing even greater control in the hands of developers. The development of previously forested areas is increasing because low-cost foreign products are depressing domestic lumber markets.[67] Forests now generate more return as a subdivision or estate development than as a working forest. The loss of managed forests leads to the loss of forestry jobs, to the detriment of rural communities.[68]

This concern is motivating forest products companies, environmental organizations, and planners to collaboratively protect forestlands. Some land-use boards have crafted different procedures for large forest-conversion projects. Combinations of working forest easements and development projects are being negotiated as part of many forestland sell-offs. These and other land-use tools protect conservation values, support a tax base, and provide jobs to the community. Sustainability standards are included in both working forest conservation easements[69] and requirements that the forested area maintain its sustainability certification. Working relationships between stakeholders are essential to the success of this approach.[70] These new procedures have been well received, and they have reduced tension in rural communities.[71]

Conclusion

Law has been a driver for sustainability over the past two decades. Much of this law, particularly environmental law, was adopted before the Rio Earth Summit. The continuing implementation of that law has had an enormous and positive effect on environmental quality and public health in the United States, though that doesn't prevent controversy about particular government or industry activities. Most of the legislation adopted over the past two decades on behalf of sustainability can fairly be characterized as economic development law—building and supporting more-sustainable forms of economic development that create jobs, foster new technologies, and help create new, innovative industries.

Governments at all levels use law to provide a variety of financial and nonfinancial incentives for sustainable development. And a variety of other laws also support more-sustainable development—laws whose very diversity illustrates the scope of needed legal changes for a more-sustainable America. The use of law on behalf of sustainability, and the fact that more-sustainable decisions are easier to make and more attractive, both reflect and contribute to public support for a variety of more-sustainable practices.

PART III

Obstacles to Further Progress

CHAPTER 11

Habits, Lack of Urgency, and Uncertainty About Alternatives

Some of the most basic challenges to sustainability are brutally practical: we behave in an unsustainable way, and we have not developed and deployed reliable sustainable alternatives. These practical obstacles can be grouped in three categories. First, and perhaps most fundamentally, there is the powerful inertial force of existing habitats and expectations. Second, a perceived lack of urgency about sustainability means that more urgent problems—which may or may not be more important—crowd sustainability off decisionmakers' agendas. Perversely, the intergenerational aspect of sustainability seems to contribute to a view that sustainability issues can be dealt with at a later time. Finally, there is considerable uncertainty about what a sustainable society would actually look like, and so it is often difficult to picture exactly where we need to be heading. While there are more-sustainable working models in some contexts (such as forestry and brownfields redevelopment), they do not exist in many other contexts. These three obstacles are mutually reinforcing. The non-existence of alternatives reinforces or solidifies existing habits. Moreover, lack of urgency means that we don't work as hard as we should to develop alternatives.

Existing Habits

A primary obstacle to sustainability is the deeply ingrained habits, objectives, practices, skills, patterns of thinking, and experiences—both good and bad—that support and carry out unsustainable actions. Governments and corporations have these entrenched tendencies, and so do individuals. Existing habits—the ways we conduct business as usual—are the default program for unsustainable behavior.

The force of existing habits begins with individual behavior, whether for personal or family reasons, on one hand, or as part of an organizational or institutional decisionmaking process on the other. We start with what we know, what others have done, and what works today. Deciding to depart from business as usual to a more-sustainable course ordinarily is not easy. It requires that we change our fixed routines, and that ordinarily takes time, thought, or money.

Set patterns of behavior are reinforced by our fixed ways of thinking about the relationship between the environment and the economy. For too many people, the default view is that environmental protection necessarily comes at the expense of the economy and job creation. Of course, as we know, there is abundant evidence of this conflict between conventional development and the environment, and so the default view is not totally unwarranted. If you describe a project that creates economic, social, and environmental benefits (recycling, green building, energy efficiency), most people will acknowledge and support its value. But all too many of us will still presume that the default view applies to everything else.

The combination of habits of acting and thinking presents a major challenge for the sustainability movement. For example, the policies underlying conventional development and urban sprawl—driven by certain unquestioned assumptions—destroy habitat and create major obstacles to biodiversity conservation. Transportation agencies at all levels of government have focused overwhelmingly on roads, cars, and trucks for roughly 60 years, and bureaucracies are resistant to change. In addition, the sprawling development of recent decades makes it very difficult for people in most places not to drive. It is what we do, so we keep on doing it.

Existing assumptions and behavior are also a problem in education, often enhancing institutional priorities that emphasize goals other than sustainability. Many institutions of higher education have a research and teaching agenda, and they divide knowledge into categories that undermine the transformational and interdisciplinary qualities of sustainability. Institutional inertia is also an obstacle for kindergarten-through-12th-grade education for sustainability. This is particularly true of the prevailing focus on teaching and testing basic reading and mathematics skills since the passage of the federal No Child Left Behind Act of 2001. Because schools are evaluated based on outcomes under this law, it is harder to integrate sustainability into education.

The power of institutional inertia also weighs heavily against sustainability in business. A common business assumption is that environmental protection, and indeed all social responsibility, is a cost that drags down the bottom line. As Chapter 8 explains, however, a well-developed body of practical experience and research demonstrates that this need not be the case and that business environmentalism can be an opportunity for growth and profitability.[1] Nonetheless, those innovative experiences struggle against conventional wisdom. The habitual focus on the short-term bottom line discourages long-term thinking about sustainability. A perception also exists that green investing is less profitable than conventional investing, a perception that survives in the face of substantial conflicting evidence.[2] The result, all too often, is the relegation of sustainability to (at best) a marginal objective—one to be pursued only when other profitable activities can pay for it.

Even among those who, if asked, would say they are concerned about the environment and sustainability, there is often a gap between awareness and action. As a result, many of us do not think about the environmental and social impacts of daily actions, engaging instead in habitual behavior that undermines sustainability efforts, even in the smallest ways—we leave lights and appliances on when not in use or throw recyclables into the trash.

Lack of Urgency

Achieving sustainability is not considered by many to be a pressing problem; other, "more practical," things seem to demand our immediate attention. Lack of good public information and education—information that would bring home the ways we affect sustainability in our everyday lives—contributes to this absence of urgency.

Other Problems Are More Urgent

There always seems to be something more pressing than sustainability. In our personal and professional lives, as well as in organizations and governments, immediate problems that may or may not be important tend to get priority over important problems that are not perceived as urgent.[3] While many understand that sustainability is important, relatively few understand its urgency. It does not help that the consequences of uncontrolled greenhouse gas emissions will primarily fall on future generations, not present voters.

As this book goes to press, there is high unemployment and a serious federal budget deficit in the United States. As important as these issues are, they can be yet another reason for Americans to focus on something other than sustainability. The 2002 World Summit on Sustainable Development in Johannesburg, South Africa, came less than a year after the 9/11 terrorist attacks. In 2007, 15 years after the 1992 Earth Summit, the United States was deeply involved in wars in Iraq and Afghanistan. There is never a convenient or appropriate time, it seems, to focus on sustainability. Pressing short-term problems push important long-term challenges aside.

The issue of immediacy is reflected on the state level by a tendency to focus on those parts of the sustainability issue that tend to have the most immediate benefits—energy efficiency and renewable energy. Those are important issues, but an overall sustainability policy framework is used by relatively few states.

At the local level, in many cases, decisionmakers often distance themselves or their community from the threat of climate change and environmental or social inequity. This distancing can be temporal ("let the next generation worry about it") or focused on a short-term political time frame, making governmental decisions with an eye towards the next election. The distancing can also be geographic ("it doesn't affect me because I don't live there"). In addition, for other decisionmakers, the economic recession trumps sustainability because sustainability is not seen as linked with economic development.

This lack of immediacy also occurs with long-standing issues on which considerable progress has been made. Many, for example, seem to feel that lead poisoning prevention is passé. Current funding for lead poisoning prevention is constrained despite the many remaining challenges that lead poisoning still presents, including leaded paint in buildings and the continued use of lead in a variety of products. Similarly, some of the enthusiasm and excitement that led to the development of many state recycling programs in the 1980s and 1990s has dissipated. While the recycling rate continues to rise nationally, Pennsylvania, which once had one of the nation's leading programs, no longer engages in significant public recycling education and no longer accurately accounts for the amount of material recycled as a result of the program.[4]

Lack of Knowledge About Sustainability Problems

The environmental history of the United States is punctuated by bold policies that have been emulated worldwide: the passage of the Clean Air Act; the creation of the Environmental Protection Agency; and the bans on DDT, lead, and chloro-fluorocarbons (CFCs). Many of these actions were preceded by dramatic rises in popular opinion that occurred in the late 1960s and early 1970s, and then again in the 1980s—what some social scientists called the first and second "miracles of public opinion."[5] Environmentalism took hold in the United States because the interests of the environmental movement coincided with prevailing opinion on the interests of the nation, especially quality of life and public health.

Sustainable development has not risen to the forefront of American conscious-ness and provoked similar populist responses. We tend to believe what we see and experience. What we don't see or experience is not as real, or not real at all. Many of the problems we observed in the early days of the environmental movement—dirty rivers, pollution from factory smokestacks and auto exhaust pipes, valleys with hundreds of rusting drums containing hazardous waste—were visible to us and are now largely controlled. Many of the remaining sustainability issues are harder for the public to understand because they are less visible.

In some cases, we even lack the basic data necessary to see or understand the sustainability issues in front of us. Our ability to fully understand the production and consumption of materials (not just recycling, but rather the entire system) is complicated by the immense diversity and scale of our economy. For any given product, one would need to track the flow of materials that begins with extraction of raw materials from the earth, the processing of those materials, transporting them for manufacture, manufacturing products from them, transporting those products again to the consumer, and finally the use and disposition of those products by the consumer. The sheer size of the system—across an enormous number of raw materi-als and products—is a real barrier to understanding fully how it works and, most importantly, how to change it. We simply cannot know how to sustain materials flows in the economy, or manage the environmental and energy impacts of those flows, without basic information about the workings of the system.

Official U.S. government accounts still do not systematically track the move-ment of materials into and out of our economy. While the U.S. Geological Survey tracks flows of individual materials, it does not conduct an overall materials flow analysis. As Chapter 2 explains, the last such analysis for the United States was done in 2008 by the World Resources Institute, a nongovernmental organization.[6] By contrast, the European Union, Japan, and several other countries have launched aggressive campaigns to reduce the materials intensity of production and to increase waste treatment and reuse. The United States has yet to adopt these measures, or to develop the data needed to support them.

A good example of how information can be used to enhance our country's long-term sustainability can be found in the case of rare-earth metals, minerals that are used in a variety of electronic goods and by the renewable energy, defense, and information technology industries. Although these metals are not rare in aggregate terms, they are widely dispersed and thus not found in economically exploitable concentrations.

Due in part to a fundamental misunderstanding of the supply of rare-earth metals and future demand, the United States did not respond when rare-earth production, once dominated by the United States, started to shift toward China in the early 1990s. Few efforts were made to decrease the environmental costs of domestic production, to keep domestic suppliers open, or to replace rare-earth components with other readily available minerals, which would reduce our need to import them. As a consequence, China now controls more than 90% of the global supply of rare-earth minerals (Figure 11.1).

Figure 11.1
Global Production of Rare-Earth Oxides, 1950–2000[7]

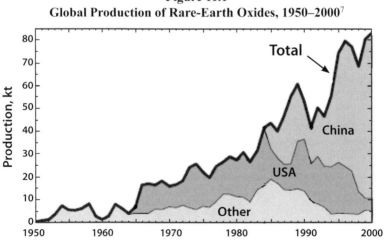

Similarly, lack of knowledge about marine species and marine ecosystems remains a barrier to achieving sustainability for oceans and estuaries. As a report from the National Oceanic and Atmospheric Administration makes clear, species remain inadequately studied even when they are commercially important, with the result that regulators are unable to determine what a sustainable population or sustainable catch would be. Interrelationships among species are even less understood, making most current attempts at ecosystem-based management difficult if not impossible. Shifting baselines also create a problem in understanding whether fish populations are increasing or decreasing. Studies of historical overfishing have made it clear that marine management, to an extent greater than other kinds of natural resource management, is subject to a "shifting baseline syndrome"—that is, a growing acceptance of unsustainable conditions as "normal."[8]

Another obstacle to achieving sustainability of marine resources is an inability in many circumstances to demonstrate real harm in a way the public can understand. Much of the important evidence of ocean sustainability is not readily perceptible to humans. People still assume that the oceans are too big for humans to damage in a permanent way. Thus, the popular protest of the 2010 Gulf oil spill has already largely dissipated, despite the fact that the long-term effects of the spill and the use of dispersant remain unknown—and much of the released oil remains unaccounted for.

The same problem occurs with climate change. We all understand day-to-day changes in the weather; they are visible and immediate. Climate, which is a reflection of weather patterns in particular places over significant periods of time, is also easy to understand in some respects; we all recognize that Minnesota and Florida have different climates. But in any one place it is harder to understand patterns over long periods. Many people simply equate climate with recent weather events, like an abnormally hot summer or a freak October snowstorm, rather than analyzing the data of many years and looking at future trajectories.

These problems are compounded by a tendency to use the term "global warming" as a synonym for climate change. Growing concentrations of greenhouse gases in the atmosphere tend to increase surface temperatures, which is why the term "global warming" is used. But higher atmospheric levels of greenhouse gases don't simply warm the atmosphere; they also cause or contribute to more frequent and intense precipitation, more frequent droughts, and other unusual weather, which Hunter Lovins, President and founder of Natural Capitalism Solutions, calls "global weirding." Because warmer air can hold greater moisture, heavy rain and snowstorms can result from human-induced climate change. Nonetheless, the February 2010 blizzard in Washington, D.C.—when the nation's capital received more than 20 inches of snow—was seen by some as demonstrating that global warming is not occurring. Even the Gallup and Pew polls described in Chapter 8 are generally based on questions about global warming, not climate change. Those who focus on warming alone miss the other consequences of climate change, and those who focus on specific weather events miss the changing pattern in which these events are occurring.

Because the climate has been relatively stable over the past 10,000 years or so, there has been little need to recognize climate change or think about what happens when it does change. As a result, there is no broadly accepted understanding or recognition of the warning signs or symptoms of climate change. Indeed, we have no experience at making a modern civilization with a very large population adapt to climate change.

Lack of transparency about institutional decisions that affect the environment is also an obstacle. Nongovernmental organizations and others are finding it more difficult to monitor multilateral banks' investment portfolios. This, in turn, makes it more difficult to ensure that these investments do no harm to local communities and are used instead to promote sustainable development. The World Bank has gradually shifted its portfolio away from its traditional practice of specifying the exact use of funds in its lending. Now, in the majority of investments the Bank provides support to broader government programs, channels funds through other financial institutions, and uses funds as general budget support for a country's treasury.[9] This policy enables borrowing governments to have a wider discretion to meet their development needs. But the environmental and social impacts of the governments' investments are difficult for nongovernmental organizations, and even the Bank, to monitor.

Uncertainty About Alternatives

Business as usual is reinforced by the presence of a wide range of problems with more-sustainable alternatives. The public may be confused about the meaning of sustainability. There might be few if any good alternatives, or some of them may have design problems, or we might lack solid information about specific programs. Market barriers may exist for sustainable alternatives, and there may be a price premium for "greener" alternatives. Consumers and investors may lack reliable information about more-sustainable products and services, and our analytical tools may be inadequate. All of these obstacles—or we might call them excuses for not acting—are discussed below.

Public Confusion About the Meaning of Sustainability

Sustainable development has been described as a concept with "broad appeal and little specificity," with little consensus on what should be sustained and developed, and for how long.[10] Even though hundreds of sustainable development initiatives exist, no common set of indicators is broadly accepted, backed by sound empirical research, and influential in policy.[11] Nor is there a widely shared vision of what sustainable development would contribute to the United States.

We have few (if any) large-scale models of sustainability. We can identify individuals, families, or small groups whose lifestyle exemplifies sustainable behavior. And we can identify governments, companies, universities, and other organizations that are taking steps toward sustainability. The first steps toward sustainability, whether for a corporation, government, community, or society, are reasonably easy to plot; they all tend to involve steadily reducing adverse environmental impacts, and steadily increasing positive environmental, social, and economic impacts at the same time. Farmers, for example, can take many immediate measures to improve their sustainability. They can employ integrated pest management, which seeks to make synthetic chemicals more of a last-resort solution to pest problems and favors the least-toxic alternatives. They can use drip irrigation and other water conservation measures. They can rotate crops in order to interrupt pest cycles and build soil fertility. And they can use cover crops to reduce soil erosion and build fertility.[12] Nevertheless, it is more difficult to see how to sustainably produce enough food for more than 300 million people in the United States, much less more than 7 billion people around the world.

A basic requirement for fostering change is to get people to recognize that the sustainability movement is advocating for true change. But it is difficult to do when the new concept—sustainability—is not well understood. Much of the public does not appear to understand that sustainability is quite different from the many conventional forms of environmentalism. The approach of systematically making environmental, social, economic, and even security goals work together, for instance, is not used by many environmentalists, who are often focused on specific issues or the protection of particular areas or values. Yet, much of the public does not understand that difference. As a consequence, sustainability appears to be understood by a very large segment of the population as more or less synonymous with environmentalism. Many of these same people understand that clean energy can create jobs and economic development. But they resist using the term sustainability or sustainable development because they don't understand it or they fear being misunderstood by others. Those who oppose change, of course, have no interest in characterizing sustainability accurately; they gladly contribute to the confusion.

On the other hand, we tend to have a better and clearer idea of what unsustainable development is, and why to oppose it. In land use, for instance, communities change their zoning and subdivision ordinances to be more environmentally sustainable because they do not like new developments. In many cases, those municipalities have no compelling vision of the kind of place they want to be; they simply know what they do *not* want to be. Abstract definitions of sustainability are simply not as attractive as a specific vision of sustainability, and these municipalities have not worked out that specific vision. "It is this failure of visualization," Prof. Jerrold Long of the University of Idaho, College of Law, says, "that most impedes attaining sustainability." The challenge, he observes, "is to accurately imagine—*before* directly witnessing—the consequences of the alternatives available to us."[13]

Lack of Alternative Models

It is easier to justify existing habits if there is a lack of demonstrated means for achieving sustainability. The quest for sustainable agriculture provides a useful illustration. The case for continuing to practice large-scale monoculture farming of annuals such as corn, rice, and soybeans is based on the fact that it actually works to feed a large population. Equally important is the fact that there are no demonstrated large-scale alternatives. Perennial polyculture farming (with multiple plant species that live several years or longer) is likely to be more sustainable, but it has not been demonstrated on a large scale. Researchers at the Land Institute reported some progress in 2010:

> In an effort to reduce soil degradation and water contamination simultaneously—something that neither no-till nor organic cropping alone can accomplish—researchers in the United States, Australia and other countries have begun breeding perennial counterparts of annual grain and legume crops . . . Initial cycles of hybridization, propagation and selection in wheat, wheatgrasses, sorghum, sunflower and Illinois bundleflower have produced perennial progenies with phenotypes intermediate between wild and cultivated species, along with improved grain production.[14]

Wes Jackson, founder of the Land Institute, points out that almost all efforts at agricultural reform are looking only at the problems *in* agriculture and not the problem *of* agriculture. Most agricultural reform efforts only ameliorate problems in the short term—for example, by using synthetic chemicals to make up for the loss of fertility in the soil—but do not deal with the underlying issue of long-term damage to soil, the basis of agriculture. These reformers ask how we can do agriculture better. Instead, Jackson would say that some problems are simply inherent in agriculture, because we are using annual crops that require us to either till the soil every year and thus expose it to erosion, or use herbicides to control weeds when we do not till. In addition, annual crops do not generate nearly as much root system as perennial crops and therefore are not as good at conserving soil, absorbing nutrients, or sequestering carbon. "Annual [crop] systems leak; they are poor micromanagers of nutrients and water," Jackson has said.[15] Perennial polyculture might prove to be a long-term solution to what ails agriculture, but we will not know that until it has been successfully demonstrated at a much larger scale.

Problems in Design and Implementation

Many sustainability programs are not fully used because, like any major effort that is still getting underway, the "kinks" have not been worked out. Start-up difficulties can be an obstacle to using new programs and so, again, become a justification for continuing existing habits.

The U.S. Green Building Council (USGBC) provides a credit toward LEED certification for wood that has been certified by the Forest Stewardship Council (FSC) as sustainably grown and harvested. The LEED credit has had the effect of both increasing and decreasing adoption of the sustainable forest certification. FSC's high standards are the only certification earning a LEED credit (though recent improvements to the Sustainable Forestry Initiative have created pressure on the USGBC to allow other certifiers to earn a credit).[16] Even with these strong standards, however, the LEED credit requires the use of 50% of certified sources only, which dampens what could be stronger demand.[17] Thus, although LEED has motivated certification, the motivation it creates is limited.

The FSC is trying to certify smaller, low-intensity forest operations. While the effort has met with some success, particularly among managers already predisposed to certify for noneconomic reasons, the demand for FSC-certified lumber is now too weak to motivate many small-forest managers to seek FSC certification. It adds little value to small-forest managers not already inclined to adopt sustainable practices.

Other problems occur because of weak consumer demand. Commitments from large buyers stimulate forest certification, as illustrated by the contrast between certified paper and certified lumber demand. The commitment of high-profile paper buyers to FSC-certified paper encourages suppliers to certify their forests.[18] To date, however, no large homebuilder or lumber contractor has made a similar commitment to certified lumber sourcing. It appears that where intermediaries stand between certified production and the consumer, consumer demand is less successful in motivating forest certification.

Market Barriers

Markets respond poorly to many of the prerequisites for sustainability. The barriers to energy efficiency are, among others, the difficulty in obtaining reliable information about the performance (energy and cost savings) of energy-efficiency measures; the relative lack of interest or knowledge among consumers, doubtless due to both the difficulty of getting reliable information and failure to understand that energy efficiency is an investment and thus has a payback period that can be calculated; principal-agent problems (the renter gains from energy efficiency but the owner makes the investment); the inconvenience and delays associated with installation of energy-efficiency measures; and the low price of energy due to subsidies and failure to internalize external costs.[19] As explained in earlier chapters, some federal and state laws have overcome these barriers in some contexts. But all too often, in other contexts, these barriers remain.

Price Premium

Green products or materials are often considered to be expensive and therefore only a niche market. A consumer survey by Mintel Oxygen Reports found that 54% of American respondents say they would buy more green products if they were less expensive.[20] The report states that while cost remains an impediment to the green market's growth, the majority of consumers are willing to pay a little extra for green products. In some cases, this price premium can be justified because of the newness of the product or service. But the perception that consumers need to pay extra for greener products and services often leads producers or sellers to charge more simply because the green market will bear a higher price.

Lack of Information, or Misinformation

Lack of information, and even misinformation, contributes to the difficulty consumers as well as investors have in making good decisions. Inadequate or wrong information also impedes the effectiveness of many sustainability programs.

The weakness of consumer demand for sustainable products also reflects the difficulty consumers face in easily getting information about the products they buy. A large number of specific certification standards exist and their content is varied. For coffee alone, there are at least eight different fair trade, organic, or sustainability certification programs and initiatives, each with different strengths and weaknesses.[21] Informed sustainability purchases are possible only by exceptionally committed consumers willing to invest an inordinate amount of time and energy in research. In the midst of busy lives, few of us have the time. While we have reasonably effective systems that regulate general consumer information, for the most part they do not include environmental or sustainability information, making the consumer's job that much more difficult.[22] Absent such information, it is likely that not enough consumers will care to begin to move the market in a sustainable direction.

Much the same is true with respect to green investors. Companies' disclosure of some environmental information is now required, and more is voluntarily supplied. Nevertheless, the regulatory systems that oversee the accuracy of information for investors reach only a small part of it, and then only inconsistently and haphazardly.[23] In sharp contrast to the regulation of financial information, environmental and sustainability information has gotten only limited and intermittent attention from either the Congress or federal agencies. We certainly know how to regulate the content and truthfulness of financial information supplied to investors; if we directed the same attention and energy to sustainability information, capital markets could be a real force for pursuing sustainability. This is particularly true for information regarding the risks of unsustainable products and processes, as well as information about the business opportunities presented by more-sustainable ones.

Where sustainability programs exist, they are often not fully used because decisionmakers are not aware of them, or they misunderstand them. Many consumers in the real estate market still know little to nothing about green buildings or their benefits, believing that green buildings are too expensive because they involve more insulation and other environmental features. In fact, a building with greater insulation in the walls, windows, and roof needs a smaller and less expensive heating, ventilation, and air-conditioning system. These kinds of cost offsets make the initial cost of a green building nearly equal to the initial cost of a conventional building. In addition, some people simply dismiss the idea of green buildings as part of a political agenda with which they disagree.

The federal and state governments, as well as nongovernmental organizations, offer many financial-incentive programs for sustainability to private forest owners, but studies analyzing the effectiveness of these programs show limited impact.

Only 12.7% of nonindustrial private forest owners in forested states participate in existing incentive programs.[24] Two barriers prevent these programs from achieving sustainability objectives. First, landowners are generally unaware of the programs. Second, those who are aware of incentive programs are usually unclear about program requirements. Many landowners misperceive program requirements or mistrust the program itself. In a number of the southern states, for example, concerns about private property rights are an impediment to sustainable forestry.[25]

Inadequate Tools

We lack many of the analytical tools and metrics needed to measure progress toward sustainability. The major conceptual obstacle to achieving sustainable biodiversity, for instance, has been the inability of the federal government or an authoritative private body to develop a uniform set of biodiversity metrics that can be used to structure programs and measure their effectiveness. Without a uniform set of metrics, it is impossible to assess the condition of biodiversity in the United States. Scientists have struggled with this obstacle for years.

Conclusion

We face many obstacles to achieving sustainability due to our personal and societal habits, and the difficulties in changing them. Many of the actions we take—as individuals, families, companies, governments, and educational institutions—are unsustainable because there is no practical alternative. Often we do not worry too much about it because sustainability issues do not seem all that urgent. There may be considerable uncertainty about whether sustainable alternatives will work, whether they really are more sustainable, and whether they are worth the extra money. These obstacles reinforce each other, tempting us back to business as usual.

CHAPTER 12

Unsupportive Law and Governance

Legal and governmental obstacles impede sustainability. An important set of governmental barriers to sustainability are laws and policies that support or codify unsustainable development, such as subsidies to the fossil fuel industries that hide the full cost of our reliance on oil, natural gas, and coal while discouraging investment in, and adoption of, more efficient and cleaner alternatives.

A second and more recent barrier is the absence within government of a bipartisan consensus on the environment. This lack of consensus can lead us to lurch back and forth from policies that support environmental protection and alternative energy development, on one hand, to policies that are less supportive and sometimes even hostile, on the other, making it extremely difficult to plan public or private investments in infrastructure over the long haul. Recently, American politics has become deeply partisan, and an ideological divide over environmental protection as an overall goal and over specific policies has increased, presenting an enormous barrier to sustainability at a time when the need for action is greatest.

A third obstacle is failures of governance: lack of governmental leadership, inconsistent responses by federal agencies to specific issues, fragmented decision-making authority over a particular issue or resource, and inadequate governmental financial support.

Laws That Support and Encourage Unsustainable Development

Many existing laws and policies prevent more-sustainable actions, or make them much more difficult. Subsidies are perhaps the most obvious example. In 1994, Maurice Strong, the organizer of the 1992 Earth Summit, noted that "for all the good things that our political leaders are saying these days about sustainable development, the economic, fiscal, and sectoral policies of government by and large continue to provide incentives and subsidies for environmentally unsound behavior."[1] Almost 20 years later, little has changed in the United States.

These problematic policies include direct and indirect subsidies for the production of energy, particularly oil, natural gas, and coal—approaches that long ago ceased to serve their purposes.[2] They range from royalty relief and the provision of tax incentives to direct payments and other forms of support for nonrenewable energy. A partial list of oil and gas subsidies gives an idea of how extensive they are:

- Enhanced oil-recovery credit, a 15% credit for certain expenses related to a project that increases the amount of recoverable domestic crude oil through the use of methods such as injecting steam or carbon dioxide.[3]
- Marginal well tax credit, a credit amount (adjusted for inflation) per unit of oil or gas extracted from a domestic well with a defined limited average production.[4]
- Expensing of intangible drilling costs, which consist of all expenses relating to the preparation of drilling a well, including labor, fuel, and supplies.[5]
- Passive-loss exception for working interests in oil and gas properties.[6] Passive-loss rules limit deductions attributable to activities in which the taxpayer is not actively engaged to the amount of income generated by the passive activity. Losses from certain working interests in oil and gas properties are not limited under the passive-loss rules.
- Percentage depletion, which is an exception to general cost recovery rules in that it permits a deduction in excess of the cost of oil and gas properties.[7]
- Domestic manufacturing deduction for oil and gas production.[8] Taxpayers with qualified oil-related production income may take a deduction of 6% of the least of its domestic oil-related production activity income, its qualified production activities income, or its taxable income.

While Congress has used the tax system to encourage conservation and renewable energy on and off since 1978, at the same time it has provided tax incentives for energy use and fossil-fuel consumption.[9] Because these subsidies have historically been greater than those for renewable energy and energy conservation, fossil fuels have long had a competitive edge in the market. The combination of perverse incentives to develop fossil fuel energy sources, such as subsidies, and a lack of sufficient incentives to develop renewable energy, distorts energy policy in ways that tilt the playing field away from renewable energy and energy efficiency.[10]

A 2009 study by the Environmental Law Institute (ELI)[11] found that the federal government provided substantially larger subsidies to fossil fuels than to renewable energy sources from 2002 to 2008. Fossil fuels received approximately $72 billion over the seven-year period, while subsidies for renewable fuels totaled only $29 billion (Figure 12.1). Moreover, more than one-half of the subsidies for renewables—$16.8 billion—are attributable to corn-based ethanol, the climate effects of which have been hotly disputed. Of the fossil fuel subsidies, nearly all went to traditional sources such as coal and oil, and only 3% went to carbon capture and storage, which is designed to reduce greenhouse gas emissions from coal-fired power plants. In sum, energy subsidies highly favored traditional energy sources that emit high levels of greenhouse gases over innovative sources that would decrease our climate footprint.

Figure 12.1
Federal Energy Subsidies 2002–2008[12]

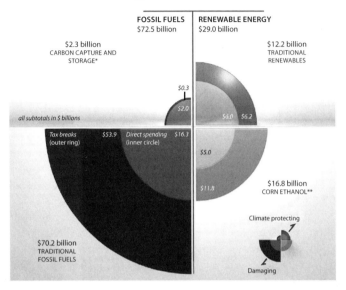

*Carbon capture and storage is a developing technology that would allow coal-burning utilities to capture and store their carbon dioxide emissions. Although this technology does not make coal a renewable fuel, if successful it would reduce greenhouse gas emissions compared to coal plants that do not use this technology.

**Recognizing that the production and use of corn-based ethanol may generate significant greenhouse gas emissions, the data depict renewable subsidies both with and without ethanol subsidies.

The ELI study also found that 61% of fossil fuel subsidies have been written into the U.S. tax code, meaning they will continue until affirmatively repealed. By contrast, all subsidies for renewable fuels expire at a set future date and therefore require congressional reauthorization to continue after the specified date. This contingency makes it more difficult for startup industries to rely on such subsidies to raise capital.

In recent years, renewable energy and energy efficiency have received relatively greater support, as Congress has increased federal financial support for alternatives to fossil fuels. The tax subsidy for fossil fuels dropped from over 60% of total tax subsidies for energy in 1997 to under 50% in 2007[13] (toward the end of the ELI study period). This is a welcome trend.[14] But as federal subsidies for renewable energy expire, this recent trend will last only if Congress reauthorizes them.

Many other government policies can have a profound stimulus on major sectors of the economy for reasons unrelated to the environment, but can provide significant incentives for unsustainable practices affecting freshwater and other resources. One example is the manner in which U.S. agricultural laws and policies encourage excess production of a limited range of commodity crops, sometimes on marginal soils or in sensitive areas, in order to stabilize prices and the farm economy generally, to maintain low food prices, and to expand export markets. Although U.S. farm policy includes some well-funded conservation programs and incentives, those efforts are overwhelmed by the better-funded counter-incentives inherent in agricultural subsidies and other production guarantees. Policies designed to promote U.S. energy security arguably have had similar unintended effects on environmental sustainability. This may be especially true for those supporting corn oil, although the corn ethanol subsidy expired at the end of 2011.

Public funding for highways creates a competitive disadvantage for energy-saving rail freight. Railroads differ from trucking companies because they own and maintain their own tracks and rights-of-way. By contrast, trucks operate on public rights-of-way that are built and maintained by taxes. Rail freight transportation is more energy-efficient and less polluting than highway freight transportation and does not contribute to highway congestion.[15]

Tax law also encourages and supports unsustainable actions—through, for example, the federal tax deduction for mortgage interest, which creates a major incentive for sprawl and, therefore, greater energy consumption.[16] As Scott Bernstein, president and cofounder of the Center for Neighborhood Technology in Chicago, explains: "Because of increasing lot sizes, home sizes, and correspondingly larger mortgage financing packages, and because the deduction is indexed to income, the deduction is worth more to borrowers in the suburbs and newer areas than in central cities and older areas."[17] At the state level, state law establishes local government boundaries and the powers and duties of those governments. State tax laws also give municipalities the power to tax property within those boundaries in ways that encourage competition for ratables (land uses that pay higher property taxes) among municipalities, including cities and their suburbs. This competition, and the absence of revenue sharing among municipalities, also contributes to sprawl.[18]

Federal public land law, the principal legal framework affecting biodiversity conservation, remains as dysfunctional as ever. Using federal land law to protect biodiversity is a classic case of trying to cram square pegs into round holes. Public land laws were enacted to reflect the utilitarian idea that all resources should be exploited to the maximum extent possible. Thus, commodity extraction remains the dominant use on public lands such as national forests, and biodiversity protection is often a secondary, marginalized use.

Other laws encourage other unsustainable activities. Federal and state water law often encourages groundwater mining and other unsustainable uses of water. In many states, there are few restraints on groundwater mining. In the western states, rights are based on the first person to put water to use. But holding a water right requires that it be actually and continuously used for a beneficial use. This often encourages wasteful practices at the expense of instream uses.[19] State and municipal zoning laws favoring single-use zoning, together with transportation laws, contribute to overdependence on personal automobile travel and sprawl and reduce quality of life in many communities.

Another obstacle is lack of clarity about when federal law preempts local action in pursuit of sustainability,[20] causing ambiguity and confusion over the authority of state and local governments to adopt and enforce particular green building standards. In a 2010 decision,[21] the federal district court of New Mexico found that stringent local construction standards for energy efficiency are preempted by energy efficiency standards for appliances under federal law.[22] However, in a similar challenge to the energy efficiency standards in Washington State, the court reached a different result. In that case, the district court upheld Washington's building code requirements because the code allowed alternative means of achieving the regulatory standards for energy efficiency.[23] Until there is better guidance on how state and local building codes can avoid federal preemption, some local governments may avoid green building in order to minimize possible exposure to litigation and liability.

Lack of Substantial and Bipartisan Consensus

President Jimmy Carter put solar collectors on top of the White House in the late 1970s; President Reagan took them down. Several administrations later, President Obama put solar collectors back on the White House roof. Will the next president take them down?

Sustainability will become a central, ongoing part of U.S. law and policy if there is a consistent bipartisan consensus supporting it. In a political system focused on two-, four-, and six-year election cycles, the only way we can maintain progress is if the major parties are all in essential agreement, just as they were about containment of communism during the Cold War. Achieving sustainability will require steady progress over more than one generation. The particular threats to sustainability are likely to change over time, but the overall challenge of sustainability will not go away.

A strong spirit of bipartisanship made possible the major federal laws that gave birth to the modern environmental movement in the late 1960s and early 1970s. Richard Nixon, a Republican, was president, and the Democratic Party controlled Congress. During this time, the Clean Air Act, the Clean Water Act, and the National Environmental Policy Act (which requires federal agencies to prepare an environmental impact statement prior to taking major actions) were signed into law. Republicans and Democrats in Congress worked together on these laws.[24] President Nixon created the Environmental Protection Agency by executive order in 1970 in order to locate in one place the various environmental protection functions that had been scattered across several agencies.[25] It may not be a coincidence that a recent Environmental Law Institute survey of environmental accomplishments of the past 40 years identified creation of EPA and the passage of the Clean Air and Water Acts as the top three.[26]

The bipartisanship that made those accomplishments possible is currently at an extremely low point. A prominent indicator of the current lack of bipartisanship is the stream of anti-environmental measures the House of Representatives passed in 2011. According to EPA Administrator Lisa Jackson, "Republicans in the House have averaged roughly a vote every day the chamber has been in session to undermine the Environmental Protection Agency and our nation's environmental laws." She adds that their efforts, if successful, would mean "an unprecedented rollback of the Clean Air Act, the Clean Water Act and our nation's waste-disposal laws."[27] Several Democratic members of the House released a report detailing 191 votes by the House in the first session of the 112th Congress to weaken environmental protections.[28] A number of Republicans have expressed concern over the party's recent environmental stance. William K. Reilly, EPA Administrator under President George H.W. Bush, has noted that "Republicans were once the party of science when environmental regulations were concerned," and warned that many Republican politicians are ignoring science and undermining the legacy of environmental progress that is "our legacy too."[29]

Although partisanship is nothing new, the divide in American politics has increased markedly in recent years, causing some to ask if the nation is governable. This is easily one of the biggest and most difficult obstacles to sustainability, and it may be the most important. Although there are still issues on which bipartisan consensus exists to some degree, common ground between the parties has eroded even in these areas. For example, support for high-speed passenger rail has traditionally been strongly bipartisan, and proposals have been advanced by members of both political parties. Yet, Republican governors elected in 2010 in Florida, Ohio, and Wisconsin rejected billions of dollars of federal funds their states had been awarded, and House Republicans successfully pushed to eliminate funding for high-speed rail in a broad spending bill for fiscal year 2012.

The reasons for this breakdown in bipartisanship, which are not limited to environmental issues, are many. But on the specific issues of sustainability, they include:

- Environmental protection is perceived by many people as indistinguishable from environmental regulation, even though regulation is only one means of protecting the environment. Regulation, in turn, is understood as a restriction on freedom. For those on the political right, environmental protection thus appears opposed to one of their core values—freedom.
- Don Elliott, an attorney and adjunct law professor at Yale, argues that polarization over the environment exists because there is no longer any serious competition between the major parties for the vote of environmentalists. He argues that "between 1970 and the 1990s, there was active competition between the two political parties on environmental issues, which resulted in many environmental accomplishments. The Democrats won the com-

petition. The environment is now their issue and as a result nothing has been accomplished for twenty years."[30] Elliott also suggests, more broadly, that polarization over the environment is just one example of the broader phenomenon of polarization in American politics and the decline of the political moderate.[31]

- The decline in market share over the past several decades of network television (ABC, CBS, NBC), which attempts to provide objective news coverage, and the emergence of advocacy-news organizations (Fox and MSNBC) contribute to the lack of a bipartisan consensus, because advocacy-news organizations accentuate the dividing points described above.

- The 2010 ruling by the Supreme Court in *Citizens United v. Federal Election Commission*[32] opened the door for wealthy individuals, privately held corporations (that do not have to deal publicly with shareholders), and others to anonymously support or oppose favored candidates or causes with very large contributions.[33] In the 2010 mid-term elections immediately after that decision, 36% of outside ads (ads not placed directly by candidates) were funded by secret sources.[34] The infusion of huge amounts of cash by small numbers of donors with special interest agendas (especially those supporting fossil fuels) is likely to make governing for sustainability even harder.

Governance Failures

Sustainable development requires governance that moves steadily and inexorably toward sustainability goals. In many cases, however, governments have failed to do what they need to do for sustainability. These failures occur in many ways.

The inability or unwillingness of governments to exercise greater leadership on sustainability is one such obstacle. As Chapter 5 indicated, leadership is an essential reason for the limited progress that the United States has made to date—at all levels of government. Because sustainable development requires significant changes from business as usual, however, the absence of governmental leadership is also a major obstacle. Political will and statesmanship are needed, but today both are in short supply.

There are other governance failures as well. Different federal agencies often treat the same or similar issues of sustainability in very different ways. At the federal, state, and local levels, fragmentation of government authority over resources and issues is an obstacle to sustainability. In addition, lack of government financial support is both significant and growing.

Lack of Governmental Leadership

The absence of constructive leadership is well illustrated by recent actions concerning U.S. energy policy. And a lack of U.S. domestic leadership at the national level on issues such as climate change has compromised our ability to engage in international leadership.

One shortcoming has been the absence of consistent and constructive federal leadership on energy policy. As previously explained, state and local governments offer mandates and incentives tailored to local jurisdictions.[35] However, there is currently no comprehensive national law or strategy for energy efficiency or renewable energy in the United States. Moreover, in some areas, such as building codes, the federal government does not have direct jurisdiction over setting energy-use standards. Rather, its role is limited to offering suggested model codes and encouraging (often with financial incentives and technical assistance) states to adopt them.[36]

On issues such as climate change, the U.S. government has not been able to provide a leadership role because its own domestic policies have fallen behind international standards. Under the Copenhagen (2009) and Cancun (2010) agreements of the parties to the Framework Convention on Climate Change, both developed and developing countries made voluntary public pledges to reduce their greenhouse gas emissions. The U.S. commitment was the weakest of all developed countries—17% below 2005 levels, or 4% below 1990 levels, by 2020. This represented the greatest level of reduction it could then hope to achieve in Congress. Yet there is a scientific consensus that emissions need to be 20% to 45% below 1990 levels by 2020 in order to avoid dangerous interference with the climate system.

The United States has refused to agree to greenhouse gas limits because, among other reasons, India and China have refused to adhere to such limits. The emissions reductions specified in the Kyoto Protocol apply only to developed countries, and the United States was the only developed country to refuse to be subject to the protocol until Canada recently announced that it is withdrawing. At the December 2011 conference of the parties to the Framework Convention on Climate Change in Durban, South Africa, all countries agreed to negotiate an agreement by no later than 2015 that would apply for the first time to both developed and developing countries. This new agreement, to come into effect and be implemented by 2020, is to cover mitigation, adaptation, finance, technology development and transfer, transparency of action, and capacity building. Despite this accomplishment, strong criticism of the Durban outcome is warranted because it is only an agreement to negotiate something that will not likely become effective until 2020. Because the Kyoto Protocol expires at the end of 2012, there will be no international agreement limiting greenhouse gas emissions for eight years. Canada, Japan, and Russia joined the United States in announcing their unwillingness to accept new emissions reduction targets under an extended Kyoto framework. Because there is a growing scientific consensus that the world is running out of time to prevent rapid or sudden warming, the Durban outcome may be seen as another lost opportunity to put the world on a path that avoids dangerous climate change.

This unwillingness or inability to exercise strong international leadership on climate change has other consequences as well. In discussions of the World Bank's approach to climate change, for example, board members representing countries such as Brazil, India, and China have frequently countered U.S. government positions on the grounds that the U.S. government has no domestic climate legislation in place; nor has it significantly restrained the growth of its own coal-fired power plants. In the U.N. climate negotiations, the United States has only recently started to make financing available to developing countries to enable their transition to sustainability, pledging $1.7 billion in 2010[37]—an amount that falls far short of the $100 billion annually that Secretary of State Hillary Clinton pledged in 2009.[38]

Inconsistency Among Federal Agencies

Federal leadership on issues of transparency and public participation varies from agency to agency. After President Obama issued a memorandum on the Freedom of Information Act creating a "clear presumption" in favor of disclosure,[39] agency responses were mixed. According to a 2010 study of 90 government agencies, 13 agencies changed their practices, 14 agencies performed staff trainings, 11 indicated a change in tone, 35 agencies stated there were no documents evidencing any change in disclosure, and 17 did not even respond to the FOIA request used to collect the data for the study.[40] While the 2011 version of the study shows some improvements, the results generally indicate that without a clear legislative mandate, transparency and participation depend on the extent to which an agency culture supports such values. On environmental issues, EPA and the Department of the Interior provide contrasting examples of agency practices.

EPA has aggressively adopted new administrative and institutional measures for openness. In EPA's strategic plan for 2011-2015, Administrator Lisa Jackson established three core values for EPA: "science, transparency, rule of law."[41] An example of the agency's commitment to transparency is its preparation for publishing information about greenhouse gas emissions online. A 2008 appropriations law requires major contributors to greenhouse gas emissions to publicly report their emissions to EPA, but did not require EPA to publish the data it received.[42] In addition to finalizing a regulation requiring the annual reporting of that data to EPA,[43] the agency has also committed to publishing this information online in 2012 (the first reports were due in September 2011, and this information was not yet published when this book went to press). EPA is anticipating the public's interest in the information, rather than waiting for individual FOIA requests to arrive.[44] EPA also recently added 16 new chemicals to the Toxics Release Inventory.[45]

By contrast, changes at the Department of Interior have been gradual, perhaps in part because of influence by some of the mining, oil and gas, logging, and grazing industries the agency is supposed to regulate. Frank Rusco, director for natural resources and the environment at the U.S. Government Accountability Office (GAO), testified to the House of Representatives that "stakeholders, including industry groups and nongovernmental organizations representing environmental, recreational, and hunting interests, expressed frustration with the transparency and timeliness of the information."[46]

The Department of the Interior's Bureau of Land Management has used its authority to exclude certain oil and gas activities from NEPA review without publicly disclosing such exemptions.[47] The GAO also found that there were not enough opportunities for public participation during the oil and gas leasing process,[48] although the secretary has announced reforms that may address the problem.[49] The Bureau of Ocean Energy Management, Regulation, and Enforcement (formerly the Minerals Management Service) also tends to be opaque with respect "to non-proprietary information regarding leases, volumes of production, production costs, audits, Environmental Impact Statements, and safety assessments."[50] Similar problems of secrecy were reported with respect to the Deepwater Horizon oil spill in 2010.[51]

For the most part, the Securities and Exchange Commission (SEC) has similarly failed to consistently support information disclosure for sustainability, as noted earlier. This agency regulates information aimed at investors, mandating disclosure of information it thinks investors need and supervising the accuracy of information that is disclosed voluntarily. For voluntarily disclosed information, securities regulators have focused their attention only on information traditionally understood to be related to financial performance, and they have tended to be skeptical of attempts to require disclosure of environmental or other social information.[52] SEC officials approach claims based on misstatement or omission of environmental information with the view that such information is beyond their core mission of investor protection and is not important to investors. To date, regulators have been slow to perceive that environmental and social information can be of great financial importance, hence the heavy burden of proof on private parties who claim violations of securities law for inaccurate or incomplete environmental information, and the history of limited enforcement by public officials.

Although companies are required to furnish a great deal of business and financial information, the law is not well developed to require environmental information. There are some limited requirements, but there are so many qualifications that companies have many options for avoiding or minimizing reporting under them. Although there have been substantial calls for the SEC to adopt greater disclosure requirements for environmental performance, in the past the agency has largely resisted.[53] SEC's recent guidance on disclosing information on climate change information and business risks may indicate the beginning of a more aggressive approach.

Governmental Fragmentation and Competition

Fragmented governmental structure is an obstacle to sustainability. In many cases, more than one department is responsible for a particular resource, each with different goals and competing for jurisdiction and funding. The several federal statutes that deal with marine resources—the Clean Water Act, the Coastal Zone Management Act, the Marine Mammal Protection Act, the Endangered Species Act, and the Magnuson-Stevens Fishery Conservation and Management Act—each regulate specific aspects of the problem without connecting the dots overall. The statutes are administered by several different federal agencies (EPA, Department of the Interior, Department of Commerce) in conjunction with a great many states and the varying businesses and nongovernmental organizations they affect. Until all of the governmental and nongovernmental entities that play a role in managing and exploiting marine resources are working toward shared goals, and until the interrelationships between land-based activities and ocean health are fully accepted at a regulatory level, sustainability of marine resources will be difficult, if not impossible, to achieve.

Problems of fragmented authority also apply on the state and local level. For example, potential improvements to a freight rail corridor as part of a public-private partnership with a railroad company may need to be undertaken in multiple states, yet the priority assigned to such a project and available funding may differ substantially among those states. The need for multistate cooperation on freight rail—and passenger rail and highway—projects has led to the creation of multistate corridor coalitions (such as the I-95 Corridor Coalition) to enhance coordination in planning and investments. Similarly, many state climate change action plans lack any mention of partnerships with local governments. Most of these plans simply focus on implementation strategies for state agencies dealing with government-owned buildings, transportation fleets, and other infrastructure and work force issues.

Inadequate Governmental Financial Support

Many sustainability efforts require some level of government support and assistance. This is true for public infrastructure, which is traditionally funded by government. It is also true for a variety of investments that the private sector does not ordinarily make but that are essential to sustainability. While governmental financial support for sustainability has always been challenging, it is even more challenging now.

The budget deficit, which has been worsened by the 2008 recession, is also a significant obstacle to sustainability programs. Government spending exceeded revenues even before 2008, and declining revenue has pushed government deficits and rising federal debt even higher. The United States ran a deficit of 10.7% of gross domestic product in 2010, and it had a public debt of 65.2% of GDP.[54]

While the budget deficit is a financial sustainability issue, and therefore beyond the scope of this book, it affects environmental sustainability in several ways. The urgency over deficit and debt issues—much of it justified—makes it harder to discuss anything else, including job creation or environmental sustainability. The budget deficit is also making it much harder to move the country in a more-sustainable direction because the necessary public funding—for clean energy, more-sustainable transportation infrastructure, spending to boost employment in green jobs—is not available. Recent budget cuts for energy efficiency and renewable energy, for instance, put a whole set of clean energy opportunities further out of reach. Efforts to shrink the federal budget threaten to reverse any progress made toward biodiversity conservation, and states have fewer resources to take on the task. It appears that over the next several years sustainability tools that involve direct or indirect public funding, including tax incentives for clean energy, will be harder to fund, much less fund at adequate levels. The federal agencies with the greatest responsibilities for environmental protection, including EPA, the Department of the Interior, and the Department of Energy, are seeing their budgets cut. It is unlikely that longstanding environmental programs will be funded at adequate levels in coming years. Some of this funding can perhaps be made up for by innovative use of private funding, but not all of it.

Even before the current economic difficulties, the lack of adequate funding created substantial impediments to sustainability. The paucity of research and development (R&D) funds for clean energy technologies—and the inconsistency of this funding from the federal government—cause inefficiency in the use of R&D funds that do exist. Unlike the private sector, the government is interested in technologies that will become mature in a period of three to five years. Thus the overall national public and private R&D effort has achieved considerably less success than it might have. The difficulty in achieving lasting public-private partnerships and close collaborations with other countries in R&D on clean-energy systems has also slowed progress in addressing achievements needed over the long term to achieve sustainability.

Freshwater sustainability provides another funding challenge. All levels of government in the United States have invested hundreds of billions of dollars in water and sewage treatment infrastructure, but future needs are enormous. If we do not maintain our existing infrastructure, health and environmental problems will worsen. EPA's most recent "clean watershed" survey identified funding needs of nearly $300 billion over the next 20 years for wastewater collection and treatment, combined sewer overflow corrections, stormwater management, and the like.[55] EPA's most recent drinking water survey identified another $335 billion in needs for treatment and distribution over the next 20 years.[56] Those two figures represent a combined total of $665 billion over the next 20 years.

Infrastructure funding is increasingly a political as well as a fiscal problem. When President Nixon first vetoed the Clean Water Act in 1972, his reason was not that the law would excessively burden industry; he objected to such significant use of federal tax dollars to subsidize infrastructure that he believed should be funded at the state and local level. The problem with that approach was that upstream communities had little incentive to internalize the costs of pollution they could send downstream across municipal or state boundaries. Congress promptly and overwhelmingly overrode Nixon's veto, sending a message that water pollution was a national rather than a local problem. We now face a heated national political debate over the proper role of the federal government in environmental and many other issues, and over the skyrocketing national debt and how to pay for it. Maintaining federal funding for water supply and sewage treatment infrastructure will be increasingly challenging in this political climate.

Sustainable transportation faces the same hurdles. Budget pressures have forced projects to be delayed or scaled back. In fact, many transit agencies have taken steps backward, raising fares and making major service cuts at a time when transit ridership had been increasing.[57]

Competition for funding is also a frequent obstacle. In public health, funding is predominantly, even overwhelmingly, directed toward communicable diseases,[58] largely stemming from the need to address AIDS and malaria, to the virtual exclusion of preventable environmental diseases such as childhood lead poisoning.[59] While efforts to address AIDS and malaria are obviously crucial, they should not be used as a zero-sum excuse to avoid environmental diseases such as lead poisoning, which debilitates society by detracting from the healthy life of individuals and destroying children's ability to learn. In particular, lead poisoning offers the opportunity for a relatively easy cure based on prevention, since we know its sources and how feasibly to control and eliminate them.

Conclusion

Unsupportive law and governance provide the second major set of obstacles to sustainability. Laws that foster and encourage unsustainable activities are not simply unsupportive; they also are antagonistic. The polarizing nature of environmental issues makes consistent governance for sustainability over time immensely more complicated, as national elections produce something of a whiplash effect between support of, and opposition to, laws and policies to protect the environment. Governance failures, particularly inconsistent policies of different agencies on the same issue, fragmentation of legal authority over particular problems, and inadequate financial support for programs that only the government is positioned to support, are also an obstacle.

These obstacles reinforce those described in Chapter 11 by making it harder to create more-sustainable alternatives that are also reliable. These obstacles also confuse the public about both the urgency of sustainability threats and the opportunities that sustainability provides.

CHAPTER 13

Political Opposition and Growing Influence of Other Countries

Existing habits, lack of urgency about sustainability, and the apparent lack of attractive alternatives provide one set of obstacles. Laws that favor unsustainable development, polarized politics over the environment and sustainability, and failures in governance provide another. A final set of obstacles reinforces the first two, but is quite different: active, direct opposition to sustainability or an explicit unwillingness to pursue more-sustainable laws and policies.

The sluggish economy we have experienced since the financial crisis of 2008 has helped to revive the old argument over the economy versus the environment because it brought strong voices (including the Tea Party movement) for reducing regulatory burdens and government spending. Antiregulatory sentiment runs much deeper than just environmental regulation and investments. But they are certainly among its most prominent targets, and those voices get greater attention than they would if the economy were stronger. In addition to these circumstances, a more active, direct opposition to sustainability comes from economic interests that see themselves as being adversely affected by such measures as the reduction of greenhouse gas emissions. And notwithstanding their international commitments to sustainable development, many nations, especially developing countries, are pursuing rapid economic growth based on conventional development.

Economic Recession and the Budget Deficit

The state of the economy provides much of the context for today's discussion of sustainability. The global economic recession that began in 2008, and which continued as an ongoing economic downturn since then, has impeded the American journey toward sustainability. As discussed at length in Chapter 3, the United States faces high levels of poverty and unemployment and a rising gap between the rich and poor. The current recession has made things worse, although it is certainly not the cause of the growing income gap.

Sustainable forest certification has suffered from the effects of the sagging economy. The Forest Stewardship Council and other certification programs require landowners to recertify their forests as sustainable on a periodic basis. The economic downturn may result in decreased certified acreage. Many acres of forest land were certified in response to paper buyer demands in 2006 and 2007, but the benefit of certification in a down economy is unclear. Lumber prices rose and fell dramatically in 2010, and buyers and sellers are unable to predict the future of the construction sector.[1] While some forest managers see the current environment as an opportunity for forest product producers to reposition themselves as environmentally friendly,[2] uncertainty in both the paper and lumber markets may dissuade many from recertifying because they see no value in it.

And a broader problem has emerged. In recent years the global financial and economic crisis has created a perception that governments must choose between the environment and jobs. After the onset of the global financial crisis, U.S. and international policymakers understandably turned their priorities to job creation and economic growth. While clean energy and environmental protection can help to promote jobs in the United States and abroad, many policymakers feel they must make a choice between jobs and the environment. Shortly after the U.S. Export-Import Bank adopted its carbon policy in 2009 to encourage climate-friendly technologies, for example, the U.S. government ordered the bank to circumvent the policy. In June 2010, the bank decided not to finance exports of machine parts by Wisconsin-based Bucyrus International to a controversial coal-fired power plant in India.[3] Arguing that the decision would result in the loss of more than 1,000 jobs, the Obama Administration ordered the bank to reverse its decision and provide financing.

Political Opposition

Direct and explicit opposition to sustainable development is principally of two kinds. One form is the economic interests that contribute to, and benefit from, unsustainable development; a visible example is industry-funded efforts to sow confusion about climate change. A second form of opposition, or perceived likely opposition, takes some sustainability issues off the table before they have even been raised; this is most especially true of questions concerning population, where even the possibility of a civil public discussion seems to be off the table because opposition from some parts of society is expected to be so fierce.

Political Power of Economic Interests

Even though sustainable development embraces both environmental protection and economic development, a significant part of the business community depends on activities that are not sustainable and shows little interest in moving in more than symbolic ways toward sustainability. Many powerful corporations have an enormous stake in the continuation of current policies and practices. Oil companies, highway construction companies, and other special interests that profit handsomely from the existing system represent a powerful institutional resistance to change.

These vested interests exert substantial political pressure to continue policies that benefit them, opposing many efforts to promote more-sustainable transportation and other sustainable activities. In representative democracies like the United States, special interests exercise significant political power, and it should come as no surprise that they would use it to keep their subsidies and otherwise prevent reforms.[4] While a growing part of the business community is moving in a more-sustainable direction, the economic interests that benefit from unsustainable development continue to exert strong resistance.

Climate change is the poster child for industry-funded disinformation campaigns. A well-organized, well-financed political opposition has been successful in blocking federal action to reduce greenhouse gas emissions for more than three decades. The difficulties at the federal level are illustrated by the failure of the American Clean Energy and Security (ACES) Act of 2009 (also known as the Waxman-Markey Bill) to become law. ACES would have required the formulation of new national mandatory building energy codes; established a national renewable portfolio standard and an energy-efficiency resource standard; dramatically increased subsidies to alternative fuel, energy efficiency, renewable energy, and carbon-sequestration technologies; and established a national cap-and-trade system for carbon emissions. A 2009 report by the Congressional Budget Office indicated that the bill would have been deficit neutral over the next decade.[5] The bill failed to obtain the needed votes in the Senate, primarily because of the language creating a cap-and-trade system for carbon dioxide emissions. Because a carbon dioxide tax was politically impossible, few if any alternatives to cap-and-trade were considered by Congress.

Scientific organizations have been warning the U.S. government about climate change since 1965, when President Lyndon Johnson's Science Advisory Committee issued a report on environmental threats that included a special section on carbon dioxide, "the invisible pollutant." The Committee concluded:

> Through his worldwide industrial civilization, Man is unwittingly conducting a vast geophysical experiment. Within a few generations he is burning the fossil fuels that slowly accumulated in the earth over the past 500 million years.... By the year 2000, the increase in atmospheric CO_2 will be close to 25%. This may be sufficient to produce measurable and perhaps marked changes in the climate, and will almost certainly cause changes in the temperature....[6]

Repeatedly (in 1977, 1979, 2001, 2004, 2010, and 2011), the U.S. National Academy of Sciences has issued warnings about climate change with increasing levels of scientific confidence.[7] All of these reports warned that human-induced climate change was a substantial and growing threat to human health and ecological systems. Nearly half a century since Americans were first warned of the enormous threat of climate change, the U.S. Congress has been unable to control or limit emissions of carbon dioxide and other greenhouse gases because of political opposition, coming mostly from fossil fuel and other business interests who fear their profitability being adversely affected by climate change legislation.

Since the 1980s, fossil fuel interests, electric utilities, and others have spent large amounts of money to convince American citizens that the mainstream scientific view of climate change is unsupportable if not an outright hoax.[8] These interests have effectively funded and publicized the work of a few scientists who sow the seeds of doubt about the reality of climatic change. Against the campaign, the environmental movement was very late in taking up climate change and did a poor job of mobilizing American support. And some Washington-based think tanks funded by oil and coal industries have been effective at undermining what support there was by raising doubts about whether climate change was human-created, whether we can do anything about it, and whether doing something about it will wreck the economy.

This kind of strategic skepticism about climate change science suggests that more and better science is needed—that we need to close the deficit of information. During the George W. Bush Administration, the U.S. government spent billions to improve the science of climate change and to close the information gap. In part because of those efforts, we can be more certain now of the mainstream view that humans cause warming and that the risks are serious. Yet, for a great many people and special interests, any amount of evidence on climate change can be safely ignored.

On October 21, 2010, John Broder of the *New York Times* reported that "the fossil fuel industries have for decades waged a concerted campaign to raise doubts about the science of global warming and to undermine policies devised to address it."[9] According to the article, the fossil fuel industry has "created and lavishly financed institutes to produce anti-global-warming studies, paid for rallies and Web sites to question the science, and generated scores of economic analyses that purport to show that policies to reduce emissions of climate-altering gases will have a devastating effect on jobs and the overall economy."

This effort convinced enough members of the House of Representatives to pass a bill in April 2011 that would prevent EPA from regulating greenhouse gas emissions from power plants, factories, and similar sources.[10] Before passing the bill, the House defeated an amendment declaring that "Congress accepts the scientific findings of the Environmental Protection Agency that climate change is occurring, is caused largely by human activities, and poses significant risks for public health and welfare."[11] Thus, in passing the bill, the House rejected EPA's scientific findings about the seriousness and risks of climate change—findings that tracked and were based on mainstream science.

The bill passed by the House included a statement expressing the "sense of Congress" that "there is established scientific concern over warming of the climate system based upon evidence from observations of increases in global average air and ocean temperatures, widespread melting of snow and ice, and rising global average sea level."[12] Although this language acknowledges "established scientific concern," the House rejected language that said that climate change is "caused largely by human activities, and poses significant risks for public health and welfare." A soft acknowledgement concerning climate change doesn't change the fact that in voting down this amendment, the U.S. House of Representatives, which is not a scientific body, categorically rejected the findings of some of the most respected scientific bodies in the world. This is particularly problematic because one of the key bodies that supplied this scientific information, the National Academy of Sciences, was created by Congress during the Civil War for the purpose of providing Congress with scientific and technological advice. Special-interest money unquestionably has confused scientific and other issues enough to prevent U.S. action to reduce greenhouse gas emissions.

Industry has also acted as an impediment to other regulation. Republicans in Congress have criticized EPA's regulatory efforts and have attempted to curb EPA efforts to regulate sources that contribute to interstate transport of air pollution that injures public health and the environment[13]—even though EPA's calculations show that the benefits of regulation would far outweigh the costs.[14]

Sometimes the constituency supporting business as usual is more subtle. Successful models for sustainable agriculture have been co-opted by industrial agriculture and altered to fit its needs. For example, much of the initial thinking behind organic agriculture has been lost during its recent ascendancy in the marketplace. Early pioneers in the organic farming movement were attempting to think ecologically by developing whole-farm approaches to farm management, rather than seeing each problem in isolation from the rest of the farming system and its neighboring wild ecosystems.[15] To a large degree, that earlier vision has been simplified down to an "input substitution" form of organic agriculture—substituting natural inputs for synthetic inputs. This allows large-scale industrial producers to call themselves organic, but only under an entirely different definition of what the term means.[16]

The U.S. Department of Agriculture has close ties to agribusiness advocates and has embraced the resource-intensive but highly productive industrial model of agriculture. The agency has not been an advocate of alternative farming systems that take a more holistic approach to farming. The land-grant system of universities, with their strong agricultural focus, has also been closely tied to agribusiness and the industrial agriculture system.[17] While the Department of Agriculture's strategic planning is supportive of sustainable agriculture, its vision of sustainable agriculture tends to be based on a modified version of the industrial model.

Many farmers involved in conventional agriculture would like to make changes in the direction of sustainability but are hamstrung by their dependence on large agricultural corporations that control markets for their products. This is particularly true in the case of farmers who raise animals under contract to large companies that can dictate the terms of the contract because of their substantial market power.[18]

For example, the top four beef packing firms controlled 81% of the market in 2001. In pork, the top four packing companies controlled 66% of the market as of 2006. In the chicken industry, the top four broiler producers controlled almost 60% of the market in 2006.[19] In the egg industry, only 180 large companies raise about 95% of the egg-laying hens in the United States, down from about 2,500 companies in 1987.[20] The level of apparent market control is so great that in 2010, the U.S. Department of Justice for the first time combined with the U.S. Department of Agriculture to hold five public hearings on "competition issues affecting the agricultural sector in the 21st century and the appropriate role for antitrust and regulatory enforcement in that industry."[21] Since the workshops concluded in December 2010, the Agriculture and Justice Departments have not done anything to directly address market concentration in agriculture.

Issues That Are off the Table

A more fundamental political objection is the refusal or unwillingness to even discuss or acknowledge certain sustainability issues because of the perception of strong opposition. This is perhaps most true of population growth, which has not been widely discussed as a coherent and discrete policy topic, even in discussions of environmental and resource pressures.

Part of the problem is that immigration reform and abortion—two policies that affect population—are politically controversial, to say the least. The most reliable data indicate that roughly one-third of U.S. annual population growth is due directly to immigration, and the generally higher birth rates of immigrants disproportionately augment the rate of natural increase. For a variety of reasons (including pressure from high-tech and other employers), in 1990, Congress revised the immigration laws for the first time since 1965. The revised law changed the pattern of immigration and allowed greater numbers of legal immigrants with special scientific and technological skills to be admitted.[22] Granting amnesty to illegal aliens has influenced population growth as well. The Immigration and Naturalization Service (INS) reports that approximately 2.7 million immigrants received permanent U.S. residence in the late 1980s and early 1990s under the Immigration Reform and Control Act of 1986, which offered retrospective amnesty.[23] By 2010, however, a new population of 11-13 million illegal aliens had replaced the pre-1986 population of illegal aliens.[24] The INS also concluded that family members moving to the United States to unite with amnestied relatives further contributed to both legal and illegal immigration as well as population growth.

Abortion is even more controversial, and public funding for abortion is accordingly quite restricted. Today, 17 states and the District of Columbia pay for medically necessary abortions for Medicaid recipients, and 32 states will cover Medicaid recipients if the mother's life is in danger or the pregnancy occurred as a result of rape or incest.[25] On the other hand, 46 states permit health care providers to refuse to participate in abortions; 18 states require counseling before an abortion;

24 states require a waiting period between the time of counseling and the abortion procedure; and 36 states require some type of parental involvement for minors.[26]

People of good will can reasonably disagree about the circumstances under which abortion should be available, and how immigration reform should be handled. But that should not prevent us from having an open and intelligent public conversation about the sustainability of our population size. For one thing, we should be able to separate our discussion of the problem from what to do about it. For another, abortion and immigration control are not the only two available approaches to this issue. Other approaches include better education about birth control, reduced per-capita environmental impact through more benign technologies, and lower use of energy, materials, and water.

Continuing Adherence to Development, Not Sustainable Development

Another major obstacle to sustainability, both within the United States and around the world, is the continuation of traditional development even under arrangements where sustainable development has been endorsed, such as within the World Trade Organization (WTO). The agenda of developing countries, which understandably emphasizes poverty reduction and economic growth, is also becoming an obstacle, especially as developing countries grow and become more economically powerful.

The WTO has failed to make significant progress on the linkage among trade, environment, and sustainable development. The reason is straightforward: the current negotiations on agricultural trade have sidelined any serious discussion of sustainability. Trade negotiations occur in "rounds," each of which focuses on a range of issues that are agreed to in advance. The current Doha Round was initiated at a WTO meeting in Doha, Qatar, in 2001. At that meeting, the trade ministers of WTO members reaffirmed their commitment to sustainable development. They agreed that two aims can be, and must be, mutually supportive: (1) upholding and safeguarding an open and nondiscriminatory multilateral trading system and (2) acting for the protection of the environment and the promotion of sustainable development. WTO members agreed to a broad negotiating agenda that includes the relationship between existing WTO rules and specific trade obligations set out in multilateral environmental agreements (such as the Montreal Protocol). They agreed to negotiate a reduction of fisheries subsidies that have encouraged overfishing and depletion of the world's fish stocks. They also agreed that one focus of this round of negotiations would be agricultural trade.

The Doha Round has focused obsessively and inconclusively on agricultural trade. In the area of agricultural subsidies, domestic and export subsidies by developed countries—in particular, by the United States and the European Union—have encouraged overproduction of field crops (primarily corn, cotton, wheat, and soybeans), which in turn has put pressure on natural resources, including water and arable land. If the Doha Round is able to secure meaningful reductions in farm subsidies, important gains for sustainable development in the agriculture sector could be achieved. Moreover, a successful Doha Round could result in duty-free treatment for environmental goods and market openings for environmental service suppliers, two areas where the United States enjoys a comparative advantage. Yet, neither the United States nor any group of nations has been able thus far to secure that result, at least in part because of opposition from agricultural interests in the U.S. and European Union that benefit from the current system.

Sustainability has not been a serious part of the Doha Round discussions, and negotiations on it have moved at a snail's pace. In August 2004, after nearly three years of stalemate, the WTO General Council issued a decision that attempted to break the logjam, outlining a work program for the remainder of the negotiations. Yet the term "sustainable development" could not be found in the General Council's decision. In 2007, in the face of, or perhaps in spite of, the lack of solid progress by the WTO committees charged with the responsibility for advancing sustainable development on the Doha Round agenda, WTO Director-General Pascal Lamy called for greater attention to sustainable development. The broad Doha agenda has also narrowed to three topics: trade in agriculture (the reduction of subsidies and tariffs), market access for industrial goods, and market access for trade in services. Barring a breakthrough in the Doha Round negotiations, the lack of any serious discussion about the interface of trade, environment, and sustainable development over the past several years may mean that no WTO ministerial-level decision will ever be issued on this vitally important subject.

The economic development agenda of developing countries—which are experiencing much larger economic growth rates than are the developed countries—is also a growing challenge to sustainability. To some degree, this is a continuing story. Tensions between the developed and developing worlds surfaced at the 1992 Rio Summit on the Environment and Development. Developing countries argued then, and continue to argue, that environmental and resource constraints will prevent them from growing to the levels of developed countries. The Rio Summit's compromise, sustainable development, was more or less premised on an understanding that developed countries would take the lead on environmental issues while developing countries worked to get their citizens out of poverty. Developing countries would try to make their development more environmentally sustainable, with assistance and support from developed countries, but developing countries' primary interest was economic and social development.

The comparatively slower economic growth of the developed countries over the past two decades has served to give developing countries an even greater voice now than they had then. The economies of developing countries are growing much more rapidly than those of the United States and other developed countries. The global remapping of economic power presents significant opportunities and challenges to U.S. policymakers and companies operating in emerging markets. By 2030, China may become the largest economy in the world. Less than one decade from now, emerging markets—primarily Brazil, China, India, Mexico, and Russia—will compose half of the world's top-10 GDP list.[27] In 2009 and 2010, two Chinese state-owned banks lent more money to developing countries than the World Bank did.[28] During the recent financial crisis, Brazil invested $10 billion in International Monetary Fund bonds, a striking example of the country's transformation from a debtor to creditor.[29] We are currently witnessing what the OECD calls "the new geography of growth"—"a 20-year structural transformation of the global economy in which the world's economic center of gravity has moved towards the East and South."[30] This transformation is often tilted toward conventional development—understandable in view of the vast poverty in developing countries, but a challenge for the goals of sustainability.

The World Bank provides an example of this shifting international influence. The World Bank's board of directors is comprised of the U.S. and other governments, which vote to approve investments and new policies. As the Bank's largest shareholder, the U.S. vote has traditionally wielded the most influence. The U.S. government's voice on the World Bank's board of directors, while still necessary, is not sufficient to promote environmental and social sustainability reforms. In some cases, the U.S. government's realization of the limitations of its power has resulted in uncomfortable confrontations. In 2009, for example, the U.S. Treasury released a guidance note for multilateral development banks on lending for coal-fired power generation. The guidelines recommended that development banks encourage demand for zero- and low-carbon energy sources, and included step-by-step procedures for doing so. Yet nine of the 25 executive directors who vote on Bank activities—representing, among others, the governments of India, China, and Saudi Arabia—wrote a letter to World Bank president Robert Zoellick protesting the U.S. attempt to use its influence to informally change Bank operations.[31] The United States, they pointed out, has not even restricted its own use of coal-fired power plants.

This confrontation at the Bank reflects a global power shift, where large emerging economies have found their voice in international policy debates. The World Bank is learning to respond to four changes in global dynamics:

- *Greater voice of developing countries.* Since 2008 many developing countries that sit on the Bank's board of directors have begun to occasionally take joint positions on complex issues such as climate change. This is in sharp contrast to board discussions of the past several decades, which were dominated by developed countries. As a result, Bank staffers are becoming more responsive to the development priorities of borrowing governments. In 2009, the High Level Commission on Modernization of World Bank Group Governance (the Zedillo Commission) produced a report with five recommendations, the first being to enhance the voice and influence of developing countries through a reallocation of voting power. In 2010, the Bank increased voting power of developing countries by 3.13 percentage points to 47.19% of the total vote.[32] The change in percentage is not enormous, but symbolically represents the more prominent voice of countries such as China, India, and Brazil in Bank deliberations. On several occasions, particularly on issues of climate change and energy, this new balance has already resulted in gridlock on the board. One example is the April 2011 discussions on the World Bank's new energy strategy, when no decision could be reached.

- *Greater competition from emerging economies.* The Bank is facing new competition from banks in emerging economies. As noted above, in 2009 and 2010, the China Export-Import Bank and the China Development Bank lent more to developing countries than the World Bank did. Financial institutions from emerging economies are providing governments with low-cost alternatives to the Bank. This has led to a sense of competition and uncertainty about the Bank's role as a leader in development finance.
- *Aftershocks of the financial crisis.* While many donor governments continue to struggle with their economies, the Bank's own budget has become more restricted. Bank management has reduced the budget for several operations and urged investments to go forward more cheaply and quickly. This has led to pressure to streamline policies as a way to cut costs. As a result, without external pressure from the U.S. government or another champion, Bank management has little incentive to strengthen environmental and social policies.
- *New types of lending.* The Bank has gradually shifted its portfolio away from its traditional lending for specific projects. Now, in the majority of investments, the exact use of funds is not specified ahead of time. Instead, borrowers pool Bank funds with other donors, channel funds to broad government programs, and use funds as general budget support for the treasury. These financing approaches allow the Bank to leverage a wider range of development activities, but their performance is more difficult to track.

Of course, these trends at the World Bank will bring both benefits and challenges for development. On the one hand, Bank management must now seek broader buy-in for reforms, where it once could engage with only a small subset of countries. Early indications are that the Bank has responded to these trends by stepping away (sometimes unintentionally) from environmental and social responsibility in its investments.[33] But it is more difficult for the public to monitor and hold the Bank accountable for its use of public funds.

Similarly, South-South financial flows are changing the nature of development finance and assistance. China is now among the world's five largest investors. Naturally, with $50 billion per year in overseas investment and a particular appetite for natural resources and infrastructure, China draws scrutiny of its operational standards in emerging and frontier countries. In June 2011, Secretary of State Hillary Clinton expressed frustration with these trends, saying:

> We don't want to see a new colonialism in Africa. We want, when people come to Africa and make investments, we want them to do well, but we also want them to do good.

We don't want them to undermine good governance. We don't want them to basically deal with just the top elites and, frankly, too often pay for their concessions or their opportunities to invest.[34]

Nongovernmental organizations (and parts of the U.S. government) are concerned that Chinese companies are investing overseas without strong environmental and social standards, and that these investments will create downward pressure on U.S. investors to lower their standards in order to compete. Others point out that Chinese companies act no differently from other multinational companies and have brought economic benefits to many countries.

The Chinese government is increasingly aware of the importance of managing its reputation overseas. The government has directed state-owned enterprises to begin to prepare corporate social responsibility reports. A recent study reports that 58% of the largest companies in China now prepare such reports, which is at the level of Spain, Italy, and the Netherlands just three years ago, and that 37% of these do some assurance on the accuracy of the reports.[35] In the coming years, we can expect greater attention to this issue. How the U.S. government will engage in this issue remains unclear. Many American companies continue to be involved in controversial international operations, and the United States has few regulations to oversee their environmental and social performance.

The U.S. government also faces obstacles in the extent to which it promotes environmental reforms for the Export Import Bank. The Obama Administration's 2010 decision to reverse the World Bank on financing Bucyrus' sale of machine parts for a controversial coal-fired power plant in India is an example of recent decisions that seem to give priority to job creation over environmental protection. The Overseas Private Investment Corporation has faced similar pressure to circumvent its new carbon policies.

In coming decades, the U.S. government is at risk of losing its global leadership, not only as the premier economic powerhouse but also as a champion of environmental and social sustainability on these particular issues. It is unclear whether an absence of U.S. leadership will lead to a lowering of standards, whether new leaders will emerge, or whether the U.S. will need to become more selective in where it exerts its leverage.

Conclusion

Much of the opposition to sustainability, particularly on the climate change issue, comes from economic interests that profit from unsustainable development. In addition, the rapidly growing economies of the developing world have made those countries more politically influential than they were two decades ago, and they seem more committed to conventional development than to sustainable development. Although many question the strength and sincerity of the U.S. international voice on sustainability, the American voice has nonetheless been stronger and more forceful than that of many other countries, and now is losing influence. The continuing sluggish economy contributes to these problems.

Outright opposition inhibits the development of more-sustainable alternatives and provides a reason for people to feel less urgency about sustainability. Outright opposition contributes to polarized politics about the environment and sustainability, especially at the national level. Outright opposition also means that government will be less supportive, if not itself opposed, to sustainability efforts. The growing influence of less sustainability-minded developing countries, in turn, provides still another excuse for the United States to do little on climate change and other sustainability issues. And so all of the obstacles described in this part of the book reinforce each other.

PART IV

Accelerating Progress, Overcoming Obstacles

CHAPTER 14

More and Better
Sustainability Choices

Achieving sustainability requires much more rapid progress than we have seen to date. Green building, for instance, needs to become the standard, rather than a niche industry. As Rob Watson, the "father" of the LEED green building program, has observed, to accomplish the goals of sustainability, "we need more savings, and faster, in order to reduce total [greenhouse gas] emissions at the necessary scale, scope and speed."[1] What needs to be done to accelerate and intensify more-sustainable development differs depending upon the policy or step in question, the level of government involved, dynamics such as the politics in a particular area, and other variables. Still, some overall themes are apparent that build on the broad patterns of progress described in Part II of this book.

Chapter 8 explained that one reason for the progress we have made over the past two decades is that more-sustainable alternatives are now available, and that employing those alternatives is more attractive for a variety of reasons, including efficiency and profitability. And better choices will likely continue to be developed. The costs of business as usual—the rising costs of raw materials, high and volatile oil prices, more intense congestion, loss of biodiversity, and the effects of climate change—will by themselves make more-sustainable alternatives attractive even if the alternatives themselves do not improve. In addition, as individuals, businesses, and governments make greater use of existing alternatives—such as LEED certification for green buildings, sustainable forest certification, voluntary cleanup programs for contaminated sites, and sustainability education programs—many of these alternatives are likely to move from being thought of as "cutting edge" into widespread use.

This chapter describes four ways to accelerate progress by providing more and better options for sustainability. First, developers of private standards and certification programs need to make these standards and programs more credible to the public. LEED green building standards are a good start, but they are a long way from zero energy standards and have been subject to some valid criticisms. Certification schemes need to be continually improved so the behavior they encourage gets closer and closer to authentic sustainability.

Second, the improved alternatives need to be more broadly available, so that there are more options for virtually any activity.

Third, government and industry need to ensure that a broader array of decision-making tools for sustainability are available and easier to use. Such tools include sustainability-based life-cycle analysis of products, approaches that enable future land-use outcomes to be spatially visualized, and government reporting on the number and kinds of green jobs, to name just a few.

Fourth, governments and the private sector need to find better ways to encourage sustainable human behaviors. Because individuals and families are responsible for a growing share of the nation's environmental footprint, it follows that changes in individual behavior could make a considerable contribution to sustainability.

More Credible and Demanding Standards

As sustainability standards gain wider use, they also draw more critical attention. An instructive example is the U.S. Green Building Council's LEED certification program.

The lesson learned from early experiences in green building is that further progress will depend on continued advancement in reducing waste and increasing efficiency in building design, construction, and operation. Through modeling, experimentation, and collaboration, the building industry succeeded in creating a market for a greener product. This success can be expanded by building on existing strategies and programs, with particular attention given to deficiencies in the early green building programs.

Yet LEED has been cast as an example of an inappropriate private involvement in the formation of regulatory standards.[2] The program has been criticized for failing to account for regional climatic conditions and for designing a merit system that is too easy to game. It must be recognized that LEED was not, at least initially, intended to provide *regulatory* standards; its point system provides builders with a set of options to achieve the points required for the different levels of certification rather than a set of requirements. Thus, adoption of the LEED system by local governments *as* a building code is fraught with problems. These problematic features of LEED standards are leading some people to conclude that all green building standards are meaningless, make no contribution to sustainability, or make no difference in how buildings impact the natural environment.

Early versions of green building standards were clearly not intended to serve as regulatory mandates.[3] The U.S. Green Building Council initially launched LEED as a marketing tool based on self-selection and voluntary compliance; architects and builders who want to portray themselves and their products as green can signify it with the LEED label.[4] However, it has been argued that the LEED standards undercut their potential contribution to sustainability: LEED certification can be achieved without too great a sacrifice. In 2010, University of Maine law professor Sarah Schindler noted that a "substantial problem with the LEED system is that the points are not weighted, and thus developers often go with the cheaper and easier points to achieve LEED certification, neglecting the more expensive yet environmentally beneficial options."[5] Although the LEED rating system has been scrutinized and constantly improved, certification under green building systems is generally awarded based on design and construction, but not after the building has proven its ability to operate efficiently, suggesting that efficiency may not be maintained or improved because "there's no incentive to do better" once a building is granted the green building seal of approval.[6] Finally, national green building schemes, which may be appropriate for requiring sustainable behaviors, have struggled with the dilemma of providing sufficient flexibility to account for regional climatic differences.[7]

Green building has caught on by now, finding its way into almost every con-versation about regulatory governance, markets, and even environmental ethics. To the extent that early iterations of the idea of green building may have been intentionally kept conservative to remain palatable to the public, it is clear that the initial skirmish for acceptance has been won. Code designers for green building can—and should—focus on optimal building performance and the use of market competition to drive up performance while driving down the cost to consumers.

Attention must be given to improving on the existing deficiencies, but made within an understanding of the breadth and varying conditions of green building. One area for obvious improvement is in energy efficiency—even the greenest structure can have its gains in energy efficiency offset by the climatic effects of its location. The regulatory drive toward uniformity can overlook the importance of locational variation. Thus, progress toward sustainability must integrate principles of location into green building principles.

Approximately 40% to 45% of U.S. energy consumption occurs in buildings, and an estimated 28% is used in transportation, presumably due to travel between buildings.[8] It is clear that we need to employ the principles of green building more broadly to encompass the locational impacts of the built environment. Some progress has been made in reducing transportation needs through effective building siting. Through sustainable site credits and LEED-ND—a relatively new certifica-tion program for neighborhood development, not just individual buildings—LEED is credited with reducing vehicle travel.[9]

Collaborative building groups must also raise green building standards to reduce the impact the built environment has on energy, water, habitat, and land. How high can green building standards go? In general, green buildings can reduce energy use by 20% to 50% (compared with conventional counterparts) by attention to design principles and building orientation. However, energy savings beyond 50% typi-cally rely on more innovative strategies in design and technology.[10] One obvious direction for progress is to incorporate passive energy design and strive for net zero energy buildings that can satisfy their own energy needs by reduction in energy needs or on-site production through solar and wind generation.[11] In the Energy Independence and Security Act of 2007, Congress set a goal of zero net energy use for all new commercial buildings by 2030 and for half of existing commercial building stock by 2040, and established the Zero-Net-Energy Commercial Building Initiative in the Department of Energy to achieve those goals.[12] California is now promoting its Zero Net Energy Action Plan for commercial buildings.[13] The plan encourages commercial building owners to "increasingly embrace zero net energy performance (including clean and distributed generation), reaching 100 percent penetration of new starts in 2030."[14] Distributed generation is energy produced at the place where it is consumed (for example, rooftop solar), as opposed to a large power plant many miles away.

Business reporting on activities to address climate change also needs to be improved, based on more demanding reporting standards. For many in the U.S. business community, climate change is a new and still somewhat contested issue, and many business environmental programs are still struggling to catch up. Many firms are now announcing policies and programs, making voluntary disclosure of their efforts and their performance, and promising more. Yet the programs are quite new, with gaps and limits in what is publicly reported. Several prominent U.S. organizations have recently published findings that today there is little depth in disclosure of climate change activities and only limited evidence of a robust corporation strategy dealing with climate change.[15]

Corporate reporting on climate change and its impact on companies involves two kinds of information. The first emphasizes the company's emissions and their impact on climate change. Many companies already report this information voluntarily, and there is every reason to expect it to increase. The second kind of information, about the business risks and business opportunities that climate change presents for a company, is of principal interest to investors. Emissions are important because they may lead to regulatory costs or influence the marketability of products. But the concerns about business risks and business opportunities go further. First, actions to respond to climate change may raise the cost of doing business. An energy-intensive company with limited direct emissions, for example, may find its energy suppliers' costs increasing, and thus its own. Further, even a company that does not emit a great deal itself may produce products that do over their lifetimes, making their products less attractive. For example, production of gas-guzzling automobiles probably does not involve substantially more emissions than production of an efficient mid-sized hybrid sedan, yet the gas-guzzler is much less popular in today's market in large part because of the environmental impact of driving it. The record shows that today company disclosure of the business risks and opportunities presented by climate change is spotty and incomplete; much more and better information will be required to meet the needs of consumers and investors.

Industry groups have undertaken several voluntary programs to improve performance on climate change. As these programs are refined, they should encourage more robust corporate reporting on climate change. One such example is the Carbon Principles, which JP Morgan Chase and other major banking corporations established in 2008 with the assistance of the Environmental Defense Fund and the Natural Resources Defense Council. The Carbon Principles seek to increase energy efficiency and the use of more-sustainable and less carbon-intensive technologies in projects for which the member banks provide financing.[16] Another example is the Climate Principles, which has been adopted by five international financial businesses, with help from the Climate Group (a nonprofit organization), as a guide to help financial and insurance institutions manage climate change risks and performance across a broad section of services and products.[17] A third example is the Climate, Community and Biodiversity (CCB) Standards, developed in 2007 by the Climate, Community and Biodiversity Alliance, a nongovernmental organization. The program offers project certification based on applying many different environmental criteria to land development and management projects.[18] The CCB standards require that projects be analyzed by third-party auditors.[19] While this program is new, as are the Carbon Principles and the Climate Principles, its broad goals, including but going beyond carbon emissions, and its requirement of third-party inspection and certification, offer real promise.

Another area where more credible and demanding standards are needed is in clear and consistent sustainability labeling, including but not limited to eco-labeling (labels that help consumers consider the environmental impact of a product). For all but a handful of products, consumers simply have no idea what is environmentally preferable, much less what is preferable from a sustainability perspective. A labeling system that enables consumers to make more informed decisions would encourage producers to make more-sustainable products and would enable consumers to choose those products with confidence. While the Federal Trade Commission provides regulations through the publication of its *Guides for the Use of Environmental Marketing Claims* (known as the Green Guides), and these are being revised, more and broader controls are needed. The guides were originally adopted in 1992 and substantially amended in 1996 and 1998. The FTC has been considering further amendments since 2007. While the guides themselves are not legally binding, failure to comply with them can result in corrective action enforcement by the FTC under its general enforcement power to prevent unfair or deceptive acts or practices.[20]

To enable informed sustainable consumption, clear eco-labels based on life-cycle assessments and environmental product declarations (EPDs) must be developed. An EPD is a "standardized ... and life-cycle analysis based tool to communicate the environmental performance of a product or system, and is applicable worldwide for all interested companies and organizations."[21] The International Standards Organization (ISO) has developed standards governing environmental labeling. ISO also provides guidelines for EPDs.[22] Certified EPDs must have an independent third-party review and provide standardized methods to enable comparison across product categories. At present, however, few labels meet ISO's criteria for such eco-labels.

Similarly, businesses should consider using concepts of industrial ecology to improve their sustainability and corporate social responsibility (CSR) initiatives, including their public reporting on those initiatives. Although it is commonplace for many of today's largest companies to produce annual reports detailing their CSR initiatives, these reports have been characterized as no more than "aggregate[d] anecdotes about uncoordinated initiatives to demonstrate a company's social sensitivity," and thus disconnected from actual business practices and strategy.[23] To provide more coherence to their CSR initiatives, businesses could examine systematically their various social and environmental impacts and determine how to translate reduced negative impacts (or better still, positive impacts) into improved business performance. Industrial ecology, with its analytical lens focused on a product's life-cycle and its emphasis on interactions between humans and the environment, can assist in this analysis. Analyses grounded in industrial ecology principles can help identify tangible areas for improving environmental perfor- mance.[24] As noted in Chapters 8 and 9, most large companies are now reporting on sustainability or corporate social responsibility, and consistent reporting standards and auditing guidance are being adopted. By applying the principles of industrial ecology, including life-cycle analysis, companies could make these reports a better tool for sustainable business.[25]

Broader Availability of Sustainability Options

Certification programs, management systems, and voluntary cleanup programs for contaminated sites all provide an alternative to business as usual. Because such tools do not exist for all sectors, it is important to design and implement sustain- able alternatives for sectors where those alternatives do not exist. Once again, the construction and renovation of buildings provides an example. While the LEED certification system was designed to change how we construct new buildings, LEED and other programs have not focused as intensely on existing buildings. This is especially problematic because of the large number of existing buildings and because they use too much energy, water, and material.

Encouragingly, there is some evidence that green building programs are having an impact on the existing-building market, primarily through retrofit guidelines offered in LEED and similar programs. This should not be too surprising, given that existing buildings need more repairs as they grow older, and spending on remodeling and retrofits has been on the rise to meet the challenge.[26] McGraw-Hill Construction reports that green building has captured 5% to 9% of the value of the retrofit and renovation market.[27] The trends suggest that the share will grow, perhaps as high as 20% to 30% by 2014.[28] Given the evidence of the benefits of green buildings, it should not be surprising to find that building owners and ten- ants are likely to do more green retrofit projects. It also should not be surprising that recent economic circumstances have motivated the inclusion of energy- and water-efficient practices in renovation projects, including energy-efficient or natural lighting, energy-efficient mechanical and electrical systems, and efficient water delivery systems.[29]

Because of the limited progress made on upgrading existing homes, they remain both a problem and a source of potential progress. In general, significant cumulative efficiencies can be accomplished by minor renovations, such as installing energy-saving lighting fixtures and upgrading mechanical and electrical systems. At present, the retrofit market is estimated to be between $2.1 billion and $3.7 billion. McGraw-Hill Construction predicts that the retrofit market will grow to between $10.1 billion and $15.1 billion by 2014.[30]

The U.S. Department of Energy's Better Buildings Initiative, which was described in Chapter 10, is intended to create a national market for more energy-efficient upgrades and retrofits. The U.S. Green Building Council estimates that retrofitting commercial and multifamily buildings could create 114,000 new jobs and save businesses more than $1.4 billion annually.[31] Whether or not LEED certification is further expanded into this area, the development of an active market for upgrades and renovations would provide more-sustainable alternatives where such alternatives are currently limited.

Green building investments, particularly for retrofits, also need to benefit low-income and affordable housing. Efforts to encourage green building in affordable housing face practical dilemmas. Although the cost of making modest upgrades is relatively small, the upfront expense of retrofitting an existing building may be too great.[32] Landlords face the problem of split-incentives because "a building owner that pays a higher cost for an energy-efficient boiler may not see the savings, which instead accrue to the tenant (if the tenant pays the utility bills). As a result, the building owner may not want to invest in higher cost green building practices."[33] The scope of this problem is far-reaching: approximately 1.2 million households live in public housing units,[34] and more than 35 million live in rental units.[35] The benefits of green building will not be distributed across all social strata unless concerted efforts are made to ensure distribution of green building benefits.

Some efforts have been made to include low-income and affordable housing within the ambit of green building. A majority of states and some federal agencies have endorsed some form of sustainability standard for subsidized housing programs, and some funding sources for affordable housing include green building requirements. Private involvement includes pioneering organizations such as Enterprise Community Partners, which has invested or secured investments in excess of $9 billion in affordable housing programs, and which has had an enormous influence on applying green building principles to affordable housing through its Green Communities Program.[36] However, despite positive steps, these efforts may provide limited results due to their reliance on voluntary measures.

Higher education could also benefit from broader and more rigorous sustainability requirements. Major funders, including federal and state agencies as well as foundations, could play a critical role by requiring grantees to meet certain standards of sustainability and by allocating a portion of their grants to sustainability-related expenses. To reach those institutions that are not yet engaged in sustainability and to accelerate sustainability efforts at others, accreditation agencies could incorporate sustainability into their school evaluations. Finally, the Association for the Advancement of Sustainability in Higher Education has worked with universities and colleges to create the Sustainability Tracking, Assessment & Rating System™ (STARS) framework.[37] Broader acceptance of this framework would likely accelerate college and university sustainability efforts, and it would provide another way to compare efforts among institutions.

Finally, sustainable products and services need to be competitively priced. Making sustainable products universally available and competitive at all price points would go a long way toward increasing the attractiveness of more-sustainable options. To some degree, this is already happening because of better economies of scale due to greater demand and product improvements. The initial investment in design and construction for LEED certification has fallen to a point where it is now at or near the cost of conventional building design and construction. Similarly, the price of solar photovoltaic energy is continuing to fall; some observers believe it will be competitive with fossil fuels within five years.[38]

Price reductions need to occur more broadly, across all the products and services that support sustainability. Government can help; a variety of state and federal laws have had the effect of reducing the price of energy efficiency and renewable energy by providing tax credits or price rebates. But ultimately the private sector must make more competitively priced and sustainable goods and services.

Better Decisionmaking Tools

Because sustainability requires the integration of social, environmental, and economic aspects of decisionmaking, it can make decisions harder than they might otherwise be. It is thus essential for government, business and industry, and nongovernmental organizations to develop, refine, and use tools that enable integrated decisionmaking to be done as simply and effectively as possible.

The federal government especially needs to finalize the creation of tools that are under development. Key instruments for assessing progress at the national level—such as EPA's use of sustainability indicators and the integration of green jobs data into the statistical reporting done by the Bureau of Labor Statistics—will make it easier to assess our progress on sustainability, to understand what the next steps should be, and to make better (more-sustainable) decisions.

Because sustainability is directed toward the future, we also need tools that enable us to understand our current course and anticipate future events. As the financial crisis, Deep Water Horizon explosion in the Gulf of Mexico, and 2011 Japanese earthquake starkly demonstrate, existing methods of anticipating crises are inadequate. It is imperative to expand our thinking and revisit assessment methods for anticipating such "Black Swan" events[39]—low-probability, high-risk events—and responding to them. One tool is scenario analysis. A scenario is not a prediction; it is instead "a plausible story about how the future might unfold from current conditions" based on specified assumptions about "biophysical processes, human behavior, policy, and institutions."[40]

Government and industry should work together to develop and use tools that address all aspects of sustainability in the production of goods, not just some aspects. Sustainable production has focused primarily on improving environmental impacts through the use of tools like life-cycle analysis, which focuses on the environment. Societal impacts are somewhat addressed by product safety, health effects, and worker safety regulations, but environmental justice and community impacts are not part of the normal equation for sustainable production. In addition, life-cycle economic costs and the impacts on the nation's economy from sustainable materials production are rarely evaluated alongside effects on environment and society. To push toward truly sustainable production, a holistic analysis of the sustainability of products and materials should be undertaken.

Other tools and programs would clear away obstacles to the making of more-sustainable decisions. Brownfields redevelopment, which involves not only cleanup but also redevelopment of the site, provides an example. Assistance with securing grant funding and other professional help can be an important factor in the success of brownfields redevelopment. Matching developers with opportunities to remediate and reuse brownfields requires careful planning, through marketing approaches and the designation of local officials as contact points to navigate complex approval processes.[41] Developers can find the brownfields redevelopment process to be overly complex.

Another challenge is developing and using tools to make sustainability-oriented programs work together more effectively. The sustainability of brownfields redevelopment depends to a great extent on the type of new development that is employed on a previously contaminated site. While there has been much progress in this area at brownfields sites, "there is still room and need for further experimentation and implementation of sustainable and green methodologies."[42] That conclusion also applies to the present relationship between green technology and brownfields redevelopment: much has been accomplished, but there are still considerable opportunities.

For colleges and universities—and likely other sectors as well—it would be helpful to have a playbook that offers a methodology for organizational change that demystifies the implementation of sustainability at an organizational level. The "newbies" entering the sustainability market of ideas and actions can't be left to make it up as they go along. They need a system that they can follow that will present a credible, understandable, and plausible path towards sustainability. Such a system will assure those entities that what they need to do is attainable. This is one of the lessons from the American College & University Presidents' Climate Commitment, which sets out a specific path for colleges and universities to reduce their climate footprint.

More Use of Behavioral Tools

New tools and technology can only bring us part of the way to a more-sustainable future. In the final analysis, the most important target for an intensified sustainability effort is our own behavior. If individuals are presented with attractive sustainable options, they are likely to choose them. And individuals can be motivated to choose more-sustainable options with the right kind of noncoercive messages, as seen in the effectiveness of the national anti-smoking effort discussed in Chapter 10. Yet for decades, U.S. government agencies have underinvested in the kind of social science research that enables us to understand human motivation and behavior. When budget cuts occur, social science programs and social scientists are the first to go.

Appeals to individuals and individual behavior for environmental purposes are not entirely new. Perhaps the strongest statement about the role of individuals is contained in the National Environmental Policy Act of 1969, where "Congress recognizes . . . that each person has a responsibility to contribute to the preservation and enhancement of the environment."[43] In addition to anti-smoking laws and various tax credits and deductions for energy efficiency and energy conservation, other laws encouraging more-sustainable human behavior include anti-litter laws and recycling laws.

In 2010, the government of the United Kingdom established a cabinet-level office, the Behavioral Insight Team, or so-called Nudge Unit, to explore ways to help citizens make better choices—such as using less household energy and eating healthier—and improving consumer choices through information sharing.[44] As one of the largest users of energy and natural resources, the United States needs to get serious about social science and educational strategies to enable more-sustainable choices by making sustainable behavior the default, or easy, choice. The challenge to public policy becomes how to develop institutions that "bring out the best in humans."[45]

The magnitude of the climate change challenge, for example, is such that all available resources are needed to address it. Put somewhat differently, if individual effort and participation are harnessed, the U.S. response to climate change will be more effective, and the pace of emissions reductions faster, than it would otherwise be.[46]

Individual behaviors are a significant contribution to U.S. greenhouse gas emissions. Household energy use is directly responsible for 38% of U.S. carbon dioxide emissions, and 8% of global emissions.[47] A major challenge in any effort to change that behavior is that consumers, and American consumers in particular, seem to equate high consumption with a high standard of living. Through much of American history, the case for living a simpler life has been heeded only by the few.[48] For most of us, the "simple life" is more appealing in theory than in practice.

There is a sizeable body of social science research on the effectiveness of various energy conservation and energy efficiency policies adopted in the 1970s and 1980s, when a variety of laws were adopted or amended to reduce energy use.[49] Much of this research indicates that these laws were often less effective than anticipated.[50] Yet, experience with these laws helped us learn a great deal about why they did not work and how laws and policies to engage individuals can be made more effective.[51] For instance, if issues are reframed so that the sustainable option is presented as the choice most people exercise, consumers are more likely to engage in sustainable behaviors. Knowledge that one's peers are doing a particular thing (recycling, using less energy) is often more effective than abstract appeals to conscience or protecting the environment.[52]

While information is important, information by itself is not enough. The focus of any effort should not simply be to provide information but to change behavior.[53] Individual behavior can be changed by increasing the benefits and reducing the obstacles of acting in a particular way, and competing behaviors can be changed by decreasing the benefits of those behaviors and increasing the obstacles.[54] Household collection of recyclables, for instance, is encouraged not just by the ready availability of good information, but also by the actual availability of convenient opportunities to recycle, such as curbside collection and the ability to mix or commingle different types of material (such as cans and bottles) in the same collection container.[55] Similarly, financial and other incentives can be used to encourage certain behaviors (such as net metering programs that enable those who install solar collectors or wind turbines to sell their extra electricity to the grid), discourage others (through higher fees), or both.[56]

Appeals to values or norms are also key to changing behavior. In the case of climate change, a variety of norms are capable of motivating appropriate individual behavior. One is self-interest. Perhaps the most obvious and immediate appeal to self-interest is to reduce energy costs through efficiency or conservation. The economic payback from efficiency and conservation, of course, varies with the type of technology being employed, but the potential for such a payback provides an incentive for its use.

Another value or norm is concern for the impact of climate change on other humans and on all life. Still another is citizenship, particularly in times of national emergency or obvious need. Climate change can also implicate deeply held moral, ethical, and even religious views. Such motivations could powerfully and positively influence any national effort if handled respectfully and in a nonsectarian manner. Social justice is an important consideration, particularly because climate change caused primarily by developed countries adversely affects people living in developing countries.

The most successful sustainability programs also recognize that there are many obstacles to behavioral change: money, available technology, convenience, and distrust of the information being provided, to name just a few. Successful programs address all of these obstacles by combining quality information, financial incentives, and convenient choices.[57] They are also based on an understanding of behavior from the individual's perspective, as well as recognition of the existence of constraining factors beyond the individual's control (such as available technology). Finally, these programs are subject to monitoring, evaluation, and adjustment to improve their effectiveness.[58]

According to a 2009 study, individual actions could reduce overall household emissions by one-fifth, an amount equal to 7.4% of U.S. carbon dioxide emissions, over the next 10 years.[59] The study assumed no changes in existing regulation or technology. Among the most effective actions for reducing energy use and carbon dioxide emissions are the use of a more fuel-efficient vehicle; home weatherization (including sealing leaks and installing insulation); use of more-efficient appliances; car pooling; and more efficient heating, ventilation, and air conditioning equipment. But how could this be made to happen? Using what has already been learned about changing human behavior, the authors of the study suggest that a combination of approaches is better than any single method. Mass-media messaging—through advertising, for example—is one necessary tool. Another is daily or continuous information about a household's energy use (such as smart grid technology that provides real-time information about electricity consumption and price), and thus the effect of energy efficiency or conservation actions. Communication about energy savings through the social networks of individuals is also useful. A multifaceted approach using all of these tools would be more effective than any one of them alone. As the authors of this study also acknowledge, it is possible to obtain even greater reductions if households respond more positively than projected, if technology improves, or if there are legal changes that provide greater incentives for certain behaviors.

Conclusion

The progress we have made in the last two decades has been driven in great part by the growing availability and attractiveness of more-sustainable alternatives to business as usual. It follows that the transition to sustainability can be accelerated by increasing the number and variety of those alternatives and by making them even more attractive. These standards need to be made continually more rigorous, and need to apply to more and more activities. In addition, there need to be more and better decisionmaking tools to enable streamlined and accurate integration of social, economic, and environmental factors in ways that enable better decisions. Finally, we need to make more effective use of behavioral tools to motivate individuals to make more-sustainable decisions.

CHAPTER 15

Law for Sustainability

As we have seen, the law of sustainability encompasses a wide variety of laws. It includes, but is emphatically not limited to, environmental regulation. Sustainability does not always require more law; in many cases, we need to repeal or modify existing laws that create barriers to sustainability. Nor does sustainability categorically require bigger government; it requires better governance, creating an enabling framework in which the many innovations required for sustainability can grow and flourish.

Sustainability does not now have an adequate legal foundation, even though many environmental and natural resources laws do exist. If we are to make significant progress toward a sustainable society, much less achieve sustainability, we will need to develop and implement laws and legal institutions that do not now exist, or that exist in a much different form.

A great many new or modified laws and policies, as well as changes in governance, are needed to accelerate the transition to sustainability. The first part of this chapter takes a thematic approach to analyzing the needed changes in law and governance. Instead of recommending what should be done in a particular sector, the chapter recommends broad approaches to law and governance that span all sectors. (Readers interested in sector-specific recommendations should consult a companion volume, *Agenda for a Sustainable America*.) We focus here on approaches to governance and lawmaking that can and should be applied across the great variety of sustainability issues that the nation confronts. The question in each case is what legal instruments or tools—or, more precisely, what combination of legal instruments and tools—are most capable of accelerating the transition to sustainability. While regulation is one approach, it is only one among many.

The second part of the chapter examines a variety of laws and policies that should be considered to address climate change. Whatever combination of laws is ultimately employed, the country needs to adopt and implement legislation that corresponds to the scale and seriousness of climate change. Climate change is arguably the most serious long-term danger we face because it affects or will affect virtually every sector of the American economy; it also presents some of the greatest opportunities.

From Environmental Law to the Law of Sustainability

At all levels of government—federal, state, and local—we need to reshape law so that it supports and drives sustainability. The legal transformation is not simply about environmental regulation, although it includes such laws. Rather, it is about all laws that may affect sustainability, including tax law, securities law, and even property law. Governments need to establish sustainability objectives for particular resources and problems and to establish short- and long-term goals and strategies for achieving those objectives. Economic development and job creation laws need to be adopted or refocused, and scaled up, to achieve environmental sustainability. Laws that support unsustainable development need to be modified or repealed. Legal incentives for sustainability need to be greatly expanded. Where state and local programs that move toward sustainability are working reasonably well, those programs need to be further improved, and their use should be extended to other governments. And in some cases, voluntary programs should be converted into mandatory programs to accelerate the transition to sustainability.

Establish Sustainability Objectives for Specific Resources

A holistic approach to particular resources—one that draws in all involved parties, both public and private, and adopts varied approaches—rather than the fragmented treatment they often are now given, is necessary for advancing sustainability. Three areas—materials consumption, biodiversity conservation, and protection of oceans and estuaries—can illustrate such a holistic approach. More generally, the establishment of targets and timetables to achieve specific goals by specific dates is a useful way of achieving the step-by-step progress that is needed.

A range of approaches could help the United States reduce materials consumption. First, we must reduce materials use through conscious individual decisions to limit personal consumption. The composition of manufactured products can be changed to incorporate more abundant materials, and they can be designed with end-of-life recycling in mind. Government and the private sector should work with upstream production processes to encourage the use of renewable materials with low environmental impacts, and incorporate efforts to reduce water and energy use all along the production supply chain. Finally, government needs to work with manufacturers and retailers so that products are reclaimed at the end of the life-cycle.[1] All of these steps would have a major impact on materials and resource sustainability in the United States. The United States addresses this issue now in bits and pieces—through state recycling laws, for example—but does not address materials consumption comprehensively.

For biodiversity, a starting point would be U.S. ratification of the Convention on Biological Diversity. The first objective of the convention is to encourage national biodiversity conservation at large scales. Ratification of the convention, by itself, will not advance biodiversity conservation in the United States because the treaty is weak and the United States meets its minimal standards. However, ratification would establish biodiversity conservation as a legal objective in the United States and stimulate the development of a comprehensive national biodiversity strategy because a ratified treaty is part of U.S. law. Also, ratification would help to focus attention on effective compliance with the convention's objectives.

At the federal level, an important step for accelerating biodiversity conservation would be congressional authorization and funding of a national commission on biodiversity conservation, with three assigned tasks. First, the commission should develop measurements and indices to track the status of biodiversity and evaluate the effectiveness of conservation programs. Second, it should review the existing legal mandates of the major federal land management and regulatory agencies to determine how well they promote biodiversity conservation and modify their mandates to the maximum extent possible consistent with due process and the sustainable use of natural resources. Third, the commission should assess the role of private land acquisition in biodiversity conservation.

The United States needs a national biological survey, similar to the U.S. Geological Survey, to inventory the nation's biodiversity heritage and to provide scientific support for the establishment of biodiversity indices and conservation performance standards. The most ambitious and closest effort to a biodiversity inventory is the 2008 Heinz Center survey of the state of our ecosystems.[2] The creation of a national biological survey should be complemented by redirecting the support provided to federal land grant universities to give biodiversity conservation research and support parity with agricultural research and support.

The challenge is similar for oceans and estuaries. As both the Pew Oceans Commission and the U.S. Commission on Ocean Policy pointed out in 2003 and 2004, respectively, authority over ocean management and regulation is fragmented between federal, state, and local governments and among multiple agencies and departments at the state and federal levels.[3] There is no overarching set of priorities for ocean management at the federal level, leaving agencies to pursue their own, often conflicting, missions. The United States must enact a national oceans act, or the equivalent, that establishes a goal of sustainability in the oceans as a national priority and to which all existing marine priorities are subordinate.

In addition to coherent and resourcewide sustainability objectives, it is also important to shape legal strategies and short-term goals that move in a more-sustainable direction. Many of the hardest problems we face at the national and international level will likely require at least a generation, if not much longer, to address with even a modicum of success. Step-by-step incremental progress over a long period will thus be needed to reach sustainability. Targets and timetables—measurable goals that are to be achieved by specific dates—are useful approaches for guiding this kind of effort. The establishment of targets and timetables identifies priorities, forces decisionmakers to clarify objectives, demonstrates commitment to sustainable development and thus gives it greater credibility, gives operational meaning to sustainable development, and clarifies the role of law. For difficult long-term objectives, the establishment of short-term or interim goals can also provide benchmarks of progress.

Two relatively common examples of such targets and timetables occur in state recycling and renewable energy portfolio standards laws. States have often set goals for increasing the recycling rate or the tonnage of materials recovered to a specified percentage or amount by a particular year. Laws mandating renewable energy portfolio standards require electric-generating companies to increase the percentage of electricity that comes from renewable sources to a specified percentage by a particular year. This approach of moving incrementally over a period of years could be applied more broadly. Indeed, a number of bills have proposed incremental national increases in renewable energy, energy efficiency, and clean energy. Congress could also consider requiring incremental increases over time in the use of certified environmental management systems by publicly traded corporations.

What such programs do less frequently, however, is continue the progress after the initial goal has been accomplished. If we were truly moving toward sustainability, lawmakers might say in advance that interim targets are meant ultimately to achieve long-term objectives such as zero waste or energy that is 100% non-fossil fuel. Success in meeting the first goal would lead automatically to a second one kicking in, a more ambitious goal to be achieved by a later date. Success in meeting the second goal would lead to a third target and timetable, and so on, until the long-term objective is fully met. Long-term objectives, of the kind that were contained in the Waxman-Markey climate change bill passed by the House of Representatives in 2010, which requires a steady reduction in greenhouse gas emissions over 40 years, represent a similar approach.

Scale Up Sustainable Economic Development and Job Creation

The single approach that perhaps most effectively demonstrates the distinctiveness of sustainability is sustainable economic development and accompanying job creation. No other approach says as clearly that sustainability is about environmental protection, economic development, and social well-being. No other approach so directly counters claims that environmental protection necessarily comes at the expense of the economy and jobs.

Bringing economic development law into the service of sustainability could help to bridge the ideological chasm in the United States on environmental policy. Because environmental regulation is the traditional vehicle for environmental protection, the policy debate tends to focus on whether we need more or less regulation. When we also employ economic development tools on behalf of environmental protection, we may find that the path to a sustainable society has broader public support. To be sure, focusing on economic development is fraught with risks. Most obviously, sustainable economic development is easily confused with what is known as *sustainable growth*—a goal of continued increases in gross domestic product or profits that has nothing to do with environmental protection.

We are referring instead to *environmentally sustainable economic development*, which maintains and improves public health, creates employment, saves money, and fosters intergenerational equity.

This issue has both international and domestic aspects. The United States needs to encourage and support environmentally sustainable economic development in developing countries through the World Trade Organization (WTO). Many economists and commentators posit that people will demand higher environmental standards as development occurs, that is, as they become wealthier. If that assumption is correct, efforts to improve the welfare of the world's poor need to be redoubled at the WTO by pushing for increased trade and development, which will ultimately lead to better use of scarce resources. Even if that assumption is not correct, we need to encourage and support more-sustainable alternatives to conventional development in developing countries. To that end, a successful completion of the Doha Round (which was discussed in Chapter 13)—with reduced developed-country agriculture subsidies and other sustainability features—is imperative. Skeptics may counter that this is unrealistic. But what are the alternatives, and are the critics' alternatives any more realistic? Critics often push for trade sanctions rather than trade promotion as a response to a country's failure to observe environmental and sustainable development norms. However, unilateralism is a two-way street. Trade barriers generally make for poor environmental policy, and the effectiveness of unilateral import bans as a means for achieving certain environmental ends is unproven. Trade sanctions may have as their primary aim trade protectionism, not environmental protection.

Within the United States, as this book has shown, there is already significant movement in the direction of sustainable economic development and job creation. In Chapter 4, we saw a shift toward sustainable economic development for the built environment—transportation, brownfields redevelopment, land use, and green building. In Chapters 3 and 5, we saw how local and state governments, as well as the federal government, are fostering economic development and job creation through the use of laws supporting renewable energy and energy efficiency, and through laws and policies supporting more-sustainable community development. Chapter 9 explored the many ways that all levels of government have been using law to require more-sustainable activities (such as recycling), to permit more-sustainable activities (such as the production of organic food), and to remove impediments to sustainable economic development. The challenge ahead is to scale up and accelerate these efforts.

While more-sustainable economic development brings the promise of green jobs, there has been some controversy about how many green jobs could actually be made available. Estimates vary, but there is considerable evidence that sustainable economic development will create more jobs than business as usual. In part, this is due to growing demand. The Brookings Institution study on green jobs described in Chapter 3 pointed out that "during the middle of the recession—from 2008 to

2009—the clean economy grew faster than the rest of the economy, expanding at a rate of 8.3 percent."[4] A study commissioned by the U.S. Conference of Mayors and the Mayors Climate Protection Center in 2008 attempted to project the potential for green jobs in the U.S. economy over a 30-year period. Based on certain assumptions—federal mandates for increases in renewable power generation, retrofitting existing residential and commercial building stock, and increased use of alternative transportation fuels—the study described a potential for 4.2 million new jobs in the U.S. economy. If the potential growth were to follow the growth pattern outlined in the Brookings Institution report, the clean economy sector would continue to be the fastest growing segment of the U.S. economy over the next several decades, and dramatically increase its share of total employment.[5]

All other things being equal, more-sustainable economic development also appears to create more jobs than conventional economic development. Recycling systems can create twice as many jobs as landfills, according to researchers at the Department of Agricultural and Resource Economics at the University of California in Berkeley.[6] Recycling creates more jobs because once material has been placed in the landfill, it loses all of its value. Reuse and recycling systems, on the other hand, provide a range of opportunities to create value and jobs. Similarly, energy efficiency creates 19 to 20 jobs for construction and services (the sectors where energy efficiency jobs are concentrated) for every million dollars invested, compared with an average of about 10 jobs per million dollars invested in the traditional energy sector.[7]

Green jobs, or those jobs requiring a specific green knowledge or skill, also tend to be higher paying than the average job—13% more, according to the Brookings Institution.[8] And jobs in the green economy tend to be more accessible to the working class; a high school education is the extent of educational attainment for almost half of all workers in the green economy, whereas 37% of workers have a high school diploma or less in the rest of the economy. In addition, the skills required for most green jobs are, in fact, traditional skills (a green building laborer still needs to know how to swing a hammer and use a level).[9] This is why embedding green skill training into traditional occupational educational programs is a high leverage and sustainable opportunity. Because businesses are increasingly looking at sustainability as a key to remaining competitive,[10] green skills are increasingly a required skill set across a range of industries and occupations. For example, already 88% of all architects say they have now had some form of training in sustainable design.[11]

But, just as with any career path, all credentials in green economy industries are not created equal. Therefore, efforts need to be made to support high-quality, industry-recognized credentials linked to emerging national standards and best practices for applying environmental technologies. Many have argued that the green economy has provided a good focal point for emphasizing the broader need for a national framework for validating credentials so they meet the needs of employers and support successful career advancement of workers.[12] Programs that are linking to these standards and also connecting into existing occupational training systems, such as skilled trade apprenticeship programs, are creating sustainable career paths for the wave of workers integrating into the green economy. The federal government and many labor and industry organizations have begun to do so for renewable power, energy efficiency, and other career pathways.[13] While green industry will for some be a dedicated and unique new career path, for the majority of workers the development of sustainability knowledge and application of environmental technology skills is a new, essential competency that needs to be incorporated as part of traditional career pathways.

All levels of government thus need to make sustainability a greater part of their economic development and job creation effort. For sustainable economic development and job creation to be achieved, there needs to be clear market demand for energy savings, cleaner and more environmentally responsible choices, locally produced goods, and the building of infrastructure for cleaner air, water, and food—resulting in an increase in jobs dedicated to a more-sustainable way of life. While this is already occurring to some degree, we have a long way to go. There also needs to be an increase in the supply of more-sustainable technologies, goods, and services.

Government policy will need to continue to play a key role in enabling the market to do what it does best—optimize supply and demand for clean technologies, goods, and services. At a time when other countries are moving fast to market more-sustainable goods and services, and growing more jobs by doing so, the United States is significantly at risk of falling behind the opportunity to meet growing world demand for more-sustainable goods and services. The federal government plainly has a role to play on climate change as well as other sustainability issues. But in the face of inaction at the federal level, regional, state, and local efforts should continue and expand.

What can government do to promote sustainable economic development and job creation? As a starting point, a green development and jobs strategy should span industries, occupations, skill levels, and regions. Second, it should also rely on sustainability-related innovation and new market opportunities as the major drivers for diverse economic growth. Third, it needs to focus on the knowledge and skills of the workers. Human capital has been the primary building block for U.S. economic success in the industrial era, and it will be even more critical to gaining a competitive edge in the 21st century.

With all of this in mind, it is possible to describe a policy framework to support sustainable economic development and green job creation:

Enable It. Federal, state, and local programs and policies need to nurture public demand for more-sustainable goods and services, making sustainability-related technologies and community-based markets more accessible to local entrepreneurs. For example, government laws, regulations, ordinances, procurement guidelines, and even staff manuals need to ensure the use of sustainable technologies and practices in public utilities and infrastructure, including the electric grid, schools, hospitals, fueling stations, and parking lots. Adoption of more-sustainable laws and policies is essential to creating and maintaining green jobs.

Build It. Provide support and incentives for high-growth and emerging sustainability-driven technologies and practices. Subsidies can be provided for those who commute by means of mass transit, procurement policies can encourage local food sourcing, and municipal building removal contracts can encourage deconstruction practices. Deconstruction is the most commonly used approach for recycling at a building demolition site. It involves salvaging as much as possible—plumbing fixtures, windows and window frames, doors and door frames, hardwood floors, appliances, and anything else of value—before a building is completely demolished. Three emerging industries—building deconstruction, energy efficiency, and local food production—have the potential to create up to 300,000 direct jobs.[14]

Support It. Level the playing field so local entrepreneurs and businesses can compete for business and satisfy demand for sustainable products and services. Examples include lowering small-business loan requirements and fees and supporting local construction firms to develop community wind demonstration projects.

Supply It. Work with employers, educational partners, and community-based organizations to ensure that education and training programs provide job seekers with the skills and credentials needed for emerging employment opportunities in sustainable industry. This includes providing alternative forms of employment and training. Examples include establishing job training centers and apprenticeship programs, and underwriting social enterprises that provide transitional jobs for high-risk workers doing energy retrofit and deconstruction work. These jobs can create pathways to careers for lower-skilled residents with disadvantaged backgrounds.

Sustain It. Efforts related to more-sustainable businesses and industry can have a greater and longer term impact when economic, community, and workforce development stakeholders are aligned and working with an integrated work plan towards a common set of goals. This kind of collective impact approach[15] not only helps public resources go further; it can also reduce risk and provide a clear signal to the private market that helps attract private sector investment. One example is the creation of publicly underwritten, private-sector loan programs that finance investments in more-sustainable technologies (such as building energy upgrades, solar installations on schools, and community-member-owned wind energy projects). Another is development of regional initiatives focused on growing a more-sustainable industry and supporting the integration of economic developers, education and workforce training providers, and community-based organizations so that employers in that region have an adequate supply of local workers with the specific skills they need, and so local residents have clear educational pathways to careers in those sustainable industries.[16]

While these steps are not simple or easy, they are a proven path to economic development and workforce preparation that contributes to a sustainable and resilient future—an economy that saves money, promotes health and equity, and incentivizes profit-making. Federal and state agencies can play an integral role in these efforts through policies and investments that support public-private partnerships between governments, businesses, philanthropies, and community-based organizations. With the right actors and policies in place, a great many new jobs could be created within two to three years.

Repeal or Modify Laws Supporting Unsustainable Development

Changes in the direction of sustainability have occurred most commonly when the total net benefits of a more-sustainable approach are demonstrated to be greater than an unsustainable alternative. Laws that support unsustainable development, including laws that authorize direct and indirect subsidies, impede the widespread use of more-sustainable alternatives by reducing the comparative benefits of those alternatives. Thus, another key ingredient in the law of sustainability is the repeal or modification of such laws.

In a convergence of top-down and bottom-up approaches that would benefit sustainability, the federal government could create a level playing field for bottom-up technological competition by eliminating or phasing out subsidies for unsustainable practices. Subsidies often lock in suboptimal technologies for decades and provide little incentive for firms to develop and commercialize alternative solutions. Ultimately, costs for green technologies need to be driven down to what venture capitalist Vinod Khosla calls the Chinidia price—the price that people in China and India could afford without any subsidies.[17]

President Obama has proposed eliminating certain oil and gas tax subsidies,[18] which would be a step in the right direction. His proposal would subject oil and gas corporations to the same tax treatment as other corporations engaging in similar activities.[19] Repealing these subsidies would help to stimulate use of renewable energy sources, and would raise about $26 billion over the next decade.[20] But the U.S. Senate recently failed to defeat a filibuster of legislation that would have eliminated several tax breaks for oil and gas companies.[21]

The rules of federal preemption, under which federal laws and regulations take precedence over state and local ones, are likely to require legislative amendment when they make it difficult for local authorities to take certain sustainability actions. Legal impediments to local green building laws appear to require amendments to the federal Energy Policy and Conservation Act and the Energy Policy Act of 1992, although such amendments would undoubtedly face opposition from the building industry lobby.

In some cases, sustainability requires amendment of laws to impose higher costs on those who exercise less-sustainable options. The National Flood Insurance Program, for example, encourages development in those often environmentally sensitive areas that have a high risk of flooding. Flood insurance that is more expensive and less widely available would impose higher costs on that development and encourage people to live and work in less risky areas. Congress is considering such legislation.[22]

Implement Existing Laws and Programs in a More-Sustainable Way

Where the agencies administering existing statutes have the discretion, they should consider implementing those statutes in a more-sustainable manner. In some cases, the continued implementation of some existing laws will, by itself, result in continued progress toward sustainability. In other cases, the agencies administering these laws should, in consultation with their many stakeholders, find ways to administer them in an even more-sustainable way.

Ongoing implementation of the Clean Air Act, for example, is likely to move the country in a more-sustainable direction. New, cleaner motor vehicles will continue to replace older, dirtier models; high-polluting processes (like nonferrous smelting, a traditional source of prodigious quantities of sulfur dioxide) may become obsolete in this country, and cleaner processes will replace the old. But much remains to be done to reach and maintain a sustainable and environmentally protective level. Further control of ground-level ozone and fine particulate matter, which cause breathing difficulties and premature death,[23] is especially important. While there has been considerable progress in dealing with ozone, the existing standard (established in 1997) is violated in 45 areas of the United States, in which almost 120 million people live[24] (about 40% of the nation's population). The Atlantic seaboard is in nonattainment from Boston to the Washington, D.C., metropolitan area—that is, from southern New Hampshire to northern Virginia. So are all but the most isolated areas of California as well as metropolitan areas scattered around the nation. Many of the same areas do not meet the standard for fine particulate matter.[25] And even worse, those existing standards for ozone or particulate matter appear insufficient to protect public health.[26]

EPA needs to establish more stringent air quality standards for these pollutants and become more vigorous in overseeing and enforcing state plans to implement those standards. EPA also needs to develop more stringent standards for new and existing sources of nitrogen oxide and sulfur dioxide emissions from electricity-generating units. These actions will be difficult; the adoption of modified standards has already been repeatedly postponed.[27] EPA and its supporters have emphasized to the public the economic and public health benefits of more stringent standards, and they need to continue to do that.

In addition to EPA's authority under the Clean Air Act and other statutes, the National Environmental Policy Act of 1969 (NEPA) provides authority to all federal agencies to move in a more-sustainable direction. Although NEPA does not use the terms *sustainable* or *sustainable development*, it mirrors perfectly what we now describe by those terms. In that act, Congress declares:

[I]t is the continuing policy of the Federal Government, in cooperation with State and local governments, and other concerned public and private organizations, to use all practicable means and measures, including financial and technical assistance, in a manner calculated to foster and promote the general welfare, to create and maintain conditions under which man and nature can exist in productive harmony, and fulfill the social, economic, and other requirements of present and future generations of Americans.[28]

The act then identifies six specific objectives that the federal government needs to accomplish to fulfill that policy:

In order to carry out the policy set forth in this Act, it is the continuing responsibility of the Federal Government to use all practicable means, consistent with other essential considerations of national policy, to improve and coordinate Federal plans, functions, programs, and resources to the end that the Nation may—

(1) fulfill the responsibilities of each generation as trustee of the environment for succeeding generations;

(2) assure for all Americans safe, healthful, productive, and esthetically and culturally pleasing surroundings;

(3) attain the widest range of beneficial uses of the environment without degradation, risk to health or safety, or other undesirable and unintended consequences;

(4) preserve important historic, cultural, and natural aspects of our national heritage, and maintain, wherever possible, an environment which supports diversity and variety of individual choice;

(5) achieve a balance between population and resource use which will permit high standards of living and a wide sharing of life's amenities; and

(6) enhance the quality of renewable resources and approach the maximum attainable recycling of depletable resources.[29]

NEPA then states that these responsibilities are in addition to existing grants of agency authority: "The policies and goals set forth in this Act are supplementary to those set forth in existing authorizations of Federal agencies."[30] NEPA thus provides some legal authority for federal agencies to implement their existing statutes in a more-sustainable manner.[31]

All government agencies can and should also use their other existing legal authorities to implement programs in a more-sustainable manner. The National Research Council's 2011 report to EPA recommended that the agency use an internal management system—similar to those used by corporations seeking to move in a more-sustainable direction—to decide how to phase in the implementation of sustainability in EPA's various programs. The report also acknowledged that EPA is already achieving significant benefits by applying sustainable development concepts in certain programs. These benefits include lower costs of compliance, greater environmental and public health improvements, more livable communities, and improved environmental justice.[32] The report noted that other federal agencies could use a similar approach to fostering sustainability without the need to expand their existing legal authority and mission.[33]

As EPA's implementation of the Clean Air Act shows, some kinds of environmental pollution and natural resources protection are still best addressed through existing forms of regulation. But, as the National Research Council report explains, more innovative strategies will also be needed. In the face of the passionately anti-regulatory views voiced by a number of Americans, it may be difficult to sustain and improve the traditional regulatory approaches that have resulted in so much of the water quality and other environmental improvement the country has enjoyed over the past several decades. Use of regulatory methods that allow or promote innovation and flexibility may be viewed as more acceptable in the current political climate than more prescriptive approaches.

At the local level, governments need to integrate sustainable development approaches into their community and areawide planning efforts. When the merits of a proposed brownfields revitalization project are being examined, for example, the project should fit within an overall development plan. Sustainability must not be an add-on to a brownfields project but integrated with it, with the community considering all of the economic, environmental, and institutional impacts, not just those of remediation.[34] As the National Association of Local Government Professionals and the Northeast-Midwest Institute noted in a 2004 report: "Communities will succeed in brownfields revitalization when they consider these properties as community and economic opportunities that happen to have an environmental challenge, and connect brownfields initiatives to their broader community vision and revitalization priorities."[35] Climate action plans (such as those developed in Portland, Oregon, and Cincinnati, Ohio[36]) can also be excellent tools for integrating brownfields redevelopment planning into communitywide agendas for sustainability, and their implementation should be done more widely.

Employ More Incentives

Incentives, especially financial incentives, are another important way to use law to accelerate the transition to sustainability. Dangling carrots is often far preferable to swinging sticks. As discussed in previous chapters, the federal government and state governments provide a variety of tax credits, deductions, and other financial incentives for renewable energy and energy efficiency. In general, these incentives should be continued and even enhanced where appropriate, so that they encourage even greater use of renewable energy and energy efficiency. Yet, the federal budget deficit and weak economy make it less likely that such incentives will be available in the near future, at least not at past levels. So, a major challenge moving forward will likely be to supplement government financial support with other kinds of incentives.

International trade provides an important opportunity for sustainable development incentives. For example, developed countries could grant improved market entry to countries that hit certain targets on environmental protection and sustainable development. In partnership with the European Union, Canada, and Japan, the United States needs to provide positive incentives to large developing countries (Brazil, Russia, India, and China—the so-called BRIC countries) to likewise adopt measures to limit and roll back greenhouse gas emissions. One tool will be incentives in the form of reduced customs duties on imports from these countries if they meet certain greenhouse gas benchmarks.

In general, World Trade Organisation (WTO) member countries are not allowed to discriminate among their trading partners in imposing tariffs or other trade barriers; all countries must be given the same treatment as a country's "most favored" trading partner. But the Generalized System of Preferences (GSP) creates an exemption to that rule by allowing lower tariffs in developed countries for imports from developing countries.[37] While developed countries must respond positively to the varied needs of developing countries, identical tariff treatment need not be accorded to all GSP beneficiaries.

Discrimination by developed countries *among* developing countries in trade preference programs is also permitted, according to a 2004 WTO Appellate Body decision,[38] so long as developing countries in similar circumstances are treated similarly. According to the Appellate Body, the response of a preference-granting country must be taken with a view to improving the development, financial, or trade situation of a beneficiary country, based on a particular need. Thus, in the Appellate Body's view, a sufficient nexus should exist between, on the one hand, the preferential treatment provided under the trade preference program and, on the other hand, the likelihood of alleviating the relevant needs of the beneficiary country. In the context of a tariff preference program implemented under the GSP, the Appellate Body explained, the particular need at issue must be such that it can be effectively addressed through tariff preferences.

In response to this decision, the European Union (EU) in 2005 adopted a replacement GSP scheme, to which it made minor technical revisions in 2008. The EU's current GSP scheme creates three separate arrangements: (1) standard GSP; (2) the Special Incentive Arrangement for Sustainable Development and Good Governance (popularly known as the GSP Plus), which offers additional preferences to support vulnerable developing countries in their ratification and implementation of relevant international conventions in the areas of human rights, labor rights, environment, and good government; and (3) Everything But Arms (EBA), which provides duty-free, quota-free access to the EU for the 48 least-developed countries on all products except arms and ammunition. Using the EU's GSP Plus program as an example, additional trade benefits could be offered to the largest greenhouse gas emitters among the developing countries in exchange for their agreement to reduce their emissions. And, of course, such additional trade preferences would not have to be limited to just hitting GHG emission benchmarks but could be expanded to cover a range of environmental and sustainable development initiatives. The United States should follow the EU's approach.

The United States may also be able to use the GSP system in other ways. Although it would be politically difficult, breaking the logjam that currently exists with China and India over greenhouse gas emissions may be possible through a quid pro quo arrangement that includes incentives. Currently, China is not a beneficiary under the U.S. GSP program, and many products of export interest to India, such as textiles and clothing, are not eligible for GSP duty-free treatment.[39] By offering these two countries special duty-free incentives on products of keen export interest to them in exchange for their agreement to reduce their greenhouse gas emissions and to meet other benchmarks in connection with sustainable development, a deal might be struck that would advance the climate change agenda.

Another approach—which has already been put to some use—is to offer regulatory rewards for better environmental performance. A number of regulatory programs offer support for companies that adopt environmental management systems. These rewards include the faster and easier granting of environmental permits, flexible emissions standards, and fewer inspections, as well as reduced penalties for violations that do occur. Similar European policies offer financial support, preferences in public procurement, and other benefits.[40] There is some evidence that the incentives in these programs improve environmental performance.[41]

A final and somewhat novel approach to incentives is the use of prizes to induce innovation, a tool that appeals to those skeptical of governmental regulation.[42] Prize money can be a relatively inexpensive way of producing breakthrough technological innovations. And prizes work. In 1714, the British Parliament established an award for inventing a way to measure longitude on ships, so they could determine how far east or west they were. Conventional wisdom was that the prize would be won by an astronomer who could discern longitude from the stars, but it went instead to a watchmaker who invented a mechanical clock that did the job. Within decades, thousands of ships around the world were using his clocks.[43] Professor Jonathan Adler of Case Western Reserve University Law School has suggested that the federal government make available $10 billion in prizes over 10 years to address specifically targeted greenhouse gas and energy efficiency problems across a range of technologies.[44] Prize programs such as this could lead to breakthroughs in the development and diffusion of energy technologies that might otherwise be unachievable. They also could appeal across the political spectrum, avoiding the ideological gridlock that has made progress on this issue difficult. Such programs do not even need to be government sponsored; indeed, some nongovernmental organizations are already offering prizes for environmental and energy achievements.[45]

Improve and Expand the Use of Programs That Work

The law of sustainability can also be built on the foundation of existing programs that are being employed to some degree at the state and local level. Many of these programs are being improved over time through experience, fine-tuning, and information sharing. Others work quite well but can be applied more widely. Two examples are pay-as-you-throw programs and smart growth.

Pay-as-you-throw programs, which began in the 1980s in the United States, have reduced the amount of landfilled waste and increased incentives to recycle by creating a financial incentive to reduce waste that requires disposal. The programs charge higher fees to households and businesses that produce more solid waste— typically based on a charge for each can or bag of waste that is placed for pickup. Pay-as-you-throw programs make sense for environmental protection, economic growth, and job creation. They reduce residential generation of municipal solid waste by about 17% by increasing the amount of waste that is recycled, by diverting waste to yard waste collection, and by reducing waste generation through other means.[46] According to a 2006 report prepared for EPA, pay-as-you-throw "is the most effective single action that can increase recycling and diversion, and can also be one of the most cost-effective."[47] Diversion of waste from landfills to recycling centers also creates more jobs, as noted earlier.[48]

While there may be concern that pay-as-you-throw will increase illegal dumping, the evidence indicates that dumping occurs in only one in five communities, ordinarily lasts no more than three months, and most frequently involves large appliances ("white goods").[49] Communities can address these problems by adopting and enforcing illegal dumping ordinances, ensuring that citizens have easily available recycling and yard waste programs, and adopting special programs for the collection of white goods.[50]

The Lincoln Institute of Land Policy published the first national evaluation of smart growth programs and outcomes in 2009.[51] This evaluation has made an important contribution to the broader and more effective use of smart growth programs. The report concluded that these programs "should be guided by a vision of sustainable and desirable development outcomes," "must be coordinated at the regional level," and "must articulate the means of achieving smart growth objectives and specify implementation mechanisms, rather than just declare objectives." The report explained that the long period required for effective implementation of smart growth programs requires an equally long governmental commitment. The report also stated that the "most successful states use a variety of regulatory controls, market incentives, and institutional policies to achieve their objectives." Analyses like this provide a foundation for improving existing programs, and for applying these lessons elsewhere. When new and unusual ideas become tried and proven through experience, they are no longer new and unusual. Sometimes, accelerating the transition to sustainability simply means deploying what works in places where those laws and programs are not yet being used.

Move From Voluntary to Legally Binding Standards

A final key ingredient in the law of sustainability is consideration of legally binding standards in areas where voluntary standards have already been employed.
Voluntary standards are an important driver of sustainability because they provide
room to experiment and encourage participation. There comes a point, however,
when sufficient experience with voluntary standards can warrant making those
standards mandatory. Mandatory standards put everyone on a level playing field,
and also improve the effectiveness of the overall sustainability effort by requiring
a minimum level of performance from all. Once again, green building provides
an example.

The initial growth of green building may be attributed in large part to the voluntary and incentivized approach of industry groups and local governments, but
the "carrot approach" provided by continued reliance on incentives and education
will not succeed in transforming the building industry. Instead, this approach may
provide only enough of a driver to create a niche industry for green builders. Until
recently, only a handful of local governments had passed ordinances requiring
builders of private projects to meet the high performance standards set in various
green building programs.[52] The time has come to require all buildings and building
improvements to meet green standards.

Are we ready to face the consequences of mandatory green building standards?
Green building mandates are the most effective means of removing unhealthy
choices and products. Objections based on the supposed higher costs of green
building compliance are, as discussed previously, contradicted by the evidence.
There is also an argument for caution in adopting, as mandatory, standards that
were intentionally crafted to be voluntary certifications. Indeed, if not done properly, mandatory standards can threaten the legitimacy of green building and may
have negative environmental consequences, particularly if those standards do not
account for regional building differences. Yet, this claim applies only against the
mechanical adoption of certification standards as regulatory standards. It does not
provide a categorical reason to oppose a green building mandate. While flexibility is needed when adapting codes to climatic and cultural variation, many local
governments that require green building have allowed builders to meet alternative
standards or adopted regional green building standards.[53]

One milestone in green building was California's adoption of the Green Building
Standards Code, also known as CALGreen. The code went into effect in 2011 and
was hailed as the first statewide green building standards code in the nation. The
code applies to newly constructed low-rise residential (three stories or less) and
most nonresidential buildings, but not to building additions, alterations, or repairs.[54]
Like its voluntary counterparts, CALGreen includes site selection considerations,
construction practices, building operation efficiencies, materials selection, and
natural resource conservation measures. Although the intent of CALGreen is to
create uniform and enforceable standards for new buildings across the state, it

does allow local jurisdictions to customize their own codes where circumstances of climate, topography, or geology justify the departure.

A second important development is a collaborative effort of professionals across the green building industry. In 2008, the American Society of Heating, Refrigerating and Air Conditioning Engineers, the Illuminating Engineering Society, and the U.S. Green Building Council began a national effort to accelerate commercial green building practices throughout the country. Standard 189, which covers criteria such as sustainability, water and energy efficiency, indoor environmental quality, and materials and resource use, provides minimum standards for building design, construction, and operation for states and local governments.[55] Soon thereafter, the International Code Council developed the International Green Construction Code (IGCC) in cooperation with the American Institute of Architects and ASTM International.[56] The IGCC "is positioned to achieve significant market transformation in those segments that are not likely to react to voluntary programs."[57] The IGCC also allows flexibility to meet regional variations in green building needs.

The adoption of these codes, and others like them, will provide a way to broaden green building practices at a more ambitious scale. They create a means to accelerate the deployment of demonstrated programs and technologies throughout the country. More generally, the movement from voluntary toward legally mandated practices might be a useful model for meeting sustainability standards in other sectors.

Climate Change

While law for sustainability requires a wide range of actions—including resource-specific frameworks and goals, economic development tools, repeals, more-sustainable implementation, incentives, expanded use of tools that work, and binding standards—it also requires us to address climate change directly and seriously. Climate change is an enormous, challenging—and controversial—problem. To understand how law can be employed to address climate change, it is first necessary to understand how sustainability can help reframe the debate over climate change.

Those who oppose climate change legislation typically focus on two points. They challenge the scientific certainty of the evidence in support of human-induced climate change, and they challenge the enormity of the government program that would be put in place to address climate change. These two assertions can be and should be contested, and there are many reasons to believe that those who deny the reality of climate change are utterly and dangerously wrong. An enormous body of scientific evidence shows that humans are already changing the climate, that these changes are almost certainly going to be greater in coming decades, and that the changes are likely to have adverse effects throughout the United States and the world. Numerous studies show that current and projected levels of greenhouse gas emissions pose a threat to the health and welfare of all.[58] And, rather than impose a large government bureaucracy, the cap-and-trade legislation that has been proposed to address climate change, and which passed the House of Representatives in 2010, is much more market-oriented than any number of other approaches.

Instead of focusing just on these two points, however, a sustainable development perspective reframes the issue of climate change in at least five different ways. First, the issue is not about certainty but about risks, including both the probability that adverse effects will occur and the magnitude of those effects. To justify the U.S.-led invasion of Iraq, President George W. Bush argued that even a 1% chance that Saddam Hussein was developing weapons of mass destruction was too great a risk for the United States to bear.[59] On climate change, we know that the risks are much greater; indeed, they are already being realized.

Second, climate change is not only an environmental issue. U.S. greenhouse gas emissions will not only adversely affect the U.S. climate but will, according to the mainstream science of climate change, have the harshest impact on many millions of people around the world, most of them already living in poverty, destabilizing countries due to famine from droughts and the rise in sea levels, and increasing the chances of armed conflict, massive refugees, and humanitarian crises. In the United States, the likely effects include more severe droughts and increased flooding and the impact of higher temperatures and heat stress, particularly on the poor and elderly. In other words, climate change puts at serious risk things we care about deeply and on which our continued well-being depends, whatever we may feel about the environment or climate in the abstract.

Third, climate change raises profound moral and religious issues. Despite the significant risks to human health and the environment, the two dominant perspectives in the conversation about climate change and sustainability are on national self-interest and economic value. Those who argue against climate change policies tend to focus on costs and benefits, economic issues such as job creation, and which options will maximize the welfare of most people. This "value-neutral" approach hides important ethical questions—for example, about how much future generations matter and whether, because accounting for costs and benefits is ordinarily based on lost income, the value of a human life lost due to climate change in a developing country should be considered less than a human life in a developed country because of the more limited earning capacity in developing countries. An economic framing of all sustainability issues can transform something that should be understood as sacred or outside market transactions into no more than commodity valuation, even on human life.

Because sustainability issues are moral matters, they entail not only self-interest but duties, responsibilities, and obligations to those who will be harmed by unsustainable behavior, including future generations. If the moral issues are hidden or obscured by the translation of value into an economic equation, reflection on the moral questions will be deferred. While these moral issues do not dictate a particular policy outcome, they make clear that policy should not be based only on quantitative assessments of national self-interest.

Fourth, climate change is also an energy security issue, as the great majority of U.S. greenhouse gas emissions result from the burning of fossil fuels. Because the United States imports a great deal of oil, often from unfriendly countries and across supply lines that require military protection (such as the Persian Gulf), it follows that climate policies that also reduce our dependence on oil will improve our energy security.

Fifth, the legal and policy tools available to reduce greenhouse gas emissions can foster economic development, create new jobs, improve U.S. economic competitiveness, lead to the development of new technologies, reduce the impact of high and fluctuating fossil fuel prices on the poor and on business, and cut emissions of health-damaging air pollutants. These measures, in short, can create opportunities that would not otherwise exist. This approach is also based on considerable evidence. The states that began renewable energy portfolio standards, net metering, energy-efficient building codes, and similar legal tools that foster renewable energy and energy efficiency more than a decade ago did so primarily because these benefits would be realized within their borders. Reduced greenhouse gas emissions, by contrast, benefit not just a state but the entire world because greenhouse gases mix so readily in the atmosphere that their concentrations at any given time are relatively the same everywhere. Thus, many of these policies and laws would make sense even if the consensus on climate science were utterly wrong.

Many states have implemented sustainable policies for economic reasons. By stressing the economic sustainability of new policies—job growth, good paying jobs associated with high technology, lower energy costs—proponents of sustainability have made limited progress to date. In Oregon, people in the major urban centers generally accept the premises of climate science and support the development of renewable energy, even if it increases prices. While rural areas tend to be suspicious of climate science, they support renewable energy development as a vital economic development strategy.[60] Convincing those in rural areas of the benefits of sustainability has required a different approach to policy framing in those areas.[61]

The Regional Greenhouse Gas Initiative (RGGI) provides a good example of the benefits of sustainability. As a collaborative effort to "support the development and implementation of each RGGI State's Carbon Dioxide Budget Trading Program,"[62] RGGI established a model cap-and-trade rule to reduce emissions from power plants by 10% by 2018. Its nine member states each establish independent regulations based on that model rule. This creates a network of individual programs functioning as a regional market. Each state auctions allowances (equal to one ton of carbon dioxide), which power plant operators can use to demonstrate compliance with the emission reduction requirement in any state's program.

Through a memorandum of understanding, each member state has agreed to allocate 25% of the program's allowances for consumer benefit or strategic energy purposes. Through 2010, proceeds from auctions of these allowances have provided over $700 million to support such programs. Over 60% of this money has been invested in energy efficiency and renewable energy programs. Collectively, these programs reduce emissions, save consumers money, and create jobs throughout the region.[63]

At the national level, the argument for some kind of price on carbon—either through cap-and-trade or a carbon tax—is also based to a considerable degree on economics. A carbon price that is stable or even increases at a predictable rate over time will permit businesses to invest in development of renewable energy and energy efficiency with confidence that their efforts, if successful, will be rewarded in the market. The winners in the market will be those who develop alternatives to carbon that people actually want to buy and use. A carbon price would, in other words, engender competition to provide the most attractive alternatives to carbon-based energy production.[64]

One can argue that higher fuel prices achieve the same result because they spur the use of renewable energy and energy efficiency. Because fuel prices tend to fluctuate over time, however, they do not give a consistent economic signal. In addition, the money paid on fossil fuels goes to foreign governments or oil companies, and (unlike a carbon tax or charge) it does not get used for renewable energy, energy efficiency, or balancing the federal budget.

A carbon tax can be quite small at first, but it can include a schedule that steadily increases the taxation rate over a decade or two, enabling businesses and individuals to gradually adjust their behavior without sudden new costs or disruptions. Indeed, many observers believe that a carbon tax would be simpler to administer, more fair, and less bureaucratic than a cap-and-trade program. Interestingly, President Obama's bipartisan deficit-reduction commission recently called for an increase of 15 cents per gallon in the gas tax.[65] Additionally, in difficult economic times, when there is a considerable federal budget deficit, a tax on carbon can also be employed to help reduce the deficit, other taxes, or both.[66] As of this writing, however, neither a tax or cap-and-trade system appears viable for setting a price on carbon. Barring some dramatic change in the political environment, Congress is unlikely to pass any bill requiring a reduction in emissions. Alternative policies thus need to be adopted, such as incentives to create a massive shift away from present fuel sources to the production of environmentally sustainable energy forms, or disincentives to the production and use of most of today's energy forms. The government has a variety of available tools, such as supporting research and development, labeling "green" products, giving recognition to the "greenest" companies, discouraging the use of the dirtiest energy forms (by requiring that they advertise the effects of their use, much like is required on cigarette packages), expanding government support and private tax write-offs for R&D on green technologies, providing incentives for green investment, and, as explained in Chapter 14, engaging individuals and households to reduce their energy use.

One particularly important approach to increasing the sustainability of our energy system is a concerted and coordinated federal effort to increase both energy efficiency and renewable energy. There would be great potential for reducing U.S. greenhouse gas emissions if the government were to adopt aggressive policies promoting renewable energy, particularly wind and solar. The United States is falling behind some other countries in installed renewable energy as a percentage of national energy use (Figure 15.1). Although the United States has more installed wind generation than any country in the world in terms of total megawatts, on a per capita basis the country is far behind several other countries.

Figure 15.1
Installed Wind per Capita as of 2010[67]

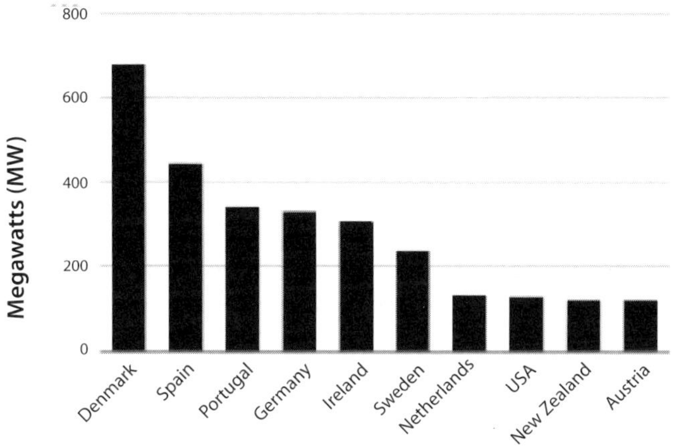

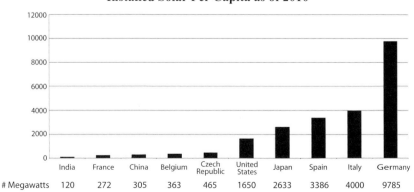

The United States is also far behind several other countries in installed solar on a per capita basis, as the following graph indicates (Figure 15.2).

Figure 15.2
Installed Solar Per Capita as of 2010[68]

	India	France	China	Belgium	Czech Republic	United States	Japan	Spain	Italy	Germany
# Megawatts	120	272	305	363	465	1650	2633	3386	4000	9785

Perhaps the most widely discussed legal tool for increasing the use of renewable energy is the renewable energy portfolio standard. As explained in Chapter 5, a renewable energy portfolio standard requires an increase in the percentage of electricity provided by renewable energy sources by a specified date. Although many states have such laws, there is no comparable standard at the federal level. If we are not going to employ a carbon fee, a federal renewable portfolio standard would be the most straightforward way to increase the use of renewable energy at the national level.

Another possibility is aggressive policies on energy efficiency. A 2010 report by the National Academy of Sciences found:

> Energy-efficient technologies for residences and commercial buildings, transportation, and industry exist today, or are expected to be developed in the normal course of business, that could potentially save 30 percent of the energy used in the U.S. economy while also saving money. If energy prices are high enough to motivate investment in energy efficiency, or if public policies are put in place that have the same effect, U.S. energy use could be lower than business-as-usual projections by 19-22 quadrillion BTUs (17-20 percent) in 2020 and by 30–36 quadrillion BTUs (25-31 percent) in 2030.[69]

The report added: "The full deployment of cost-effective, energy-efficient technologies in buildings alone could eliminate the need to add to U.S. electricity generation."[70] These policies include, but are not limited to, more stringent fuel-efficiency standards for motor vehicles, more stringent efficiency standards for household appliances and industrial equipment, more widespread and ambitious energy efficiency standards in building codes, greater use of the Energy Star program, and more ambitious and wider use of energy efficiency programs for utilities at the state level.[71] Such policies can significantly improve U.S. performance on moving to sustainable energy and save money at the same time. Moreover, a strong case can be made that policies on energy efficiency should be at the top of U.S. energy policy as an ethical matter, in light of the high per capita U.S. energy consumption.[72]

Because of the difficulty in achieving significant policy reforms at the federal level, a second-best solution may be new and strengthened programs and policies to reduce greenhouse gas emissions at the state and local level. As explained in Chapter 5, California and New York have been able to keep per capita electricity consumption more or less stable since the early 1970s, even though overall U.S. per capita electricity consumption has risen by about 50%. Both states have used a combination of legal and policy tools to achieve that result.

Another measure of the potential significance of the state contribution is based on the laws and policies contained in 20 state climate change action plans. In these plans, states identify a range of measures that they intend to implement to reduce greenhouse gas emissions and quantify the reductions that implementation of these measures can achieve. If the legal and policy measures contained in 20 existing state climate change action plans were made applicable at the national level, the United

States could reduce its greenhouse gas emissions by 10% below 1990 levels by 2020. This state planning process, if required of all states by national legislation, also provides an opportunity to achieve cheaper, faster, and greater emissions reductions than federal legislation or regulation alone would achieve.[73] These plans will achieve emissions reductions in a many key sectors, including transportation and land use; low carbon fuels; energy supply; renewable, advanced, and low-emitting generation for heat and power; residential, commercial, and industrial energy use; agriculture, forestry, and waste; and land protection and conservation practices. These policies as a whole, if scaled up from 20 states to the entire country, would produce economywide cost savings of $85 billion by 2020 and cumulative savings of hundreds of billions between now and 2020.

There is, nonetheless, a limit on what states can achieve by themselves. They have limited authority to enact measures that can address other significant sources of greenhouse gas emissions, such as standards for appliance efficiency and auto fuel economy. California is one state that has done a great deal to reduce greenhouse gas emissions through the Global Warming Solutions Act of 2006, a cap-and-trade program for greenhouse gases, and other measures described in Chapter 5. New York, Connecticut, and Michigan have also mounted aggressive programs.[74] But relatively few states have the resources or the political will to create policy vehicles that move them significantly in the direction of sustainable energy.

Because state and federal financial support for renewable energy and energy efficiency likely will be limited in the foreseeable future, it is important to design mechanisms that encourage innovative financing. A relatively new but rapidly growing approach is a property assessed clean energy (PACE) program. In a PACE program, a municipality provides loans for solar energy, energy efficiency, and other clean energy improvements to homeowners and businesses within its jurisdiction. In return, the borrower agrees to an individual tax or other assessment on its real property sufficient to repay the loan plus interest over the term of the loan. As of this writing, 27 states and the District of Columbia have adopted laws authorizing PACE programs.[75] All of these jurisdictions have adopted PACE programs since 2008 (with the exception of Hawaii, which relies on preexisting legal authority for its program). Regrettably, the Federal Housing Finance Authority (FHFA) has announced that a PACE assessment will disqualify a home from receiving a Fannie Mae or Freddie Mac mortgage.[76] This announcement has deterred many homeowners from taking advantage of a PACE program and has inhibited the passage of new authorizing legislation in other states.

While the FHFA announcement is being contested, there is considerable interest in private investment in the energy efficiency upgrade of commercial buildings under PACE programs. In such an arrangement, private investment companies, rather than municipalities, would finance the PACE improvements, making substantially more capital available. Some municipalities, like Miami and Sacramento, may provide a private company with a five-year exclusive license to offer

PACE upgrades in that community. The loan repayment agreements for individual properties would be bundled into long-term bonds that are marketed like other bonds. This approach, if replicated across the country, could lure tens of billions in private investment to renovate and upgrade commercial buildings and result in much greater energy savings.[77] Approaches like this, involving a blend of public and private action, are an important way of overcoming both policy gridlock at the federal level and the limitations of public financing.

In addition to reducing greenhouse gas emissions, the United States also needs to adapt to climate change that is already occurring and anticipate future climate change that to some significant degree is inevitable. Biodiversity conservation is a good example of the challenges. Federal agencies have already prepared an interagency report containing recommendations for a climate change strategy that recognizes the need to protect biodiversity[78] and have drafted a separate plan to address climate change impacts on water resources.[79] Global climate change threatens to render impossible the biodiversity conservation of many reserves. Thus we need a national adaptation policy for biodiversity along the lines of the program included in the Waxman-Markey climate change bill. At the present time, the best strategy seems to be to conserve and expand, whenever possible, the existing mix of public and private land that shelters biodiversity. Our stock of public and private reserves provides some buffer against risks such as species loss and migration.

Modest but creative biodiversity conservation strategies will also be needed. One example is an experiment comprising Indian tribes, the federal and local governments, and private parties to ensure that the Nisqually River in western Washington can continue to support the Chinook salmon runs that are important to the Nisqually Indians.[80] Scientists predict a warmer summer river, which is not good for the Chinook. Restored wetlands may be inundated as the Pacific Ocean rises. The groups are working to increase associated groundwater infiltration to counter the expected decreases in the river's flow and to create deeper, cooler pools for the fish. Others argue that we must anticipate the risks of species extinction and try to prevent them by assisted migration. Assisted migration challenges "foundational tenets of conservation law and ethics that seek to preserve and restore preexisting biological systems and shield them from human interference."[81] But these same biological systems, left unaided in the face of climate change, are unlikely to maintain Chinook salmon runs on the Nisqually River.

At the present time, the best tool available to run experiments like this is adaptive management, or learning by doing—trying a particular approach, monitoring for results, and improving or changing the approach based on what has been learned.[82] The impacts of climate change on biodiversity reserves and waterways must be assessed to the extent possible under existing data and models. After this is done, a series of adaptation experiments need to be constructed and implemented. Climate change adaptation will involve not only learning by doing but also managing for somewhat different purposes.

Conclusion

Law can provide a strong and sure foundation for achieving sustainability. The United States needs to move from relying mostly on environmental regulation as a means of protecting the environment to a greater variety of legal tools, including economic development, job creation, incentives, tax law, and the like.

Reframing climate change as a sustainability issue may help to defuse some of the contentious political wrangling that has occurred and provide a means for reasonable people in both major political parties to find a way to proceed. State renewable energy and energy efficiency programs, which enjoy strong bipartisan support, provide a useful model for the national government. By adopting legislation to reduce greenhouse gas emissions and adapting better to climate change, we can accelerate the transition to sustainability. All of these steps, taken together, will make more-sustainable decisions even more attractive and further accelerate this transition.

CHAPTER 16

Visionary and Pragmatic Governance

In order to accelerate the transition to sustainability, we need government at all levels to combine the seemingly dissonant strains of vision and pragmatism. We need visionary governance to help us see a more-sustainable and positive future, to figure out how to realize that future, and to help lead the way. We need pragmatic governance because that vision must be tempered by a strong sense of the real world, the limits of governmental power, and the trial-and-error quality of the sustainability journey.

Visionary and pragmatic governance is necessary to move law in a more-sustainable direction, as described in the previous chapter, on climate change and a range of other issues. Visionary and pragmatic governance for sustainability also requires a compelling public narrative about how the United States can face the challenges and seize the opportunities of sustainability, as well as a national strategy to guide the nation's efforts over many decades. All levels of government need to do a better job of educating the public about sustainability and engaging the public in decisions that move the nation in a more-sustainable direction. Finally, because the development and deployment of new and more-sustainable technologies will be essential, the federal government in particular needs to make appropriate incentives and direction for such efforts a high priority.

A Bipartisan Narrative and Strategy

The United States needs to develop a sustainability narrative and strategy on sustainability that can survive national electoral changes without major reversals of the kind we have seen on many issues in the past several decades. There will be 10 presidential elections between 2012 and 2050. Whatever else the strategy and narrative do, their basic elements must command the active support of the major political parties (and independents) to ensure continuity.

Sustainability should be able to provide a bridge across the partisan chasm because it is both pro-business and pro-environment and because it focuses on two of our greatest concerns: our security and our children. Building a bridge across the bipartisan chasm may simply take time and repeated effort. Because the pressures created by unsustainable activity are inexorable and physical, their impacts on the United States will become clearer over time. Sooner or later, the scripts of both political parties will have to change. In that sense, the question is not whether the bridge will be built but when and who will bear the cost if the bridge is built later rather than sooner.

As a starting point, the United States needs to adopt a national strategic *narrative*. The idea of a strategic narrative is explained in an important recent paper by Navy Captain Wayne Porter and Marine Corps Colonel Mark Mykleby, strategic advisors in the office of the Joint Chiefs of Staff. The paper, which was released by the Woodrow Wilson Center, says that a strategic narrative is needed "to frame our National policy decisions regarding investment, security, economic development, the environment, and engagement well into this century."[1] A narrative is a story that has public resonance and provides a coherent explanation of the past, present, and future; a national strategy, by contrast, is written by and for specialists.

Our strategic narrative during the Cold War, Porter and Mykleby write, was that "the United States was the leader of the free world against the communist world; that we would invest in containing the Soviet Union and limiting its expansion while building a dynamic economy and as just and prosperous a society as possible."[2] This narrative governed much of U.S. policy from 1946 until 1989, through both Democratic and Republican administrations, until the fall of the Berlin Wall and the collapse of the Soviet Union. It meant continued public and governmental attention to the threat of nuclear war, prompted the U.S. manned space program, provided justification for the interstate highway system (named the National Defense Highway System), and led to a focus on mathematics and science in education. The September 11, 2011, terrorist attacks resurrected the Cold War narrative in a different form, with al-Qaeda and its allies replacing the Soviet Union as a universally understood threat. But that narrative has not carried the same public resonance. As we move deeper into the 21st century, then, there remain basic questions about our role in the world, to which Americans want answers. These questions, explains Ann-Marie Slaughter, a professor of politics and international affairs at Princeton University, are:

> Where is the United States going in the world? How can we get there? What are the guiding stars that will illuminate the path along the way? We need a story with a beginning, middle, and projected happy ending that will transcend our political divisions, orient us as a nation, and give us both a common direction and the confidence and commitment to get to our destination.[3]

There is now no such story, and certainly no narrative that deeply integrates sustainability. Sustainability can be at the core of that new narrative because it provides a framework for integrating "decisions regarding investment, security, economic development, the environment, and engagement"; because it furthers our values and strengthens the country; and because it responds to the actual threats and opportunities in front of us. This narrative could include the following elements, many of which were described in the introduction: Sustainability's ultimate objectives—freedom, opportunity, and quality of life—are also among the values we hold most dear as a nation, values for which we have fought hot and cold wars.

- Sustainability would strengthen the economy and our security, create jobs, and enable us to use our resources more efficiently because we would be treating our environmental, security, economic, and social goals as mutually reinforcing. Some would argue that we cannot afford sustainability because the costs would make us uncompetitive with other countries. The truth is likely just the opposite; our very high energy and materials consumption will almost certainly make it harder to compete in a world of rising competition for resources, greater risks of losing access to resources, and higher prices for those that are available. And the economic advantages of countries that do not proceed sustainably are not as great as they appear. An international team of experts working with the World Bank has calculated the economic cost of China's considerable air and water pollution. The public health, agriculture, and water availability costs alone are an amount equal to nearly 6% of China's GDP[4]—a figure that very likely underestimates the costs of Chinese environmental policy.
- Sustainability's implicit message of paying for more than one thing at once (not just environmental protection but also economic development, public health, resource conservation, job creation, and national security) makes financial sense. This is particularly true in weaker economic times.
- Sustainability would lead to a safer and more secure world because it addresses problems like climate change that are likely to be deeply destabilizing and, because of the historical U.S. contribution to atmospheric concentrations of greenhouse gases, likely to cause deep and lasting resentment in developing countries that are adversely affected.
- Technological innovation and diffusion, core strengths of the United States, are essential for sustainability.
- Because sustainability is the right thing to do—for ourselves, for others, and for those who follow us—it is consistent with how America sees itself.

All of these can be major threads in a new national strategic narrative. They help explain much of what is going on in the world, and what we need to do, both now and for the foreseeable future. Such a narrative could provide the public face for a national sustainability strategy.

A sustainability *strategy* would provide an analytical and policy basis for realizing the vision contained in the narrative. A sustainability strategy—better described as a strategic process—would provide deeper insight into the relationships among the social, environmental, economic, and security challenges that the United States faces, a more accurate early warning system of potential problems, a more sophisticated ability to prevent problems before they occur, and an increased opportunity to take economic advantage of foreseeable trends. It will also provide a means of integrating our analysis of a variety of potential threats to the nation's well-being, including not only the budget deficit and climate change but also such issues as international competitiveness.[5] All too often, the analyses of such issues are conducted separately, with relatively little discussion of the relationships among them. A national strategic process would enable U.S. decisionmakers to understand these relationships, would provide them with better options, and would enable them to make better choices. As Chapter 5 explained, the United States is moving toward a more comprehensive strategic process; the national government needs to complete the transition.

Most developed countries, as well as the European Union (EU), have sustainability strategies.[6] Such strategies provide a mechanism for integrating national environmental, social, and economic objectives; are based on a long-term vision and perspective; involve stakeholders in their development and implementation; set targets and use indicators to measure progress; and incorporate mechanisms for monitoring, evaluation, and modification.

The EU's sustainable development strategy,[7] adopted in 2001, states that sustainable development is a "fundamental objective" of the European Union.[8] Sustainable development offers "a better quality of life for everyone, now and for generations to come," the EU statement says, by offering "a vision of progress that integrates immediate and longer-term objectives" and by regarding "social, economic and environmental issues as inseparable and interdependent components of human progress."[9] The strategy has these priorities: climate change and clean energy, sustainable transport, sustainable consumption and production, conservation and management of natural resources, public health, social inclusion, demography and migration, and global poverty and sustainable development challenges.[10] The EU also regularly evaluates progress under the strategy. The 2009 review highlighted that "the EU has taken the lead in the fight against climate change and the promotion of a low-carbon economy," but noted unsustainable trends in many areas: "Significant additional efforts are needed to curb and adapt to climate change, to decrease high energy consumption in the transport sector and to reverse the current loss of biodiversity and natural resources."[11]

A similar U.S. strategy could also help prioritize policymaking concerning sustainability and focus the country's attention on its most important challenges and opportunities over an extended period of time. It could provide a way of guiding policy from administration to administration, enabling the United States to pursue a steadier course over time. A regular review mechanism could provide a way of assessing progress and making adjustments.

Improved Public Education and Engagement

Municipalities, state governments, and the federal government all need to enhance public engagement and education on behalf of sustainability. Among the most important tasks are educating the public about the risks and opportunities of sustainability, enabling the comparability of data from different databases, fostering greater public involvement and participation, and documenting the results of more-sustainable efforts.

Public Education and Information

Public education about sustainability is a basic responsibility of government at all levels. But it is a challenge to draw public attention to long-term potential problems when so many immediate issues demand our attention. Although the sustainability framework has become clearer to many Americans, much of the public thinks of sustainability as a secondary issue to the pressing problems of unemployment, the federal budget deficit, and other, seemingly more important, problems.

The federal government in particular needs to lead a public education effort to:

- Explain the importance of reducing our environmental and carbon footprint if the country is to prosper on a finite planet with a growing population and economy. (To be fair, the Obama Administration has argued the point repeatedly, particularly on renewable energy and energy efficiency.) The federal government needs to enhance and strengthen that message, under both Democratic and Republican administrations.

- Explain that environmental issues are "not just environmental issues." For example, Americans need to better understand the economic and social values of their marine resources and the fragility of those resources in the face of pollution, overfishing, and climate change. Similarly, Americans should understand that clean energy and environmental protection can help to create jobs.[12]

- Provide the public with basic information about our progress toward sustainability. The key indicators effort described in Chapter 5, which is intended to provide a broader and more accurate statement of the nation's well-being than GDP alone, appears likely to produce something akin to the sustainability indicators employed by the European Union.

- Educate the American public about what environmental laws have achieved over the past several decades. Support for regulation may be waning due to the very success of regulatory efforts of earlier decades. Because most Americans no longer face some of the visible and acute environmental harms that led to adoption of those measures—such as polluted rivers and dirty air—it is possible that people now see only the costs and do not recognize the benefits.

- Provide information and tools that are tailored to specific communities, states, and regions. The impacts of climate change need to be localized to particular coastal communities so they can engage in scenario-building to understand the possible range of impacts as ocean levels rise. Many coastal communities in the United States, such as New York City, have begun to engage in such adaptation planning, but communities (and the states and the federal government) need to have a scientific basis for understanding the much broader impacts of climate change on the sustainability of their

communities and on their ability to continue to depend on marine resources
and marine ecosystem services in the future.

- Encourage individuals and families to take actions that would reduce their
  environmental or carbon footprint. The challenge of sustainability is too
  daunting to focus simply on large polluters, and there is considerable reason
  to believe that individuals and families can make a significant contribution.

The federal government also needs to develop data, or make existing data
available, to enable a better public understanding of how sustainable—or unsustainable—the United States actually is and what our priorities should be. The data
on materials use that we have now, for example, provide only limited assistance in
setting these priorities. As indicated in Chapter 11, the data indicate only certain
effects of the most environmentally intensive materials like hazardous wastes and
other highly toxic materials; they tell us only generally which production, use, and
disposal practices are egregious. It is more difficult to compare large-scale patterns
of materials use. Only a national materials flow analysis, like the World Resources
Institute study published in 2008, will enable policymakers, industrial leaders, and
average citizens to work together toward comprehensive materials sustainability.

Similarly, greater investment in basic and applied scientific research on a variety
of issues related to sustainability is also needed. Any future hope of improved sustainability for marine resources, for example, depends on greater understanding of
the oceans and marine ecosystems and the changes they are undergoing. After 20
years, the National Oceanic and Atmospheric Administration still does not know the
status of dozens of commercially important major stocks of fish. Nor, as the recently
completed international Census of Marine Life made clear, do we know the status
of thousands of species that have no known or measurable value whatsoever.[13]

Government agencies can also improve public education and information by
enabling data from different databases to be compared. They can build upon the
progress made in giving the public access to environmental information over the
Internet by collecting and cataloging information with an eye toward maximizing
opportunities to link data from different databases through "mashups"—webpages
or applications that combine data from two or more databases.[14] At present, it
is difficult to link data from different data sets because there are few common
identifiers. For example, it is difficult to verify that Acme, Inc. (a hypothetical
company) in one database is the same Acme, Inc. in another database. However,
if all data related to environmental leasing, licensing, permitting, and compliance
had common identifiers, not only for an individual facility but also for corporate
headquarters and a corporate family, a mashup could generate a compliance history for a corporation across media and facilities throughout the nation, including
across different government agencies and different levels of government. Extending
this idea to ecosystem-based identifiers could allow environmental information to
be processed across media by ecosystem (the Chesapeake Bay, perhaps). These
technological developments and related building blocks should be made permanent

with legislation to safeguard the public availability of these databases. Such legislation would ensure that the collection and dissemination of complete information
continues regardless of changes in agency leadership.

More generally, the federal government needs to standardize the vastly varying
interpretations by government agencies of the Freedom of Information Act and
other laws. For instance, Congress should amend the FOIA to require disclosure
and electronic publication of public information, putting the burden on agencies
to justify why they cannot affirmatively disseminate such information. This would
make the FOIA request process a fall-back, rather than the primary, and often difficult, means of securing information.

Improved Public Participation

Public participation improves the quality of government decisionmaking for
sustainability because citizens bring information and issues to the government's
attention that might otherwise be given insufficient attention or even overlooked.
Public participation also means that a government's decision will likely be more
publicly credible because issues that might otherwise have been neglected will be
addressed and resolved.

Brownfields redevelopment provides an example of the usefulness of public
participation. Public participation is not always required in planning for brownfields site remediation, and the level of participation can be less than meaningful
even when public meetings or other means of involvement are conducted. Yet,
according to the National Association of Local Government Professionals and the
Northeast-Midwest Institute, active participation by the affected community "is
one of the most important ingredients for a successful brownfields project."[15] And
EPA has stated that "by creating a dialogue among all stakeholders in a brownfields
project, community engagement enhances the final reuse of the property and the
long-term success of the project."[16] This approach recognizes several realities of
typical brownfields sites. First, sites are often in areas of cities where residents
have "traditionally been left out of the planning process,"[17] and their support
can be key to a project's success. Second, brownfields sites often "dramatically
impact the health and economy of the nearby communities,"[18] making community
outreach important.

The redevelopment and cleanup of the Assunpink Greenway, a 99-acre park
along the Assunpink Creek in Trenton, New Jersey, illustrates the value of an
engaged public. After poor attendance at public meetings, a group of nonprofit
organizations stepped in and, according to Prof. Justin Hollander, "became a critical component of the project." Hollander notes that the East Trenton Collaborative
was "successful in informing and engaging the community."[19] The group led a
neighborhood planning process and conducted fieldwork to assess building, street,
and landscape conditions in the greenway area, all of which provided input to the
redevelopment and cleanup process.

Public officials can and should encourage community residents themselves to engage with sustainability issues and take positive action. As the Assunpink story illustrates, communities need "buy in" from residents for sustainability planning to work and become institutionalized. Individual residents can and should be encouraged to contribute new ideas and lead the way in creating support for sustainability in their neighborhoods.

Electronic communication and the Internet provide another opportunity to promote greater public participation. Using the Internet, government agencies can foster exchanges of information both with and among interested stakeholders. Currently, the federal Administrative Procedure Act requires government agencies only to give notice of their actions and to accept written comments.[20] Because stakeholders tend to file their written comments at the last minute, they have no opportunity to respond to one another's comments. Agencies are experimenting with an electronic dialogue that involves more public participation.[21] For example, agencies have partnered with the Cornell e-Rulemaking Initiative (CeRI) to post proposed rules at Regulationroom.org, which hosts moderated discussions of regulations to develop public comments.[22] CeRI also uses social media to encourage stakeholders to participate who might not otherwise be heard.[23] Such mechanisms could provide for wider public discussions on a range of sustainability issues.

Better Documentation of Results

Better documentation of projected results before a project begins, and final results after it is completed, will add to the credibility of sustainability efforts. Successful projects will be replicated, and unsuccessful ideas will be set aside or modified. This is about more than data; it is also about collaborative processes for sharing data and alternatives to shape a more-sustainable future.

For sustainable transportation projects, for instance, the following steps would be helpful:

- Develop data and articulate the benefits of sustainable transportation steps. Change can be accelerated if the public is provided studies that compare the cost to taxpayers of providing services to sprawling, auto-dependent development and the cost of more-sustainable development patterns; case studies on the economic return on investment in light-rail projects; data on the health benefits and cost savings of reduced pollution; and information on the money saved by purchasing fuel-efficient vehicles.
- Use graphics such as maps that show how a region will look under both sprawl and more compact development, simulations of how a declining corridor would look if it were made more pedestrian-friendly and if mass transit and transit-oriented development were added, and images of a large parking lot if trees were planted and other steps were taken to reduce and filter runoff.
- Create a vision for a community or region through an open and collaborative process that includes decisionmakers, the business community, and the

public. Scenario planning, for example, can produce information and allow participants to explore a variety of alternatives to meet future population and economic growth in an area.

- Develop indicators and performance measures to assess transportation proposals and progress toward greater sustainability. Such measures would include reduced oil consumption; lower greenhouse gas emissions; and number of roads, bridges, and transit systems in good repair.

Prioritize Transformational Technology Research

The argument for new and better technologies to foster sustainability has been repeated for years by a variety of people with very different political points of view. Many supporters *and* opponents of federal climate change legislation, for example, support the development and deployment of new renewable energy and energy efficiency technologies. In other words, technology is an issue on which there can be bipartisan agreement. A coordinated effort to use technology to reduce energy, materials, and water consumption will be an enormous contribution toward sustainability in the United States.

While the private sector has an important role to play in research and development for more-sustainable products and services, the federal government must also give high priority to research for sustainability. Achieving more-sustainable production systems will require the savvy management of a research and development portfolio that balances some sure bets with investment in more transformational research, and that addresses needs and opportunities that private-sector investment will not or cannot reach. The government has historically played an important role in spurring new transformational technologies like the Internet, airplanes, and computers. Because some clean energy technologies are not yet viable for the marketplace, federal government investment will continue in the short run to be critical to the invention and commercialization of many clean technologies. Government remains a key investor and bridge builder over what is commonly known as the "valley of death" between invention of a technology and the full-scale commercial rollout of products in the marketplace.[24]

At the moment, no single agency in the federal government is in charge of overall portfolio management and decisions regarding investments in science and technology for sustainability. This lack of alignment around strategic goals leads to suboptimal allocation of scare resources, to counterproductive investments, or to no investments at all. Though there has been some investment in greening emerging technologies like nanotechnology, the funding is orders of magnitude too low. Some of the needed strategy shifts are outlined in Figure 16.1.

Figure 16.1
Strategy Shifts Needed for Sustainable Technologies

Individual technologies		Systems of technologies
Key technologies inside your realm of interest	→	Key technologies outside your traditional realm of interest
Reactive responses to serious impacts	→	Greater foresight to prevent impacts, seize opportunities
By-products of Production → Products of Production →		Production (of almost everything) • How we produce • Where we produce • Whether we produce

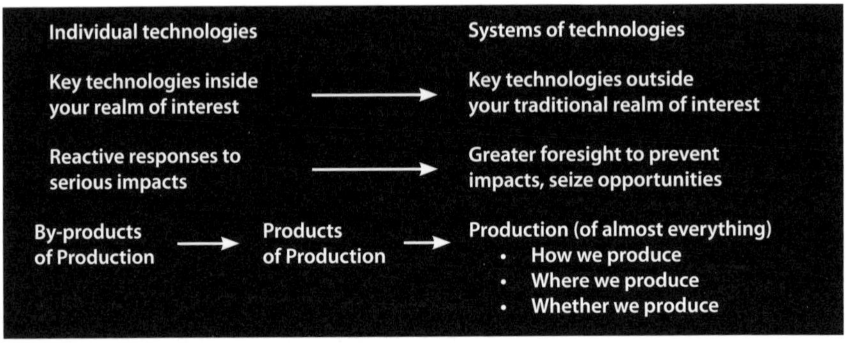

It is easy to hope for a technological "silver bullet" and to spend large sums looking for one, forgetting that we are surrounded by technologies that remain dramatically suboptimal by current standards in terms of the efficiency with which they use energy and materials. We are very much captives of what English historian David Edgerton called "the shock of the old." Our strategic arsenal, for example, still relies on the B-52 bomber (in service since 1955), machetes and small arms kill most people in wars, and climate change is driven by a suite of old-fashioned technologies and practices.[25] We have spent decades cleaning up leftover toxins and trying to nudge technological artifacts like the internal combustion engine and steam-powered dynamo, both inventions of the late 19th century, into a more environmentally friendly state. Francis Bacon, the 16th-century pioneer of the scientific method, understood the importance of scientific and technological research. "He that will not apply new remedies, must expect new evils," he said, "for Time is the greatest innovator."

In addition to maintaining outdated technologies, we think about technology in a simple and outdated way. Our approach to technological change tends to ignore one of the basic tenets of complex systems behavior—that in a system you can never do just one thing. We focus on one class of solutions, with one type of innovation strategy, put one institution in charge, but fail to seek out and manage for synergies. Yet, synergies among our environmental, security, economic, and social goals are precisely what sustainability requires. As the Indian physicist and environmental activist, Vandana Shiva, has noted, global sustainability is undermined by "monocultures of the mind" that focus on a single entity or goal.[26]

In too many cases, the greening agenda has become synonymous with small-step, continuous change, when what is needed is creative destruction—the continuous displacement of unsustainable technologies as new sustainable technologies become available.[27] The goal of this effort is to escape the well-navigated neighborhoods and predictable expectations shaped by technologies of the past, change the frames of reference for investments, and create new opportunities to radically reduce energy and resource needs. We must have a more systematic search for game-changing innovations that have the potential to (1) improve performance (such as energy efficiency) 5 to 10 times beyond existing products or processes, (2) reduce costs by 30% to 50%, or (3) have what some term "new to the world" performance features.[28]

What is needed is multiple forms of innovation—incremental, combinatorial, modular, and radical. Figure 16.2 visualizes a portfolio-based sustainable technology strategy driven by these four types of innovation.

Figure 16.2
Forms of Technological Innovation[29]

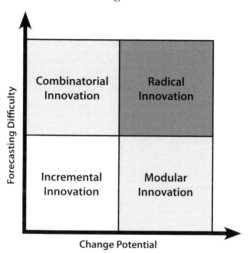

Incremental innovation increases the efficiency and utilization of old technologies and systems of old technologies. One can refocus strategies for incremental innovation on areas that significantly boost the speed and efficiency of processes. In such cases, rapid quantitative change, though incremental, can lead to qualitative shifts and, ultimately, to a new market for a product that completely displaces the old product. For example, improvements in computer processing speeds—doubling computational speed per unit cost every 18 months—have underpinned disruptive innovations in multiple products and industries for three decades because new products rapidly become preferable to even slightly older products. A similar phenomenon is now occurring in biotechnology because of rapid decreases in the cost of sequencing DNA.

There are some relatively simple fixes, though these require us to take a novel approach and view wastes as unutilized or underutilized resources. Combined heating and power units with district heating have some of the highest efficiencies and lowest carbon footprints because they produce both electricity and heat and because the heat is used to warm businesses and residences near the power plant. A traditional power plant, by contrast, produces only electricity, and the heat is wasted. The technology for combined heating and power units—largely pipes and valves—is proven and simple. Still, the United States has largely abandoned the technology. In Minnesota, in the 1950s, there were about 40 district steam systems, but today only a few remain. In Denmark, district heating provides more than 60% of space and water heating needs; in Finland, 50%. Prague, Vienna, Copenhagen, Hamburg, and Berlin have large district heating systems, and the approach is supported by the European Union's Combined Heat and Power Directive. Technological solutions focused on recovering or retrieving wasted energy flows should be given high priority in the sustainability portfolio. They will not require massive investments in basic or applied science.

Combinatorial innovation involves merging existing technologies. The power of combinatorial innovation is well known. When the DC-3 aircraft rolled out on the runway in 1936 to revolutionize commercial air transport, it combined multiple innovations like hydraulic control systems, retractable landing gear, the radial-cooled engine, and monocoque fuselage construction (which use the external skin of the plane to help hold it together). In essence, the combination was the innovation.

Combinatorial innovations put together existing ideas in new ways—for instance, combining cell phones with the Internet to create citizen monitoring networks to track deforestation or map biodiversity, or combining genomics and robotics technologies to develop high-throughput screening systems for chemicals. More recently, the Prius hybrid automobile has achieved significant gains in fuel efficiencies by combining a number of old technologies: the Atkinson cycle engine, developed in 1882, which provides efficiency at the expense of power density; regenerative braking, which converts mechanical power into electricity during braking, and was common on streetcars in the early 1900s; and aerodynamic body design, which can be traced back to Leonardo da Vinci, if not further.

Combinatorial innovation for sustainability is key in a world where parts need to be integrated into complex platform technologies, but it is not easy. Intellectual property regimes often thwart integration efforts and contribute to an inability to find and assemble the pieces into a holistic solution. The not-invented-here syndrome found in many organizations, including government bureaucracies, also undermines the ability to find synergies. Steve Jobs' old adage, "we steal ideas shamelessly," is a principle used in many highly creative learning organizations.[30] Weaving together existing technologies into a novel package is dependent not on massive investments in science and technology but on the design of organizations, creating effective incentives, and addressing intellectual property barriers. It also means finding the right kind of people; generalists are often better at these tasks.

Modular innovation combines emerging technologies with old technologies. For example, we could better recover waste heat flows with new technologies that convert heat directly into electricity. More than 8 quadrillion BTUs of heat flow from internal combustion engines in the United States annually. Both Volkswagen and BMW are developing thermoelectric generators for their cars, which will replace the standard alternator, converting waste heat directly into electricity and improving fuel efficiency by 4% to 5%.

Nano-scale surface engineering has allowed companies like Mazda to reduce the amount of precious metals used in catalytic converters by 70% to 80% while maintaining or increasing capacity for emissions reduction. (Catalytic converters are used in cars to reduce air pollution.) Generally, increasing the efficiency of catalytic conversion processes can have significant impacts on both the environment and economy. The economic impact of industrial catalysis has been estimated at $10 trillion annually, and the value of catalytic conversion in the United States is estimated at over 17% of GDP.[31]

Networks of micro- or nano-scale sensors installed in computer server farms or industrial facilities can provide significant increases in efficiencies and are examples of what some have termed an emerging cyber-physical infrastructure. Verizon recently used a mesh network of temperature sensors in 24 data centers to reduce its annual energy consumption for cooling by 55 million kilowatt-hours, reducing carbon dioxide emissions by 66 million tons per year.[32] Research by McKinsey has indicated that integrating smart control systems in power grids, buildings, and logistics systems could reduce greenhouse gas emissions by an amount equal to the greenhouse gas emissions produced by the intellectual technology industry (including computers, data centers, telecommunications, and cell phones).[33]

These are examples of using emerging technological capabilities to reduce energy and materials requirements of existing technologies or systems of production. In many cases, optimization processes enabled by this approach also improve product quality and system reliability (for instance, reducing maintenance costs). A more intensive research program for sustainability would likely produce many more such examples.

Radical innovation produces novel results. In the long run, we are going to need new ideas. As Stanford University economist Paul Romer once noted about innovation, "It springs from better recipes, not just more cooking." Radical innovations—such as nuclear fission, the transistor, and recombinant DNA—are the most difficult to anticipate. In some cases, though, they occur when the performance limits of existing technologies are understood and new solutions are consciously sought.[34] Sustainable development will depend on scientific advances that provide humankind with some paradigm-shifting options, such as viable alternatives to the internal combustion engine, ways to cheaply produce protein without the need for conventional livestock, or cost-effective solar technologies with conversion factors of more than 40%.

Our increasing ability to visualize, simulate, and control matter at a molecular scale, including biological matter, is a game changer. Stan William, who directs quantum science research at Hewlett Packard Labs, observed that "every industry that involves manufactured items will be impacted. . . . Everything can be made in some way better—stronger, lighter, cheaper, easier to recycle—if it's engineered and manufactured at the nanometer scale." As Neri Oxman at the MIT Media Lab recently noted, the biological world at the microscopic level "is displacing the machine as a general model of design." Higher efficiencies in resource use and transitions from a hydrocarbon economy will be built on more precise control of matter. We are entering what some have termed the molecular economy, based on our increasing ability to see, simulate, and manipulate matter at a biologically relevant nanometer scale.

Early signs of the transition can be found at the intersection of nanotechnology and synthetic biology. In Angela Belcher's laboratory at MIT, she and her colleagues are building parts for highly efficient rechargeable batteries by using viruses that have been engineered to coat themselves with iron and then attach to ultra-thin carbon wires to form a conductive network. At the University of California in Berkeley, chemical engineer Jay Keasling has created cellular factories using modified yeast that produce biofuels and drugs (the first commercial product is artemisinin, a key ingredient in the drug used to treat malaria).

Moving from a hydrocarbon economy to one that is biologically based is not without risks. If we begin to engineer life, these activities will raise a myriad of ethical, social, legal, and environmental issues—as well as possible unintended consequences that will need to be addressed. In many cases, we have neither the institutional capacity nor the political will to do so, and new organizational solutions are required to deal with impact assessment and risk management. As Princeton historian Edward Tenner once noted: "There is a tendency for advanced technologies to promote self-deception."

This emerging molecular economy can be directed toward greater sustainability—or not. It could be green, or brown; equitable, or unjust. However, virtually nobody is paying attention to the environmental and social implications of this profound transformation of our industrial production systems. The ETC Group recently created two lapel buttons that capture this tension and the choices we now face: "It's the Bio-economy, Stupid" and "It's the Stupid Bio-economy."

Approaches with the highest potential to bring change will likely place the highest demands on organizational learning, leadership, and the rethinking of innovation dynamics. As some recent observers have pointed out, radical innovations increasingly appear from networks of multiple actors operating in nonmarket systems, fed by high flows and exchanges of information. As Steven Johnson, author of *Where Good Ideas Come From: The Natural History of Innovation*, has put it: "The more government thinks of itself as an open platform instead of a centralized bureaucracy, the better it will be for all of us, citizens and activists and entrepreneurs alike."[35]

From a technology standpoint, we need strategies that are similar to a multisided business model in that they combine approaches to stimulate incremental change and discontinuous change simultaneously. Unfortunately, this often requires contradictory structures, processes, and cultures that are not found in most bureaucracies. Agility and flexibility should be critical components of public-sector strategy, but the challenge of promoting them is significant. At a minimum, we need to focus on strategies to nudge the innovation system. The best place to put the fulcrum is at the front edge of technological advance. The sustainable development community needs to mount a major expedition to the technological frontier, where the change potential is the greatest.

Public deliberation on scientific and technological research could help accelerate the needed investments. Achieving sustainable development requires the consideration of social and economic impacts of science and technology investments early in the R&D process, not after the fact. Otherwise, as Langdon Winner once put it, "powerful technologies emerge from the lab and go looking for uses."[36] Unlike many European countries, the United States has no official or formal mechanisms for supporting public deliberation involving science and technology investments using public funds.

Fortunately, methods for initiating a dialogue around our technological choices already exist and can be applied at virtually any scale, from local to global. Participatory technology assessment would benefit sustainable development practices by giving people a voice in technological innovation. Its use thus far in the United States, however, has been very limited.[37] Greater use of science cafes (events where scientists discuss research with the lay public), consensus conferences, and other deliberative mechanisms would help support sustainability goals and ensure more responsible development of emerging technologies, as well as mitigating unintended social consequences. A recent Europe-wide survey made the point that "harnessing the winds of change into the design of particular emerging technologies will necessitate listening and accommodating to the public's voice(s)."[38]

Willingness to Discuss and Act on Hard Issues

Governmental leadership means a willingness to discuss, or at least openly participate in a discussion of, the very hardest sustainability issues, the issues that might seem to be politically off limits. The U.S. government cannot claim that it is taking steps toward sustainability without first analyzing, through a formal review, the country's environmental resource base and developing policies to ensure that the population does not exceed its carrying capacity, including its ability to draw on foreign resources. This review should include considerations of equity in a globalizing and increasingly competitive world, as well as the possible tightening of constraints on global resources such as petroleum and certain minerals essential for future technologies.[39] The review should also include an assessment of population in areas vulnerable to climate change, including coastal areas that are likely to be affected by sea-level rise.

The United States has thus far failed in this admittedly difficult and complex obligation. Piecemeal analyses have been undertaken by scientists in universities and research institutes, often supported with government funds, but there has been no government-sponsored attempt to make such an assessment on a comprehensive national scale for at least three decades. In some cases, Congress or the executive branch has even attempted to discourage any such research by cutting budgets for work by government agencies on such relevant topics as renewable energy or a national inventory of biodiversity. Nor has any government-sponsored research been conducted on a desirable population size for the United States from an environmental standpoint, although the President's Council on Sustainable Development in the Clinton Administration at least raised the question.

This type of analysis and the valuable public debate it would engender would be difficult, to be sure, but it is certainly possible. Australia conducted just such an exercise nearly a decade ago, sparking a nationwide debate over the population size it should aim toward in the 21st century.[40] While the conclusions of that report were controversial, it sparked serious discussion over how access to fresh water, for example, could or should limit population growth, not only at a national level but at regional and municipal levels as well.

The federal government also needs to exercise international leadership on population. In late 2011, the world's population climbed over 7 billion. Given an increasingly economically and environmentally integrated world, it is essential that we deepen the nation's commitment to the international agreements on population, development, and the environment that we have signed and ratified. Taken together, these agreements add up to a common understanding that population stability, environmental integrity, prudent resource use, and equity considerations must all be inextricably linked in any design for a sustainable human future.

Continued State and Local Policy Innovation

State and local governments also need to fill the innovation gap that is still being left by the federal government. Historically, state and local governments have been a fertile testing ground for effective sustainability policies. Indeed, Justice Louis Brandeis famously characterized the states as "laboratories" for experimentation.[41]

The innovations made by one state can serve as models for other states to emulate. Political scientists have long argued that states are inclined to adopt a policy of a neighboring state if it appears to be productive.[42] Prof. Christopher Mooney of the University of Illinois has described the process of policy diffusion, in which a state adopts a neighboring state's policies:

> Early in diffusion, little information is available to help policymakers reduce uncertainty in decisionmaking. The policy may be untested and its long-term consequences unknown. Having the policy recently adopted by a neighbor increases the information available about both its policy and political consequences. Policy entrepreneurs may

seize the opportunity to enhance their own careers by championing the "reform," playing up the positive aspects of it that citizens in neighboring states are enjoying.[43]

The development of regional climate action plans, discussed in Chapter 5, is an example of state policy diffusion. Northeastern states have already initiated a cap-and-trade program for greenhouse gases, known as the Regional Greenhouse Gas Initiative, which is designed to reduce carbon dioxide emissions from electricity generation by 10% by 2018.[44] California's leadership led to the Western Climate Initiative, which now includes California and four Canadian provinces.[45] California's cap-and-trade program for greenhouse gases is even sparking interest in states that tend to be unsupportive of legislation to address climate change because entrepreneurs in those states see opportunities to generate profits from offsets.[46] (Offsets in this context are reductions at unregulated facilities that are sold and used to reduce the control obligations of regulated facilities.) Quebec, one of the Canadian provinces in the Western Climate Initiative, recently adopted a cap-and-trade program that is intended to work together with California's program.[47] This kind of partnership suggests the possibility of a North American cap-and-trade program that is built from coordinated state and provincial programs.

California and the Northeast are not typical of America, as coal is rarely used to generate electricity in those areas; by contrast, nearly half of America's electricity comes from burning coal.[48] Nonetheless, these programs could do a great deal to show the feasibility of a cap-and-trade approach combined with suitable safeguards. Greenhouse gas control is perhaps the one area in which there is the greatest need for innovative programs to be tested and refined. It is particularly important that we find out whether an emissions offset program—of the kind that California is employing—is workable.

Conclusion

Governance for sustainability must be both visionary and pragmatic, positive and forward looking but also attentive to facts on the ground and willing to make adjustments that do not compromise the ultimate objective. The federal government should employ a strategic process for sustainability to identify priorities and threats and determine the best means of addressing them. Governments at all levels must also provide the public with more information related to sustainability, and encourage broader public participation in decisions related to sustainability. The federal government also needs an aggressive and well-funded effort to develop and deploy new technologies for sustainability.

None of this necessarily requires bigger government or more regulation. What it requires instead is a willingness to explicitly acknowledge the challenges before us as well as the opportunities. And it requires a governmental commitment to work hard on these issues, day after day, decade after decade. This governmental commitment will make it more likely that laws are adopted, modified, and implemented to foster sustainability. And both supportive laws and governance will speed up the availability and attractiveness of more-sustainable options.

CHAPTER 17

An American Sustainability Movement

To achieve sustainability, the United States needs a committed and engaged pub-lic—the kind of widespread support that once fought World War II or, without its excesses, that fought communism during the Cold War. Half measures, symbolic commitments, and political gestures simply will not do. There is enormous work to do, the time is limited, and the stakes are high for us as well as for future genera-tions. Yet, the hard reality is that we do not now have that level of near-universal commitment on issues of sustainability. Without a powerful constituency across much of the country and a consensus on the need for strong actions—without, in short, a broad national movement for sustainability—the required full-bore effort will be difficult to muster.

As this book shows, the sustainability movement in the United States has already begun. The movement's existence is reflected in the fact that much of the progress made on sustainability over the past two decades has been from the bottom up. Hundreds of corporations are using less energy and water and are selling more-sustainable products and services. Large and small communities are becoming more livable and attractive. Schools, particularly colleges and universities, are greening their operations and teaching their students about the connections between the environment and everything else we care about. The built environment is in many ways becoming more sustainable because of the greater use of brownfields redevelopment and green building. And religious organizations are becoming more active in what they teach and do, affecting not only their members but the broader public. These efforts have been driven by citizens, voters, landowners, customers, students, parents, and many other stakeholders. Local governments, businesses, educational institutions, and religious leaders—all of whom are closer to many of the problems of unsustainable activities than is the national government—have strong incentives to pay attention to what these people want. To a great degree, in fact, that is why sustainability efforts have gained traction.

This emerging sustainability movement includes related movements that have also been described in this book, most notably the environmental movement that took off in the late 1960s and early 1970s. It includes other movements as well—environmental justice, smart growth, green development, climate change, climate justice, education for sustainability, sustainable agriculture, and organic farming.[1] It also must draw lessons from some of the most important movements in this nation's history—the abolition of slavery, women's suffrage, and civil rights.

The emerging movement for sustainability is based on millions of like-minded people seeking greater sustainability in their communities, businesses, and their own lives, as well as in the states and nation. It is inner-directed (toward the homes, organizations, institutions, and businesses where people live and work) as well as outer-directed (toward the decisions made by communities, states, and the national government). It involves the scientific and technological community, business and industry, educational institutions, religious organizations, farmers, lawyers, and labor unions. It involves leaders, followers, and more independently minded individuals and organizations who pursue sustainability for their own reasons but will neither lead nor be led. The affiliations between and among individuals, organizations, and governments can be formal or informal, loose or tight.

This emerging American sustainability movement is part of a global movement based on more than a million nongovernmental organizations that the environmental writer Paul Hawken says are "working toward ecological sustainability and social justice."[2] What he says in his book *Blessed Unrest* about the global movement is also true of the emerging sustainability movement in the United States:

> By any conventional definition, this vast collection of committed individuals does not constitute a movement. Movements have leaders and ideologies. People *join* movements, study their tracts, and identify themselves with a group. They read the biography of the founder(s) or listen to them perorate on tape or in person. Movements, in short, have followers. This movement, however, doesn't fit the standard model. It is dispersed, inchoate, and fiercely independent. It has no manifesto or doctrine, no overriding authority to check with. It is taking places in schools, farms, jungles, villages, companies, deserts, fisheries, slums—and yes, even fancy New York hotels. One of its distinctive features is that it is tentatively emerging as a global humanitarian movement that is arising from the bottom up.[3]

The movement's political base can become huge—not merely a majority but a base that is "party blind" and includes the middle 60% to 80% of the American population. And it needs to expand now. This expanding movement will better mobilize rural, urban, and suburban citizens, interest groups, and the media. It will also put greater pressure on local, state, and national political leaders for meaningful and effective policies to promote sustainability. While there are numerous groups and individuals currently involved in the effort to promote sustainability, and there is widespread support among the lay public for many policies that promote sustainability in the abstract, these groups and individuals will have a major additional challenge: they will have to engage a disconnected and nonparticipating public. The process may be both long and difficult.

What needs to happen for this movement to become a major force in American society and politics? Sociologists and political scientists have identified characteristics of successful movements. The remainder of this chapter discusses some key characteristics of a successful American sustainability movement.

A Widely Shared Mobilizing Framework

A mobilizing framework is a worldview that allows people to simplify and make sense of an issue. In this case, the mobilizing framework is the central philosophy of sustainability—the view that we must find ways to achieve our social, economic, environmental, and security goals in an integrated manner, both for our present quality of life and for that of future generations. Of equal importance, we all have a role to play, in our personal and work lives, in fostering sustainable development.

Within that broad definition of sustainability, several points can serve as the practical focus for action. These include a demand for more-sustainable and attractive choices across the entire range of decisions that individuals, businesses, governments, and others make on a daily basis; an insistence on laws that support and encourage sustainable development, including environmentally sustainable economic development; and a demand (even in the face of public cynicism and pessimism about government) for the kind of visionary and pragmatic governance needed to ensure our prosperity and that of our descendants. They also include the willingness of each individual, business, institution, and government to accept a fair share of the responsibility to reduce his, her, or its environmental impact and move toward sustainability.

Because sustainable development is directed toward quality of life, freedom, and opportunity, it does not accept the false distinction between the economy and the environment. Sustainability is not about choosing people first or the environment first; it is about putting people *and* the environment first. Unlike their counterparts in the rest of the world who have a better understanding of sustainability, however, Americans tend to see sustainability through "green-tinted lenses," as synonymous with environmental protection alone—or more derisively, saving polar bears and spotted owls.[4] An essential task for this movement is to clarify that sustainability is oriented to the needs of people and their quality of life. It is practical and hard-headed—anything but tree-hugging.

Hopeful Expectations, Based on Evidence

When participating in a movement, people want to feel they are joining ranks with large numbers of like-minded people and that their own participation will contribute to the success of the movement. For sustainability, this hopeful expectation can be promoted in two ways.

One way is through the development of vision statements for localities, corporations, states, and even the nation that are both optimistic and pragmatic. At the community level, for instance, the vision should link an individual's "own desires for the future and ideas about the best way to achieve that future" with those of the community and provide a basis for informing and motivating people.[5] Yet, the particulars of that vision will differ for each community, based on its geography, history, and culture. The particular sustainability vision of a corporation, similarly, will depend on the particular goods or services that it provides. At the national level, President Clinton's Council on Sustainable Development, an advisory body that issued its primary report in 1996, crafted this vision statement:

> Our vision is of a life-sustaining Earth. We are committed to the achievement of a dignified, peaceful, and equitable existence. A sustainable United States will have a growing economy that provides equitable opportunities for satisfying livelihoods and a safe, healthy, high quality of life for current and future generations. Our nation will protect its environment, its natural resource base, and the functions and viability of natural systems on which all life depends.[6]

All too often, our impetus for action can be negative—to resist or change something we do not want. But it is difficult to move coherently over a long period driven by ad hoc reactions to undesirable developments or activities. If there is to be a journey toward sustainability, there must be a vision with a destination, an aspiration for what people want their communities and their institutions to look like, around which a great many and varied acts can be undertaken and coordinated. An affirmative statement of positive environmental welfare, for example, can strengthen support for regional ecosystem restoration programs. In higher education, clearer models of what sustainable colleges and universities look like and how they operate will help higher education institutions plan more effectively for their role in a more-sustainable future.

In fashioning a vision, we need to be alert to the great difference between "strong" and "weak" models of sustainability. Weak sustainability allows the degradation or depletion of natural capital (forests, for example) as long as it is used to make products of equal value (lumber or paper). Strong sustainability, by contrast, maintains the existing stock of natural capital because a forest cannot be replaced and its actual value is difficult to accurately measure in economic terms. Strong sustainability is also consistent with religious and ethical justifications for sustainability. If a vision is not based on strong sustainability, strategies and steps to "move toward sustainability" will continue to stumble or will fail to elicit wide support, while generating comfortable illusions of progress.

In addition to a positive vision, the second basis for a hopeful expectation is growing evidence that a more-sustainable future is actually achievable. The track record thus far with more-sustainable alternatives—in green building, forest certification, reductions in pollution and waste, among other things—indicates that there are many tried-and-true alternatives that are preferable to business as usual. Our ability to develop and implement those alternatives also indicates that even more alternatives can be created—that there is an empirical basis for believing a more-sustainable future, even a truly sustainable future, is achievable.

Compelling Reasons to Participate

In many movements, the compelling reasons to join are based on dramatic spot-lighting, in which events that lead to public outrage are highlighted for the media and potential participants. Because most Americans receive information through television, the most effective appeal to emotions concerning sustainable policies would have to be visual and compelling. The plight of some Arctic animals, such as polar bears encountering declining habitat, has generated much media atten-tion on climate change and individual carbon footprints. A national campaign that uses powerful images on behalf of sustainability could be conducted jointly with educational programs. Citizen knowledge of environmental issues and support for environmental protection go hand in hand. Recent research on sustainable ocean and coastal fisheries found that the enhancement of citizen knowledge is critical to the development of public support for protective measures.[7]

But for sustainability to grow and endure as a movement, something more than memorable images and public education will be needed. People participate in a movement when they understand that the values of the movement align with their own values. For this to happen, the message of the movement must be clear and attractive, and fit easily within people's value system.[8] This process of lining up movement messages with individual values, called frame alignment, is needed for the sustainability movement. Three deeply resonant messages, frames with which most of us can align our own values, should encourage people to participate over the long term.

First, sustainability will lead to higher quality of life. While we can analyze environmental, social, and economic issues separately, we improve the quality of life by making all three mutually reinforcing. Conversely, we reduce quality of life when we further economic and social goals without regard to the resulting envi-ronmental harm or without considering the effect that environmental harm has on our economic and social goals. This book is replete with examples of communities and organizations that have moved in a more-sustainable direction to make their localities more attractive for existing and prospective residents, to create more livable and attractive buildings, to convert contaminated and unused lots back into attractive properties, and to provide healthier food.

Second, sustainability is economically attractive. As we look ahead to a more crowded world with increased economic activity and growing environmental threats, the only economic activity that will be durable, profitable, and job creating is that which is environmentally sustainable. This is a statement of fact rather than optimism; it simply reflects the reality in which we live. Out of necessity, unsus-tainable activities will, sooner or later, be more heavily regulated and otherwise limited. Again, this book contains many illustrations of environmentally sustainable economic development, and many of these also directly improve human quality of life—for example, certification of organic food, green building, smart growth, and more-sustainable transportation and land-use practices in communities.

For problems that are less amenable to traditional regulation, such as those caused by population growth in specific places, communities need to be convinced that economic incentives and other measures are desirable to promote their long-term continuing community welfare. One example is making appropriate use of scarce water resources across a region. A challenge in this regard is to convince communities facing acute short-term problems of unemployment and budget deficits that investments in long-term sustainability will benefit the community enough in the future to sacrifice some short-term benefits. One possible strategy in this regard is to use the best available efforts to catalog and value (in monetary or other terms) the benefits of ecosystem services provided by aquatic and other ecosystems, so that the public and decisionmakers understand the benefits of restoring and protecting those systems for their economic as well as their intrinsic value.

To be sure, sustainability is not financially attractive to businesses that depend on unsustainable practices. But it is important not to confuse those businesses with the business community as a whole. Some of these businesses may also be willing and able, with the right persuasion, to change their practices in a significantly more-sustainable direction.

Third, sustainability is the right thing to do. Sustainability links ancient ethical and religious teachings that are almost universally held, including the duty not to harm innocent beings, with environmental protection and restoration, which is not ordinarily recognized as part of conventional ethical or religious beliefs. The key factual premise is that sooner or later environmental damage will hurt other humans, including humans who are not yet born. When people come to understand that, they often begin to see sustainable alternatives as aligned with their beliefs and attitudes, as expressions of who they are and what they want.

A common feature of many personal commitments to the sustainability movement is the "aha" moment, the instant when someone connects the dots, seeing for the first time that his company's actions, his personal actions, or her vote in Congress could help, or harm, the world in which his or her grandchildren will grow up. It is when someone sees for the first time that actions that damage the environment also hurt other people, offend the God that created everything, or both. In these stories, nothing changes except an individual's understanding of his or her place in the world, and yet that makes all the difference.

Among corporate executives, few were better known for their sustainability leadership than Ray Anderson, the chair and founder of Interface, the world's largest producer of modular carpeting. Anderson understood that doing the right thing can be far from sacrifice. Under his leadership, the company rented carpet rather than selling it, and then later replaced and recycled worn-out carpet pieces instead of throwing them away. Through recycling, reduced energy use, and lower greenhouse gas emissions, the company saved hundreds of millions of dollars. Before his death in August 2011, Anderson spoke tirelessly and with an evangelical zeal about what Interface had done. He once told a conference of business executives:

"We are all part of the continuum of humanity and life. We will have lived our brief span and either helped or hurt that continuum and the earth that sustains all life. It's that simple. Which will it be?" Anderson attributed his change of attitude to another Paul Hawken book, *The Ecology of Commerce*, which he read after he was already running Interface. "I got it," he said. "I was a plunderer of Earth, and that is not the legacy one wants to leave behind."[9] When Anderson died, he was described as "the greenest CEO in America."[10]

The moral dimension of sustainability is being understood and applied with greater seriousness across a range of religious and nonreligious communities.[11] It includes an understanding of the importance of care for creation as well as the need to care for people who are adversely affected by unsustainable actions. There is also a growing sense that environmentally unsustainable activities are putting our children and future generations at risk. Such perspectives have informed a growing interest in the moral aspects of specific sustainability issues; climate ethics is perhaps the most prominent of these.[12] Such perspectives, however, do not yet appear to be informing broader public thinking and attitudes about sustainability, or what the public expects from governmental officials.

Although a growing number of religious institutions are participating in policy dialogues about sustainability, they need to identify more clearly how the language used to frame sustainability problems can hide many of the central ethical issues. Much of the discourse on sustainability is framed by scientific and economic descriptions of sustainability problems and their solutions. To go beyond this framework, religious people working with ethicists can help identify the deep ethical questions that often go unnoticed when technical discourse alone frames policy options. Some cost-benefit analyses, for example, deeply discount costs to future generations. Environmental organizations also need to better articulate the ethical dimensions of policymaking. Many environmental organizations fail to identify these ethical questions, and instead advocate on behalf of sustainability using the same economic and scientific framing that is being used by opponents of sustainability practices.

The sustainability movement should foster a national dialogue on the ethics of sustainability through conferences and meetings that invite the media and leaders of environmental organizations and businesses, as well as religious leaders and ethicists, to identify the ethical dimensions of sustainability issues. A promising contribution to this effort is the National Climate Ethics Campaign, which in late 2011 was seeking signatures for a statement on "our nation's moral obligation to address climate change."[13]

A recent book by Princeton philosophy professor Kwame Anthony Appiah[14] suggests an interesting but so far unrealized possibility for building on this ethical and religious sensibility. Appiah argues that some of the most important moral revolutions in recent centuries have come about because people see a particular action as not merely morally right but also as bringing honor or esteem to those

who support that action, and shame or loss of esteem to those who do not. Historically, privileged classes supported some practices, such as dueling (Europe, United
States) or foot binding (China), until these practices no longer brought esteem but
instead brought ridicule or shame. While there were longstanding arguments that
these practices were immoral or wrong, those arguments were ultimately not successful until they were linked with loss of honor or social esteem.

Could Appiah's insights help support a sustainability movement? In both developed and developing countries, there is a tendency for the wealthiest people to
consume more than poorer people, and for consumption to be a symbol of status.
Higher status tends to be linked to bigger cars, bigger houses, and more property
and other luxuries. Imagine, in contrast, that being carbon neutral, or having a small
ecological footprint, is seen as a source of honor or esteem, and that high consumption is a source of ridicule or shame. That change in perception could enhance the
moral and religious urgency for a sustainability movement.

Finally, the issues that have ethical dimensions are not limited to the environment. Many of today's political problems—the budget deficit, the economic
recession, and climate change—all have a common root: a tendency to act in
ways that privilege today over tomorrow, and ourselves over our children and
our grandchildren, even as we declare that their well-being is our most important responsibility. Jonas Salk, the inventor of the Salk polio vaccine, said: "Our
greatest responsibility is to be good ancestors."[15] That is precisely the worldview
required for intergenerational equity. The sustainability movement needs to foster
a national conversation about what it would really mean to leave the country and
the world in better shape than we found it. That would at least be a start toward a
discussion of what it would mean, as an American, to be a good ancestor. And it
would be the right thing to do.

Absence of Crosscutting Cleavages

Sustainability is neither a conservative nor a liberal concept, but contains elements of both. Sustainability is built around a need to maintain our collective and
individual bearings in an ever-changing world. Throughout history, humans have
found their collective and individual bearings through institutional memberships
and shared principles. While conservatives and liberals may each place differing
emphases on some institutions and principles, both desire to maintain core democratic values and are eager to sustain the institutions that give life to those values.

The sustainability movement in the United States is not strongly tied to the
ideological predispositions of the two major national political parties. The companies, industries, institutions, government agencies, individuals, and families that
participate in sustainable activities do so for their own reasons—to save money, to
remain competitive, to please their customers, to improve their public image, to
create jobs and better working conditions, to produce a better or cheaper product,

to gain market share, to attract prospective students, or to better honor their own values. They are driven by scientific evidence and organizational, personal, or family needs. Although they also may have ideological values, those values do not necessarily drive the decisions they make in a specific context. While national policy matters to sustainability, this movement will almost certainly continue to grow regardless of the result of any particular election.

Still, the values and purposes of sustainability should command bipartisan political support. Environmental protection, social well-being, economic development, and national security are important to Republicans, Democrats, and independents. The ultimate goals of sustainability—freedom, opportunity, and quality of life— are important to both parties and to those who do not affiliate with either party. Because sustainability embraces a broad range of legal and policy tools, and both public and private action—and is not limited to regulation—Republicans should in theory find it easier to embrace. Because hundreds of corporations are making efforts to move toward sustainability, business-oriented Republicans should find sustainability attractive. Although there is more bipartisan support for sustainability at the local and state levels, such bipartisan support has not worked its way into national politics.

Conversely, some liberals see sustainability as a watering down of environmental protection and ecological integrity in environmental law. They see sustainability as enabling the resurrection of old claims that economic development matters more than anything else. False and misleading environmental and sustainability claims by corporations are, for these people, especially damaging to the credibility of sustainability as a concept. They also see sustainability's twin goals of development and environmental protection as both confusing and difficult to achieve in practice. To win over these critics, it is important to demonstrate genuine improvements in environmental quality, energy efficiency, job creation, and greenhouse gas emissions reduction, and the potential for still more.

On an issue-by-issue basis, there can and should be room for bipartisan agreement on a variety of sustainability issues. For sure, movements are messy, and partisans are involved on both sides of many sustainability issues. Yet promoting sustainability should not be seen simply within a framework of conflict—as rural versus urban, conservative versus liberal, and environmentalist versus industry. Such crosscutting cleavages lead to political gridlock and undermine efforts at building a large and effective movement. Any successful movement will have to operate in a large tent and focus on common goals. One successful effort was the expansion of Michigan's bottle bill in the 1980s, which imposed a mandatory deposit on certain nonreturnable containers, and required the deposit to be refunded to the consumer when the container is returned. The legislation reduces litter, as people are less likely to throw these containers on the roadside, and also increases recycling. To pass this legislation, hunting, fishing, conservation, and environmental groups put their differences aside and focused on increasing and expanding beverage container deposits. This movement crossed not only ideological lines but also some very different views on resource management.

In any given situation, part of the challenge is finding vocabulary to express values that are shared across a wide range of perspectives and backgrounds. One approach is to develop and frame the sustainability proposals in ways that will make them more appealing to politically conservative voters and decisionmakers.[16] Appeals based on thrift, green jobs, conservation for future generations, less dependence on foreign oil, and care for creation are more likely to work than appeals based on climate change, where disinformation campaigns and suspicion of mainstream science have created a wide gap that may be too wide to bridge at this time.[17]

Another approach is to use language that conveys the meaning of sustainability without using the word itself. Emphasizing energy security, for instance, brings together the challenges of fossil fuel prices, fuel availability, sources of fuel diversity, the trade deficit, energy efficiency, and climate change.[18] Other terms that appear to capture the sustainability concept and that appear to resonate as more immediate concerns include food security,[19] water security, green jobs, and green economy. Taken together, all of these terms capture a significant part of the sustainability framework. It would be valuable to explore this and other vocabulary based on recent research on what make ideas "sticky" and socially contagious.[20]

An outreach effort of this kind may require many organizations to change their approach and the tone of their message. Fred Krupp, President of the Environmental Defense Fund, has suggested that the failure to adopt climate change legislation may rest to some extent within the environmental movement.[21] Krupp characterizes environmental supporters of legislation as "having an air of disdain for their opponents" and an attitude that "we have all the answers." In explaining his remarks, Krupp has said that the environmental community needs "to do a better job of engaging with the public, rather than just lecturing," and that "we need to do a better job of listening, and of connecting to needs as the public sees them, rather than just telling them what they ought to be worried about."[22] Krupp's comments have been criticized as too harsh on the environmental community, but the desired attitude they express is right on target.

Capable and Competent Leadership

Across the sustainability movement, articulate and charismatic leaders and organizers are essential. Strong and principled leadership has been and will continue to be a primary factor in building support for sustainability. Leadership is especially important because sustainability requires alternatives to business as usual, breaking old habits and going in a new direction. Still, if leaders are identified as being too partisan or allied too closely with a particularly divisive interest group, then their ability to lead a broad-based movement is diminished.

"Sustainability and leadership are two great and intertwined themes of our time," says James Strock, founding secretary of California's Environmental Protection Agency and former assistant administrator for enforcement of the U.S. Environmental Protection Agency.[23] He has asked: "If we look ahead 30 years, are we going to see the world stay as it is, but just more of it?" Or are we going to see the world "that could be?" This, he said, is where leadership and sustainability come together.[24]

Strock argues that leadership for sustainability is based, first and foremost, on ethics. Doing the ethical thing, he asserts, is "increasingly the practical thing" for businesses and others to do. Because the global availability of information makes it virtually impossible for businesses to hide bad practices, doing the right thing can give a business a competitive advantage.

The disconnect that Ray Anderson saw—between how he had been acting and his regard for the future—goes to the heart of the sustainability challenge. He made a decision, in short, to *act as if tomorrow matters.* Leadership for sustainability almost invariably requires a departure from fixed ways of doing things, a willingness to experiment and take risks, the ability to persuade others to join or follow, and a hard-nosed will to find ways of making environmental protection, economic development, and social well-being work together.

Other individual leadership examples abound. The development of the U.S. Green Building Council's LEED certification program required both vision and an ability to translate that vision into specific, technically feasible standards that could actually be implemented. Robert Watson, who has been called the "father of LEED," combined those two qualities when he chaired the U.S. Green Building Council from its inception in 1993 until 2006. He founded LEED, he says, because "the construction and operation of buildings is the most resource intensive and environmentally-damaging of all human activities—approximately 50 percent of global energy and material resources are consumed by the construction and operation of buildings."[25] Watson now runs EcoTech International, a consulting firm that promotes green building around the world.

In the area of environmental justice, early leadership emerged in the late 1970s and 1980s from grassroots movements formed to draw attention to environmental racism in the siting of otherwise locally unwanted land uses such as hazardous waste facilities, landfills, and industrial uses in close proximity to communities of color.[26] Dr. Robert Bullard, who is now director of the Environmental Justice Resource Center at Clark Atlanta University, has been a leader from the movement's early days, collecting data for a Houston, Texas, lawsuit to prove the existence of environmental racism. He has since authored, coauthored, or edited more than a dozen books on environmental justice. Bullard has also played a prominent advocacy role, helping to persuade EPA to integrate environmental justice into its work. Other environmental justice leaders include the United Church of Christ's Commission for Racial Justice, which issued a landmark report in 1987 that documented a significant relationship between the location of hazardous waste facilities and toxic waste sites, on one hand, and race, on the other.[27] Today, EPA, under the direction of Administrator Lisa Jackson, has assumed a leadership role in institutionalizing environmental justice principles throughout EPA and in partner agencies. The chair of EPA's advisory committee, the National Environmental Justice Advisory Council (NEJAC), is attorney/advocate Elizabeth Yeampierre, who is the Executive Director of UPROSE (The United Puerto Rican Organization of Sunset Park), the oldest Latino community-based organization in Brooklyn, New York.[28]

One of the visionaries of sustainable agriculture is plant breeder Wes Jackson, who takes a systems-based approach to solving agriculture problems. He applies the philosophy of biomimicry to his work, as he mimics the prairie in designing what he calls perennial polyculture—agriculture based on plant species that live three or more seasons and puts two or more plant species on a single plot of land. Jackson notes that our agricultural practices are not what one finds in nature; nature does not plow and does not deal in monocultures. So, in 1976, he founded the Land Institute in Salina, Kansas, with the intention of designing a perennial polyculture that mimics the prairie and could replace our current system of agriculture.

Many companies are also playing leadership roles. Recently, Wal-Mart decided to ban polybrominated flame retardants from its products and told its suppliers to come up with alternatives. Whole Foods recently decided to ban bisphenol A (BPA), which is linked to several different adverse health effects, from baby products. Lately, Google is acting more like a public sector entity, with its recent investment in an underwater transmission line for off-shore wind energy along the Atlantic coastline. Hewlett Packard's initiative to create a Central Nervous System for the Earth involves a "planetwide sensing network using billions of tiny, cheap, tough and exquisitely sensitive detectors" to monitor not only traffic conditions but also an enormous variety of environmental conditions, providing data about weather and climate that we do not now have. This is the kind of audacious, let's-put-a-man-on-the-moon, goal that used to come from the public sector.[29] Nike recently created GreenXchange, a creative commons system to allow sharing of sustainable technological innovations between companies.[30] To be sure, many corporate claims about sustainability are greenwash, and it is entirely possible that, as many have argued, sustainability will ultimately require deeper changes in the way that corporations are managed. Still, these examples, individually and collectively, show corporate leadership on sustainability, and indicate the constructive role that corporations can play in the sustainability movement.

These leaders need to come from every other walk of life, organization, and discipline. Chicago is consistently ranked as one of the top sustainable cities in the United States largely due to the efforts of former Mayor Richard Daley, who often said his goal was to "make Chicago the greenest City in America." Individual citizens also need to be sustainability leaders, raising issues about quality of life or environmental justice in their communities, developing and sharing information, advocating specific legal or policy changes, acting on behalf of nongovernmental organizations or leading those organizations.

Leadership at the national level—from both the president and Congress—can play a key role as well. Much of recent progress at the national level has occurred because of increased presidential commitment to sustainability concepts. President Barack Obama's support for higher fuel efficiency for motor vehicles, as a combined policy of economic development, environmental protection, and job creation is one of several examples of the administration's sustainable energy policy.

In taking these actions, the Obama Administration is building on preexisting agency commitments toward sustainability under the Government Performance and Results Act as well as environmental and energy legislation. It must also be remembered that the George H.W. Bush Administration committed the United States to the global plan of action for sustainability (Agenda 21) at the 1992 U.N. Conference on Environment and Development in Rio de Janeiro—an act of greater political leadership in retrospect than it appeared to be at the time.

Leaders have also emerged in international financial institutions. At the World Bank from 1995 to 2005, President James Wolfensohn championed several reforms, leading the Bank to focus more on poverty reduction, environmental protection, anticorruption, good governance, and human rights.[31] Staff members at the World Bank have also acted as champions for specific environmental and human rights reforms. The Bank hired Dr. Robert Goodland, for example, as its first ecologist in the 1970s. In the 1980s, he drafted and persuaded the Bank to apply environmental and social safeguards to its lending, undertaking dozens of workshops, conferences, publications, guest lectures, and meetings with internal committees. These policies were the first at the Bank to take into account the environment, indigenous peoples, involuntary resettlement, and other key issues, and later served as models for other international institutions.[32]

A Micro-Mobilization Approach

Organizing small groups at the local level, all connected to a much larger network or coalition, is an important component of a successful movement. Interacting at the local level increases interest in issues and thus levels of participation. At the same time, there must be a connection to a larger movement; people are more likely to participate if they believe large numbers of others are also participating.[33] Examples of successful movements that modeled this organizational structure are the women's suffrage movement as well as the environmental movement in the 1960s and 1970s.

The emerging U.S. sustainability movement already operates to a large degree as "bottom up." As various individual pieces of the sustainability movement grow, and those who have been affected by them reach out to other sustainability networks, the impetus for even more progress can become much greater.

Diverse and Effective Communications Network

Successful movements have communication networks that connect large and diverse numbers of people. The greater the number and diversity of people actively participating in the network, the more likely the movement will be successful. The communication network needs to connect individuals, organizations, businesses, and other participants in the movement with each other, with mass media and policy makers, and with potential new participants.

This communications network should include social media such as Facebook, LinkedIn, Twitter, and YouTube. Given the widespread use of the Internet among youth and the rapid spread of connectivity in both workplace and home settings, social media are a promising source of such information.

The accessibility and widespread use of sources like Facebook and Twitter have created an alternative outlet to the mainstream media. The Egyptian uprising in spring 2011 is sometimes referred to as the "Twitter Revolution" because of that site's role in publicizing demonstrations and mobilizing people to the streets. As one activist tweeted, "We use Facebook to schedule the protests, Twitter to coordinate, and YouTube to tell the world."[34] The United States also saw the effects of social media during the Occupy Wall Street protests. For the first week, the protesters attracted very little mass media attention. It was dedicated messaging in social media that first brought the movement into national focus; mainstream media attention snowballed when a video of a police officer pepper spraying protesters went viral on YouTube.

Scientists also have an important role to play in this network. Research scientists need to engage more frequently in policy debates, working closely with citizens, interest groups, and decisionmakers. The principle reason why decisionmakers and the attentive public look to science for information and guidance is confidence that it produces reliable knowledge. Climate disinformation notwithstanding, there is still considerable confidence in scientists as truth-seekers, strongly committed to the professional methods and norms of scientific inquiry, and to collecting and analyzing evidence independent of any special interests.[35]

Sufficient Financial Resources

Financial resources are pivotal to success in policymaking. This is particularly true for a national movement that is based on hundreds if not thousands of local movements throughout the country. The resources necessary to wage a strong campaign to promote sustainability policies would have to go beyond mere membership dues. They would also need to include resources from allied industries, such as renewable energy, and foundations. This is particularly important for sustainability proposals that are opposed by the substantial resources of the affected industry. In most parts of the United States, conservation and environmental groups rely heavily on membership dues and volunteers, while industry related groups have fewer members but more substantial financial resources.[36]

Fortunately for sustainability, many businesses, business organizations, and other nongovernmental organizations are already supportive of various sustainability proposals—the renewable energy and energy-efficiency industries, the U.S. Business Council on Sustainable Development, the U.S. Green Building Council, to name just a few. Many environmental organizations, including the Environmental Defense Fund, Friends of the Earth, and the Natural Resources Defense Council, are now emphasizing sustainability in their work. A newer organization, 350. org, founded by environmentalist and author Bill McKibben and others, works to reduce atmospheric concentrations of carbon dioxide below 350 parts per million, which climate scientists say is needed to prevent dangerous human interference with the climate system (the level is now about 392 parts per million). A great many organizations, such as Sustainable Seattle, are advocating sustainability at the local level. In Pennsylvania, sustainability is advocated by groups as diverse as the Pennsylvania Association for Sustainable Agriculture, which provides support and technical assistance for farmers, and Citizens for Pennsylvania's Future, an environmental advocacy organization that has registered a trademark for its motto, "Every environmental victory grows the economy." As these and other groups work together on shared sustainability goals, they can bring growing resources to the sustainability movement.

People and Organizations With Prior Experience

Experienced and skilled staff and leaders are more likely than others to know which strategies work and which do not. They are also more likely to be connected to affected communities and know the political landscape. Among other things, that helps in the recruitment of participants. As the previous section suggests, many environmental and other organizations currently involved in promoting sustainability existed before sustainability became a widely used term. These organizations also include community groups, labor organizations, and environmental justice organizations.

If this movement is to be successful, however, we must also rely on the creative energy and ideas of younger people and people who are new to environmental issues. This is true not only because younger people tend to be more aware of, and sensitive to, the challenges and opportunities of sustainability. It is also true because more traditional approaches to environmental protection have not been fully successful, and because people unhindered by decades of experience with other approaches may see things that more senior people do not. The best approach, in fact, is likely to blend the strengths of all generations.

Active Participation

While numerous public opinion surveys show support for policy change on many sustainability issues, the overwhelming majority of these people do nothing politically to change the current situation. As with other issues in the political sphere, there are many free riders—people who support a policy position but are willing to sit back and watch others take action. This must change, at the state, local, and national levels, if sustainability is to be promoted. Individuals will have to take political action (writing letters, attending public meetings, voting for pro-sustainability candidates, joining groups, donating money) and change their personal behaviors (decrease their use of energy, recycling, and so on) if we are to have meaningful change. Businesses, nongovernmental organizations, and others must move toward sustainability in their own operations and, when appropriate, support changes in law and policy. This broad participation also needs to include the poor, the unemployed, and people of color. If they have no voice, it is unlikely that new policies and actions will address their needs and concerns.

Conclusion

The emerging sustainability movement builds on the many local, state, regional, organizational, corporate, and environmental justice movements that already exist, and melds them into something of much greater influence. This movement will lead to a greater variety of attractive and sustainable alternatives to business as usual. It will support legal changes that will prevent or inhibit unsustainable actions and make more-sustainable decisions more attractive. It will encourage forms of governance that will enable the United States to grow and prosper in coming decades, and pass that prosperity along to our children and grandchildren.

This movement is not just about avoiding or preventing problems, or about seizing opportunities—though it is partly that. Nor is it only about changing law, policy, or behavior, though it is partly that as well. More fundamentally, a movement for sustainability is about our most cherished beliefs as individuals and citizens. It is about our ethical and religious responsibilities to others, including future generations, as well as to the environment. It is about our belief in freedom, opportunity, and the quality of life—values we hold dear as Americans. And, deep down, we know that tomorrow matters.

Endnotes

Preface

1   John Dernbach & the Widener University Law School Seminar on Law and Sustainability, *U.S. Adherence to Its Agenda 21 Commitments: A Five-Year Review*, 27 ELR 10504 (Oct. 1997).
2   STUMBLING TOWARD SUSTAINABILITY (John C. Dernbach ed., ELI Press 2002).
3   AGENDA FOR A SUSTAINABLE AMERICA (John C. Dernbach ed., ELI Press 2009).

Introduction

1   *See, e.g.,* AGENDA FOR A SUSTAINABLE AMERICA (John C. Dernbach ed., ELI Press 2009); STUMBLING TOWARD SUSTAINABILITY (John C. Dernbach ed., ELI Press 2002).
2   NATIONAL RESEARCH COUNCIL, SUSTAINABILITY AND THE U.S. ENVIRONMENTAL PROTECTION AGENCY 1 (Nat'l Acad. Press 2011) (footnote omitted).
3   ANDREA WULF, FOUNDING GARDENERS: THE REVOLUTIONARY GENERATION, NATURE, AND THE SHAPING OF THE AMERICAN NATION (Knopf 2011).
4   James Madison, *Address to the Agricultural Society of Albemarle, Virginia, in* 3 LETTERS AND OTHER WRITINGS OF JAMES MADISON 63, 76-77 (1884).
5   U.N. Conference on Environment and Development (UNCED), Agenda 21, U.N. Doc. A/CONF.151.26 (1992), *available at* http://www.un.org/esa/dsd/agenda21/.
6   UNCED, Rio Declaration on Environment and Development, U.N. Doc. A/CONF.151/5/Rev.1, 31 I.L.M. 874 (June 3-14, 1992), *available at* http://www.unep.org/Documents.Multilingual/Default.asp?documentid=78&articleid=1163.
7   *Idea: Triple Bottom Line*, THE ECONOMIST, Nov. 17, 2009, *at* http://www.economist.com/node/14301663.
8   Rio Declaration, *supra* note 6, princ. 24.
9   WORLD COMMISSION ON ENVIRONMENT AND DEVELOPMENT, OUR COMMON FUTURE 43 (1987), *available at* http://www.un-documents.net/wced-ocf.htm.
10   Rio Declaration, *supra* note 6, princ. 16.
11   *Id.* princ. 10.
12   OUR COMMON FUTURE, *supra* note 9, at 43.
13   RUMU SARKAR, INTERNATIONAL DEVELOPMENT LAW: RULE OF LAW, HUMAN RIGHTS, AND GLOBAL FINANCE xvi (Oxford Univ. Press 2009).
14   *Id.* at 32.
15   AMARTYA SEN, DEVELOPMENT AS FREEDOM 3 (Knopf 1999).
16   NATIONAL RESEARCH COUNCIL, OUR COMMON JOURNEY: A TRANSITION TOWARD SUSTAINABILITY 7 (Nat'l Acad. Press 1999).

Chapter 1

1   NATIONAL RESEARCH COUNCIL, SUSTAINABILITY AND THE U.S. ENVIRONMENTAL PROTECTION AGENCY (Nat'l Acad. Press 2011).

2   U.S. EPA, OUR NATION'S AIR: STATUS AND TRENDS THROUGH 2010, at 5 (2012), *available at* http://www.epa.gov/airtrends/2011/report/fullreport.pdf.

3   U.S. EPA, OUR NATION'S AIR: STATUS AND TRENDS THROUGH 2008, at 31 (2010), *available at* http://www.epa.gov/airtrends/2010/report/no2coso2.pdf.

4   U.S. EPA, Green Book, Carbon Monoxide Information, http://www.epa.gov/oaqps001/greenbk/cindex.html.

5   Clean Air Act Amendments of 1990, Report of the Committee on Energy and Commerce, U.S. House of Representatives, 101st Cong. 2d Sess. 148 (1990).

6   Craig N. Oren, *Is the Clean Air Act at a Crossroads?*, 40 ENVTL. L. REV. 1231, 1235–36 (2010).

7   U.S. EPA, National Emissions Inventory Air Pollutant Emissions Trends Data: 1970–2011 Average Annual Emissions, All Criteria Pollutants in MS Excel (2011), *available at* http://www.epa.gov/ttn/chief/trends/trends06/nationaltier1upto2011basedon2008v1_5.xls.

8   Oren, *supra* note 6, at 1236.

9   *See* U.S. EPA, ACID RAIN PROGRAM RESULTS: 2009, at 4, *available at* http://www.epa.gov/airmarkets/progress/ARP09_downloads/ARP2009Results.pdf.

10   *Id.; see also* 40 C.F.R. Part 81; U.S. EPA, Green Book, Sulphur Dioxide Nonattainment Areas as of August 30, 2011, http://www.epa.gov/oaqps001/greenbk/snc.html (list of nonattainment areas) (last visited Oct. 15, 2011).

11   Oren, *supra* note 6, at 1237.

12   U.S. EPA, THE BENEFITS AND COSTS OF THE CLEAN AIR ACT FROM 1990 TO 2020 (2011), *available at* http://www.epa.gov/air/sect812/feb11/fullreport.pdf; *see also* U.S. EPA, Benefits and Costs of the Clean Air Act Amendments of 1990 (2011), *at* http://www.epa.gov/air/sect812/feb11/factsheet.pdf (summary of report).

13   Oren, *supra* note 6, at 1237.

14   *Id.* at 1237–38.

15   *Id.* at 1239.

16   John M. Broder, *Re-election Strategy Tied to Shift on Smog*, N.Y. TIMES, Nov. 16, 2011, *at* http://www.nytimes.com/2011/11/17/science/earth/policy-and-politics-collide-as-obama-enters-campaign-mode.html?scp=2&sq=obama%20ozone&st=cse.

17   U.S. EPA, High Production Volume (HPV) Challenge: Basic Information, http://www.epa.gov/hpv/pubs/general/basicinfo.htm.

18   Charles W. Schmidt, *TOX 21: New Dimensions of Toxicity Testing*, 117 ENVTL. HEALTH PERSPECTIVES A348-53 (2009), *available at* http://ehp03.niehs.nih.gov/article/info%3Adoi%2F10.1289%2Fehp.117-a348.

19   Kim G. Harley et al., *PBDE Concentrations in Women's Serum and Fecundability*, 118 ENVTL. HEALTH PERSPECTIVES 699 (2010).

20   U.S. EPA, Existing Chemicals: Bisphenol A (BPA) Action Plan Summary, http://www.epa.gov/oppt/existingchemicals/pubs/actionplans/bpa.html.

21   ARTHUR GRUBE ET AL., U.S. EPA, BIOLOGICAL AND ECONOMIC ANALYSIS DIVISION, OFFICE OF PESTICIDE PROGRAMS, PESTICIDES INDUSTRY SALES AND USAGE: 2006 AND 2007 MARKET ESTIMATES (EPA 733-R-11-001) (2011), *available at* http://www.epa.gov/opp00001/pestsales/07pestsales/market_estimates2007.pdf.

22   U.S. EPA, America's Children and the Environment (ACE): Measure B1: Lead in the Blood of Children, http://www.epa.gov/ace/body_burdens/b1-graph.html (last visited Nov. 23, 2011).

23   JOHN E. IKERD, CRISIS & OPPORTUNITY: SUSTAINABILITY IN AMERICAN AGRICULTURE (2008).

24   U.S. EPA, Ag 101: Major Crops Grown in the United States, http://www.epa.gov/agriculture/ag101/cropmajor.html.

25   L. Horrigan, P. Walker & R.S. Lawrence, *How Sustainable Agriculture Can Address the Environmental and Public Health Harms of Industrial Agriculture,* 110 ENVTL HEALTH PERSP. 445 (May 2002), *available at* http://ehp.niehs.nih.gov/members/2002/110p445-456horrigan/horrigan-full.html.

26   U.S. EPA, Ag 101: Demographics, http://www.epa.gov/agriculture/ag101/demographics.html.

27   U.S. DEP'T OF AGRICULTURE, NATURAL RESOURCES CONSERVATION SERVICE, 2007 NATIONAL RESOURCES INVENTORY: SUMMARY REPORT (2009), *available at* http://www.nrcs.usda.gov/Internet/FSE_DOCUMENTS//stelprdb1041379.pdf.

28   U.S. Dep't of Agriculture, Farm Service Agency, Conservation Programs, http://www.fsa.
usda.gov/FSA/webapp?area=home&subject=copr&topic=crp (last visited Nov. 23, 2011).

29   U.S. DEP'T OF AGRICULTURE, NATURAL RESOURCES CONSERVATION SERVICE, SOIL EROSION ON
CROPLAND 2007 (2010), *available at* http://www.nrcs.usda.gov/wps/portal/nrcs/detail/national/technical/
nra/nri/?&cid=stelprdb1041887.

30   Conservation Technology Information Center, 2006 Crop Residue Management Survey: A
Survey of Tillage System Usage by Crops and Acres Planted (n.d.), *at* http://www.ctic.purdue.edu/media/
pdf/2006 CRM summary.pdf.

31   U.S. EPA, Ag 101: Crop Production, http://www.epa.gov/agriculture/ag101/printcrop.
html#nutbmps.

32   NATIONAL RESEARCH COUNCIL, TOWARD SUSTAINABLE AGRICULTURAL SYSTEMS IN THE 21ST
CENTURY 570 (Nat'l Acad. Press, 2010), *available at* http://www.nap.edu/openbook.php?record_
id=12832&page=1 [hereinafter TOWARD SUSTAINABLE AGRICULTURAL SYSTEMS].

33   *Id.* at 519.

34   MARC RIBAUDO ET AL., U.S. DEP'T OF AGRICULTURE, NITROGEN IN AGRICULTURAL SYSTEMS:
IMPLICATIONS FOR CONSERVATION POLICY (2011).

35   U.S. Dep't of Agriculture, Economic Research Service, Irrigation and Water Use, http://www.
ers.usda.gov/Briefing/WaterUse/ (last visited Feb. 24, 2012).

36   U.S. Geological Survey, High Plains Aquifer Water-Level Monitoring Study Area-Weighted
Water-Level Change, Predevelopment to 1980, 2000 Through 2009, *at* http://ne.water.usgs.gov/ogw/
hpwlms/tablewlpre.html (last modified June 17, 2011).

37   *Id.*

38   Center for Geospatial Technology, Texas Ogallala Summary (n.d.), http://www.gis.ttu.edu/
OgallalaAquiferMaps/TXOgallalaSummary.aspx.

39   Glenn D. Schaible & Marcel P. Aillery, *Irrigation Water Management in* AGRICULTURAL
RESOURCES AND ENVIRONMENTAL INDICATORS (USDA Economic Research Service 2006).

40   D. Tilman et al., *Agricultural Sustainability and Intensive Production Practices*, 418 NATURE
671 (Aug. 8, 2002).

41   CHARLES BENBROOK, THE ORGANIC CENTER, IMPACTS OF GENETICALLY ENGINEERED CROPS
ON PESTICIDE USE IN THE UNITED STATES: THE FIRST THIRTEEN YEARS (2009), *available at* http://oacc.
info/Docs/OrganicCenterUSA/EXSUM_13Years20091116.pdf.

42   Robert Howarth, *Coastal Nitrogen Pollution: A Review of Sources and Trends Globally and
Regionally*, 8 HARMFUL ALGAE 14 (2008); Robert J. Diaz & Rutger Rosenberg, *Spreading Dead Zones
and Consequences for Marine Ecosystems*, 321 SCIENCE 926 (Aug. 2008).

43   Wes Jackson, *Tackling the Oldest Environmental Problem: Agriculture and Its Impact on Soil*,
in THE POST CARBON READER: MANAGING THE 21ST CENTURY'S SUSTAINABILITY CRISES 552 (Richard
Heinberg & Daniel Lerch eds., 2010).

44   Marc Ribaudo & Noel Gollehon, *Animal Agriculture and the Environment, in* AGRICULTURAL
RESOURCES AND ENVIRONMENTAL INDICATORS (USDA Economic Research Service 2006), *available at*
http://www.ers.usda.gov/publications/arei/eib16/Chapter4/4.5/.

45   PEW COMMISSION ON INDUSTRIAL FARM ANIMAL PRODUCTION, PUTTING MEAT ON THE TABLE:
INDUSTRIAL FARM ANIMAL PRODUCTION IN AMERICA (2008), *available at* http://www.ncifap.org/_images/
PCIFAPFin.pdf.

46   MARTIN C. HELLER & GREGORY A. KEOLEIAN, UNIVERSITY OF MICHIGAN CENTER FOR SUS-
TAINABLE SYSTEMS, LIFE CYCLE-BASED SUSTAINABILITY INDICATORS FOR ASSESSMENT OF THE U.S. FOOD
SYSTEM (2000), *available at* http://css.snre.umich.edu/css_doc/CSS00-04.pdf.

47   RANDY SCHNEPF, ENERGY USE IN AGRICULTURE: BACKGROUND AND ISSUES (Congressional
Research Service 2004), *available at* http://www.nationalaglawcenter.org/assets/crs/RL32677.pdf.

48   TOWARD SUSTAINABLE AGRICULTURAL SYSTEMS, *supra* note 32, at 43.

49   Ian Harrison, Melina Laverty, & Eleanor Sterling, *Definition of Biodiversity*, CONEXIONS
(2004), http://cnx.org/content/m12151/latest/.

50   U.N. Food & Agriculture Organization, What Is Happening to Agrobiodiversity? (2004),
http://www.fao.org/docrep/007/y5609e/y5609e02.htm.

51   U.S. Dep't of Agriculture, Natural Resources Conservation Service, Wildlife Habitat Incentive Program, http://www.nrcs.usda.gov/wps/portal/nrcs/main/national/programs/financial/whip.

52   U.S. Dep't of Agriculture, Natural Resources Conservation Service, Farm and Ranch Lands Protection Program, http://www.nrcs.usda.gov/wps/portal/nrcs/main/national/programs/easements/farmranch.

53   U.S. Dep't of Agriculture, Natural Resources Conservation Service, Grassland Reserve Program, http://www.nrcs.usda.gov/wps/portal/nrcs/main/national/programs/easements/grassland.

54   42 U.S.C. §§6901-6992.

55   U.S. EPA, CLEAN WATERSHED NEEDS SURVEY, 2008 REPORT TO CONGRESS (2010) *available at* http://water.epa.gov/scitech/datait/databases/cwns/upload/cwns2008rtc.pdf.

56   U.S. EPA, FUNCTIONS AND VALUES OF WETLANDS 1 (2001), *available at* http://www.epa.gov/owow/wetlands/facts/fun_val.pdf.

57   42 U.S.C. §§9601-9675.

58   United States v. Atlantic Research Corp., 551 U.S. 128 (2007).

59   *See* Asset Conservation, Lender Liability, and Insurance Protection Act of 1996, Subtitle E, The Omnibus Consolidated Appropriations Bill for Fiscal Year 1997, Pub. L. No. 104-208 (Sept. 30, 1996).

60   U.S. EPA, Analyzing Generation and Management of Priority Chemicals 2005–2007: The National Priority Chemicals Trends Report, http://www.epa.gov/wastes/hazard/wastemin/trend.htm (last visited Nov. 29, 2011).

61   U.S. EPA, TRI Explorer, Release Reports, http://www.epa.gov/triexplorer/tri_release.chemical (calculation of all 2010 releases) (last visited Dec. 30, 2011).

62   U.S. GAO, CHEMICAL REGULATION: OPTIONS EXIST TO IMPROVE EPA'S ABILITY TO ASSESS HEALTH RISKS AND MANAGE ITS CHEMICAL REVIEW PROGRAM (2005), *available at* http://www.gao.gov/products/GAO-05-458; Lynn R. Goldman, *Preventing Pollution? U.S. Toxic Chemicals and Pesticides Policies and Sustainable Development*, 32 ELR 11018 (Sept. 2002).

63   National Oceanic & Atmospheric Administration, Office of Sustainable Fisheries, Status of U.S. Fisheries, http://www.nmfs.noaa.gov/sfa/statusoffisheries/SOSmain.htm.

64   U.S. Geological Survey, The Gulf of Mexico Hypoxic Zone, http://toxics.usgs.gov/hypoxia/hypoxic_zone.html.

65   *See, e.g.,* U.S. GLOBAL CHANGE RESEARCH PROGRAM, GLOBAL CLIMATE CHANGE IMPACTS IN THE UNITED STATES (Cambridge Univ. Press 2009), *available at* http://downloads.globalchange.gov/usimpacts/pdfs/climate-impacts-report.pdf.

66   NATIONAL RESEARCH COUNCIL, ADAPTING TO THE IMPACTS OF CLIMATE CHANGE (Nat'l Acad. Press 2011).

67   J.B. Ruhl, *Climate Change and the Endangered Species Act: Building Bridges to the No-Analog Future*, 88 B.U. L. REV. 1 (2008), *available at* http://papers.ssrn.com/sol3/papers.cfm?abstract_id=1014184.

68   U.S. GLOBAL CHANGE RESEARCH PROGRAM, *supra* note 65, at 71.

69   FREDERICK L. KIRSCHENMANN, CULTIVATING AN ECOLOGICAL CONSCIENCE: ESSAYS FROM A FARMER PHILOSOPHER (Univ. Press of Kentucky 2010).

70   United Nations Framework Convention on Climate Change, Status of Ratification of the Convention, http://unfccc.int/essential_background/convention/status_of_ratification/items/2631.php (last visited Nov. 24, 2011).

71   United Nations Framework Convention on Climate Change, art. 2, May 9, 1992, S. Treaty Doc No. 102-38, 1771 U.N.T.S. 107.

72   *Id.* art 3.1.

73   *Id.* pmbl.

74   E-Mail from Edward J. Sonnenberg, Research Librarian, Widener University Law School, to John C. Dernbach (Nov. 30, 2011), containing calculation based on World Resources Institute, Climate Analysis Indicators Tool, *available at* http://cait.wri.org/ (calculation available from John C. Dernbach).

75   INTERGOVERNMENTAL PANEL ON CLIMATE CHANGE, WORKING GROUP III REPORT: MITIGATION OF CLIMATE CHANGE 39, 90, & 776 (2007).

76   For a discussion of the meaning of "equity" under the UNFCCC, see L. Meyer & D. Roser, *Distributive Justice and Climate Change, The Allocation of Emissions Rights.*, 28 ANALYSE & KRITIK 223 (2006); Sonja Klinsky & Hadi Dowlatabadi, *Conceptualizations of Justice in Climate Policy*, 9 CLIMATE POLICY 88 (2009).

77   Kyoto Protocol to the United Nations Framework Convention on Climate Change, Dec. 10, 1997, U.N. Doc FCCC/CP/1997/7/Add.1, 37 I.L.M. 22 (1998).
78   *Id.* art. 3.1 & Annex B.
79   United Nations Framework Convention on Climate Change, Status of Ratification of the Kyoto Protocol, http://unfccc.int/kyoto_protocol/status_of_ratification/items/2613.php (last visited Nov. 25, 2011).
80   U.S. EPA, INVENTORY OF U.S. GREENHOUSE GAS EMISSIONS AND SINKS: 1990–2009 (2011), *available at* http://www.epa.gov/climatechange/emissions/downloads11/US-GHG-Inventory-2011-Complete_Report.pdf.
81   *Id.*
82   *Id.*
83   *Id.*
84   *Id.*
85   *See* Donald A. Brown, Penn State Rock Ethics Institute, Climate Ethics, The World Waits in Vain for US Ethical Climate Change Leadership as the World Warms (2011), http://rockblogs.psu.edu/climate/2011/02/the-world-waits-in-vain-for-us-ethical-climate-change-leadership.html.
86   For an insightful account of these events, see ERIC POOLEY, THE CLIMATE WAR: TRUE BELIEV-ERS, POWER BROKERS, AND THE FIGHT TO SAVE THE EARTH (Hyperion 2010).
87   Massachusetts v. EPA, 549 U.S. 497 (2007).
88   *Id.*
89   Endangerment and Cause or Contribute Findings for Greenhouse Gases Under Section 202(a) of the Clean Air Act, 74 Fed. Reg. 66496 (Dec. 15, 2009).
90   EPA's Denial of the Petitions to Reconsider the Endangerment and Cause or Contribute Findings for Greenhouse Gases Under Section 202(a) of the Clean Air Act, 75 Fed. Reg. 49556 (Aug. 13, 2010).
91   Pub. L. No. 94-163, tit. III.
92   U.S. EPA, OFFICE OF TRANSPORTATION & AIR QUALITY, LIGHT-DUTY AUTOMOTIVE TECHNOL-OGY AND FUEL ECONOMY TRENDS: 1975 THROUGH 2005 (2005).
93   John M. Broder, *U.S. Issues Limits on Greenhouse Gas Emissions From Cars*, N.Y. TIMES, Apr. 1, 2010, *at* http://www.nytimes.com/2010/04/02/science/earth/02emit.html.
94   Bill Vlasic, *Obama Reveals Details of Gas Mileage Rules,* N.Y. TIMES, July 29, 2011, *at* http://www.nytimes.com/2011/07/30/business/energy-environment/obama-reveals-details-of-gas-mileage-rules.html.
95   2017 and Later Model Year Light-Duty Vehicle Greenhouse Gas Emissions and Corporate Average Fuel Economy Standards, 76 Fed. Reg. 74854 (Dec. 1, 2011).
96   *Id.* at 74859.
97   Greenhouse Gas Emissions Standards and Fuel Efficiency Standards for Medium- and Heavy-Duty Engines and Vehicles, 76 Fed. Reg. 57106 (Sept. 15, 2011).
98   Reconsideration of Interpretation of Regulations That Determine Pollutants Covered by Clean Air Act Permitting Programs, 75 Fed. Reg.17004 (Apr. 2, 2010).
99   Action to Ensure Authority to Issue Permits Under the Prevention of Significant Deterioration Program to Sources of Greenhouse Gas Emissions: Finding of Failure to Submit State Implementation Plan Revisions Required for Greenhouse Gases, 75 Fed. Reg. 81874 (Dec. 29, 2010).
100   PSD and Title V Permitting Guidance for Greenhouse Gases, 75 Fed. Reg. 70254 (Nov. 17, 2010) (notice of availability and public comment period); U.S. EPA, PSD AND TITLE V PERMITTING GUI-DANCE FOR GREENHOUSE GASES (2010), *at* http://www.eenews.net/assets/2010/11/10/document_gw_04.pdf.
101   New York v. EPA, No. 06-1322 (D.C. Cir. 2010) (settlement reached Dec. 23, 2010).
102   American Petroleum Institute v. EPA, No. 08-1277 (D.C. Cir. 2010) (settlement reached Dec. 23, 2010).
103   U.S. EPA, Greenhouse Gas New Source Performance Standard for Electric Generating Units, http://yosemite.epa.gov/opei/rulegate.nsf/byRIN/2060-AQ91 (last visited Mar. 31, 2012).
104   U.S. EPA, Nanoscale Materials Stewardship Program and Inventory Status of Nanoscale Substances Under the Toxic Substances Control Act; Notice of Availability, 72 Fed. Reg. 38083 (July 12, 2007).

105   U.S. EPA, Office of Pollution Prevention and Toxics, Control of Nanoscale Materials Under the Toxic Substances Control Act, http://www.epa.gov/oppt/nano/index.html#snur.

106   Pesticides; Policies Concerning Products Containing Nanoscale Materials; Opportunity for Public Comment, 76 Fed. Reg. 35383 (June 17, 2011).

107   Memorandum from John P. Holdren, Assistant to the President for Science and Technology Policy et al., to Heads of Executive Departments and Agencies, Concerning Policy Principles for the U.S. Decision-Making Concerning Regulation and Oversight of Applications of Nanotechnology and Nanomaterials (June 9, 2011), *available at* http://www.whitehouse.gov/sites/default/files/omb/inforeg/for-agencies/nanotechnology-regulation-and-oversight-principles.pdf.

108   Energy Information Administration, Annual Energy Review 2010, Table 10.1: Renewable Energy Production and Consumption by Primary Energy Source, 1949-2010 *available at* http://www.eia.gov/totalenergy/data/annual/showtext.cfm?t=ptb1001.

109   *Id.*

110   RALPH SIMS ET. AL., INTERNATIONAL ENERGY AGENCY, FROM 1ST TO 2ND GENERATION BIOFUEL TECHNOLOGIES: AN OVERVIEW OF CURRENT INDUSTRY AND RD&D ACTIVITIES, (Nov. 2008), *available at* http://www.iea.org/papers/2008/2nd_Biofuel_Gen_Exec_Sum.pdf.

111   ENERGY INFORMATION ADMINISTRATION, ALTERNATIVES TO TRADITIONAL TRANSPORTATION FUELS 2009, at 32 (Table C1. Estimated Consumption of Vehicle Fuels in the United States, by Fuel Type, 2005-2009) (2011), *available at* ftp://ftp.eia.doe.gov/alternativefuels/afv-atf2009.pdf.

112   Alexander Farrell et al., *Ethanol Can Contribute to Energy and Environmental Goals*, 331 SCIENCE 506 (Jan. 27, 2006); Kenneth G. Cassman & Adam J. Liska, *Food Based Fuel for All: Realistic or Foolish?*, 1 BIOFUELS, BIOPRODUCTION, & BIOREFINING 18 (2007); Bruce A. Babcock & Jacinto F. Fabiosa, Center for Agricultural & Rural Development, Iowa State University, The Impact of Ethanol and Ethanol Subsidies on Corn Prices: Revisiting History (2011), http://www.card.iastate.edu/policy_briefs/display.aspx?id=1155; Jason Hill et al., *Environmental, Economic and Energetic Costs and Benefits of Biodiesel and Ethanol Fuels*, 103 PROC. NAT'L. ACAD. SCI. 11206 (2006).

113   Energy Independence and Security Act of 2007, Pub. L. No. 110-140 (2007).

114   Robert Pear, *After Three Decades, Tax Credit for Ethanol Expires*, N.Y. TIMES, Jan. 1, 2012, *at* http://www.nytimes.com/2012/01/02/business/energy-environment/after-three-decades-federal-tax-credit-for-ethanol-expires.html?_r=1.

115   Press Release, International Energy Agency, The Time Has Come to Make the Hard Choices Needed to Combat Climate Change and Enhance Global Energy Security, Says the Latest IEA World Energy Outlook (Nov. 10, 2009), *at* http://www.iea.org/press/pressdetail.asp?PRESS_REL_ID=294.

116   *See, e.g.*, Hannah Wiseman, *Regulatory Adaptation in Fractured Appalachia*, 21 VILL. ENVTL. L.J. 229 (2010).

117   *See, e.g.*, Pa. Dep't of Cons. and Natural Res., Marcellus and Utica Shale Research in Pennsylvania, *at* http://www.dcnr.state.pa.us/topogeo/econresource/oilandgas/marcellus/index.htm; Pa. Dep't of Cons. and Natural Res., The Process of Natural Gas Extraction From the Marcellus Shale, *at* http://www.dcnr.state.pa.us/ucmprd2/groups/public/documents/document/dcnr_007598.pdf (instructor's lesson plan for course on Marcellus Shale).

Chapter 2

1   MATHIS WACKERNAGEL & WILLIAM E. REES, OUR ECOLOGICAL FOOTPRINT: REDUCING HUMAN IMPACT ON THE EARTH 13, 88–91 (New Soc'y Pub. 1996).

2   P.R. Ehrlich & J. Holdren, *The Impact of Population Growth,* 171 SCIENCE 1212 (1971); Amit Kapur & Thomas E. Graedel, *Production and Consumption of Materials, in* STUMBLING TOWARD SUSTAINABILITY 63, 67 (John C. Dernbach ed., ELI Press 2002).

3   Arnold W. Reitze Jr., *Environmental Policy—It Is Time for a New Beginning,* 14 COLUMB. J. ENVTL. L. 111 (1989).

4   P.M. Vitousek et al., *Human Domination of Earth's Ecosystems,* 277 SCIENCE 494 (1997).

5   University of Michigan Center for Sustainable Systems, U.S. Energy System Factsheet (2011), *available at* http://css.snre.umich.edu/css_doc/CSS03-11.pdf.

6   Grecia Matos & Lorie Wagner, *Consumption of Materials in the United States, 1900–1995*, 23 ANN. REV. ENERGY & ENV'T 107 (1998) (figure of one-third in 1995 may now be lower because of economic activity in China and elsewhere.).

7   Population Resource Center, Population and Climate Change: Key Facts and Trends, *at* http://www.prcdc.org/globalpopulation/Population_and_Climate_Change/ (last visited Dec. 20, 2011).

8   Energy Information Administration, Annual Energy Review 2010, Table 2.1a Energy Consumption Estimates by Sector, Selected Years, 1949–2010, at 40 [hereinafter AER 2010], *at* http://www.eia.gov/totalenergy/data/annual/pdf/aer.pdf (total primary energy use) (2009 data are preliminary) (AAGR = Average Annual Growth Rate (%)).

9   *Id.* (total primary energy use excluding imported electricity) (wood, waste, and biofuels are components of biomass).

10   Press Release, Electric Reliability Council of Texas (ERCOT), ERCOT Regional Electricity Use Up 3.5% in 2010, Wind Energy Almost 8 Percent of Total (Jan. 10, 2011), *available at* http://www.ercot.com/news/press_releases/show/356; U.S. DEP'T OF ENERGY, 2010 WIND TECHNOLOGIES MARKET REPORT, TABLE 2. UNITED STATES WIND POWER RANKINGS: THE TOP 20 STATES 9 (2011), *available at* http://www1.eere.energy.gov/wind/pdfs/51783.pdf.

11   Christopher Head, The Energy Collective, The Curious Case of the Texas Wind Industry (Feb. 9, 2011), *at* http://theenergycollective.com/terynnorris/51416/curious-case-texas-wind-industry.

12   AER 2010, *supra* note 8.

13   U.S. Energy Information Administration, International Energy Statistics, *at* http://www.eia.gov/cfapps/ipdbproject/IEDIndex3.cfm?tid=44&pid=44&aid=2 (last visited Dec. 28, 2011).

14   KURT VONNEGUT, PLAYER PIANO (1952).

15   AER 2010, *supra* note 8 (total final energy use) (2005 dollars).

16   ROBERT U. AYRES & BENJAMIN WARR, THE ECONOMIC GROWTH ENGINE: HOW ENERGY AND WORK DRIVE MATERIAL PROSPERITY (Edward Elgar 2009).

17   AMERICAN COUNCIL FOR AN ENERGY-EFFICIENT ECONOMY, PEOPLE-CENTERED INITIATIVES FOR INCREASED ENERGY SAVINGS (Karen Ehrhardt-Matinez & John A. "Skip"Laitner eds., 2010); L.D. DANNY HARVEY, ENERGY AND THE NEW REALITY (Earthscan 2010).

18   Clifford Krauss, *In North Dakota, Flames of Wasted Natural Gas Light the Prairie*, N.Y. TIMES, Sept. 26, 2011, *at* http://www.nytimes.com/2011/09/27/business/energy-environment/in-north-dakota-wasted-natural-gas-flickers-against-the-sky.html?pagewanted=all.

19   AER 2010, *supra* note 8 (U.S. Residential and Commercial Sector Total Energy Consumption Estimates by Major Source, 1949–2010).

20   These variations across several energy sectors are helpfully tracked and evaluated on an annual basis by the American Council for an Energy-Efficient Economy, in their State Energy Efficiency Scorecard series.

21   AER 2010, *supra* note 8.

22   *Id.*

23   *Id.* (The five lowest states were Kentucky, Missouri, South Dakota, Iowa, and Nebraska (ranging from 3% to 17%)).

24   *Id.*

25   U.S. Geological Survey, Circular 1344, Estimated Use of Water in the United States in 2005 (2009) [hereinafter Circular 1344].

26   PETER H. GLEICK, THE WORLD'S WATER 2000–2001: THE BIENNIAL REPORT ON FRESHWATER RESOURCES 26, 199–202 (2000).

27   THE WATER ENCYCLOPEDIA, HYDROLOGIC DATA AND INTERNET RESOURCES, Table 7B.11, at 7–26 (Pedro Fierro, Jr. & Evan K. Nyer eds., 3d. ed. 2007) [hereinafter THE WATER ENCYCLOPEDIA].

28   David W. Moody, *Freshwater Resources of the United State*s, NAT'L GEOGRAPHIC RES. & EXPLORATION, Nov. 1993, at 81 (U.S. renewable supplies 15 times larger than consumptive annual use).

29   Circular 1344, *supra* note 25, at 4 & fig. 1.

30   *Id.* at 42–44.

31   Peter H. Gleick & Meena Pallaniappan, *Peak Water Limits to Freshwater Withdrawal and Use,* 107 PROC. OF THE NAT'L ACAD. SCI. 11115 (2010), *available at* http://www.pnas.org/content/107/25/11155.full.pdf.

32   THE WATER ENCYCLOPEDIA, *supra* note 27, at 7-22 to 7-29, Table 7B.11.

33   John L. Sabo et al., *Reclaiming Freshwater Sustainability in the Cadillac Desert*, 107 PROC. NAT'L ACAD. SCI. 21263 (2010), *available at* http://www.pnas.org/cgi/doi/10.1073/pnas.1009734108.

34   JOHN OPIE, OGALLALA: WATER FOR A DRY LAND 5–6, 162–65 (1993); DONALD E. KROMM & STEPHEN E. WHITE, CONSERVING WATER IN THE HIGH PLAINS 1–3 (1990); V. L. McGuire, U.S. Geological Survey, Fact Sheet FS-078-03: Water-Level Changes in the High Plains Aquifer, Predevelopment to 2001, 1999 to 2000, and 2000 to 2001 (2003), *available at* http://pubs.usgs.gov/fs/FS078-03/pdf/FS078-03.pdf.

35   Martin Hoerling & Jon Eischeid, *Past Peak Water in the Southwest*, SOUTHWEST HYDROLOGY, Jan.–Feb. 2007, at 18; Gregory J. McCabe & David M. Wolock, *Warming May Create Substantial Water Supply Shortages in the Colorado River Basin*, 34 GEOPHYSICAL RES. LETTERS L22708, at 3 of 5 (2007).

36   Joseph W. Dellapenna, *Interstate Struggles Over Rivers: The Southeastern States and the Struggle Over the 'Hooch*, 12 N.Y.U. ENVTL. L. J. 828 (2005).

37   JOSEPH L. SAX ET AL., LEGAL CONTROL OF WATER RESOURCES 8 (4th ed. 2006).

38   *See generally* NATIONAL RESEARCH COUNCIL, ADAPTING TO THE IMPACTS OF CLIMATE CHANGE 32, 34, fig. 2.3 (2010); U.S. EPA, OFFICE OF WATER, NATIONAL WATER PROGRAM STRATEGY, RESPONSE TO CLIMATE CHANGE, EPA 800-R-08-10-11 001 (2008) [hereinafter NATIONAL WATER PROGRAM STRATEGY]; U.S. GLOBAL CHANGE RESEARCH PROGRAM, GLOBAL CLIMATE CHANGE IMPACTS IN THE UNITED STATES 41–45 (Thomas R. Karl et al. eds., 2009), *available at* http://downloads.globalchange.gov/usimpacts/pdfs/climate-impacts-report.pdf.

39   U.S. Geol. Survey, Circular No. 1347, Water—The Nation's Fundamental Climate Issue: A White Paper on the U.S. Geological Survey Role and Capabilities (2010).

40   Circular 1344, *supra* note 25, at 4 & fig. 1.

41   Amit Kapur & Thomas E. Graedel, *Resource Use and Sustainability*, 33 ELR 10143 (Feb. 2003); University of Michigan Center for Sustainable Systems, Factsheets: U.S. Material Use, *at* http://css.snre.umich.edu/css_doc/CSS05-18.pdf.

42   Amit Kapur & Thomas E. Graedel, *Materials: From High Consumption to More Sustainable Resource Use, in* AGENDA FOR A SUSTAINABLE AMERICA 159 (John C. Dernbach ed., ELI Press 2009) (citing President's Council on Sustainable Dev., Population & Consumption Task Force Report (1996)).

43   DONALD ROGICH ET AL., WORLD RESOURCES INSTITUTE, MATERIAL FLOWS IN THE UNITED STATES: A PHYSICAL ACCOUNTING OF THE U.S. INDUSTRIAL ECONOMY (2008), *available at* http://pdf.wri.org/material_flows_in_the_united_states.pdf.

44   *Id.*

45   Thomas D. Kelley et al., U.S. Geological Survey, Historical Statistics for Mineral and Material Commodities in the United States (Version 2010), *at* http://minerals.usgs.gov/ds/2005/140/.

46   *Id.*

47   Population Reference Bureau, 2010 World Population Data Sheet (2010) [hereinafter Population Data Sheet], *available at* http://www.prb.org/pdf10/10wpds_eng.pdf.

48   *Id.*

49   *Id.*

50   If a previously growing population reaches replacement level, the population will continue to grow for roughly a lifetime—about 70 years. This is known as the momentum of population growth.

51   U.S. Census 2010, *available at* http://2010.census.gov/2010census; PAUL R. EHRLICH & ANNE H. EHRLICH, ONE WITH NINEVEH: POLITICS, CONSUMPTION, AND THE HUMAN FUTURE (Island Press 2004).

52   Population Data Sheet, *supra* note 47.

53   The Population Reference Bureau projects a U.S. population size of 423 million in 2050, a 37% increase over the 2010 population of 309 million. *See* Population Data Sheet, *supra* note 47. The United Nations Population Division projects a U.S. population of 478 million by 2100. Justin Gillis & Celia Dugger, *U.N. Forecasts 10.1 Billion People by Century's End*, N.Y. TIMES, May 3, 2011, *at* http://www.nytimes.com/2011/05/04/world/04population.html.

54   Population Connection, Factsheet: The Demographic Facts of Life, *at* http://www.populationconnection.org/site/DocServer/2011_Dem_Facts.pdf?docID=2362. This is a substantial reduction from the 1950s and 1960s.

55   L.A. Jacobsen & M. Mather, Population Reference Bureau, *U.S. Economic and Social Trends Since* 2000, 65 POPULATION BULL., No. 1, Feb. 2010, *available at* http://www.prb.org/pdf10/65.1unitedstates.pdf.

56   *Id.*

57 *See* U.S. Department of Commerce, Economics and Statistics Administration, U.S. Census Bureau, The Foreign-Born Population in the United States, March 2000 (2001); U.S. Department of Commerce, Economics and Statistics Administration, U.S. Census Bureau, The Foreign-Born Population in the United States, March 1999, at 1–2 (2000), *available at* http://www.census.gov/prod/2000pubs/p20-519.pdf.

58 T.E. Graedel, *On the Concept of Industrial Ecology*, 21 Ann. Review Energy & Env't 69, 76–78 (1996).

59 Executive Office of the President, National Science and Technology Council, Bridge to a Sustainable Future: National Environmental Technology Strategy (1995) [hereinafter Bridge to a Sustainable Future]; Executive Office of the President, Technology for a Sustainable Future (1994).

60 Bridge to a Sustainable Future, *supra* note 59, at 21.

61 John Gibbons, Chairman, Welcoming Remarks at the White House Conference on Environmental Technology 3–5 (Dec. 11–13, 1994), *in* White House Conf. on Envtl. Tech.: Working Papers of the Conf. Held in Washington, D.C. at the Grand Hyatt Hotel.

62 Bridge to a Sustainable Future, *supra* note 59, at 20.

63 U.S. EPA, Technology for a Sustainable Environment Grant Program: A Decade of Innovation (2006), *available at* http://www.epa.gov/ncer/science/tse/decade_innovation.pdf.

64 National Science Foundation, Environmental Research and Education, SEES Portfolio, http://www.nsf.gov/geo/sees/sees_portfolio.jsp (last visited Dec. 22, 2011).

65 U.S. EPA, Office of Research and Development, Chemical Safety for Sustainability Research, http://www.epa.gov/ord/priorities/chemicalsafety.htm (last visited Dec. 22, 2011).

66 National Research Council, Sustainability and the U.S. Environmental Protection Agency (Nat'l Acad. Press 2011).

67 National Academy of Sciences, Sustainability Linkages in the Federal Government, http://sites.nationalacademies.org/PGA/sustainability/linkages/index.htm.

68 Energy Information Administration, Direct Federal Financial Interventions and Subsidies in Energy in Fiscal Year 2010 35–38 (2011), *available at* http://www.eia.gov/analysis/requests/subsidy/pdf/subsidy.pdf.

69 *Id.*

70 U.S. Dep't of Energy, Report on the First Quadrennial Technology Review (2011), *available at* http://energy.gov/sites/prod/files/ReportOnTheFirstQTR.pdf.

71 *Id.* at ix.

72 *Id.* at vii–xi.

Chapter 3

1 World Commission on Environment and Development, Our Common Future 4-8 (1987), *available at* http://www.un-documents.net/wced-ocf.htm.

2 U.S. Census Bureau, Highlights of Income, Poverty and Health Insurance in the United States (2010), http://www.census.gov/hhes/www/poverty/data/incpovhlth/2010/highlights.html.

3 Poverty statistics in the U.S. Census Bureau's American Community Survey adhere to the standards specified by the Office of Management and Budget Statistical Policy Directive No. 14 (1978), *available at* http://www.census.gov/hhes/povmeas/methodology/ombdir14.html. The Census Bureau uses a set of dollar-value thresholds that vary by family size and composition to determine who is in poverty.

4 U.S. Census Bureau, Historical Poverty Tables-People, http://www.census.gov/hhes/www/poverty/data/historical/people.html.

5 Carmen DeNavas et al., U.S. Census Bureau, Income, Poverty, and Health Insurance Coverage in the United States: 2010, Current Population Report No. P60-239: Consumer Income (2011), tbl. A-3, at 41, *available at* http://www.census.gov/prod/2011pubs/p60-239.pdf.

6 *Id.*

7 Central Intelligence Agency, The World Factbook (as of Jan. 26, 2012), https://www.cia.gov/library/publications/the-world-factbook/fields/2172.html.

8   See, e.g., CONGRESSIONAL BUDGET OFFICE, TRENDS IN THE DISTRIBUTION OF HOUSEHOLD INCOME BETWEEN 1979 AND 2007 (2011), available at http://cbo.gov/ftpdocs/124xx/doc12485/10-25-HouseholdIncome.pdf; AVI FELLER & CHAD STONE, CTR. ON BUDGET & POLICY PRIORITIES, TOP 1% OF AMERICANS REAPED TWO-THIRDS OF INCOME GAINS FROM LAST ECONOMIC EXPANSION (2009), available at http://www.cbpp.org/files/9-9-09pov.pdf; EMMANUEL SAEZ, STRIKING IT RICHER: THE EVOLUTION OF TOP INCOMES IN THE UNITED STATES (2010), available at http://www.econ.berkeley.edu/~saez/saez-UStopincomes-2008.pdf (updated with 2008 estimates).

9   ARLOC SHERMAN & CHAD STONE, CTR. ON BUDGET & POLICY PRIORITIES, INCOME GAPS BETWEEN VERY RICH AND EVERYONE ELSE MORE THAN TRIPLED IN THE LAST THREE DECADES, NEW DATA SHOW 1 (June 25, 2010), http://www.cbpp.org/cms/?fa=view&id=3220 (last visited Jan. 22, 2012).

10   U.S. Census Bureau, Income Inequality, tbl. F-1, http://www.census.gov/hhes/www/income/data/historical/inequality/index.html.

11   U.S. Census Bureau, Income Inequality, tbl. IE-2, http://www.census.gov/hhes/www/income/data/historical/inequality/IE2.xls.

12   Id.

13   JONATHAN BARRY FORMAN, MAKING AMERICA WORK 31 (2006).

14   Michael B. Gerrard, Environmental Justice and Local Land Use Decisionmaking 126, in TRENDS IN LAND USE LAW FROM A TO Z: ADULT USES TO ZONING (Patricia E. Salkin ed., 2001).

15   U.S. EPA, Environmental Justice, http://www.epa.gov/compliance/environmentaljustice/index.html.

16   See Patricia Salkin, Albany Law School Environmental Justice and Land Use Planning, PAS Quick Notes, No. 26 (June 2010).

17   COMMISSION FOR RACIAL JUSTICE, UNITED CHURCH OF CHRIST, TOXIC WASTES AND RACE IN THE UNITED STATES: A NATIONAL REPORT ON THE RACIAL AND SOCIO-ECONOMIC CHARACTERISTICS OF COMMUNITIES WITH HAZARDOUS WASTE SITES xiii–vi (1987), available at http://www.ucc.org/about-us/archives/pdfs/toxwrace87.pdf; U.S. GAO, SITING OF HAZARDOUS WASTE LANDFILLS AND THEIR COR-RELATION WITH RACIAL AND ECONOMIC STATUS OF SURROUNDING COMMUNITIES (RCED 83-168) (1983), available at http://archive.gao.gov/d48t13/121648.pdf.

18   See U.S. EPA, Environmental Justice, National Environmental Justice Advisory Council, http://www.epa.gov/environmentaljustice/nejac/index.html.

19   Exec. Order No. 12898, 59 Fed. Reg. 32 (Feb. 11, 1994), available at http://www.archives.gov/federal-register/executive-orders/pdf/12898.pdf.

20   U.S. EPA, Plan EJ 2014, http://epa.gov/environmentaljustice/plan-ej/index.html.

21   Id.

22   U.S. EPA, ENVIRONMENTAL JUSTICE SMALL GRANTS PROGRAM FACT SHEET (2011), available at http://www.epa.gov/environmentaljustice/resources/publications/factsheets/fact-sheet-ej-small-grant-01-2011.pdf.

23   See E. Donald Elliott, A Cabin on the Mountain: Reflections on the Distributional Conse-quences of Environmental Protection Programs, 1 KAN. J.L. & PUB. POL'Y 5, 7 (1991) ("In my judgment, minorities and the poor probably benefit disproportionately from environmental protection measures."); William K. Reilly, Environmental Equity: EPA's Position, 18 EPA J. 18, 22 (1992) ("It is undeniable that minorities usually benefit from—are, indeed, the chief beneficiaries of—more general efforts to protect the environment."), available at http://heinonline.org/HOL/LandingPage?collection=journals&handle=hein.journals/epajrnl18&div=11.

24   Richard J. Lazarus, Pursuing "Environmental Justice:" The Distributional Effects of Envi-ronmental Protection, 87 NW. U. L. REV. 787, 792 (1992).

25   Id. at 795.

26   Id. at 798 (citing Michael Gelobter, Toward A Model of "Environmental Discrimination," in THE PROCEEDINGS OF THE MICHIGAN CONFERENCE ON RACE AND THE INCIDENCE OF ENVIRONMENTAL HAZARDS 92 (Bunyon Bryant & Paul Mohai eds., 1990) ("all changes in exposure have been regressively distributed since 1970 (the year in which the Clean Air Act was adopted)"); F. Reed Johnson, Income Distributional Effects of Air Pollution Abatement: A General Equilibrium Approach, 8 ATLANTIC ECON. J. 10, 17 (1980) (While environmental policy "costs are approximately proportional to income," data from previous studies "tends to confirm the supposition that environmental policy incidence is regressive, with only the top two income classes obtaining positive net benefits.") (summarizing results of a Swedish study on the income distributional effects of air pollution control). See also David Harrison Jr. & Daniel

L. Rubinfeld, *The Distribution of Benefits From Improvements in Urban Air Quality*, 5 J. ENVTL. ECON. & MGMT. 313, 314 (1978) ("The absolute level of benefits, measured in dollars . . . rises consistently and substantially with income. Only when expressed as a percentage of income are air quality benefits pro-poor.").

27 H. SPENCER BANZHOF & RANDALL P. WALSH, DO PEOPLE VOTE WITH THEIR FEET: AN EMPIRICAL TEST OF ENVIRONMENTAL GENTRIFICATION 24–25 (2006), *available at* http://www.rff.org/rff/documents/rff-dp-06-10.pdf.

28 *Id.* at 25.

29 Peter J. Hotez, *Neglected Infections of Poverty in the United States of America,* 2 PLoS NEGLECTED TROPICAL DISEASES e256 (2008), *available at* http://www.plosntds.org/article/info:doi/10.1371/journal.pntd.0000256.

30 BROOKINGS INSTITUTION, SIZING THE CLEAN ECONOMY (2011), *available at* http://www.brookings.edu/~/media/Files/Programs/Metro/clean_economy/0713_clean_economy.pdf.

31 *Id.* at 4, 16.

32 *Id.* at 5.

33 *Id.* at 4.

34 *Id.* at 21.

35 *Id.* at 22.

36 *Id.* at 4.

37 *Id.* at 23–24.

38 THE PEW CHARITABLE TRUSTS, THE CLEAN ENERGY ECONOMY (2009), *available at* http://www.pewcenteronthestates.org/uploadedFiles/Clean_Economy_Report_Web.pdf.

39 Christina C. DiPasquale & Kate Gordon, Center for American Progress, Top 10 Reasons Why Green Jobs Are Vital to Our Economy (Sept. 7, 2011), http://www.americanprogress.org/issues/2011/09/top_ten_green_jobs.html.

40 COLLABORATIVE ECONOMICS, 2010 CALIFORNIA GREEN INNOVATION INDEX 50 (2010), *available at* http://www.coecon.com/Reports/GREEN/CAGreen_2010.pdf.

41 *Id.*

42 Jack Lyne, *Wind-Energy Giant Gamesa Bringing U.S. HQ, Up to 1,000 Jobs to Pennsylvania*, SITE SELECTION, Oct. 25, 2004, *at* http://www.siteselection.com/ssinsider/pwatch/pw041025.htm.

43 Teresa Albano, Pittsburgh Labor Media Center, A Wind Farm Grows in Pennsylvania, Fuels Green-Collar Union Jobs, http://ilcaonline.org/content/wind-farm-grows-pennsylvania-fuels-green-collar-union-jobs (last visited Dec. 22, 2011).

44 American Recovery and Reinvestment Act of 2009, Pub. L. No. 111-5, 123 Stat. 115, 138 *available at* http://www.gpo.gov/fdsys/pkg/PLAW-111publ5/pdf/PLAW-111publ5.pdf.

45 U.S. Dep't of Energy, American Recovery and Reinvestment Act, http://www1.eere.energy.gov/recovery/ (last visited Oct. 25, 2011).

46 FRED SISSINE ET AL., CONG. RESEARCH SERV., ENERGY PROVISIONS IN THE AMERICAN RECOVERY AND REINVESTMENT ACT OF 2009 (Pub. L. No. 111-5) 2–3 (2009), *available at* http://vcresearch.siuc.edu/R40412.pdf.

47 John C. Dernbach et al., *Energy Efficiency and Conservation: New Legal Tools and Opportunities*, NAT. RESOURCES & ENV'T, Spring 2011, at 7, *available at* http://papers.ssrn.com/sol3/papers.cfm?abstract_id=1766089.

48 123 Stat. 115, 214. *See also* Where the Money Goes/Selected Programs From the $789.2 Billon Bill, WALL ST. J., http://s.wsj.net/public/resources/documents/WSJ_Stimulus_021209.pdf.

49 123 Stat. 115, 208.

50 EXECUTIVE OFFICE OF THE PRESIDENT, COUNCIL OF ECONOMIC ADVISORS, THE ECONOMIC IMPACT OF THE AMERICAN RECOVERY AND REINVESTMENT ACT OF 2009, EIGHTH QUARTERLY REPORT (2011), *available at* http://www.whitehouse.gov/sites/default/files/cea_8th_arra_report_final_draft.pdf.

51 NAT'L HIGHWAY TRAFFIC SAFETY ADMINISTRATION, CONSUMER ASSISTANCE TO RECYCLE AND SAVE ACT OF 2009: REPORT TO THE HOUSE COMM. ON ENERGY AND COMMERCE, THE SENATE COMM. ON COMMERCE, SCIENCE, AND TRANSP. AND THE HOUSE AND SENATE COMMS. ON APPROPRIATIONS 2 (2009), *available at* http://www.cars.gov/files/official-information/CARS-Report-to-Congress.pdf; Marianne Tyrrell & John C. Dernbach, *The "Cash for Clunkers" Program: A Sustainability Evaluation*, 42 TOL. L. REV. 467 (2011).

52   U.S. Dep't of Labor, Bureau of Labor Statistics, Green Jobs, http://www.bls.gov/green/ (last visited Dec. 22, 2011).

53   Notice of Comments Received and Final Definition of Green Jobs, 75 Fed. Reg. 57511 (Sept. 21, 2010).

54   *Id.* at 57512.

55   U.S. Dep't of Labor, *supra* note 52.

56   UNITED NATIONS DEVELOPMENT PROGRAMME (UNDP), HUMAN DEVELOPMENT REPORT 2007/2008, FIGHTING CLIMATE CHANGE: HUMAN SOLIDARITY IN A DIVIDED WORLD (2007), *available at* http://hdr.undp.org/en/media/HDR_20072008_EN_Complete.pdf.

57   *Id.*

58   WORLD HEALTH ORGANIZATION, CLIMATE CHANGE AND HEALTH (Jan. 2010), *available at* http://www.who.int/mediacentre/factsheets/fs266/en.

59   U.S. EPA, Climate Change Science, Future Precipitation and Storm Changes, http://www.epa.gov/climatechange/science/futurepsc.html (last visited Dec. 22, 2011).

60   The author of this paragraph, Donald A. Brown, has attended most of the Conferences of the Parties (COPs) under the United Nations Framework Convention on Climate Change and has organized programs on climate change justice at most of the COPs. He has observed growing interest in justice issues every year at the COPs.

61   NAACP, About the NAACP Climate Justice Initiative, http://www.naacp.org/pages/climate-justice-initiative-about (last visited Dec. 22, 2011).

62   Pub. L. No. 102-550, Title X.

63   U.S. EPA, Environmental Justice, State Environmental Justice Cooperative Agreements, http://www.epa.gov/environmentaljustice/grants/ej-sejca-grants.html (last visited Dec. 22, 2011).

Chapter 4

1   *See* Trip Pollard, *Transportation: Challenges and Choices*, *in* AGENDA FOR A SUSTAINABLE AMERICA 365 (John C. Dernbach ed., ELI Press 2009); Trip Pollard, *Driving Change: Public Policies, Individual Choices, and Environmental Damage*, 35 ELR 10791 (Nov. 2005); Trip Pollard, *Smart Growth and Sustainable Transportation: Can We Get There From Here?*, 29 FORDHAM URB. L.J. 1529 (2002) (each offering further discussion of the sustainability of current transportation patterns and policies). This section focuses on surface transportation, especially cars and trucks, since it is responsible for the bulk of transportation usage and impacts in the United States.

2   *See, e.g.,* ELIZABETH RIDLINGTON & GIGI KELLETT, MARYPIRG FOUNDATION, RAIL TRANSIT WORKS: LIGHT RAIL SUCCESS STORIES FROM ACROSS THE COUNTRY (2003), *available at* http://cdn.publicinterestnetwork.org/assets/rFsE5gAMlHxLZWdbowE1hg/MD-Rail-Transit-Works-text.pdf. *See also* TODD LITTMAN, VICTORIA TRANSIT POLICY INSTITUTE, RAIL TRANSIT IN AMERICA: A COMPREHENSIVE EVALUATION OF BENEFITS (2011), *available at* http://www.vtpi.org/railben.pdf (providing further discussion of the environmental benefits of such systems).

3   MATTHEW DICKENS & JOHN NEFF, AMERICAN PUBLIC TRANSPORTATION ASSOCIATION, PUBLIC TRANSPORTATION FACT BOOK, Table 5, at 10 (2011), *available at* http://www.detroittransit.org/UserFiles/APTA_2011_Fact_Book(1).pdf.

4   News Release, American Public Transportation Association, Ridership on Public Transportation Continues to Rise in 2011 (Oct. 3, 2011), *available at* http://www.apta.com/mediacenter/pressreleases/2011/Pages/111003-Ridership.aspx; *see* AMERICAN PUBLIC TRANSPORTATION ASS'N, TRANSPORTATION FOR AMERICA, STRANDED AT THE STATION: THE IMPACT OF THE FINANCIAL CRISIS IN PUBLIC TRANSPORTATION (2009), *available at* http://www.t4america.org/docs/081809_stranded_at_thestation.PDF.

5   News Release, Amtrak, Amtrak Ridership Rolls Up Best-Ever Records (Oct. 13, 2011).

6   News Release, NYC.gov, Mayor Bloomberg and Transportation Commissioner Sadik-Khan Announce 14 Percent Growth in Commuter Bike Riding Compared to Last Spring (July 28, 2011).

7   *Norfolk Southern Opens Heartland Corridor*, RAILWAY GAZETTE INT'L (Sept. 9, 2010), *at* http://www.railwaygazette.com/nc/news/single-view/view/norfolk-southern-opens-heartland-corridor.html.

8   COMMONWEALTH OF VA. DEP'T OF RAIL & PUBLIC TRANSP., ECONOMIC ASSESSMENT OF A
ROANOKE REGION INTERMODAL FACILITY, FINAL REPORT (2008), *available at* http://www.drpt.virginia.
gov/special/files/Economic%20Assessment%20of%20Roanoke%20Intermodal%20Facility%20-%20
Final%20Report%201-07-08.pdf.

9   *See, e.g.,* ROBERT CERVERO ET AL., TRANSP. RESEARCH BOARD, TRANSIT COOPERATIVE
RESEARCH PROGRAM REPORT 102: TRANSIT-ORIENTED DEVELOPMENT IN THE UNITED STATES: EXPERI-
ENCE, CHALLENGES, AND PROSPECTS (2004), *available at* http://onlinepubs.trb.org/onlinepubs/tcrp/
tcrp_rpt_102.pdf; Jeffrey Tumlin & Adam Millard-Ball, *How to Make Transit-Oriented Development
Work*, PLANNING (May 2003), *at* http://www.sonic.net/~woodhull/sctlc/PDF/How%20to%20Make%20
TOD%20Work.pdf; U.S. EPA, OUR BUILT AND NATURAL ENVIRONMENTS: A TECHNICAL REVIEW OF THE
INTERACTIONS BETWEEN LAND USE, TRANSPORTATION, AND ENVIRONMENTAL QUALITY (2001), *available
at* http://www.epa.gov/smartgrowth/pdf/built.pdf.

10   ROBERT CERVERO ET AL., *supra* note 9, at 235.

11   *Id.* at 246-47.

12   JOE CORTRIGHT, PORTLAND'S GREEN DIVIDEND, CEOS FOR CITIES (July 2007), *available at*
http://www.ceosforcities.org/files/PGD%20FINAL.pdf.

13   *See* U.S. EPA, OFFICE OF SUSTAINABLE COMMUNITIES, PARTNERSHIP FOR SUSTAINABLE COM-
MUNITIES: A YEAR OF PROGRESS FOR AMERICAN COMMUNITIES (2010) [hereinafter PARTNERSHIP FOR
SUSTAINABLE COMMUNITIES], *available at* http://www.epa.gov/smartgrowth/pdf/partnership_year1.pdf;
see also Partnership for Sustainable Communities website, http://www.sustainablecommunities.gov/
index.html (last visited Dec. 27, 2011).

14   Partnership for Sustainable Communities website, http://www.sustainablecommunities.gov/
index.html (last visited Dec. 27, 2011).

15   PARTNERSHIP FOR SUSTAINABLE COMMUNITIES, *supra* note 13.

16   Neil Pierce, *The 52-Cent Case for 'Sustainability,'* WASH. POST, Dec. 4, 2011, *at* http://www.
postwritersgroup.com/archives/peir111204.htm.

17   For links to many of these provisions, visit U.S. Dep't of Energy, Alternative Fuels &
Advanced Vehicles Data Center, Federal and State Incentives and Laws, http://www.afdc.energy.gov/
afdc/laws (last visited Dec. 27, 2011).

18   *See, e.g.,* NATIONAL GOVERNORS ASS'N CENTER FOR BEST PRACTICES, GREENER FUELS,
GREENER VEHICLES: A STATE RESOURCE GUIDE (Feb. 22, 2008), *available at* http://www.nga.org/
cms/home/nga-center-for-best-practices/center-publications/page-eet-publications/col2-content/main-
content-list/greener-fuels-greener-vehicles-a.html.

19   *See, e.g.,* U.S. Dep't of Transp., Federal Highway Administration, Context Sensitive Solutions.
org, *at* http://contextsensitivesolutions.org (last visited Dec. 27, 2011).

20   *See, e.g.,* U.S. DEP'T OF TRANSP., FEDERAL HIGHWAY ADMINISTRATION, FLEXIBILITY IN
HIGHWAY DESIGN (1997), *available at* http://contextsensitivesolutions.org/content/reading/flexibility/
resources/flex_full/ (a landmark guide that has had a significant impact in promoting more innovative,
less destructive project design).

21   *See, e.g.,* Donald C. Shoup, *Free Parking or Free Markets*, ACCESS No. 38 (Spring 2011),
at http://shoup.bol.ucla.edu/FreeParkingOrFreeMarkets.pdf; DONALD C. SHOUP, THE UNIVERSITY OF
CALIFORNIA TRANSPORTATION CENTER, THE HIGH COST OF FREE PARKING (2005), *available at* http://www.
uctc.net/papers/351.pdf (reprint); U.S. DEP'T OF TRANSP., FEDERAL HIGHWAY ADMINISTRATION OFFICE OF
TRANSPORTATION MANAGEMENT, CONGESTION PRICING: A PRIMER (2006), *available at* http://www.ops.
fhwa.dot.gov/publications/congestionpricing/congestionpricing.pdf.

22   U.S. DEP'T OF TRANSP., FEDERAL HIGHWAY ADMINISTRATION, OFFICE OF HIGHWAY POL-
ICY INFORMATION, TRAFFIC VOLUME TRENDS (2010), *available at* http://www.fhwa.dot.gov/ohim/
tvtw/10dectvt/10dectvt.pdf. Data in this paragraph on vehicle miles traveled was calculated from this
report and from the Office of Highway Policy Information's Highway Statistics series. Population growth
was calculated using data from the U.S. Census Bureau.

23   *See* ROBERT PUENTES & ADIE TOMER, METROPOLITAN POLICY PROGRAM AT BROOKINGS, THE
ROAD ... LESS TRAVELED: AN ANALYSIS OF VEHICLE MILES TRAVELED TRENDS IN THE U.S. (2008), *available at* http://climate.dot.gov/documents/brookings_2008_vehicle_miles_traveled_report.pdf.

24   Calculated from U.S. DEP'T OF TRANSP., RESEARCH AND INNOVATIVE TECHNOLOGY ADMINIS-
TRATION, BUREAU OF TRANSPORTATION STATISTICS, NATIONAL TRANSPORTATION STATISTICS 2011, tbl. 4-46,
available at http://www.bts.gov/publications/national_transportation_statistics/pdf/entire.pdf.

25   *Id.*, tbl. 4-53.

26   *See generally* U.S. EPA, About Smart Growth, http://www.epa.gov/smartgrowth/about_ sg.htm (last visited Dec. 28, 2011); Smart Growth Online website, http://www.smartgrowth.org/ (last visited Dec. 28, 2011).

27   AMERICAN PLANNING ASS'N, GROWING SMART LEGISLATIVE GUIDEBOOK (Stuart Meck ed., 2002), *available at* http://www.planning.org/growingsmart/guidebook/print/index.htm.

28   Patricia E. Salkin, *Implementation of the APA Growing Smart Legislative Guidebook: Beginning to Benchmark Success*, 33 REAL ESTATE L.J. 339 (Winter 2004).

29   U.S. EPA, Smart Growth website, http://www.epa.gov/smartgrowth/index.htm (last visited Dec. 28, 2011).

30   U.S. EPA, Smart Growth, Smart Growth Network, http://www.epa.gov/smartgrowth/sg_network.htm (last visited Dec. 28. 2011).

31   EPA, Smart Growth, HUD-DOT-EPA Partnership for Sustainable Communities, http://www.epa.gov/smartgrowth/partnership/index.html (last visited Dec. 28, 2011).

32   *See* Patricia E. Salkin, *Smart Growth and Sustainable Development: Threads of a National Land Use Polic*y, 36 VALPRAISO L. REV. 381 (Spring 2002).

33   Eark Blumenauer website, Livable Communities Task Force, http://blumenauer.house.gov/ index.php?option=com_content&task=view&id=1555&Itemid=167 (last visited Dec. 28, 2011).

34   Craig Pittman, *Powerful Interests Checkmated Florida's Growth Management Agency,* TAMPA BAY TIMES, May 22, 2011, *at* http://www.tampabay.com/news/powerful-interests-checkmated-floridas-growth-management-agency/1171063.

35   GREGORY K. INGRAM ET AL., LINCOLN INSTITUTE OF LAND POLICY, SMART GROWTH POLICIES: AN EVALUATION OF PROGRAMS AND OUTCOMES 146 (2009), *available at* http://www.lincolninst.edu/pubs/ Smart-Growth-Policies-Ch-9-Summary.pdf.

36   *Id.* at 207, *available at* http://www.lincolninst.edu/pubs/Smart-Growth-Policies-Ch-14-Colorado.pdf.

37   *See* CHRISTOPHER B. LEINBERGER, THE OPTION OF URBANISM (2008); ARTHUR C. NELSON, TOWARD A NEW METROPOLIS: THE OPPORTUNITY TO REBUILD AMERICA (2004); Arthur C. Nelson, *Leadership in a New Era*, 72 J. AM. PLAN. ASS'N 136 (Autumn 2006), *available at* http://law.du.edu/images/ uploads/rmlui/conferencematerials/2007/Thursday/DrNelsonLunchPresentation/NelsonJAPA2006.pdf.

38   PRICEWATERHOUSE COOPERS & URBAN LAND INSTITUTE, EMERGING TRENDS IN REAL ESTATE 2009 at 12 (2008).

39   In one survey, 61% of prospective homebuyers preferred a neighborhood with a shorter commute, sidewalks, and shopping, restaurants, and public transportation within walking distance over a larger lot, a sprawling neighborhood, and a longer commute and limited options for walking. BELDEN RUSSONELLO & STEWART, 2004 NATIONAL COMMUNITY PREFERENCE SURVEY (2004), *available at* http:// www.smartgrowthamerica.org/documents/national-community-preference-survey.pdf (conducted for National Association of Realtors and Smart Growth America).

40   WILLIAM H. LUCY, FORECLOSING THE DREAM: HOW AMERICA'S HOUSING CRISIS IS RESHAPING OUR CITIES AND SUBURBS (2010); Christopher B. Leinberger, *The Death of the Fringe Suburb*, N.Y. TIMES, Nov. 25, 2011, *at* http://www.nytimes.com/2011/11/26/opinion/the-death-of-the-fringe-suburb. html.

41   PRICEWATERHOUSE COOPERS & URBAN LAND INSTITUTE, EMERGING TRENDS IN REAL ESTATE 2010 at 12 (2009).

42   Each of the four volumes may be accessed via the IPCC website, http://www.ipcc.ch/publications_and_data/publications_and_data_reports.shtml#1 (last visited Dec. 29, 2011).

43   549 U.S. 497 (2007).

44   Massachusetts Executive Office of Energy and Environmental Affairs, Greenhouse Gas Emissions Policy (Apr. 23, 2007). *See also* Massachusetts Executive Office of Energy and Environmental Affairs, Revised MEPA Greenhouse Gas Emissions Policy and Protocol (2010), *available at* http://www. env.state.ma.us/mepa/downloads/GHG%20Policy%20FINAL.pdf.

45   New York State Dept. of Envtl. Conservation, Assessing Energy Use and Greenhouse Gas Emissions in Environmental Impact Statements (July 15, 2009).

46   California Governor's Office of Planning & Research website, http://www.opr.ca.gov/index. php?a=ceqa/index.html (last visited Dec. 29, 2011).

47   Patricia E. Salkin, *Can You Hear Me Up There? Giving Voice to Local Communities Impera-tive for Achieving Sustainability*, 4 HOUSTON ENVTL.ENERGY L. & POL'Y J. 256 (2009).

48   ARIZ. REV. STAT. ANN. §11–821(c)(4) (2007).

49   N.J. STAT. ANN. §40:55D–28(b)(16) (2009).

50   Mayors Climate Protection Center, List of Participating Mayors, http://www.usmayors.org/climateprotection/list.asp (last visited Dec. 29, 2011).

51   U.S. CONFERENCE OF MAYORS, MAYORS CLIMATE PROTECTION CENTER, U.S CONFERENCE OF MAYORS CLIMATE PROTECTION AGREEMENT (2005), *available at* http://www.usmayors.org/climateprotection/documents/mcpAgreement.pdf.

52   International Council for Local Environmental Initiatives (ICLEI) Local Governments for Sustainability, ICLEI Climate Program, http://www.iclei.org/index.php?id=800 (last visited Dec. 29, 2011).

53   Conservation Leaders Network, Cool Counties, http://www.conservationleaders.org/cool.counties.htm (last visited Dec. 29, 2011).

54   42 U.S.C. §9601(39)(A) (2002).

55   NAT'L ASS'N OF LOCAL GOV'T PROFESSIONALS & NORTHEAST-MIDWEST INST., UNLOCKING BROWNFIELDS: KEYS TO COMMUNITY REVITALIZATION 3 (2004) [hereinafter UNLOCKING BROWNFIELDS].

56   U.S. EPA, INVESTING IN PARTNERSHIP, POSSIBILITY, AND PEOPLE: A REPORT TO STAKEHOLDERS (MOVING FORWARD) 31 (2005).

57   Evans Paull, Northeast-Midwest Institute, Environmental and Economic Benefits of Brownfields Redevelopment, Slide 9 (2009), *available at* http://www.eswp.com/brownfields/Present/Paull%204A.pdf.

58   Western Pa. Brownfields Ctr., Assessing Brownfield Sustainability: Life Cycle Analysis and Carbon Footprinting, http://www.cmu.edu/steinbrenner/brownfields/Current%20Projects/sustainability.html (last visited Mar. 21, 2011).

59   42 U.S.C. §§9601(35) & 9607(a)(1).

60   Joel B. Eisen, *Brownfields at 20: A Critical Reevaluation*, 34 FORDHAM URB. L.J. 101, 101 (2007).

61   Liability protection was accomplished through the Small Business Liability Relief and Brownfields Revitalization Act of 2002, 42 U.S.C. §§9604-05, 9607, 9622, 9628, and a rule promulgated in 2005 by EPA that protects brownfields developers if they make "all appropriate inquiries" (including environmental investigation and remediation activities, if necessary) before acquiring ownership of brownfields sites. Standards and Practices for All Appropriate Inquiries, 40 C.F.R. §312. EPA's "All Appropriate Inquiries" page is located at http://www.epa.gov/brownfields/aai/index.htm (last visited Mar. 22, 2011).

62   Evans Paull, Northeast-Midwest Institute, Environmental and Economic Benefits of Brownfields Redevelopment, Slide 9 (2009), *available at* http://www.eswp.com/brownfields/Present/Paull%204A.pdf.

63   U.S. EPA, Brownfields Success Stories, http://epa.gov/brownfields/success/index.htm (last visited Mar. 21, 2011).

64   UNLOCKING BROWNFIELDS, *supra* note 55, at 2.

65   *Id.*

66   JUSTIN HOLLANDER, NIALLL KIRKWOOD, & JULIA GOLD, PRINCIPLES OF BROWNFIELD REGEN-ERATION: CLEANUP, DESIGN, AND REUSE OF DERELICT LAND 2–3 (2010).

67   Joel B. Eisen, *Brownfields at 20: A Critical Reevaluation*, 34 FORDHAM URB. L.J. 101, 129 (2007); Bernard Van Heusden, *Brownfield Redevelopment in the European Union*, 34 B.C. ENVTL. AFF. L. REV. 559 (2007); GERNOT PAHLEN, RESCUE: REGENERATION OF EUROPEAN SITES IN CITIES AND URBAN ENVIRONMENTS (2004), *available at* http://www.grc.engineering.cf.ac.uk/events/rescue2/pdfs/R2-MS2-GP.pdf (describing the European "RESCUE" program).

68   JONATHAN P. DEASON, GEORGE WILLIAM SHERK, & GARY A. CARROLL, PUBLIC POLICIES AND PRIVATE DECISIONS AFFECTING THE REDEVELOPMENT OF BROWNFIELDS: AN ANALYSIS OF CRITICAL FAC-TORS, RELATIVE WEIGHTS AND AREAL DIFFERENTIALS, 8.1 (Areal Differentials) (2001), *available at* http://www.gwu.edu/~eem/Brownfields/.

69   *Id.*

70   U.S. EPA, ESTIMATING 2003 BUILDING RELATED CONSTRUCTION AND DEMOLITION MATERIALS AMOUNTS (2009), *available at* http://www.epa.gov/osw/conserve/rrr/imr/cdm/pubs/cd-meas.pdf.

71   U.S. ENERGY INFORMATION ADMINISTRATION, ANNUAL ENERGY OUTLOOK 2009 EARLY RELEASE, tbls. 2, 4, 5, and 18 (Dec. 2008), *available at* http://www.eia.doe.gov/oiaf/aeo/aeoref_tab. html; U.S. Dept. of Energy, 2009 Buildings Energy Databook, tbl. 1.1.1., http://buildingsdatabook. eren.doe.gov/TableView.aspx?table=1.1.1. In addition, the U.S. Energy Information Agency (EIA) has estimated that 60% of the nation's electrical production is utilized to operate commercial buildings. *See* U.S. Energy Information Administration, Commercial Buildings Energy Consumption Survey, http:// www.eia.doe.gov; GREG KATS, GREENING OUR BUILT WORLD: COSTS, BENEFITS, AND STRATEGIES 171 (2010) (buildings account for 45% of U.S. energy consumption).

72   *See* KATS, *supra* note 71, at 73–78 (discussing the increasing market preferences for green buildings).

73   U.S. EPA, Green Building, http://www.epa.gov/greenbuilding/pubs/about.htm.

74   At present, the most widely employed standard in state and local legislation is the LEED certification, first promulgated by the U.S. Green Building Council as a pilot program in 1998. *See* CHRIS W. SCHEUER & GREGORY A. KEOLEIAN, NAT'L INST. OF STANDARDS & TECH., EVALUATION OF LEED USING LIFE CYCLE ASSESSMENT METHODS 16–17 (2002), *available at* http://www.bfrl.nist.gov/oae/publications/ gcrs/02836.pdf.

75   The Green Globes program was developed by the Green Building Initiative (GBI), a non-profit organization that has as its purpose the implementation of healthier and more-sustainable building practices. *See* Green Bldg. Initiative, About GBI, http://www.thegbi.org/about-gbi/.

76   *See* Energy Star, About Energy Star, http://www.energystar.gov/index.cfm?c=about.ab_ index.

77   *See* NAT'L ASS'N OF HOME BUILDERS, NAHB MODEL GREEN HOME BUILDING GUIDELINES 1–4 (2006), *available at* http://www.nahbgreen.org/content/pdf/nahb_guidelines.pdf.

78   INTERNATIONAL CODE COUNCIL, INTERNATIONAL GREEN CONSTRUCTION CODE (IGCC) (PUBLIC VERSION 2.0) ii (2010), *available at* http://www.iccsafe.org/cs/IGCC/Pages/IGCCDownloadV2.aspx.

79   *See* CalRecycle, Local Government Construction and Demolition Guide, http://www.calre-cycle.ca.gov/LGCentral/Library/canddmodel/instruction/faq.htm#GreenBuild.

80   *See* KATS, *supra* note 71, at 93–97 (discussing the relationships between green buildings and green communities). *See also* Keith H. Hirokawa, *At Home With Nature: Early Reflections on Green Building Laws and the Transformation of the Built Environment*, 39 ENVTL. L. 507, 547 (2009) (discussing the need to integrate community needs and operations into building); Trip Pollard, *Building Greener Communities: Smarter Growth and Green Building*, 27 VA. ENVTL. L. REV. 125, 137–39 (2009) (same).

81   Press Release, U.S. Green Building Council, One Billion Square Feet of LEED Certified Green Building Projects Worldwide (Nov. 10, 2011), *available at:* http://www.usgbc.org/News/Press-Releases.aspx?PageID=97&CMSPageID=163.

82   *Id. See also* Ariel Schwartz, *U.S. Green Building Market Will Balloon to $173.5 Billion by 2015*, FAST COMPANY (July 6, 2010), *at* http://www.usgbc.org/News/USGBCInTheNewsDetails. aspx?ID=4456 ("U.S. green building market value will balloon from $71.1 billion now to $173 billion by 2015. Commercial green building is expected to grow by 18.1% annually during the same time period from $35.6 billion to $81.8 billion. In this case, green building is defined as building with resource use and employee productivity in mind.").

83   AMERICAN INSTITUTE OF ARCHITECTS, LOCAL LEADERS IN SUSTAINABILITY: GREEN BUILDING POLICY IN A CHANGING ECONOMIC ENVIRONMENT 4 (2009).

84   *See* ROB WATSON, GREEN BUILDING MARKET AND IMPACT REPORT (2010), *available at* http:// www.greenbiz.com/green-building-market-and-impact-report-2010/download (although records of construction completions with LEED certification suggest that green building is slowing).

Chapter 5

1   John C. Dernbach, *Navigating the U.S. Transition to Sustainability: Matching National Governance Challenges With Appropriate Legal Tools*, 44 TULSA L. REV. 93 (2008).

2   NATIONAL RESEARCH COUNCIL, OUR COMMON JOURNEY: A TRANSITION TOWARD SUSTAINABILITY 7 (Nat'l. Acad. Press 1999) (emphasis added) [hereinafter OUR COMMON JOURNEY].

3   *See, e.g.,* America's Climate Security Act of 2007, S. 2191, 110th Cong. (2007) (as reported by S. Comm. on Env't and Pub. Works, Dec. 5, 2007).

4   OUR COMMON JOURNEY, *supra* note 2, at 3.

5   *Id.* ("[T]wo generations is a realistic time frame for scientific and technological analysis that can provide direction, assess plausible futures, measure success—or the lack of it—along the way, and identify levers for changing course.").

6   G.A. Bradshaw & Jeffrey G. Borchers, *Uncertainty as Information: Narrowing the Science-policy Gap*, 4 ECOLOGY & SOC'Y (2000), *available at* http://www.consecol.org/vol4/iss1/art7/; J.R. Lukey et al., *Effect of Ecological Uncertainty on Species at Risk Decision-Making*, 14 ANIMAL CONSERVATION 151 (2011); Robert S. Pindyck, *Irreversibilities and the Timing of Environmental Policy*, 22 RES.& ENERGY ECON. 233 (2000).

7   *See* Habiba Gitay, *Intrelinkages: Governance for Sustainability*, *in* UNITED NATIONS ENVIRONMENT PROGRAMME, GLOBAL ENVIRONMENTAL OUTLOOK 4, ENVIRONMENT FOR DEVELOPMENT 361, 377 (2007).

8   John C. Dernbach, *Achieving Sustainable Development: The Centrality and Multiple Facets of Integrated Decisionmaking*, 10 IND. J. GLOBAL LEGAL STUD. 247 (2003).

9   RICHARD N.L. ANDREWS, MANAGING THE ENVIRONMENT, MANAGING OURSELVES: A HISTORY OF AMERICAN ENVIRONMENTAL POLICY 4 (2d ed. 2006).

10   Jonathan D. Weiss, *Local Governance and Sustainability*, *in* AGENDA FOR A SUSTAINABLE AMERICA 43 (John C. Dernbach ed., ELI Press 2009).

11   PRESIDENT'S COUNCIL ON SUSTAINABLE DEVELOPMENT, SUSTAINABLE COMMUNITIES TASK FORCE REPORT vi (1997).

12   SustainLane, 2008 US City Rankings, http://www.sustainlane.com/us-city-rankings/articles/study-overview/LTLZYA787TN23RUSSPNM8CBZR98X.

13   AMY MORSCH, NICHOLAS INSTITUTE FOR ENVIRONMENTAL POLICY SOLUTIONS, DUKE UNIVERSITY, PROFILING LOCAL CLIMATE CHANGE GOVERNANCE IN THE SOUTHEASTERN UNITED STATES (2011).

14   Jonathan D. Weiss, *Local Governance and Sustainability: Major Progress, Significant Challenges*, *in* AGENDA FOR A SUSTAINABLE AMERICA 43 (John C. Dernbach ed., ELI Press 2009).

15   U.S. CONFERENCE OF MAYORS, MAYORS CLIMATE PROTECTION CENTER, U.S CONFERENCE OF MAYORS CLIMATE PROTECTION AGREEMENT (2005), *available at* http://www.usmayors.org/climateprotection/documents/mcpAgreement.pdf.

16   JOAN FITZGERALD, EMERALD CITIES: URBAN SUSTAINABILITY AND ECONOMIC DEV. (Oxford Univ. Press 2010).

17   *Id.* at 55–59.

18   U.S. GENERAL ACCOUNTABILITY OFFICE, ENERGY EFFICIENCY AND CONSERVATION GRANT BLOCK GRANT RECIPIENTS FACE CHALLENGES MEETING LEGISLATIVE AND PROGRAM GOALS AND REQUIREMENTS (2011), *available at* http://www.gao.gov/new.items/d11379.pdf; INTERNATIONAL COUNCIL FOR LOCAL ENVIRONMENTAL INITIATIVES (ICLEI), HOW 38 LOCAL GOVERNMENTS FUND SUSTAINABILITY STAFF AND OPERATIONS (2011) *available at* http://www.icleiusa.org/library/documents/north-star-network-events/ICLEI_Sustainability_Funding_Fact_Sheet.pdf/view.

19   Jonathan D. Weiss & Girair Simon, *Smart Growth and Sustainability*, *in* ENVIRONMENTAL ASPECTS OF REAL ESTATE TRANSACTIONS: FROM BROWNFIELDS TO GREEN BUILDINGS (James B. Witkin ed., 2011).

20   Kirsten H. Engel & Marc L. Miller, *State Governance: Leadership on Climate Change*, *in* AGENDA FOR A SUSTAINABLE AMERICA 441, 442 (John C. Dernbach ed., ELI Press 2009).

21   Greenopia, *at* http://www.greenopia.com/LC/state_search.aspx?category=State&Listpage=0&input=Name-or-product&subcategory=Nonehttp://www.greenopia.com/LC/state_search.aspx?category=State&Listpage=0&input=Name-or-product&subcategory=None (last visited Nov. 24, 2011).

22   Brian Wingfield & Miriam Marcus, *America's Greenest States*, FORBES, Oct. 17, 2007, *at* http://www.forbes.com/2007/10/16/environment-energy-vermont-biz-beltway-cx_bw_mm_1017greenstates.html.

23   Kirsten H. Engel & Marc L. Miller, *State Governance: Leadership on Climate Change*, *in* AGENDA FOR A SUSTAINABLE AMERICA 441, 444–48 (John C. Dernbach ed., ELI Press 2009).

24   M.A. Delmis & M.J. Montes-Sancho, *U.S. State Policies for Renewable Energy: Context and Effectiveness*, 39 ENERGY POLICY 2273–88 (2011).

25   U.S. Department of Energy, Database of State Incentives for Renewables & Efficiency (DSIRE), http://www.dsireusa.org/ (last visited Nov. 24, 2011).

26   Center for Climate and Energy Solutions, U.S. States and Regions–Climate Action, http://www.c2es.org/states-regions (last visited Jan. 27, 2012).

27   Center for Climate and Energy Solutions, Table of All State Initiatives (Version 01/27/2009), http://www.c2es.org/docUploads/AllStateInitiatives-01-27-09-a_0.pdf.

28   U.S. Dept. of Energy, Database of State Incentives for Renewables & Efficiency, Summary Maps, http://www.dsireusa.org/summarymaps/index.cfm?ee=1&RE=1 (follow RPS Policies hyperlink) (last visited Nov. 24, 2011).

29   Center for Climate and Energy Solutions, Energy Efficiency Standards and Targets, http://www.c2es.org/what_s_being_done/in_the_states/efficiency_resource.cfm (last visited Mar. 1, 2012).

30   Center for Climate and Energy Solutions, Decoupling Policies, http://www.c2es.org/what_s_being_done/in_the_states/decoupling (last visited March 31, 2012).

31   ELIZABETH DORIS ET AL., ENERGY EFFICIENCY POLICY IN THE UNITED STATES—OVERVIEW OF TRENDS AT DIFFERENT LEVELS OF GOVERNMENT (2009), available at http://www.nrel.gov/docs/fy10osti/46532.pdf .

32   Center for Climate and Energy Solutions, Public Benefit Funds, http://www.c2es.org/what_s_being_done/in_the_states/public_benefit_funds.cfm (last visited Mar. 31, 2012).

33   U.S. Dep't of Energy, Database of State Incentives for Renewables & Efficiency, Financial Incentives for Renewable Energy, http://www.dsireusa.org/summarytables/finre.cfm (last visited May 1, 2012).

34   Id.

35   NATIONAL RESEARCH COUNCIL, REAL PROSPECTS FOR ENERGY EFFICIENCY IN THE UNITED STATES 282–83 (Nat'l Acad. Press, 2010).

36   Id. at 284–89.

37   Id. at 279.

38   John Byrne et al., American Policy Conflict in the Greenhouse: Divergent Trends in Federal, Regional, State, and Local Green Energy and Climate Change, 35 ENERGY POLICY 4555, 4559 (2007).

39   Center for Climate and Energy Solutions, Table of All State Initiatives (Version 01/27/2009), http://www.c2es.org/docUploads/AllStateInitiatives-01-27-09-a_0.pdf.

40   CENTER FOR CLIMATE AND ENERGY SOLUTIONS, CLIMATE CHANGE 101: STATE ACTION 1 (2011), available at http://www.c2es.org/docUploads/climate101-state.pdf.

41   CAL. HEALTH & SAFETY CODE §38500 (2007).

42   Id.

43   See CAL. CODE REGS. tit. 17, §§95801-96023.

44   See CAL. HEALTH & SAFETY CODE §38560.

45   See CAL. CODE REGS. tit. 17, §§95480-95490 (2009).

46   See Rocky Mountain Farmers Union v. Goldstene, No. 09-cv-02234 (E.D. Cal. Dec. 29, 2011).

47   See CAL. PUB. UTIL. §§8340-8341.

48   Regional Greenhouse Gas Initiative, http://www.rggi.org/homehttp://www.rggi.org/home (last visited Mar. 13, 2012).

49   John C. Dernbach, National Governance, in STUMBLING TOWARD SUSTAINABILITY 723, 724–25 (John C. Dernbach ed., ELI Press 2002).

50   U.N. Secretary-General, Plan of Implementation of the World Summit on Sustainable Development, ¶ 162 (b), U.N. Doc. A/CONF. 199/20 (Sept. 4, 2002).

51   50 U.S.C. §404a. See PRESIDENT OF THE UNITED STATES, NATIONAL SECURITY STRATEGY (2010), available at http://www.whitehouse.gov/sites/default/files/rss_viewer/national_security_strategy.pdf.

52   10 U.S.C. §118(a).

53   U.S. DEP'T OF HOMELAND SECURITY, QUADRENNIAL HOMELAND SECURITY REVIEW REPORT (2010), available at http://www.dhs.gov/xlibrary/assets/qhsr_report.pdf.

54   U.S. DEP'T OF STATE & U.S. AGENCY FOR INTERNATIONAL DEVELOPMENT, LEADING THROUGH CIVILIAN POWER: THE FIRST QUADRENNIAL DIPLOMACY AND DEVELOPMENT REVIEW (2010), available at http://www.state.gov/documents/organization/153108.pdf. For a critique, see ANTHONY H. CORDESMAN, CENTER FOR STRATEGIC AND INTERNATIONAL STUDIES, THE QUADRENNIAL DIPLOMACY AND DEVELOPMENT REVIEW (QDDR): CONCEPTS ARE NOT ENOUGH (2010), available at http://csis.org/files/publication/101221_QDDR_Review.pdf.

55   EXECUTIVE OFFICE OF THE PRESIDENT, PRESIDENT'S COUNCIL OF ADVISORS ON SCIENCE AND TECHNOLOGY, REPORT TO THE PRESIDENT ON ACCELERATING THE PACE OF CHANGE IN ENERGY TECHNOLO-GIES THROUGH AN INTEGRATED FEDERAL AGENCY POLICY v (2010), *available at* http://www.whitehouse. gov/sites/default/files/microsites/ostp/pcast-energy-tech-report.pdf.

56   U.S. DEP'T OF ENERGY, REPORT ON THE FIRST QUADRENNIAL TECHNOLOGY REVIEW (2011), *available at* http://energy.gov/sites/prod/files/ReportOnTheFirstQTR.pdf.

57   10 U.S.C. §118(g).

58   GENERAL ACCOUNTABILITY OFFICE, CLIMATE CHANGE: IMPROVEMENTS NEEDED TO CLARIFY NATIONAL PRIORITIES AND BETTER ALIGN THEM WITH FUNDING DECISIONS 35-6 (2011), *available at* http:// www.gao.gov/new.items/d11317.pdf.

59   President's Council on Sustainable Development, http://clinton2.nara.gov/PCSD/http:// clinton2.nara.gov/PCSD/ (last visited Nov. 30, 2011).

60   John C. Dernbach, *National Governance, in* STUMBLING TOWARD SUSTAINABILITY 723, 730–39 (John C. Dernbach ed., ELI Press 2002).

61   David Rejeski, *Any Big Ideas Left?*, ENVTL. FORUM, Sept./Oct. 2001, at 36, 38.

62   *Government Performance and Results Act of 1993*, Pub. L. No. 103-62, 107 Stat. 285.

63   5 U.S.C. §306(a).

64   5 U.S.C. §306(c).

65   31 U.S.C. §1116.

66   GPRA Modernization Act of 2010, H.R. 2142, 111th Congress, *available at* http://www.gpo. gov/fdsys/pkg/BILLS-111hr2142enr/pdf/BILLS-111hr2142enr.pdf.

67   This table was constructed from agency GPRA plans as of July 2011: U.S. DEP'T OF AGRICULTURE, STRATEGIC PLAN FY 2010-2015 at 1-33 (2010), *available at* http://www.ocfo.usda.gov/ usdasp/sp2010/sp2010.pdf; U.S. DEP'T OF COMMERCE, STRATEGIC PLAN: FY 2007-2012 at 5-62 (2006), *available at* http://www.osec.doc.gov/bmi/budget/07strplan/DOC07strplan.pdf; U.S. DEP'T OF DEFENSE, QUADRENNIAL DEFENSE REVIEW REPORT 5-88 (2010), *available at* http://www.defense.gov/qdr/images/ QDR_as_of_12Feb10_1000.pdf; U.S. DEP'T OF EDUC., STRATEGIC PLAN 2007-2012 at 7-33 (2007), *available at* http://www2.ed.gov/about/reports/strat/plan2007-12/2007-plan.pdf; U.S. DEP'T OF ENERGY, STRATEGIC PLAN v (2011), *available at* http://www.energy.gov/media/DOE_StrategicPlan.pdf; U.S. EPA, 2011-2015 STRATEGIC PLAN: ACHIEVING OUR VISION 6-24 (2010), *available at* http://nepis.epa.gov/ Adobe/PDF/P1008YOS.Pdf; U.S. DEP'T OF HOUSING & URBAN DEV., HUD STRATEGIC PLAN FY 2010-2015 at 12-45 (2010), *available at* http://portal.hud.gov/hudportal/documents/huddoc?id=DOC_4436. pdf; U.S. DEP'T OF THE INTERIOR, STRATEGIC PLAN FOR FISCAL YEARS 2011-2016 at 9-38 (2011), *available at* http://www.doi.gov/bpp/data/PPP/DOI_StrategicPlan.pdf; U.S. DEP'T OF TRANSP., STRATEGIC PLAN FISCAL YEARS 2006-2011: NEW IDEAS FOR A NATION ON THE MOVE 11-51 (2006), *available at* http:// www.dot.gov/stratplan2011/dotstrategicplan.pdf.

68   U.S. DEP'T OF STATE & U.S. AGENCY FOR INT'L DEV., STRATEGIC PLAN FISCAL YEARS 2007-2012: TRANSFORMATIONAL DIPLOMACY 26-8 (2007), *available at* http://www.state.gov/documents/ organization/86291.pdf.

69   NATIONAL RESEARCH COUNCIL, SUSTAINABILITY AND THE U.S. ENVIRONMENTAL PROTECTION AGENCY (Nat'l Acad. Press 2011).

70   *Id.* at 36–49.

71   Exec. Order No. 13514, 74 Fed. Reg. 52117, §2 at 52118 (Oct. 9, 2009). This executive order strengthens a 2007 executive order by President George W. Bush on the same subject. (Exec. Order No. 13423, 72 Fed. Reg. 3919 (Jan. 26, 2007)).

72   Exec. Order No. 13514, *supra* note 71, §8 at 52122.

73   *Id.* §8(c). *See* White House, Council on Environmental Quality, Federal Agency Strategic Sustainability Performance Plans, *available at* http://www.whitehouse.gov/administration/eop/ceq/ sustainability/plans (last visited Dec. 5, 2011).

74   Exec. Order No. 13514, *supra* note 71, §4(b) at 52121.

75   *Id.* §16 at 52124.

76   WHITE HOUSE COUNCIL ON ENVIRONMENTAL QUALITY, INSTRUCTIONS FOR IMPLEMENTING CLI-MATE CHANGE ADAPTATION PLANNING IN ACCORDANCE WITH EXECUTIVE ORDER 13514 (2011), *available at* http://www.whitehouse.gov/sites/default/files/microsites/ceq/adaptation_final_implementing_instruc-tions_3_3.pdf. *See also* WHITE HOUSE COUNCIL ON ENVIRONMENTAL QUALITY, PROGRESS REPORT OF THE INTERAGENCY CLIMATE CHANGE ADAPTATION TASK FORCE: RECOMMENDED ACTIONS IN SUPPORT OF

A NATIONAL CLIMATE CHANGE ADAPTATION STRATEGY (2010), *available at* http://www.whitehouse.gov/sites/default/files/microsites/ceq/Interagency-Climate-Change-Adaptation-Progress-Report.pdf.

77   White House, Council on Environmental Quality, OMB Sustainability and Energy Scorecards, http://www.whitehouse.gov/administration/eop/ceq/sustainability/omb-scorecards (last visited Dec. 14, 2011).

78   Federal Reports Elimination and Sunset Act of 1995, Pub. L. No. 104-66, 109 Stat. 707, 734-35, §3003, 31 U.S.C. §1113 (note) (repealing 42 U.S.C. §4341).

79   U.S. EPA, EPA's Report on the Environment (2003 Draft), *available at* http://cfpub.epa.gov/ncea/cfm/recordisplay.cfm?deid=56830 (last visited Dec. 14, 2011).

80   U.S. EPA, EPA'S REPORT ON THE ENVIRONMENT 2008 (2008), *available at* http://www.epa.gov/roe/docs/roe_final/EPAROE_FINAL_2008.PDF.

81   U.S. EPA, Report on the Environment, *available at* http://www.epa.gov/roe/ (last visited Dec. 14, 2011).

82   Joy E. Hecht, Can Indicators and Accounts Really Measure Sustainability? Considerations for the U.S. Environmental Protection Agency (2007), *available at* http://www.scribd.com/doc/1841126/Environmental-Protection-Agency-hechtepaordpaper.

83   U.S. EPA, Indicators, http://www.epa.gov/greenkit/indicator.htm#sustain (last visited Dec. 14, 2011).

84   U.S. INTERAGENCY WORKING GROUP ON SUSTAINABLE DEVELOPMENT INDICATORS, SUSTAINABLE DEVELOPMENT IN THE UNITED STATES: AN EXPERIMENTAL SET OF INDICATORS (1998).

85   The State of the USA, About, http://www.stateoftheusa.org/about/ (last visited Dec. 14, 2011).

86   The State of the USA, History, http://www.stateoftheusa.org/about/history/ (last visited Dec. 14, 2011).

87   GENERAL ACCOUNTABILITY OFFICE, KEY INDICATOR SYSTEMS: EXPERIENCES OF OTHER NATIONAL AND SUBNATIONAL SYSTEMS OFFER INSIGHTS FOR THE UNITED STATES 12 (2011), *available at* http://www.gao.gov/new.items/d11396.pdf.

88   Patient Care and Affordable Care Act, Pub. L. No. 111-148, 124 Stat. 119, §5605 at 680 (2010) (codified at 36 U.S.C. §150303), *available at* http://www.gpo.gov/fdsys/pkg/PLAW-111publ148/pdf/PLAW-111publ148.pdf.

89   The State of the USA, Congress Appoints Key National Indicators Commission (Dec. 16, 2010), http://www.stateoftheusa.org/content/commission-on-key-national-ind.php.

90   The State of the USA, History, http://www.stateoftheusa.org/about/history/ (last visited Mar. 2, 2012).

91   ORGANIZATION FOR ECONOMIC COOPERATION AND DEVELOPMENT, OECD ENVIRONMENTAL PERFORMANCE REVIEWS: UNITED STATES (2005).

92   *Id.* at 25.

93   *Id.* at 26.

94   *Id.*

95   Center for Environmental Law and Policy, Yale University & Center for International Earth Science Information Network, Columbia University, Environmental Performance Index 2010, *at* http://epi.yale.edu/ (last visited Dec. 14, 2011).

96   Center for Environmental Law and Policy, Yale University & Center for International Earth Science Information Network, Columbia University, Country Scores, http://epi.yale.edu/Countrieshttp://epi.yale.edu/Countries (last visited Dec. 14, 2011).

97   Center for Environmental Law and Policy, Yale University & Center for International Earth Science Information Network, Columbia University, United States of America, http://epi.yale.edu/Countries/UnitedStatesOfAmerica (last visited Dec. 14, 2011).

98   *See* MARY JANE ANGELO ET AL., RECLAIMING GLOBAL ENVIRONMENTAL LEADERSHIP: WHY THE UNITED STATES SHOULD RATIFY TEN PENDING ENVIRONMENTAL TREATIES (2012), *available at* http://www.progressivereform.org/articles/International_Environmental_Treaties_1201.pdf.

Chapter 6

1   United Nations Conference on Environment and Development, Rio Declaration on Environment and Development, Principle 10, U.N. Doc. A/CONF.151/5/Rev.1, 31 I.L.M. 874 (June 3-14,

1992), *available at* http://www.unep.org/Documents.Multilingual/Default.asp?documentid=78&articl
eid=1163.

2   NATIONAL WILDLIFE FEDERATION, CAMPUS ENVIRONMENT 2008: A NATIONAL REPORT CARD ON
SUSTAINABILITY IN HIGHER EDUCATION (2d ed. 2008), *available at* http://www.nwf.org/campusEcology/
docs/CampusReportFinal.pdf.

3   ASSOCIATION FOR THE ADVANCEMENT OF SUSTAINABILITY IN HIGHER EDUCATION, HIGHER
EDUCATION SUSTAINABILITY STAFFING SURVEY 2010 (2010–2011), *available at* http://www.aashe.org/
files/2010_staffing_survey_final.pdf.

4   American College & University Presidents' Climate Commitment, http://www.presidentscli-
matecommitment.org (last visited Feb. 20, 2012).

5   Sustainable Endowments Institute, The College Sustainability Report Card: Transportation (2011), http://www.greenreportcard.org/report-card-2011/categories/transportation; Sustainable
Endowments Institute, The College Sustainability Report Card: Food & Recycling (2011), http://www.
greenreportcard.org/report-card-2011/categories/food-recycling.

6   Association for the Advancement of Sustainability in Higher Education, Academic Programs,
http://www.aashe.org/resources/academic-programs (last visited Feb. 20, 2012) (showing growing list
of hundreds of environmental and sustainability degree programs in the U.S. and Canada).

7   *See* Green Studies: The Fastest Growing Program, EDU in Review, http://www.eduinreview.
com/blog/2010/01/green-studies-the-fastest-growing-degree-program/ (last visited Feb. 20, 2012).

8   Proceedings of the Nat'l Acadamy of Sciences of the United States of America, Sustainability
Science, http://www.pnas.org/misc/sustainability.shtml (last visited Dec. 17, 2011).

9   American University, Washington College of Law, Sustainable Development Law & Policy,
http://www.wcl.american.edu/org/sustainabledevelopment/ (last visited Dec. 17, 2011).

10   *See, e.g.*, Allegheny College, Allegheny College's Center for Economic and Environmental
Development, http://ceed.allegheny.edu/ (last visited Dec. 17, 2011).

11   Elizabeth Coleman, Address given at the National Association of Independent Schools annual
conference, Feb. 25, 2011, *available at* www.nais.org/files/ac/2011/11AC%5FElizabethColemanSpeech.
pdf.

12   Harvard Law School-Green Living Program, http://green.harvard.edu/hls/green-living (last
visited Dec. 17, 2011).

13   Marian Burros, *Fresh Gets Invited to the Cool Table*, N.Y. TIMES, Aug. 24, 2005, *at* http://
www.nytimes.com/2005/08/24/dining/24school.html.

14   Recyclemaniacs website, http://www.recyclemaniacs.org (last visited Dec. 17, 2011).

15   THE PRINCETON REVIEW, THE PRINCETON REVIEW'S GUIDE TO 311 GREEN COLLEGES (2011),
available at http://apps.olin.wustl.edu/mba/casecompetition/PDF/Princeton%20Reviews%20Guide%20
to%20Green%20Colleges.pdf.

16   Carmela Federico & Jaimie Cloud, *Kindergarten Through Twelfth Grade Education: Frag-
mentary Progress in Equipping Students to Think and Act in a Challenging World, in* AGENDA FOR A
SUSTAINABLE AMERICA 109, 112–13 (John C. Dernbach ed., ELI Press 2009).

17   Putnam/Northern Westchester BOCES Curriculum Center, Education for Sustainability,
http://www.pnwboces.org/efs/ (last visited Mar. 12, 2012); Jaimie P. Cloud, *Educating for a Sustainable Future, in* CURRICULUM 21: ESSENTIAL EDUCATION FOR A CHANGING WORLD 168, 174 (Heidi Hayes
Jacobs ed., ASCD (formerly the Ass'n for Supervision & Curriculum Development) 2010).

18   Sustainable Jersey, About Sustainable Jersey, http://www.sustainablejersey.com/about.php
(last visited Dec. 17, 2011).

19   Sustainable Jersey, Education for Sustainability Programs, http://www.sustainablejersey.com/
actiondesc.php?arr_num=11&id_num=1!10 (last visited Dec. 17, 2011).

20   J. Moore, *Barriers and Pathways to Creating Sustainability Education Programs: Policy,
Rhetoric and Reality*, 11 ENVTL. EDUCATION RESEARCH 537 (2005); J. Bebbington & R. Gray, *An Account
of Sustainability: Failure, Success and a Reconceptualization*, 12 CRITICAL PERSPECTIVES ON ACCOUNTING
557 (2001).

21   E. BARRAT HACKING, B. SCOTT, & E. LEE, EVIDENCE OF IMPACT OF SUSTAINABLE SCHOOLS
(Dep't for Children, Schools & Families 2010), *available at* http://publications.teachernet.gov.uk/
eOrderingDownload/00344-2010BKT-EN.pdf; R. Becker-Klein et al., *Long-Term Associations of
Homelessness With Children's Well-being*, 51 AMERICAN BEHAVIORAL SCIENTIST 789 (2008).

22   The World Wide Web Consortium, A Little History of the World Wide Web, http://www.
w3.org/History.html.
23   Video: Eric Qualman, Socialnomics, Social Media Revolution Video (Refreshed) (2010),
http://www.socialnomics.net/2010/05/05/social-media-revolution-2-refresh/.
24   U.S. EPA, Process for Setting up Wikis and Blogs at EPA, http://yosemite.epa.gov/OEI/
webguide.nsf/socialmedia/wikisandblogs.
25   U.S. EPA, MyEnvironment Environmental Information for My Area, http://www.epa.gov/
myenvironment/ (last visited Dec. 16, 2011); *see also* U.S. EPA, Envirofacts, http://www.epa.gov/enviro/
(last visited Dec.16, 2011).
26   U.S. General Services Admin., Data.gov, http://www.data.gov/ (last visited Dec. 16, 2011).
27   For example, in 1998, Environmental Defense launched Scorecard, which is now owned by
Green Media Toolshed. Scorecard, The Pollution Information Site, http://scorecard.goodguide.com/ (last
visited Dec. 16, 2011).
28   *But see* N.Y. ENVTL. CONSERV. L. §8-0109 (4), (6), *available at* http://law.onecle.com/new-
york/environmental-conservation/ENV08-0109_8-0109.html (requiring draft environmental impact
statements prepared under the New York State Environmental Quality Review Act to be posted online).
29   OFFICE OF MGMT. & BUDGET, CIRCULAR NO. A-130 REVISED, *available at* www.whitehouse.
gov/omb/circulars_a130_a130trans4.
30   OFFICE OF MGMT. & BUDGET, OPEN GOVERNMENT DIRECTIVE (2009), *available at* http://www.
whitehouse.gov/open/documents/open-government-directive.
31   44 U.S. C. §3501 (note).
32   Memorandum from Attorney General John Ashcroft to Heads of All Fed. Dep'ts and Agencies
re: Freedom of Information Act (Oct. 12, 2001) (on "sensitive, but classified information"), *available at*
http://www.doi.gov/foia/foia.pdf. *See also* Memorandum from White House Chief of Staff Andrew Card
Jr. to Heads of All Fed. Dep'ts and Agencies re: Action to Safeguard Information Regarding Weapons
of Mass Destruction and Other Sensitive Documents Related to Homeland Security (Mar. 19, 2002),
available at http://www.dod.gov/pubs/foi/dfoipo/docs/cbrn_wh_memo.pdf.
33   RIGHT TO KNOW COMMUNITY, MOVING TOWARD A 21ST CENTURY RIGHT-TO-KNOW AGENDA:
RECOMMENDATIONS TO PRESIDENT-ELECT OBAMA AND CONGRESS 14 (Nov. 2008), *available at* http://www.
ombwatch.org/files/21strtkrecs.pdf.
34   PATRICE MCDERMOTT & AMY FULLER, OPENTHEGOVERNMENT.ORG, SECRECY REPORT CARD
2008: INDICATORS OF SECRECY IN THE FEDERAL GOVERNMENT 2, *available at* http://www.openthegovern-
ment.org/sites/default/files/otg/SecrecyReportCard08.pdf.
35   *Id.*
36   The White House Blog, Change has come to WhiteHouse.gov (2009), http://www.white-
house.gov/blog/change_has_come_to_whitehouse-gov/ (last visited Dec. 16, 2011). *See also* SEAN
MOULTON & GAVIN BAKER, OMBWATCH, ASSESSING PROGRESS: TOWARD A 21ST CENTURY RIGHT TO
KNOW 6 (2011), *available at* http://www.ombwatch.org/files/info/21strtkrecsassessment.pdf.
37   Memorandum from Admin. of Barack H. Obama to Heads of Exec. Dep'ts and Agencies
re: Transparency and Open Government (Jan. 21, 2009), *available at* http://www.gpoaccess.gov/pres-
docs/2009/DCPD200900010.pdf.
38   Memorandum from the President to Heads of Exec. Dep'ts and Agencies re: Freedom of
Information Act (Jan. 21, 2009), 74 Fed. Reg. 4435 (Jan. 26, 2009), *available at* http://edocket.access.
gpo.gov/2009/pdf/E9-1773.pdf.
39   OMB WATCH, ASSESSMENT OF SELECTED DATA FROM THE ANNUAL AGENCY FREEDOM OF
INFORMATION ACT REPORTS 2, 4–5 (2011), *available at* http://www.ombwatch.org/files/info/fy2010foia-
analysis.pdf.
40   PATRICE MCDERMOTT & AMY FULLER, SECRECY REPORT CARD 2010: INDICATORS OF SECRECY
IN THE FEDERAL GOVERNMENT 2 (2010).
41   Spencer S. Hsu, *Obama Invokes 'State Secrets' Claim to Dismiss Suit Against Targeting of
U.S. Citizen al-Aulaqi*, WASH. POST., Sept. 25, 2010, *at* http://www.washingtonpost.com/wp-dyn/content/
article/2010/09/25/AR2010092500560.html.
42   Memorandum from Attorney General Eric Holder to Heads of Exec. Dep'ts and Agencies/
Heads of Dep't Components re: Policies and Procedures Governing Invocation of the State Secrets
Privilege (Sept. 23, 2009), *available at* http://www.justice.gov/opa/documents/state-secret-privileges.
pdf.

43   Press Release, Department of Justice Office of Public Affairs, Attorney General Establishes New State Secrets Policies and Procedures (Sept. 23, 2009), *available at* http://www.justice.gov/opa/pr/2009/September/09-ag-1013.html.

44   Lujan v. Defenders of Wildlife, 504 U.S. 555 (1992).

45   *Id.* at 560–61.

46   *See, e.g.*, Steel Co. v. Citizens for a Better Env't, 523 U.S. 83 (1998) (citizens sued over a company's failure to file its reports under the Emergency Planning and Community Right-to-Know Act (EPCRA), but because the company filed the reports after the suit was filed, the plaintiffs were found to lack standing because their injuries could no longer be redressed by the Court's decision).

47   Friends of the Earth v. Laidlaw, 528 U.S. 167, 183–84 (2000) (granting standing based on the plaintiff's decision not to use the local river for recreational purposes based on their "reasonable concerns" about exposure to defendant's discharges of mercury).

48   Massachusetts v. EPA, 549 U.S. 497 (2007).

49   Summers v. Earth Island Inst., 555 U.S. 488, 490–98 (2009) (holding that the plaintiff's standing to sue ceased to exist once the particular tract of land that the plaintiff used was no longer part of the dispute).

50   5 U.S.C. §504(a)(1).

51   H.R. 1, 112th Cong. §4007 (2011), *available at* http://www.gpo.gov/fdsys/pkg/BILLS-112hr1eh/pdf/BILLS-112hr1eh.pdf (moratorium on the payment of funds under the Equal Access to Justice Act that passed in the House, but was removed in the final budget). *See* H.R. 1473, 112th Cong. (2011) (as passed in both House and Senate), *available at* http://www.gpo.gov/fdsys/pkg/BILLS-112hr1473enr/pdf/BILLS-112hr1473enr.pdf.

52   *Compare* Soc'y of the Plastics Indus. v. County of Suffolk, 573 N.E.2d 1034 (N.Y. 1991) (the injury to a plaintiff in SEQR litigation must be "different in kind or degree from that of the public at large"), *and* Save Our Main Street Buildings v. Green County Legislature, 740 N.Y.S.2d 715 (N.Y. App. Div. 2002), *lv. denied*, 98 747 N.Y.S.2d 409 (2002) (antique shop owner two blocks from proposed demolition of 10 buildings in historical district denied standing), *with* Save the Pine Bush, Inc. v. Common Council of the City of Albany, 918 N.E.2d 917 (N.Y. 2009) (requiring a demonstration that a plaintiff's use of a resource is more than that of the general public).

53   For Maryland, see Univ. of Md. School of Law, 2010 Joint Chairmen's Report (JCR) on the Univ. of Md. School of Law's Environmental Law Clinic R30.B21, p.34, *available at* http://dlslibrary.state.md.us/publications/JCR/2010/2010_134.pdf; Md. Dep't of Legislative Serv's, Report on the State Operating Budget (SB 140) and the State Capital Budget (SB 142) and Related Recommendations by the Chairmen of the Senate Budget and Taxation Committee and House Appropriations Committee, 133–34 (2010), *available at* http://mlis.state.md.us/2010rs/budget_docs/all/JCR.pdf. For Louisiana, see Louisiana Senate Bill 549 (2010), *available at* http://www.legis.state.la.us/billdata/byinst.asp?sessionid=10RS&billtype=SB&billno=549 (summary only); Adam Babich & Brandon David Souza, *Protecting Public Participation*, ENVTL. FORUM, May/June 2011.

Chapter 7

1   Royal C. Gardner & Ezequiel Lugo, *Official Development Assistance: Toward Funding for Sustainability*, *in* AGENDA FOR A SUSTAINABLE AMERICA 400-01 (John C. Dernbach ed., ELI Press 2009).

2   All data on development finance are from the AidData data set. For discussion on categorization methods, see ROBERT L. HICKS ET AL., GREENING AID? UNDERSTANDING THE ENVIRONMENTAL IMPACT OF DEVELOPMENT ASSISTANCE (Oxford Univ. Press 2008). For updated data after 1999, see Michael J. Tierney et al., *More Dollars Than Sense: Refining Our Knowledge of Development Finance Using AidData*, 39 WORLD DEV. 1891 (2011).

3   *Id.*

4   *Id.*

5   RICHARD K. LATTANZIO, THE GLOBAL CLIMATE CHANGE INITIATIVE (GCCI): BUDGET AUTHORITY AND REQUEST, FY2008-FY2012 (Congressional Research Service 2011), *available at* http://www.fas.org/sgp/crs/misc/R41845.pdf; White House, President Obama's Development Policy and the Global Climate Change Initiative (n.d.), *available at* http://www.whitehouse.gov/sites/default/files/Climate_Fact_Sheet.pdf; Graciela Kincaid & Graciela and J. Timmons Roberts, No Talk but Some Walk: Obama

Administration Rhetoric on Climate Change and International Climate Spending (to be presented at the American Sociological Association meeting, Aug. 2012).

6   *See, e.g.,* The Equator Principles Ass'n, Equator Principles, http://www.equator-principles. com.

7   *See, e.g.* Leonardo A. Crippa, *Multilateral Development Banks and Human Rights Responsibility*, 25 AM. U. L. REV. 531 (2010).

8   United Nations Conference on Environment and Development, Rio Declaration on Environment and Development, Principle 3, U.N. Doc. A/CONF.151/5/Rev.1, 31 I.L.M. 874 (June 3-14, 1992), *available at* http://www.unep.org/Documents.Multilingual/Default.asp?documentid=78&articl eid=1163.

9   Robert B. Zoellick, *Why We Still Need the World Bank: Looking Beyond Aid*, FOREIGN AFFAIRS, Mar./Apr. 2012, at 66.

10   Jonathan Peterson, *World Bank OKs Moving Chinese to Tibet/U.S. Objects to Relocating 58,000 Farmers*, L.A. TIMES, June 25, 1999, *at* http://www.sfgate.com/cgi-bin/article.cgi?f=/c/a/1999/06/25/ MN1850.DTL; Jonathan Peterson, *World Bank Cancels Chinese Resettlement Project/Plan Criticized by U.S. and Other Nations for Its Impact on Tibet*, L.A. TIMES, July 8, 2000, *at* http://articles.sfgate. com/2000-07-08/news/17652481_1_damaging-internal-audit-tibetan-influence-and-culture-controver-sial-development-effort.

11   For examples of recent controversial World Bank activities, see the websites of the Bank Information Center, http://www.bicusa.org, and the Bretton Woods Project, http://www.brettonwoods-sproject.org.

12   *See, e.g.,* JANET REDMAN ET AL., INST. FOR POLICY STUDIES, DIRTY IS THE NEW CLEAN: A CRITIQUE OF THE WORLD BANK'S NEW STRATEGIC FRAMEWORK FOR DEVELOPMENT AND CLIMATE CHANGE (Oct. 2008), *available at* http://www.ips-Dc.org/reports/dirty_is_the_new_clean.

13   Athena Ballesteros, Will Climate Finance Mean a New Path for the World Bank? (May 17, 2010), http://blogs.worldbank.org/climatechange/will-climate-finance-mean-new-path-world-bank.

14   The ADB also committed to provide $2 billion annually to the clean energy project beginning in 2013, a doubling of such investments based on 2008 lending. News Release, Asian Development Bank, New ADB Policy Targets Secure, Clean Energy for Asia (June 19, 2009), *available at* .adb.org/ media/Articles/2009/12917-asian-clean-enegy-policies.

15   Smita Nakhooda, Word Resources Institute, The World Bank Eskom Support Program (Mar. 8, 2010), http://www.wri.org/stories/2010/03/world-bank-eskom-support-program.

16   WORLD BANK GROUP, ESKOM INVESTMENT SUPPORT PROJECT: QUESTIONS & ANSWERS (Apr. 14, 2010), *available at* http://www.sitesources.worldbank.org/INTSOUTHAFRICA/Resources/Q_A_ Eskom_Investment_Support_Project_031810.pdf.

17   DAVID HALLOWES, THE WORLD BANK AND ESKOM: BANKING ON CLIMATE DESTRUCTION (2009), *available at* http://www.bicusa.org/en/Project.Resources.10520.aspx; Bobby Peek, Bretton Woods Project, Eskom Loan Blackens the World Bank's Name (Apr. 16, 2010), http://www.brettonwoodsproject. org/art-566122; Bank Info. Ctr., World Bank Approves $3.75 Billion Loan to Eskom (Apr. 8, 2010), http://www.bicusa.org/en/Article.11838.aspx.

18   U.S. Dep't of the Treasury, Treasury Department Statement on the U.S. Position on the World Bank's Eskom Investment Support Project (Apr. 8, 2010).

19   ATHENA BALLESTEROS ET AL., POWER, RESPONSIBILITY, AND ACCOUNTABILITY: RE-THINKING THE LEGITIMACY OF INSTITUTIONS FOR CLIMATE FINANCE (2010), *available at* http://pdf.wri.org/power_ responsibility_accountability.pdf.

20   Overseas Private Inv. Corp., Our Mission, http://www.opic.gov/about/mission.

21   Press Release, Friends of the Earth, Landmark Global Warming Lawsuit Filed (Feb. 6, 2009), *available at* http://action.foe.org/t/6545/pressRelease.jsp?press_release_KEY=486.

22   Press Release, Export-Import Bank of the United States, Export-Import Bank Adopts Carbon Policy to Encourage Renewable Energy and Climate-Friendly Technologies (Nov. 3, 2009) [hereinafter Export-Import Bank], *available at* http://www.exim.gov/pressrelease.cfm/BC0AA512-EF10-91BF-A6F1508E016C9E5E/.

23   Settlement Agreement, Exhibit B, Friends of the Earth v. Spinelli, No. 02-4106 (N.D. Cal. Feb. 6, 2009), *available at* http://www.climatelaw.org/cases/case-documents/us/opic.pdf.

24   Export-Import Bank, *supra* note 22.

25   Settlement Agreement, Exhibit B, *supra* note 23.

26   Statement of Jonathan Sohn, Hearing on The Reauthorization of the Overseas Private Inv. Corp. Before Subcomm. on Terrorism, Non-Proliferation, and Trade (May 24, 2007), *available at* http://pdf.wri.org/070524_sohn_testimony_housefa.pdf.

27   Org. for Econ. Co-Operation and Dev., Revised Council Recommendation on Common Approaches on the Environment and Officially Supported Export Credits (2007), *available at* http://www.oecd.org/officialdocuments/displaydocumentpdf?cote=TAD/ECG(2007)9&doclanguage=en.

28   WORLD SUMMIT ON SUSTAINABLE DEVELOPMENT, PLAN OF IMPLEMENTATION OF THE WORLD SUMMIT ON SUSTAINABLE DEVELOPMENT ¶ 98 (2002), *available at* http://www.un.org/esa/sustdev/documents/WSSD_POI_PD/English/WSSD_PlanImpl.pdf.

29   Marrakesh Agreement Establishing the World Trade Organization, pmbl., Apr. 15, 1994, 1867 U.N.T.S. 154, 33 I.L.M. 1144 (1994).

30   HÅKAN NORDSTRÖM & SCOTT VAUGHAN, TRADE AND ENVIRONMENT (WTO Secretariat Special Studies No. 4) (1999).

31   North American Free Trade Agreement, pmbl., U.S.-Can.-Mex., Dec. 17, 1992, *reprinted in* 32 I.L.M. 289 (entered into force Jan.1, 1994).

32   North American Agreement on Environmental Cooperation, art. 14, U.S.-Can.-Mex., Dec. 17, 1993, *reprinted in* 32 I.L.M. 1480 (1993) [hereinafter NAAEC].

33   *Id.* art. 14.1. The Secretariat maintains a registry of submissions on enforcement matters at www.cec.org.

34   The Dominican Republic-Central America-United States Free Trade Agreement, Annex 10-C, ¶ 4(b), *available at* http://www.ustr.gov/trade-agreements/free-trade-agreements/cafta-dr-dominican-republic-central-america-fta/final-text.

35   United States-Peru Trade Promotion Agreement, art. 18.11(1)-(2) (2011); United States-Colombia Trade Promotion Agreement, art. 18.11(1)-(2) (2011). The texts of these agreements are available at http://www.ustr.gov/trade-agreements/free-trade-agreements.

36   Environmental Review of Trade Agreements, Exec. Order No. 13141, 64 Fed. Reg. 63169 (Nov. 16, 1999). *See also* The Guidelines for Implementation of Exec. Order No. 13141, 65 Fed. Reg. 79442 (Dec. 19, 1999), *available at* http://www.ustr.gov/environment/environmental.shtml.

37   Bilateral Investment Treaty, U.S.-Uru., Nov. 4, 2005, *available at* http://www.state.gov./documents/organization/56650.pdf.

38   *Id.* at Annex B, ¶ 4(b).

39   Jamie Lincoln Kitman, *The Secret History of Lead*, THE NATION, Mar. 20, 2000, *at* http://www.thenation.com/article/secret-history-lead?page=full.

40   *See generally* Newser, News About: Lead Poisoning, http://www.newser.com/tag/4636/1/lead-poisoning.html.

41   TRUST FOR LEAD POISONING PREVENTION [ORIGINALLY ALLIANCE TO END CHILDHOOD LEAD POISONING], MYTHS AND REALITIES OF PHASING OUT LEADED GASOLINE (1997), *available at* http://global-leadnet.com/89/myths-and-realities-of-phasing-out-leaded-gasoline.

42   R.L. Jones et al., *Trends in Blood Lead Levels and Blood Lead Testing Among U.S. Children Aged 1 to 5 Years, 1988–2004*. 123 PEDIATRICS e376 (2009).

43   K.W. James Rochow, *Lead Poisoning and Prevention: Opportunities for Internationalized Solutions*, *in* AGENDA FOR A SUSTAINABLE AMERICA 425, 432 (John C. Dernbach ed., ELI Press 2009).

44   PARTNERSHIP FOR CLEAN FUELS AND VEHICLES & U.N. ENVIRONMENT PROGRAM, LEADED PETROL PHASE-OUT: GLOBAL STATUS (2011), *available at* http://www.unep.org/transport/PCFV/PDF/MapWorldLead_January2011.pdf.

45   *See, e.g.*, M.A.S. Laidlow & G. M. Filipelli, *Resuspension of Urban Soils as a Persistent Source of Lead Poisoning in Children*, 23 APPLIED GEOCHEMISTRY 2021 (Aug. 2008); J.O Nriagu et al., *Lead Levels in Blood and Saliva in a Low-income Population of Detroit, Michigan*, INT'L J. HYGIENE & ENVTL. HEALTH 109–21 (2006). *See generally*, ROBERT D. BULLARD ET AL., ENVIRONMENTAL HEALTH AND RACIAL EQUITY IN THE UNITED STATES, *esp.* Preface at xii & Ch. 1 (2011).

Chapter 8

1   Riley E. Dunlap, *Trends in Public Opinion Toward the Environment: 1965–1990*, in AMERI-
CAN ENVIRONMENTALISM: THE U.S. ENVIRONMENTAL MOVEMENT 1970–1990 (Riley E. Dunlap & Angela
G. Mertig eds., 1992).
2   A. Kohut & J. Shriver, *Environment Regaining a Foothold on the National Agenda*, GALLUP
REPORT (1989).
3   RILEY E. DULAP ET AL., THE HEALTH OF THE PLANET: RESULTS OF A 1992 INTERNATIONAL
ENVIRONMENTAL OPINION SURVEY OF CITIZENS IN 24 COUNTRIES (George Gallup International Institute
1992), *available at* http://www.conpsychmeasures.com/CONPSYCHMeasures/Measures/Gallup/Gal-
lup.html; G. Heuber, *Americans Report High Levels of Environmental Concern, Activity*, GALLUP POLL
MONTHLY (Apr. 1991); Lydia Saad & Riley E. Dunlap, *Americans Are Environmentally Friendly, but
Issue Not Seen as Urgent Problem*, GALLUP NEWS SERVICE (Apr. 17, 2000), *available at* http://www.
gallup.com.
4   Jeffrey M. Jones, *Americans Increasingly Prioritize Economy Over Environment*, GALLUP
POLITICS (Mar. 17, 2011), *at* http://www.gallup.com/poll/146681/americans-increasingly-prioritize-
economy-environment.aspx.
5   Jeffrey M. Jones, *In U.S., Many Environmental Issues at 20-Year-Low Concern*, GALLUP POLI-
TICS (May 16, 2010), *at* http://www.gallup.com/poll/126716/environmental-issues-year-low-concern.
aspx.
6   Jones, *supra* note 4.
7   Lydia Saad, *In U.S., Expanding Energy Output Still Trumps Green Concerns*, GALLUP
POLITICS (Mar. 6, 2011), *at* http://www.gallup.com/poll/146651/Expanding-Energy-Output-Trumps-
Green-Concerns.aspx (click on link, "View methodology, full question results, and trend data").
8   Frank Newport, *Americans' Global Warming Concerns Continue to Drop*, GALLUP POLITICS
(Mar. 11, 2010), *at* http://www.gallup.com/poll/126560/americans-global-warming-concerns-continue-
drop.aspx.
9   Pew Research Center, Little Change in Opinions About Global Warming (Oct. 27, 2010),
http://www.people-press.org/2010/10/27/little-change-in-opinions-about-global-warming/.
10   *Id.*
11   *Id.*
12   *Id.*
13   Newport, *supra* note 8.
14   *See, e.g.*, ANTHONY LEISEROWITZ, CLIMATE CHANGE RISK PERCEPTION AND POLICY PREF-
ERENCES: THE ROLE OF AFFECT, IMAGERY AND VALUES (2006), *available at* http://glennumc.org/
clientimages/41359/etf_risk_perception.pdf; M. Thompson & S. Rayner, *Cultural Discourses, in*
HUMAN CHOICE AND CLIMATE CHANGE (S. Rayner & E. Malone eds., 1998); MARY DOUGLAS & AARON
WILDAVSKY, RISK AND CULTURE: AN ESSAY ON THE SELECTION OF TECHNOLOGICAL AND ENVIRONMENTAL
DANGERS (Univ. of Calif. Press 1982).
15   MIKE HULME, WHY WE DISAGREE ABOUT CLIMATE CHANGE: UNDERSTANDING CONTROVERSY,
INACTION AND OPPORTUNITY 208 (Cambridge Univ. Press 2009).
16   J.C. Pierce et al., *Knowledge, Culture and Public Support for Renewable Energy Technology
Policy in Oregon*, 7 COMP. TECH. TRANSFER & SOC'Y 270–86 (2009); C.A. Simon, *Cultural Constraints
on Wind and Solar Energy in the U.S. Context*, 7 COMP. TECH. TRANSFER & SOC'Y 251–69 (2009); S.S.
White et al., *Planting Food or Fuel: Developing an Interdisciplinary Approach to Understanding the
Role of Culture in Farmers' Decisions to Grow Second-Generation, Biofuel Feedstock Crops*, 7 COMP.
TECH. TRANSFER & SOC'Y 287–302 (2009).
17   J.C. Pierce et al., Cultural Considerations in the Adoption of Renewable Energy Technologies:
An Oregon and Washington Case Study (2011) (paper delivered at the Western Energy Policy Research
Conference, Boise, Idaho).
18   Pew Research Center, Little Change in Opinions About Global Warming, *supra* note 9.
19   PEW RESEARCH CENTER, LIFE IN 2050: AMAZING SCIENCE, FAMILIAR THREATS 6 (2010), *available at* http://people-press.org/http://people-press.org/files/legacy-pdf/625.pdf.
20   *Id.*

21   Russell Dalton, The Good Citizen: How a Younger Generation Is Reshaping American Politics (CQ Press 2009); M. Winograd & M.D. Hais, Millennial Makeover: MySpace, YouTube and the Future of American Politics 93 (Rutgers Univ. Press 2009).

22   Pew Research Center, *supra* note 19, at 7.

23   *Id.*

24   Dalton, *supra* note 21; Winograd & Hais, *supra* note 21.

25   American Lung Association, American Lung Association Bipartisan Poll Shows Strong Public Support for Lifesaving Clean Air Act (Feb. 16, 2011), http://www.lung.org/press-room/press-releases/bipartisan-clean-air-poll.html.

26   *See, e.g.,* James J. Parsons, *On "Bioregionalism" and Watershed Consciousness*, 37 Prof. Geographer 1 (1985); Donald Alexander, *Bioregionalism: Science or Sensibility?*, 12 Envtl. Ethics 161 (1990); Eric Freyfogle, *Ownership and Ecology*, 43 Case W. Res. L. Rev. 1269, 1291 (1993).

27   *See* Robert W. Adler, *Addressing Barriers to Watershed Protection*, 25 Envtl. L. 973, 1000–03 (1995).

28   Haya El Nasser, *Community Involvement Important Across Demographic Lines*, USA Today, Dec. 8, 2010.

29   *Id.*

30   Transportation for America, Future of Transportation National Survey 2010, http://t4america.org/resources/2010survey/.

31   Christopher Simon et al., State and Local Government: Sustainability in the 21st Century (Oxford Univ. Press 2010).

32   Sarah Crow & Cecilia Danks, *Why Certify? Motivations, Outcomes and the Importance of Facilitating Organizations in Certification of Community-Based Forestry Initiatives*, 9 Smallscale Forestry 195, 205–06 (2009).

33   Forum on Religion and Ecology, Yale School of Forestry & Environmental Studies, Religions of the World and Ecology Series Description, http://fore.research.yale.edu/publications/books/book_series/cswr/index.html (last visited Mar. 5, 2012) (listing the titles, editors, and publication dates of 10 volumes, published between 1997 and 2004 by Harvard University Press, that explore visions of human-earth relations and implications for environmental ethics expressed in the beliefs, rituals, attitudes, doctrines, and moral teachings of Buddhism, Christianity, Confucianism, Daoism, Hinduism, Indigenous Traditions, Islam, Jainism, Judaism, and Shinto).

34   Holmes Rolston III, *Saving Creation: Faith Shaping Environmental Policy*, 4 Harv. L. & Pol'y Rev. 121 (2010), *available at* http://hlpronline.com/2010/02/rolstoD_faith/.

35   Paul Hawken, Blessed Unrest: How the Largest Movement in the World Came Into Being and Why No One Saw It Coming 2 (Viking Penguin 2007).

36   MIT Sloan Management Review and Boston Consulting Group, Sustainability Nears a Tipping Point, Research Report (2012), *available at* http://sloanreview.mit.edu/feature/sustainability-strategy/.

37   *Id.* at 6–7 (noting that 25% of the companies cite interest in product information and 22% cite interest in business model and process information, both sustainability matters of particular interest to institutional investors).

38   *Id.* at 7–9.

39   *See* Kurt A. Strasser, Myths and Realities of Business Environmentalism: Good Works, Good Business or Greenwash? 917 (Edward Elgar 2011). *See also* KPMG, International Survey of Corporate Responsibility Reporting 2011 (2011), *available at* http://www.kpmg.com/PT/pt/IssuesAndInsights/Documents/corporate-responsibility2011.pdf [hereinafter KPMG 2011] (most recent comprehensive survey by KPMG of the corporate responsibility reporting practices of the largest 250 companies in the world) *and* KPMG International Survey of Corporate Responsibility Reporting 2008 (2008), *available at* http://www.kpmg.com/Global/en/IssuesAndInsights/ArticlesPublications/Documents/International-corporate-responsibility-survey-2008.pdf hereinafter KPMG 2008 [hereinafter KPMG 2008].

40   *See* KPMG 2011, *supra* note 39; KPMG 2008, *supra* note 39.

41   KPMG 2011, *supra* note 39, at 11, 7, respectively.

42   KPMG 2008, *supra* note 39, at 12–20. *See also* Strasser, *supra* note 39; Corporate Register.com, CRRA Reporting Awards '07: Global Winners and Reporting Trends 30-34 (2008)

[hereinafter Reporting Awards 07]; *and* Ans Kolk, *Sustainability, Accountability and Corporate Governance: Exploring Multinationals' Reporting Practices,* 18 BUS. STRAT. ENV. 1 (2006).

43   GLOBAL REPORTING INITIATIVE, SUSTAINABILITY REPORTING GUIDELINES, VERSION 3.0, at 28–29 (2006) [hereinafter GRI], *available at* https://www.globalreporting.org/resourcelibrary/G3-Sustainability-Reporting-Guidelines.pdf.

44   *Id.* at 29–33.

45   Kolk, *supra* note 42 (describing details of governance in Table 2, at 6). *See also* GRI, *supra* note 43, at 8.

46   KPMG 2011, *supra* note 39, at 19; KPMG 2008, *supra* note 39, at 19; STRASSER, *supra* note 39, at 13–15.

47   Sylvie Bertholet et al., *Environmental Disclosure Research: Review & Synthesis,* 22 J. ACCOUNTING LIT. 1 (2003) (review of empirical literature finding that such reporting was not shown to be associated with better environmental performance). *See also* David Hess, *Social Reporting and New Governance Regulation: the Prospects of Achieving Corporate Accountability Through Transparency,* 17 BUS. ETHICS Q. 453 (2007).

48   Peter Clarkson et al., *Revisiting the Relations Between Environmental Performance and Environmental Disclosure: An Empirical Analysis,* 33 ACCOUNTING, ORGS. & SOC'Y 303, 325 (2007). *See also* STRASSER, *supra* note 39, at 15–17.

49   Chris Van Staden & Jill Hooks, *A Comprehensive Comparison of Corporate Environmental Reporting and Responsiveness,* 39 BRITISH ACCOUNTING REV. 197 (2007).

50   Charles Davis & Katherine Hoffer, Federalizing Energy: Agenda Change and the Politics of Fracking (2011) (paper presented at the Western Energy Policy Conference, Boise, Idaho), *available at* http://epi.boisestate.edu/media/8415/15_charles%20davis%20(paper)_federalizing%20energy,%20agenda%20change%20and%20politics%20of%20fracking.pdf.

51   *See* Kurt Strasser, *Do Voluntary Corporate Efforts Improve Environmental Performance? The Empirical Literature,* 35 B.C. ENVTL. AFF. L. REV. 533, 546–54 (2008).

52   International Council of Chemical Associations, Responsible Care, http://www.responsiblecare.org (last visited May 6, 2008); *see also* Sustainable Forestry Initiative, http://www.sfiprogram.org/ (last visited Mar. 4, 2012). *See also* Errol Meidinger, *Multi-Interest Self-Governance Through Global Product Certification Programmes, in* RESPONSIBLE BUSINESS: SELF-GOVERNANCE AND THE LAW IN TRANSNATIONAL ECONOMIES, ch. 9 (Hart Pubs. 2008).

53   *See* STRASSER, *supra* note 39, ch. 7.

54   DOUG COGAN ET AL., CORPORATE GOVERNANCE AND CLIMATE CHANGE: CONSUMER AND TECHNOLOGY COMPANIES 3 (Ceres 2008), *available at* http://www.ceres.org/resources/reports/corporate-governance-and-climate-change-2008.

55   *Id.* at 24-28 (describing specific targets of individual companies—e.g., Texas Instruments goal of 48% PFC reduction in 1998, achieved it in 2007, and Dell Computer's goal of companywide carbon neutrality).

56   STRASSER, *supra* note 39, at 19–33; Thomas P. Lyon & John W. Maxwell, *Environmental Public Voluntary Programs Reconsidered,* 35 POL'Y STUD. J. 723, 729 (2007) (surveying 60 government-sponsored programs and the available literature to conclude that "overall, the empirical results suggest that participation in these PVP's [public voluntary programs] had little or no impact on firm's environmental performance"; *see also* Dinah A. Koehler, *Effectiveness of Voluntary Environmental Programs, in* VOLUNTARY ENVIRONMENTAL PROGRAMS 522 (Peter de Leon and Jorge Rivera, eds., Lexington Books 2009).

57   Andrew King & Michael Lennox, *Industry Self-Regulation Without Sacrifice: The Chemical Industry's Responsible Care Program,* 43 ACAD. MGMT. J. 678–716 (2000).

58   MAGALI DELMAS & MARIA MONTES-SANCHO, VOLUNTARY AGREEMENTS TO IMPROVE ENVIRONMENTAL QUALITY: ARE LATE JOINERS FREE RIDERS? (2007), *available at* http://www.epa.gov/ncer/events/calendar/2008/jan14/delmas_011408_paper.pdf.

59   Magali Delmas & Arturo Keller, *Free Riding in Voluntary Environmental Programs: The Case of U.S. EPA WasteWise Program,* 38 POL'Y SCI. 91 (2005).

60   Michael Lenox & Jennifer Nash, *Industry Self-Regulation and Adverse Selection: A Comparison Across Four Trade Association Programs,* 12 BUS. STRATEGY & ENV. 343 (2003).

61   Press Release, U.S. Dep't of Agriculture, Forest Service, Forest Legacy Program Reaches 2 Million Acre Milestone in Protecting Threatened Private Forests (Nov. 23, 2010), *available at* http://

www.usda.gov/wps/portal/usda/usdahome?contentidonly=true&contentid=wps/portal/usda/!ut/p/
c5/&contentid=2010/11/0618.xml.

62   ROB ALDRICH & JAMES WYERMAN, LAND TRUST ALLIANCE, 2005 NAT'L LAND TRUST CENSUS
REPORT 6 (2006), *available at* http://www.landtrustalliance.org/land-trusts/land-trust-census/2005-report.
pdf.

63   Benjamin M. Leoni, *Resolving Disputes in the Northern Forests: Lessons From the Connecticut and Moosehead Lakes*, 35 VT. L. REV. 295 295–96, 311, 315 (2010).

64   Press Release, Friends of the Earth, Landmark Global Warming Lawsuit Settled (Feb. 6,
2009), *available at* http://action.foe.org/t/6545/pressRelease.jsp?press_release_KEY=486.

65   WORLD BANK INSPECTION PANEL, ACCOUNTABILITY AT THE WORLD BANK: THE INSPECTION
PANEL AT 15 YEARS 88–89 (2009), *available at* http://siteresources.worldbank.org/EXTINSPECTION-
PANEL/Resources/380793-1254158345788/InspectionPanel2009.pdf.

66   Association for the Advancement of Sustainability in Higher Education, www.aashe.org.

67   The U.S. Partnership for Education for Sustainable Development, www.uspartnership.org.

68   Disciplinary Associations Network for Sustainability, www.aashe.org/dans.

69   Thanks to Dave Newport, Director of the Environmental Center at University of Colorado
at Boulder, for this observation.

70   KPMG 2011, *supra* note 39, at 18–19.

71   TRUST FOR LEAD POISONING PREVENTION [ORIGINALLY ALLIANCE TO END CHILDHOOD LEAD
POISONING], MYTHS AND REALITIES OF PHASING OUT LEADED GASOLINE (1997), *available at* http://
globalleadnet.com/89/myths-and-realities-of-phasing-out-leaded-gasoline; TRUST FOR LEAD POISONING
PREVENTION, INTERNATIONAL ACTION PLAN FOR PREVENTING LEAD POISONING (3rd ed. 2001), *available
at* http://www.globalleadnet.org/policy_leg/policy/intlactionplan.cfm.

72   U.S. EPA Partnership Programs: List of Programs, *http://*www.epa.gov/partners/programs/
index.htm#product (last visited Sept. 27, 2011).

73   BlueGreen Alliance, About the BlueGreen Alliance, http://www.bluegreenalliance.org/
about_us?id=0001.

74   United States Climate Action Partnership, Welcome to the U.S. Climate Action Partnership
(USCAP) Web Site, http://www.us-cap.org/.

75   United Nations Environment Programme, Partnership for Clean Fuels and Vehicles, http://
www.unep.org/pcfv/.

76   U.N. Envtl. Program & World Health Org., Global Alliance to Eliminate Lead Paint, http://
www.chem.un.ch/Lead_in_paint/.

77   Press Release, Mintel Oxygen Reports, Mintel Finds Fewer Americans Interested in Going
"Green" During Recession (Feb. 2009), *available at* http://www.mintel.com/press-centre/press-
releases/325/mintel-finds-fewer-americans-interested-in-going-green-during-recession.

78   Fred Kirschenmann, *A Brief History of Sustainable Agriculture*, 9 NETWORKER No. 2 (Mar.
2004) (Science & Environmental Health Network), *available at* http://www.sehn.org/Volume_9-2.
html#a2.

79   Local Harvest, Community Supported Agriculture, http://www.localharvest.org/csa/; Steven
McFadden, Rodale Institute, The History of Community Supported Agriculture, Part II: CSA's World of
Possibilities, http://newfarm.rodaleinstitute.org/features/0204/csa2/part2.shtml.

80   WALLACE CENTER, WINROCK INTERNATIONAL, CHARTING GROWTH TO GOOD FOOD: DEVEL-
OPING INDICATORS AND MEASURES OF GOOD FOOD (2009), *available at* http://www.wallacecenter.org/
our-work/current-initiatives/sustainable-food-indicators/sustainable-indicators-report/CHARTING
GROWTH BOOK final with charts.pdf.

81   U.S. DEP'T OF AGRICULTURE, AGRICULTURAL MARKETING SERVICE, FARMERS' MARKET
GROWTH: 1994–2011 (2011), *available at* http://www.ams.usda.gov/AMSv1.0/ams.fetchTemplateData.
do?template=TemplateS&leftNav=WholesaleandFarmersMarkets&page=WFMFarmersMarketGrowth
&description=Farmers Market Growth&acct=frmrdirmkt.

82   GENERAL ELECTRIC CO., SOLUTIONS FOR THE WORLD'S TOUGHEST CHALLENGES: ECOMAGINA-
TION 2010 ANNUAL REPORT (2011), *available at* http://files.gecompany.com/ecomagination/progress/
GE_ecomagination_2010AnnualReport.pdf.

83   European Commission, REACH, http://ec.europa.eu/environment/chemicals/reach/reach_
intro.htm (last visited Oct. 22, 2011).

Chapter 9

1   Federico Cheever & Ward J. Scott, *Sustainable Forestry: Moving From Concept to Consistent Practice, in* AGENDA FOR A SUSTAINABLE AMERICA 285, 293 (John C. Dernbach ed., ELI Press 2009).

2   SUSTAINABLE FORESTRY INITIATIVE & FOREST STEWARDSHIP COUNCIL, SFI AND FSC CERTIFI-CATION IN NORTH AMERICA—A SUMMARY COMPARISON (2010), *available at* http://www.glatfelter.com/files/sustainability/SFIvFSC.pdf.

3   V. ALARIC SAMPLE ET AL., PINCHOT INSTITUTE FOR CONSERVATION, NATIONAL FOREST CERTI-FICATION STUDY: AN EVALUATION OF THE APPLICABILITY OF FOREST STEWARDSHIP COUNCIL (FSC) AND SUSTAINABLE FORESTRY INITIATIVE (SFI) STANDARDS ON FIVE NATIONAL FORESTS 11 (2007), *available at* http://pinchot.org/NFCertificationStudy_PIC.pdf.

4   KATHRYN FERNHOLZ ET AL., DOVETAIL PARTNERS, INC., FOREST CERTIFICATION: A STATUS REPORT (2010), *available at* http://www.dovetailinc.org/files/DovetailCertReport0310b.pdf.

5   *Id.* at 11.

6   KATHRYN FERNOLZ ET AL., DOVETAIL PARTNERS, INC., DIFFERENCES BETWEEN THE FOREST STEWARDSHIP COUNCIL (FSC) AND SUSTAINABLE FORESTRY CERTIFICATION STANDARDS FOR FOREST MAN-AGEMENT (2011), *available at* http://www.dovetailinc.org/files/DovetailFSCSFIComparison32811.pdf.

7   Ruben N. Lubowski et al., *Major Uses of Land in the United States, 2002,* ERS REPORT SUM-MARY (May 2006) *available at* http://www.ers.usda.gov/publications/EIB14/eib14_reportsummary.pdf.

8   WASHINGTON STATE DEP'T OF NATURAL RESOURCES, WASHINGTON'S "GREEN" CERTIFIED STATE TRUST FORESTS 1 (2010), *available at* www.dnr.wa.gov/Publications/frc_fsc-sfi_certification_factsheet.pdf.

9   Minn. Dep't of Natural Resources, Minnesota Forest Certification Data, http://www.dnr.state.mn.us/forestry/certification/certifiedforest_data.html (last visited Mar. 8, 2011).

10   WIS. DEP'T OF NATURAL RESOURCES DIVISION OF FORESTRY, WISCONSIN CERTIFIED ACRES (Jan. 9, 2009), *available at* http://dnr.wi.gov/topic/TimberSales/documents/WI_Forest_Acres_Certified_2009.pdf.

11   Press Release, Mich. Dep't of Natural Resources, Michigan's State Forests Maintain Dual Forest Sustainability Certification (Jan. 18, 2011), *available at* http://www.michigan.gov/dnr/0,1607,7-153-10371_10402-249687--,00.html.

12   Pa. Dep't of Conservation and Natural Resources, Forest Sustainability, http://www.dcnr.state.pa.us/forestry/naturalgasexploration/sustainability/index.htm (last visited Mar. 4, 2012).

13   MD. DEP'T OF NATURAL RESOURCES, SUSTAINABLE FOREST MANAGEMENT PLAN, PUBLIC SUM-MARY FOR POCOMOKE STATE FOREST, SUSTAINABLE FORESTS FOR PEOPLE AND THE BAY (2010) *available at* http://www.dnr.state.md.us/forests/pdfs/PSF_SP_Summary.pdf.

14   Press Release, N.Y. Dep't of Envtl. Conservation, N.Y. Joins Elite Company With Certified "Green" Forests, State Owned Forests Meet Highest Requirements for Protection, Sustainability (Mar. 10, 2008), *available at* http://www.dec.ny.gov/press/42552.html.

15   Mass. Division of Fisheries and Wildlife, Forest Certification, http://www.mass.gov/dfwele/dfw/habitat/management/bdi/forest_mgt/green_certification.htm (last visited Oct. 17 2011).

16   News Release, Ohio Dep't of Natural Resources, Growing Green—Ohio's State Forests Certi-fied as Sustainably Managed (Dec. 27, 2010), *available at* http://ohiodnr.com/home_page/NewsReleases/tabid/18276/EntryId/2065/Growing-Green-Ohio-s-State-Forests-Certified-as-Sustainably-Managed.aspx.

17   SAMPLE ET AL., *supra* note 3, at 11.

18   Press Release, Rainforest Alliance, Rainforest Alliance's SmartWood Program Certifies Largest Forestry Group to FSC Standards (Dec. 19, 2008), *available at* http://rainforest-alliance.org/newsroom/news/group-certification.

19   Energy Policy Act of 2005, Pub. L. No. 109-58, §131, 119 Stat. 594, 620 (2005) (codified at 42 U.S.C. §6294a).

20   U.S. Environmental Protection Agency & U.S. Dep't of Energy, ENERGY STAR, History of ENERGY STAR, http://www.energystar.gov/index.cfm?c=about.ab_history (last visited Sept. 2, 2011).

21   GOVERNMENT ACCOUNTABILITY OFFICE, ENERGY STAR PROGRAM: COVERT TESTING SHOWS THE ENERGY STAR PROGRAM CERTIFICATION PROCESS IS VULNERABLE TO FRAUD AND ABUSE 1 (2010), *available at* http://www.gao.gov/new.items/d10470.pdf.

22   U.S. Environmental Protection Agency & U.S. Dep't of Energy, ENERGY STAR, About ENERGY STAR, *available at* http://www.energystar.gov/index.cfm?c=about.ab_index (last visited Sept. 2, 2011).

23   ENERGY STAR, ENERGY STAR® OVERVIEW OF 2010 ACHIEVEMENTS 1 (2011), *available at* http://www.energystar.gov/ia/partners/publications/pubdocs/2010%20CPPD%204pgr.pdf.

24   *Id.* at 2.

25   42 U.S.C. §15821 (2007).

26   U.S. Dep't of Energy, Rebates for ENERGY STAR® Appliances, http://www.energysavers. gov/financial/70020.html (last visited Mar. 4, 2012).

27   *See, e.g.*, KPMG SUSTAINABILITY SERIES, 2006 SURVEY OF INTEGRATED SUSTAINABILITY REPORTING IN SOUTH AFRICA 1 (2006).

28   KPMG, INTERNATIONAL SURVEY OF CORPORATE RESPONSIBILITY REPORTING 2011, 21 (2011), *available at* http://www.kpmg.com/PT/pt/IssuesAndInsights/Documents/corporate-responsibility2011. pdf [hereinafter KPMG 2011]. *See also* Oren Perez, *The New Universe of Green Finance: From Self-Regulation to Multi-Polar Governance, in* RESPONSIBLE BUSINESS: SELF-GOVERNANCE AND LAW IN TRANSNATIONAL ECONOMIC TRANSACTIONS, at 162–67 (Olaf Dilling et al. eds., 2007) (excellent introduction to the GRI guidelines).

29   Yong Ting Aw et al., The Impact of Assurance on the Quality of Voluntary Environmental Disclosures: An Empirical Analysis. Paper presented at the 2009 Accounting and Finance Association of Australia and New Zealand conference, Adelaide, South Australia, *available at* http://epublications. bond.edu.au/business_pubs/239/.

30   *See* KURT A. STRASSER, MYTHS AND REALITIES OF BUSINESS ENVIRONMENTALISM: GOOD WORKS, GOOD BUSINESS OR GREENWASH? 11–13 (Elgar 2011),

31   KPMG 2011, *supra* 28, at 28 (the 2005 percentages being 30% and 33%, respectively).

32   KPMG, INTERNATIONAL SURVEY OF CORPORATE RESPONSIBILITY REPORTING 2008, 65 (2008), *available at* http://www.kpmg.com/Global/en/IssuesAndInsights/ArticlesPublications/Documents/ International-corporate-responsibility-survey-2008.pdf [hereinafter KPMG 2008].

33   *Id.* at 60 (reporting that 27% of the reporting G250 companies and 18% of the largest 100 in each country use this approach).

34   American Bar Association Section of Environment, Energy, and Resources, ABA-EPA Law Office Climate Challenge, http://www.americanbar.org/groups/environment_energy_resources/ projects_awards/aba_epa_law_office_climate_challenge.html (last visited Aug. 26, 2011).

35   American Bar Association Section of Environment, Energy, and Resources, Law Firm Sustainability Framework, http://www.americanbar.org/groups/environment_energy_resources/proj-ects_awards/model_law.html (last visited Aug. 26, 2011).

36   Massachusetts Bar Association, The MBA Lawyers Eco-Challenge, http://www.massbar. org/about-the-mba/initiatives/lawyers-eco-challenge (last visited Sept. 28, 2011); Massachusetts Bar Association, About CLF, http://www.massbar.org/about-the-mba/initiatives/lawyers-eco-challenge (last visited Mar. 4, 2012).

37   State Bar of California, Voluntary State Bar of California Lawyers Eco-Pledge and Voluntary Law Office Sustainability Policy (2008), *available at* http://calbar.ca.gov/calbar/pdfs/bog/special/Eco-Pledge-Policy.pdf.

38   Pennsylvania Bar Association, Pennsylvania Lawyers United for Sustainability (PLUS) Program, http://www.pabar.org/public/sections/envco/plusprogram.asp (last visited Aug. 26, 2011).

39   OREGON LAWYERS FOR A SUSTAINABLE FUTURE, MODEL LAW OFFICE SUSTAINABILITY POLICY (2006), *available at* http://sustainablelawyers.org/assets/sustainability_policy.pdf.

40   International Council of Chemical Associations, Responsible Care, http://www.responsiblec-are.org (last visited Mar. 4, 2012).

41   *See* Andrew King & Michael Lennox, *Industry Self-Regulation Without Sacrifice: The Chemical Industry's Responsible Care Program*, (2000) 43 ACAD. MGMT. J. 678 (2000); STRASSER, *supra* note 30, at 17–20.

42   American Chemistry Council, Responsible Care® Performance Results, http://responsiblec-are.americanchemistry.com/Performance-Results/default.aspx (last visited Mar. 4, 2012).

43   Bicycling, America's Top 50 Bike-Friendly Cities, http://www.bicycling.com/news/ advocacy/1-minneapolis-mn (last visited Oct. 22, 2011).

44   U.S. CONFERENCE OF MAYORS, RECYCLING AMERICA'S LAND: A NATIONAL REPORT ON BROWN-FIELDS REDEVELOPMENT (1993-2010) 13 (2010), *available at* http://www.usmayors.org/pressreleases/uploads/November2010BFreport.pdf.

45   *See generally* PETER CALTHORPE, URBANISM IN THE AGE OF CLIMATE CHANGE (2010).

46   JUSTIN HOLLANDER, NIALLL KIRKWOOD, & JULIA GOLD, PRINCIPLES OF BROWNFIELD REGENER-ATION: CLEANUP, DESIGN, AND REUSE OF DERELICT LAND 86 (2010) (discussing the Assunpink Greenway in Trenton, NJ).

47   *Id.* at 54–55.

48   City of Brockton, Brockton Brightfields, http://www.brockton.ma.us/government/depart-ments/Planning/BrocktonBrighfields.aspx (last visited Mar. 21, 2011).

49   *See, e.g.,* U.S. Green Building Council, http://www.usgbc.org/ (last visited Mar. 21, 2011), U.S. Environmental Protection Agency, Green Building, http://www.epa.gov/greenbuilding/ (last visited Mar. 21, 2011).

50   WILLIAM SARNI, GREENING BROWNFIELDS: REMEDIATION THROUGH SUSTAINABLE DEVELOP-MENT 144 (2009).

51   GREG KATS, GREENING OUR BUILT WORLD: COSTS, BENEFITS, AND STRATEGIES (2010); U.S. GREEN BUILDING COUNCIL, BUILDING MOMENTUM: NATIONAL TRENDS AND PROS-PECTS FOR HIGH-PERFORMANCE GREEN BUILDINGS (2002), *available at* http://www.usgbc.org/Docs/Resources/043003_hpgb_whitepaper.pdf.

52   CATHY TURNER & MARK FRANKEL, NEW BUILDINGS INSTITUTE, ENERGY PERFORMANCE OF LEED FOR NEW CONSTRUCTION BUILDINGS 31 (2008), *available at* http://www.usgbc.org/ShowFile.aspx?DocumentID=3930.

53   ROB WATSON & GREEN BIZ GROUP, GREEN BUILDING MARKET AND IMPACT REPORT (2010), *available at* http://www.greenbiz.com/sites/all/themes/greenbiz/doc/GBMIR_2010.pdf.

54   GREG KATS, GREENING AMERICA'S SCHOOLS: COSTS AND BENEFITS (2006), *available at* http://www.usgbc.org/ShowFile.aspx?DocumentID=2908.

55   *E.g.,* BUILDING DESIGN & CONSTRUCTION, GREEN BUILDINGS AND THE BOTTOM LINE 7 (2006), *available at* http://www.bdcnetwork.com/bdc-white-paper-2006-green-buildings-and-bottom-line; GREG KATS, THE COSTS AND FINANCIAL BENEFITS OF GREEN BUILDINGS: A REPORT TO CALIFORNIA'S SUSTAINABLE BUILDING TASK FORCE 12 (2003), *available at* http://www.capitalmarketspartnership.com/UserFiles/Admin%20Building%20Design%20Construction%202006%20White%20Paper.pdf.

56   BUILDING DESIGN & CONSTRUCTION, WHITE PAPER ON SUSTAINABILITY 1 (2003), *available at* https://www.usgbc.org/Docs/Resources/BDCWhitePaperR2.pdf.

57   *See, e.g.,* GREEN BUILDINGS AND THE BOTTOM LINE, *supra* note 55, at 4.

58   KATS, *supra* note 55, at 12.

59   THE AMERICAN INSTITUTE OF ARCHITECTS, LOCAL LEADERS IN SUSTAINABILITY GREEN BUILD-ING POLICY IN A CHANGING ECONOMIC ENVIRONMENT 63 (2009), *available at* http://www.aia.org/aiaucmp/groups/aia/documents/document/aiab081614.pdf.

60   KATS, *supra* note 55, at 12.

61   U.S. GREEN BUILDING COUNCIL, MAKING THE BUSINESS CASE FOR HIGH PERFORMANCE GREEN BUILDING (2003), *available at* https://www.usgbc.org/Docs/Member_Resource_Docs/makingthebusi-nesscase.pdf.

62   U.S. DEP'T OF ENERGY, BUILDING REGULATORY PROGRAMS MULTI-YEAR PROGRAM PLAN 12 (2010), *available at* http://apps1.eere.energy.gov/buildings/publications/pdfs/corporate/regulatory_pro-grams_mypp.pdf.

63   NATIONAL RESEARCH COUNCIL, SUSTAINABILITY AND THE U.S. ENVIRONMENTAL PROTECTION AGENCY 120 (Nat'l Acad. Press 2011).

64   Press Release, Dow Chemical Co., Dow Enhances Global Energy Efficiency and GHG Reduction Leadership (June 7, 2011), http://www.businesswire.com/news/home/20110607005063/en/Dow-Enhances-Global-Energy-Efficiency-GHG-Reduction; E-Mail from Dawn L. Shiang, Associate Director, Sustainable Technologies & Innovation Sourcing, Dow Chemical Co., to John Dernbach (Mar. 20, 2012, 16:37:56 EDT) (on file with author).

65   FERNHOLZ ET AL., *supra* note 4.

66   Donald H. Schepers, *Challenges to Legitimacy at the Forest Stewardship Council*, 92 J. BUS. ETHICS 279, 286 (2010).

67   Wis. Dep't of Natural Resources, Wis. Statewide Forest Assessment 2010, Criterion 6 (2010), http://dnr.wi.gov/forestry/assessment/strategy/conclusions.asp?id=6 (last visited Oct. 6, 2011).

68   DINA COVER & TD ECONOMICS, WHAT'S NEXT FOR LUMBER PRICES 1 (2010), *available at* www.td.com/economics/special/dc0710_lumber.pdf.

69   *Id.*

70   William E. Rees, *Consuming the Earth: The Biophysics of Sustainability*, 29 ECOLOGICAL ECON. 23 (2009).

71   ROBERT PRESCOTT-ALLEN, THE WELLBEING OF NATIONS: A COUNTRY-BY-COUNTRY INDEX OF QUALITY OF LIFE AND THE ENVIRONMENT (2001).

72   WOLFGANG SACHS, PLANET DIALECTICS: EXPLORATIONS IN ENVIRONMENT AND DEVELOPMENT (1999).

73   BOSTON FOUNDATION, THE WISDOM OF OUR CHOICES: BOSTON INDICATORS OF PROGRESS, CHANGE AND SUSTAINABILITY (2000), *available at* http://www.tbf.org/uploadedFiles/Title%20Pages.pdf.

74   John Dernbach and the Widener University Law School Seminar on Climate Change, *Next Generation Recycling and Waste Reduction: Building on the Success of Pennsylvania's 1988 Legislation*, WIDENER L. J. (forthcoming), *available at* http://papers.ssrn.com/sol3/papers.cfm?abstract_id=1808911.

75   Carl J. Circo, *Using Mandates and Incentives to Promote Sustainable Construction and Green Building Projects in the Private Sector: A Call for More State Land Use Policy Initiatives*, 112 PENN ST. L. REV. 731, 735 (2007–2008).

76   Robert McNally & Michael Levi, *A Crude Predicament: The Era of Volatile Oil Prices*, FOREIGN AFFAIRS, July/Aug. 2011, at 100, 107.

77   Ira Robert Feldman, *Business and Industry: Transitioning to Sustainability in* AGENDA FOR A SUSTAINABLE AMERICA 71, 72 (John C. Dernbach ed., ELI Press 2009). *See also* STRASSER, *supra* note 30, ch. 7 (review of what corporate climate change programs and what they are reporting about them).

78   Center for Climate and Energy Solutions, Climate Action Plans, http://www.c2es.org/what_s_being_done/in_the_states/action_plan_map.cfm (last visited Mar. 4, 2012).

79   NAT'L PARKS CONSERVATION ASS'N, THE STATE OF AMERICA'S NATIONAL PARKS 20 (2011), *available at* http://www.npca.org/cpr/sanp/SANP-long-WEB.pdf.

80   U.S. DEP'T OF THE INTERIOR, U.S. GEOLOGICAL SURVEY, CIRCULAR 1344, ESTIMATED USE OF WATER IN THE UNITED STATES IN 2005 at 45 (2009).

81   K.W. James Rochow, *Lead, in* STUMBLING TOWARD SUSTAINABILITY 433, 434–35 (John C. Dernbach ed., ELI Press 2002).

82   Gretchen Daily et al. *Ecosystem Services: Benefits Supplied to Human Societies by Natural Ecosystems*, 2 ISSUES IN ECOLOGY 1, 2 (1997); Robert Costanza et al., *The Value of the World's Ecosystem Services and Natural Capital*, 387 NATURE 253 (1997); MILLENNIUM ECOSYSTEM ASSESSMENT, ECOSYSTEMS AND HUMAN WELL-BEING: SYNTHESIS at v (2005).

83   EPA SCIENCE ADVISORY BOARD, VALUING THE PROTECTION OF ECOLOGICAL SYSTEMS AND SERVICES 8 (2009), *available at* http://yosemite.epa.gov/sab/sabproduct.nsf/WebBOARD/SAB-09-012/$File/SAB%20Advisory%20Report%20full%20web.pdf.

84   Geoffrey Heal et al., *Protecting Natural Capital Through Ecosystem Service Districts*, 20 STAN. ENVTL. L.J. 333, 336–37 (2001); Robert Costanza & Herman E. Daly, *Natural Capital and Sustainable Development*, 6 CONSERVATION BIOLOGY 37, 39 (1992).

85   MILLENNIUM ECOSYSTEM ASSESSMENT, *supra* note 82.

86   John Porter et al., *The Value of Producing Food, Energy, and Ecosystem Services Within an Agro-Ecosystem*, 38 AMBIO 186, 186 (2009).

87   Gretchen C. Daily et al., *Ecosystem Services in Decision Making: Time to Deliver*, 7 FRONTIERS ECOL. & ENV'T 21, 23 (2009).

88   TERHI MAJANEN ET AL., ECOAGRICULTURE PARTNERS, INNOVATIONS IN MARKET-BASED WATERSHED CONSERVATION IN THE UNITED STATES: PAYMENTS FOR WATERSHED SERVICES FOR AGRICULTURAL AND FOREST LANDOWNERS 6, 9 (2011), *available at* http://ecoagriculture.org/documents/files/doc_362.pdf.

89   42 U.S.C. §§9601–9675. *See also* Natural Resource Damage Assessments—Type A Procedures, 61 Fed. Reg. 20560 (May 7, 1996); Natural Resource Damage Assessments, 59 Fed. Reg. 14262 (Mar. 25, 1994); 43 C.F.R. §§11.13(e)(2), 11.25(e)(2), 11.38(c)(2)(i), 11.70.

90   33 U.S.C. §§2701–2761. *See also* 15 C.F.R. §§990.10, 990.11, 990.21; EPA, Proposed Rules, 40 C.F.R. Parts 50 and 58 National Ambient Air Quality Standards for Ozone (Jan. 19, 2010), 75 Fed. Reg. 2938.

91   Pub. L. No. 110–246. *See also*, U.S. Dep't of Agriculture, Forest Service National Forest System Land Management Planning, 74, Fed. Reg. 67165–01 (Dec. 18, 2009).

92   U.S. EPA, Ecosystem Services Research, http://www.epa.gov/ecology (last visited Oct. 6, 2011).

93   U.S. DEP'T OF AGRICULTURE, SECRETARY'S MEMORANDUM 1056-001: ESTABLISHMENT OF THE OFFICE OF ECOSYSTEM SERVICES AND MARKETS (2008), *available at* http://www.ocio.usda.gov/directives/doc/SM1056-001.pdf.

94   S.B. 513, 75th Leg., Reg. Sess. (Or. 2009), *available at* http:www.leg.state.or.us/09reg/measpdf/sb0500.dir/sb0513.intro.pdf.

95   I.K. WERNICK & F.K. IRWIN, MATERIAL FLOWS ACCOUNTS: A TOOL FOR MAKING ENVIRON-MENTAL POLICY (2005), *available at* http://pdf.wri.org/WRI_MFA_Policy.pdf; EMILY MATHEWS ET AL., WORLD RESOURCES INSTITUTE, THE WEIGHT OF NATIONS: MATERIAL OUTFLOWS FROM INDUSTRIAL ECONOMIES (2000), *available at* http://pdf.wri.org/weight_of_nations.pdf.

96   M.M. MEKONNEN & A.Y. HOEKSTRA, 1 NATIONAL WATER FOOTPRINT ACCOUNTS: THE GREEN, GREY, AND BLUE WATER FOOTPRINT OF PRODUCTION AND CONSUMPTION (2011), *available at* http://www.waterfootprint.org/Reports/Report50-NationalWaterFootprints-Vol1.pdf.

97   T.E. GRAEDEL & B.R. ALLENBY, INDUSTRIAL ECOLOGY AND SUSTAINABLE ENGINEERING (2010).

98   Daniel C. Esty & Michael E. Porter, *Industrial Ecology and Competitiveness: Strategic Implications for the Firm*, 2 J. INDUSTRIAL ECOLOGY 35 (1998).

99   DANIEL C. ESTY & P.J. SIMMONS, THE GREEN TO GOLD BUSINESS PLAYBOOK: HOW TO IMPLE-MENT SUSTAINABILITY PRACTICES FOR BOTTOM-LINE RESULTS IN EVERY BUSINESS FUNCTION (2011).

100   Marian R. Chertow, *Industrial Symbiosis: Literature and Taxonomy*, 25 ANN. REV. ENERGY & ENVT. 313 (2000).

101   U.N. Environment Programme & Society of Environmental Toxicology and Chemistry (SETAC), Life Cycle Initiative: International Life Cycle Partnerships for a Sustainable World, http://lcinitiative.unep.fr/ (last visited Oct. 19, 2011).

102   Governor of California, Exec. Order No. S-1-07 (2007), *available at* http://www.arb.ca.gov/fuels/lcfs/eos0107.pdf.

103   European Commission, Proposal for a Directive of the European Parliament and of the Council amending Directive 98/70/EC as regards the specification of petrol, diesel and gas-oil and introducing a mechanism to monitor and the introduction of a mechanism to monitor and reduce green-house gas emissions from the use of road transport fuels and amending Council Directive 1999/32/EC, as regards the specification of fuel used by inland waterway vessels and repealing Directive 93/12/EEC, COM/2007/0018 final - COD 2007/0019 (2007), *available at* http://ec.europa.eu/prelex/detail_dossier_real.cfm?CL=en&DosId=195322.

104   U.K. Department of Transport, Office of the Renewable Fuels Agency, Renewable Transport Fuel Obligations Order 2007.

105   Government of British Columbia, Greenhouse Gas Reduction (Renewable and Low Carbon Fuel Requirements) Act, BILL 16 — 2008, *available at* http://www.leg.bc.ca/38th4th/3rd_read/gov16-3.htm.

106   42 U.S.C. §7545(o).

107   Regulation of Fuels and Fuel Additives: Changes to Renewable Fuel Standard Program, 75 Fed. Reg. 14670 (Mar. 26, 2010) (codified at 40 C.F.R. Part 80).

108   Martyn Poliakoff et al., *Green Chemistry: Science and Politics of Change*, 297 SCIENCE 807 (Aug. 2, 2002).

109   *See* STRASSER, *supra* note 30, at 24–31; Cary Coglianese & Jennifer Nash, *Management-Based Strategies: An Emerging Approach to Environmental Protection, in* LEVERAGING THE PRIVATE SECTOR: MANAGEMENT-BASED STRATEGIES FOR IMPROVING ENVIRONMENTAL PERFORMANCE 3 (Cary Coglianese & Jennifer Nash eds., 2006). *See also* Cary Coglianese & David Lazer, *Management-Based Regulation: Prescribing Private Management to Achieve Public Goals*, 37 L. & SOC. REV. 691 (2003) (excellent theoretical discussion of the policy issues and choices in using such management systems as regulatory policy).

110   INTERNATIONAL STANDARDS ORGANIZATION, ENVIRONMENTAL MANAGEMENT: THE ISO 14000 FAMILY OF INTERNATIONAL STANDARDS (2009) (introduction to ISO system); Susan Summers Raines & Christian Haumeser, *ISO 14001 in the United States: Good News on the Question of Hype Versus Hope*, 4 ENVTL. PRAC. 163 (2002).

111   STRASSER, *supra* note 10, at 24–31.
112   NATIONAL RESEARCH COUNCIL, *supra* note 63.
113   KARL-HENRIK ROBERT, THE NATURAL STEP: A FRAMEWORK FOR ACHIEVING SUSTAINABILITY IN OUR ORGANIZATIONS (1997).
114   Strategic Approach to International Chemicals Management, http://www.saicm.org/index. php?ql=h&content=home (last visited Feb. 3, 2012).
115   U.S. EPA, Regional Vulnerability Assessment (ReVA) Program, http://amethyst.epa.gov/ revatoolkit/Reva.jsp (last visited June 15, 2011).

Chapter 10

1   United Nations Conference on Environment and Development, Rio Declaration on Environment and Development, princ. 16, U.N. Doc. A/CONF.151/5/Rev.1, 31 I.L.M. 874 (June 3-14, 1992), *available at* http://www.unep.org/Documents.Multilingual/Default.asp?documentid=78&articl eid=1163.
2   CELIA CAMPBELL-MOHN, *Objectives and Tools of Environmental Law, in* ENVIRONMENTAL LAW: FROM RESOURCES TO RECOVERY §4.1 (Celia Campbell-Mohn et al. eds., 1993).
3   *Id.*
4   *See generally,* Dennis D. Hirsch, *Green Business and the Importance of Reflexive Law: What Michael Porter Didn't Say*, 62 ADMIN. L. REV. 1063 (2010).
5   U.S. EPA, FY 2011–2015 EPA Strategic Plan, http://www.epa.gov/planandbudget/strategic-plan.html (last visited Feb. 4, 2012).
6   Residential Lead Based Paint Reduction Act of 1992, Pub. L. No 102–550, Title X (1992).
7   U.S. Dep't of Energy, Net Metering Programs by State, http://www.eere.energy.gov/green-power/resources/maps/netmetering_map.shtml (last visited Feb. 23, 2011); *see also* Valerie J. Faden, *Net Metering of Renewable Energy: How Traditional Electricity Suppliers Fight to Keep You in the Dark*, 10 WIDENER J. PUB. L. 109, 119–20 (2000).
8   *Id.* at 123.
9   Organic Trade Association, Industry Statistics and Projected Growth, http://www.ota.com/ organic/mt/business.html (last visited Apr. 1, 2012); Carolyn Dimitri & Lydia Oberholtzer, U.S. DEP'T OF AGRICULTURE, ECONOMIC RESEARCH SERVICE, MARKETING U.S. ORGANIC FOODS: RECENT TRENDS FROM FARMS TO CONSUMERS 1 (2009), *available at* . http://www.ers.usda.gov/Publications/EIB58/ EIB58_ReportSummary.pdf (report summary).
10   THOMAS L. FRIEDMAN, HOT, FLAT, AND CROWDED: WHY WE NEED A GREEN REVOLUTION— AND HOW IT CAN RENEW AMERICA 384 (2008).
11   *See* Tax Relief Act of 1997, Pub. L. No. 105–34, §312, 111 Stat. 788, 836 (1997) (codified as amended at 26 U.S.C. §121 (2006)).
12   TRIP POLLARD, *Transportation: Challenges and Choices, in* AGENDA FOR A SUSTAINABLE AMERICA 365, 368 (John C. Dernbach ed., ELI Press 2009).
13   *See, e.g.*, Keith Schneider, *Midwest Emerges as Center for Clean Energy*, N.Y. TIMES, Dec. 1, 2010, at B8, *available at* http://www.nytimes.com/2010/12/01/business/energy-environment/01solarcell. html?pagewanted=1&_r=1 (describing a new solar shingle manufacturing facility that is being built with help from "federal manufacturing tax credits" and "various state aid programs").
14   Jack Lyne, *Wind-Energy Giant Gamesa Bringing U.S. HQ, Up to 1,000 Jobs to Pennsylvania*, SITE SELECTION, Oct. 25, 2004, *at* http://www.siteselection.com/ssinsider/pwatch/pw041025.htm.
15   JOHN C. DERNBACH & MARIANNE TYRRELL, *Federal Energy Efficiency and Conservation Laws, in* THE LAW OF CLEAN ENERGY: EFFICIENCY AND RENEWABLES 25 (Michael Gerrard ed., 2011).
16   U.S. Dep't of Energy, Rules, Regulations & Policies for Energy Efficiency, Database of State Incentives for Renewables & Efficiency (DSIRE), http://www.dsireusa.org/summarytables/rrpee.cfm (last visited Feb. 26, 2011).
17   U.S. DEP'T OF ENERGY, 2009 BUILDINGS ENERGY DATA BOOK 2–24, 3–18 (2009), *available at* http://buildingsdatabook.eren.doe.gov/.
18   MARILYN A. BROWN ET AL., TOWARDS A CLIMATE-FRIENDLY BUILT ENVIRONMENT 14 (2005), *available at* www.pewclimate.org/docUploads/Buildings_FINAL.pdf.

19   MIDDLE CLASS TASK FORCE, COUNCIL ON ENVTL. QUALITY, RECOVERY THROUGH RETROFIT 1
(2009), *available at* http://www.whitehouse.gov/assets/documents/Recovery_Through_Retrofit_Final_
Report.pdf.
20   *Id.*
21   U.S. Dep't of Energy, Better Buildings, http://www.eere.energy.gov/betterbuildings/ (last
visited October 4, 2011).
22   *Id.*
23   Bradley Karkkainen, *Information as Environmental Regulation: TRI and Performance
Benchmarking, Precursor to a New Paradigm?*, 89 GEO. L.J. 257 (2000); KURT STRASSER, MYTHS AND
REALITIES OF BUSINESS ENVIRONMENTALISM: GOOD WORKS, GOOD BUSINESS OR GREENWASH? 76–79, (E.
Elgar 2011).
24   U.S. EPA, 2010 TRI NATIONAL ANALYSIS QS AND AS 8 (2011), *available at* http://www.epa.
gov/tri/tridata/tri10/nationalanalysis/qanda/2010_TRI_National_Analysis_Qs_and_As_final.pdf.
25   FY2008 Consolidated Appropriations Act, Pub. L. No. 110–161, 121 Stat 1844, 2128 (2008).
26   74 Fed. Reg. 56260 (Oct. 30, 2009).
27   16 C.F.R. §§260.1–2 (2006). The guides were originally adopted in 1992 and substantially
amended in 1996 and 1998. The FTC has been considering further amendments since 2007. While the
guides themselves are not legally binding, failure to comply with them can result in enforcement by the
FTC under its general power to prevent unfair or deceptive acts or practices. *See* STRASSER, *supra* note
23, at 103–10.
28   STRASSER, *supra* note 23, at 115–28.
29   Commission Guidelines Regarding Disclosure Related to Climate Change, 75 Fed. Reg.
6290 (Feb. 8, 2010). *See also Push for Disclosure of Environmental Risks Expected to Lead to New SEC
Requirements*, 40 ENVTL. REP. 1800 (July 24, 2009).
30   *See generally* Pub. L. No. 111–32, §1302, 123 Stat. 1859, 1909 (2009).
31   *Id.*
32   *See* Marianne Tyrrell & John C. Dernbach, *The "Cash for Clunkers" Program: A Sustainability Evaluation*, 42 U. TOL. L. REV. 467 (2011).
33   *Id.* at 487–91.
34   American Recovery and Reinvestment Act of 2009, Pub. L. No. 111–5, 123 Stat. 115, 208
(2009).
35   *Id.* §203. Other allocations in the Act, which are reported to total $8.4 billion, support related
efficiency measures. *See, e.g.,* Where the Money Goes/Selected Programs From the $789.2 Billon Bill,
WALL ST. J., http://s.wsj.net/public/resources/documents/WSJ_Stimulus_021209.pdf.
36   American Recovery and Reinvestment Act of 2009, §139.
37   U.S. EPA, INVESTING IN PARTNERSHIP, POSSIBILITY, AND PEOPLE: A REPORT TO STAKEHOLDERS
33 (2005), *available at* http://www.epa.gov/brownfields/overview/05Stakeholder/StakeholderReport_
MovingForward.pdf. *See also* U.S. CONFERENCE OF MAYORS, RECYCLING AMERICA'S LAND: A NATIONAL
REPORT ON BROWNFIELDS REDEVELOPMENT (1993–2010) 11 (2010), *available at* http://www.usmayors.
org/pressreleases/uploads/November2010BFreport.pdf ("Cities were asked to identify the most useful
tools to redevelop brownfield sites. The top four, in order, were: EPA Assessment Funding, Private Sector
Investment, EPA Clean-Up Funds, and State programs such as the State Voluntary Clean-Up Programs.").
38   NAT'L ASS'N OF LOCAL GOV'T PROFESSIONALS & NORTHEAST-MIDWEST INST., UNLOCKING
BROWNFIELDS: KEYS TO COMMUNITY REVITALIZATION 5 (2004).
39   JUSTIN HOLLANDER ET AL., PRINCIPLES OF BROWNFIELD REGENERATION: CLEANUP, DESIGN,
AND REUSE OF DERELICT LAND 14 (2010).
40   This chart is derived from programs described in U.S. EPA, A GUIDE TO FEDERAL TAX
INCENTIVES FOR BROWNFIELDS REDEVELOPMENT (2011), *available at* www.epa.gov/brownfields/tax/
tax_guide.pdf.
41   *Id.* at 31; NAT'L ASS'N OF LOCAL GOV'T PROFESSIONALS & NORTHEAST-MIDWEST INST., *supra*
note 38, at 7.
42   *See generally* Joel B. Eisen, *Brownfields at 20: A Critical Reevaluation*, 34 FORDHAM URB.
L.J. 101, 101 (2007).
43   *See, e.g.,* Baltimore County, Md., Code art. 11, §11-2-203.2 (2008), http://www.amle-
gal.com/nxt/gateway.dll/Maryland/baltimore_co/baltimorecountycode?f=templates$fn=default.
htm3.0vid=amlegal:baltimoreco_md (three-year tax credit for LEED-Silver certified residential

construction on a sliding scale, depending on the achieved certification level, and a 10-year tax credit for commercial construction).

44   N.Y. Tax Law §19(a) (McKinney 2008); N.Y. COMP. CODES R. & REGS. tit. 6, §§638.1-638.14 (2008), http://www.dec.ny.gov/regs/4475.html#17896.

45   HARRIS COUNTY COMM'RS COURT, GUIDELINES & CRITERIA FOR GRANTING TAX ABATEMENT IN A REINVESTMENT ZONE CREATED IN HARRIS COUNTY 6 (2008), *available at* http://www.co.harris. tx.us/CmpDocuments/103/Economic%20Development/2008-05-20%20Approved%20Tax%20Abatement%20Guidelines.pdf.

46   Cincinnati, Ohio, Ordinance 182-2007 (May 16, 2007), *available at* http://city-egov.cincinnati-oh.gov/Webtop/ws/council/public/child/Blob/20406.pdf?rpp=-10&m=2&w=doc_no%3D'200700567'.

47   A.B. 3 (Nev. 2005), http://www.leg.state.nv.us/22ndSpecial/bills/AB/AB3_EN.pdf.

48   Tax Break Pulled "Out of the Air" Could Cost State $900 million, LAS VEGAS SUN (May 20, 2007), *available at* http://www.lasvegassun.com/news/2007/may/20/tax-breakpulled-out-of-the-air-could-cost-state-9.

49   NEV. REV. STAT. 701A.110 (2007).

50   Green Infrastructure Digest, Chicago Green Roofs: Seven Million Square Feet and Growing (Nov. 13, 2009), http://hpigreen.com/2009/11/13/chicago-green-roofs-seven-million-square-feet-and-growing/.

51   Green Chicago, Green Roofs, http://www.explorechicago.org/city/en/about_the_city/green_chicago/Green_Roofs_.html (last visited May 1, 2012).

52   *See, e.g.*, HAW. REV. STAT. §46-19.6 (2008) (requiring counties to give priority application processing for projects that achieve LEED Silver or equivalent).

53   Santa Monica, Cal., Mun. Code §8.108.050 (2008), *available at* http://www.qcode.us/codes/santamonica/index.php?topic=8-8_108-8_108_050 (for registration with LEED for New Construction, LEED for Homes, and LEED for Core and Shell); *see also*, Sarasota County, Fla., Res. 2006-174 (Aug. 22, 2006), *available at* https://building.scgov.net/OSG/Sarasota/Green%20Building/Resolution_2006-174.pdf .

54   CITY OF PASADENA, GREEN BUILDING ORDINANCE AND PROGRAM AGENDA REPORT 10 (2005), *available at* http://cityofpasadena.net/councilagendas/2005%20agendas/Dec_19_05/5A1.pdf (Pasadena, California, offers grants to private developers of $15,000 for LEED Certified; $20,000 for Silver; $25,000 for Gold; and $30,000 for Platinum); Miami Lakes, Fla., Ordinance 07-92 (July 10, 2007), *available at* http://webform.townofmiamilakes.com/public/Ordinances/ORD%2007-92.pdf (grants for residential buildings achieving compliance with LEED for New Construction and Major Renovations (LEED NC), LEED for Building Cores and Shells (LEED CS) and LEED for Existing Buildings (LEED EB), as well as homeowners who comply with LEED for Homes).

55   Gainesville, Fla., Code of Ordinances ch. 6, art. I.5, §6-12(2) (2008), *available at* http://www. municode.com/resources/gateway.asp?pid=10819&sid=9.

56   *See, e.g.*, Arlington County, Va., Zoning Ordinance §36.H.7.b (2009), *available at* http://www. arlingtonva.us/departments/CPHD/planning/zoning/pdfs/Ordinance_Section36.pdf (allowing additional height for proposals that meet a minimum LEED certified status); Pittsburgh, Penn., Ordinance 2006-0540 (Dec. 19, 2007) (projects that earn LEED NC or LEED CS certification are entitled to a density bonus of an additional 20% FAR and a variance on 20% of applicable height restrictions).

57   Gainesville, Fla., Code of Ordinances ch. 6, art. I.5, §6-12 (3) (2008), *available at* http://www. municode.com/resources/gateway.asp?pid=10819&sid=9 (offering several "green building awards" and a variety of free marketing incentives for private green projects). *See also*, Sarasota County, Fla., Res. 2005-048 (Mar. 15, 2005), *available at* http://www.scgov.net/Sustainability/documents/Green-Bldg2005048.pdf.

58   NORTH CAROLINA TOBACCO PREVENTION AND CONTROL BRANCH EPIDEMIOLOGY AND EVALUATION UNIT, THE NORTH CAROLINA SMOKE FREE RESTAURANTS AND BARS LAW AND EMERGENCY DEPARTMENT ADMISSIONS FOR ACUTE MYOCARDIAL INFARCTION: A REPORT TO THE NORTH CAROLINA STATE HEALTH DIRECTOR (2011), *available at* http://tobaccopreventionandcontrol.ncdhhs.gov/smokefreenc/docs/TPCB-2011SFNCReport-SHD.pdf (collecting studies showing the linkage between anti-smoking laws and reduced heart attacks).

59   Brian S. Armour et al., *State-Level Medicaid Expenditures Attributable to Smoking*, 6 PREVENTING CHRONIC DIS. A84 (2009), *available at* http://www.ncbi.nlm.nih.gov/pmc/articles/PMC2722402/.

60   Rob Goszkowski, *Among Americans, Smoking Decreases as Income Increases: Gradual Pattern Is Consistent Across Eight Earnings Brackets*, GALLUP WELL-BEING, Mar. 21, 2008, *at* http://www.gallup.com/poll/105550/among-americans-smoking-decreases-income-increases.aspx.

61   SUSHEELA SINGH ET AL., GUTTMACHER INSTITUTE, ADDING IT UP: THE COSTS AND BENEFITS OF INVESTING IN FAMILY PLANNING AND MATERNAL AND NEWBORN HEALTH (2011), *available at* http://www.guttmacher.org/pubs/AddingItUp2009.pdf.

62   Population Institute, Family Planning Faces Uphill Fight in 112th Congress (Jan. 12, 2011), http://www.populationinstitute.org/newsroom/press/view/37/.

63   LARRY NOWELS, CONG. RESEARCH SERV., POPULATION ASSISTANCE AND FAMILY PLANNING PROGRAMS: ISSUES FOR CONGRESS (2005), *available at* http://pdf.usaid.gov/pdf_docs/PCAAB323.pdf.

64   Justin Gillis & Celia Dugger, *U.N. Forecasts 10.1 Billion People by Century's End*, N.Y. TIMES, May 3, 2011, *at* http://www.nytimes.com/2011/05/04/world/04population.html.

65   Center for Health and Gender Equality, http://www.genderhealth.org/the_issues/family_planning/.

66   *Id.*

67   Lynda V. Mapes, *New Strategy to Save Forests: Logging*, SEATTLE TIMES, Aug. 3, 2009, *at* http://seattletimes.nwsource.com/html/localnews/2009588406_forest03m.html.

68   Thomas Brendler & Henry Carey, *Community Forestry, Defined*, J. FORESTRY, Mar. 1998, at 21, 22.

69   BRENDA LIND, LAND TRUST ALLIANCE, TRENDS IN WORKING FOREST CONSERVATION EASEMENTS (2001), *available at* http://www.privatelandownernetwork.org/plnpro/trendsinworkingforestces.pdf.

70   Brendler & Carey, *supra* note 68; Benjamin M. Leoni, *Resolving Disputes in the Northern Forests: Lessons From the Connecticut and Moosehead Lakes*, 35 VT. L. REV. 295, 330 (2010).

71   Leoni, *supra* note 70, at 310–11, 317–22.

Chapter 11

1   DANIEL C. ESTY & ANDREW S. WINSTON, GREEN TO GOLD: HOW SMART COMPANIES USE ENVIRONMENTAL STRATEGIES TO INNOVATE, CREATE VALUE, AND BUILD COMPETITIVE ADVANTAGE (2006) (most analytical book in a very large literature).

2   KURT A. STRASSER, MYTHS AND REALITIES OF BUSINESS ENVIRONMENTALISM: GOOD WORKS, GOOD BUSINESS OR GREENWASH? 137 (2011).

3   STEPHEN R. COVEY ET AL., FIRST THINGS FIRST 36–39 (1994).

4   John Dernbach & the Widener University Law School Seminar on Climate Change, *Next Generation Recycling and Waste Reduction: Building on the Success of Pennsylvania's 1988 Legislation*, WIDENER L.J. (forthcoming 2012), *available at* http://papers.ssrn.com/sol3/papers.cfm?abstract_id=1808911.

5   Hazel Erskine, *The Polls: Pollution and Its Costs*. 39 PUBLIC OPINION Q. 120 (Spring 1972); Riley E. Dunlap & Rik Scarce, *Poll Trends: Environmental Problems and Protection*, 55 PUBLIC OPINION Q. 651 (Winter 1991).

6   DONALD ROGICH ET AL., WORLD RESOURCES INSTITUTE, MATERIAL FLOWS IN THE UNITED STATES: A PHYSICAL ACCOUNTING OF THE U.S. INDUSTRIAL ECONOMY (2008), *available at* http://www.wri.org/publication/material-flows-in-the-united-states.

7   GORDON B. HAXEL ET AL., U.S. GEOLOGICAL SURVEY, RARE EARTH ELEMENTS—CRITICAL RESOURCES FOR HIGH TECHNOLOGY (2002), *available at* http://pubs.usgs.gov/fs/2002/fs087-02/fs087-02.pdf.

8   National Oceanic & Atmospheric Administration, Office of Sustainable Fisheries, Status of U.S. Fisheries, http://www.nmfs.noaa.gov/sfa/statusoffisheries/SOSmain.htm (last visited Nov. 24, 2011); J.B.C. Jackson et al., *Historical Overfishing and the Recent Collapse of Coastal Ecosystems*, 293 SCIENCE 629 (2001); C. Sheppard, *The Shifting Baseline Syndrome*, 30 MARINE POLLUTION BULL. 766 (1995).

9   *See, e.g.*, VINCE MCELHINNY, BANK INFORMATION CENTER, THE WORLD BANK AND DPLS: WHAT MIDDLE INCOME COUNTRIES WANT (2011), *available at* http://www.bicusa.org/en/Article.12351.aspx.

10	T.M. Parris & R.W. Kates, *Characterizing and Measuring Sustainable Development*, 28 ANN. REV. ENV'T & RESOURCES 559 (2003).

11	*Id.*

12	NATIONAL RESEARCH COUNCIL, TOWARD SUSTAINABLE AGRICULTURAL SYSTEMS IN THE 21ST CENTURY 570 (Nat'l Acad. Press 2010).

13	Jerrold A. Long, *Private Lands, Conflict, and Institutional Evolution in the Post-Public-Lands West*, 28 PACE. ENVTL. L. REV. 670, 759 (2011).

14	T.S. Cox et al., *Progress in Breeding Perennial Grains*, 61 CROP & PASTURE SCI. 513 (2010).

15	Wes Jackson, *Tackling the Oldest Environmental Problem: Agriculture and Its Impact on Soil in* THE POST CARBON READER: MANAGING THE 21ST CENTURY'S SUSTAINABILITY CRISES 552 (Richard Heinberg & Daniel Lerch eds., 2010).

16	Leslie Guevarra & Greener World Media, *USGBC Wood Policy Stands*, REUTERS, Dec 9, 2010, *at* http://www.reuters.com/article/idUS182811819420101209.

17	Donald H. Schepers, *Challenges to Legitimacy at the Forest Stewardship Council*, 92 J. BUS. ETHICS 279, 286 (2010).

18	KATHRYN FERNHOLZ ET AL., DOVETAIL PARTNERS, INC., FOREST CERTIFICATION: A STATUS REPORT 11 (2010), *available at* http://www.dovetailinc.org/files/DovetailCertReport0310b.pdf.

19	NATIONAL RESEARCH COUNCIL, REAL PROSPECTS FOR ENERGY EFFICIENCY IN THE UNITED STATES (2010).

20	Press Release, Mintel Finds Fewer Americans Interested in Going "Green" During Recession, Mintel Oxygen Reports (Feb. 2009), *available at* http://www.mintel.com/press-centre/press-releases/325/.

21	International Coffee Organization, Sustainability Initiatives, http://www.ico.org/sustaininit. asp (last visited Apr. 1, 2012).

22	STRASSER, *supra* note 2 at 101–15.

23	*Id.* at 115–28.

24	Michael G. Jacobson et al., *Incentive Programs' Influence in Promoting Sustainable Forestry in the Northern Region*, 26 NORTHERN J. APPLIED FORESTRY 61, 65 (2009).

25	Michael G. Jacobson et al., *Influence and Effectiveness of Financial Incentive Programs in Promoting Sustainable Forestry in the South*, 33 SOUTHERN J. APPLIED FORESTRY 35, 41 (2009).

Chapter 12

1	M.F. Strong, In the Trenches: Building on Rio's Blueprint for a Sustainable World, Remarks at the Annual Meeting of the Environmental Business Council of New England, Boston, Mass. (May 4, 1994).

2	ENVTL. LAW INST., ESTIMATING U.S. GOVERNMENT SUBSIDIES TO ENERGY SOURCES: 2002–2008 (2009), *available at* http://www.elistore.org/Data/products/d19_07.pdf; Roberta Mann, *Subsidies, Tax Policy and Technological Innovation, in* GLOBAL CLIMATE CHANGE AND U.S. LAW 565, 576–83 (Michael B. Gerrard ed., 2007); DAVID SANDALOW, FREEDOM FROM OIL: HOW THE NEXT PRESIDENT CAN END THE UNITED STATES' OIL ADDICTION 125 (2007) (describing "large literature on externalities related to oil use, as well as on government subsidies that promote oil use"); Doug Koplow & John Dernbach, *Federal Fossil Fuel Subsidies and Greenhouse Gas Emissions: A Case Study of Increasing Transparency for Fiscal Policy*, 26 ANN. REV. ENERGY & ENV'T 361, 364–71 (2001).

3	I.R.C. §43.

4	I.R.C. §613A.

5	I.R.C. §263(c).

6	I.R.C. §469.

7	I.R.C. §§611–13.

8	I.R.C. §199.

9	*See* Roberta F. Mann & Mona L. Hymel, *Getting Into the Act: Enticing the Consumer to Become "Green" Through Tax Incentives*, 36 ELR 10419, 10422 (June 2006) [hereinafter Mann & Hymel, *Getting Into the Act*].

10	Koplow & Dernbach, *supra* note 2 at 371.

11	ESTIMATING U.S. GOVERNMENT SUBSIDIES TO ENERGY SOURCES: 2002–2008, *supra* note 2.

12   Envt'l Law Inst., Energy Subsidies Black, Not Green (2011), *available at* http://www.eli. org/pdf/Energy_Subsidies_Black_Not_Green.pdf (graphic accompanying release of ESTIMATING U.S. GOVERNMENT SUBSIDIES TO ENERGY SOURCES: 2002–2008, *supra* note 2).

13   Gilbert E. Metcalf, *Taxing Energy in the United States: Which Fuels Does the Tax Code Favor?*, ENERGY POL'Y. & ENV'T REP. 13. (Jan. 2009), *available at* http://www.manhattan-institute.org/html/eper_04.htm.

14   *See* CRAIG HANSON & DAVID SANDALOW, GREENING THE TAX CODE (2006), *available at* http://pdf.wri.org/greening_the_tax_code.pdf.

15   *See* ASS'N OF AMERICAN RAILROADS, OVERVIEW OF AMERICA'S FREIGHT RAILROADS 7 (May 2008), *available at* http://www.aar.org/PubCommon/Documents/AboutTheIndustry/Overview.pdf.

16   *See generally* Roberta F. Mann, *The (Not So) Little House on the Prairie: The Hidden Costs of the Home Mortgage Interest Deduction*, 32 ARIZ. ST. L.J. 1347 (2000); *see also* Jonathan D. Weiss, *Local Governance*, *in* STUMBLING TOWARD SUSTAINABILITY 683, 689 (John C. Dernbach ed., ELI Press 2002) (describing how the "federal mortgage deduction favors wealthier home buyers over those who are less wealthy, renters, multifamily property owners, and people who rehabilitate existing structures.").

17   John C. Dernbach & Scott Bernstein, *Pursuing Sustainable Communities: Looking Back, Looking Forward*, 35 URB. LAW. 495, 505 (2003).

18   Weiss, *supra* note 16, at 696–97.

19   Dan Tarlock, *Do Water Law and Policy Promote Sustainable Water Use?*, 28 PACE ENVTL. L. REV. 642 (2011).

20   *See* Rachel Rawlins & Robert Paterson, *Sustainable Building and Communities: Climate Change and the Case for Federal Standards*, 19 CORNELL J.L. & PUB. POL'Y 335 (2010) (arguing that a federal program of building code mandates is essential).

21   Air Conditioning, Heating & Refrigeration Inst. v. City of Albuquerque, No. 1:2008cv08-633 (D.N.M. Sept. 30, 2010).

22   The federal laws at issue included the Energy Policy and Conservation Act, Pub. L. No. 94-163, 89 Stat. 871 (1975), as amended by the National Appliance Energy Conservation Act of 1987, Pub. L. No. 100-12, and the Energy Policy Act of 1992, Pub. L. No. 102-486, 42 U.S.C. §6297.

23   Building Industry Ass'n of Washington v. Washington State Building Code Council, 2011 WL 485895 (W.D. Wash. Feb. 7, 2011), *available at* http://lawoftheland.files.wordpress.com/2011/02/building-industry.pdf.

24   David Rejeski, *Any Big Ideas Left?*, ENVTL. FORUM, Sept./Oct. 2011, at 36, 37.

25   Reorganization Plan No. 3 of 1970 (codified at 5A U.S.C).

26   Rejeski, *supra* note 24, at 38–39.

27   Lisa P. Jackson, Editorial, *"Too Dirty to Fail"? House Republicans' Assault on our Environmental Laws Must be Stopped*, L.A. TIMES, Oct. 21, 2011, *at* http://articles.latimes.com/2011/oct/21/opinion/la-oe-jackson-train-act-20111021.

28   Minority Staff, U.S. House of Representatives Committee on Energy and Commerce, The Anti-Environment Record of the U.S. House of Representatives, 112th Cong., 1st sess. (2011), *available at* http://democrats.energycommerce.house.gov/sites/default/files/image_uploads/_Anti-Environment%20Report%20Final.pdf.

29   Jeremy P. Jacobs, *Former EPA Chief Reilly Blasts GOP for Ignoring Science*, ENV'T & ENERGY DAILY, Nov. 8, 2011.

30   E. Donald Elliott, *Politics Failed, Not Ideas*, ENVTL. FORUM, Sept./Oct. 2011, at 42, 43.

31   *Id.* at 43.

32   130 S. Ct. 876 (2010).

33   BILL DEBLAZIO, PUBLIC ADVOCATE FOR THE CITY OF NEW YORK, CITIZENS UNITED AND THE 2010 MIDTERM ELECTIONS 2 (Dec. 2010), *available at* http://advocate.nyc.gov/files/12-06-10CitizensUnitedReport.pdf.

34   *Id.* at 3.

35   ELIZABETH DORIS ET AL., NATIONAL RENEWABLE ENERGY LABORATORY, ENERGY EFFICIENCY POLICY IN THE UNITED STATES: OVERVIEW OF TRENDS AT DIFFERENT LEVELS OF GOVERNMENT (2009), *available at* http://www.nrel.gov/docs/fy10osti/46532.pdf.

36   *Id.*

37   WORLD RESOURCES INSTITUTE, SUMMARY OF DEVELOPED COUNTRY FAST-START CLIMATE FINANCE PLEDGES 5 (2011), *available at* http://pdf.wri.org/climate_finance_pledges_2011-05-09.pdf.

38   Lisa Friedman & Darren Samuelsohn, *Hillary Clinton Pledges $100B for Developing Countries*, N.Y. TIMES, Dec. 17, 2009, *at* http://www.nytimes.com/cwire/2009/12/17/17climatewire-hillary-clinton-pledges-100b-for-developing-96794.html.

39   President Barack Obama, Memorandum of January 21, 2009: Freedom of Information Act. 74 Fed. Reg. 4683 (Jan. 26, 2009), *available at* http://edocket.access.gpo.gov/2009/pdf/E9-1773.pdf; Attorney General Eric Holder, Memorandum for the Heads of Executive Departments and Agencies: The Freedom of Information Act (FOIA) (Mar. 19, 2009), *available at* www.justice.gov/ag/foia-memo-march2009.pdf.

40   NATE JONES ET AL., NATIONAL SECURITY ARCHIVE & GEORGE WASHINGTON UNIVERSITY, SUNSHINE AND SHADOWS: THE CLEAR OBAMA MESSAGE FOR FREEDOM OF INFORMATION MEETS MIXED RESULTS—THE NATIONAL SECURITY ARCHIVE FOIA AUDIT 6–10,(2010), *available at* http://www.gwu.edu/~nsarchiv/NSAEBB/NSAEBB308/2010FOIAAudit.pdf.

41   U.S. EPA, FY 2011–2015 EPA STRATEGIC PLAN: ACHIEVING OUR VISION II (Sept. 20, 2010), *available at* http://nepis.epa.gov/EPA/html/DLwait.htm?url=/Adobe/PDF/P1008YOS.PDF.

42   FY2008 Consolidated Appropriations Act, Pub. L. No.110–161, 121 Stat. 1844, 2128 (2008).

43   74 Fed. Reg. 56260 (Oct. 30, 2009) (codified at 40 C.F.R. Part 98).

44   Proposed Confidentiality Determinations for Data Required Under the Mandatory Greenhouse Gas Reporting Rule and Proposed Amendment to Special Rules Governing Certain Information Obtained Under the Clean Air Act, 75 Fed. Reg. 39094, 39097 (July 7, 2010), *available at* http://edocket.access.gpo.gov/2010/pdf/2010-16317.pdf.

45   Addition of National Toxicology Program Carcinogens; Community Right-to-Know Toxic Chemical Release Reporting, 75 Fed. Reg. 72727 (Nov. 26, 2010), *available at* http://www.epa.gov/tri/lawsandregs/ntp_chemicals/NTPchemicals_final_Rule11262010.pdf.

46   Frank Rusco, Oil and Gas Management: Key Elements to Consider for Providing Assurance of Effective Independent Oversight, Testimony Before the Subcommittee on Energy and Mineral Resources, Committee on Natural Resources, House of Representatives, at 2 (June 17, 2010), *available at* http://www.gao.gov/new.items/d10852t.pdf.

47   *Id.* at 8–9.

48   *Id.* at 9.

49   MEMORANDUM FROM ROBERT ABBEY, DIRECTOR, U.S. DEP'T OF INTERIOR, BUREAU OF LANDS MGMT, INSTRUCTION MEMORANDUM 2010-117: OIL AND GAS LEASING REFORM—LAND USE PLANNING AND LEASE PARCEL REVIEWS 11–4, (May 17, 2010), *available at* http://www.blm.gov/wo/st/en/info/regulations/Instruction_Memos_and_Bulletins/national_instruction/2010/IM_2010-117.html.

50   Testimony of Danielle Brian, Executive Director, Project on Government Oversight (POGO) Before the Subcommittee on Energy and Mineral Resources, The Deepwater Horizon Incident: Proposals to Split Up the Minerals Management Service (June 17, 2010) *available at* http://www.pogo.org/pogo-files/alerts/natural-resources/nr-ogr-20100414.html.

51   NATIONAL COMMISSION ON THE BP DEEPWATER HORIZON OIL SPILL AND OFFSHORE DRILLING, THE AMOUNT AND FATE OF THE OIL: STAFF WORKING PAPER NO. 3 (Jan. 11, 2011), *available at* http://www.oilspillcommission.gov/sites/default/files/documents/Updated%20Amount%20and%20Fate%20of%20the%20Oil%20Working%20Paper.pdf.

52   *See, e.g.*, Cynthia Williams, *The Securities and Exchange Commission and Corporate Social Transparency*, 112 HARV. L. REV. 1197, 1246–92 (1998–1999); John Bagby et al., *How Green Was My Balance Sheet? Corporate Liability and Environmental Disclosure*, 14 VA. ENVTL. L.J. 225, 265–87 (1994–1995). *But see* United Paperworkers Int'l Union v. Int'l Paper Co., 85 F.2d 1190 (2d Cir. 1993) (one of relatively few examples of successful suit by private plaintiff).

53   *See* Williams, *supra* note 52; Perry Wallace, *Disclosure of Environmental Liabilities Under the Securities Laws: The Potential of Securities-Market-Based Incentives for Pollution Control*, 50 WASH. & LEE L. REV. 1093 (1993). *See also* KURT A. STRASSER, MYTHS AND REALITIES OF BUSINESS ENVIRONMENTALISM: GOOD WORKS, GOOD BUSINESS OR GREENWASH? ch. 6 (2011).

54   Simon Rogers National Debt and Deficit Date for Every OECD Country (2010), Datablog, (May 27, 2010), http://www.guardian.co.uk/news/datablog/2010/may/27/debt-deficit-oecd-countries-data#data (last visited Oct. 2, 2011). *See also* Google docs, OECD Country Debts and Deficits, https://spreadsheets.google.com/ccc?key=0AonYZs4MzlZbdDZsU2k2VEQ2elkwcnNDOTNHS3ZwRkE&hl=en#gid=0 (last visited Oct. 2, 2011); International Monetary Fund, Data and Statistics: World Economic

Outlook Database (2011), http://www.imf.org/external/pubs/ft/weo/2011/01/weodata/weoselgr.aspx (last visited Oct. 2, 2001).

55   U.S. EPA, CLEAN WATERSHED NEEDS SURVEY 2008, REPORT TO CONGRESS v (2010), *available at* http://water.epa.gov/scitech/datait/databases/cwns/upload/cwns2008rtc.pdf.

56   U.S. EPA, DRINKING WATER INFRASTRUCTURE NEEDS SURVEY AND ASSESSMENT, FOURTH REPORT TO CONGRESS (2009), *available at* http://www.epa.gov/ogwdw/needssurvey/pdfs/2007/report_needssurvey_2007.pdf.

57   Marisol Bello, *Ridership Up on Mass Transit Shows More People Are Working*, USA TODAY, Dec. 8, 2011, *at* http://www.usatoday.com/news/nation/story/2011-12-07/mass-transit-ridership/51720984/1; TRANSPORTATION FOR AMERICA & TRANSPORTATION EQUITY NETWORK, STRANDED AT THE STATION: THE IMPACT OF THE FINANCIAL CRISIS IN PUBLIC TRANSPORTATION (2009), *available at* http://www.t4america.org/docs/081809_stranded_at_thestation.PDF.

58   *E.g.,* BILL & MELINDA GATES FOUNDATION, GLOBAL HEALTH STRATEGY OVERVIEW 1, 2 (2010) ("Our top priority is the development and delivery of vaccines for infectious diseases . . . ."), *available at* http://www.gatesfoundation.org/global-health/Documents/global-health-strategy-overview.pdf.

59   *See, e.g., Global Health: Less Mary Poppins*, THE ECONOMIST, Nov. 11, 2006 (arguing that the World Health Organization should focus on infectious diseases in the developing world rather than "lifestyle" diseases (arising from personal choice) without recognizing the impediment that environmental diseases such as childhood lead poisoning pose to sustainable development—especially in the developing world).

Chapter 13

1   DINA COVER & TD ECONOMICS, WHAT'S NEXT FOR LUMBER PRICES (2010), *available at* http://www.tdbank.com/investments/exc/pdfs/dc0710_lumber.pdf.

2   Press Release, Minn. Wood Education Project, New Certification Program Will Assist Minnesota Producers, Manufacturers and Distributors of Forest-Based Products (Jan. 5, 2009), *available at* http://forest.nrri.umn.edu/industry-news/press-clips/new-certification-program-will-assist-minnesota.

3   Michelle Chan, *U.S. Taxpayer-Funded Bank, Under Pressure From Obama Administration, Gives Green Light to Giant Dirty Coal Plant in India*, HUFFINGTON POST, July 15, 2010, *at* http://www.huffingtonpost.com/michelle-chan/us-taxpayer-funded-bank-u_b_648174.html; James R. Hagerty & Amol Sharma, *Employment, Environment at Odds: U.S. Agency Won't Back Sale of Coal Equipment; Company Says That Costs Jobs*, WALL ST. J., June 28, 2010, *at* http://online.wsj.com/article/SB100014 24052748704846004575332810145193160.html.

4   *See, e.g.,* JAMES M. BUCHANAN & GORDON TULLOCK, THE CALCULUS OF CONSENT (1962); DANIEL A. FARBER & PHILIP P. FRICKEY, PUBLIC CHOICE AND PUBLIC LAW (1997).

5   CONGRESSIONAL BUDGET OFFICE, COST ESTIMATE: H.R. 2454, AMERICAN CLEAN ENERGY AND SECURITY ACT OF 2009 (2009), *available at* http://www.cbo.gov/sites/default/files/cbofiles/ftpdocs/102xx/doc10262/hr2454.pdf.

6   ENVIRONMENTAL POLLUTION PANEL, PRESIDENT'S SCIENCE ADVISORY COMMITTEE, RESTORING THE QUALITY OF OUR ENVIRONMENT (Nov. 5, 1965), *available at* http://dge.stanford.edu/labs/caldeiralab/Caldeira%20downloads/PSAC,%201965,%20Restoring%20the%20Quality%20of%20Our%20Environment.pdf.

7   Donald A. Brown, Penn State Rock Ethics Institute, Climate Ethics, The U.S. Academy of Sciences' Reports on Climate Change and the U.S. Moral Climate Change Failure (May 25, 2011), http://rockblogs.psu.edu/climate/2011/05/praise-and-ethical-criticism-of-the-united-states-academy-of-sciences-reports-on-climate-change.html.

8   For descriptions of this campaign, see JAMES HOGAN & RICHARD LITTLEMORE, CLIMATE COVER-UP, THE CRUSADE TO DENY GLOBAL WARMING (2009); NAOMI ORESKES & ERIK W. CONWAY, MERCHANTS OF DOUBT, HOW A HANDFUL OF SCIENTISTS OBSCURED THE TRUTH ON ISSUES FROM TOBACCO SMOKE TO GLOBAL WARMING (2010); and ERIC POOLEY, THE CLIMATE WAR, TRUE BELIEVERS, POWER BROKERS, AND THE FIGHT TO SAVE THE EARTH (2010).

9   John Broder, *Climate Change Doubt Is Tea Party Article of Faith*, N.Y. TIMES, Oct. 20, 2010, *t* http://www.nytimes.com/2010/10/21/us/politics/21climate.html?pagewanted=1.

10   H.R. 910, 112th Cong. (passed House of Representatives Apr. 7, 2011).

11   Ben Geman, *Amendment That Says Climate Change Is Occurring Fails in House*, E2 Wire, The Hill's Energy and Env't Blog, Apr. 6, 2011, *at* http://thehill.com/blogs/e2-wire/677-e2-wire/154445-house-votes-down-climate-science-amendment (last visited Oct. 2, 2011).

12   H.R. 910, 112th Cong. §4(1) (2011).

13   *See* Matthew L. Wald, *New Air Quality Rules for Power Plants in Dispute*, N.Y. TIMES, Dec. 2, 2011, *at* http://www.nytimes.com/2011/12/02/science/earth/dispute-over-new-air-pollution-rules-for-power-plants.html.

14   *See* News Release, U.S. EPA, EPA Reduces Smokestack Pollution, Protecting Americans' Health From Soot and Smog/Clean Air Act Protections Will Cut Dangerous Pollution in Communities That Are Home to 240 Million Americans (July 7, 2011), *available at* http://www.epa.gov/airtransport.

15   Lady Eve Balfour, Speech to the International Federation of Organic Agriculture Movements: Towards a Sustainable Agriculture—The Living Soil (1977), *available at* http://www.soilandhealth.org/01aglibrary/010116Balfourspeech.html.

16   Peter M. Rosset & Miguel A. Altieri, *Agroecology Versus Input Substitution: A Fundamental Contradiction of Sustainable Agriculture*, 10 SOC'Y. & NAT'L. RES. 283 (1977).

17   John Ikerd, Sustaining People Through Agriculture: Opportunities for Graziers,7th Ann. Okla. Grazing Lands Conf. (Okla. City, 2008), *available at* http://web.missouri.edu/~ikerdj/papers/Oklahoma%20Grazing%20Lands%20--%20Sustaining%20People.htm.

18   PEW COMMISSION ON INDUSTRIAL FARM ANIMAL PRODUCTION, PUTTING MEAT ON THE TABLE: INDUSTRIAL FARM ANIMAL PRODUCTION IN AMERICA (2008), *available at* http://www.ncifap.org/_images/PCIFAPFin.pdf.

19   MARY HENDRICKSON & WILLIAM HEFFERNAN, CONCENTRATION OF AGRICULTURAL MARKETS (Apr. 2007), *available at* http://www.foodcircles.missouri.edu/07contable.pdf.

20   United Egg Producers, General U.S. Stats (Oct. 2011), http://www.unitedegg.org/General-Stats/default.cfm.

21   U.S. Dep't of Justice, Agriculture and Antitrust Enforcement Issues in Our 21st Century Economy, http://www.justice.gov/atr/public/workshops/ag2010/index.html.

22   CHRISTINE M. MATTHEWS, CONG. RESEARCH SERV., FOREIGN SCIENCE AND ENGINEERING PRESENCE IN U.S. INSTITUTIONS AND THE LABOR FORCE 2, 11 (2010), *available at* http://www.fas.org/sgp/crs/misc/97-746.pdf.

23   *Immigration and Emigration*, N.Y. TIMES, Jan. 19, 2012, *at* http://topics.nytimes.com/top/reference/timestopics/subjects/i/immigration-and-emigration/index.html.

24   *Id.* (although it should be noted that this is a disputed and necessarily inexact estimate).

25   GUTTMACHER INSTITUTE, STATE POLICIES IN BRIEF: STATE FUNDING OF ABORTIONS UNDER MEDICAID (2012), *available at* http://www.guttmacher.org/statecenter/spibs/spib_SFAM.pdf.

26   GUTTMACHER INSTITUTE, STATE POLICIES IN BRIEF: AN OVERVIEW OF ABORTION LAWS (2012), *available at* http://www.guttmacher.org/statecenter/spibs/spib_OAL.pdf.

27   ORGANIZATION FOR ECONOMIC COOPERATION AND DEVELOPMENT, PERSPECTIVES ON GLOBAL DEVELOPMENT (2010).

28   Xiaomei Tan, World Resources Institute, Emerging Actors in Development Finance: A Closer Look at Chinese and Brazilian Overseas Investments n.2 (June 7, 2011), *at* http://www.wri.org/stories/2011/06/emerging-actors-development-finance-closer-look-chinese-and-brazilian-overseas-inves#fn:1.

29   *Id.*

30   ORGANIZATION FOR ECONOMIC COOPERATION AND DEVELOPMENT, PERSPECTIVES ON GLOBAL DEVELOPMENT 2010: SHIFTING WEALTH 15 (2010).

31   Bretton Woods Project, The World Bank's Conflicted Role in Energy: Controversy Among the Bank's Directors (Feb. 15, 2010), http://www.brettonwoodsproject.org/art-565914.

32   DEVELOPMENT COMMITTEE (JOINT MINISTERIAL COMMITTEE OF THE BOARDS OF GOVERNORS OF THE BANK AND THE FUND ON THE TRANSFERS OF REAL RESOURCES TO DEVELOPING COUNTRIES), MODERNIZING THE WORLD BANK GROUP: AN UPDATE (2011), *available at* http://siteresources.worldbank.org/DEVCOMMINT/Documentation/22885417/DC2011-0005%28E%29Modernization.pdf.

33   WORLD BANK, INDEPENDENT EVALUATION GROUP, SAFEGUARDS AND SUSTAINABILITY POLICIES IN A CHANGING WORLD: AN INDEPENDENT EVALUATION OF WORLD BANK GROUP EXPERIENCE (2010), *available at* http://siteresources.worldbank.org/EXTSAFANDSUS/Resources/Safeguards_eval.pdf.

34   Simon Lester, *Is Chinese Investment in Africa Neo-Colonialism?*, Int'l Law and Policy Blog, June 12, 2011, *at* http://worldtradelaw.typepad.com/ielpblog/2011/06/is-chinese-investment-in-africa-neo-colonialism.html?utm_source=feedburner&utm_medium=feed&utm_campaign=Feed%3A+ielpbl og+%28International+Economic+Law+and+Policy+Blog%29 (last visited Oct. 2, 2011).
35   KPMG INTERNATIONAL COOPERATIVE, KPMG INTERNATIONAL SURVEY OF CORPORATE RESPONSIBILITY REPORTING 2011, at 10, 21 (2011), *available at* http://www.kpmg.com/PT/pt/IssuesAndInsights/Documents/corporate-responsibility2011.pdf.

Chapter 14

1   ROB WATSON, GREEN BUILDING MARKET AND IMPACT REPORT 2010, at 34 (2010), *available* at http://www.greenbiz.com/sites/all/themes/greenbiz/doc/GBMIR_2010.pdf.
2   *See generally* Sarah B. Schindler, *Following Industry's LEED®: Municipal Adoption of Private Green Building Standards*, 62 FLA. L. REV. 285 (2010).
3   *Id.* at 327.
4   *Id.* at 310–11.
5   *Id.* at 348.
6   Mireya Navarro, *Some Buildings Not Living Up to Green Label*, N.Y. TIMES, Aug. 30, 2009, *available at* http://www.nytimes.com/2009/08/31/science/earth/31leed.html.
7   Schindler *supra* note 2, at 322.
8   GREG KATS, GREENING OUR BUILT WORLD: COSTS, BENEFITS, AND STRATEGIES 89 (2010); REID EWEING ET AL., GROWING COOLER: THE EVIDENCE OF URBAN DEVELOPMENT AND CLIMATE CHANGE 4 (2008), *available at* http://postcarboncities.net/files/SGA_GrowingCooler9-18-07small.pdf.
9   WATSON, *supra* note 1, at 16–17 (2010) (reporting an estimated 1.4 billion vehicle miles traveled in 2010, with an apparent 20% shift toward location efficiency consideration since 2007).
10   KATS, *supra* note 8, at 26–32.
11   Press Release, Cal. Public Utilities Comm'n, CPUC and Business Leaders Launch Zero Net Energy Action Plan; Goal of Efficient, Clean Energy Powered Buildings by 2030 (Sept. 1, 2010), *available at* http://docs.cpuc.ca.gov/PUBLISHED/NEWS_RELEASE/122911.htm.
12   42 U.S.C. §17082.
13   Press Release, Cal. Public Utilities Comm'n, *supra* note 11; *see also* Cal. Public Utilities Comm'n, Energy Efficiency Strategic Plan, http://www.cpuc.ca.gov/PUC/energy/Energy+Efficiency/eesp/ (last modified Mar. 5, 2012).
14   CALIFORNIA ENERGY EFFICIENCY STRATEGIC PLAN, ZERO NET ENERGY ACTION PLAN: COMMERCIAL BUILDING SECTOR 2010–2012, at 7 (2010), *available at* http://www.cpuc.ca.gov/NR/rdonlyres/6C2310FE-AFE0-48E4-AF03-530A99D28FCE/0/ZNEActionPlanFINAL83110.pdf; Press Release, Cal. Public Utilities Comm'n, *supra* note 11.
15   TRUCOST & NSF INTERNATIONAL, CARBON EMISSIONS—MEASURING THE RISKS: AN ANALYSIS OF GREENHOUSE GAS EMISSIONS AND COSTS (2009), *available at* http://www.nsf.org/business/sustainability/SUS_NSF_Trucost_Report.pdf; KEVIN L. DORAN ET AL., CENTER FOR ENERGY AND ENVIRONMENTAL SECURITY, RECLAIMING TRANSPARENCY IN A CHANGING CLIMATE: TRENDS IN CLIMATE RISK DISCLOSURE BY THE S&P 500 FROM 1995 TO THE PRESENT (2009), *available at* http:// cees.colorado.edu/10K_Report_Final_May_27.pdf; CERES & ENVIRONMENTAL DEFENSE FUND, CLIMATE RISK DISCLOSURE IN SEC FILINGS: AN ANALYSIS OF 10-K REPORTING BY OIL AND GAS, INSURANCE AND ELECTRIC POWER COMPANIES (2009), *available at* http://www.ceres.org/resources/reports/climate-risk-disclosure-2009/view. *But see Companies Show Little Awareness of Climate Change Risks, Report Finds*, GREENBIZ.COM, June 3, 2009, *at* http://www.climatebiz.com/print/25557.
16   Press Release, JP Morgan, Leading Wall Street Banks Establish the Carbon Principles: Guidelines to Strengthen Environmental and Economic Risk Management in the Financing and Construction of Electricity Generation (Feb. 4, 2008), *available at* http://www.morganstanley.com/about/press/articles/6017.html.
17   *Id.*
18   CCB Standards: The Climate, Community & Biodiversity Alliance, Landmark Certification of Forestry Projects That Combat Climate Change, Feb. 26, 2007, http://www.climate-standards.org/news/news_feb2007.html.

19   *Id. See also* Kelly Levin et al., *Can Non-State Certification Systems Bolster State-Centered Efforts to Promote Sustainable Development Through the Clean Development Mechanism?*, 44 WAKE FOREST L. REV. 777, 783 (2009) (discussion of the "Gold Standard" program related to the Kyoto Protocol).

20   16 C.F.R. §§260.1–2 (2006). *See also* KURT A. STRASSER, MYTHS AND REALITIES OF BUSINESS ENVIRONMENTALISM: GOOD WORKS, GOOD BUSINESS OR GREENWASH? 103–10 (2011).

21   Environmental Product Declarations, Introduction, http://www.environmentalproductdeclarations.com/ (last visited Feb. 24, 2012).

22   Environmental Product Declaration, The International EPD System—A Communication Tool for International Markets, http://www.environdec.com (last visited Oct. 19. 2011).

23   Michael E. Porter & Mark R. Kramer, *Strategy & Society: The Link Between Competitive Advantage and Corporate Social Responsibility*, 84 HARV. BUS. REV. 78, 81 (2006).

24   *Id.*

25   STRASSER, *supra* note 20, at 15–17.

26   *See generally*, JOINT CENTER FOR HOUSING STUDIES OF HARVARD UNIVERSITY, FOUNDATIONS FOR FUTURE GROWTH IN THE REMODELING INDUSTRY (2007) (indicating that owners of homes built before 1970 spent an average of $500 on energy efficiency related improvements in 2005), *available at* http://www.jchs.harvard.edu/sites/jchs.harvard.edu/files/r07-1.pdf.

27   MCGRAW-HILL CONSTRUCTION, GREEN BUILDING RETROFIT & RENOVATION: RAPIDLY EXPANDING MARKET OPPORTUNITIES THROUGH EXISTING BUILDINGS (2009), *available at* http://mts.sustainableproducts.com/Capital_Markets_Partnership/BusinessCase/MHC%20Green%20Building%20Retrofit%20%26%20Renovation%20SMR%20(2009).pdf.

28   Charles Lockwood, *Building Retro*, URBAN LAND 46, 54 (Nov./Dec. 2009), *available at* http://www.esbnyc.com/documents/sustainability/uli_building_retro_fits.pdf.

29   *"Green" Building Retrofits to Be 20–30% of Commercial Projects by 2014*, ENVTL. LEADER, Oct. 23, 2009, *at* http://www.environmentalleader.com/2009/10/23/green-building-retrofits-to-be-20-30-of-commercial-projects-by-2014.

30   MCGRAW-HILL CONSTRUCTION, *supra* note 27.

31   LANE BURT, U.S. GREEN BUILDING COUNCIL ET AL., A NEW RETROFIT INDUSTRY: AN ANALYSIS OF THE JOB CREATION POTENTIAL OF TAX INCENTIVES FOR ENERGY EFFICIENCY IN COMMERCIAL BUILDINGS AND OTHER COMPONENTS OF THE BETTER BUILDINGS INITIATIVE (2011), *available at* http://www.usgbc.org/ShowFile.aspx?DocumentID=9531.

32   STOCKTON WILLIAMS, ENTERPRISE COMMUNITY PARTNERS, BRINGING HOME THE BENEFITS OF ENERGY EFFICIENCY TO LOW-INCOME HOUSEHOLDS: THE CASE FOR A NATIONAL COMMITMENT 8 (2008), (noting that "utility bills often impose a financial hardship on very low-income households, forcing many to make desperate tradeoffs between heat or electricity and other basic necessities."), *available at* http://www.practitionerresources.org/redir.html?id=66381&topic=Weatherization&doctype=Spreadsheet&url=http%3A%2F%2Fwww.practitionerresources.org%2Fcache%2Fdocuments%2F663%2F66381.pdf.

33   GENERAL ACCOUNTABILITY OFFICE, GREEN AFFORDABLE HOUSING: HUD HAS MADE PROGRESS IN PROMOTING GREEN BUILDING, BUT EXPANDING EFFORTS COULD HELP REDUCE ENERGY COSTS AND BENEFIT TENANTS 11 (2008), *available at* http://www.gao.gov/new.items/d0946.pdf; JAY CARLIS ET AL., A PRIMER ON GREEN BUILDING: THE CURRENT LANDSCAPE FOR HOMEOWNERS AND DEVELOPERS, INCLUDING A DISCUSSION OF USING GREEN BUILDING TACTICS IN AFFORDABLE HOUSING DEVELOPMENTS 17 (2006), *available at* http://www.slideshare.net/BizArchitect/unc-mba-a-primer-on-green-building.

34   U.S. Dep't of Housing and Urban Development, HUD's Public Housing Program, http://portal.hud.gov/hudportal/HUD?src=/topics/rental_assistance/phprog (last visited Mar. 7, 2012).

35   U.S. Census Bureau, American Housing Survey, Frequently Asked Questions, http://www.census.gov/housing/ahs/about/faq.html#Q9 (last visited Mar. 7, 2012).

36   *See* Ellen McGirt, *Edward Norton's $9,000,000,000 Housing Project (That's $9 Billion)*, FAST COMPANY, Nov. 25, 2008, *at* http://www.fastcompany.com/magazine/131/edward-nortons-9000000000-housing-project-thats-9-billion.html. *See also*, Enterprise Community Partners, Enterprise Green Communities, http://www.greencommunitiesonline.org/ (last visited Mar. 7, 2012).

37   Ass'n for the Advancement of Sustainability in Higher Education's Sustainability Tracking, Assessment & Rating System, Overview, *at* https://stars.aashe.org/pages/about/ (last visited July 13, 2011).

38   Creating American Jobs by Harnessing Our Resources: U.S. Offshore and Renewable Energy Production: Hearing Before the Nat. Resources Comm., 112th Cong. (Sept. 8, 2011) (Remarks by Rep. Edward Markey & Shayle Kann, Managing Director, Solar Program, GTM Research), *available at* http://www.youtube.com/watch?v=cnT6vynquiY.

39   NASSIM NICHOLAS TALEB, THE BLACK SWAN: THE IMPACT OF THE HIGHLY IMPROBABLE (2007).

40   NATIONAL RESEARCH COUNCIL, SUSTAINABILITY AND THE U.S. ENVIRONMENTAL PROTECTION AGENCY 65 (Nat'l Acad. Press 2011).

41   Catherine Finneran, *Attracting Development to Brownfields Sites: A Local Challenge,* PUB. MGMT. 8, Nov. 2006.

42   GREG LEWIS, NORTHEAST-MIDWEST INSTITUTE, BROWN TO GREEN: SUSTAINABLE REDEVELOPMENT OF AMERICA'S BROWNFIELD SITES 15 (2008), *available at* http://www.nemw.org/images/issues/brownfields/2008-12-26%20-%20Green%20brownfield%20issue%20brief.pdf.

43   National Environmental Policy Act of 1969, Pub. L. No. 91-190, §101(c), 83 Stat. 852, 853 (1970); 42 U.S.C. §4331(c) (2000).

44   *See* Cabinet Office, Behavioural Insight Team Annual Update, http://www.cabinetoffice.gov.uk/resource-library/behavioural-insight-team-annual-update (last visited Mar. 7, 2012) (annual review of team's work).

45   Elinor Ostrom, Beyond Markets and States: Polycentric Governance of Complex Economic Systems, Nobel Lecture (Dec. 8, 2009), *available at* http://www.nobelprize.org/nobel_prizes/economics/laureates/2009/ostrom-lecture.html.

46   Michael P. Vandenbergh & Ann C. Steinemann, *The Carbon-Neutral Individual*, 82 N.Y.U. L. REV. 1673 1739-40 (2007) (efforts directed at individuals could "buy time for new technologies or regulatory measures, create incentives for the development of these measures in the first place, and make them more effective when they are adopted").

47   Thomas Dietz et al., *Household Actions Can Provide a Behavioral Wedge to Rapidly Reduce U.S. Carbon Emissions*, 106 PROC. NAT'L ACAD. OF SCI. 18452 (2009).

48   *See, e.g.*, DAVID SHI, THE SIMPLE LIFE: PLAIN LIVING AND HIGH THINKING IN AMERICAN CULTURE (1985).

49   Paul C. Stern, Director, Committee on the Human Dimensions of Global Change, National Research Council, Why Social and Behavoral Science Research Is Critical to Meeting California's Climate Challenges (Dec. 12, 2006) (PowerPoint presentation to the California Energy Commission, on file with John Dernbach).

50   *Id.*

51   *Id. See also* GERALD T. GARDNER & PAUL C. STERN, ENVIRONMENTAL PROBLEMS AND HUMAN BEHAVIOR (2d ed. 2002) (textbook on environmental behavior).

52   *See, e.g.,* Noah J. Goldstein et al., *Invoking Social Norms: A Social Psychology Perspective on Improving Hotels' Linen-Reuse Programs*, 48 CORNELL HOTEL & REST. ADMIN. Q. 145 (2007).

53   Deborah L. Rhode & Lee Ross, *Environmental Values and Behaviors: Strategies to Encourage Public Support for Initiatives to Combat Global Warming*, 26 VA. ENVTL. L.J. 161 (2008).

54   DOUG MCKENZIE-MOHR & WILLIAM SMITH, FOSTERING SUSTAINABLE BEHAVIOR 5 (1999).

55   Ann E. Carlson, *Recycling Norms*, 89 CAL. L. REV. 1231, 1265–66 (2001).

56   MCKENZIE-MOHR & SMITH, *supra* note 54, at 103–15.

57   Stern, *supra* note 49.

58   *Id.*

59   Dietz et al., *supra* note 47.

Chapter 15

1   Amit Kapur & Thomas E. Graedel, *Materials: From High Consumption to More Sustainable Resource Use, in* AGENDA FOR A SUSTAINABLE AMERICA 159, 167–68 (John C. Dernbach ed., ELI Press 2009).

2   H. JOHN HEINZ III CTR. FOR SCI., ECON. & ENV'T, THE STATE OF THE NATION'S ECOSYSTEMS: MEASURING THE LANDS, WATERS, AND LIVING RESOURCES OF THE UNITED STATES (2008).

3   U.S. COMM'N ON OCEAN POLICY, AN OCEAN BLUEPRINT FOR THE 21ST CENTURY: FINAL REPORT (2004); PEW OCEANS COMM'N, AMERICA'S LIVING OCEANS: CHARTING A COURSE FOR SEA CHANGE: SUMMARY REPORT (2003).

4   MARK MURO ET AL., SIZING THE CLEAN ECONOMY 21 (Brookings Inst. 2011), *available at* http://www.brookings.edu/~/media/Files/Programs/Metro/clean_economy/0713_clean_economy.pdf.

5   U.S. CONFERENCE OF MAYORS, CURRENT AND POTENTIAL GREEN JOBS IN THE U.S. ECONOMY (2008), *available at* http://www.usmayors.org/pressreleases/uploads/greenjobsreport.pdf.

6   George Goldman & Aya Ogishi, Department of Agricultural and Resource Economics, Univ. of California, Berkeley, The Economic Impact of Waste Disposal and Diversion in California vi-ix (2001), *available at* http://are.berkeley.edu/extension/EconImpWaste.pdf.

7   American Council for an Energy-Efficient Economy, Energy Efficiency in a Clean Energy Standard, http://www.aceee.org/files/pdf/fact-sheet/Clean-Energy-Standards-Facts.pdf.

8   MURO ET AL., *supra* note 4, at 4.

9   SARAH WHITE & JASON WALSH, CENTER ON WISCONSIN STRATEGY ET AL., GREENER PATHWAYS: JOBS AND WORKFORCE DEVELOPMENT IN THE CLEAN ENERGY ECONOMY (2008), *available at* http://www.cows.org/pdf/rp-greenerpathways.pdf.

10   LISA NEUBERGER, UNITED NATIONS GLOBAL COMPACT, A NEW ERA OF SUSTAINABILITY: U.N. GLOBAL COMPACT-ACCENTURE CEO STUDY 2010 (2010), *available at* http://www.unglobalcompact.org/news/42-06-22-2010.

11   AUTODESK & AMERICAN INSTITUTE OF ARCHITECTS, 2008 AUTODESK/AIA GREEN INDEX 14 (2008), *available at* http://images.autodesk.com/adsk/files/2008_autodesk-aia_green_index_report_final.pdf.

12   MURO ET AL., *supra* note 4.

13   U.S. Dep't. of Energy, Guidelines for Home Energy Professionals, http://www1.eere.energy.gov/wip/retrofit_guidelines.html (last visited Mar. 7, 2012); CENTER FOR ENERGY WORKFORCE DEVELOPMENT, WORKFORCE DEVELOPMENT AND CAREER PATHWAYS FOR SKILLED ENERGY TECHNICIANS AND ENGINEERS (2012), *available at* http://www.cewd.org/mem_resources/CEWDGetIntoEnergyBooklet.pdf.

14   Michael DiRamio et al., Community-Based Job Creation: Creating Fertile Economic Gardens and Empowering Resident Entrepreneurs in Tough Times (forthcoming 2012 at www.bigideasforjobs.org).

15   John Kania & Mark Kramer, *Collective Impact*, STAN. SOCIAL INNOVATION REV., Winter 2011, at 36, *available at* http://www.ssireview.org/images/articles/2011_WI_Feature_Kania.pdf.

16   Corporation for a Skilled Workforce, A Summary of State Sector Strategies (2010), http://www.sectorstrategies.org/sites/all/files/Summary%20of%20State%20Sector%20Activity%20-%20Oct%202010.docx.

17   Brain Scan, *Betting on Green*, THE ECONOMIST, Mar. 10, 2011, *at* http://www.economist.com/node/18304172.

18   U.S. DEP'T OF THE TREASURY, GENERAL EXPLANATIONS OF THE ADMINISTRATION'S FISCAL YEAR 2010 REVENUE PROPOSALS 59–69 (2009) [hereinafter GREENBOOK].

19   For a comparison of the tax treatment of oil companies to those in other industries, see Roberta Mann, *Waiting to Exhale?: Global Warming and Tax Policy*, 51 AM. U. L. REV. 1135, 1164–67 (2002).

20   GREENBOOK, *supra* note 18, at 128 (calculating $31.5 billion total less $5.3 billion levy on offshore oil and gas production).

21   Drew Pierson, *Senate Defeats Bill to Repeal Oil Industry Tax Incentives*, 131 TAX NOTES 795 (May 23, 2011).

22   Bruce Alpert, *Flood Insurance Premiums Likely to Rise if Federal Legislation Passes*, TIMES-PICAYUNE (New Orleans, La.), July 23, 2011, *at* http://www.nola.com/politics/index.ssf/2011/07/flood_insurance_premiums_likel.html.

23   Air Now, Particle Pollution and Your Health, http://www.airnow.gov/index.cfm?action=particle_health.page1#3 (particulate pollution); Air Now, Ozone, http://www.airnow.gov/index.cfm?action=aqibasics.ozone.

24   U.S. EPA, 8-Hour Ozone Nonattainment Areas as of Aug. 30, 2011, http://www.epa.gov/oaqps001/greenbk/gntc.html (last visited Mar. 14, 2012).

25   U.S. EPA, PM-2.5 Nonattainment Areas (2006 Standard), http://www.epa.gov/oaqps001/greenbk/mappm25_2006.html (last visited Mar. 14, 2012).

26   *See* National Ambient Air Quality Standards for Ozone, 75 Fed. Reg. 2938 (Jan. 19, 2010) (proposed tightening of rule for ozone); Andrew Childers, *Air Quality Standards: EPA Says More Protective Standards Needed for Fine Particulate Matter*, 42 ENV'T REP. (BNA) 845 (2011).

27   Andrew Childers, *Upton, Inhofe, Question EPA Decision to Re-Think Air Quality Standards for Ozone*, 42 ENV'T REP. (BNA) 477 (2011).

28   42 U.S.C. §4331(a).

29   *Id.* §4331(b).

30   *Id.* §4335.

31   ENVTL. LAW INST., REDISCOVERING THE NATIONAL ENVIRONMENTAL POLICY ACT: BACK TO THE FUTURE (1995).

32   NATIONAL RESEARCH COUNCIL, SUSTAINABILITY AND THE U.S. ENVIRONMENTAL PROTECTION AGENCY 114-15 (Nat'l Acad. Press 2011).

33   *Id.* at 9.

34   WILLIAM SARNI, GREENING BROWNFIELDS: REMEDIATION THROUGH SUSTAINABLE DEVELOPMENT 84–85 (2009).

35   NAT'L ASS'N OF LOCAL GOV'T PROFESSIONALS & NORTHEAST-MIDWEST INST., UNLOCKING BROWNFIELDS: KEYS TO COMMUNITY REVITALIZATION 6 (2004).

36   Portland Bureau of Planning and Sustainability, 2009 Climate Action Plan, http://www.portlandonline.com/bps/index.cfm?c=41896 (last visited Mar. 21, 2011); City of Cincinnati, Climate Protection—Green Cincinnati Plan, http://www.cincinnati-oh.gov/cmgr/pages/-17659-/ (last visited Mar. 21, 2011).

37   *See* U.N. Conference on Trade and Development, About GSP, http://www.unctad.org/Templates/Page.asp?intItemID=2309&lang=1 (last visited Mar. 7, 2012).

38   Appellate Body Report, European Communities—Conditions for the Granting of Tariff Preferences to Developing Countries, WT/DS246/AB/R (Apr. 7, 2004), *available at* http://www.wto.org/english/tratop_e/dispu_e/246abr_e.doc.

39   OFFICE OF U.S. TRADE REP., U.S. GENERALIZED SYSTEM OF PREFERENCES (GSP) GUIDEBOOK (May 2011), *available at* http://www.ustr.gov/webfm_send/2880.

40   KURT A. STRASSER, MYTHS AND REALITIES OF BUSINESS ENVIRONMENTALISM: GOOD WORKS, GOOD BUSINESS OR GREENWASH? Ch. 5 (2011).

41   CARY COGLIANESE & JENNIFER NASH, GOVERNMENT CLUBS: THEORY AND EVIDENCE FROM VOLUNTARY PROGRAMS (Corporate Social Responsibility Initiative, Working Paper No. 50) (2008), *available at* http://www.hks.harvard.edu/m-rcbg/CSRI/publications/workingpaper_50_coglianese_nash.pdf.

42   Jonathan H. Adler, *Eyes on the Climate Prize: Rewarding Energy Innovation to Achieve Climate Stabilization*, 35 HARV. ENVTL. L. REV. 1 (2011).

43   DAVID SOBEL, LONGITUDE (1995).

44   Adler, *supra* note 42, at 42–45.

45   *See, e.g.*, XPrize Foundation, Energy & Environment Prize Group, http://www.xprize.org/prize-development/energy-and-environment (last visited Feb. 24, 2012).

46   LISA A. SKUMATZ & DAVID J. FREEMAN, SKUMATZ ECONOMIC RESEARCH ASSOCIATES, PAY AS YOU THROW (PAYT) IN THE U.S.: 2006 UPDATE AND ANALYSES: FINAL REPORT 1, 7 (2006), *available at* http://www.epa.gov/osw/conserve/tools/payt/pdf/sera06.pdf.

47   *Id.* at 1.

48   *Id.* at 9.

49   *Id.*

50   *Id.*; U.S. EPA, Illegal Diversion, http://www.epa.gov/epawaste/conserve/tools/payt/top8.htm (last visited Apr. 3, 2011).

51   GREGORY K. INGRAM ET AL., SMART GROWTH POLICES (Lincoln Institute, 2009), *available at* http://www.lincolninst.edu/pubs/smart-growth-policies.aspx.

52   *See, e.g.*, Gaithersburg, Md., Ordinance O-11-08 (Sept. 15, 2008) (requiring LEED certification for all buildings equal to or larger than 10,000 square feet, and LEED Silver certification for buildings larger than 99,999 square feet).

53   *See, e.g.*, West Hollywood, Cal., Ordinance 07-762, §6 (July 16, 2007), *available at* http://www.weho.org/media/File/GreenbuildingOrdinance.pdf.

54   Cal. Dep't of Housing & Community Development, CALGreen, http://www.hcd.ca.gov/CALGreen.html (last visited Mar. 7, 2012).

55   ANSI/ASHRAE/USGBC/IES, Standard 189.1, Standard for the Design of High-Performance Green Buildings, Except Low-Rise Residential Green Buildings, http://www.ashrae.org/greenstandard (last visited Mar. 7, 2012).

56   INTERNATIONAL CODE COUNCIL, INTERNATIONAL GREEN CONSTRUCTION CODE (IGCC) SYNOPSIS ii (2010), *available at* http://www.iccsafe.org/cs/igcc/documents/publicversion/igcc_pv2_synopsis.pdf.

57   *Id.* at 2.

58   For a summary, see Endangerment and Cause or Contribute Findings for Greenhouse Gases Under Section 202(a) of the Clean Air Act: Final Rule, 74 Fed. Reg. 66496 (Dec. 15, 2009).

59   RON SUSKIND, THE ONE PERCENT DOCTRINE (2006); Thomas L. Friedman, *Going Cheney on Climate*, N.Y. TIMES, Dec. 8, 2009, *at* http://www.nytimes.com/2009/12/09/opinion/09friedman.html.

60   J.C. Pierce et al., *Knowledge, Culture and Public Support for Renewable Energy Technology Policy in Oregon*, 7 COMP. TECH. TRANSFER & SOC'Y 270 (2009); Yao Yin, Is Wave Energy Comparatively Sustainable in Oregon?, Master of Public Policy Essay (June 10, 2009) (unpublished M.P.P. thesis, Oregon State University), *available at* http://ir.library.oregonstate.edu/xmlui/bitstream/handle/1957/12116/yaoyin.pdf?sequence=1; FAXEN CONWAY ET AL., SCIENCE AND KNOWLEDGE INFORMING POLICY AND PEOPLE: THE HUMAN DIMENSIONS OF WAVE ENERGY GENERATION IN OREGON, REPORT TO THE OREGON ENERGY TRUST (2009), *available at* http://ir.library.oregonstate.edu/xmlui/bitstream/handle/1957/13499/HDWE%20Final%20Report%20OWET.pdf?sequence=1 Report to the Oregon Energy Trust.

61   Kirsten Winters, Methods for Engaging Leaders in Climate Science and Providing Local Decision Support (Feb. 17, 2011) (unpublished M.P.P. thesis, Oregon State University), *available at* http://ir.library.oregonstate.edu/xmlui/bitstream/handle/1957/20531/winters.pdf?sequence=1.

62   Regional Greenhouse Gas Initiative, RGGI, Inc., http://www.rggi.org/rggi (last visited April 25, 2012).

63   REGIONAL GREENHOUSE GAS INITIATIVE, INVESTMENT PROCEEDS FROM RGGI CO$_2$ ALLOWANCES (2011), *available at* http://www.rggi.org/docs/Investment_of_RGGI_Allowance_Proceeds.pdf.

64   FRED KRUPP & MIRIAM HORN, EARTH: THE SEQUEL: THE RACE TO REINVENT ENERGY AND STOP GLOBAL WARMING (2008).

65   NATIONAL COMMISSION ON FISCAL RESPONSIBILITY AND REFORM, THE MOMENT OF TRUTH 24 (2010), *available at* http://www.fiscalcommission.gov/sites/fiscalcommission.gov/files/documents/TheMomentofTruth12_1_2010.pdf.

66   *See, e.g.,* CONGRESSIONAL BUDGET OFFICE, REDUCING THE DEFICIT: SPENDING AND REVENUE OPTIONS 191–92, 205–06 (2011), *available at* http://www.cbo.gov/sites/default/files/cbofiles/ftpdocs/120xx/doc12085/03-10-reducingthedeficit.pdf (estimating the revenue that could be raised from raising the gasoline excise tax or imposing a tax on greenhouse gases).

67   Zachary Shahan, Installed Wind Power Capacity Per Capita (Country Comparisons) (Apr. 11, 2011), http://cleantechnica.com/2011/04/11/installed-wind-power-capacity-per-capita-country-comparisons/.

68   Green Earth, Top Ten Countries Using Solar Power 2010, http://feelthephoton.blogspot.com/2010/09/top-10-countries-using-solar-power.html (last visited Mar. 7, 2012) (table derived from data posted at this source).

69   NATIONAL RESEARCH COUNCIL, REAL PROSPECTS FOR ENERGY EFFICIENCY IN THE UNITED STATES 262 (Nat'l Acad. Press 2010).

70   *Id.* at 263.

71   *Id.* at 264–78.

72   John C. Dernbach & Donald A. Brown, *The Ethical Responsibility to Reduce Energy Consumption*, 37 HOFSTRA L. REV. 985 (2009).

73   John C. Dernbach et al., *Making the States Full Partners in a National Climate Change Effort: A Necessary Element for Sustainable Economic Development*, 40 ELR 10597 (June 2010).

74   For a good summary of programs at the state and local level, see U.S. EPA, State and Local Climate and Energy Program, at http://www.epa.gov/statelocalclimate/index.html (last visited Oct. 7, 2011).

75   U.S. Dep't of Energy, Database of State Incentives for Renewables & Efficiency, Property Assessed Clean Energy (PACE), http://www.dsireusa.org/documents/summarymaps/PACE_Financing_Map.ppt (last visited Oct. 7, 2011).

76   Federal Housing Finance Authority, FHFA Statement on Certain Energy Retrofit Loan Programs (July 6, 2010), http://www.fhfa.gov/webfiles/15884/PACESTMT7610.pdf. *See also* Prentiss Cox, *Keeping PACE?: The Case Against Property Assessed Clean Energy Financing Programs*, 83 U. COL. L. REV. 83 (2011) (arguing that PACE programs should be substantially restructured).

77   Justin Gillis, *Tax Plan to Turn Old Buildings "Green" Finds Favor*, N.Y. TIMES, Sept. 19, 2011, *at* http://www.nytimes.com/2011/09/20/business/energy-environment/tax-plan-to-turn-old-buildings-green-finds-favor.html.

78   WHITE HOUSE COUNCIL ON ENVIRONMENTAL QUALITY, PROGRESS REPORT OF THE INTERAGENCY CLIMATE CHANGE TASK FORCE: RECOMMENDED ACTIONS IN SUPPORT OF A NATIONAL CLIMATE CHANGE ADAPTATION STRATEGY (2010), *available at* http://www.whitehouse.gov/sites/default/files/microsites/ceq/Interagency-Climate-Change-Adaptation-Progress-Report.pdf.

79   INTERAGENCY CLIMATE CHANGE ADAPTATION TASK FORCE, DRAFT NATIONAL ACTION PLAN: PRIORITIES FOR MANAGING FRESHWATER RESOURCES IN A CHANGING CLIMATE (2011), *available at* http://www.whitehouse.gov/sites/default/files/microsites/ceq/napdraft6_2_11_final.pdf.

80   Leslie Kaufman, *Seeing Trends, Coalition Works to Help a River Adapt*, N.Y. TIMES, July 20, 2011, *at* http://www.nytimes.com/2011/07/21/science/earth/21river.html?pagewanted=all.

81   Alejandro E. Camacho, *Assisted Migration: Redefining Nature and Natural Resources Law Under Climate Change*, 27 YALE J. REG. 171, 176 (2010).

82   *See* CENTER FOR PROGRESSIVE REGULATION, MAKING GOOD USE OF ADAPTIVE MANAGEMENT (2010), *available at* http://www.progressivereform.org/articles/Adaptive_Management_1104.pdf.

Chapter 16

1   MR. Y, A NATIONAL STRATEGIC NARRATIVE 5 (2011), *available at* http://www.wilsoncenter.org/events/docs/A%20National%20Strategic%20Narrative.pdf. (Mr. Y is a pseudonym for Wayne Porter and Mark Mykleby, as explained *id*. at 13.)

2   *Id*. at 2.

3   Ann-Marie Slaughter, *Preface, in id.* at 2.

4   WORLD BANK, COST OF POLLUTION IN CHINA: ECONOMIC ESTIMATES OF PHYSICAL DAMAGES (2007), *available at* http://siteresources.worldbank.org/INTEAPREGTOPENVIRONMENT/Resources/China_Cost_of_Pollution.pdf.

5   NATIONAL RESEARCH COUNCIL, RISING ABOVE THE GATHERING STORM, REVISITED: APPROACHING CATEGORY 5 (Nat'l Acad. Press 2010).

6   ORGANIZATION FOR ECONOMIC CO-OPERATION AND DEVELOPMENT, GOOD PRACTICES IN THE NATIONAL SUSTAINABLE DEVELOPMENT STRATEGIES OF OECD COUNTRIES 10 (2006), *available at* http://www.oecd.org/dataoecd/58/42/36655769.pdf.

7   EUROPEAN COMMISSION, A SUSTAINABLE EUROPE FOR A BETTER WORLD: A EUROPEAN UNION STRATEGY FOR SUSTAINABLE DEVELOPMENT (2001), *available at* http://eur-lex.europa.eu/LexUriServ/site/en/com/2001/com2001_0264en01.pdf.

8   COUNCIL OF THE EUROPEAN UNION, BRUSSELS EUROPEAN COUNCIL 14 DECEMBER 2007: PRESIDENCY CONCLUSIONS 2 (2008), *available at* http://www.consilium.europa.eu/ueDocs/cms_Data/docs/pressData/en/ec/97669.pdf.

9   European Commission, Sustainable Development, http://ec.europa.eu/environment/eussd/ (last visited Oct. 21, 2011).

10   *Id.*

11   *Id.*

12   *See, e.g..*, PEW CHARITABLE TRUSTS, THE CLEAN ENERGY ECONOMY: REPOWERING JOBS, BUSINESSES AND INVESTMENTS ACROSS AMERICA (2009), *available at* http://www.pewcenteronthestates.org/uploadedFiles/Clean_Economy_Report_Web.pdf [hereinafter CLEAN ENERGY ECONOMY].

13   University of Rhode Island, Graduate School of Oceanography, Census of Marine Life, http://www.coml.org/ (last visited Mar. 7, 2012).

14   *See* Data.gov, A Se-mash Hit, http://www.data.gov/communities/node/116/view/119 (last visited Mar. 7, 2012).

15   NAT'L ASS'N OF LOCAL GOV'T PROFESSIONALS & NORTHEAST-MIDWEST INST, UNLOCKING BROWNFIELDS: KEYS TO COMMUNITY REVITALIZATION 6 (2004).

16 *See* U.S. EPA, BUILDING VIBRANT COMMUNITIES: COMMUNITY BENEFITS OF LAND REVITALIZA-TION (2009), *available at* http://www.epa.gov/brownfields/policy/comben.pdf.

17 DANIEL M. SPEISS, PUBLIC PARTICIPATION IN BROWNFIELDS CLEANUP AND REDEVELOPMENT: THE ROLE OF COMMUNITY ORGANIZATIONS 43 (2008), *available at* http://deepblue.lib.umich.edu/handle/2027.42/60850.

18 NAT'L CTR. FOR NEIGHBORHOOD & BROWNFIELDS REDEVELOPMENT, BUILDING CAPACITY: BROWNFIELDS REDEVELOPMENT FOR COMMUNITY-BASED ORGANIZATIONS I-1 (2008), *available at* http://policy.rutgers.edu/brownfields/projects/Manual_Building_Capacity.pdf.

19 JUSTIN HOLLANDER ET AL., PRINCIPLES OF BROWNFIELD REGENERATION 88–89 (2010).

20 5 U.S.C. §553(b) (on notice); 5 U.S.C. §553(c) (on participation).

21 Council on Environmental Quality, CEQ NEPA Pilot Program, http://www.whitehouse.gov/administration/eop/ceq/initiatives/nepa/nepa-pilot-project (last visited Mar. 7, 2012); Memorandum from Nancy H. Sutley, Chair, Council on Environmental Quality, to interested parties and heads of federal departments and agencies (Mar. 17, 2011) (calling for innovative pilot project proposals to improve implementation of the National Environmental Policy Act), *available at* http://www.whitehouse.gov/sites/default/files/microsites/ceq/final_soliciation_with_signature.pdf.

22 Cornell E-Rulemaking Initiative, Regulation Room: About Regulation Room, http://regula-tionroom.org/about/ (last visited Mar. 7, 2012.

23 Annie Lipowicz, *Will E-Rulemaking Catch on?*, GOV'T COMPUTER NEWS, Feb. 2011, *at* http://gcn.com/articles/2011/02/28/home-page-gov-20-dot-erulemaking.aspx.

24 MARK MURO ET AL., SIZING THE CLEAN ECONOMY 37 (Brookings Inst. 2011), *available at* http://www.brookings.edu/~/media/Files/Programs/Metro/clean_economy/0713_clean_economy.pdf; CLEAN ENERGY ECONOMY, *supra* note 12.

25 DAVID EDGERTON, THE SHOCK OF THE OLD: TECHNOLOGY AND GLOBAL HISTORY SINCE 1900 (2006).

26 Vandana Shiva, *Equity: The Shortest Way to Global Sustainability*, in EUROPEAN RESEARCH ON SUSTAINABLE DEVELOPMENT (Carlo C. Jaeger et al. eds., 2011).

27 Stuart L. Hart & Mark B. Milstein, *Global Sustainability and the Creative Destruction of Industries*, SLOAN MGMT REV., Fall 1999, at 23.

28 Mark P. Rice et al., *Managing Discontinuous Innovation*, 41 RES. TECH. MGMT. 52 (2009).

29 This matrix is adapted from Rebecca M. Henderson & Kim B. Clark, *Architectural Innova-tion: The Reconfiguration of Existing Product Technologies and the Failure of Established Firms*, 35 ADMIN. SCI. Q. 9 (Mar. 1990).

30 DAVID A. GARVIN, LEARNING IN ACTION: A GUIDE TO PUTTING THE LEARNING ORGANIZATION TO WORK (2000).

31 *See* Pacific Northwest National Lab., Inst. For Integrated Catalysis, Research Areas, http://iic.pnnl.gov/research/index.stm (last visited Mar. 7, 2012); *see also* North American Catalysis Society, Who We Are, http://www.nacatsoc.org/who.asp (last visited Mar. 7, 2012).

32 Personal Communication between David Rejeski and Dr. Kris Pister, Dust Networks (Aug. 24, 2011).

33 Giulio Boccaletti et al., *How IT Can Cut Carbon Emissions*, MCKINSEY Q. (Oct. 2008), *available at* http://www.mckinseyquarterly.com/How_IT_can_cut_carbon_emissions_2221.

34 *See, e.g.*, EDWARD W. CONSTANT, THE ORIGINS OF THE TURBOJET REVOLUTION (1980).

35 STEVEN JOHNSON, WHERE GOOD IDEAS COME FROM: THE NATURAL HISTORY OF INNOVATION (Riverhead Books 2010).

36 Langdon Winner, Testimony to the Committee on Science of the U.S. House of Representa-tives on the Social Implications of Nanotechnology (Apr. 9, 2003).

37 RICHARD SCLOVE, REINVENTING TECHNOLOGY ASSESSMENT: A 21ST CENTURY MODEL (2010), *available at* http://www.wilsoncenter.org/sites/default/files/ReinventingTechnologyAssessment1.pdf.

38 George Gaskell et al., *The 2010 Eurobarometer on the Life Sciences*, 29 NATURE BIOTECH. 113 (Feb. 2011).

39 Gretchen C. Daily & Paul R. Ehrlich, *Population, Sustainability, and Earth's Carrying Capacity*, 42 BIOSCIENCE 761 (NOV. 1992).

40 *See, e.g.*, PETER MCDONALD & REBECCA KIPPEN, POPULATION FUTURES FOR AUSTRALIA: THE POL-ICY ALTERNATIVES (1999), *available at* https://digitalcollections.anu.edu.au/html/1885/41933/2000rp05.htm.

41 New State Ice Co. v. Liebmann, 285 U.S. 262, 311 (1932) (dissenting opinion).

42   Frances Stokes Berry & William D. Berry, *Innovation and Diffusion Models in Policy Research, in* THEORIES OF THE POLICY PROCESS 169 (Paul A. Sabatier ed., 2d ed. 2007); Christopher Z. Mooney & Mei-Hsien Lee, *Legislating Morality in the American States: The Case of Pre-Roe Abortion Regulation Reform*, 39 AM. J. POL. SCI. 599 (1995).

43   Christopher Z. Mooney, *Modeling Regional Effects on State Policy Diffusion*, 54 POL. RES. Q. 103, 119 (2001).

44   Regional Greenhouse Gas Initiative, Welcome, http://www.rggi.org/home (last visited Mar. 7, 2012).

45   Western Climate Initiative, History, http://www.westernclimateinitiative.org/history (last visited Dec. 23, 2011).

46   Felicity Barringer, California Adopts Limits on Greenhouse Gases, N.Y. TIMES, Oct. 20, 2011, *at* http://www.nytimes.com/2011/10/21/business/energy-environment/california-adopts-cap-and-trade-system-to-limit-emissions.html.

47   Carolyn Whetzel, *Western Climate Initiative Works to Link California, Quebec Trading Programs*, INT'L ENVTL. REP. (BNA), Jan. 18, 2012, *at* http://0-news.bna.com.libcat.widener.edu/ieln/IELNWB/split_display.adp?fedfid=24276158&vname=inernotallissues&wsn=500752000&searchid=16754303&doctypeid=1&type=date&mode=doc&split=0&scm=IELNWB&pg=0.

48   U.S. ENERGY INFORMATION ADMINISTRATION, ANNUAL ENERGY OUTLOOK 2012 EARLY RELEASE OVERVIEW 2 (2012), *available at* http://www.eia.gov/forecasts/aeo/er/pdf/0383er(2012).pdf.

Chapter 17

1.   *See also* Frances Moore Lappé, *The Food Movement: Its Power and Possibilities*, THE NATION, Oct. 3, 2011, *at* http://www.thenation.com/article/163403/food-movement-its-power-and-possibilities.

2   PAUL HAWKEN, BLESSED UNREST: HOW THE LARGEST MOVEMENT IN THE WORLD CAME INTO BEING AND WHY NO ONE SAW IT COMING 2 (2007).

3   *Id.* at 2–3.

4   Michael P. Healy, *The Sustainable Development Principle in United States Environmental Law,* J. ENERGY & ENVTL. L. 19 (Summer 2011), *available at* http://groups.law.gwu.edu/jeel/ArticlePDF/2-2-Healy.pdf.

5   Jerrold A. Long, *From Warranted to Valuable Belief: Local Government, Climate Change, and Giving Up the Pickup to Save Bangladesh*, 49 NAT. RESOURCES J. 743, 799 (2009).

6   PRESIDENT'S COUNCIL ON SUSTAINABLE AMERICA, SUSTAINABLE AMERICA: A NEW CONSENSUS iv (1996).

7   Brent Steel et al., *Correlates and Consequences of Public Knowledge Concerning Ocean Fisheries Management Issues*, 33 COASTAL MGMT. 37 (2005).

8   David A. Snow et al., *Frame Alignment Processes, Micromobilization, and Movement Participation*, 51 AM. SOC. REV. 464 (1986).

9   *Id.*

10   *Ray Anderson, "Greenest CEO in America," Dies at 77*, WASH. POST, Aug. 11, 2011, *at* http://www.washingtonpost.com/local/obituaries/ray-anderson-greenest-ceo-in-america-dies-at-77/2011/08/10/gIQAGoTU7I_story.html; Paul Vitello, *Ray Anderson, Businessman Turned Environmentalist, Dies at 77*, N.Y. TIMES, Aug. 10, 2011, *at* http://www.nytimes.com/2011/08/11/business/ray-anderson-a-carpet-innovator-dies-at-77.html?_r=1.

11   Dieter T. Hessel, *Religion and Ethics Focused on Sustainability*, *in* AGENDA FOR A SUSTAINABLE AMERICA 129 (John C. Dernbach ed., ELI Press 2009).

12   *See, e.g.*, CLIMATE ETHICS: ESSENTIAL READINGS (Stephen Gardiner et al. eds., 2010); Penn State Rock Ethics Institute, Climate Ethics: Ethical Analysis of Climate Science and Policy, http://rockblogs.psu.edu/climate/ (last visited June 23, 2011).

13   National Climate Ethics Campaign, Statement of Our Nation's Moral Obligation to Address Climate Change, http://climateethicscampaign.org/statement/ (last visited Dec. 23, 2011).

14   KWAME ANTHONY APPIAH, THE HONOR CODE: HOW MORAL REVOLUTIONS HAPPEN (W.W. Norton 2010).

15   Jonas Salk, *as quoted in* LIAM FAHEY & ROBERT M. RANDALL, LEARNING FROM THE FUTURE: COMPETITIVE FORESIGHT SCENARIOS 332 (1998).

16   Anna Clark, *Corporate Responsibility: How to Create Green Change in a Conservative Culture*, MATTER NETWORK, Mar. 19, 2010, *at* http://featured.matternetwork.com/2010/3/how-create-green-change-conservative.cfm (last visited Mar. 8, 2012).

17   Leslie Kaufman, *In Kansas, Climate Skeptics Embrace Cleaner Energy*, N.Y. TIMES, Oct. 18, 2010, *at* http://www.nytimes.com/2010/10/19/science/earth/19fossil.html?pagewanted=1.

18   BIPARTISAN POLICY CENTER, ENERGY SECURITY: GOALS, METRICS, AND ACCOUNTABILITY: BPC ENERGY PROJECT STAFF BACKGROUND PAPER (2011), *available at* http://www.bipartisanpolicy.org/sites/default/files/Staff%20Paper.pdf.

19   ORGANIZATION FOR ECONOMIC COOPERATION AND DEVELOPMENT & FOOD AND AGRICULTURAL ORGANIZATION, AGRICULTURAL OUTLOOK 2011–2020 (2011) (summary available at http://www.oecd.org/dataoecd/13/2/48186214.pdf).

20   CHIP HEATH & DAN HEATH, MADE TO STICK: WHY SOME IDEAS SURVIVE AND OTHERS DIE (2008).

21   Colin Sullivan, *EDF Chief: "Shrillness" of Greens Contributed to Climate Bill's Failure in Washington*, N.Y. TIMES, Apr. 5, 2011, *at* http://www.nytimes.com/gwire/2011/04/05/05greenwire-edf-chief-shrillness-of-greens-contributed-to-37964.html.

22   Joe Romm, Exclusive: *EDF's Fred Krupp on "How We Begin to Rebuild Public Support for Climate Action and the Political Will to PassClimate Legislatio*n, THINK PROGRESS, Apr. 6, 2011, *at* http://thinkprogress.org/romm/2011/04/06/207837/edf-fred-krupp-rebuild-public-support-for-climate-action-political-will-pass-climate-legislation/ (quotation).

23   James Strock, Sustainability and 21st Century Leadership, Address at St. Thomas University Law School Distinguished Speaker Series, Miami Gardens, Fla. (Oct. 11, 2011) (transcript available from John Dernbach).

24   *Id.*

25   Robert K. Watson, EcoTech International, Letter from the CEO, http://www.ecotech-intl.com/ceoletter.html (last visited Dec. 15, 2011).

26   CLIFFORD RECHTSCHAFFEN ET AL., ENVIRONMENTAL JUSTICE: LAW, POLICY & REGULATION 3 (2d ed. 2009).

27   COMMISSION FOR RACIAL JUSTICE, UNITED CHURCH OF CHRIST, TOXIC WASTES AND RACE IN THE UNITED STATES: A NATIONAL REPORT ON RACIAL AND SOCIO-ECONOMIC CHARACTERISTICS OF COMMUNITIES WITH HAZARDOUS WASTE SITES (1987), *available at* http://www.ucc.org/about-us/archives/pdfs/toxwrace87.pdf.

28   National Environmental Justice Advisory Council, Brief Summary of Member Biographies (2010), http://www.epa.gov/compliance/ej/resources/publications/nejac/members-exec-council-bios.pdf.

29   *See* Hewlett Packard, Shell to Use CeNSE for Clearer Picture of Oil and Gas Reservoirs, http://www.hpl.hp.com/news/2009/oct-dec/cense.html?aoid=35252 (last visited Mar. 8, 2012).

30   *See* Nike, Inc., NIKE, Inc. & Creative Commons Create a System for Sharing Innovation, *at* http://www.nikebiz.com/crreport/content/environment/4-4-0-case-study-greenxchange.php (last visited Mar. 8, 2012).

31   SEBASTIAN MALLABY, THE WORLD'S BANKER (2004).

32   Marie T. Zenni, World Bank Group, Oral History Program, Transcript of Interview with Robert Goodland, Jan. 26, 2005, Washington, D.C.

33   DAVID BORNSTEIN, HOW TO CHANGE THE WORLD: SOCIAL ENTREPRENEURS AND THE POWER OF NEW IDEAS (2004).

34   Philip N. Howard, *The Arab Spring's Cascading Effects*, MILLER-McCUNE, Feb. 23, 2011, *at* http://www.miller-mccune.com/politics/the-cascading-effects-of-the-arab-spring-28575/.

35   Arild Underdal, *Science and Politics: The Anatomy of an Uneasy Partnership, in* SCIENCE AND POLITICS IN INTERNATIONAL ENVIRONMENTAL REGIMES 10 (Steinar Andresen et al. eds., 2000).

36   Brent Steel & Denise Lach, *Environmental Policy, in* OREGON STATE AND LOCAL POLITICS 225 (Univ. of Neb. Press 2005).

Index